PHILOSOPHY, POLICIES, AND PROGRAMS FOR EARLY ADOLESCENT EDUCATION

PHILOSOPHY, POLICIES, AND PROGRAMS FOR EARLY ADOLESCENT EDUCATION

An Annotated Bibliography

Compiled by Dale A. Blyth
and
Elizabeth Lueder Karnes

GREENWOOD PRESS
WESTPORT, CONNECTICUT • LONDON, ENGLAND

Library of Congress Cataloging in Publication Data

Blyth, Dale A.
  Philosophy, policies, and programs for early adolescent
education.

  Includes indexes.
  1.   Junior high schools.   2.   Middle schools.
3.   Adolescence.   I.   Karnes, Elizabeth Lueder. II.   Title.
LB1623.B49   373.2'36   81-4237
ISBN 0-313-22687-3 (lib bdg.)   AACR2

Library of Congress Catalog Card Number: 81-4237
ISBN: 0-313-22687-3

First published in 1981

Greenwood Press
A division of Congressional Information Service, Inc.
88 Post Road West, Westport, Connecticut 06881

Printed in the United States of America

10 9 8 7 6 5 4 3 2 1

Contents

Preface   *vii*

Acknowledgments   *ix*

Introduction   *xi*

    Organization and Content of the Chapters   *xiv*

    Author and Subject Indices   *xviii*

    General Comments on Entry Format and

    Locating Materials   *xviii*

1. Philosophy and Theory of Schools for Early Adolescents   3
2. Prescriptions for and Descriptions of Middle Schools   139
3. Prescriptions for and Descriptions of Junior High Schools   201
4. Guidance Programs   225
5. Design and Renovation of Schools for Middle Years Education   249
6. Internal Organization of Schools for Early Adolescents: Team Teaching, Departmentalization, and Related Concepts   275
7. Development and Implementation of Curriculum   307
8. Development and Implementation of Cocurricular and Extracurricular Activities   393
9. Policy Analyses Concerning Schools for Early Adolescents   413
10. Research on Organizational Patterns and the Effects of Schools on Early Adolescents   431
11. Teacher Preparation and In-Service Training   569

12.   Discipline and Problem Behavior in Schools for
      Early Adolescents   623

      Author Index   *641*
      Subject Index   *673*

Preface

The genesis of this book goes back to the winter of 1978 when I was directing a series of research studies under the umbrella title "Schools and Adolescent Development." Dr. Roberta Simmons and I had just been awarded money from the William T. Grant Foundation to conduct a study of middle schools and their effects on the social and psychological development of early adolescents. At that time we were already involved with a five-year longitudinal study of the effects on students of attending an elementary school (kindergarten through eighth grade) versus a junior high school. As I began to prepare for the middle schools research project, it became increasingly clear that we needed to get a handle on the similarities and differences in philosophy and implementation of middle school and junior high school programs for early adolescents.

Fortunately, it was at this time that I was introduced to Dr. Elizabeth Karnes, who had been working in early adolescent education for ten years. She had taught courses on the history and philosophy of middle schools and junior high schools which many teachers needed in order to obtain the middle grades endorsement on their teaching certificates in Nebraska. She was then serving as Media Specialist at the Wegner Middle School on the Boys Town campus. Over the course of the project she became the Supervisor of Curriculum and Instruction for the Boys Town School System.

Late in the winter of 1978 with the help of a small grant from the Boys Town Center for the Study of Youth Development we began to collaborate on a review of the literature dealing with the history and philosophy of schools for the middle grades and the research on what effect different arrangements had on the social and psychological development of students. Over the first few months of our collaboration, we increased the scope of our project in three ways. First, having the perspectives of both a psychologist and an educator led us to add a number of topics to our original outline. Second, we decided to be more comprehensive within each area. Rather than simply exploring the philosophy and research in an area, we also wanted descriptions of programs in the field. Finally, the expansion in the topics and in comprehensiveness required a considerably expanded time frame. Although we went through several attempts to reduce one or more of these expanded dimensions, we ultimately decided to seek additional support for our work.

The William T. Grant Foundation of New York, which had provided much support for our earlier research, was approached about the possibility of funding the development of a comprehensive annotated bibliography in the area of schools for early adolescents. It is the expansion of their support to this project which has permitted the full-scale effort necessary to produce the book now before you. Without their support, we would never have been able to pull together all the material we had been collecting over the first year, nor would we have been able to initiate new searches based on a more refined outline. For their contribution to this work we are extremely grateful.

In the last year as we have tried to pull the various pieces together, we have kept in mind three basic tenets. First, we believed the book should be organized and written so that it would be optimally useful to a variety of educational practitioners and researchers. Second, we felt the book should contain a wide spectrum of materials, both published and unpublished, because so much of the useful and descriptive material on how to create programs and implement them is simply not available in the published literature. Finally, we felt it was necessary to present information from a variety of perspectives rather than synthesize these perspectives into conclusions about what should be done. We did not want to create a book which advocated a particular style of education for early adolescents. The great diversity of early adolescents, of their communities, and of those who work with them suggested the need for one book that would accurately describe the wide variety of materials we found in the literature.

This book is the culmination of two years of collaborative work. It is our hope that it will be used creatively to help educate and facilitate the development of early adolescents.

Acknowledgments

In addition to the indispensable resources and support provided by the William T. Grant Foundation, we would like to thank the Boys Town Center for the Study of Youth Development and particularly Lu Otto for providing the start-up funds and the environment and resources which made it possible for us to think about a comprehensive bibliography. The orientation of the Center—an interdisciplinary institution devoted to disseminating research in such a way that those in the field can apply it—encouraged us to address a broad issue with relevance to a wide spectrum of educators and researchers.

The Boys Town Center also provided the library personnel who worked so closely with us in searching out the initial material and then, through several computerized searches, did major work in updating and expanding the scope of the project. A special thanks to Jim Sweetland and Donna Richardson, who helped us design and ultimately executed these search strategies. Their contribution is reflected in the more than 1,600 entries from diverse published and unpublished sources in this bibliography. In addition, we would like to thank Betty Schnase, Ann Potter, Diane Huerta, and Cathy Bifaro, who worked along with Jim and Donna to obtain the necessary materials and helped us double check and clean up problems in citing the material. Their capable, good-natured, and enthusiastic help made it possible to continue our work.

The Research Computing Division directed by Dr. Edmund Meyers at the Boys Town Center also provided resources and expertise which were quite helpful. A special thanks to John Evans and Leo Collins, who wrote all of the programs to alphabetize and merge the materials together as well as create the subject and author indices which make this work more useful. Another part of the Computing Division which was essential to this document's preparation is the Word Processing Department under the able direction of Mary Pat Roy. Mary Pat along with Vickie Kuehn and Marilyn Pittillo spent long hours correcting the manuscript and working with us in making it as clean and attractive as possible. It was their efforts and expertise that made it possible to create a camera-ready copy that would speed up the publication of this book.

In working on this project, we had the good fortune to locate two competent and enthusiastic professional editors who worked with us in cleaning up both the style of the entries and the clarity of the annotations. To Judy Timberg and Sandy Wendel we wish to extend a special thanks, since it was their work in the final months that made this book more consistent, concise, and much more readable.

Most importantly, however, both of us would like to acknowledge with applause (which is difficult when writing) the unending and unselfish contributions of Connie Finnell to this project. She has probably put in more hours than everyone else put together in making this book a reality. She transcribed the endless tapes for all the annotations which form the core of this book. She worked with the editors and the authors in organizing the consistent style of the entries and the accuracy of the information. Finally, she did much of the proofing and cleaning which is so necessary but so difficult in a project of this magnitude. It is safe to say that had it not been for Connie's presence and persistence over the two years of this project, we would never have made it to the end. For all this and for her help in so many other projects as well, we wish to thank her.

In any project of this magnitude it is necessary to have the full support and backing of one's family. We both would like to thank our spouses and our children for their understanding and support for this endeavor. They allowed us the time necessary to create this book. We hope our own children will someday benefit from the materials it contains.

Finally, although it is unusual, we would like to thank each other for the time, consideration, and enthusiasm which was brought to this project. Liz worked very hard and long on reviewing and annotating the volumes of materials which we discovered. I served primarily as a resource person, critic, and managing editor. Truly collaborative work is never easy. It requires a willingness to share the joys and the frustrations of creating something new. We have shared both throughout the two years of this project and remain friends and colleagues.

Dale A. Blyth
Elizabeth L. Karnes

Introduction

Before 1900 most early adolescents were either outside the formal educational process or included only in the upper levels of the elementary school. Around the turn of the century, pressure began to build for considering early adolescence as a separate stage of life needing its own type of education. The development of junior high schools and junior/senior high schools grew throughout the first half of the century, but it was not until the late 1940s that most schools housing early adolescents were organized as entities separate from the elementary schools. During this time early adolescents came to be seen less as elementary school students and more as secondary students.

During the last twenty years there has been renewed interest in redefining early adolescent education as neither elementary nor secondary but rather as a unique task requiring special educational tools and structures. While this movement is most often associated with the middle school ideology, we believe it extends beyond a concern with what grades should be included in a particular building. In fact, one can look at the long history of junior high schools and find much of the philosophy that is currently espoused by the middle school movement.

The development of a new philosophy for educating early adolescents, when combined with such factors as desegregation, declining enrollments, and financial pressures resulting from the so-called tax revolt, creates new opportunities for better meeting the needs of this special age group. As with most opportunities, however, there is a tremendous need for information about what has already been done, what effects these programs and schools have had, and finally, what might be done to better serve the needs of early adolescents. Without such information, it is possible to reinvent the wheel and, perhaps more dangerously, to reinvent dysfunctional wheels. As more and more school districts consider the reorganization of their grade level patterns and the types of programs offered within those patterns, it is helpful to have a comprehensive and systematic overview of what other school districts have tried, and what different authors believe to be the important issues in educating this age group. It is to this end that we have developed this annotated bibliography. We hope it will serve as a resource to both those who are contemplating changing or evaluating their current educational program for early adolescents as well as those who are attempting to better understand what the effects of these programs are on the educational, psychological, and social development of early adolescents.

To meet the need for this information, we began with the material each of us had used in the past five to ten years. On the one hand this included research evidence on the effects of different grade level patterns on the development of early adolescents, and on the other hand it included material on the philosophy and history of junior high schools and middle schools. From this beginning, we developed, with the cooperation of Jim Sweetland, the Boys Town Center's Public Service Librarian, a general search for material on schools for early adolescents. This involved working with several computerized data bases, including ERIC (Educational Resources Information Center), Psychological Abstracts, Sociological Abstracts, and Dissertation Abstracts. In the process of obtaining and reading this material, we delineated twelve basic issues which we felt were most important in understanding schools for early adolescents. At this point we also began to look at the references in the materials we were annotating to further expand the coverage of the bibliography.

Since each of these areas was now more specific and refined than the original literature searches we had performed, we enlisted the help of Donna Richardson of the Boys Town Center Library to creat special computerized searches in each area. Once again, the searches covered several different computerized data bases. The material turned up through this process was then reviewed for inclusion in the bibliography. At the same time that these specific searches were being undertaken, we also did a general update of our original computer searches to see if any new material had been forthcoming. These searches were completed in April of 1980, so most of the available material through 1979 and some from the first half of 1980 has been included.

In going over the material which resulted from these searches, we discovered that certain areas were not covered as fully as we had hoped. This was particularly true with respect to analyses of what school districts had done when faced with different pressures concerning reorganization. In order to get better information in this area and in the general area of schools for early adolescents, we sent out letters to each State Department of Education, to all districts with more than ten thousand students, and to a sample of districts with an enrollment between five thousand and ten thousand. In these letters, which were mailed in the spring of 1980, we requested information on how the districts had organized their schools for early adolescents and any documents concerning the process they went through to reach this conclusion. Although many districts did not respond, those that did fit primarily into two categories, those which shared materials with us and those which were in the process of reviewing what their district was doing for early adolescents and what information they needed in this area. The materials we received were screened for their potential applicability to a wider audience and, if deemed appropriate, were annotated and included in the bibliography. At this point we wish to acknowledge the cooperation of those who sent us material and hope they will benefit from this book. To those who noted the need for information in this area we hope the book is not too late to be of service.

Given this process for locating and screening information to be included, it is appropriate to say a few words about the comprehensive nature of the final product. In general, the comprehensiveness of this book is limited by three factors. First, because the search for materials depended so much on the computerized data bases using both key words and open-field searching, the results will be no better than the accuracy of these data bases in capturing the relevant literature and indexing it appropriately. Unfortunately, some of the data bases do not do very well at indexing the literature for schools in the middle grades. It is our hope that this will improve over time as these schools gain greater recognition and independence from both the elementary and secondary schools. A second factor which has limited the comprehensiveness of this volume is simply the greater knowledge and experience of the authors in some areas rather than others. For example, neither of the authors is experienced in counseling or architecture, so the sections of the book dealing with guidance programs for early adolescents and facilities for early adolescents are less comprehensive than those on the philosophy and theory of such schools. Finally, in a task of this magnitude, some limitations develop as a result of sheer size. For example, we were unable to examine each entry's reference section to determine if we had already examined all of the material cited. We did this only for what we believed were key references in each of the areas. Size also limited us in the discussion of curriculum. Although we did individual literature searches for each subject (e.g., math, science, English, reading), it was ultimately not possible to include much of this material. Instead, we decided to include only those materials which gave an overview of what the curriculum ought to be like in a given subject area.

The unpublished nature of many of the materials we located suggest that probably another volume worth of materials has been written on this subject. Many of these materials are not easily accessible and were occasionally left out of this volume if we believed it would be impossible for the interested reader to obtain copies. In general, however, we leaned in the direction of including these materials and annotating them as fully as possible in order to make their presence known more widely. If you are aware of any material that we have left out, please feel free to write us about it so that we may include it in future work. We also located some films and filmstrips in the process of our search, but we did not specifically search for or preview any of these materials. If we located them in the process of our work, we did include them in the bibliography. Thus, this annotated bibliography does not contain a systematic search of all available training films and filmstrips on the topic of schools for early adolescents.

In annotating the materials included in this book, we tried to keep in mind two basic goals. The first is that the interested reader ought to learn from the annotations themselves. That is, we felt that wherever possible the annotations should be complete enough to communicate the nature of the work and any conclusions drawn by the author. Second, we wanted to provide the best base possible for interested readers to judge which selections they would want to obtain for themselves. Because we had these goals, the annotations are longer than usual for a book of this type. We are grateful to the publisher for permitting us to include the annotations in this form.

In conclusion, we have spent two years compiling what we hope will be a useful and systematic presentation of literature on a variety of topics concerned with schools for early adolescents. The book contains over 1,600 entries organized around twelve basic themes. In the next section, we briefly discuss the types of materials included in each chapter and discuss the author and subject indices and how they were created. Finally, we discuss some of the conventions used in citing material and give suggestions for obtaining material from the source.

ORGANIZATION AND CONTENT OF THE CHAPTERS

This book has been organized around twelve central issues, each of which constitutes a separate chapter. Although a number of entries could well have been placed in multiple chapters, we selected that chapter which we felt captured the primary emphasis of the material and then provided subject indices which would permit the interested reader to locate it. The entries within a chapter are listed alphabetically by author. Each entry is numbered consecutively within the chapter and has been assigned a prefix which designates the chapter number. For example, entry no. 10123 is the 123rd entry in Chapter 10. The digits in the thousands always refer to chapters making it easy to determine what chapter the entry is in. The system also permits for the expansion of the material in each of the twelve chapters at some point in the future.

Rather than provide a review or synthesis of the material to be found in each chapter, we have decided simply to describe the types of material the reader will find in each chapter. This is consonant with our belief that an annotated bibliography should present the authors' ideas and not those of the compilers.

1   Philosophy and Theory of Schools for Early Adolescents.

This section includes articles and books on the historical development, philosophy, and objectives of schools for early adolescents. Articles deal with the junior high versus middle school controversy, questions regarding the best educational plan for students in this age range, theoretical and practical aspects of these schools, recommendations for grade reorganization, and issues identified as significant at this level of schooling. Lists of advantages and disadvantages are included as well as entries on early adolescence in general and the development of young people at this stage.

2   Prescriptions for and Descriptions of Middle Schools.

3   Prescriptions for and Descriptions of Junior High Schools.

These two chapters present articles on model schools and programs of the two primary types that exist in the United States today. Additional material on student evaluation, school evaluation, administration, articulation, school organization, scheduling, and accreditation is also included. In general, material in chapter three refers to schools that contain ninth graders while chapter two refers to schools without ninth graders.

4   Guidance Programs.

The special role of counseling and guidance in schools for early adolescents is discussed and illustrated in this chapter. Comprehensive guidance programs are described including the goals of the guidance counselor and the role of teachers as counselors.

5   Design and Renovation of Schools for Middle Years Education.

This chapter includes floor plans, descriptions of buildings, and explanations of the components of a school's physical plant. Trends in educational spaces and innovations in planning functional school buildings are discussed. Articles consider what administrators and teachers believe to be important ingredients in educational facilities for early adolescents. Also included are articles dealing with the question of remodeling versus constructing a new building and the best facilities for flexible scheduling, team teaching, large-group and small-group instruction, and the development of instructional media centers.

6   Internal Organization of Schools for Early Adolescents: Team Teaching, Departmentalization, and Related Concepts.

This chapter discusses the variety of ways in which schools are internally organized with respect to students, teachers, time, and facilities. The following concepts are included: team teaching, staff utilization and deployment, interdisciplinary teams, tutorial programs, flexible modular scheduling, educational parks, house plans, and nongraded plans. The controversy surrounding self-contained classrooms, semidepartmentalization, and full departmentalization for classes of early adolescents is included as well as many other articles on student grouping.

7   Development and Implementation of Curriculum.

This chapter includes descriptions of curricular plans for both middle schools and junior high schools. It includes articles on core curriculum, curriculum evaluation, curriculum planning, and specialized curricula in health, science, home economics, math, English, social studies, and reading. A few references are also included on physical education, music, career education, and drama.

8   Development and Implementation of Cocurricular and Extracurricular Activities.

This chapter deals with activities and athletics in school programs for early adolescents. Descriptions of model cocurricular, extracurricular, and exploratory activities are presented. Intramural vs. interscholastic athletics are discussed. Position papers from various youth-serving organizations are included.

9   *Policy Analyses Concerning Schools for Early Adolescents.*

This chapter presents articles about policies developed by various school systems for reorganizing their middle grades education. Articles cite budgetary and financial concerns, philosophical considerations, student population shifts, integration, and improvement of the education program as primary reasons for changing school structure.

10   *Research on Organizational Patterns and the Effects of Schools on Early Adolescents.*

This chapter includes studies of individual schools as well as studies comparing different grade patterns. Articles report on research in the following areas of student development: self-concept, self-esteem, attitudes toward school, educational performance, morale, behavior, social maturity, emotional maturity, physical maturity, achievement, and attendance. Also included are studies on articulation problems, organization of the school day, grouping patterns, pupil evaluation, the effects of departmentalization, teacher attitudes toward students, and staffing and curriculum revisions. In addition, we have included national and regional surveys of the prevalence of different grade patterns and reviews of research in these general areas.

11   *Teacher Preparation and In-Service Training.*

In this chapter teacher competencies, teacher certification, teacher performance, and teacher selection are all discussed. Pre- and in-service programs are included, as well as surveys that identify the teacher training institutions and state departments of education that are addressing the issues of middle grades preparation and certification.

12   *Discipline and Problem Behavior in Schools for Early Adolescents.*

This chapter was one of the last to be developed in the process of creating this bibliography and as such is probably less comprehensive than the rest. Nonetheless, we felt it was important to provide information on delinquency, discipline, and general problem behaviors of early adolescents in schools. We hope the material which is included here will provide a useful beginning for those working in this area.

AUTHOR AND SUBJECT INDICES

At the back of the book are two indices. The first of these is an author index, indicating the items by an author using the entry numbers. All authors of a given entry (when they were specified) are included in the index, not simply the first authors. Since we use initials rather than first names of authors, it was sometimes impossible to distinguish between two potentially different authors. In general, we kept authors with almost identical names (e.g., H. Jones, H. C. Jones, Jr.) separate unless we knew the initials referred to the same person.

The subject index at the back of the book was developed jointly by the authors after all annotations had been written. The key words were refined over a period of several months. The subject index also includes cross-references so that words which are similar in nature to those we decided to use will indicate the terms which were actually used. In addition, related terms are usually cited so that the user may expand upon his or her search.

Subject key words were assigned to each entry based on a reading of the annotation by the authors. Then a computer program produced the index by compiling all the entries associated with each key word.

The major limitation of the subject index is that it was developed after the annotations were finished, so that main points which were missed in the annotation were also missed in the indexing. In addition, the indexing system is based upon our view of the field and may therefore be limited.

GENERAL COMMENTS ON ENTRY FORMAT AND LOCATING MATERIALS

As in most bibliographies, each entry contains two principal components. The first is the full reference for locating the article if further information is desired. The second is the annotation of that material. The annotations were developed either from reading the original source or from quoting an abstract, such as that available through ERIC. If the second course was used, a note is included in the annotation.

In the reference section of each entry we have included as much information as we had available on how to locate the material. In a few cases where the publisher's address was given on the title page of an unpublished work, we included this in our reference for the reader's convenience. In other cases, we attempted to signal both the national association that was responsible for the material as well as the committee or subcommittee that generated the material. In those cases where material was not published elsewhere, we tried to include the ERIC number so that one could obtain it directly through ERIC Resource Centers. The same is true for doctoral dissertations that are available through University Micro-films.

In general, we have tried to organize this bibliography to maximize its utility to the reader and to provide as many different ways of using it as possible. We hope you will find it meets your needs. Please feel free to comment on how useful you find it. Your comments would be greatly appreciated.

PHILOSOPHY, POLICIES, AND PROGRAMS FOR EARLY ADOLESCENT EDUCATION

1

Philosophy and Theory of Schools for Early Adolescents

1001. Adams, J. F. Understanding Adolescence: Current Development in Adolescent Psychology. Boston: Allyn and Bacon, 1976.

Contains chapters on: 1) Adolescents in an Age Acceleration. 2) Theories of Adolescence. 3) A Cross Cultural View. 4) Nature and Nurture. 5) Physiological Development. 6) Development and Dynamics of the Self. 7) Moral Development. 8) Cognitive Development and Learning. 9) Sex Role Development. 10) Creativity. 11) Educational Institutions. 12) Culturally Disadvantaged Youth. 13) Adjustment and Maladjustment. 14) Contemporary Drug Issues Involving Youth. 15) Youth and the Counter Culture. 16) A Cognitive Approach to Sex Education. 17) Emotions and Sex Education. 18) Career Development. Note Chapter 11 deals with schooling and adolescence and covers functions for students and society, goals in American schools, empirical research, national findings, a broad set of objectives, social and psychological forces in the development of objectives, the effects of schooling, education and success, research on school differences and school effects, dropouts, and implications for change. The chapter attempts to explain the high observability of some outcomes, the varying political efficacy of recent groups, the public controversy surrounding certain issues, the absence of organizational or curriculum structure to support some objectives, the lack of certain types of teacher training, the dangers involved in social experimentation, the effect of psychological and social forces on schools, and the correlation of success and educational attainment.

1002.   Ahrens, M. R. "The junior high school is not a stepchild." Educational Leadership, 14(1957):466.

The integrative function of the junior high school is significant and desirable. For students to experience optimum growth, the junior high school must direct pupils toward objectives of education and provide opportunities for them to solve problems. This approach to integration gives purpose to subject matter by relating it to real life situations. Integration cannot adequately be achieved in highly departmentalized programs. Hence, the core or block program has become a common element in junior high school program design: the teacher better understands the special needs of early adolescents for guidance and integration. The junior high school is a distinctive general educational institution.

1003.   Alexander, W. M. "What educational plan for the inbetweenager?"   National Education Association Journal, 55(1966):30-32.

Author observes that the junior high school tends to precipitate adolescent behavior; thus, he is a proponent of the middle school. Preadolescents and early adolescents who attend junior high schools with fully developed, sophisticated teenagers pick up unfortunate mannerisms and behavior patterns. This premature growing up has disastrous effects. The good middle school could avoid some of this danger by easing the transition from childhood to adolescence and by making it the gradual process it naturally is, rather than a precipitous shift that society has forced. The middle school is ideally suited for a nongraded organizational pattern because of the wide age differences in children, programs of diagnostic services, frequent teacher/student conferences, and much individualized instruction to help children achieve optimum progress without arbitrary grade-level expectations. Some pupils might move through the middle school in three years while others might need a fourth year. Article speaks to the issues: 1) How could the program be made intellectually stimulating? 2) How should learning skills be taught and emphasized?   3) What common or general studies are to be provided? 4) What exploratory experiences and activity programs should be provided? 5) What would be the best way to bring about sound personal development?   To ensure the success of a middle school, the reorganization should provide varied learning opportunities so that each pupil, whether 10 or 14 years old, boy or girl, advantaged or disadvantaged, can find some success and challenge to stimulate further learning. The plan should include instruments for rigorous evaluation of results.

1004.   Alexander, W. M. and Kealy, R. P. "From junior
high school to middle school." High School Journal,
53(1969):151-163.

Suggests that the middle school focus on the following: 1) provide a program especially adapted to the
wide range of individual differences and special
needs of the "inbetweenager," 2) create a school
ladder to promote continuity of education from school
entrance to exit, and 3) introduce needed innovations
in curriculum and instruction.   The authors ask these
questions to measure middle school curriculum: 1) Is
the curriculum balanced?   2) Is continuity provided?
3) Is the curriculum plan flexible?   4) Is curriculum
individualization provided?   Results of a 1967-68
survey of 1,101 middle schools indicated that few of
the middle schools had changed curriculum from their
previous organization.   Most were middle school by
grade-level groupings only; their program descriptions reflected little concern for middle school
rationale.   Survey findings testify to the discrepancies between middle school theory and middle school
practice: 1) These schools were most often established to eliminate crowded conditions in other
schools.   2) The middle schools that aimed to remedy
the weaknesses of the junior high had programs which
did not differ markedly from typical junior high
programs in regard to interscholastic athletics,
departmentalized organization, and curriculum opportunities in general.   3) More than half the schools
that include grade 5 maintained at this grade the
typical elementary self-contained classroom arrangement.   4) About three fourths or more of the schools
used the junior high school departmentalized organization for grades 7 and 8, and few of these schools
had an extensive offering of exploratory electives,
especially in grades 5 and 6.   5) Relatively few
schools used the back-to-back and other team teaching
plans or large group/small group instructional procedure.   6) Schedules with five to seven daily periods,
uniform in length, were used in more than 70 percent
of the schools; less than 5 percent used any type of
modular schedule.   7) Sharing a faculty and program
opportunities to promote articulation between the
middle school and other schools was almost nonexistent.   8) Only 20 percent scheduled independent study
time.

1005.   Alexander, W. M. and Williams, E. L. "Schools for
the middle school years." Educational Leadership,
23(1965):217-223.

Margaret Mead claims, "Junior highs have resulted
inadvertently in classifying together boys and girls
when they vary most within each sex, between the
sexes, and are least suited to a segregated social

existence." Dacus, in his dissertation study, states, "On a criterion measure of social, emotional, and physical maturity, and on opposite sex choices, the least differences were found between pupils in grades 6 and 7 and pupils in grades 9 and 10. Yet, it is between these grades that our present 6-3-3 plan divides children." Alexander would choose a different educational plan for the inbetweenager: take boys and girls from the years of upper childhood and see some 85 percent of them through to early adolescence, that is, keep grades 5 to 8, ages 10 to 14 together. The article discusses the 6-3-3 plan-- the proposal for a model middle school--with these guidelines: A true middle school should be designed to serve the needs of the older children, preadolescents, and early adolescents, and it should promote the long-held ideal of individualized instruction. A middle school program should place primary emphasis on intellectual components of the curriculum and skills of continued learning, and it should provide a rich program of exploratory experiences. A program of health and physical education should be designed especially for boys and girls. An emphasis on values should underline all aspects of the middle school program. The curriculum should be organized around the special skills and interests of the staff members at that school. The curriculum plan of a real middle school would consist of planned programs in three phases: learning skills, general studies, and curriculum development. The organization for instruction would be based on a homeroom unit, a wing unit, a vertical unit, and a special learning center. The key to the implementation of a successful middle school program is a staff of uncommon talents and abilities. The teachers must be knowledgeable in their chosen academic fields, and they must have training in the guidance and counseling of children of middle school age. A program of selection, recruitment, and training would be necessary to develop a staff with these special qualifications.

1006.   Anastasiow, N. J., et al. "Educational implications of earlier sexual maturation." Phi Delta Kappan, 56,3(1974):198-200.

In the last twenty years the age of menarche has dropped from 13.5 years in 1950 to a mean age of 11.5 in 1970. Authors urge educators to address the social and physical consequences of the physiological revolution on contemporary America, and they suggest a potential role for schools to help solve the problem. Child rearing should be taught in junior high school. See ERIC Abstract #EJ 105 857.

1007.   Atkins, N. P. "Rethinking education in the middle." Theory Into Practice, 9(1968):118-119.

Both the middle school and the junior high school should serve a transitional function. The purpose of that transition for the middle school is not merely anticipatory (looking toward high school) but enabling (deriving from the developmental characteristics of the learners of this age). This shift in interpretation has led to constructive rethinking about the nature of the educational experiences these pupils need. Article answers these questions: In this pioneering and developing stage, what are some of the characteristics which differentiate the middle school from the elementary and the high school? What features promise to distinguish it as a uniquely appropriate institution for the children it serves? Article discusses attitudinal stance--a matter of attitude, expectation, sensitivity, and perception, rather than organization, courses, grouping, scheduling, or staffing. The mission of the school is neither remedial nor preparatory. The middle school is characterized organizationally by flexibility, environmentally by sensitivity to changing needs, and instructionally by individualization. The middle school is distinguished by the shift in emphasis from mastery to practical use of knowledge, that is, supporting the pupil's efforts to move from dependence to independence as a learner. Recapture for the student the sense of inquiry, curiosity, and commitment to learning and values when choosing from alternative plans of action. The middle school should not crystallize into a single pattern of organization or into a common format of operation. The middle school movement poses new questions for which old answers are worthless. It challenges some of the instructional folklore that has found acceptance, undermines some of the institutional rituals and shakes some stereotypical thinking about how and what children of this age should learn. It is hoped that the middle school ideal retains its viability, excitement, and relevance to pupils.

1008.   Atkins, T. A. "It's time for a change, or is it?" National Elementary Principal, 48,4(1969):46-48.

Schools must continue to respond to the needs of the changing society. To avoid the mistakes of the past and to respond adequately to the challenges of the future, change must not only continue to occur, it must proceed in a more efficient and orderly manner. The demand that leadership be provided by the elementary school principal has never been greater. He must be able to foresee the implications and consequences of proposed changes in relation to the goals and structures of the school. He must monitor an orderly change process, based on fairly supported and adequately tested proposals. To avoid change for the sake of change and to proceed with a needed reform movement based on rationality, the values and goals of the school must be continually reviewed and revised in relation to the needs of children and society. To do less would be to inhibit the patient pursuit of excellence so necessary in the interests of youth and society.

1009.   Barker, R. G. and Gump, P. V. Big School: High School Size and Student Behavior. Palo Alto, Calif.: Stanford University Press, 1964.

Empirical research on school size indicates: 1) Persons in small groups, other social organizations, and ecological units a) are absent less often, b) quit jobs less often, c) are more punctual, d) participate more frequently when participation is voluntary, e) take positions of responsibility in a wider range of activities more often, f) are more productive, g) demonstrate more leadership behavior, h) are more important to the groups and setting, i) have broader role conceptions, j) are more frequently involved in roles directly relevant to the group task, and k) are more interested in the affairs of the group.   2) Small groups and other ecological and social units give rise to a) greater individual participation and communication in social interaction and less centralization of the communication around one or a few persons, b) more greeting and social transactions per person, c) increased communication skills, d) greater group cohesiveness and camaraderie, and e) greater ability to identify outstanding persons.   3) Persons in smaller groups a) receive more satisfaction, b) speak more of participation having been valuable and useful, c) are more familiar with the setting, d) report being more satisfied with teams and the result of discussion, and e) find their work more meaningful.

1010.   Barnett, L. J., Handel, G. and Weser, H. The School in the Middle: Divided Opinion on Dividing Schools. New York: Center for Urban Education, 1968.

Presents a range of views, guidelines for innovation, experiments in intermediate education, and an overview of trends. Parts I, II, and III are journal articles. Part III presents a case study of New York City. The first article--"Excellence for the Schools of New York City"--is the Board of Education's 1965 Statement of Policy which calls for a new program in which the child will be taught basic skills and how to use these skills to gather information. "One of the most important phases of his education in this period will be his introduction to other children who are different from those with whom he associated in his elementary school....This means that curriculum must be developed to...introduce children to the

sensitive relationships." The second article--
"Primary School, Intermediate School, Four-Year
Comprehensive High School"--describes a middle school
plan in the context of an educational program ranging
from the primary through the high school years.
Three separate but related committee recommendations
for total system reorganization are made. Goals,
curriculum, staffing, professional growth, buildings,
and equipment are discussed. The next article--
"Action for Excellence"--presents the recommendations
of Superintendent Donovan for changes in grade level
organization based on his response to the committee's
findings and proposals. Of interest is the chief
administrator's pragmatic as well as theoretical
justification for the changes he recommends. He
makes clear that the practicing school administrator
must insert into his deliberations considerations
that may appear to the uninitiated as weakly connected, remote, or even extraneous. Donovan's
recommendations suggest a real engagement with
educational purpose, coupled with an equally real
mastery of the art of concession and compromise. In
the next article--"Grade Level Reorganization"--the
Board of Education responds to Donovan's recommendation. A careful study reveals the subtle but
decisive changes that occur in the evolution from
proposals to policy. Several hundred New York City
junior high school principals represented by the
Association prepared a "Response to Memorandum:
Advantages of Establishment of Four-Year High School
Policy," a critical rejection of the four-year high
school proposal.

1011.   Barratt, B. B. "Training and transfer in combinatorial problem solving: the development of formal
reasoning during early adolescence." Developmental
Psychology, 11,6(1975):700-704.

Explores the emergence of combinatorial competence as
an aspect of the development of formal reasoning during early adolescence and examines the effectiveness
of training procedures based on the principles of
programmed discovery. Eighty subjects aged 12 to 14
participated in a pretest, two training sessions, an
immediate posttest and a posttest two months later.
Significant increases in combinatorial skill with age
were shown, and it was found that the expression of
this skill is significant if problems involved concrete material of low complexity. With the older
subjects, training produced significant improvements
in performance on combinatorial tasks that were
markedly different from the training items in both
content and modality, especially over time and with
practice.

1012.   Baruchin, F. "Middle school for elementary youngsters?" New York State Education, 54(1967): 44-47.

Despite much implementation, debate of the pros and cons of middle schools is becoming heated, for in actuality there seems to be little consensus over what constitutes a middle school. The educational justification is debatable because the middle school presently takes many forms. The respective characteristics of middle school and junior high (program, faculty preparation and retraining, administration, supervision, curricula, methods, and the real behavioral needs of the children) lie virtually unexplored. How can we possibly debate the issues before we isolate the characteristics of the different institutions? The article suggests that the argument for linking the elementary grades to the middle school may not be as justified and as scientifically based as its proponents make it seem. The impetus for the middle school emanates from three primary sources: 1) In cities it will aid integration by sending youngsters from neighborhood schools to centrally located middle schools. 2) Overcrowded situations will be relieved by a realignment of grade levels. 3) The junior high school is judged as falling short of its original purposes and the middle school is considered to be the panacea. Article suggests that a formal effort be made to base our assertions in favor of, or against, this new organizational pattern. This study would isolate the actual differences between middle and junior high schools and identify the characteristics peculiar to each, and it would determine whether the middle school offers more promise to elementary youngsters in terms of improved academic achievement in the basic studies, improved social development, better self-concept, and more positive and sustained attitudes toward school--all of which should compose the real justification for including these youngsters in the new organizational unit in the first place.

1013.   Batezel, W. G. "The middle school: philosophy, program, organization." Clearinghouse, 43(1968): 487-490.

A carefully thought-out philosophy serves as a guide: 1) A good middle school ought to provide for a gradual transition from the typical self-contained classroom to the highly departmentalized high school. 2) Provision should be made for each student to become well known by at least one teacher. 3) The middle school ought to exist as a distinct, flexible, and unique organization tailored to the special needs of preadolescent and early adolescent youth, not to be an extension of the elementary nor seek to copy

the high school.   4) The middle school ought to
provide an environment where the child, not the
program, is more important, where the opportunity to
succeed exists.   The article describes a model
program for sixth, seventh, and eighth graders with
ideas for organization and staffing plus all types of
classes and curricula.   The program should be consistent with the aims expressed in the philosophy and
should strive for the following attributes: 1) close
coordination and cooperation between teachers in
developing programs tailored for the needs of the
youngsters involved, 2) close, warm, and wholesome
relationship between teacher and student, 3) flexibility to provide for thoughtful innovation, 4) a new
concept of evaluation designed to lessen anxiety
about grades and increase self-esteem of the pupils,
5) individual programming for each youngster according to the level of his ability.

1014.   Battlick, D. H. "What do we believe about the
exploratory function of the junior high school?"
Bulletin of the National Association of Secondary
School Principals, 46(1962):9-10.

Exploration provides each student a breadth of experience that will broaden his horizons, develop his
interests, and identify his attitudes, strengths, and
weaknesses in vocational, educational, and avocational pursuits.

1015.   Bauer, F. C. "Causes of conflict." Bulletin of the
National Association of Secondary School Principals,
49,300(1965):15-17.

The basic conflict of adolescence is the struggle
between his need to become independent and the
equally strong tendency to remain dependent.   In 1965
the adolescent is fundamentally no different from the
adolescent of previous generations.   Why, then, are
his problems more numerous and acute?   This question
is more logically answered by examining our radically
different social structure than by postulating change
in the nature of the adolescent.   We have indeed pro-
pelled our children toward maturity and independence
and insisted that they assume responsibilities before
they are ready for it.   When we reflect on the dis-
arming statistic that in our society one of every
four marriages terminates in divorce, thereby removing the most important source of stability in childhood, it becomes easier to appreciate why so many
youngsters are overwhelmed by the challenge of
adolescence.   If we recognize that in at least two of
the three remaining marriages, the parents have
abdicated their position of authority and have joined
the adolescent they should be leading, we're still
closer to an understanding of the problem.   Human

nature is the one constant in an ever-changing universe. Human nature has the unique capacity to effect change and to adapt to change without changing itself in the process. Consequently, if we are concerned with the adolescent, we must consider him as not essentially different from his predecessors. We must consider rather those changes which make him appear different from other adolescents at other times in other settings.

1016.   Baughman, M. D. "Perceptions beyond the retina." Teachers College Journal, 39(1967):51.

The middle school is proposed as an alternative organization to the junior high school as a means of providing more appropriate educational experiences for learners in the preadolescent and early adolescent stages of development. The author is not necessarily for or against the middle school concept. It is his thesis that the junior high school need not be scrapped. Many quality junior high schools should be kept. The number of junior high schools as well as the number of early adolescents enrolled in them is ample evidence that this truly American idea is accepted as a segment of our educational ladder.

1017.   Benish, J. A Comprehensive Middle School Bibliography. Charleston: West Virginia State Department of Education, Bureau of Learning Systems, Division of Instructional Learning Systems, 1978.

Document should be valuable to junior high school educators. Section I includes a comprehensive list of books, articles (journals and magazine), pamphlets and booklets, ERIC documents, papers, theses, dissertations and reports, newspaper articles, bulletins, and newsletters. Section II includes resources reviewed and categorized under major topics found in "A Programmatic Definition from Middle Schools in West Virginia." These include: rationale, needs assessment, instruction, staff, management, evaluation, facilities, budget, students, organization, curriculum, communication, and philosophies and goals. Section III includes addresses where the material cited may be obtained.

1018.   Berman, S. "As a psychiatrist sees pressures on middle class teenagers." National Education Association Journal, 54(1965):17-24.

Berman sees the changes from elementary to junior high school as quite poorly timed and declares that "in the midst of deciding who they are, they should not have to waste any energy finding out where they are." During the highly volatile years--age 11 to 13 and 14--youngsters should have a familiar background in which to operate.

1019.   Bernard, J. "Teenage culture: an overview." Annals of the American Academy of Political and Social Science, 338(1961):1-12.

Class pervades all aspects of teenage culture, from clothes, to taste in movies, to hangouts, to activities. Teenage culture is a product of affluence: we can afford to keep a large population in school through high school, where the culture of younger adolescents is characteristically lower class, and that of older teenagers is upper middle class. The material traits of teenage culture include certain kinds of clothes, automobiles, and the paraphernalia of sports and recreation. Teenagers constitute an important market; advertisers join them in a coalition that supports teenage consumption if parents protest. The nonmaterial culture traits include a special language and a greater emphasis on fun and popularity. Popular songs reflect the preoccupation of teenagers with love in its various stages. Political concern is not characteristic of teenage culture but, when asked for their opinions, teenagers reflect those of their class background. In teenage society, as in the larger world, a substantial proportion is alienated. At the college level, the old "rah-rah" culture is giving way to more serious vocational and academic cultures. If this trend continues, teenage culture may end with high school graduation; at the college level, young people will be more adult. At the same time, however, it appears that children enter teenage culture at an earlier age. So long as we can afford to support a large leisure class of youngsters, teenage culture in some form or another will continue.

1020.   Bondi, J. C., Jr. "Programs for emerging adolescent learners." In Leeper, R. (Ed.), Middle School in the Making, pp. 17-18. Washington, D.C.: Association for Supervision and Curriculum Development, 1974.

Much progress in American school districts has occurred since 1964 in developing and implementing new programs for pre- and early adolescents. Middle grades education in many school districts has represented a dramatic break from the past. Building on growing research on the needs and characteristics of emerging adolescent learners, innovative programs include a wide range of learning opportunities for use in the middle grades. Although many of these programs are housed in new organizational structures called middle schools, such programs can be found in some upper elementary grades as well as in junior high schools and secondary schools. The argument over the name or grade structure of the middle unit of schools has largely disappeared. The Association for Supervision and Curriculum Development established a working group on the middle school and the emerging adolescent learner in 1974. The working group grew out of a Council on the Emerging Adolescent Learner appointed by ASCD in 1969 and subsequent formal and informal working groups established between 1969 and 1974. The ASCD Council urged this working group to contact representatives of the National Association of Secondary School Principals, National Association of Elementary School Principals, and the National Middle School Association in an effort to establish a joint task force to prepare a working paper dealing with school for the middle years. Article discusses teacher preparation for middle school grades, education of emerging adolescents, and the role of ASCD in dealing with the middle school students.

1021.   Bough, M. "Theoretical and practical aspects of the middle school." Bulletin of the National Association of Secondary School Principals, 53(1969):8-13.

Administrators whose school corporations are in the process of structural reorganization and/or school building construction should consider three factors justifying the middle school in the 4-4-4 plan of internal organization: human growth and development, current social unrest, and facilities. What about the school district that has an established system of junior high schools complete with adequate facilities? What will happen to those facilities not needed in a middle school? These are questions to be considered by administrators who are tempted to jump on the middle school bandwagon. Time to weigh the "middle school or junior high school" question is needed. Some concerns are general and will need to be studied by all administrators; others will be unique to certain school districts. Those who resist the temptation to jump and who pause to study the problem in relation to their own situations will be taking wise action.

1022.   Bough, M. E. and Hamm, R. L. (Eds.). The American Intermediate School. Danville, Ill.: Interstate Printers and Publishers, 1974.

Book contains the following sections: 1) The Beginnings of the Junior High School: How the Junior High School Came to Be. New Light on Junior High School History. Junior High School: The Uniquely American Institution. The Junior High Mystique. 2) The Junior High School Student: The Early Adolescent in Today's American Culture and Implications for Education. Do Junior High School Youth Grow Up to

Fast?   The Awkward Age.   The Junior High School: A
Psychologist's View.   3) The Junior High School
Curriculum: A General Point of View.   Curricular
Changes in Junior High Schools.   What Educational
Program is Needed in the Junior High School?   Some
Problems of the Junior High School.   Survey of the
Junior High School Curriculum.   4) Teaching-Learning
in the Junior High School: Junior High School
Priorities.   The Open Classroom.   The Junior High
School Differs.   Methods of Teaching and Learning in
the Junior High School.   5) Administering the Junior
High School: Another Look at the Junior High School
Principalship.   Organization and Administration of
the Modern Junior High School.   Evaluation and
Accreditation of Junior High Schools.   6) A Forward
Look.   The Growing Edge: Are Junior High Schools the
Answers?   Junior High School: Yesterday and Tomor-
row.   The Junior High School Today and Tomorrow.   An
Unfinished Dream: The Junior High School.   Recent
Trends in Junior High School Practices, 1954-64.   7)
Middle School or Junior High?   Theoretical and Prac-
tical Aspects of the Middle School.   Some Questions
Surrounding the Middle School.   The Middle School:
Alternative to the Status Quo.   The Middle School
Child in Contemporary Society.   Teacher Education for
the Middle School: A Framework.

1023.   Boutwell, W. V. "What's happening in education:
what are middle schools?" PTA Magazine, 60(1965):14.

Discusses why middle schools are being proposed and
how they can be tailored to the needs of preadolescents.   Author cited Tompkin and Roe's survey of
seventh and eighth grade junior high principals
indicating that 64 percent would prefer a three-year
school rather than their present two-year school.
Most principals prefer to add the ninth grade, with
"some few stating that the three-year school should
be grades 6, 7, 8."   The author attacks junior highs
by saying they were created to fill a need which no
longer exists--combating dropouts--and they do not
fit the particular needs of that strange, loveable,
but exasperating character--the preadolescent.
Boutwell writes, "What do we need as a school for
early adolescents?   We need a school tailored to the
preadolescent.   In the fifth grade he is a joy to his
teachers and parents.   He loves to learn.   In the
sixth grade, he is often another being, his grades
may go down.   He is always in action; he hates sitting at a desk.   He is more interested in his fellow
students than adults, any adults.   To the preadolescent, sitting hour after hour in the traditional egg-
crate classroom is a pain in the neck.   He isn't old
enough to relate the hard work of learning to the
life aims he hasn't yet formed."   Since preadolescence ends with pubescence, educators see middle

schools organized for children from 10 to 14 years old. They see schools with movable partitions for flexible programs; team teaching and carrels and a library at the heart of the school; specialization introduced gradually, beginning with art and music and moving toward science and shop. They see students learning in action rather than sitting, reading, and reciting.

1024.   Brandt, R. "The middle school in a nongraded system." Journal of Secondary Education, 43(1968): 165-170.

General summary quotes various authors on middle schools versus junior high schools, including quotations from Strickland's study of two Florida schools and quotes from Campbell, Cunningham and McPhee, Heathers, Wattenberg, and Popper. There is general agreement on the need for a school which specializes in preadolescent education but disagreement as to when it should begin and end, specifically as to which grades should be included in the school. Discusses such terms as grade, elementary, and secondary education and quotes from Gastwirth, Margaret Mead, amd Downey. The article also discusses Nisbet and Entwistle's review of British education and students moving from elementary to secondary education. If we change our schools today we should change them in the direction of what we want them to be tomorrow. In the meantime, we should not allow ourselves to be sidetracked by meaningless controversy. If progress is to be made in defining the middle school, attention should be focused not on grades but on individuals. The article talks about the difference of various students in, for example, the sixth grade and the importance of having a nongraded system. Support is given to the idea that as part of the total school system the middle school would have its own set of objectives to establish performance criteria for each student. The student's progress toward maturity would be evaluated periodically by his teachers, his parents, and himself to determine whether or not the objectives continue to be appropriate and to measure progress toward meeting them. At certain preestablished check points, consideration would be given to the student's readiness for a transfer to a higher level school. The article reviews some of the criteria school districts use as a basis for transfer from one level school to the next, including age, number of years at school attended, academic achievement, physical development, and social and psychological maturity.

1025.   Breckenridge, M. E. and Vincent, E. L. Child Development. 5th ed. Philadelphia: W. B. Saunders Co., 1965.

A comprehensive discussion based on exhaustive research on studies of physical and psychological growth through adolescence. Contains an extensive bibliography and list of pertinent films and filmstrips.

1026.   Briggs, T. H. The Junior High School. Boston: Houghton-Mifflin, 1920.

A good reference on the early junior high school movement. Helpful in understanding the ideas of the forerunners in the movement.

1027.   Brimm, R. P. "Middle school or junior high?" Man/Society/Technology: A Journal of Industrial Arts Education, 31,1(1971):6-8.

Article discusses the background and rationale of industrial arts and the middle school and includes a section on better college preparation, reorganization in 1918, the mimicry of high school, the opportunity to mix ethnic groups, the middle school and puberty, imitation and absorption.

1028.   Brimm, R. P. "Middle school or junior high?--background and rationale." Bulletin of the National Association of Secondary School Principals, 53(1969): 1-7.

Discusses better college preparation of a junior high, reorganization in 1918, mimicry of high school, the opportunity to mix ethnic groups, the middle school and puberty, imitation and absorption.

1029.   Brodinsky, B. "Tell us: what logic puts fifth graders in some junior highs?" Updating School Board Policies, 10,3(1979):1-3.

Article includes a brief account of the history and present trends of grade organization patterns, with emphasis on the development of the middle school. See ERIC Abstract #EJ 199 456.

1030.   Budde, R. "(5)-6-7-8, the middle school of the future." Michigan Journal of Secondary Education, 6(1964):43-51.

For the 1970s the 7-8-9 junior high school is no longer a defensible unit of school organization. It has made its contribution; it has had its day. The 6-7-8 or the 5-6-7-8 middle school is a better answer for grouping students between elementary school and the four-year high school. The article looks at several educational realities which support these contentions: 1) The foundation ideas on which the

7-8-9 junior high school is based, originally formu-
lated by L.V. Koos and Thomas H. Briggs in 1920, are
no longer valid. The ideas were revised and restated
as functions in 1947 by William T. Gruhn and Harl R.
Douglass. By making the ninth grade part of the
junior high, this would reduce dropouts. When this
was proposed in the 1920s, large numbers of boys and
girls were quitting school at the end of eighth
grade. The dropout problem is no longer as crucial.
The 7-9 junior high, although it has differentiated
its curriculum to assist the potential dropout, no
longer has a distinctly specific role which would
justify a ninth grade being part of an intermediate
union. Besides that, vocational education was one of
the original tasks of the 7-8-9 junior high school.
One of the original dreams of the 7-8-9 junior high
unit was that its existence would enable guidance
services to be extended to a lower age group. This
function is no longer valid for the 7-8-9 junior high
or for secondary schools. Although one of the continuing functions of the 7-8-9 junior high school is
helping the young person understand himself and
develop his powers and his personality during the
difficult years of adolescence, one recent study has
found that basic developmental tasks such as learning
an appropriate sex role, achieving emotional independence of parents and other adults, and getting along
with age mates are accomplished by the age of 13. 2)
Many 7-8-9 junior high schools have become JUNIOR
high schools lacking a sound philosophical basis.
Many 7-8-9 junior high schools are finding their
place in the educational design by becoming JUNIOR
high schools literally. 3) Growth and research
studies by Stewart, Melony, Jones, and Harris support
placing ninth graders in the senior high school.

1031.   Buell, C. E.   "What grades in the junior high
school?"   Bulletin of the National Association of
Junior High School Principals, 46(1962):14-22.

Gives some excellent arguments for continuing the
organizational pattern of 6-3-3 in urban areas and
the 6-6 pattern in rural and small urban areas.

1032.   Bulletin of the National Association of Secondary
School Principals.   "What do we believe about grades
to be included, desirable size, appropriate loca-
tions, and the facilities for junior high schools?"
Bulletin of the National Association of Secondary
School Principals, October 1962:5-7.

The three-year junior high school, grades 7, 8, and
9, provides a desirable, separate environment for
young adolescents aged 12 to 15--a very special group
in terms of growth and development. About half of
the entering seventh grade pupils are adolescents,

about two thirds of the girls and one third of the
boys. As the school term progresses, more and more
of these pupils will enter adolescence. The junior
high school provides a separate school organization
for the young adolescent and separates him from the
younger pupils as well as from the more sophisticated
actions of the senior high school student. On the
other hand, grade 6 should remain in the elementary
school because the majority of the pupils in this
grade are not adolescents. In grade 9 the great
majority of the pupils are adolescents while a few
are still children by nature. The senior high school
is not designed for the pupil who is still in this
period of transition from childhood. An important
function of the junior high school is to develop
social qualities and leadership in pupils. The
junior high school provides more adequate guidance
facilities and is staffed with teachers with subject
matter specialties who have a comprehension and
understanding of the young adolescent. The junior
high school should be a neighborhood-type school,
centrally located relative to feeder elementary
schools. The junior high school is a unique school
for unique pupils who differ from each other in
height, weight, rate of growth, development of
internal organs, sexual and social maturity, academic
skills and interests; and they are changing rapidly
in all these areas. The early adolescents seek to
belong and conform to their peer group and to withdraw from adults. They have some special fears and
problems. At the same time they are idealists; they
are concerned about ideals and ethical concepts; and
they are eager for social service. Putting all of
these items together, it is most important that there
be a particular school--the junior high school--
available for boys and girls in grades 7, 8, and 9.

1033. California State Department of Education. Handbook
for California Junior High Schools. Sacramento,
Calif., 1949.

California junior high school administrators reformu-
lated the imperative needs for youth at the junior
high school level. All junior high school youth need
1) to explore their own aptitudes and to have experiences basic to occupational proficiency, 2) to
develop and maintain abundant physical and mental
health, 3) to be participating citizens of their
school and community, with increasing orientation to
adult citizenship, 4) experiences and understanding
appropriate to their age and development, which are
the foundations of successful home and family life,
5) to develop a sense of values of material things
and of the right of ownership, 6) to learn about the
natural and physical environment and its effects on

life and to have opportunities for using the scientific approach in the solution of problems, 7) the enriched living which comes from appreciation of and expression in the arts and from experiencing the beauty and wonder of the world around them, 8) to have a variety of socially acceptable and personally satisfying leisure time experiences which contribute either to their personal growth or to their development in wholesome group relations, or to both, 9) experiences in group living which contribute to the personality and character development; they need to develop respect for other persons and their right to grow in ethical insights, and 10) to grow in their ability to observe, listen, read, think, speak, and write with purpose and appreciation.

1034.   Canadian Teachers' Federation. "Junior High and Middle Schools." Bibliographies in Education, no. 50. Ottawa, Ontario: ERIC Doc. ED 105 607, February, 1975.

Bibliography of books, articles, theses and dissertations.   Sources include the Cumulative Book Index, the Current Index to Journals in Education, the Education Index, the Directory of Education Studies in Canada, Research in Education, Research Studies in Education, the Subject Guide to Books in Print, and the Subject Guide to Canadian Books in Print.   See ERIC Abstract #ED 105 607.

1035.   Cantlon, R. J.   "A Current Interpretation of the Functions of the Junior High School Derived from Historical and Developmental Antecedents."   Dissertation, University of Colorado, 1968.

Integration as a function of the junior high school is that endeavor which makes possible the pupil's understanding of the ways that elements of his environment and his being are, or may be, interrelated, and which develop competence in processes required for: the explanation of phenomena which he perceives, the interpretation of one's own behavior and values, and appreciation for the plurality of intellectual approaches which may be used in the pursuit of problem solving.   Integrative activity, which is self-motivating, should help the pupil perceive that each learning experience contributes toward a new and satisfying unity of knowledge, such unity emanating from and contributing to the dynamism of his personal growth and to his interaction with his environment.   Integration should be inherent with the organization of the curriculum, planning for instruction, and teacher/pupil interaction.   Integration may be inferred from the pupil's striving for a more meaningful organization of experience, his

attainment of individual objectives, and the satisfaction which he derives from the attainment of such
goals.

1036.   Caplan, G. (Ed.).   Prevention of Mental Disorders
in Children: Initial Explorations.   New York: Basic
Books, 1961.

Chapter 16 entitled "Primary Prevention in a School
Setting" by Eli M. Bower includes sections on the
school as a social institution: education as primary
prevention, resistive factors in school and community, culture conflicts in prevention, the concept
of primary prevention, and difficulties of preventive
action in the school.   A second section outlines a
research program and primary prevention: research
beginnings, mental health indexes, research findings,
present research, program possibilities and primary
prevention, use of the index of relatability, alienation by teachers, consultation to teachers by mental
health specialists, parent-group counseling, and
child care contact.   The author finds it surprising
that at no point in the formal education of adolescents are there planned educational experiences aimed
specifically at helping one understand the basic
rudiments of human behavior.   The opportunity of
close alliances of middle grade and junior high
children with nursery, and child-care programs can be
developed into profitable experiences for both the
school and nursery children.   Girls who have failed
in other school enterprises and future mothers and
fathers experience the behavior of children and
relate their thoughts and feelings about themselves
in a socially acceptable, individually helpful
manner.

1037.   Cardellichio, T. C. "The school in the middle is
not an accordion." English Journal, 66,4(1977):38-41.

Article asks these questions: Do students of middle
school and junior high school age have unique educational needs?   At what point or ages are these needs
manifested?   What programs are necessary to meet the
needs of children at this age?   Author shows how a
middle school program must be developed.   His intent
is not to develop a comprehensive program, but rather
to sketch the way educators must progress if they are
going to have middle and junior high schools which
are founded on a solid educational base.   He believes
that a school which is rooted in a conceptual framework will be less susceptible to administrative and
political tampering.   Author hopes that a school will
stress that a middle and junior high school child
with particular needs will have a unique type of
educational program carefully analyzed to fit the
special requirements of the child.   So designed, the

program can prove to have intrinsic worth and necessity.

1038.   Carefoot, J. "The Middle School." Research paper prepared by the Mid-Continent Regional Educational Laboratory at the request of the Lincoln Catholic Diocese for the MCREL Lincoln Area Center Lincoln, Nebr., 1967.

The advantages of a junior high school, a 6-3-3 over the 5-3-4, include: 1) The most salient and compelling advantage is logistics. More communities have junior high schools than they have or are contemplating middle schools. 2) Closely related is the question of economy. A complete switch to middle schools involves building new schools. Existing arrangements may be converted, but this is most likely to prove unsatisfactory. Ideal arrangements for a middle school are found in Saginaw, Michigan, and Amory, Mississippi. 3) Grade organization is important and clearly defines the junior high. Proponents of a middle school criticize the junior high: 1) Junior highs are thought to be out-moded. 2) The emphasis is on preparation for senior high school. 3) The junior high school tends to be dominated by the ninth grade. 4) Junior high school has taken the teaching cast-offs from the elementary and senior high schools. 5) The junior high school, like the senior high, frequently develops a star system, that is, an elite or superior group of pupils who become the core of the junior high. 6) The junior high tends to precipitate adolescent behavior.

1039.   Carlson, R. "Stability and change in the adolescent's self-image." Child Development, 36(1965): 659-666.

A longitudinal study of the self-image of forty-nine students in the sixth grade and again as high school seniors. Self and ideal self descriptions obtained on parallel forms (preadolescent and adolescent) of a questionnaire designed to control several response sets provided measures of self-esteem and social and personal orientation. Over the six-year period, as predicted, girls showed an increase in social orientation while boys increased in personal orientation, reflecting the different processes of personality development for adolescent boys and girls. Self-esteem, however, was independent of sex role. Adolescents low in self-esteem more frequently characterized others in terms of personal reference and/or derogatory attitudes on the role construct repertory tests.

1040.   Center for Early Adolescence.   "Learning Environments: Selected Readings."   University of North
Carolina, Suite 223, Carr Mill Mall, Carrboro, N. C.
27510, 1979.

Bibliography discusses how a healthy learning environment helps communication, access to information
and experimentation, and intentionally respects human
needs while it defines, limits, directs and expands
behavioral choices.   Includes newsletters, monographs, articles, and books.

1041.   Center for Early Adolescence.   "General Reading on
Early Adolescence."   University of North Carolina,
Suite 223, Carr Mill Mall, Carrboro, N. C. 27510,
1980.

Sources include articles, books, government documents, and pamphlets.

1042.   Center for Early Adolescence.   "Community Services
for Young Adolescents."   University of North
Carolina, Suite 223, Carr Mill Mall, Carrboro, N. C.
27510, 1980.

Helpful readings for developing philosophy and
setting policy along with programs that provide ideas
or are models that can be adapted to meet needs of
young adolescents and their families.   Resources for
training, technical assistance, and materials are
included.

1043.   Chall, J. S. and Mirsky, A. F. (Eds.).   Education
and the Brain.   77th Yearbook of the National Society
for the Study of Education, Part II.   Chicago: University of Chicago Press, 1978.

Program permits early identification, forecasting,
and remediation of educational difficulties and
should help develop a teaching effort and program
designed on each child's growth and maturity, talents
and weaknesses, and not on the basis of average
values that fit any single pupil.   Chapter 10--
"Growth Spurts During Brain Development: Implications for Educational Policy and Practice" by Herman
T. Epstein--includes an introduction, stages in
intellectual development, brain growth and mental
growth from birth to maturity, perturbations of brain
and mind development, implications of phrenoblysis
and further comments.   Study this chapter in relationship to schooling for the early years of adolescence (pp. 343-370).   Chapter 11 by Chall and Mirsky
discusses the implications for education.   They
identify and comment briefly on those themes that
emerge from the information given in the book, the
empirical findings, the provocative hypotheses and

theories, and the implications contained in the chapters for education.

1044.   Clarke, H. H. and Clarke, D. H. "Social status and mental health of boys as related to their maturity, structural, and strength characteristics." Research Quarterly of the American Association of Health, Physical Education and Recreation, 32(1961): 326-334.

Authors studied personal and social adjustment of boys 9 to 14 years old by using a sociometric questionnaire and an inventory-tape instrument: The Mental Health Analysis. The experimental variables consisted of skeletal age, various anthropometric tests, and selected strength test formulas and batteries. When the sociometric questionnaire was used, positive relationships between peer status and body size and muscular strength were found. However, when the inventory-type instrument was used, the results were conflicting.

1045.   Clear Creek Independent School District. "A Plan for Reorganization of the Clear Creek Schools." League City, Tex., 1965.

Calls for a school-within-a-school organization. Because the school district found it undesirable for ninth graders to be closely associated with more mature eleventh and twelfth graders, the administrative staff recommended a four-year high school, but with arrangements for appropriate distinctions to separate ninth and tenth graders from eleventh and twelfth graders.

1046.   Coe, T. R. "What grades should constitute the junior high school?" American School Board Journal, 112(1946):42.

Presents arguments for certain grade groupings with special consideration for systems in the state of Washington.

1047.   Cole, L. Psychology of Adolescence. 4th ed. New York: Rhinehart, 1954.

Contains these sections: 1) Physical Development. 2) Emotional Development. 3) Social Development. 4) Moral Development. 5) Intellectual Development. Of special interest are Chapter 8, Emotions in the School, and Chapter 12, The Social Life of the School. Chapter 8 includes sections on the teacher: 1) the teacher's personality, 2) the rating of teachers, 3) control of the class, 4) discipline and punishment, 5) emotional involvements and a section on mental hygiene: a) fears caused by schoolwork, b) discrimination, c) the problems of boys and girls, d) provisions for emotional outlets, e) instruction in mental hygiene, and f) recognition of maladjustment. Chapter 12 deals with the social life of the class: 1) social anatomy of the classroom, 2) use of sociograms, and 3) relation of teacher to class. Chapter 12 also deals with the cocurricular program: 1) nature and type of activity, 2) distribution of cocurricular activities, and 3) the non-academic program.

1048.   Coleman, J. S. "The competition for adolescent energies." Phi Delta Kappan, 42(1961):231-235.

The primacy of the school can no longer be taken for granted, and formal education must take its place alongside the other activities which compete for an adolescent's energy. Adolescent energies can be successfully captured for learning if those responsible for the program will plan it that way. The adolescent no longer faces the barriers of illiteracy, inarticulateness, and inability to comprehend which focused his energies and forced him to learn as a child. These fundamental hurdles overcome, his energies may spread themselves in directions our affluent society pulls. The article presents sections on The Limbo We Call Adolescence, The Importance of Athletics, "Right" Crowd, Energy Goes in Jockeying for Status, Parents Make School a Social Cosmos, and Some Alternative Solutions.

1049.   Coleman, J. S. "Social change: impact on the adolescent." Bulletin of the National Association of Secondary School Principals, 49,300(1965):11-14.

A number of changes have combined to make the family a less cohesive, less effective agent within which to raise children. These include large numbers of women entering the labor force, fewer families that have relatives--aunts, uncles, grandparents--living in the household, greater geographic mobility of families, and the shift of the father's work in the home or neighborhood to a distant office or factory. The consequences of weakened family ties are increased going steady among adolescents and earlier age of dating and interest in the opposite sex. Shifts of adolescent values derive only in part from weakened family ties. Changes in society bring about early social sophistication among adolescents. Urban and suburban living, television and other mass media, the money they now have to spend, their better educated parents, and the school itself have made adolescents more wise in the ways of the world. Of all the recent changes in adolescents, this early desire for sophistication poses perhaps the greatest problem and the greatest challenge for secondary schools.

Teenagers are less willing to respond to the junior
or senior high school teacher just because he is a
teacher. They are more responsive if their imagination is captured, more able and willing to respond to
a real challenge. The school's task is more difficult, for it cannot take the adolescent's interest
for granted; it must find new ways of capturing this
interest and energy. It has no other alternative but
to accept these more sophisticated adolescents and
turn their sophistication to the advantage of
education.

1050.   Coleman, J. S. "The children have outgrown the
schools." Psychology Today, February 1972:72-82.

Discusses the elements of change in our society's
communication structure related to information
richness but not a necessary consequence of it. New
institutions must resist the temptation to direct
themselves mainly to teaching the child so they can
fruitfully redirect their goals. One of these goals
must be the development of strategies for coping with
an information rich and institutionally complex
society; another must be the use of external activities where children are not students but contributors
to a larger enterprise.

1051.   Commission on the Reorganization of Secondary
Education. "Cardinal principles of secondary education." U. S. Bureau of Education Bulletin, 35(1918):
12-13.

The highly influential report of the Commission on
the Reorganization of Secondary Education in 1918 set
forth the famous Cardinal Principles of Secondary
Education: We recommend a reorganization of the
school system whereby the first six years should be
devoted to elementary education designed to meet the
needs of pupils approximately 6 to 12 years of age;
and the second six years to be secondary education
designed to meet the needs of pupils approximately
12 to 18 years of age.   The six years to be devoted
to secondary education may well be divided into two
periods which may be designed as a junior and senior
period.   In the junior period, emphasis should be
placed on the attempt to help the pupil explore his
own aptitudes and make at least provisional choice of
the kinds of work to which he shall devote himself.
In the senior period, emphasis should be given to
training in the fields thus chosen.   This distinction
lies at the basis of the organization of the junior
and senior high schools.   In the junior high school
there should be a gradual introduction of departmental instruction, some choice of subjects under
guidance, promotion by subject, pre-vocational
courses, and a social organization that calls for

initiative and develops a sense of personal responsibility for the welfare of the group."

1052.   Committee on Adolescence, Group for the Advancement of Psychiatry. Normal Adolescence: Its Dynamics and Impact. Vol. 6, pp. 799-816. Publications
Office, Group for the Advancement of Psychiatry, 419
Park Avenue, South, New York 10016, February 1968.

In early adolescence those features of behavior characteristics of preadolescence are still in evidence
and even more marked. The increased activity,
increased aggressiveness, decreased dependence upon
the adult (especially parental) world, and the
greater scope of social interaction continue to mount
with no sharp demarcation between preadolescence and
adolescence. Sections include the impact of puberty,
the move toward independence, the peer group, mastur-
bation, menstruation, the new body and self-image,
action and impulsive behavior, the capacity for
thought, boy-girl relationships, and the resolution
of early adolescence. The major characteristics of
early adolescent development are as follows: 1)
Rebellion against and withdrawal from adults and
their values. Initially the rebellion is mainly
verbal, but it becomes more action oriented as
adolescence progresses. The detachment from parents
is impelled by guilt over the oedipal fantasies
reawakened now in the threatening context of near-
adult capability for sexual and aggressive behavior
and by the need to discover individual identity,
which is felt to be jeopardized by too close an
attachment to the adult with his strongly established
identity. The need for guidance from adults and for
adult models for identification persists, but attachment even to adults other than the parent usually is
transitory. 2) Intense narcissism, with a strong
preoccupation with one's own body and self. 3) The
peer group is of vital importance, serving as a way
station during the transition from childhood to
adulthood. 4) Sexual urges and feelings become
intense and gain expression, at first in fantasies
and then in masturbatory and other sexual activities
as the adolescent moves into beginning heterosexual
relationships. 5) Marked increase in aggressive
urges, now supported by a corresponding increase in
physical size and strength. 6) Marked increase in
emotional and intellectual capabilities with a
parallel broadening of interests and activities. 7)
Attitudes and behavior in general are characterized
by unpredictable changes and much experimentation.

1053.   Compton, M. "The middle school: alternative to
the status quo." Theory Into Practice, 7(1968):
108-110.

Reasons why a middle school is favored over the adoption of a junior high school.

1054.   Conant, J. B.   A Memorandum to School Boards: Recommendations for Education in the Junior High School Years.   Princeton, N. J.:   Educational Testing Service, 1960.

Fourteen recommendations from visits to 237 schools in twenty-three states.   Because of wide diversity in school organization and professional disagreement, the place of grades 7, 8, and 9 in the organization of a school system is of less importance than the program provided for adolescent youth.

1055.   Constant, G. A.   "Adolescence: Its perspective and problems."   Journal of the Mississippi State Medical Association, 4(1963):16-18.

Ignored for generations, adolescent medicine has drawn concentrated interest since the mid-1950s.   In this paper presented to general practitioners, the author says the family physician is in the best position to take care of the adolescent.   Author discusses the physician's role in solving problems peculiar to the adolescent.

1056.   Cook, D. H. "The three R's of socialization in the middle school."   Middle School Journal,   11,2(1980): 10-11.

Any worthwhile learning experience must recognize the differing levels of mastery attainment which exist among early adolescents.   From a procedural stand-point, the middle school must promote continuous, positive, social development through a program focus-ing on three components: restoration, renewal, and reinforcement.   Sections on each of these three areas conclude that social skills must be learned by the individual and can be done so in a school setting. The middle school must create an educational environ-ment conducive to the progressive development of social skills by the emerging adolescent.

1057.   Coppock, N. and Hale, N.   "Middle Schools."   ACSA School Management Digest, series 1, no. 4, 1977. Association of California School Administrators. Also ERIC/CEM Research Analysis Series, no. 31. Eugene: University of Oregon, ERIC Clearinghouse on Educational Management, ERIC Doc. ED 137 896, 1977.

Booklet contains sections on The Middle School Pupil, Historical Roots and Present Trends, History of Intermediate Education, Patterns of Organization, A Slowing Trend, The Middle School Philosophy, Student Growth Characteristics, Reforming the Junior High

School, A Synthesis of Programs, The Middle School
Program, Curricular Theory, Curricular Practices, The
Middle School Staff: Need for Special Training,
Teachers, Principals, Counselors, Conclusion,
Bibliography.

1058.   Corbally, J. E., Jensen, J. T., and Staub, F.
Educational Administration: Secondary School. Boston:
Allyn and Bacon, 1961.

Since biblical times man has recognized the "turning
point" that comes at early adolescence. Psychologists and physiologists have supplied us with
evidence of the nature of this change. Sociologists
have described the cultural change that takes place
at the junior high school age. This growth process
is continuous, but there are certain modal points
readily recognized.

1059.   Croft Educational Services. "The Case for the
Middle School." Public relations supplement to
monthly newsletter, For School Board Members. New
London, Conn., 1967.

Historically, the junior high appeared in 1896 when
Indiana switched from 8-4 to a 6-2-4 plan. Columbus,
Ohio, generally gets credit for purposefully revising
both structure and curriculum to create an intermediate school designed to meet the special problems
of preadolescents in 1909. In 1918, the junior high
idea won endorsement of the highly influential Commission on the Reorganization of Secondary Education.
In a historic statement on the "Cardinal Principles
of Secondary Education" the Commission said the six
years to be devoted to secondary education may well
be divided into two periods which may be designated
as the junior and senior periods. The most common
organization is 6-3-3 but variations include 6-2-2-2,
5-3-4, 7-5, 7-2-3, and 6-6. Reasons for keeping the
ninth grade with the senior high school include: 1)
The permanent academic record consists mainly of the
school work in grades 9 through 12. 2) The ninth
grader of 1967 has much more in common with senior
high school students than with the seventh or eighth
graders of the typical junior high school. 3) In the
academic program, a distinct break occurs after grade
8, even in a 7-9 junior high school. In almost every
school, no matter how organized, true secondary
education begins in grade 9. 4) Accrediting programs
affect only ninth grade and above, not grades 7 and
8. 5) Within any one junior high class, there is apt
to be an age spread of almost one year. This means
that the full age range in grades 7 to 9 is quite
likely to be from 11 to 15. 6) Physical maturity in
the typical junior high school is wide ranging. The
more this range is narrowed, as in the middle school,

the better the education all the pupils will receive.
7) Some critics say that instead of the one gap
inherent in the 8-4 plan, the junior high school
creates two gaps. Emotional changes--sometimes
violent--can take place in the child when he enters
the junior high and, again, when he enters the senior
high. 8) Credit requirements set by state officials
and colleges have become so rigid that many junior
high schools are geared primarily toward transforming
intermediate children into slavish scholars by the
time they reach grade 9. Many junior highs have
become places where young children are lectured to,
given large doses of homework, and expected to learn
masses of material. 9) Whether a school district has
a junior high is often determined by the kind and
amount of space available.

1060.   Crow, L. D.   "Teenage traits, interests, and
worries." Educational Forum, 20(1956):423-428.

In a study of early adolescent boy-girl relationships, Crow stressed physical growth changes as
determinants of certain attitudes held by girls
toward group membership and pointed out that it is
folly to try to build an effective school system
while ignoring the physical and emotional differences
between early and late adolescents.

1061.   Curtis, T. E. "Crucial times for the junior high
school." New York State Education, 53(1966):14-15.

Functions, principles, and philosophies which are
accepted by a strong majority of educators, principals, and teachers have not entirely succeeded
because of certain structural inadequacies in the
educational system. With the advent of the middle
school movement, a second opportunity has come to
those interested in the education of youngsters of
this age. It may now be possible to seize the
initiative in the achievement of objectives which
have been the goals of educators for years, and
which, with the inception of the experimentally
minded middle school, have become a practical
possibility rather than philosophical statements
impossible to achieve in the traditional junior high
school. The primary differences between the middle
school and the junior high school might not be in the
administrative changes and the implications inherent
in them but rather in the attitude with which these
changes are approached. At last, the philosophy of
the education for early adolescents can possibly be
implemented through a transitional school with an
experimental orientation: the middle school.

1062.   Curtis, T. E. "Middle school: the school of the
future." Education, 88(1968):228-231.

Educational theorists question the increase in numbers of middle schools springing up throughout the country. The middle school, grades 6-8, being an evolution from the junior high school, requires of all interested in American education a serious and dispassionate consideration of the purposes of education for early adolescents and how these purposes may best be achieved. If grades 6-8 can be presumed to be a more valid ideal instructional and curriculum pattern because of the deletion of the Carnegie Unit with its college preparatory connotations, and emphasis on the traditional aspects along with experimental approaches to early adolescent education in the middle school, then increased attention will be given to this new grade arrangement. Intense interest is being displayed in various areas of the country, particularly in New York, Ohio, Michigan, and Texas. Educational theorists, administrators, teachers, and laymen should continue to observe objectively the development of this new grade arrangement to determine if the middle school may well become the school of the future.

1063.   Darien Public Schools. "Toward the Middle School: A Position Paper." Darien, Conn., 1968.

Presents an historical perspective of the junior high and middle school; the study committee looks into the middle school, gives a philosophical statement and advantages and objectives of the middle school with grades 6, 7, and 8.

1064.   Darling, G. "The changing junior high: an urgency in education." Minnesota Journal of Education, 47(1966):10-12.

Supports the idea of a middle school rather than the traditional junior high.

1065.   Davis, R. B. "The Madison project's approach to a theory of instruction." Journal of Research in Science Teaching, 2(1964):146-162.

The methods of the traditional school and the objectives of the materials are normally at war with one another. The author thinks the new middle school conflict points to a hopeful direction in resolving the war, it is precisely at this age level that the war is most accute. The experiences should be appropriate to the age of the child. This sounds like a truism, but in ordinary education seems honored mainly by noncompliance. Fifth graders (about 10 years old) are natural intellectuals and can enjoy choosing a set of algebraic axioms, including a variety of algebraic theorems from them. (This topic was formally encountered in college or in graduate school.) By contrast, seventh and eighth graders are not intellectuals; they are engineers at heart. For them the usual school regime of sitting at desks, reading, writing, and reciting seems to ignore the basic nature of the child at this age. He wants to move around physically to do things, to explore, to take chances, to build things. The importance of this question should not be overlooked. Neither the author nor most of his contacts with psychologists attach much special importance to the fifth-sixth-eighth-grade developmental pattern. Yet, for virtually every one of the "new curriculum" projects in mathematics and science which deal experimentally with this age range, this is the single decisive, elusive, and discouraging phenomenon. The fifth grader is very good at mathematics and science. The same child at grade 6, begins to perform less well. In grades 7 and 8 he is usually a total loss--he will perform routine tasks to a mediocre standard, but in situations calling for greater creativity, he usually creates chaos. Alternative explanations from psychoanalysts, teachers, physiologists, and parents include: 1) the sex theory, 2) the energy theory, 3) the metabolic theory, 4) the noise theory, 5) the nobody loves junior high school theory, 6) the pure group theory, 7) the neo-Pareto theory, 8) the finding yourself theory, 9) the finding reality theory, and 10) the poor self-concept of the junior high teacher theory.

1066.   DesJarlais, L., et al. Needs and Characteristics of Students in the Intermediate Years, Aged 12 to 16. A Comprehensive Review of the Literature 1930-1974 with Recommendations for Educational Practice. Faculty of Education, Ottawa University, Ottawa, Ontario. Toronto: Ontario Department of Education, 1975.

Authors present a synthesis of information based on quality research studies concerning the physical, intellectual, social and emotional characteristics of intermediate adolescents. They provide material to bring teachers greater awareness of the necessity for implementing educational processes compatible with the needs and characteristics of early adolescents. Document serves as a reliable basis for decision-making relative to educational programs intended for the intermediate division. Chapter on the Overview of Adolescent Growth and Development includes: 1) the meaning of adolescence, 2) theories and other important points of view, 3) goals of adolescence, 4) psychological consequences of biological change, 5) psychological effect of physiological changes, 6) psychological effect of changes in cognitive functioning, and 7) the need for curriculum reform based on knowledge of adolescence. Chapter 2--Growth in

Other Physiological Levels and Events in Adolescents:
1) introduction, 2) growth in adolescents, 3) other
physiological levels and events, 4) childbearing in
adolescence, 5) biorhythmicity of consciousness, and
6) summary of educational implication. The third
chapter--Early Adolescent Cognitive Functioning in
Intellectual Growth: 1) introduction, 2) quantitative aspects of cognitive development during early
adolescence, 3) qualitative aspects of cognitive
functioning during early adolescence, and 4) impact
of percepto-cognitive styles on adolescent cognitive
functioning. Chapter 4--Empirical Base for the Emotional and Social Development of Normal Adolescents:
1) general introduction, 2) emotional development,
and 3) social development. A bibliography is
included. Schools should be acutely aware of the
needs and characteristics of emerging adolescents.
The early adolescent's intellect is undergoing pro-
found and lasting changes from ages 12 to 16 and
unless educators understand some of the dynamics and
expressions of the evolution of the adolescent's
intellect and are successful in confronting him with
a well-planned challenge, only miseducation can take
place.

1067.   DiVirgilio, J.   "Switching from junior high to
middle school?" Clearinghouse, 44(1969):224-226.

Outlines five considerations for any district seriously contemplating the change from junior high to
middle school: 1) Coordinator-Supervisor should be
chosen to serve as a continuing consultant. This
position can be gradually phased out once the school
has been established and seems to be developing into
a true middle school.   2) Budget should be established that permits the coordinator and other personnel to: a) purchase new and varied materials and
supplies, b) hire outside consultants, c) develop in-
service programs, d) travel to other middle schools,
e) increase teacher ratio or paraprofessionals if
needed.   3) Facility changes need not be done in advance of the opening of the middle school. It should
be the result of a thorough study by middle school
teachers and administrators working with the advice
of architects.   4) Internal organization changes
should start with cooperative teaching and evolve
toward team teaching by including a) teachers who are
specialists in their disciplines, b) reading teachers
who have graduate work in reading, c) special area
teachers, d) guidance personnel trained to understand
the preadolescent and who can help teachers become
aware of the sociological and emotional needs of
children, and e) media specialists.   5) Negative pre-
cautions: a) no interscholastic athletics, b) no
marching bands, c) no night activities, d) no formal
dances, e) no published honor rolls, f) no final

exams, and g) no formal club programs. Instead a
middle school should have a special interest program
developed around student interests which encourages
students to move from activity to activity.

1068.   Drash, A. "Variations in pubertal development and
the school system: A problem and a challenge."
Transescence: The Journal of Emerging Adolescent Education, 4(1976):14-26.

The professional who spends a significant amount of
time working with adolescents is aware of many characteristics that are relatively unique or are of
special importance to this age group.   Success in
relating to the adolescent, whether it be in the area
of education, athletic activity, counseling or health
supervision, is dependent, at least in part, on an
understanding of the physical and emotional changes
that characterize the transition from childhood to
full physical maturity.   The purposes of this article
are: 1) to review the factors involved in the
control of physical growth and sexual maturation,
including the variability in normal rates of progression, 2) to provide information regarding techniques
available for grading levels of sexual maturation, 3)
to identify those extremes of the maturational process which should lead to medical supervision, and 4)
to discuss possible application of this information
in the educational setting.   School personnel working
in junior high schools and middle schools, and to a
lesser extent high schools, are confronted daily with
students in the same classroom who may vary from preadolescent to fully developed and sexually mature.
Differences of six to eight inches in height and
forty to sixty pounds are common.   The physical variability is further confounded by remarkable differences in emotional maturity, attentiveness, interests, and intellectual ability.   One might ask
whether this extraordinary variability makes a difference and if anything can be done.   Studies stress
the importance of maturational level on the development of personality characteristics during adolescence and the persistence of these characteristics
into adult life.   The problems of variability in rate
of growth and sexual maturation are most dramatically
accentuated in athletics.   The development of school
teams, based on age and grade placement, almost
invariably means the small, later maturer is quickly
relegated to non-competitive status.

1069.   Eckstein, W. "Ninth graders: where do you put
them?" Clearinghouse, 48,9(1974):519-523.

Based on the single criterion of student achievement,
studies emphasize that it does not really matter
where ninth graders attend.   If we can accept this as

a fact, then we can determine their environmental placement by other factors such as overcrowded buildings, class size and availability of finances. Put ninth graders wherever it is expedient and work towards the goal of providing them with the best education possible. Having done this, educators can rest assured that students will not suffer academically. Author cites various educators with different opinions and does not feel the problem is severe.

1070.   Eichhorn, D. H.   "Rationale for Emergence: A Look at the Middle School." Paper presented at the Conference on the Middle School: Rationale and Development, University of Pittsburgh, ERIC Doc. ED 017 977, December 11, 1967.

The existing organizational structure of our educational system is inadequate for 10-to-14-year-olds who are experiencing extensive physical, emotional and cognitive changes. It is necessary to adopt the middle school design to meet the emerging needs of the child. The author discusses the question: Is the middle school merely another regrouping of grades in what appears to be an endless series of stratagems or is the middle school a concept involving substance and fundamental purpose?   The paper analyzes certain basic assumptions that can be investigated in light of current knowledge providing some basis for a middle school rationale. 1) Youngsters in the 10-to-14-year age group constitute a distinct stage of development involving similar physical, emotional and mental characteristics.   2) In 1967 students age 10 to 14 possess growth characteristics which are significantly different from the growth characteristics of the same age students during the early decades of this century.   3) Societal forces suggest a new pattern of organization for the middle years.   4) Current and former organization models no longer adequately serve the transescent.

1071.   Eichorn, D. H.   "Variations in growth rate." Childhood Education, 44,5(1968):6.

Addresses these topics: 1) measurement of developmental rates from conception to adolescence--chronological age becomes a progressively poor predictor of a child's size, shape, and behavior; increasing differences with age and developmental status hence the concept of rate of maturing, 2) skeletal age, 3) mental age, 4) correlation, 5) girls maturing earlier than boys, 6) accelerated rate of maturation in succeeding generations, 7) preadolescence and adolescence, 8) problems of variations in maturation rates a) during the junior and senior high school period, groups of youths of the same chronological age will usually have a range of at least six years in maturational age, and b) the secular trend of greater maturity of children for a given age was typical for adults who supervise them.

1072. Eichhorn, D. H. "Middle School: Promise of the Future." Paper presented at Southeast Missouri State College, ERIC Doc. ED 033 4444, March 13, 1969.

Article contains sections on the various facets of the middle school program including environment, analytical, personal dynamics, self-expression, student grouping, activity programs, scheduling, and guidance. The paper is based on the premise that a separate maturation level exists for youngsters in the middle school demonstrated through research data that middle school youth possess similar physical, social, mental, and emotional characteristics.

1073. Eichhorn, D. H. "The Controversy of the Middle School." Forum address presented at the National Conference of the Association for Supervision and Curriculum Development, Chicago, ERIC Doc. ED 033 481, March 17, 1969.

Author makes two assumptions: 1) The philosophy of the middle and/or the junior high school which states that school bridges the elementary and high school levels has been organizationally accepted by American education. 2) The uniqueness of the youngster aged 10 to 14 has not been accepted as a basic concept for program development. Author discusses student grouping and climate for instruction. He feels that the differences in maturation rates for children of this age necessitates the development of programs for the middle school which differ from elementary and high school approaches. He discusses the rate of student growth both mentally and physically, socially and emotionally. He states that a flexible school can be encouraged by staff attitudes that permit consider- able freedom of action to youngsters and also by flexible scheduling.

1074. Eichhorn, D. H. "Middle school: the beauty of diversity." Middle School Journal, 8(1977):1.

Article gives students' impressions of the middle school and outlines the challenges ahead: 1) to keep the movement dynamic, 2) to develop schools which excite and inspire, 3) to create instructional pro- grams which expect students to learn and curriculum which challenges their intellect, 4) to broaden the base of knowledge regarding physical characteristics of middle school students, and 5) to focus on the transescent as the foundation. The author puts the middle school student into perspective by suggesting that educators consider the middle school journey

further, that educators need the courage and vision
to start with the characteristics of students to
develop programs. The student, rather than the organization, is unique in middle schools and classrooms,
and schools should be judged by how effectively they
mesh with what students are like.

1075.   Elkind, D.   Children in Adolescence: Interpreta-
tive Essays on Jean Piaget.   New York: Oxford University Press, 1970.

Essays at three levels of difficulty include popular
pieces directed toward a lay audience to provide a
general introduction to Piaget's work and its significance for modern thinking about child development.
More advanced essays relate Piaget's work in education to educators such as Montessori.   Psychological
studies attempt to relate certain Piagetian concepts
such as egocentrism to personality.   Throughout, the
aim of the essays is not merely to summarize Piaget's
work, but rather to relate that work to well-known
concepts in this country.

1076.   Elkind, D.   A Sympathetic Understanding of a Child
6 to 16.   Boston: Allyn and Bacon, 1971.

Introduction on observing classroom groups, observing
pupil roles, and observing the individual child.
Part 1--The Child: facets of growth and development,
sociocultural change, general characteristics of middle and late childhood, the world of self, home, and
community, the child in relation to adults, adults in
relation to children, parent-child contrasts, the
development of mental abilities, the growth of knowledge, and age profiles of the 6-to-11-year-old.   Part
2--The Adolescent: facets of growth and development,
sociocultural change, general characteristics, the
world of self, home, and community, adolescents in
relation to adults, adults in relation to adolescents, mental development, and age profiles of the
12-to-16-year-old.   Also includes an annotated bibliography.   Sample age profiles follow.   Age 9:   a
refinement of behaviors exhibited at age 8, gives the
impression of steadfastness and responsibility that
will be the benchmarks of later maturity, an
increased awareness of sex and sex appropriate behaviors, tendency to organize and budget time, parental
relationships are friendly and accommodating, begins
strengthening close friendships with peers, academic
achievement is of prime importance because it is the
major way in which he is evaluated.   Age 10:   girls
are slightly more advanced sexually than boys, fears
and anxieties are minimal, increasing interests in
parents, teachers, and peers, self-accepting, sex
differences in friendship patterns emerge, active
participation in organized group activities, likes

school and is a responsible student. Age 11: activity level shows a decisive increase, anxious for new experiences and curious about the world, quarrelsome, tends to be disciplined, seeds of independence from parental influence show, friendships are formed around mutual interests and temperament, more definite interests in the opposite sex. Age 12: outgoing, enthusiastic, generous, begins to assert that he is no longer a child, relate successfully to peers and adults, new competitiveness with parents, both in athletics and intellectual games, girls begin verbalizing their romantic interests in boys.

1077.   Elkind, D.   "Cognitive structure and experience in children and adolescents."   In Elkind, D. (Ed.), Children and Adolescents.   New York: Oxford University Press, 1974.

In their definitive work on adolescent thinking, Piaget and Inhelder pointed out some ways that adolescent thought differs from that of the child. The adolescent is capable of combinatorial logic and can deal with problems in which many factors operate at the same time. The adolescent has the ability to use a second symbol system: a set of symbols for symbols. Still a third characteristic of adolescent thinking is the capacity to construct ideals or contrary-to-fact situations and proceed with the argument as if the premise were correct. In addition to expanding the adolescent adaptive potential, these aspects of adolescent thinking pave the way for new experiences and reactions unknown to children.

1078.   Elliott, R. W.   "New problems in articulation." American School Board Journal, 142(1961):11.

Advocates a K-3-3-3-3 plan with a great deal of ungraded organization.   "Traditional grades from 1 to 12 may be abandoned. In their place there will be four areas of instruction, each embracing a three-year block."

1079.   Epstein, H. T.   "A neuroscience framework for restructuring middle school curricula."   Transescence: The Journal of Emerging Adolescent Education, 5(1977):6-11.

Author states there is already enough hard information about brain growth to inform new kinds of educational experimentation.   Shows that brain growth in humans takes place in stages.   Thus, the growing child is not to be thought of as being at some particular place in his developmental program which can be a little ahead or a little behind other children. A child who has not yet experienced a brain growth spurt at a particular age is qualitatively less capable of absorbing new kinds of intellectual inputs; he is a very different child from what he and others will be when they have experienced the next brain growth spurt. The author assumes that a different brain development is evidence for a qualitatively different mental development. He shows two ways that brain growth spurts are correlated with mental growth spurts. The author describes the first wave as biological and the second wave by analyzing the data in the literature to see if mental age measures increase steadily or in a stage-wise fashion. Based on hypotheses presented from the data, one would examine the performances of middle school students to see if such students are unable to acquire new intellectual skills. If so, the author suggests that the reason is biological because of connection with slow brain growth rather than with puberty. If the characterization is correct, curriculum should be altered to avoid the novelties and to include a much larger component of experience and practice of skills. Middle school children should be given massive doses of interaction with nature, society, and people; for example, remove children from school most of the week and put them to work in public service projects, nature reclamation projects, helping with old age homes, and day care centers. Retain schooling for a couple of days each week, but put emphasis on developing already initiated skills. Mathematics should be taught in terms of applications to human problems like filling out tax forms. History should be taught as a collection of dates, places, and names, thereby filling the mind with the factual data needed for creative human existence. Author would teach English as a tool of expression, omitting most of the literature study. Children of this age can profitably learn the facts of law, politics, and human relations.

1080.   Epstein, H. T. and Toepfer, C. F., Jr. "A neuroscience basis for reorganizing middle grades education." Educational Leadership, 36,8(1978):656-659.

Scientific findings strongly urge reappraisal of the traditional approaches to cognitive learning in the learning school years. While puberty is inevitable, there is a great variance in the time at which individuals experience this phase. School programs have not traditionally been responsive to the needs of individuals during puberty.

1081.   Espenschade, A. and Meleny, H. E. "Motor performance of boys and girls." Research Quarterly of the American Association of Health, Physical Education and Recreation, 32(1961):187.

Study compared youngsters in the same school in
1934-35 and again in 1958-59. Author found that
girls in the latter sample were one inch taller and
six pounds heavier and that the boys in the more
recent study were over two inches taller and ten
pounds heavier. The 1958-59 youngsters were superior
in the areas of jump and reach, the dynamometric
strength pull test and the boys excelled in throw for
distance, the brace test, and grip strength.

1082.   Farris, L. P. "Compensating values of a five-year
school."   California Journal of Secondary Education,
16(1941):470-72.

Lists objections to the six-year school and states
that 90 percent of the valid objections to the combined junior-senior high school are removed if the
seventh grade is not included.   Objects to the
association of immature with somewhat more mature
youth.   Also discusses advantages of a five-year
secondary school.

1083.   Faust, M. S.   "Developmental maturity as a determinant of prestige in adolescent girls."   Child
Development, 31(1960):173-184.

Tryon's Guess Who Test, including an additional pair
of items to measure prestige, was administered to 731
girls in the sixth, seventh, eighth, and ninth
grades.   Correlations between prestige and the other
twenty traits were computed for each grade separately, and the correlations were tested for significance.   Results showed that precocious physical
development tends to be a detriment to prestige during sixth grade, while it tends to become a decided
asset during the three succeeding years.   Level of
development is not a single factor in determining a
girl's status in the group, but it is an important
part of a composite of factors in creating a girl's
reputation during adolescence.   The discrepancy
between rate of developmental change and rate of
change in prestige was interpreted in terms of different meanings which early and late development have
for girls at differing times during adolescence.

1084.   Fenwick, J. J.   "Insights into the middle school
years." Educational Leadership, 37,7(1977):528-531.

A critical period to form a rational, positive, personal value system.   Psychological insights are given
that have implications for school organization, curriculum design, and staff preparation.   Describes
characteristics of middle school students: The student experiences turbulent, shifting and frequently
conflicting emotions.   Lacks self-confidence, appears
moody and introspective; there is often a quest for

answers to the big question "Who am I?" The opinions
of one's peers are cause for joy or for dismay. The
norm of conformity to peer behavior can result in
intolerance of others' apparent differences, especially when these do not meet peer standards. There
is often an unpredictability in the student's
response to adult affection with a strong tendency to
show either rejection or ambivalence. The impact of
rapid physical growth and accelerated hormone changes
can produce skewed responses in individual student
behavior patterns. Personal values and attitudes
tend to be questioned and frequently rejected.
"Other imposed" values gradually give way to one's
own value system. The student is able to grasp moral
and ethical subtleties such as reality, truth, and
goodness. There is a developing sense of social
responsibility beyond self, family, and one's immediate peer group. The student can become fiercely
idealistic. The student establishes a clearly
defined feminine or masculine sex role and ordinarily
seeks meaning for that role in heterosexual settings.
Hormonal changes, acceptance by peers, and influences
of the mass media contribute heavily to the student's
self-concept in regard to his or her sex role. The
middle school years typically represent a tenuous
transition from childhood to adolescence and young
adulthood accentuated by value conflicts within a
highly pluralistic society.

1085.   Ferguson, W. J.   "Junior high school issues identified by a state study."   Bulletin of the National
Association of Secondary School Principals,   40,3
(1967):152-157.

A California study identified areas of concern which
must be addressed in either a middle school or junior
high.   1) Curriculum change: How should junior
high/middle school curriculum be modified to cope
with recent societal changes and accelerated differences in adolescents? 2) Communication: How can we
better communicate regarding the junior high school
with the state department, state board of education,
state legislature, and the local community?   3)
Evaluation: How can we accurately and objectively
measure and evaluate the effectiveness of the junior
high school in meeting educational needs?   4)
Finance: How can we obtain better financial support
for the junior high school?   5) Teacher training:
How can we harmonize the teacher training program of
colleges so that junior high/middle schools will be
staffed with well-qualified and well-trained teachers?   6) Organization: What grade organizational
pattern is best suited to the educational needs?   7)
Legislation: How can we insure that educational
legislation, including credentialing, mandating programs, and curriculum revisions, will support

instructional programs and will meet legal and professional responsibilities?

1086.   Fine, B.   "Junior high school: is it needed?"
Education Forum, Omaha World Herald,   July 26, 1970:
15.

Although the junior high schools have been in existence for more than half a century they have served
their purpose and are no longer needed. Times have
changed.   Children are more sophisticated.   Colleges
accept students at an earlier age.   The high school
guidance counselor under the 6-3-3 system has the
student in his school for only two years before he
has to prepare a transcript and determine the qualifications of the individual. This is not enough time
for an appraisal. The new program, the middle school
based on a 4-4-4 system, has proven successful, but
even a return to the 8-4 method is desirable.   The
junior high school is the stepchild of the school
system.   Usually, it attracts the poorest teachers
and has little more than a makeshift program.
Students frequently find they are in limbo, caught
between the lower grade and the high school.

1087.   Ford, E. A.   "Organizational pattern of the
nation's public secondary schools."   School Life,
42(1960):10-12.

Describes patterns for junior highs, middle schools,
intermediate schools, and high schools in the United
States.

1088.   Fox, J. H., Jr.   "Middle schools and high schools:
a collision course for the '80s?" Transescence: The
Journal on Emerging Adolescent Education,   8,1(1980):
18-21.

Author discusses the history of the middle school and
makes suggestions to narrow the gap between the middle school and the senior high school. At the college level, departments of early and middle childhood
education are being formed, often in isolation from
departments of secondary education.   That must end.
High school teachers in preparation must be exposed
to middle school philosophy, and middle school teachers must also be exposed to both elementary and high
school philosophies concerning the teacher-learner
relationship.   At teacher preparation institutions, a
focus must be placed on the needs of the learner. A
person is unique, whatever the level of experience.
Within school districts in-service programs must be
developed to give the senior high school teacher an
understanding of the philosophy of middle school as
well as its strategies, many of which are transfer-
able to the high school scene.   At the same time,

middle school teachers need in-service to understand the objectives of the high school. School boards and central office personnel must receive in-service at each level. The central office leadership should support a K-12 continuum of learning activities, not separate programs. Educators in the 80s will see the beginning of an organizational revolution at the high school level.

1089.   Frank, L. K., Harrison, R., Hellersberg, E., Machover, K., and Steiner, M. "Personality development in adolescent girls." Monographs of the Society for Research in Child Development, 41(1951):205-206.

The school often demands academic achievement and expects active interest in various subject matters just before and after puberty. Most girls are least capable of meeting those demands then, except by sacrifice at a crucial time in their maturation and at possible psychological cost.

1090.   Frazier, G. W. "The junior high is an educational problem." California Journal of Secondary Education, 27(1952):112-115.

Traces the history of junior high schools and discusses the extent to which they have either achieved their reasons for being or have changed them.

1091.   Gastwirth, P. "Questions facing the middle school." High Points, 44(1966):40-47.

Faces problems of definition. What is a middle school? What should be the organizing principle of the middle school? Grade organization? Chronological age of pupils? Social and psychological maturity of pupils? The logistics of building space within the system? The demands of political groups? The demands for desegregation? An administrative convenience? Economy? Grade organization is a vital factor in the development of both curricular and cocurricular learning experiences. The article describes the basic features of a middle school, the problem of identification, the superficial criticism of the junior high school, the trends of grades 5 and 6, the problems of personnel, pre-service and in-service training, and other considerations. The author attacks the middle schools on separate points aimed at discounting the need for middle schools when quite adequate junior high schools are already in existence. Some of the criticisms could be considered major disadvantages of the middle school: 1) The middle school faces the problem of identification and definition--there is much confusion as to what a middle school is. It needs identification, more stability, a unique philosophy, and an organizing principle. 2) The problems of the junior high school are also present in the middle school. The two are not very different, and the middle school will eventually evolve into the junior high school. 3) There is no need to include grades 5 and 6 in the middle school with grades 7 and 8, because organizational changes taking place in the upper elementary school will provide these grades with the instructional equivalent of the middle school without the organizational upheaval accompanying it. In the nongraded school of the future, the concept of grade organization will be replaced by the concept of age level organization.

1092.   Gastwirth, P.   "Questions facing the middle school." Clearinghouse, 41(1967):472-475.

In a report issued by the Educational Facilities Laboratories entitled "Middle Schools," six types of grade organization are mentioned: 7-8, 7-8-9, 6-7-8, 6-7-8-9, 5-6-7-8, and 5-6-7-8-9. In this article Gastwirth addresses the same questions listed in entry 1091.

1093.   Gaumnitz, W. H. and Hull, J. D.   "Junior high schools vs. the traditional 8-4 high school organization."   Bulletin of the National Association of Secondary School Principals, 38(1954):112-121.

Lists advantages of the traditional junior high school and uses tables to interpret statistical trends of high school reorganization.

1094.   Gaumnitz, W. H., et al. Strengths and Weaknesses of the Junior High School. U.S. Office of Education, Circular 441. Washington, D.C.: Government Printing Office, 1955.

Contains texts of major addresses presented to a national conference held in Washington, D.C.

1095.   Gay, G.   "Ethnic identity in early adolescence: some implications for instructional reform." Educational Leadership, 35,8(1978):649-655.

Educators must know and respond to the ethnic identification process as they design programs in middle and junior high schools for maximum social growth and educational success. See ERIC Abstract #EJ 179 250.

1096.   George, P. S.   "Unresolved issues in education for the middle years." Clearinghouse, 47,7(1973):417-419.

Sections cover each unresolved issue: 1) Open space: good, bad, or indifferent? 2) Team teaching:

interdisciplinary or disciplinary? 3) Which ages or grades for the middle school? 4) Teachers for the middle school, what should they be like? 5) Other issues--sex education, competition, academic offerings, and middle school versus junior high school.

1097.   Georgiady, N. P. and Romano, L. G. "The middle school: is it a threat to the elementary school?" Impact, Winter 1967-68:14-18.

Presents a definition of a middle school, failures of the junior high school, conditions leading to the development of a middle school, and principles in the middle school concept. Those principles are as follows: 1) to recognize the unique physical, emotional, social, and psychological characteristics of children in this age group, 2) to use knowledge concerning those characteristics for developing school programs, 3) to develop a curriculum not necessarily modeled after the high school or the elementary school program but articulated with both, 4) to provide greater opportunity for student self-direction and responsibility for learning, 5) to provide opportunities for the students to understand and appreciate democratic principles by practicing democratic skills. The article suggests possible negative and positive effects and implications.

1098.   Gesell, A., Ilg, F., and Anes, L. Youth: The Years from Ten to Sixteen. New York: Harper and Row, 1956.

From a state of relative calm, the transescent begins a period of accelerated development in late childhood. Most transescents have not had such a rapid growth spurt since infancy. They had been able to adjust to the regular growth patterns of early and middle childhood. The child at this stage of development is the "picture of equipoise" and seems to be "a finished product of nature's handwork." However, most transescents enjoy this fine state of physical adjustment only briefly. The onset of puberty brings an abrupt end to the stability prepubescents enjoyed. With it an upheaval in their life actions becomes commonplace, and a period of adjustment to a chain of events begins which will ultimately result in the child becoming an adult.

1099.   Gibson, J. T. "The middle school concept: 'an albatross?'" Journal of Teacher Education, 29, 5(1978):17-19.

Includes differences between the structure and educational philosophy of middle schools and traditional junior high schools. Characteristics of school organization which are sensitive to the needs of preadolescent youth are discussed. See ERIC Abstract #EJ 191 489.

1100.   Glass, J. M. "Tested and accepted philosophy of the junior high school movement." Clearinghouse, 7(1933):334.

Describes a sound philosophy founded on the psychology of early adolescence.

1101.   Glatthorn, A. and Manone, C. "The 9-10 school: A novelty or a better answer?" Educational Leadership, 23(1966):285-289.

Article describes advantages and disadvantages of a 9-10 building and answers these questions: 1) How would a varsity sports program be organized? 2) How are ties coordinated between the 9-10 building and the 11-12 building? 3) How is the curriculum coordination assured? 4) Do guidance counselors move with the student or stay with the building? 5) How are the two buildings administered? 6) What happens if students fail key subjects? Adolescents need to develop a sense of independence. Many junior high schools thwart this need by placing pupils in a school situation that is too structured. Students need to develop leadership abilities and gain a sense of status. The 14-and-15-year-olds need the security of being with age mates at a similar stage of physical development. They need a sense of involvement, participation, and activity.

1102.   Glines, D. E. "The junior high school: progress report on educational change." Bulletin of the National Association of Secondary School Principals, 51(1967):144-151.

Neither the middle school nor the junior high is significantly better. It depends on the following areas which are discussed at length: philosophy, teaching strategy, curriculum, organization, and facilities.

1103.   Gorwood, B. "9-13 middle schools: a local view." Education 3-13, 6,1(1978):15-18.

Author questions the similarity of middle schools and compares them to middle schools for 9-to-13-year-olds in England. See ERIC Abstract #EJ 182 801.

1104.   Gray, R. and Seagren, A. "Junior High School vs. The Middle." Region for Education 343, Teachers College, University of Nebraska at Lincoln, 1966.

States the following advantages of the middle school over the junior high: 1) The middle school makes a

four-year high school possible. 2) There is a better
chance for sameness of students. 3) The middle
school eliminates the semantic difficulties of
"junior." 4) There is more opportunity for flexible
experimentation of programs. 5) The fifth and sixth
graders have a greater span of interest and acquaintances. 6) There is a more gradual transition from
elementary to secondary. 7) A better division of
grades allows for specialized teacher training.

1105. Groden, A. F. "Who will win? Junior high vs.
middle school vs. adolescents." Bulletin of the
National Association of Secondary School Principals,
60,396(1976):109-112.

It is impossible to distinguish clearly between
junior highs and middle schools, and the proponents
of both should give up their fight and work together
in harmony. The article promotes a middle school
position based on six factors: 1) an increasing dissatisfaction with the essence of the junior high concept, 2) appropriate placement of grades 6 through 9
on the educational ladder, 3) a re-emphasis of the
special needs of preadolescents and adolescents, 4)
administrative feasibility in facing the problems of
increasing enrollments, integration and neighborhood
shifts in reorganization, 5) appropriate replacement
of antiquated or abandoned school buildings, and 6)
pressures from high school administrators and
teachers to restore the four-year high school. In
looking at these positions, the author states that
proposed programs for educational improvement may or
may not emerge in practice as they exist on paper or
in the minds of their creators. The social and/or
professional status of an individual or group is a
reliable predictor of the acceptance or rejection of
educational programs. Class consciousness exerts a
strong influence on the direction of educational
institutions.

1106. Grooms, A. "The middle school and other innovations." Bulletin of the National Association of
Secondary School Principals, 40,3(1967):158-160.

Grade arrangements have been based on the idea that
educational experiences can be neatly packaged into a
single-year program, and then somehow can be integrated into a total package. Hence, it really hasn't
made too much difference how the organization is
structured. The advocates of a given grade arrangement are hard pressed to identify the differences
among elementary, intermediate, middle, and junior
high school programs. The author feels that none of
the foregoing arrangements is adequate for the education of the 10-to-14-year-old student, and includes
that the middle school must provide a solution to the

problem of a dull, uninteresting, and unchallenging program. The school must be dedicated to each pupil who enters, so that each may discover his own talents for learning, for growth, and for service. Planning for the middle school must exercise the work of the individual, enable students to begin to accept responsibility for their own learning, recognize student involvement with change, provide for opportunities to participate in decision making, prepare learning situations most conducive to student growth, and establish growth criteria and a program for acquiring data which can be measured quantitatively. Education of the 10-to-14-year-old requires a professional in a given discipline who possesses skill and knowledge in learning theory, social psychology, and public relations. Where the elementary school uses the generalist as a scientist, mathematician, social scientist, and communications expert, the junior high school requires attention to subject rather than a discipline. The middle school professional always operates within his discipline, but the student interactions are likely to cover a spectrum of his expertise. The professional staff of a middle school should be a team of teachers--a learning coordinator, a teacher-counselor, and a discipline generalist for science, math, social sciences, and language arts. The middle school must foster the student's rate of growth with respect to a given discipline, not in the absolute quantity of growth. Secondary school principals are challenged to develop measuring devices for student growth rates and student effectiveness based on growth rates for expenditure of resources.

1107.   Grosse Point, Michigan, Public School System. "Middle Schools in Action." Education Research Circular 2. Arlington, Va.: American Association of School Administrators, 1969.

Delineates specific differences between a middle school and a junior high school: A middle school program is designed to recognize the uniqueness of the growth stage spanning the transition from childhood to adolescence. The junior high has evolved into exactly what the name has implied--"junior" high school. Here are specific differences.

Middle School Emphasizes:	Junior High Emphasizes:
A child-centered program	Subject-centered program
Learning how to live	Acquiring a body of information
Creative exploration	Skill and concept mastery
A belief in one's self	Interstudent competition
Skilled guidance for student	Conformance to the teacher-made, self-direction lesson plan
Teacher responsible for student learning	Students responsible for their own learning

Student independence	Control by the teacher
A flexible schedule	A six-period day
Students plan the schedule	Administrators plan the schedule
Variable group size	Standard classroom
Use of team teaching	One teacher per class
Students learning at different rates, self-pacing	All students at the same place at the same time, textbook approach

1108.   Gruhn, W. T.   "An Investigation of Relative Frequency of Curriculum and Related Practices Contributing to the Realization of the Basic Function of the Junior High School."   Dissertation, University of North Carolina at Chapel Hill, 1940.

Distinguishes between the cultural mission of the American middle school and the basic functions in its organization which are required to fulfill that mission.

1109.   Gruhn, W. T. "What's New and Interesting in Junior High School Education." Paper presented at the Southwest Regional Junior High School Conference, Stillwater, Okla., November 11-13, 1959.

Makes ten observations: 1) The basic purpose and philosophy of the junior high school has remained basically the same since its inception: to provide the best possible education for boys and girls in the early adolescent years. 2) Changes in the curriculum in the junior high school have been made more rapidly from 1954 to 1959 than in any previous period to accomodate all boys and girls at all levels of abilities, not just those at each extreme. 3) The quality of the instructional program can be improved as we find more effective ways for teachers and pupils to work together in a learning situation. 4) We are not adequately using all the available information on each pupil to make teaching more effective. 5) The problem of articulation has increased greatly as secondary school subjects are being pushed downward for more able pupils and in some areas (such as reading) are being pushed upward into the high school for the less able student.   We need more articulation upward, cooperative articulation with all levels, and teachers from all levels working together in workshops.   6) Some progress is being made in developing a well-integrated program of education for early adolescents by using cooperative planning time in a team approach to teaching. 7) The counselor's work in the junior high school is undergoing change because of pressure on the junior high school: selecting pupils for honor classes, evaluating work of these pupils, counseling for college admissions.   8) Return to a form of ability grouping for a specific purpose

instead of previous rigid block grouping. Pupils are
grouped in terms of individual needs and abilities,
with some special classes for extremes but keeping
these pupils integrated into the total school program. 9) The needs of the gifted are not being met;
counselors must identify every gifted youngster. 10)
Junior high school principals do not have sufficient
administrative, supervisory, and clerical staffs.

1110.   Gruhn, W. T. "Major issues in junior high school
education."   Bulletin of the National Association of
Secondary School Principals, 45(1961):18-24.

We should examine the basic philosophy of the junior
high school, the essential purposes it is to serve,
and the nature of the junior high school pupil. Then
we will not make changes in the junior high school as
a result of social, political, and international
pressures. The author examines the following questions: 1) Should we continue to be concerned with
all aspects of child growth and development in the
junior high school, or should we be concerned with
the intellectual growth of boys and girls? 2) Should
the program of the junior high school continue to be
general education, or should pupils begin to specialize for future educational and vocational goals? 3)
Should we exert strong pressures for academic
achievement on boys and girls as early as the junior
high school, or should we delay such pressures until
pupils are more mature physically, physiologically,
and emotionally? 4) Should extracurricular activities continue to be a significant part of the educational program or should activities be cut back to
provide more time for the classroom program? 5)
Should we continue to think of the junior high as a
three-year school which ordinarily includes grades 7,
8, and 9, or should we reorganize it on a K-6-2-4
basis or some other grade plan? 6) Should we continue to think of the junior high school as providing
a unique educational program which is designed primarily for early adolescents, or should the junior
high school become increasingly a downward extension
of the senior high school?

1111.   Gruhn, W. T. "What's right with junior high and
middle school education?"   Bulletin of the National
Association of Secondary School Principals,   54,346
(1970):139-145.

Author discusses those characteristics of junior high
schools and middle schools which he considers to work
well. The philosophy, purposes, and objectives of
junior high and middle school education have always
been well defined and widely accepted by American
educators. In harmony with the philosophy, a broad
curriculum recognizes the interests, needs, and

abilities of young adolescents. The junior high and
middle school throughout their history have been
genuinely concerned with pupils as individuals rather
than as a group. The junior high and middle school
have responded to the need for experimentation, innovation and change in educational methods, materials,
and programs characterized by dedicated, imaginative,
and resourceful leadership at the local level.

1112. Gruhn, W. T. and Douglass, H. R.   The Modern
Junior High School. 2d ed. New York: Ronald Press,
1956.

Text for the study of junior high school with the
following sections: History and Philosophy: growth
of the junior high school, philosophy of the junior
high school, and advantages and limitations of the
junior high school. The Instructional Program: curriculum trends and organization, the core curriculum,
curriculum fields (industrial arts, health and
physical education, mathematics, art, home economics,
language arts, foreign languages, social studies,
music, business education, and science), directing
learning activities, meeting individual differences.
Guidance and Extra-Class Activities: the guidance
program, the homeroom, extra class activities.
Evaluating, Reporting, and Recording Pupil Progress:
problems of organization and articulation, staff
problems. Looking Ahead: problems facing the junior
high school.

1113. Gruhn, W. T. and Tompkins, E. "What is the best
combination." National Education Association Journal, 45(1965):496-498.

Authors did not feel that any grade below the seventh
grade was emerging into a transitional school. They
did not mention either 5-3-4 or 4-4-4 in this report.

1114. Gulf School Researcher magazine. "Texas survey."
Gulf School Researcher, 9,3(1962):19.

Junior high school principals in Texas agree that 1)
existing facilities play an important role in the
grade level distribution of students, 2) the Carnegie
Unit System is a controlling factor in the present
and planned ninth grade placement in many districts,
3) the effect of grade level placement on students is
so important (affecting their school spirit, leadership roles, boy-girl relations) that it must be taken
more seriously, 4) the placement of ninth grade
students presents the most difficult problems, 5) the
extent of many activity programs depends on the
location of the ninth grade, 6) a saving of money on
special facilities, such as laboratories, would
result from the placement of the ninth grade in the

senior high school, 7) the total growth through counseling services is greater when the ninth grade is in the junior high school, 8) transition for students is easier in the 7-8-9 system, 9) there may be duplicate offerings in the ninth and tenth grades when the ninth grade is in the junior high school. The principals disagree concerning 1) the grade level at which children should be placed in the junior high school, 2) the relative maturity of the children of the sixth grade compared to seventh and eighth grades, 3) the difficulty of flexible programming under the different grade combinations, and 4) teachers available for grade placement combinations.

1115.   Hale, C. J.   "Changing growth patterns of the American child." Education, 78(1958):467-470.

American children are maturing faster. Outstanding advances in medicine, an increased knowledge of nutrition, and the control of our environment may be primary factors. Antibiotics and vaccines control many childhood diseases like dyptheria, small pox, whooping cough, malaria, typhoid fever, and scarlet fever. The vitamin fortified and balanced diets everyone can afford provide for optimum growth. Education must not overlook the fact that these great advances may have effected a change in its own product, the country's most valuable resource, the American child.

1116.   Hanson, N. G.   "Changing the junior high to a middle school." Bulletin of the National Association of Secondary School Principals, 63,427(1979):66-72.

Article provides a list of do's and don'ts for grade level reorganization. Do develop a good public relations program.   Do involve the community in your planning. Do involve your staff on committees and in visitations to other schools.   Do invite consultants to meet with your staff.   Do establish a timetable for all activities. Do invite the parents of incoming fifth and sixth graders to your buildings.   Do become knowledgeable about state certification requirements for middle schools.   Don't assume all staff members are interested.   Don't forget to involve the Board of Education.   Don't assume that the community will accept the philosophy and rationale of a middle school.   Don't assume your present program needs to be changed or modified entirely. Examples taken from the Austin, Minnesota, school district.

1117.   Hargreaves, A. and Warwick, D.   "Attitudes to middle schools." Education 3-13, 6,1(1978):19-23.

Article includes sections on the sociology, the economic and social role, and the ideology of middle schools. Authors propose that the contradictions between educational theory and practice as seen in educational institutions are a product of the social and historical location of middle schools, and that alternative conditions are possible. They refer to expressions of attitudes against middle schools made by those involved in their creation, provision, and organization and to the social basis of these conditions. See ERIC Abstract #EJ 182 802.

1118.   Harvey, J. P. "An Act of Creation: A Chronicle of the Creation of a Small School Dedicated to Holistic Development for Students Aged 9 through 13 Years." Alameda, Calif.: The Wright Institute, 1974.

Study of an experimental educational institution where the focus is on a total program including physical, intellectual, emotional, social, perceptual, and spiritual dimensions. Goals and structure emerged along with the interplay of biographies (the use of the school as a stage in which participants express their drive toward self-actualization or individualization). Tension, strain, and exhaustion also emerged. The developmental needs of students influenced what was possible and appropriate for inclusion in this open system.

1119.   Havighurst, R. J. Developmental Task and Education. New York: David McKay, 1952.

For transcents, school emphasis should center on social/emotional areas. "The period from 12 to 18 is primarily one of physical and emotional maturing.... The principle lessons are emotional and social, not intellectual."

1120.   Havighurst, R. J. "Do junior high school youth grow up too fast?" Bulletin of the National Association of Secondary School Principals, 47(1963): 151-163.

Socially, adolescence is a moratorium between childhood and adult roles, during which a youth slowly acquires adult roles by a process of trial and error with the help of schools and peers. Psychologically, adolescence is a period of time during which a youth acquires identity. He narrows and focuses his personal, occupational, sexual, and ideological commitments to the point where he is perceived by others to be an autonomous adult. If the new generation of adolescents is to measure up to the challenge of the contemporary society, it will need to combine a world-wide system of efforts with the traditional

American values of instrumental activism, in which
responsibility, autonomy, and individualism are
motives, and achievement is best demonstrated through
work.   Young people may be divided into three groups
with respect to their attitudes toward assuming adult
responsibilities: 1) The ego-involved leaders of
this society.   Perhaps 35 percent will be highly productive people who enjoy work for its own sake.   2)
The maintainers of the society.   They are less activ-
istic, have less achievement drive, are more content
to accept the status quo, and are less creative
intellectually.   3) The alienated, perhaps 15 percent
of the total youth group.   They do not accept a commitment to work for the social welfare, and do not
accept norms of society.   Discussion of adolescence
has focused on the older adolescent who is in the
senior high school or college.   The younger adolescent in junior high school is at the age when the
unquestioned life ends for youth as the dividing
point between early and later adolescence.   Early
adolescence is considered as the age range from about
11 or 12 to 15 or 16--the junior high school.   The
junior high school age is both a stage of life and a
form of living.   As a stage of life, it is a crucial
period.   The body develops into adult form and characteristics, which may be sources of pride or
inferiority throughout the remainder of life.   The
mind develops with adult capacity, capable of any
kind of learning, and it is more subtle than it will
be in later years.   The personality takes on adult
outlines during this stage.   The qualities that
should be developed through the family, the school,
and youth organizations are associated with achievement of the developmental tasks of early adolescence.
The task of industry, according to Erikson, is the
center path of early adolescence.

1121.   Havighurst, R. J.   "Lost innocence--modern junior
high school youth."   Bulletin of the National Association of Secondary School Principals, 49(1965):1-4.

Biologically, adolescence is the same in all races
and in all the countries where we have knowledge of
human development.   Nature's built-in time clock
controls the changes of puberty, their order, and
their timing.   Sexual maturity comes perhaps a year
earlier than it did one hundred years ago, but this
change came slowly.   Socially, adolescence is a
moratorium between childhood and adult roles during
which a youth slowly acquires adult roles by a process of trial and error with the help of schools and
peers.   Each generation must find a way of life that
grows out of its childhood and fits into what it
perceives to be the historical process leading to the
future.   Psychologically, adolescence is a period of
time during which a youth acquires an identity.   He

narrows and focuses his personal, occupational, sexual, and ideological commitments to the point where he is perceived by others to be an autonomous adult. Junior high school can contribute in an important way to the process of becoming an adult. The school might work in three ways: 1) To give boys and girls opportunities to be of service to the society. Contributing to the welfare of society cements the bonds of loyalty and interest; at the same time, it increases one's self-esteem to do something which is valued by others. 2) To teach about the heros and heroines of a modern self-renewing society. In their courses in literature and social studies, boys and girls may study contemporary scientists, business persons, and statesmen who have committed themselves to making the world more productive and peaceful. 3) To study and analyze contemporary social problems with an emphasis on positive solutions.

1122.   Havighurst, R. J., Robinson, M. Z., and Dorr, M. "The development of the ideal self in childhood and adolescence." Journal of Educational Research, 40,4 (1946):241-257.

Self-reports during childhood and adolescence describe the development of the ideal self or the ego-ideal. Boys and girls wrote a brief essay on the subject, "The Person I Would Like To Be Like." The ideal self commences in childhood as an identification with a parental figure, moves during middle childhood and early adolescence through a stage of romanticism and glamour, and culminates in late adolescence as a composite of desirable characteristics which may be symbolized by an attractive, visible young adult or simply an imaginary figure. Evidence suggests that the ideal self is deeply influenced by association with people who are in positions of prestige because they are older, more powerful, and better able to get the desirable things of life than the child or adolescent who observes them. A boy or girl combines qualities of parents with qualities of attractive, successful young adults into a composite ego-ideal. Schools, churches, and youth-serving agencies influence the ideals of youth as much or more by the presence and behavior of teachers, clergy, and youth group leaders than through their verbal teaching.

1123.   Hedgecock, L. "Eighth grade rebel." National Educational Association Journal, 56(1967):19.

Written by an eighth grade student, the paper explains an early adolescent's feelings in relation to an excellent teacher who is trying to help the student through some common early adolescent problems.

1124.   Heffernan, H. and Smith M.   "The young adolescent."   California Journal of Elementary Education, 28(1959):70.

Don't assume education can be "poured into" a child's mind while ignoring the needs of the early adolescent, although there has been a great deal of "pitcher filling in the junior high schools." Subject matter properly presented with sincere and sympathetic understanding of adolescence will focus all efforts on goals and standards so intrinsic to his needs that each student will "soak up more basic skills in fundamental subject matter like a sponge."

1125.   Heilbron, P. D.   "My search for the middle school 'mind': an open letter to all middle school educators."   Transescence: The Journal of Emerging Adolescent Education, 8,1(1980):22-25.

Search for more information about the cognitive development of the early and middle adolescent to refute Conrad Toepfer who suggested the brains of most children between the ages of 12 and 14 virtually cease to grow.   Gives specific implications for the teaching of mathematics.   Author's research suggests: 1) increases in brain weight, 2) development of negative neural networks, 3) fluid intelligence, 4) relationship between physiological and cognitive development, 5) attainment of formal stage functioning, 6) stage development--retrogressive traits, and 7) existence of a fifth stage.

1126.   Heironomous, N. C.   "Is this the earliest known junior high school?"   Clearinghouse, 14(1940):518.

In 1895, Richmond, Indiana, had a distinct unit of the city school set apart for seventh and eighth graders.

1127.   Heller, R. W.   "Needed: A rational rationale for the middle school."   New York State Education, 53 (1969):35-36.

Describes the controversies surrounding the middle school concept.

1128.   Herriott, M. E.   "Organizing the junior high school."   Bulletin of the National Association of Secondary School Principals, 35(1951):15-19.

All junior high school youth need 1) to explore their own aptitudes and to have experiences basic to occupational proficiency, 2) to develop and maintain

physical and mental health, 3) to be participating
citizens of their school and community, with increasing orientation to adult citizenship, 4) to have
experiences and understandings appropriate to their
age and development, which are the foundation of
successful home and family life, 5) to develop a
sense of values of material things and the right of
ownership, 6) to learn about the natural and physical
environment and its effect on life and to have
opportunities for using the scientific approach in
the solution of problems, 7) to enriched living which
comes from appreciation of an expression in the arts
and from experiencing the beauty and wonder of the
world, 8) to have a variety of socially acceptable
and personally satisfying leisure time experiences
which contribute to their personal growth and to
their development in wholesome group relationships,
9) experiences in group living which contribute to
personality and character development, to develop
respect for other persons and their rights and to
grow in ethical insights, 10) to grow in their
ability to observe, listen, read, think, speak, and
write with purpose and appreciation.

1129.   Hillson, M.   Change and Innovation in Elementary
School Organization. New York: Holt, Rhinehart and
Winston, 1965.

Reorganization includes the upper grades, departmentalized and semi-departmentalized grouping plans,
team teaching, team learning, coordinate and collaborative teaching, dual progress and multi-age or
multi-grade grouping plan, and nongrading.   Contains
much material on nongraded programs which are useful
in developing middle school programs.

1130.   Hines, V. and Alexander, W.   "Evaluating the
middle school."   National Elementary Principal, 48,4
(1969):32-36.

The middle school organization is whittling away the
upper grades--grade 6 or grades 5 and 6--of the elementary school and is tending to replace the traditional junior high school plan throughout the United
States.   Evaluation of the middle school seeks to
provide answers to two related questions: 1) How
well are we achieving our goals and purposes? 2) How
can we improve what we are doing or do it better
another time?   The article gives answers to these
questions--Why evaluate the middle school?   Who
develops and evaluates the design? and What hypotheses are to be tested?   The authors argue for development of adequate evaluation plans for new middle
schools.   While embracing new efforts to provide
greater continuity in educational programs, educators
have no data to tell which plans work best for whom.

The article emphasizes the need for getting these
data as new school organizations go into operation
and suggests some essentials in the data gathering
process.

1131.   Hobbs, M. E. "The middle school." Hoosier Schoolmaster, November 1958:17-20.

Asks three basic questions in establishing a middle
school program: 1) What philosophy and objective
should prevail for the middle school? 2) What should
be taught to this age group? 3) What instructional
procedures and materials will best teach what we wish
to teach? The middle school is usually limited to
three years of a student's educational program;
therefore, it should not accept a task beyond the
realm of a single institution. Like other educational progress, it deals with ideas, knowledge,
intellectual skills, and physical development.

1132.   Horrocks, J. E.   The Psychology of Adolescence:
Behavior and Development. Boston: Houghton-Mifflin
Co., 1962.

A chapter outline: The Adolescent Period--includes
nature of adolescence. The Adolescent and His
Relation to Others--discusses the adolescent and his
family, social adjustment, friendship and personal
acceptability, heterosexual relationships, adolescent
groups and group memberships. Delinquent Behavior.
Development and Growth--outlines physical, physiological, structural, and intellectual development.
Bases of Behavior. Adolescent Activities and
Interests--nature and social aspects, personal
aspects, attitudes and ideals, vocational interests
and abilities.

1133.   Horrocks, J. E. and Buker, M.   "A study of the
friendship fluctuations of preadolescents." Journal
of Genetic Psychology, 78(1951):131-144.

An inquiry into the stability of friendships among
children, particularly as it changes or remains from
year to year, should serve as a step toward understanding the development of social behavior, one of
the more important aims of education. Earlier
studies of interpersonal relationships were concerned
with the development of methods of observing the
social behavior of the child. Recently, the emphasis
shifted to the observation and measurement of the
child's acceptance by his contemporaries and interaction in the social groups. Friendship as one form
of acceptance plays an important role in group interaction. Friendship fluctuation was determined by
pupil choices using sociometric tests. The subjects
were asked to list their three best friends on two

occasions, fourteen days apart, and again four weeks later. The data showed a trend toward greater stability and friendship with increasing chronological age and a corresponding higher grade placement. The means of the friendship fluctuation indices for chronological age groups comparing two studies formed a continuous curve, showing a downward trend in friendship fluctuation from age 5 to age 18.

1134.   Howard, A. W.   "Which years in junior high?" Clearinghouse, 33(1959):405-408.

The appeal of a four-year high school plus changing practices of junior high toward the senior high have "caused many people to feel that it is worthwhile to consider a 7-8 or 6-7-8 organization. Whatever dividing lines in grade divisions are finally established should be set in terms of pupil need and good educational practices, not tradition."

1135.   Howard, A. W. and Stoumbis, G. C. The Junior High and Middle School: Issues and Practices.   Scranton, Pa.: Intext Educational Publishers, 1970.

The book includes sections on the history and function of the junior high, adolescence, guidance and counseling, administration, and physical facilities. Describes instructional programs in common learning, health, physical education, and exploratory areas. Discussion follows of the what and why of middle schools, criticisms and conflict determining which grades in the middle school, and middle school curricula and programs. The book discusses staffing the junior high school, junior high school student activities and athletics, curricular designs, ability grouping, evaluation, testing and recording, student unrest and behavior. Discussed are the changing patterns of instruction including flexible scheduling, team teaching, and nongraded schools. A model evaluation program for a junior high school is described.

1136.   Howell, B. "The middle school: is it really any better?" North Central Association Quarterly, 43 (1969):281-287.

Reviews a documentary report, "Making a Middle School"--a chronology covering a two-year span and explaining the program realignment of a traditional junior high school to that of a middle school. The community middle school of Eagle Grove, Iowa, began its second year as a revamped junior high school in 1969. This program has been one faculty's attempt to better meet the needs of 600 students in a school district serving a community of seven thousand.

Developing the middle school resulted in the following conclusions at Eagle Grove: 1) organize a school
for transitional students from ages 11 to 15 (or
grades 6-9), 2) incorporate a nongraded structure
with a continuous progress learning model, 3) maintain the major objectives of teaching students how to
learn and develop attitudes of receptivity toward
learning, 4) focus on the individual, his achievement, and his needs.   New innovations at Eagle
Grove's middle school included: 1) A quest period--a
daily period during which students used a contract
plan to explore topics of interest.   2) Independent
study--academic contract plan where students worked
to achieve ends they helped to determine. 3) Advisor
program--each staff member was assigned a limited
number of student advisees in a variety of age
levels, thus insuring the same advisor during the
four-year span and providing parents with a school
contact.   4) Mutual planning in teaching time--skills
teams were scheduled or unscheduled at the same time,
thus providing some time to interact and coordinate.
5) Educational media center--a considerable increase
in multimedia equipment and materials promoted
interests and encouraged diversified approaches.   6)
Continuous progress--a nongraded format in all basic
skills permitted students to advance at their own
rate.   This required the development of a learning
alternatives model and a program based on individual
prescription.

1137.   Huber, J. D.   "How innovative is the middle
school?" Clearinghouse, 49(1975):103-105.

The article describes grades 5-8 or 6-8 as the best
grade organizational pattern for a school for transescents.   It compares the middle school favorably to
the one-room schoolhouse because of independent
study, tutorial programs, family-type atmosphere,
openness, space and structured freedom.

1138.   Hull, J. H.   "The junior high school is a poor
investment." Nation's Schools, 65(1960):78-81.

Hull claims that the junior high school puts the
unstable child in a situation more appropriate for
older youth.   A typical junior high school program
includes the following elements to some degree: 1)
teachers more concerned with subject matter than with
children, 2) teachers who want to be senior high
school teachers, 3) poor teachers who have been
demoted from the high school, 4) some good teachers,
but trained in elementary education, 5) teachers
marking time until they can get a better teaching
job, 6) parents, teachers, and administrators imitating the high school program, even to competitive
interscholastic sports, 7) many teachers who cannot

handle disciplinary problems even in their special
subject areas, 8) the student body almost out of
control, 9) students imitating high school students,
10) students shuttled from room to room all day, 11)
students not really responsible to anyone in particular, 12) teachers not responsible for any particular
group of students, 13) parents rather frightened with
the often ineffective process, 14) the cost of
education higher than it would be in a self-contained
elementary program with poorer results, 15) lost
seventh and eighth graders hopelessly in a quandary,
16) students who have learned to go the limit with
each teacher. They will arrive at senior high school
with a crass and arrogant attitude toward teachers
and school in general. The article also contains a
section on what research says about the junior high
school. In 1927 there was evidence that the junior
high school was not living up to its promises. A
comprehensive study by J. Orin Powers compared
instructional achievement in Minneapolis, where there
were some new junior high schools, some old junior
high schools, some junior-senior high schools, and
schools in an elementary school organization through
grade 8. Schools having the highest degree of
departmentalization ranked uniformly lowest on
standardized tests. Of the groups compared, the non-
junior high school is the highest, and junior-senior
high school is the lowest. A study at Harvard
University by Bancroft Beatley in 1932 found that the
junior high school takes time away from the academic
subjects.

1139.   Hull, J. H. "Are junior high schools the answer?"
Educational Leadership, 23(1965):213-216.

The junior high school is one of America's educational blunders because of imitating the high school,
departmentalization, competitive athletic programs,
huge enrollment, frequent class changes, teachers
meeting 150 students a day, and students being
jostled about with strangers every forty minutes. We
want to develop and recognize the variablity of our
future citizens. Mass production education will
perhaps develop the likenesses we want, but perhaps
it may be used to develop diversity if the right
goals are set up to achieve it, supported with
adequate resources. Yet, some educators still prefer
to work toward the idea of taking a more gradual and
less sophisticated step in the upper elementary
school as a transition to the high school program.
This is not an argument for holding children back, it
is an argument for a little less pushing, less
imitating of the high school, and more appropriate
tailoring of the program to the particular student.

1140.   Hunt, J. T.   "The adolescent: his characteristics
        and   development."   Review of Educational Research,
        30(1960):13-21.

        Sections cover physical development, mental develop-
        ment, family relationships, social and emotional
        adjustment,   social   class   and   behavior,   social
        attitudes, values, relationships, vocational inter-
        ests, and aspirations.   An extensive bibliography is
        included.

1141.   Hunter, M.   "Current   Organizational   Patterns."
        Middle   School   Portfolio,   Leaflet   4.   Washington,
        D.C.:   Association for Childhood Education Interna-
        tional, 1968.

        Educators must resist the temptation to accept the
        dazzling complexity of organizational patterns as
        educational ends in themselves.   These patterns serve
        only as passageways to enable educators to more
        efficiently traverse the route leading to the only
        end that is appropriate in education--increased
        learning by each individual in the areas deemed
        appropriate by school and society.   The article dis-
        cusses nongrading, team teaching, and teacher-learner
        relationships.   Diagnostic information is needed
        first on middle school students from five areas of
        the   learner's   development: mental,   physical,
        emotional, educational, and social.   Based on this
        information, a prescription for the student will
        include the most appropriate teacher, the group of
        boys and girls with whom he or she will best learn,
        the type of classroom organization that will propel
        learning, and an appropriate educational program
        within that classroom.   The most important single
        factor in a student's learning at school is his
        teacher's ability to promote learning.

1142.   Hurlock, E. B.   Adolescent Development.   New York:
        McGraw-Hill, 1955.

        Book contains the following chapters: 1) Adoles-
        cence, Age of Transition.   2) Puberty Changes.   3)
        Psychological Significance of Body Changes.   4)
        Emotions in Adolescence.   5) Social Behavior.   6)
        Social Adjustment.   7) Adolescent Interests.   8)
        Personal Interests.   9) Adolescent Recreations.   10)
        Religious Beliefs and Attitudes.   11) Moral Concepts
        and Behavior.   12) Sex Interests.   13) Dating and
        Courtship.   14) Family Relationships.   15) Personal-
        ity.   The book includes a visual bibliography.

1143.   Illinois State University.   "A Reexamination of
        the Function of the Junior High School."   Normal,
        Ill., 1962.

The junior high school, an American reality, is an educational program designed to meet the needs, interests, and abilities of boys and girls during early adolescence. It serves as a transition between childhood and later adolescence and between the organizational patterns of self-contained classrooms and departmentalization. The curriculum is a flexible aggregate of exploratory experiences in group and individual activities. These experiences are provided to meet the unique developmental needs of every early adolescent in the areas of esthetic, emotional, mental, physical, social, and spiritual growth. The junior high school is preferably a three-year program within grades 6-9.

1144.   Inhelder, B. and Piaget, J.   Growth of Logical Thinking from Childhood to Adolescence: An Essay on the Construction of Further Operational Structures. New York: Basic Books, 1971.

Researchers say that the social environment acts as a variable in stage development of mental operations. The development of the ability to conform formal thinking, to deal with abstractions, and to conceptualize, which children in the past acquired somewhere between age 12 and 14, can be and has been appearing at an earlier age due largely to the experience found within the social environment. Since the cultural and educational conditions are variables which may be slowed or stepped up, it follows that earlier development of mental ability is possible and even probable--cultural factors directly affect the rate of mental maturation.

1145.   Isacksen, R. O.   "Assessing new issues in junior high school organization."   Bulletin of the National Association of Secondary School Principals, 45(1961): 104-105.

Foresaw the 1970s, as the third phase in the junior high school development, to be a period of experimentation. The name junior high school is dropped in favor of middle school.

1146.   Jennings, W. "The middle school? No!" Minnesota Journal of Education, 47(1967):73-74.

The key to better education is not slicing the pie differently but altering classroom practices, developing a curriculum significant for life, and preparing competent staff within the junior high framework. The middle school offers no real merit over the well established junior high system. There is much important work to be done in making schools for young adolescents effective without setting up another school organization that is slightly different.

1147.   Jensen, K.   "Physical growth."   Review of Educational Research, 25(December 1955):369-414.

Comparative statistics in child growth suggest that advances in medical science, better diet, and greater control of environmental conditions affect the rate of physical development.

1148.   Jersild, A. T.   The Psychology of Adolescence.   2d ed. New York: Macmillan, 1963.

Chapter 16--"The Adolescent at School"--contains material on attitudes toward school, teachers' and pupils' perceptions of causes of failure, qualities adolescents like and dislike in their teachers, adolescents who drop out of school, academic, utilitarian, and personal aspects of education for adolescents' problems, the problem of personal meaning, educating for self-understanding, resources for promoting knowledge of self, and premises underlying education for knowledge of self. Most persons move from childhood and adolescence into adulthood with a burden of unresolved personal problems, many of which are linked with the inevitable adversaries of human existence. But an education designed to help young adolescents to use their minds effectively should aim to help students take a thoughtful view of their personal concerns. Strictly from a scholarly point of view, the full meaning and value of many academic subjects (such as literature, history, biology, health, and physical education) can be achieved only if the student can relate what is taught to his own personal experience. Education can offer adolescents something more meaningful to them, as persons, than the usual impersonal academic routine. This can make an important difference in their lives, even though the teacher who tries to provide such instruction does not offer, or pretend to provide, the more intensive kind of self-scrutiny from psychotherapy. Self-examination is more profitable when a person is in the process of making crucial decisions than after such decisions have been made. Adolescents have more desire and capacity for self-inquiry than has been recognized in the kind of education they usually receive.

1149.   Joan, D. R.   "Pressures and adolescents."   Educational Leadership, 23,3(1965):209-211.

Pressure comes from parents who wish the best for their children, and social pressure comes from peers who push the idea of conformity to meet the demands of the right crowd. Homework and grades add additional pressures. What should be done: 1) Teachers and teaching must be improved. The teacher should be an educated person who has love and understanding for adolescent children and realizes that he can help youngsters solve their problems. 2) Problems of adolescence must be detected early and given attention by the guidance counselor. 3) Pressure of college preparation and accelerated programs should be balanced. 4) It is mandatory that leadership and membership roles be studied, understood, and practiced in the junior high school. As the curriculum is revised to meet the crisis of the junior high school level, it is not a matter of trying out new ideas, but rather of applying basic principles of learning and teaching to help improve the program. With love and understanding, the adolescent can survive this period of "transition and chaos."

1150.   Johnson, E. W.   How to Live Through Junior High School: A Practical Discussion of the Middle and Junior High School Years for Parents, Students, and Teachers. Philadelphia: J. B. Lippincott Co., 1975.

Chapters are: 1) The Passage from Childhood to Adulthood. 2) The Ages 10-15. 3) Grades 5-9. 4) Learning How to Learn: Study Habits, Homework, Marks. 5) Reading and Mathematics. 6) Underachievement and Boredom. 7) Social Life at Home and at School. 8) Sexual Development and Behavior. 9) The Use and Abuse of Drugs, Alcohol, and Tobacco. 10) Living with Parents and Teachers. 11) Adolescence and the Future. The author suggests fiction books that students in grades 5-9 would enjoy.

1151.   Johnson, M. "The adolescent intellect." Educational Leadership, 23,3(1965):200-204.

The junior high school should give greater emphasis to the adolescent intellect. Underlying such transformation is a basic change in the climate of the school. Some junior high schools are characterized by a repressive rigidity and stagnation, others by a sentimental indulgence of the frivolous and trivial. Neither type is a result of ideas or inquiry. Teachers and the school policies should give clear indications that intellectual pursuits are valued above all others. Equally important for adolescents' intellectual development in the junior high school is an appropriate quality in the elementary school. Children must, at an early age, come to view reading primarily as a source of ideas and information, and second as a means of recreation. By the time they reach the junior high school, the majority of students should be ready for formal operation. They should then regularly engage in explaining definitions, identifying a substance, dealing with cause and effect relations, classifying individual phenomena, and determining necessary and suspicious conditions for a conclusion. In short, they should, in

the terms of Robert Ennis' definition of critical
thinking, be able to assess statements correctly.
Charles Armstrong and Ethyl Cornell found that most
individuals have two cycles of mental growth, the
second beginning around puberty, often after a
plateau period of relatively little progress.
Possibly this plateau is a result of the school's
failure to confront the young adolescent with a
timely challenge to his changing intellect. It seems
unlikely that the physiological and emotional aspects
of maturing at that stage take so great a proportion
of some fixed reserve of psychic energy that little
is left for intellectual activity. Indeed, when an
individual is putting away childish things, he is
anxious to think about various matters. The adolescent intellect deserves more respect and greater
expectations.

1152.   Johnson, M. (Ed.).   Toward Adolescence: Middle
School Years.   79th Yearbook of the National Society
for the Study of Education. Chicago: University of
Chicago Press, 1980.

Perhaps the best available collection of viewpoints,
this book compiles sixteen articles by leading
authors in several fields dealing with adolescents
and their development. Sections deal with the age
group and its milieu, some areas of intervention,
approaches to research, and tasks for the school in
the middle.

1153.   Johnson, M., Jr. "School in the middle: junior
high--education's problem child."   Saturday Review,
45(1962):40-42.

In a world in which adults say one thing and do
another, in which schooling and economic dependence
are prolonged, and in which social life is largely
outside the family, the value of the junior high as a
haven is readily recognized. Unfortunately, not all
junior high schools are havens. Johnson describes
the middle school controversy versus the junior high,
discusses what constitutes a good junior high school
teacher, and describes the curriculum in a middle
school. The significant question is who will teach
early adolescents and what will they be taught.
Their teachers need to be well versed in their
respective subject fields and know and appreciate the
relative immaturity of these pupils, their transitional status, and their diversity. Junior high
school teachers must be willing and able to help
pupils become students, equipping them with the tools
and procedures for a lifetime of study, rather than
assume they can acquire the ability to study effectively and independently. Changes in curriculum
should put greater emphasis on significant ideas as

opposed to inert facts, greater continuity of intellectual development, greater flexibility of programming, particularly in the area of the arts and at
least as much attention to independence and study and
thinking as in the social and emotional spheres. If
teachers could provide a junior high curriculum which
would engage students' attention more fully, they
might then be distracted from many of their physical,
social and emotional problems. A Cornell study of
600 teachers found that those teaching grades 7 and 8
were much less satisfied with the level of their
assignment than were teachers in the grades both
above and below. An analysis of the stated reasons
for dissatisfaction indicated that the nature of the
curriculum rather than the nature of the pupils at
this level seems to be predominant. Teachers who
enjoy teaching many subject areas cannot do so in the
junior high school nor can those who enjoy teaching
advanced content.

1154.   Johnson, M., Jr. American Secondary Schools. New
York: Harcourt, Brace and World, 1965.

Contains sections on the goals and functions of
secondary schools, organization, program of studies,
academic subjects, practical subjects, student
activities, student personnel services, instructional
techniques, management and control, tradition and
innovation. The defenders of a three-step plan--
elementary, junior high, and senior high--contend
that just as children in adolescence differ sufficiently to warrant different educational treatment,
students need to be treated still differently during
the transition from childhood to adolescence. Furthermore, in this period of uncertain developmental
status, students achieve a sense of identity from
sharing in a school unit of their own. The argument
for a middle school unit is weakened because the
timing of this transition differs greatly from
individual to individual and between the sexes. Any
middle school will inevitably contain a mixture
consisting of immature children, primarily boys;
relatively mature young people, primarily girls; and
those of both sexes who are at the inbetween stage.
No institutional arrangement designed for groups can
be completely appropriate for every individual. By
serving the group with maximum diversity, the middle
unit permits the elementary school to cater primarily
to children, and the senior high school mainly to
adolescents. Although there will probably always be
variations in the organizational pattern, it seems
unlikely that the distinction between elementary and
secondary education will disappear entirely or that
any grades will be returned to the elementary school.
Rather, the secondary school will probably begin at
an even lower grade, thus making a middle school even

more essential if a manageable age range is to be
maintained. But whether this middle school includes
grades 6-8 or 5-8 or continues to serve grades 7-9,
it must have well-defined purposes and its own
identity and at the same time assure continuity with
the adjacent units.

1155. Johnson, M., Jr. "The junior high mystique."
Junior High School Newsletter, 3,3(1965):1.

Junior high students--lively, questioning, full of
curiosity--possess both the basic tools of learning
and an impetus to abandon childish attitudes and
modes of thinking. The junior high school is in a
better position to improve than either of the other
two levels. The elementary school is limited by the
lack of maturity and skills of its pupils, and the
senior high school is plagued by the attractive
nuisance of premature vocational training. The
junior high school is the last bulwark of the general
education and is in a position to offer its students
a vigorous, exciting, and challenging introduction to
all the major areas of organized knowledge. Only the
mystique prevents this, by turning attention inward
on adolescents rather than outward on the frontiers
of scholarship and by stressing the realization of
false group goals rather than of precious individual
potential.

1156. Johnson, S. C. "Middle Schools." Educational
Management Review Series 7. Eugene: University of
Oregon, ERIC Clearinghouse on Educational Management,
ERIC Doc. ED 066 778, July, 1972.

Article contains sections on the identity of middle
schools, the present status of the junior high and
middle school, future prospects for the middle
school, assessment of middle schools, and references.
The middle school movement is discussed as the mechanism of educational reform through grade level
reorganization.

1157. Joint Commission on Mental Health of Children,
Committees on Education and Religion. Mental Health
of Children. Report of Task Forces 1, 2, and 3. New
York: Harper and Row, 1973.

Note especially these chapters: Studies of Children
from Kindergarten through Eighth Grade, Studies of
Adolescents and Youth, Education and Mental Health.
Of specific interest--"Mental Health in the School
Environment"--these articles detail an expanded role
for growth of the school, recommendations for an
upper elementary school model, and developmental
processes as educational goals. Learning can be
considered optimal when it takes shape as independent

pursuit by an actively involved child: 1) A positive learning environment presents the child with varied possibilities to observe, discover, invent, and choose; it avoids complete dependence on verbal vicarious transmissions of information and emphasizes processes of search in which the child identifies his power and competence in being the author of inquiry and the initiator of action. 2) Learning is incomplete from the developmental view unless it encompasses both cognitive and affective domains and uses the forces--the cumulated meanings, feelings, wishes, conflicts--of the inner life of impulse and affect. It is essential that children have opportunity to express feelings directly in their relations to people in school and that they have opportunity to express in symbolic form the affective elements of their encounter with the outer world. 3) The organization of learning tasks should make maximum use of one of the major developmental trends of the elementary and middle school years, namely, the tendency to turn to the peer group both as refuge and as authority. 4) The maintenance of a rational authority structure in a school is a cornerstone in establishing an open climate for learning; its effectiveness depends on the extent to which the relations of those in superior positions to teachers are consistent with what is expected of teachers.

1158. Jones, M. C. "Comparison of attitudes and interests of ninth grade students over two decades." Journal of Educational Psychology, 51,4(1960):178.

Ninth graders of the 1950s are more mature than ninth graders of the 1930s. "One fact is outstanding in our results. In the more recent tests boys and girls in the ninth grade marked items in such a way as to indicate greater maturity and greater social sophistication." Fourteen-year-olds in 1953 and 1959--compared to 14-year-olds in 1935--are more studious, interested in the contemporary scene, more tolerant in their social attitudes, and inclined to value controlled behavior and disapprove irresponsible behavior in others. The 14-year-olds of the 50s show greater maturity, are more serious about heterosexual interests, and are more tolerant of social issues.

1159. Jones, M. C. and Bayley, N. "Physical maturing among boys as related to behavior." Journal of Educational Psychology, 41(1950):129-148.

The problems of adjustment during the adolescent period center around the youth's need to develop heterosexual interests, to select a vocation, and, in general, to acquire the status of adulthood in the eyes of his peers and of his elders. The impetus for the attainment of maturity is undoubtedly related to the adolescent's physical changes, but the process of growing up is so complex and so interwoven with cultural factors that we have not been able to demonstrate more than a general relationship between physical and psychological phases of development. The report deals with two groups of boys who were on opposite ends of a normal sample based on one developmental characteristic: skeletal age. The physically accelerated boys are usually accepted and treated by adults and other children as more mature. They appear to have relatively little need to strive for status. From their ranks come the outstanding student body leaders in senior high school. In contrast, the physically retarded boys exhibit many forms of relatively immature behavior, perhaps in part because others tend to treat them as the little boys they appear to be. Furthermore, a fair proportion of these boys tries to counteract the physical disadvantage in some way--usually by greater activity and striving for attention, although in some cases by withdrawal. The findings show the effect of physical maturity on behavior. Perhaps of greater importance, however, is the repeated demonstration of the many factors, psychological and cultural as well as physical, which contribute to the formation of basic personality patterns.

1160.   Josselyn, I. M. "Social pressures in adolescence." Social Casework, 39,5(1952):187-193.

Up to the junior high school level, the adolescent has had his teacher as a parent substitute to guide him in the learning process. The junior high school deprives him of the daily relationship with one teacher. The school experience now is geared primarily to subject matter, and the teacher becomes an instrument for teaching the subject. His contact with the teacher is limited in most instances to his classwork. The school system attempts to meet this problem by providing advisors, deans, and vocational counselors. Usually, such specialists are not an integral part of the everyday school life of the child; he views them as persons set apart, filling a special role. The adolescent's school experience-- subject matter rather than personal relationships to the faculty--comes at a time when an impersonal relationship is gratifying to him because it allows him to retreat, but it can be frustrating if he wants help. He may find a member of the faculty who will serve as a supporting person because of his own seeking or through the initiative of a particular teacher, not because it is inherent in the educational program.

1161.   Josselyn, I. M.   "Psychological changes in adolescence."   Children, 6,2(1959):43-47.

"One of the best tools for dealing with adolescents is nothing derived from complicated ideas about them, but is merely a feeling of being comfortable in working with them. If we have this, the attitude will show that you are not afraid and so will not tend to increase their panic. If we are calm--though not indifferent in dealing with them--they at least will feel that we offer the kind of stable baseline they cannot see in themselves." The article includes these sections: Wanted: A Framework, Roots of Confusion, Acting Out, Struggling for Freedom, and Effect of Peers.

1162.   Journal of School Health. "Children: bigger and better." Journal of School Health, 27(1957):267-268.

The article presents findings of studies that say children are larger, stronger, and healthier. This information is important when considering grade arrangements for early adolescents.

1163.   Jurenas, A. C. "Junior high to middle school: one school's conversion." Middle School Journal, 11,2 (1980):26.

Follows the changes made when a junior high was converted to a middle school at the O.W. Huth Upper Grades Center in Matteson, Illinois. The article describes the way the school was operated before the change, leads up to the planning, and finally discusses the process of change on the staff and on the community.

1164.   Kagan, J. "A conception of early adolescence." Daedalus, Fall 1971:27-35.

Argues that maturational development, though still not completely understood, prepares the mind of a 12-year-old to examine sets of propositions for logical consistency. This competence, when applied to his own premises, can produce new assumptions if it is catalyzed by encounter with experiences that jolt the mind into using this capacity. Puberty is one such inducing event in all cultures. Western society adds local phenomena surrounding school, drugs, sexuality, authority, and family--each of which generates uncertainty that the child must resolve. In so doing, he creates new beliefs. The specific form of the conflict and its resolution depend on the belief clash that initially generated the uncertainty, as well as the community in which the child lives. Middle-class, American 15-year-olds are waging war against feelings of isolation, commitment to action and belief, loyalty to others, and capacity for love. Earlier generations grappled with the theme of social status and financial security. Each era is marked by

one or two social problems that give substantive
direction to the brooding. Racial strife, density of
population, and more important, lack of a central
ideology loom as the potential capacities of the
future.

1165.   Kagan, J. and Moss, H. A.   Birth to Maturity: The
Fels Study of Psychological Development.   New York:
Wiley, 1962.

This investigation uncovered several new ideas about
developmental sequences that were not emphasized by
theorists in the early 1960s. Chapters include: 1)
The Introduction. 2) Methods of Assessment. 3) The
Stability of Behavior: Passivity and Dependency. 4)
The Stability of Behavior: Aggression. 5) The Stability of Behavior: Achievement and Recognition. 6)
The Stability of Behavior: Sexuality, Social Interaction, and Selected Behaviors. 7) Maternal Practices and the Child's Behavior. 8) Sources of
Conflict and Anxiety. 9. Summary and Conclusions.

1166.   Kerr, R. D.   "Let's play change."   School and
Community, 56(1969):26-27.

The middle school concept is the best new educational
innovation since the 1920's.

1167.   Kindred, L. W.   The Intermediate Schools.   Englewood Cliffs, N.J.:   Prentice-Hall, 1968.

Book presents these sections: 1) Introduction:
Intermediate Schools Today. 2) Educational Foundations: Developmental Background. Nature of the
Learner. Instructional Processes. Underlying View-
points. 3) The Instructional Program: Curriculum
Designs. Program of Studies. Special Education
Programs. Daily Schedules. Instructional Resource
Centers. Instructional Aids. Instructional Policies. Instructional Improvement. Student Activities
Programs. 4) Related Services: Pupil Personnel Services. Special Services. 5) Organization and Administration: Organizational Structures. Administrative Services. Staff Personnel Practices. School
Plant design. Relations with the Community. Evaluating the Program.

1168.   Kittel, J. E.   "Changing patterns of education:
the middle school years."   College of Education
Record, 30(1967):62-68.

The evidence for junior highs or middle schools is as
yet much too spotty, too subjective, and too meager
for firm conclusions. It is questionable whether
states will establish special training programs for

the middle school teacher; programs have been inadequate for junior high teachers in the past. Teachers
must be made an integral part of any educational
innovation. There are other possible grade groups
such as 6-6, 8-4, nursery and kindergarten, 3-3-4-4,
grades 10-14. Each is advocated by a significant
number of educators. Most of the problems now
plaguing existing grade organizations will not be
solved by merely shifting grades one way or the
other. No single plan of organization will solve all
problems, and the middle school is no exception. A
real imperative is the individualization of education
for preadolescence, and any age or grade grouping
that effectively meets this need should be seriously
considered. The middle school concept appears to
offer one new and promising method. If it does no
more than focus educators' attention on the increasing problems of pubescence, it will serve a useful
function. In 1967 there were over three hundred
middle schools which fit the 5-3-4 or 4-4-4 pattern
of organization with an additional 150 estimated in
the process of shifting. This article also dealt
with the organizational patterns of departmentalization, special courses, appropriate facilities,
special services and activities, and administrator
reactions.

1169. Kohen-Raz, R. The Child From 9 to 13: The
Psychology of Preadolescence and Early Puberty.
Chicago: Aldine-Atherton, 1971.

Offering fresh insights into the problems of normal
and disturbed children, this work is the first to
consider the interval between the end of childhood
and the beginning of puberty as an entirely independent, critical, and formative stage in human development. Instead of viewing adolescence as an extension
of childhood or an intermediate link between the
child and the adult, the author identifies this
period as the beginning of a second phase of life.
Kohen-Raz defines the onset and end of preadolescence
and early puberty and describes the motor, mental,
perceptual, emotional, and social development of this
stage in the life process. He demonstrates that preadolescence and early puberty are characterized by
antagonistic tendencies of physical, mental, and
emotional development. While preadolescence is shown
to be a phase of relatively quiet physical maturation, motor, intellectual, and social activity inten-
sify. Early puberty, in contrast, is characterized
by abrupt physiological changes, introversion, and
social withdrawal. Topics covered include: preadolescence in primitive societies, educational problems
of the normal preadolescent, and the psychopathology,
psychotherapy, and problems of special education of
this group. Chapter 6 deals with the educational

problems of the normal preadolescent, with sections
on general changes in scholastic attitudes and
aptitudes, the basic curriculum, mathematics and
geometry, humanities, natural science, art education,
preadolescent reading preferences, social interaction
in the classroom, the role of the teacher, and the
educational role of the parent. The main task of the
school in educating preadolescents and early adolescents is the transmission of universal values and the
presentation of impersonal social demands.

1170.   Kohl, J. W., Caldwell, W. E., and Eichhorn, D. H.
Self-appraisal and Development of the Middle School:
An In-service Approach. University Park: Pennsyl-
vania School Study Council, 1970.

The middle school attempts to provide for the stage
of development (transescence) which begins prior to
the onset of puberty and extends through the early
stage of adolescence by 1) developing a unique
program adapted to the needs of transescents, 2)
providing a wide range of intellectual, social, and
physical experiences, 3) providing opportunities for
exploration and for development of skills involved in
individual learning patterns, 4) maintaining an
atmosphere of basic respect for individual differences, 5) creating a climate that enables students to
develop abilities, to find facts, to weigh evidence,
to draw conclusions, to determine values, and to keep
their minds open to new facts, 6) recognizing and
understanding the students' needs, interests, backgrounds, motivations, goals, and especially their
stresses, strains, frustrations, and fears, 7) providing smooth educational transitions from the elementary school to the high school while recognizing
the physical and emotional changes taking place, 8)
providing an environment where the child, not the
program, is more important, 9) providing an environment where the opportunity to succeed is insured for
all students, 10) offering guidance to the pupil in
the development of mental processes and attitudes
needed for contributing constructive citizenship and
in the development of lifelong competencies and
appreciations required for effective use of leisure
time, 11) providing competent teachers who will
strive to understand the students they serve and who
will develop professional skills to teach the transescent, and 12) providing facilities and a flexible
use of time to allow students and teachers to best
meet the goals of the program.

1171.   Koos, L. B.   The Junior High School.   New York:
Harcourt, Brace and Co., 1920.

This very early text presents a complete history of
the junior high school and describes the movement for

reorganization, the specific functions of the junior high, and the original program of study.

1172.   Koos, L. B.   "Educational news and editorial comment."   School Review, 44,3(1956):101-107.

In Independence, Kansas, the school system switched from a 6-3-3-2 grade pattern to a 6-4-4. The article analyzes the advantages of this plan and gives reasons for its slow growth nationally.

1173.   Kuhlen, R. G. and Collister, E. G.   "Sociometric status of sixth and ninth graders who fail to finish high school."   Educational and Psychological Measurement, 12(1952):632-637.

Students who failed to complete high school were less acceptable socially to their classmates and were judged by their classmates to possess traits showing personal and social maladjustment.

1174.   Kuhlen, R. G. and Lee, B. J.   "Personality characteristics and social acceptability in adolescence." Journal of Educational Psychology,   34,6(1943):321-340.

Social acceptability scores and peer judgments on personality characteristics of seven hundred sixth, ninth, and twelfth graders were studied to determine trends during adolescence and to compare the relationship between social acceptability (in the study, social acceptability among one's own sex) and the various personality traits.   The study found these insights with social development: 1) Emerging interest in heterosexual relationships in all study participants was clearly evident, in terms of percentage choosing and being chosen by the opposite sex as possible companions for various activities.   2) Heterosexual adjustment was far from general even at the twelfth grade--35 percent not being chosen by the opposite sex and about 25 percent making no opposite sex choices.   3) Girls showed increased liking for the opposite sex, enjoyed jokes on self, wanted to be popular with others, and were willing to take a chance.   Girls were considered to show greater interest in the opposite sex and less interest in active games as they grew older.   4) Sex differences indicated boys to be more restless, talkative, active in games, to enjoy a joke, to enjoy fighting, to be more willing to take a chance, and to seek attention more than girls.   Girls were considered to act older than their ages more frequently than boys.   5) The evidence suggested that in early adolescence (ninth grade) the girls tend to be more active socially (are more often judged to be sociable and to initiate activities), but by later adolescence (twelfth grade) boys tend to dominate the social scene. Boys were judged more frequently than girls to be popular and to initiate games and activities.

1175.   Landers, J. and Mercurio, C. "Improving curriculum and instruction for the disadvantaged minorities." Journal of Negro Education, 34(1965):342-365.

Establishes guidelines for educational programs and assistance to disadvantaged youth and gives examples of useful programs. The article includes sections on New Standards of Evaluation, Social Skills for Dis- advantaged Youth, Vocational Education, The Civil Rights Struggle and Learning, Implications for Organizations, Specific Programs, Reading and Lan- guage Arts, A Description of the Program in New York City, The Frostig Program, Guidance and Motivation, Discussion of the Cultural Emphasis for Disadvantaged Youth, Community School Programs, Programs in Cleveland, Philadelphia, Wilmington, Milwaukee, and St. Louis, Pre-service and In-service Training Pro- grams in Philadelphia, Cleveland, and New York City, Programs for Potential Dropouts in Chicago and Cleveland, Materials for Instruction, Programmed Instruction, Team Teaching, Auxiliary Programs Such as After-School Study Centers, Volunteers, All-Day Neighborhood Schools, and The Homework Helper Program.

1176.   Launchner, A. H. "What are the characteristics of a modern junior high school?" Bulletin of the National Association of Secondary School Principals, 34(1950):10-16.

Points out how and why the junior high school has accomplished its purposes.

1177.   Lawrence, G. "Do programs reflect what research says about physical development?" Middle School Journal, 11,2(1980):12-14.

Article discusses eight facts of physical development and tells what middle schools can do about them: 1) Muscle size and strength increase, but more for boys than girls, making boys able to do heavier work and run faster and longer. 2) The sequence of adolescent changes remains constant. In general, girls develop two years ahead of boys, but individuals differ con- siderably in the timing of puberty. 3) Although the sequence of adolescent development remains constant, the age of the onset of puberty has been changing for both boys and girls. 4) The growth spurt in muscle occurs at the same time and rate as the spurt in skeletal growth because the same hormones are respon- sible for both. 5) Relative freedom from illness is typical of this age group, but the diet and sleeping habits of many transescents are poor. 6) The adolescent growth spurt occurs at a different tempo for various parts of the body. 7) The duration of the maturation cycle differs widely. 8) The first signs of puberty differ, causing some confusion among children and parents.

1178.   Leipold, L. E.   "Young, energetic, and going places." Clearinghouse, 29(1955):408-409.

The article describes the strong points of the junior high school and presents some of the beliefs of principals, superintendents, and teachers as to why this grade organizational pattern is best for young adolescents.

1179.   Leonard, J. P.   "Frontiers in junior high school education." Bulletin of the National Association of Secondary School Principals, 44(1940):112-119.

Departmentalization is out of harmony with what we know about development of early adolescent youth. Junior high youth do not quickly adjust from guidance of one person to the assignments of five or more teachers, shifting from a unified emphasis to a specialized interest.

1180.   Lewis, G. M. "I am - I want - I need. Preadolescents look at themselves and their values." Childhood Education, 46,4(1970):186-194.

In class and small group discussions, individual interviews, anonymous writing, and teacher observation, students freely expressed their health interests, concerns, and problems. The project included more than five thousand students in four selected Connecticut school systems, grades K-12, representing inner-city, suburban, rural, and high economic communities. The study reports misconceptions, misinformation, half-truths, and facts these young people have learned from their surroundings. Clues abound for teachers in all grades who wish to help boys and girls in their "now" needs. Evidence related to approximately two thousand students in grades 5 to 8 has been extracted from the total report. Middle school educators will find this partial report of special use. For example, the sharp difference in questions raised by 10-year-olds and by 11- to 13-year-olds raises some doubt about the advisability of the grade 5 to 8 grouping and indicates the care educators must take to make such a grouping profitable for 10-year-olds. The responses show the strong preadolescent character of fifth graders, with a few students (usually girls) embarrassed by early maturation; the greater mixture of pre- and young adolescents in the sixth grade, with many concerned about indications of puberty; the greater number of young adolescents in the seventh grade, with a few worried and uncomfortable about late maturation; and the more homogeneous development in the eighth grade, with a few very late maturers.

1181.   Lipsitz, J. S. "Schooling for Young Adolescents: A Key Time in Secondary Education." Testimony prepared for the Subcommittee on Elementary, Secondary, and Vocational Education, Carl D. Perkins, Chairman, U.S. House of Representatives, January 24, 1980.

Early adolescence, a crucial time in human development, is often overlooked. Despite the critical importance of this age group, (10-to-15-year-olds) the intellectual and economic resources of our country are not being allocated to these young people. The testimony emphasizes these points: 1) The early years of secondary education, the junior high years, desperately need the national attention that the early elementary grades and later years of secondary schooling receive. 2) Why should educators and researchers turn their attention to young adolescents? Like early childhood, adolescence is a time of such remarkable growth and change that positive prevention and intervention are possible. Unlike early childhood, adolescence cannot be overlooked because the personal and societal losses that result from our neglect can no longer be ignored. 3) Policies and techniques that are effective with other age groups don't work in intermediate school life. One must look at each educational issue as it relates specifically to the developmental characteristics of this age group. We cannot assume that what works at the elementary or senior high levels (for instance, compensatory education, basic skills, desegregation, programs for the handicapped, vocational education, the arts, or professional development) is also effective in schools for young adolescents. 4) The shift to thinking abstractly is a crucial developmental phenomenon that most people are unaware of. 5) Because adolescence is generally viewed as a healthy time in life, we fail to do the screening necessary to insure that we have in our schools the one undeniable prerequisite for successful learning: an intact child. 6) Programs that select individual students for special attention or services will not be as attractive as programs that work with the peer group. 7) Young adolescents need to be with a diverse mix of adults. 8) We need to get more young people out of the schools to learn. 9) We have an image of young teenagers as being irresponsible, and therefore we do not trust them with meaningful work, yet they are the babysitters of our nation. Lipsitz is the Director of the Center for Early Adolescence at the University of North Carolina at Chapel Hill.

1182.   Livingston, H. "The middle school: can it survive the claims of its supporters?" Illinois Education, 30(1968):345-347.

Describes the controversies surrounding the middle
school concept.

1183.   Loomis, M. J. The Preadolescent: Three Major
Concerns. New York: Appleton-Century-Crofts, 1959.

Part I deals with aspirations to greater independence. Its four chapters are concerned with assessing developmental needs for increasing independence,
pacing teacher guidance through value guided action,
situational accounts, and creative approaches to
fostering desirable independence. Part II focuses on
preadolescents striving for sexual identification.
Part III looks ahead to junior high school and adolescent living. Because the social aspects of readiness for junior high school compete with academic
readiness, they merit special investigation and analysis. Teachers and parents who view sympathetically
the importance which preadolescents attach to interrelationships are in a better position to help guide
the children in the direction of behavior based on
value-guided action. The attitudes and behavior of
preadolescents in aspiring to greater independence,
striving for sexual identification, and looking ahead
to junior high school living are frequently the most
puzzling to adults and children.

1184.   Loomis, M. J. "Early adolescence (ages 11-14)."
Chapter 4 in Mary Jane Loomis (Ed.), How Children
Develop. Columbus: Ohio State University, 1964.

The chapter covers these areas: 1) Personal health
and healthful living can be achieved by meeting needs
of rest, diet, and by promoting freedom from infec-
tion, optimal physical and organic development, and
engaging in suitable recreational activities. 2)
A sense of security can be maintained by gaining and
holding affection, confidence, esteem, and status,
and by developing a social personality. 3) To
develop and maintain a sense of achievement one must
feel personal adequacy and control over the environment as well as sensitivity to the opposite sex. 4)
Intellectual and aesthetic interests and appreciations develop along with social values and respect
for the cultural heritage.

1185.   Loost, W. R. "Perceptions across the life span of
important information sources for children and adolescents." Journal of Psychology, 78(1971):207-211.

Persons of all ages were asked whom they perceive to
be the most important transmitters of information to

children and adolescents. Parents were perceived to be most significant for children. Peers were named more often as being prime transmitters for adolescents, although parents was a frequent response. The late adolescent/young adult samples perceived less importance of parents than did any other age group. Of lesser importance were the mass media, schools, teachers, and churches.

1186.   Lounsbury, J. H. "What has happened to the junior high school?" Educational Leadership, 13(1956): 368-369.

Describes the history of the junior high school, and relates how its functions and characteristics have changed in this century.

1187.   Lounsbury, J. H. "Junior high school education: renaissance and reformation." High School Journal, 43(1960):143-150.

Points out critical decisions being made about junior high school education following renewed interest in the 1950s.

1188.   Lounsbury, J. H. "How the junior high school came to be." Educational Leadership, 18(1960):145-147.

Many factors caused the inauguration and early success of the crusade to reorganize secondary education. The original impetus came from the colleges and was concerned with economy of time and with college preparation. Discussions about reorganization became linked with other school problems (dropouts and retardation).

1189.   Lounsbury, J. H. and Vars, G. F. "The middle school: fresh start or new delusion?" National Elementary Principal, 51,3(1971):12-19.

The appearance of the middle school should be viewed, not as a new answer, a new solution, but as a new opportunity, a new rallying point, a fresh start. The educational tools and techniques available to achieve these goals are the same; the vehicles in which we travel are almost the same; and the roadblocks to be removed or skirted confront all who travel this way. All concerned must work together to provide vital and appropriate educational experiences for youth in the critical transitional years. Authors argue for the middle school in these areas: 1) precocity of the learner, 2) homogeneity of the age group, 3) curricular autonomy, 4) specialized instruction, 5) individualization, flexibility, and innovation, 6) guidance, 7) staff, 8) school desegregation, and 9) buildings and finances.

1190.   Low, C. M.   "Tasting their teens in the junior
         high school."   National Education Association Jour-
         nal, 42(1953):347-349.

         Statement describes the nature and characteristics of
         early adolescents of both sexes and gives a brief
         description of a good teacher for this school level.

1191.   Macauly, G.   "What grades should be included when
         opening a new high school?"   Journal of Secondary
         Education, 43(1968):326-331.

         Two factors should be considered when opening a new
         high school and if deciding to include grade 9 or
         not. These factors are: 1) slow, predictable growth
         of student population, and 2) insufficient district
         funds to build the complete plant at once. Once the
         decision has been made to open with grade 9 or grade
         10, administrators involved in the planning and
         operation of the new school should take care to do
         the following things: 1) The curriculum should be
         the same as the curriculum in established high
         schools in the district. 2) Club activities should
         not be overextended. 3) The athletic program should
         be appropriate to the age of the students and the
         size of the student body. 4) Efforts should be made
         to develop potential leadership from a broader base
         of students than the leadership group in office when
         school opens. 5) Until the school is well estab-
         lished, student leaders should be elected each
         semester. 6) The public relations program should be
         telling parents that small schools can provide an
         educational program of the same quality as larger
         schools. 7) The minimum first year ratio of library
         books per student should be six. 8) The principal
         should begin early to influence long-range plans for
         building and grounds development.

1192.   Manitoba Department of Education.   "Education in
         the Middle Years." Manitoba, Canada, 1977.

         Intended for discussion of education in the Manitoba
         schools, the paper outlines these areas: the junior
         high school, the middle years child (cognitive, phys-
         ical, social, emotional, and moral characteristics),
         schools in the middle years (the program, strategy,
         school climate, discipline, and organizational pat-
         tern), the middle years educators (characteristics,
         needs, teacher training, pre-service and in-service,
         teacher attitudes, teacher competencies), the middle
         years school in the community, community expecta-
         tions, relationship between school and community, use
         of community resources, a book list, and resources.

1193.   Manlove, D. C. and Mowrey, L. Junior High School/
Middle School Evaluative Criteria.   Arlington, Va.:
National Study of School Evaluation, 2201 Wilson
Blvd., Arlington, Va. 22201, ERIC Doc. ED 043 671,
1970.

The study develops criteria and provides directions
for their use.   The sections on school and community
and on philosophy and objectives form the foundation
for the entire evaluation process. Formal aspects of
an educational program, educational commitments, the
organization of the curriculum, student activities,
learning media services, student services, administration, instructional staff, and auxiliary staff,
school plant and facilities are also discussed in
this report. See ERIC Abstract #ED 043 671.

1194.   Manone, C. J. and Glatthorn, A. J.   "The 9-10
school: a novelty or a better answer?" Educational
Leadership, 23(1966):285-289.

Interest increases in the 6-2-2-2 or 5-3-2-2 or
4-4-2-2 plan where the high school is in two sections: grades 9-10 in "lower high" or "mid-high" and
grades 11-12 in "upper high."

1195.   Martin, E. C.   "Reflections on the early adolescent in school." Daedalus, 100,4(1971):1087-1103.

The early adolescent expresses attitudes toward a
middle school or junior high school in sections with
these headings: 1) on being a twitch, 2) on being
full of enthusiasm, 3) dump--an in-depth example, 4)
the beginning of discontent, 5) the power of a touch,
6) on being with one's peers, 7) on classrooms and
teachers.

1196.   Martinson, F. M.   "Sexual knowledge, values, and
behavior patterns of adolescents."   Child Welfare,
47(1968):405-410.

A study of seven hundred middle-class adolescents in
Minnesota indicates that these adolescents aren't
bound by social rules saying premarital sex is wrong.
Young people do want help, especially from parents,
in how to handle sexual relationships. They say that
parents, church, and school have failed to help. The
article is divided into sections on sexual behavior
and values, claims on adolescence, dating patterns,
methods of birth control, and available sex
education.

1197.   Maryland State Department of Educational Curriculum Studies. "Some Developmental Characteristics of
Junior High Pupils." Baltimore. (No year given.)

Presents important aspects of physical, intellectual, social, and overall personal development with implications for the school program.

1198.   Maybee, G. D. (Ed.). "What do we believe: position paper on junior high." Bulletin of the National Association of Secondary School Principals, 46(1962): 5-7.

Middle school advocates point out that the National Association of Secondary School Principals took a stand for a three-year junior high school (grades 7-9).

1199.   McCormick, M. J. "The junior high school should be eliminated." Instructor, 75(1965):27.

The junior high school is a valuable asset to our school system; it aids in caring for the developmental processes of our boys and girls, in providing the guidance needed to solve the problems of early adolescence, in making it possible to provide a broader curriculum, in simplifying administration, and in making better use of the physical plants. In spite of several problems, the junior high school must stay if educational organization is to be most successful. In these middle years when youngsters are in a difficult adjustment time, specialized guidance, understanding, and counseling can help to solve the problems confronting them. The junior high school is definitely needed and it serves a purpose that no other unit can serve as well. It should be nourished. The speed of social maturity is the basic reason for the development of junior high schools. Adolescence occurs in every child; physical growth cannot be fought. A child will grow regardless of his environment. Maturity and independence, however, are learned aspects of behavior. Here is where the school plays an integral part in helping youth to grow into self-sufficient adults.

1200.   McGlasson, M. "The Middle School: Whence? What? Whither?" Fastback Series, no. 22. Phi Delta Kappa Educational Foundation, 8th and Union, Box 789, Bloomington, Ind. 47401, ERIC Doc. Ed 085 897, 1973.

Booklet discusses how middle schools may be described in terms of grades--grades 5 or 6 through 8--or in terms of program--one that assists boys and girls to move from elementary to secondary education with greatest success. The author traces historical roots of middle schools, examines the variety of middle schools, discusses them in terms of grade structure, administration, and program, and compares their roles to those of traditional junior high schools. Middle

schools of the future are discussed.   See ERIC
Abstract #ED 085 897.

1201.   McGlasson, M. and Pace, V.   "A history of NCA
accreditation of junior high schools." North Central
Association Quarterly, 45,2(1970):253-258.

The interest of the North Central Association of
Colleges and Secondary Schools in the junior high
school as a special unit of school organization and
as a program of studies for early adolescents dates
back to 1909.   The article presents a chronology of
NCA accreditation from 1959-1970.

1202.   McMahon, M. P.   "Intellectual capabilities of the
preadolescent."   In Thornburg, H. (Ed.), Preadolescent Development.   Tucson: University of Arizona
Press, 1974.

The concept of intelligence has been defined in a
variety of ways by educators and researchers.   Intelligence or intellectual capacity is considered to be
the effective adaptation to situations in the
individual's environment.   This capability is present, in some degree, in all individuals.   The article
presents a brief summary of intellectual development
from the Piagetian viewpoint and then discusses the
developmental characteristics, interests, and abilities of the preadolescent.   To show the preadolescents' increasing intellectual capabilities, the last
section examines the subject areas of science,
mathematics, and social studies.   Comparisons and
contrasts are drawn among the various grade levels
associated with this developmental period.   These
three subjects require the same basic capabilities
from the student: the ability to classify, discriminate, form concepts and rules, and apply the
knowledge in solving the problems.   The five grade
levels, fourth through eighth, have also used these
same intellectual capabilities in an increasing level
of complexity as the grade level increased.   It is
important to note that even though these capabilities
are a part of the preadolescent's intellectual
development, it is very necessary for the teacher to
actively guide the student in the proper sequential
development of these intellectual capabilities and to
ensure that the proper content is presented.

1203.   McNassor, D.   "The night world of preadolescence."
Childhood Education, 51,6(1975):312-318.

The middle school years mark a new stage in psychological growth.   Biological developments have prepared the child for changes in cognitive styles,
interests, and behaviors.   A mysterious mechanism
alters a child's psychic competence so that he is

able to react to events, tasks, and people in new
ways. The early adolescent requires teaching, counseling, and experiences that are different from what
is considered developmentally proper in the elementary school or in high school. The article comprises
sections on the nature of the new cognitive competence, thinking in multiple dimensions, searching for
inconsistencies, new thoughts--fresh patterns, developing individual interests, searching for new relationships, teachers as friends, other adults "outside," mutual peer testing, the future generations of
early adolescents, tomorrow's school: obsolescent or
regenerative, and signs of the future.

1204.   McNassor, D. J. "Future of the junior high school:
a reappraisal of the development in education in
early adolescence." California Journal of Secondary
Education, 33(1958):71-75.

In August 1957, sixty junior high school principals,
teachers, and supervisors met to study the behavior
and fundamental needs of young adolescents, the
cultural realities of their times, and the present
operation of the junior high school. The school
leaders reviewed the major basic research on adolescent development in the junior high school years.
Strong ideas emerged: 1) The early adolescent boy
and girl need the junior high school, either as a
separate institution or as a distinctive program, in
their unsure reach for responsibility, new creations,
and independence. 2) In the interest of the mental
development and mental health of young adolescents,
certain aspects of the junior high school program
appear vulnerable and should be the basis for
research and experimental or pilot programs. 3) How
are we going to change the direction of junior high
organization from that of a large personal collective
of two thousand early adolescents to one of a group
of several learning communities in one school? The
small integrated community for the student would be a
group of two or three hundred students with its own
faculty, administrative leadership, program of
studies, exploratory activity, and guidance personnel. This small school faculty would operate as a
team and would come to know well all the students in
their unit. A great motivation in learning would
result from settings where students could be closely
supervised and supported in their education and human
development. Teachers would also find more gratification in their work. They would no longer individually have to assume total responsibility for unknown
pupils with an unknown future who come and go each
day. According to this conference the future of the
junior high school's effectiveness will depend on how
sensitive and informed the teachers are regarding

early adolescents and the cultural realities that are shaping their views and confidence.

1205. McNeil, E. B. Human Socialization. Belmont, Calif.: Brooks-Cole Publishing Co., 1969.

Of particular interest are Part IV--the nature of education, the teacher, the child in school, discipline, emotional disturbance, theories of frustration, emotional and behavior problems, and trends toward educational mental health--and Part V--the socialization of youth, rites of passage, developmental tasks and needs, peer group influence on personality, the youth culture, and conflict between the generations.

1206. McNeil, E. B. "The changing children of preadolescence (or the questionable joy of being pre-anything)." Childhood Education, 46,4(1970):181-185.

The emerging adolescent is unclear as to how he should feel and behave and what societal or moral pressures may result. Comments are pointed toward teachers of preadolescents, although parents and other adults will find the material relevant. The author challenges the reader to look at the changing preadolescent and the new social behaviors and pressures with which he must contend in addition to increasing pressure on the preadolescent to be thinking about and looking forward to adolescence. The author contends there is no defined latency, and that more than half of fifth and sixth grade children have definite interests in members of the opposite sex.

1207. McQueen, M. "The rationale of the middle school: not just another label for junior high." Education Digest, 37(1972):10-13.

The emphasis and spirit of the middle school program are much more important than a new name. The hope is to give each student confidence that he can learn and the knowledge that learning is really worthwhile. The author criticizes the junior high and sees the middle school as a fresh approach with a new organizational plan, balanced curriculum, individualization and personal development, exploratory experiences, teachers, flexibility, and physical facilities.

1208. Mead, M. "Are we squeezing out adolescence?" PTA Magazine, 55,1(1960):4-6, and Educational Digest, 26: 5-8.

Every responsible community and school should help early adolescents in these ways. First, emphasize the special abilities of boys rather than recognize their greater waywardness and variability. Second, a determined effort should be made to reduce social activities at the junior high level, to encourage solitary activity and to promote separate activities for boys and girls. (All of which are discouraged today by parents and teachers). Third, adolescent social affairs should cut across high school and college lines. Fourth, there should be a serious exploration of the advantages of growing up slowly. The long days of adolescence will never return those days in which both boys and girls have their last leisure to search their souls and to try, without commitment, the many possible roles they may take in the world.

1209.   Mead, M. "The early adolescent in today's American culture and implications for education." Junior High School Newsletter, 1(1963):6.

The junior high school was set up to protect young adolescents, to provide for their transition, to give them things the elementary school could not do at a time when they are too young for the senior high school.

1210.   Mead, M. "Early adolescence in the United States." Bulletin of the National Association of Secondary School Principals, 49(1965):5-10.

The grades included in junior high were postulated on age and not on size, strength, or stage of puberty. So when junior highs, designed to cushion the shock of change in scholastic demands, became the focus of the social pressures once exerted in senior high school, problems multiplied. The emphasis on earlier and earlier participation in adult activities is incongruent with the junior high school movement. The appropriate experiences of the early teens are pair friendships with members of their own sex; an emerging recognition that the other sex can be interesting; admiration and emulation of adult models, heros, and ideals (who reincarnate the early childhood sense that the parents and teachers were all knowing and wise); and enormous curiosity about the outside world, about their own changing bodily responses, and about their shifting sense of identity. The dull routine of school, in which children learn a tenth of what they could, blunts the curiosity that might carry them through junior high school. Social circumstances condemn millions of adolescents to learn very little at school and to live a life in which their potential is practically unrealized. The specific smaller tragedies are dropouts in high school, after high school, and in college; early marriage, early parenthood; and underachievement for one third of our young people.

Corrective measures are on the horizon: more differentiation by special interests within junior high schools; more association of junior high school students with younger and older students; consciously diversified summer experiences; and not the least important but with possibilities for great good and great harm, the increasing strength of the organization for junior high school teachers, principals, and curriculum specialists. If this increasing organizational strength (once treated as transitional with little sense of special status and identity), is used to increase sensitivity to the problems of junior high school students, good changes may be expected.

1211.   Mehit, G.   "The middle school: a new design for learning holds promise for the education of early adolescence." Ohio Schools, 44(1966):23-24.

Although each school system must develop its own middle school philosophy, all middle schools follow a "basic philosophy of transition" from dependent childhood to self-directed adolescence.

1212.   Meleny, H. E.   "Motor Performance of Adolescent Girls as Compared with Those of 24 Years Ago." Masters Thesis, University of California, 1959.

The researcher found no striking difference between motor abilities but did find that girls in 1959 were significantly taller and heavier than girls in 1935.

1213.   Merz, W. R.   "Education and the process of change." Educational Leadership, 24(1967):561-569.

Discusses eight aspects which are unique to the change process (junior high to a middle school) in education: 1) Most changes in practice require changes in the attitudes, skills, and values of the practitioners.   2) Most significant innovations in education remain invisible, undocumented, and inaccessible to many potential users.   3) Under some conditions, educators are expected to be their own inventors, while under others, their colleagues and their administrators would disapprove.   4) Education lacks a professional network of communicators and change agents.   5) Colleagues often are afraid to try innovations.   6) Creative working relationships among social scientists are lacking.   7) Educators need feedback mechanisms to reinforce change efforts and to measure success.   8) Administrators and curriculum coordinators feel that the community will react against experimentation.   Will education continue to be buffeted about by the demand placed on it by society or will schools meet the challenges of a rapidly changing society?   Models such as those

presented by Brickell, Clark and Guba, and Fox may be
useful conceptual schemes in organizing for change.

1214.   Metz, M. H.   "Order in the Secondary School:
Variations on a Theme."   Paper presented at the
Annual Meeting of the American Sociological Associa-
tion, September 6, 1977.

Examines sources of continuing threats to order in
public and secondary schools. The means of control
available to principals and teachers are analyzed,
and the consequences of control strategies are
considered as they interact with strategies for
academic education.   Order often requires mutually
contradictory action supported by different organizational structures, especially when incoming students
challenge the usefulness of the school's academic
goals.   Four junior high schools in two districts
illustrated the interaction. School staff, the study
concluded, are preoccupied with order because order
is constantly threatened. The ordinary school building and school routine are constructed so that even
small amounts of innocent restless activity can dis-
rupt academic efforts or endanger a child.   Inten-
tional attack on classroom concentration or on prop-
erty or persons can easily take place.   Adolescent
energy and discontented students who feel forced to
attend supply the impetus for potential disruption.
In some schools, student discontent with some aspect
of the school or its context is sufficient to cause
disruption.   The school is inadequately prepared to
face these threats.   Whether it tries to control
using normative commitment (the exchange of extrinsic
rewards for cooperation) or coercion, its resources
will often be unequal to the task.   Schools can
easily control through reliance on students' naive
acceptance of the inevitability of passing cooperatively through an institution which contains everyone
of their age in the transformation from child to
adult.   When students do not believe such a passage
is either inevitable or useful, the school may
control them by underscoring its legal and social
mandate to regulate their lives and by appearing to
possess more coercive resources than it could in fact
muster.

1215.   Michigan Association of School Boards. "The Middle
School." Lansing, Mich., 1965.

There is no ideal breaking point in the growth
(maturity) characteristics within the thirteen-year
span from ages 5 to 17. Nonetheless, analysis of all
the characteristics and implications shows significant areas of similarity for the 11- to 13-year-old
age group, usually grades 6, 7, and 8.   Relevent
literature reveals at least 320 physical, mental,

emotional, and social growth characteristics for boys
and girls from K-12. Some 130 (about 41 percent) of
those characteristics apply to 10- to 13-year-olds.
The environment created by the middle school nurtures
growth characteristics. The middle school is a
school for growing up, and it serves more effectively
the educational needs of this age group. The ideal
instructional program, with flexibility to meet the
individual needs of a learner, enables the boy or
girl to move securely from one class group with one
teacher to many groups, large and small, of his peers
and more teachers. Middle school students have the
opportunity to become increasingly self-directing.

1216.   Milwaukee Public Schools, Office of the Superintendent of Schools. "A Working Draft for the Plan
for the Transition to the Middle School." Milwaukee,
Wis., November 9, 1978.

This report to the Milwaukee Board of School
Directors and the community defines the middle school
program which had been developed to meet needs of
early adolescents, ages 10 to 14 in grades 6-8. A
multiyear plan includes staff, parents, pupils, central office personnel, and community residents. This
structure was designed for: 1) the needs of early
adolescent pupils, 2) transition from elementary
school to high school, 3) shared decision making, 4)
a modified pupil day to enhance the instructional
program, 5) pupil-advisor opportunities, 6) block-
time scheduling, 7) team planning time, 8) flexible
use of time, space, materials, and grouping of
pupils, 9) staff in-service, and 10) an enrollment
range from 600 to 960 pupils. The instructional program was based on a mastery of basic skills, skill
and appreciation of fine and applied arts, a feeling
of self-worth, responsible citizenship, individual
programming, exploratory experiences, competency in
communication, and positive social interactions. The
philosophy of the school system is that each student
is an individual with intellectual, emotional,
social, physical, and psychological differences. A
humanistic environment is stressed in which students
realize their full potential in the cognitive, affective, and psychomotor areas. Students will have an
environment in which they can continue to work on the
basic skills as well as explore many new areas of
knowledge and skills. This report includes sections
on philosophy and rationale, nature of the middle
school child, key elements of the middle school,
background information, exceptional education,
organization, staffing, and curriculum overview.

1217.   Mitchell, J. J. Human Life: The Early Adolescent
Years.   Toronto: Holt, Rhinehart and Winston of
Canada, 1974.

Contains the following information 1) physical, mental, social, moral, and psychological development during early adolescence, 2) profiles adolescents at age 10, 11, 12, 13, 14, and 15, 3) overview of early adolescence--the change in the body, the expanding intellect, the advancing morality, the inward journey, the outward parade, the anguish and joy of early adolescence.

1218.   Morse, W. C. and Wingo, G. M.   Classroom Psychology: Readings in Educational Psychology.   Glenview, Ill.:   Scott Foresman and Co., 1971.

Articles on adolescents appear in Chapter 5.   Other sections of interest in this bibliography are Chapter 4, Elementary School Children; Chapter 7, Learning in the Classroom; Chapter 8, Kinds of Learning; Chapter 9, Group Aspects of Learning; Chapter 10, What Pupils Bring to Learning; Chapter 11, Discipline: The Learning of Self Management; Chapter 12, Social and Emotional Problems in the Classroom.

1219.   Mosher, R. L. (Ed.)   Adolescents' Development in Education: A Janus Knot.   McCutchan Publishing Corp., 1979.   Available from the Association for Supervision and Curriculum Development, 225 N. Washington St., Alexandria, Va. 22314, 1979.

Book is an anthology of information for teachers, psychologists, and parents.

1220.   Moss, T. C.   "The middle school comes--and takes another grade or two."   National Elementary Principal, 48(1968):37-41.

Elementary schools are losing 11-year-olds (sixth graders) and sometimes 10-year-olds (fifth graders) to the middle schools which number well over one thousand with more being established each year.   Does this indicate a significant trend toward middle schools?   Can the needs of 10- and 11-year-olds be better met in a middle school or in an elementary school?   What effects will these newer organizational units have on what remains of the elementary school? This article seeks answers.   Throughout the United States, there are many junior high schools that have consistently done an excellent job of meeting the needs of early adolescents.   Should they be abolished in favor of middle schools?   Since Sputnik, American education has undergone many changes--some desirable and some not.   Confronted by pressures to integrate, to accelerate, to harden the curriculum, and to automate instruction, will the middle school better serve the needs of children and early adolescents? Each school system should thoroughly examine the needs of students from nursery school through high

school.   Then, after developing an N-12 sequential
curriculum, educators can select the organizational
pattern that seems best for these students.

1221.   Moss, T. "The 7-9 junior high school may triumph
after all!"   Bulletin of the National Association of
Secondary School Principals, 58(1974):82-85.

Using birth statistics to predict school enrollment
trends, the author describes a hypothetical case in
which a system returns to the junior high arrangement
after trying the middle school.   The author specu-
lates that this may be the model for tomorrow.   The
author hopes the middle school experience will make
those reinstated junior high schools more student-
centered and relevant to contemporary society.   If
districts do revert to the 7-9 junior high school,
the author hopes that they will not take a step
backward by using the programs which lead initially
to the revolt against the junior high school.

1222.   Murphy, L. B.   "Enjoying preadolescence--the
forgotten years."   Childhood Education, 46(1970):
179-180.

This editorial overview calls for a fresh look at the
inbetween years of 10 to 14 and their distinctive
problems and pleasures.

1223.   Murray, J. N. "The marginal child--which way will
he go?" Education, 96,1(1975):68-77.

The marginal child is described as one who is experiencing a number of potentially serious problems.   If
these problems are not attended to, they will move
the child into predelinquent or delinquent categories. See ERIC Abstract #EJ 130 520.

1224.   Muus, R. E. Theories in Adolescence. 3d ed. New
York: Random House, 1975.

Presents famous theories and educational implications
of each in the following chapters: 1) The Philosophical and Historical Roots of Theories of Adolescence.
2) The Psychoanalytic Theory of Adolescent Development. 3) Erik Erikson's Theory of Identity Development.   4) A Geisteswissenschaftliceh Theory of Adolescence.   5) Cultural Anthropology and Adolescence.
6) Field Theory and Adolescence.   7) Social Psychology and Adolescence.   8) Arnold Gesell's Theory of
Adolescent Development.   9) Central European Stage
Theories of Adolescent Development.   10) Jean
Piaget's Cognitive Theory of Adolescent Development.
11) Lawrence Kohlberg's Cognitive-Developmental

Approach to Adolescent Morality.   12) The Implications of Social Learning Theory for an Understanding of Adolescent Development.

1225.   National Association of Secondary School Principals, Committee on Junior High School Education. "Recommended grade organization for junior high school education." Bulletin of the National Association of Secondary School Principals,   43,248(1959): 40-42.

What should be considered when deciding to use the 6-3-3 plan, the 6-6 plan, the 6-2-4 plan, or the 8-4 plan: 1) administrative and legal provisions that establish grade organization by law such as regional, consolidated, township, and county districts, 2) the size of the community and the potential enrollment for grades 7-12, 3) the growth of the school population in grades 7-12 during the next ten to fifteen years, 4) The present school buildings in the community and problems in adapting those buildings to expanding enrollments and new types of educational programs, especially as these affect the program for grades 7-12, 5) the distance that pupils must be transported to centers where schools might be built. The Committee recommends that when the pupil enrollment is sufficiently large, the three-year junior high including grades 7,8, and 9 is the most appropriate school for early adolescents.   The three-year junior high can: 1) provide adequate time for principals, counselors, and teachers to become more acquainted with pupils, 2) make it possible to have a principal, counselor, and teachers primarily for working with adolescents, 3) make it easier to concentrate on developing educational programs especially suited to early adolescents, 4) bring together a large number of pupils to justify the facilities, equipment, and specialized staff for a variety of educational offerings, 5) make it possible to offer more challenging opportunities for talented people, 6) bring together a large number of pupils to provide experiences for early adolescents in social skills, leadership activities, and citizenship responsibility.   The Committee also recommends that in communities with smaller enrollments in grades 7-12, the best type of grade organization is a combined junior/senior high school.   The two-year junior high school may be justified in communities where current conditions make it difficult or impossible to have three-year junior high schools.

1226.   National Association of Secondary School Principals, Committee on Junior High School Education. "Recommended grades or years in junior high or middle schools."   Bulletin of the National Association of Secondary School Principals, 51(1967):68-70.

With earlier pubescence, the 11-year-old or sixth
grader in 1967 may be just as ready for junior high
or middle school as seventh graders were in previous
years. The committee recommended that the middle
unit incorporate grades 7-9 or grades 6-9. The
separately organized and administered middle unit
provides pupils with valuable opportunities to participate in and lead activities designed especially
for this age group. The Committee states that only
two years or two grades in a middle school are not
enough to provide stability and to fulfill the stated
educational goals of these schools. It suggests
three years as the best alternative. The key to an
effective middle grade unit is that administrative
organization needs to be determined on educational
grounds, rather than on building expediency, economy,
or racial imbalance. Nor is a special reorganization
of units essential for encouraging needed educational
reforms. Any middle school or junior high school can
and should engage in innovative teaching and learning
programs. The Committee urges the importance of
research on present levels of physical and social
maturation of pupils, in determining quality in educational programs and on the special characteristics
of existing grade organizations.

1227.   National Education Association, National School
        Public Relations Association. Farewell to Junior
        High. National Education Association, 1201 16th St.,
        N.W., Washington, D.C. 20036, April 29, 1965.

        Discusses the nation's largest school system, New
        York City, and its decision to phase out junior high
        school beginning in 1966 and to be fully carried out
        by 1972-73. The city educators foresaw, within the
        intermediate pattern of a middle school, fulfillment
        of the obvious need for special testing and guidance
        services, for remedial work, for subject matter spe-
        cialists, and for human relations consultants. New
        textbooks and instructional materials were developed,
        and the buildings provided necessary space and flexi-
        bility to accommodate the concept. The article dis-
        cusses the cost involvement, teacher disapproval, and
        desegregation.

1228.   National Study of Secondary School Evaluation.
        Evaluative Criteria for Junior High and Middle
        Schools. Washington, D.C.: National Study of
        Secondary School Evaluation, 1963.

        Self-evaluation instrument developed for use in the
        junior high and middle school.

1229.   New Hampshire State Department of Education. "Proposed Standards and Guidelines for Middle/Junior High Schools." Bicentennial ed. ERIC Doc. Ed 148 010, February, 1976.

The publication is based on the idea of organizing junior high and middle school instruction so it motivates and challenges early adolescents to develop informed and responsible behavior. The guidelines cover the following sections: Meet the Student, Organizing Learning and Instruction, Art Education, Business Education, Career Education, Foreign Languages, Guidance Services, Health Education, Health Services, Home Economics, Industrial Arts, Language Arts and Reading, The Media Center, Mathematics, Music, Physical Education, Safety Education, Science Education, Social Studies, Services for Educationally Handicapped Students, Staffing, A Philosophy for Middle-Junior High Schools.

1230.   New Jersey State Department of Education. "The numbers game." Secondary Schools Bulletin, 21,6 (March 1965):Whole Issue.

The New Jersey junior high schools (grades 7-9) demonstrated their effectiveness in providing for the young adolescent. Within a ten-year period, the number of junior high schools doubled. The basic functions of transition, exploration, guidance, orientation, and socialization continue to be important in a new grade arrangement. Controversy usually centers around the placement of the ninth grade. Those who have worked with pupils in this age under various organizational patterns agree that the ninth grade experience in a junior high school is most productive because of these advantages: 1) Curricular offerings are designed to provide for a smooth transition between the elementary and high schools. 2) Cocurricular activities are more suitable to the age group. 3) Exploration in the fine and practical arts is continuous. 4) Opportunities for student participation and leadership are increased. The failure rate for pupils enrolled in junior high schools was significantly lower through grade 10 than the rate of failure in other organizational patterns.

1231.   Nickerson, N. C., Jr. Junior High Schools Are on the Way Out. Danville, Ill.: Interstate Printers and Publishers, 1966.

The pamphlet provides an historical perspective on the grade organizational patterns of schools for transescents. Junior high schools attempt to meet the following objectives: 1) The school environment must suit adolescents who are at a similar stage of physiological and social development. 2) Seventh and eighth grade students are provided a broad curricular program that accommodates individual differences. 3) Young adolescents have better opportunities to participate in and develop leadership in extra-class activities. 4) Students have an opportunity to study with teachers who are prepared in special subjects. 5) Junior highs generally have better guidance facilities and personnel than do elementary schools. 6) The transition from the self-contained classroom of elementary school to the departmentalized secondary school is made by pupils with less difficulty if an intermediate unit is provided. Havighurst says that children are maturing earlier now than they used to. If this is the case, ninth graders are ready for the senior high school and should be with the upper three grades and not with seventh and eighth graders. The evidence indicates that the ninth grader is closer to a twelfth grader than he is to the seventh grader in his development. The junior high deals with exploration and remedial help, particularly for the seventh and eighth graders. Some schools do explore and offer remedies, and some don't. Most junior highs force exploration by mandating what subjects the students will take. The seventh and eighth graders usually have few or no electives through which to pursue their individual differences. Youngsters in a junior high have an opportunity to work with teachers who are better trained in the subject matter areas than elementary teachers, but these same teachers are not trained in the methods of handling the transescent. The regional accrediting associations forced the senior highs into providing enough guidance counselors, but the junior highs as yet do not have enough.

1232.   Noar, G. E.   "Movement emerges."   Educational Leadership, 14(1957):468-472.

In 1892 a committee suggested that secondary education begin at grade 7. Seven years later the Committee on College Entrance Requirements reaffirmed the philosophy that seventh grade should be the dividing line between elementary and secondary education.

1233.   Noar, G. The Junior High School: Today and Tomorrow. 2d ed. Englewood Cliffs, N.J.: Prentice-Hall, 1961.

Book concentrates on four major areas: 1) A functioning junior high school is built on basic ideas which include the functions of the junior high school, meeting the needs of youth, the role of human relations, and some applications of the nature of the learning process. 2) The responsibility for creating the program is shared by the principals, the teachers, and the community. 3) Modern curriculum and technique include the multiperiod or core class, the language arts program, techniques of instruction, classroom management, discipline, and meeting the needs of slow and gifted pupils. 4) Resource materials for the teacher include a glossary of terms, resource unit outlines, and reports of classroom work.

1234.   Odell, W. R.   "Educational Survey Report for the Philadelphia Board of Public Education."   Philadelphia: Board of Public Education, February 1, 1965.

Chapter 6 deals with the junior high school; specifically, the report describes the scope of the junior high school task, the program of instruction in grades 7 through 9, pupil accomplishment, problems of instructional improvement, plan for improved instruction, and the portal school.   The issue in the Philadelphia schools was not how to achieve optimum academic, personal, and social development through curriculum based on exploration and analysis of life problems or the needs of youth of previous generations.   Rather, the issue was how to build curriculum based on new approaches and disciplines, while at the same time coping with the problems of the culturally disadvantaged, the demands of increased academic excellence for all pupils (especially the gifted), and the requirements of youth employment.   How to deal with these problems without surrendering commitment to the goal of discovering, motivating, and unleashing the potential--personal and social as well as intellectual--of young adolescents magnified the task of the contemporary junior high school.   Two different activities in Philadelphia junior high schools represented a modest beginning to meet these new demands.   The first was the upward extension from the elementary school of the educational improvement program aimed at educationally disadvantaged youth. At the secondary level, the educational improvement program was unabashedly a corrective operation.   The compensatory features of the improvement program at the elementary school level should eventually remove the need for an elaborate parallel in the junior and senior high school.   At the other end of the continuum, a few junior high schools and combined junior-senior high schools offered foreign language study in grades 7 and 8.   Also, at least one junior high school established an accelerated mathematics program which enabled selected pupils to start the study of algebra in grade 8.

1235.   Oestreich, A. H.   "Middle school in transition." Clearinghouse, 44(1969):91-95.

Seeks to answer the question: How do we plan the organization of instruction and content of the subject matter?

1236.   Ogletree, E. J. "Intellectual growth in children and the theory of bioplasmic forces." Phi Delta Kappan, 55,6(1974):407-412.

A new theory of energy developed in the USSR suggests that academic learning before a child is maturation-ally ready will reduce his learning potential. Mid-dle years education is accused of trying to teach content to students before they are ready to learn it. Conventional approaches--pouring knowledge into the child, fitting him into a curriculum that is foreign to his nature--must cease. The bioplasmic or growth forces theory supports development of a cur-riculum and methods compatible with the child's unfolding stages of growth. It explains human growth, the development of thinking children, and the rationale for readiness. The theory implies that the educational process should help the child to sustain and develop his bioplasmic body, his forces of growth. The bioplasmic theory may be the key to human and child development that could revolutionize education.

1237.   Ohles, J. F. "Guidelines for early secondary programs." New York State Education, 53(1966):14.

The educational subdivision between elementary and secondary levels is generally accepted as a transi-tional experience, although there is confusion about whether the bridge is to be built between social and physical groupings or educational experiences. The junior high school is a failure as this transitional unit. Let the intermediate school be a totally ungraded institution with social groupings on an age basis and with physical education, art, music, and all academic subjects structured on an aptitude-achievement basis. All similar activities take place in the same time periods for all youngsters. Teach-ers for the intermediate school will require special training in team teaching techniques with major and minor specialities in particular subjects. They would serve in turn as team leaders, first assis-tants, and assistant teachers in several subjects. For example, an English teacher might be a first assistant social studies teacher and assistant teacher in science and mathematics. The fiction indulged in by many schools that youngsters do move from one group to another may become a reality where scheduling is not an actual problem. It is time to plan for a new intermediate school with a unified academic program. The junior high has failed because it was set up mainly as a separating institution for ministering to physical, psychological, and emotional stresses of early adolescence. If the division continues to take place after the eighth grade, the junior high is bound to fail.

1238.   Otto, H. A. and Otto, S. T.   "A new perspective on the adolescent."   Psychology in the Schools, 4,1 (1967):76-81.

Society often has a problem accepting the current generation of adolescents. Young people are seen as moving away from adult values rather than moving toward conformity. The authors attribute this picture to a cultural conspiracy, largely the work of the mass media, which has led to a false image of youth. The article outlines some of the major developmental tasks of this age period and discusses ways in which the characteristics of adolescents can serve as a catalyst for the good of society: 1) The adolescent is fully engaged in clarifying and developing his identity--he issues the challenge that identity formation is a lifelong undertaking. 2) The adolescent symbolizes active commitment to self-realization. 3) The adolescent is a growth catalyst. 4) The adolescent represents a force for social and institutional regeneration. 5) The adolescent's healthy body and capacity for sensory awareness indicate individual potential. True understanding of the interrelationship among man must lead to the development of a new perspective of the teenager which more accurately reflects his real function and contribution. The adolescent is the active symbol of man's unfolding possibilities--the human potential.

1239.   Ovard, G. F.   Administration of the Changing Secondary School. New York: Macmillan, 1966.

Brief discussion on the organizational patterns with emphasis on the 8-4, 6-3-3, and 6-6. The following arguments support the 8-4 organization: 1) The junior high school takes one year away from the high school program. Colleges are interested in student records from grades 9-12, and guidance counselors cannot evaluate the college potential of students in only three years.   2) Good teachers trained for junior high teaching are hard to find. As a result, school systems must rely on teachers trained either for elementary school or for high school. 3) Students would have to make two adjustments--from elementary to junior high and from junior to senior high school. 4) It is more expensive to operate the 6-3-3 program. 5) Rural, one-room schools need the financial benefit from keeping grades 7 and 8. 6) Better discipline can be maintained in an elementary program than in a junior high school. 7) Students grow up too soon in junior high. The following arguments support the 6-3-3 organization: 1) The junior high school meets the needs of early adolescents better than any other plan of school organization. 2) It provides a varied curriculum and provides opportunities for students to choose electives on the basis of their interests and abilities. 3) It lends itself to grouping according to ability, so that subject matter can be presented more effectively. 4) It is possible to establish effective health and physical education programs geared to the needs of this age group. 5) Junior highs make it possible to organize special education programs for mentally retarded, emotionally disturbed, and socially maladjusted students. 6) It permits the gradual transition from the one-teacher system of the elementary school to the departmentalization of the senior high school. 7) Rural students have an opportunity to participate in activities that are not available to them in small schools.

1240.   Pansino, L. P. (Comp.) The Middle School: A Selected Bibliography with Introduction. Urbana: University of Illinois at Urbana, Bureau of Educational Research, ERIC Doc. ED 029 714, April, 1969.

Two books are reviewed: The American Middle School: An Organizational Analysis by Samuel H. Popper and Perspectives on the Middle School by M. Ann Grooms. A selected bibliography includes books, journal articles, and reports.

1241.   Paparella, P.   "They are your children.   And mine." Educational Leadership, 37,2(1979):169-170.

This graduation speech clearly shows the feelings of an early adolescent student. See ERIC Abstract #EJ 210 974.

1242.   Parker, F.   "Fifty years of the junior high school: Preface to a bibliography of 131 doctoral dissertations." Bulletin of the National Association of Secondary School Principals, 46(1962):435.

The junior high school evolved as a bridge across the adolescent years. This bridge rests on the uncertain ground of an awkward age, as full of opportunity as it is of peril. This article describes the historical background of the junior high school with information on William Torrey Harris and Charles William Eliot, two founding fathers. The article discusses the sociological elements of the junior high school, the first junior high school, and present prospects and future hopes. A bibliography lists 131 doctoral dissertations on junior high schools.

1243.   Partin, C. S. "To sample--or to explore." Educational Leadership, 23,3(1965):194-199.

This article deals with the junior high students'
search for meaning, how the self is important, the
need to explore feelings, the need to know what one
values, the need for a time, a place, and a group.
Since its inception, the junior high school has
justified its existence by saying it meets the
educational needs of adolescents. Educators often
state that a special program is needed for and
special health is required by the student. They hold
that students experiencing the transition from childhood to young adulthood should, in addition to the
general educational experiences, be provided an
opportunity to identify their specific talents and
abilities. The junior high school student needs to
explore his world. He is becoming more aware of
himself as a person and is concerned with questions
about himself and about his identity. He is concerned about attaining objectives that are important.
A comprehensive exploratory program, under optimum
conditions, can give students an opportunity to find
their way. It can provide them opportunity to
develop a realistic view of self and a positive
regard for others. It can give them an opportunity
to scan the world of work and the world of values.
It can provide them a time, a place and a group where
they can feel emotionally safe and personally
esteemed. An exploratory program may become the
medium through which both student and teacher discover the means at the student's disposal for the
achievement of their joint enterprise.

1244.   Passow, A. H. "American Secondary Education: The
Conant Influence. A Look at Conant's Recommendations
for Senior and Junior High Schools." Reston, Va.:
National Association of Secondary School Principals,
ERIC Doc. ED 145 580, 1977.

Author examines three of Conant's major works on
American education: 1) The American High School
Today: A First Report to Interested Citizens.   2)
"Education in the Junior High School Years." 3) The
Comprehensive High School: A Second Report to Interested Citizens. Schools in metropolitan areas are
discussed, with attention to the education of
teachers and educational policy. Recommendations for
high schools and junior highs are listed in the
appendix. See ERIC Abstract #ED 145 580.

1245.   Patterson, F. "The adolescent citizen and the
junior high school." Bulletin of the National Association of Secondary School Principals, 46,274(1962):
69-79.

In a certain sense, American youth are exiles, and
they know it. Adults have successfully excluded
youth from significant roles and have placed youth in

a social vacuum with nothing to measure themselves except standardized academic achievement scores and peer standards that are shaped by advertising, consumer persuasion, and the disc jockey. The chief remaining roles for youth are those of passive students, consumers, dependents, and bored observers of the adult rat race. Identity is an essential quest for adolescents, but the quest for identity is increasingly stalled and carried unfulfilled into adulthood. The questions of adolescence, the crucial ones asked in the junior high school years--"Who am I?" "Where am I going?" "What is the meaning of life?"--become harder and harder to answer in ways that are stable, satisfying, and socially constructive.

1246.   Pitkin, V. E. "What kind of education for early adolescents?" School and Society, 86(1958):113.

Compares the 8-4 with the 6-3-3 and 6-6, but does not consider other organizational patterns.

1247.   Plutte, W. "Going into junior high school: bugaboo or big adventure?" Instructor, 68(1954):11.

The changes a child must make in his daily routine when he enters junior high school may be characterized as follows: "Imagine yourself in a similar situation. You have never been away from home, and suddenly you are placed in a huge city with instructions to find six or seven houses during the day and remember everything that happens. You will have a confusing time finding your way about the city. Hesitant to ask questions of unsmiling strangers and worried lest you be late, you have to face the stares of more strangers as you walk to the front of a great hall."

1248.   Popper, S. H. "The paramount middle school goal." In Popper, S. H. (Ed.), The American Middle School: An Organizational Analysis. Waltham, Mass.: Blaisdell Publishing Co., 1967.

The middle school was adopted as a result of administrative disenchantment with the cultural rigidities of the six-year high school. The middle school established a special unit for the education of early adolescents in a protective psychological environment which neither the elementary school nor the high school could provide. The paramount goal of the middle school is the psycho-social and cognitive development of the adolescent. The psycho-social component is the most difficult challenge for middle school administration. The principal must understand the middle school's function and make sure that a functional balance of instrumental and expressive values is attained in the school environment.

1249.   Popper, S. H. The American Middle School: An Organizational Analysis. Waltham, Mass.: Blaisdell Publishing Co., 1967.

What is at issue? It's not whether there shall be a junior high school or a middle school (a semantic distinction without a difference), but rather which grades are functionally appropriate for this unit of public school organization. From the perspective of organization theory, and out of concern for the human condition in American society and early adolescence, a meaningful resolution begins with a rigorous definition of what is expected of a middle school. This book presents a theoretical perspective of the American middle school. The organization of the middle school is projected as a mechanistic system, a psychological system, and a cultural system. The middle school is presented in an overview as a functionally differentiated unit of the public school system. It emerged in the public school system about 1910 as a direct consequence of secondary differentiation: early adolescent pupils were now defined as a special category of public school clients. Functional value is then used as a bridging theme in a treatment of the middle school as a social system which is structured as a formal organization. A treatment of the middle school program--the technology with which a middle school organization attains its goal--is set within an evolutionary context. Several chapters reaffirm the social value of the American middle school in the following topic areas: 1) the first middle schools, 2) aspects of the social system, 3) the paramount middle school goal (see bibliographic entry 1248 for a full review of this chapter), 4) the institutional aspect, 5) the changing society and social Darwinism, 6) the changing society and liberal Darwinism, 7) the changing society and public education, 8) committees dealing with middle grade education, 9) reforms within the middle school movement, 10) aspects of the formal educational organization, 11) dysfunctions and instability, 12) a middle school program evolves, 13) adolescence in American society, 14) the turn ahead, and 15) the middle school of tomorrow.

1250.   Popper, S. H. "Institutional integrity in middle school organization." Journal of Secondary Education, 43(1969):184-191.

"As we ponder the cultural meaning of early adolescent education in the United States, Emile Durkheim's dictum comes to mind. Durkheim held the source of all school life is the society. This is another way

of saying that the bond between school and society is
a powerful and inseparable bond. It is powerful and
inseparable because, at the level of cultural values,
one is an extension of the other. For example, out
of habit, one seldom speaks of school or society, but
one makes frequent references to school and society.
Consequently, we find that evaluative standards of
American public school systems mesh in a remarkable
close fit with the dominant values of American
society.   These dominant values provide sanctioned
orientations to social behavior and they form a
pattern--that is to say, they crystallize a value
pattern--which Parsons has defined as one of 'instrumental activism'."   Does it matter whether a middle
school is of grades 5-8 or any other combination of
grades?   "The legitimation of the American middle
school from the first has been as a school for early
adolescents.   Grades 7-9 were assigned to the school
not out of accommodation or change, but because the
years from 12 to 15 were defined by the science of
that age as the transitional period between late
childhood and postpubescent adolescence. And society
wastes its resources in unrewarding duplication when
a middle school is diverted from the paramount goal
of early adolescent education."

1251.   Popper, S. H.   "Why don't elementary school principals raise some hell?"   National Elementary Principal, 49,5(1970):59-62.

Principals of elementary schools are given reasons
why they should keep grades 5 and 6 in their grade
school.   The author uses historical records concerning the junior high and middle school to ask the
overriding question: When does childhood education
end and early adolescent education begin?   The 6-8
and the 5-8 organizational pattern are not supported
by scientific knowledge of child growth and
development.

1252.   Post, R. L.   "Middle school: a questionable
innovation." Clearinghouse, 43(1968):484-486.

A reaction to Eugene Reagan--"The junior high school
is dead" (November, 1967 Clearinghouse, see entry
1257). This author makes a strong statement in favor
of the junior high, emphasizing that individual
instruction, independent study, progressive curricula, team teaching, and flexible scheduling can be
just as effective in a junior high as in a middle
school.

1253.   Prescott, D. A.   "Factors that Influence Learning." Horace Mann Lecture, University of Pittsburgh,
1958.

Educators often feel that the child is a mechanism to whom learning occurs chiefly as a result of something that is done to him from the outside. Educators have a responsibility to consider the transescent's needs as the "engine" and not the "caboose" of the educational "train."

1254. Pumerantz, P. (Ed.) The Emerging Adolescent Learner in the Middle Grades. Springfield, Mass.: Educational Leadership Institute, 1973.

This multimedia program is designed for administrators and teachers and considers alternative teaching/learning styles applicable to early adolescents. Six lectures and filmstrips featuring leading junior high/middle school educators cover the following topics: Implications of the Curriculum: Boyce Medical Study (Donald Eichhorn); Educating Emerging Adolescents: Some Operational Problems (Conrad Toepfer); The Nature of the Emerging Adolescent (Mary Compton); Learning Strategies for the Emerging Adolescent (Bruce Howell); Adult Models for the Emerging Adolescent (Thomas Sweeney); The Impact of Social Forces on Children (James Phillips).

1255. Purkey, W. W. Self-Concept and School Achievement. Englewood Cliffs, N. J.: Prentice-Hall, 1970.

During the middle school years, the additional educational experiences which lead to affective growth results enhance cognitive growth as well. Poor self-concept correlates with lack of cognitive achievement. Experiences that reverse poor self-concept and improve this perception bring about a similar improvement in cognitive achievement.

1256. Putnam, R. The Organization and Functions of Oregon Junior High Schools. Salem, Ore.: State Department of Education, Superintendent of Public Instruction, 1959.

Block-time scheduling encourages integration and articulation and contributes to guidance. By reducing the number of teachers a student must face, and the total number of students a teacher must meet, a closer student/teacher relationship can be achieved than is possible under a departmentalized program. Many authorities feel that the child who was educated in the self-contained classroom of the typical elementary school is not prepared for an abrupt break to a completely departmentalized program. In many schools the block-time classes become the framework for a homeroom program for activities such as student participation in school management and social affairs, thus encouraging socialization. A program

of unit teaching within the block may directly contribute to further exploration and differentiation.

1257.   Reagan, E. E.   "The junior high school is dead."
Clearinghouse, 42(1967):150-151.

The middle school, unencumbered by requirements of
the high school, has the opportunity to develop an
identity that is characteristic of the boys and girls
it serves.   The middle school is only required to
meet the needs of early adolescence.   Flexible
scheduling, large and small groups, modular scheduling, and programming for basic skills development can
take place without concern for the Carnegie Unit in
grade 9.   For a rebuttal to Reagen, see Post, entry
1252.

1258.   Redl, F.   "Preadolescents: what makes them tick?"
Child Study, 21(1944):44-48.

Explains the personality shake-up of preadolescents,
extending even to age 13 or grade 8:   "During preado-
lesence the well-meant pattern of a child's personality is broken up or loosened, so that adolescent
changes can be built into it, and so that it can be
modified into the personality of an adult.   During
preadolescence, it is normal for youngsters to drop
their identification with adult society and establish
a strong identification with a group of their peers.
Most referrals to child guidance clinics occur around
this preadolescent age."

1259.   Redl, F.   "Some Psychological Facts About Junior
High School Children, Strengths and Weaknesses of the
Junior High School."   Circular 441. Washington, D.C.:
U.S. Office of Education, 1955.

This speech is an analysis of a pupil group.   It
stresses the phenomena of organismic disorganization
and the group psychological break.

1260.   Riggs, N. D.   "Organization for instruction."
Clearinghouse, 44(1969):45-49.

Schools doing organizational innovations were identified in all fifty states by reputable education
sources.   Based on the data from educators surveyed
in the study, the following criteria are being
employed in the substructure of junior high school:
1) The vice-principal is the principal's immediate
subordinate.   2) The department head is the second
level of authority below the principal.   3) The
department head is selected for his leadership ability, enthusiasm for work, and his knowledge and
understanding of students.   4) The department head is

responsible to the principal. 5) Approval of innovative practices must be obtained from the department
head and/or principal. 6) The counselor is the third
level of authority under the principal. 7) The counselor's primary duty is face-to-face counseling. 8)
The principal's administrative span of control is
among three and eight positions. 9) The student
council is the principal's primary channel of communication with the student body.   10) A student
government advisor acts as a liaison between the students and the principal. 11) Inter-school visits are
used to broaden the vision of teachers. 12) Subject
matter workshops and departmental study sessions are
the techniques used to influence a curriculum.   13)
Line officer/teacher consultations are used to
improve instruction. 14) Ability grouping is used to
meet individual differences of the student. 15) Team
teaching is the staff pattern used for independent
progress of students. 16) Team leaders are the level
of authority under the department head.   17) The
position of vice-principal should be employed when
the enrollment of a junior high school reaches 750.
18) The vice-principal's major responsibility should
be student-personnel administration. 19) A curriculum coordinator should be provided to serve as a
subject matter generalist for the entire school.

1261.   Ritz, J. M. "Integrating home economics, art, and
industrial arts at the middle grades." Man/Society/
Technology, 37,3(1977):24-26.

Studies show that middle grade learners differ in
needs from the elementary and high school learners.
Incorporating subject areas in a unified teaching
approach will make learning a more meaningful
experience. See ERIC Abstract #ED 173 027.

1262.   Robinson, G.   "Principals' opinions about school
organization." National Elementary Principal, 41
(1961):39-42.

Fifty-one percent of principals polled voted in favor
of K-6-3-3, although 721 principals were not offered
choices of either 4-4-4 or 5-3-4.

1263.   Romano, L. G., Hedberg, J. D., and Lulich, M.
"Developmental characteristics of preadolescents and
their implications." In Romano, L., Georgiady, N.,
and Heald, J. (Eds.), The Middle School: Selected
Readings on an Emerging School Program, pp. 185-214.
Professional Technical Series. Chicago: Nelson-Hall,
1973.

Presents a chart of physical development, emotional
and social characteristics, mental growth characteristics, and implications for the preadolescent (ages

11 to 14), for the curriculum, and for the teacher.
The chart guides the middle school educator in
planning learned activities consistent with the growing needs of these children.   Physical development
refers to body growth, health, and body management.
Emotional and social characteristics include emotional status, feelings for self and others, tendency
to have fears, personal ideals and values, independence, responsibility and sensitivity, and play.
Mental growth characteristics comprise intellectual
development, interests, and creative ability and
appreciation.

1264.   Rowe, R. N.   "Why we abandoned our traditional
junior high." Nation's Schools, 79(1967):74.

Every community should reanalyze its educational
program, including the grade structure of its
schools.   If integration is important to the community, traditional grade structure should not be
allowed to interfere.   Although grouping of children
into various age levels or in traditional elementary,
junior high school, and high school campuses may be
administratively convenient, and may in some communities be educationally sound, we must not be
wedded to such convenience.   If the nongraded concept
relieves anxiety of young people and improves their
learning opportunities, we should abandon grades.   If
the educational park solves an integration problem
and improves educational opportunities for all, let
our children go to school in parks.   And as progress
is made, if the traditional junior high falls by the
wayside, let it fall.

1265.   Sandefur, W.   "The mouse race."   Clearinghouse,
50,1(1976):23-24.

A parent reviews his son's first days in a junior
high school.   He questions the amount of work
assigned students and its effect on a student's
morale.   See ERIC Abstract #EJ 152 966.

1266.   Sanders, S. G.   "Challenge of the middle school."
Educational Forum, 32(1968):191-197.

Sections cover these areas: 1) factors influencing
acceptance of the junior high, 2) challenges by other
grade combinations, 3) The ninth grade problem, 4)
changing developmental patterns of children and
youth, 5) tradition and the proponents of the junior
high school.

1267.   Sawyer, D. J.   "Linguistic and cognitive competencies in the middle grades."   Language Arts, 52,8
(1975):1075-1079.

In the broadest sense, competence refers to 1) the
level of physical development children have reached,
2) the level of reasoning ability and memory they are
capable of demonstrating in both receptive and
expressive situations, 3) the level of language
development they have achieved, 4) the level of
independence they are able to demonstrate along with
the degree and variety of approaches they are able to
apply in problem solving situations.   To determine
student readiness in academic subjects, teachers at
the middle school level must determine individual
levels of cognitive competencies.   If the teacher
carefully observes the performance of each student in
areas of language ability and thinking skills, uses
the performance to assess individual competencies,
and adjusts learning tasks and teacher expectations
for achievement, then an effective individualized
program for students will be realized.

1268.   Schmuck, R.   "Concerns of contemporary adolescents."   Bulletin of the National Association of
Secondary School Principals, 49,300(1965):19-28.

The adolescent has problems when he tries to integrate the simultaneous and often inconsistent demands
of three groups of people: parents, teachers, and
peers.   Adolescents view parents as the most significant teacher in their lives.   They usually refer to
parents whenever important decisions have to be made.
Youngsters report 65 percent of their concerns
involve their parents: 1) parents not discussing
with the adolescent what he or she considers important, 2) parents demanding that the adolescent's
thoughts and activities be public, 3) parents
restricting dating patterns, and 4) adolescent lacking respect for and trust in parents.   Teachers are
the second most common group of people with whom adolescents have major concerns: 1) teachers not getting to know the student, 2) teachers lacking interest in teaching and youth, and 3) teachers showing
partiality for certain students.   Major concerns with
peers include personal values clashing with those of
friends, and difficulty in obtaining friends and popularity.   The most basic issue for the adolescent is
the attempt to achieve a sense of autonomy and individuality.   The interpersonal concerns of this period
are heightened by the adolescent's physical develop-
ment--biologically he is an adult during the high
school years.   He looks to parents and teachers as
models for expectation about and ways of expressing
his maturing urges.   Observations and interviews
collected over the last five years indicate that
working- and middle-class adolescents are not alienated from adults.   They are not retreating from or
rebelling against adult society; they are not against
school achievement and the core values of the

society.   Adolescents are, however, struggling with the integration of the interpersonal messages and appraisals of parents, teachers, and peers. They are attempting to pull these diverse implements together into an autonomous and consistent picture of themselves.

1269.   Schoo, P. H.   "Optimum Setting for the Early Adolescent: Junior High or Middle School?"   Paper presented at the Meeting of the North Central Association for Colleges and Schools, Chicago, March, 1973.

Suggests answers to the following questions: 1) What do critics say about schools for early adolescents? 2) What does research indicate about the physical, social, and emotional growth of early adolescents? 3) What is the most appropriate size of the school for early adolescents?   4) What grades should be housed in a school for early adolescents?   5) What type of curriculum should be offered to early adolescents?   The two school settings are more similar in terms of practice.   The middle school exists more in an ideal than in reality. Research evidence in physiological and sociological areas conflicts; therefore it cannot be used to support either grade organization.   In general, research findings support the view that early adolescents are physically, emotionally, and socially more sophisticated than previous generations were at the same age. A review of this literature supports the following: 1) Early adolescents are physically larger and mature at an earlier age than youngsters during the early years of this century when the junior high school movement began.   2) Both boys and girls who are early physical maturers experience less difficulty adjusting to their environment than their late maturing peers.   3) Earlier physical maturation is accompanied by a greater interest in heterosexual activities than previous generations.   4) The peer group is a major force in determining the attitudes and behavior of early adolescents.   5) Ninth grade students tend to be physically and socially more like senior high school students than their seventh and eighth grade classmates. 6) Sixth grade students tend to be more easily influenced by older adolescents.   7) If social, emotional, and physical maturity, and opposite sex choices are measured, students in grades 6 and 7 are more alike as are students in grades 9 and 10.

1270.   School Executive magazine.   "Types of high school organization: their advantages and disadvantages." School Executive, 68(1948):63-76.

Seven school authorities discuss the merits of the common forms of grade reorganization, such as the 6-3-3, 6-6, and 6-4-4.

1271.   Schutter, C. H.   "Should we abolish the seventh
and eighth grade?" School Executive, 74(1955):53.

The author suggests that grades 7 and 8 be eliminated
because they primarily review material and waste
time, and proposes that schools adopt a four-year
secondary pattern similar to some European schools.

1272.   Scrofani, E. A.   "Diminishing adolescent inequali-
ties."   Bulletin of the National Association of
Secondary School Principals, 41(1957):45-47.

The distinct differences between the adolescent boy
and the adolescent girl cause major problems in
secondary schools.   Most educators are confronted
with behavior problems, unbalanced proportions of the
sexes on the honor rolls, and social or emotional
problems requiring formal guidance.   The present
general policy of equal age requirement, except for
children with proven maturity, puts the normal male
student in an unfavorable competitive position.   By
creating a school society that does not recognize
physical differences which act as springboards to
social and emotional trouble, we perpetuate adolescent problems that can be avoided.

1273.   Shane, H. G. "Grouping in the elementary school."
Phi Delta Kappan, 41(1960):313-319.

The article describes thirty-two plans for grouping
elementary and junior high school students.   Special
terms growing out of these plans include ungraded
groups, primary and intermediate groups, grade grouping, intra-subject field grouping, multiple track
grouping, the Dolpin plan, and the Woodring plan.
For example, Woodring suggested that K-8 be divided
between an ungraded primary school and a middle
elementary school.   The more able children would
spend as few as two years in the primary, moving to
the middle school as early as age 7.   The less able
might remain in the ungraded primary through age 9.
He envisioned the bright children leaving elementary
school at age 11, the others leaving at perhaps age
13.

1274.   Sheviakov, G. and Redl, F. (Revised by Richardson,
S. K.) "Discipline for Today's Children and Youth."
Washington, D. C.:   National Education Association,
1956.

Sections dealing with discipline in the classroom are
entitled: Thinking Straight About Discipline, What
Kind of Discipline Do We Want? Growth Toward Self
Guidance, Democratic Principles to Guide our
Practices, Teacher's Role in Educating for Self-
Discipline, The Three Main Headaches, Studying and

Minimizing Discipline Problems, What Most Frequently
Goes Wrong in School Groups, Know your Groups, Discipline in Teacher Personality, Before You Go Back to
Your Classroom--Remember This.   Here, briefly, are
the four democratic principles and a statement of how
they are applied in the classroom: 1) Faith in the
worth and dignity of every human being is the key
value of a democratic society.   Teachers use positive
ways of guidance which communicate this belief in the
value of each personality, rather than negative ways
which undermine self-confidence and self-esteem.   2)
As a nation, we have confidence in the capacity of
all to learn cooperation and mutual respect.   Our
schools provide a climate in which mutual respect and
trust are possible.   Teachers build understanding and
communication between individuals and groups.   3) We
believe in the right of people to have a voice in
plans and policies which directly affect them.
Teachers help children to understand the reasons for
standards and rules and to foresee the consequences
of their own behavior.   Schools provide for children's growth in self-government in which they share
increasingly in planning their own activities.   4) We
have trust in the rational approach to human problems
and in the ability of human intelligence to resolve
conflicts.   Teachers study children's behavior scientifically, searching for causes and formulating
hunches and hypotheses about how changes may be made.
Teachers help young people to understand the reasons
for their own and others' behavior and to develop
more effective ways of meeting common conflicts.

1275.   Shipp, F. T.   "4-4-4-3: new plan for school
organization."   School Executive, 71(1951):62.

An early proposal recommended the 4-4-4-3 plan, which
would include the kindergarten and the first three
grades (ages 4-8) in the primary school; grades 4-7
(ages 9-13) in the intermediate school; grades 8-11
(ages 13-17) in the high school, and grades 12-14
(ages 18-20) in the community college.   The author
believes that the proposed four-year units retain the
values of the older patterns, are more efficient to
administer, and are more economical than traditional
schemes.   But most important, the organizational plan
provides for similar age groups and their needs,
since each unit circles a common growth period.
Especially considered was the difficulty encountered
under the 6-3-3 system for seventh graders making a
sudden shift from one teacher to a multi-teacher-
departmental relationship in the junior high school.
The author believes it is better to detain the
socially accelerated girls, who mature somewhat
earlier than boys do during this period, than to
advance the boys, who frequently are not ready for
seventh grade in the junior high school.

1276.   Shirts, N. A. "Ninth grade: curriculum misfits?"
Bulletin of the National Association of Secondary
School Principals, 41(1957):135-137.

The earliest printed plea for a reevaluation of the
traditional junior high school organization was this
author's query in 1957: "Could it be that the 6-3-3
plan is 'corseting' our ninth grade group, restricting their normal development, and imposing an ill-
fitting administrative structure on their basic needs
and demands? Why not investigate a 5-3-4 or a 6-2-4
plan?"

1277.   Skogsberg, A. H. and Johnson, M., Jr. "The magic
numbers of 7-8-9: is the structure really the best
for the junior high school?" National Education
Association Journal, 52(1963):50-51.

Both sides of the coin are considered. Skogsberg
discusses child development, society's vocational and
avocational requirements, readiness for subject
matter, personal needs in our culture, time necessary
for certain maturational changes, and relevancy of
operation to purposes leading to this conclusion:
Young people in what are commonly called grades 7, 8,
and 9 belong in the junior high school. Conversely,
Johnson states that there is no reason to believe
that the junior high school must be composed of
grades 7, 8, and 9. He believes that the decision
will have to be made on practical grounds and on the
basis of social and administrative viability. Any
pattern is satisfactory that gives identity to youth
during early adolescence, that includes at least
three grades for stability, and brackets those grades
in which significant numbers of pupils reach
pubescence.

1278.   Smith, B. F. "A further look at manifest anxiety
of urban junior high school students." Journal of
Secondary Education, 45,2(1970):66-81.

Junior high school students, particularly blacks,
experience excessive inner conflict, because they
lack social skills and confidence. These feelings of
insecurity stem mainly from an awareness of social
exile. In general, the black eighth grader is
unhappy and is experiencing difficulty in controlling
his social relationships. These students appear
impulsive, immature, and academically sluggish.

1279.   Smith, M., Standley, L. L., and Hughes, C. L.
Junior High School Education, Its Principles and Procedures. New York: McGraw-Hill, 1942.

Brings together experimental evidence about pupils
and the survey data that bear on the problem of

junior high school education. Sections cover these
areas: 1) the introduction to junior high school
education, 2) physical growth and development, 3)
mental growth, 4) the adolescent in society.   5)
adjustment through the guidance program. 6) adjustment of exceptional children.   7) the program of
studies, 8) teacher planning, 9) enriching instruction through extra-class activities, 10) enriching
instruction through the library, 11) objective aids
to instruction, 12) appraising and reporting pupil
progress, 13) the principal and staff, 14) democra-
tizing school administration, 15) scheduling school
activities, 16) interpreting the school to the
public, 17) the functioning school plant, and 18)
looking into the future.

1280.   Spaights, E.   "Accuracy of self-estimation of
junior high school students." Journal of Educational
Research, 58,9(1965):416-419.

This study examined the relationship between actual
and perceived achievement levels of junior high
school students.   Pupils are generally unable to
reasonably estimate their own achievement level.
Theoretically, there is an actual self and a perceived self. When these selves are nearly equal, an
individual is said to be congruent. An incongruent
relationship exists where the self-estimate deviates
greatly from a measured level.   Incongruent relationships between actual and perceived selves have long
been of interest to research investigators.   The
eighty pupils studied were from four ability groups
of a seventh grade in a junior high school--twenty
from each group. The revised Stanford-Binet Intelligence Test was administered.   The findings of the
study suggest the following conclusions: 1) Bright
pupils tend to rate themselves less accurately than
their less intelligent peers.   Most of the pupils in
the able learner group felt they were performing
school work equal to the grade level on which they
had been placed.   2) Mentally retarded children in a
class of slow learners are more accurate predictors
of their academic ability than are mentally retarded
children in the modified classes.   A pupil assigned
to a class for slow learners soon discovers that his
academic performance is not consistent with the grade
level on which he has been placed.   This discovery
may result from self-introspection, conversations
with peers, or teacher conferences.   In any case,
special class pupils have more insight into the
nature and extent of their disability than mentally
retarded children found in modified classes.   3) Boys
compared to girls show no significant difference in
achievement level prediction.   Each sex has life
experiences which result in an equivalent amount of
academic self-perception.   4) Junior high school

pupils predict their grade placement score in reading more accurately than they predict their scores in arithmetic or language arts.

1281.   Spaulding, F. T., Frederick, O. I., and Koos, L.B. "The Reorganization of Secondary Education." National Survey of Secondary Education, Monograph 5. Washington, D.C.: United States Office of Education, Bulletin 17, 1932.

Compares common types of grade patterns in terms of scope and consistency of internal organization, and the 6-6 and 6-3-3 stand out. The separate three-year junior and senior high schools seem to owe whatever advantage they have to the size of their enrollments.

1282.   Spencer, H. B. "Community meets junior high school needs through plans of organization." Bulletin of the National Association of Secondary School Princi-pals, 42(1958):309-312.

Urges continuation of the three-year junior high school, doesn't mention the possibility of a downward extension to include grade 6, yet is openly opposed to removing ninth grade.

1283.   Stanavage, J. A. "Beyond the middle school: a review and a prospect." American Secondary Educa-tion, 2,2(1972):5-10.

Lists attributes of a junior high and a middle school but outlines faulty assumptions in the middle school concept, these being: 1) the misconception that adolescence is primarily physiologically determined, 2) the assumption that the best way to educate young people is in an age-segregated school; 3) mistaken belief that school grade layering is the most effec-tive organizational plan for learning. The article describes a viable alternative and how it would work better. Small clusters of children and young people would come together in learning settings of no more than five hundred, ranging from nursery school through twelfth grade.

1284.   Stephens, W. R. "Stephens sheds new light on junior high school history." Junior High School Newsletter, 5,2(1967):1.

The junior high school emerged in twentieth century America not as a result of the new child study move-ment as some have argued, but primarily as a result of the progressing reform forces that honored the values of efficiency and economy. These values appeared in the schools in the form of more practical education for business and industry.

1285.   Stephens, W. R.   "The junior high school, a product of reformed values, 1890-1920."   Teachers College Journal, 39(1967):52-60.

This article presents an historical perspective of the junior high school. The excellent footnotes are helpful.

1286.   Stone, J. and Church, J.   Childhood and Adolescence. 2d ed. New York: Random House, 1969.

A comprehensive, well-written, and highly readable text on child psychology that integrates the cognitive approach of Piaget with the dynamic approach of Freud.

1287.   Storen, H. S.   "Junior high school priorities." Clearinghouse, 35(1960):67-71.

Try to develop in each young person an enthusiasm for learning and a curiosity for further knowledge about the world. Help each boy and girl develop an awareness of and a sensitivity to beauty in nature, in literature, in music, in decoration of home and community. This paper has not tried to delineate how we shall do these things, but simply makes a plea for educators to lend their best efforts toward establishing some new priorities. Although other priorities may be justified, in a world of confusion and tension, a love of learning and an appreciation of beauty are stable values that will serve our children well throughout their lives. If these values are not developed in early adolescence, they may never have a chance to grow.

1288.   Stoumbis, G. and Howard, A.   Schools for the Middle Years: Readings. Scranton, Pa.: International Book Co., 1969.

A collection of articles on the junior high and the middle school is organized in the following five areas: 1) the junior high school, 2) the middle school, 3) controversy and problems, 4) changing patterns of instruction, and 5) curriculum.

1289.   Strang, R.   The Adolescent Views Himself: A Psychology of Adolescence. New York: McGraw-Hill, 1957.

Two sections of this book are especially appropriate to the study of middle school youth. The section on achieving scholastic success deals with academic problems, the meaning of school success, the role of interest in learning, how adolescents feel about tests, marks, and report cards, how marks affect pupil-teacher relations, what makes studying easy or difficult for adolescents, age differences and responses, and the role of intelligence and motivation. A second section discusses favorable learning conditions: personal factors affecting concentration, cooperation and assistance in study, time and place for studying, suitable assignments, appropriate curriculum, effective teaching methods, constructive teacher-student relations, and teacher personality.

1290.   Strickland, J. H. and Alexander, W. "Seeking continuity in early and middle school education." Phi Delta Kappan, 40(1969):397-400.

These suggestions would help coordinate planning and programming in public schools: 1) Interested groups should develop alternative models of schooling which use closely coordinated programs and staffing patterns in school levels previously labeled as preschool, prechildhood, elementary, intermediate, middle, and junior high. 2) School faculties should construct curriculum sequences which allow for human variance in the development of communication skills, cognitive processes, concept formulation, creativity, values and attitudes, and individuality. 3) All levels should jointly and efficiently use special programs and facilities such as the library, laboratories, the materials center, the health clinic, and the psychological and social services center. 4) Teacher education should provide early and extended team work opportunities with children of several age levels before beginning specialization in any function, area, and level. 5) Program planning for early childhood, later childhood, and preadolescent education--even adolescent education--should draw heavily on family and community involvement. Continuing attention should be given to the common effort made by school, home, and community in focusing on the developing learner and his successive learning experiences rather than on separate levels and educational organizations.

1291.   Strickland, V. E. "Role and significance of the junior high school in the total school program." Bulletin of the National Association of Secondary School Principals, 46(1962):69-77,

Several understandings seem to be basic goals for junior high education: 1) Background and tradition is more important than ever before. Boys and girls cannot understand their world neighbors unless they understand themselves. There should be a renewed emphasis on democracy--American style. Young people should be taught to be proud and steadfast in their own heritage. 2) Changing the curriculum does not necessarily mean throwing out to make room for something new. It does mean a careful appraisal of what

is taught in terms of usefulness to Americans. 3)
Raising standards is necessary to help pupils learn
more in a given time period. Talented pupils should
be given an opportunity to advance as their capacities permit. If intelligence is a real resource, it
must be carefully identified and deliberately nourished. 4) The growing need for pupils to learn more
facts, to develop broader understandings, to achieve
new attitudes, and to acquire new skills will require
lengthening the period of learning--the school day
and school year. Specific goals for junior high
school students are these: 1) know how to accept
others and be accepted, 2) make decisions with guidance and accept increasing responsibility, 3) know
academic things (reading and writing, listening and
talking, competence in arithmetic, and science--
scientific method and problem solving), 4) make
opportunities for leadership, 5) explore many interests, 6) seek vocational information and suggestions,
7) arrive at conclusions relating to personal-social
issues, 8) have at least one adult friend, 9) carry a
job to completion, 10) understand the physiology of
one's body, 11) understand society and its institutions, 12) understand the philosophy of democracy,
13) implement moral and spiritual values, 14) participate in and accept change, 15) understand some of
the cultural background of our society, 16) experience creativity, 17) experience both success and
failure.

1292.   Stuart, H. C. "Normal growth and development during adolescence." In Seidman, J. (Ed.), The Adolescent: A Book of Readings, pp. 86-115.   New York:
Holt, Rhinehart and Winston, 1960.

Boys in the United States, both Caucasian and black,
are 68 percent taller and 12 to 15 percent heavier
than boys were a half century ago.

1293.   Tanner, J. M. Growth at Adolescence.   Oxford,
England: Blackwell Scientific Publications, 1962.

The trend toward earlier physical growth is accompanied by earlier sexual maturity. Children in the
early 1960s are markedly taller and heavier than
those born in the earlier decades of this century.
For example, nine-year-olds are as large as ten-
year-olds were thirty years ago. Chapters are
presented on the following topics: 1) physical
growth at adolescence, 2) the development of the
reproductive system, 3) sex differences in physique
arising at adolescence, 4) developmental age and the
concept of physiological maturity, 5) factors affecting the time and character of the adolescent spurt,
6) physiological changes at adolescence, 7) the
endocrinology of adolescence, 8) motor development at

adolescence, 9) changes in mentality and behavior at adolescence.

1294.   Tegarden, R. S. "Implications of the middle school for elementary, secondary education." Bulletin of the National Association of Secondary School Principals, 60,402(1976):86-92.

Considering the move toward a school in the middle, the author addresses these questions: Where have we been? What should they do? and Where do we go from here? Middle level programs must be based on goals; failure to accomplish these goals during transescence will stifle growth and self-actualization which results in personal unhappiness in the future.

1295.   Teicher, J. D. "Normal psychological changes in adolescence." California Medicine, 85,3(1956): 171-176.

Adolescents are different; they have a vast capacity for change and often exhibit the sickest kind of behavior, which may be very frightening to us and to them. Physicians should not be panicked by the turbulence, confusion, and contradiction that mark adolescent behavior. This is relatively normal behavior in the drive toward maturation and adulthood. The adolescent has to cope with his sexual drive which is continually frustrated; he has to cope with the problems of emancipation from parental authority; he has to cope with an aggressive drive to achieve and to dominate. Parents, too, have to be understanding and ready to render unselfish support, for they continue to be the source of strength and security, and even the source of healthy restrictions. Adults must be aware that the adolescent struggles with his conscience and its dictates. Cliques, groups, and clubs act as a healthy assistance in the preservation of standards, ethics, and morals.

1296.   Tepper, S. S. "The Problem with Puberty...The Problem With Your Body." Denver: Rocky Mountain Planned Parenthood, 1852 Vine St., Denver, Colo. 80206, ERIC Doc. ED 161 830 (Document not available from EDRS), 1976.

The physical and mental problems facing the adolescent male are discussed. See ERIC Abstract #ED 161 830.

1297.   Thomas-Tindal, E. V. and Myers, J. D. V. Junior High School Life. New York: Macmillan, 1924.

"The establishment of the junior high school throughout the country marks the greatest advance yet made

toward the realization of the ideal of equal opportunity in education."

1298.   Thornburg, H. "Adolescence: a reinterpretation."
Adolescence, 5,20(1970):463-484.

Rapid social and technological changes that have been
taking place in society since World War II call for a
reevaluation of adolescent developmental tasks. The
article presents discussion on the following tasks:
1) learning appropriate relationships with peers, 2)
learning the appropriate masculine and feminine
social role, 3) learning acceptance and use of one's
own body, 4) behavioral and emotional independence of
parents and other adults, 5) striving toward economic
independence, 6) vocational election and preparation,
7) preparing and accepting the role of marriage and
family life, 8) developing a social and civic intelligence, 9) acquiring personal values and ethics.

1299.   Thornburg, H. D.   "Learning and maturation in
middle school aged youth." Clearinghouse, 45(1970):
150-155.

Discussion focuses on the physical, intellectual, and
social development of 10- to 13-year-olds during
their transitional period from childhood to adolescence. Six maturational and learning tasks occur.
Learning to cope with bodily changes, exercising a
new mode of intellectual functioning, and taking
steps to be a person in his own right present a
tremendous challenge to the youngster. The challenge
is just as great to the emerging middle school to
develop and implement an educational program which
will foster greater maturation and learning. Developmental and learning tasks which youth encounter
during preadolescence are presented to give proponents of the movement a basis to meet student needs:
1) developing and organizing knowledge and concepts
necessary for everyday functioning, 2) accepting
changes in one's physique, 3) learning new social-sex
roles, 4) developing friendships with peers, 5)
becoming an independent person, 6) developing elementary moral concepts and values.

1300.   Thornburg, H. D. (Ed.) Preadolescent Development.
Tucson: University of Arizona Press, 1974.

This book contains the following chapters: The Preadolescent Years. Physical Growth. Sex Differences.
Preadolescent Intelligence. Emerging Values. Discipline and the Preadolescent. Drugs and the Preadolescent. Sexuality in Preadolescence. Toward
Adolescence.

1301.   Thornburg, H. "Can the middle school adapt to the needs of its students?" Colorado Journal of Educational Research, 19,1(1979):26-29.

Three categories of development are discussed: 1) The nature of human development. What are the characteristics of preadolescents, and how do they interface with the school? 2) The nature of learner characteristics. How do these preteens learn, and how may their environment influence their development? 3) The nature of teacher characteristics. To what extent are classroom teachers aware of the developmental and learning needs of their students? Thornburg states, "The extent to which the middle school becomes a viable educational alternative to traditional school models is directly proportional to the ability of middle school educators and researchers to identify and investigate the developmental needs and learning capacities of the students which it serves."

1302.   Thornburg, H. D.   The Bubblegum Years: Sticking with Kids from 9-13. Tucson, Ariz.: H.E.L.P. Books, 1979.

Book contains the following chapters: 1) The Bubblegum Years--What is Preadolescence? 2) Choosing Your Flavor--Preteen Emotions.   3) Don't Swallow It--Physical Growth. 4) Spearmint or Tutti-Frutti--New Social Roles. 5) Save the Wrapper--Preteens and the Family. 6) Snapping to It--Going to School. 7) Sticking Together--Having Friends. 8) Chomping at the Bit--Becoming Independent. 9) Bursting the Bubble--Preteen Delinquency.   10) Double Your Pleasure--Preteen Sexual Behavior.   11) A Sticky Situation--Preteen Drug Use. 12) Two Sticks at a Time--Entering Adolescence. Chapter 6, Snapping to It--Going to School, is of special interest. This chapter contains the following sections: how smart are they? what is a good school? activity experiences, common expectations, honest relationships, basic skills, relevance, values, counseling, what can teachers do? are schools to blame? and the role of TV in a preadolescent's world. The preadolescent's ability to problem solve is presented as well as the ability to discriminate. A 9-year-old's reasoning skills are compared to those of a 13-year-old's. A good general characteristic of a school for early adolescents would be "one which has enough flexibility to meet the personal needs of its students, even though those needs may change from year to year." Teachers are encouraged to let students plan many of their own learning activities. Learning must include understanding, social contact, and responsibility. Much student achievement is related to gaining status with friends. Students should not be expected to conform to everything at school.

1303.   Thornburg, H. D. "Is the Beginning of Identity the End of Innocence?" Keynote address at the Western Regional Middle/Junior High Consortium Conference, January, 1980.

If professionals are going to respond adequately to the needs of middle school/junior high school aged youngsters, they should consider the following observations. Professionals don't understand early adolescent development. The school environment is still not conducive to positive growth for these youngsters nor does it act as an arena where they can act out their new energies and desires. Professionals fail to take a contemporary stance when ascertaining the needs of early adolescents. The author discusses these areas of concern which affect individuals moving out of the stage of innocence, childhood, and moving toward the age of identity, adolescence. Thornburg contends that identity is beginning earlier than ever before, and as a source of self-understanding, identity is more ambiguous than in previous generations. Regarding this contemporary identity search, the author posits four major reasons why identity pursuits have been accelerated in early adolescents. First, he states that development is occurring earlier than ever before, and second, peers are becoming more formalized at earlier ages. Third, parents are spending less time with children, and fourth, the media have influenced social awareness.

1304.   Thornburg, H. D. "Developmental Characteristics of Middle Schoolers and Middle School Organization." Paper presented at American Educational Research Association symposium entitled Relationships Between Developmental Research and Curriculum and Instruction Design for Middle Schools, Boston, April 7-11, 1980.

Human development at the middle school level emphasizes developing friendships and becoming aware of increased physical changes. The teacher must remember that learning must be functional to the student and emphasizes the importance of allowing preteens to show interest in planning many of their own learning experiences. Teachers must not actively compete with students' friends or with powerful external influences such as the media, yet teachers must present relevant issues.

1305.   Tiffany, B. E. "Let's listen to the students." Journal of NAWDAC, 40,3(1977):116-117.

Students in a 7-9 junior high school with an enrollment of one thousand were asked to comment on their
classes and their school activities.   See ERIC
Abstract #EJ 161 868.

1306.   Toepfer, C. F., Jr. "The middle school: implications for elementary and secondary education."
Impact, Winter 1967-68:3-5.

School systems considering a move to a middle school
should identify what the middle school approach can
do more effectively. If no such evidence develops, a
change seems worthless. The second step is to plan
for a systematic move to a middle school organization. Failure of earlier innovative patterns to plan
change has raised apprehension that the middle school
may turn out to be just another administrative whim
to which early adolescents will be subjected. It is
not difficult to find junior high school administrators who contend that all we need to do to achieve
the unfulfilled objectives of the junior high school
is to replace it with a middle school. This entire
issue features opinions by experts in the field of
early adolescent education including Thomas Curtis,
Dorothy Rosenbaum, Nicholas Georgiady, Louis Romano,
Mary Compton, Edward McHugh, and Harold Rankin. They
address the problems concerning the middle school as
an effective curricular pattern for early adolescents
and identify its place in the balance between
elementary and secondary education.

1307.   Toepfer, C. F., Jr. "The Process of the Middle
School." Paper presented at the Annual Conference of
the National Middle School Association, St. Louis,
November, 1976.

Includes a basic bibliography of sources documenting
brain growth periods and its impact on transescent
learners. The author gives addresses of persons who
have information on brain growth.

1308.   Toepfer, C. F., Jr. "A Realistic Expectation for
Cognitive Growth During Transescence."   Paper pre-
sented at the Annual Meeting of the Association for
Supervision and Curriculum Development, Houston,
March, 1977.

Cautions educators against high expectations for
rapid cognitive growth during middle school years and
urges a rethinking of curriculum for those years,
based on neurological data concerning brain growth
patterns. Research indicates that brain growth
corresponds to increases in body size during five
distinct periods of growth occurring in the age
intervals 3 to 10 months, 2 to 4 years, 6 to 8 years,
10 to 12 years, and 14 to 16 years. Brain growth

ceases for 85 percent of youngsters between the ages
of 12 and 14. Predictions concerning abilities for
cognitive growth potential for ages 2 to 4 and 6 to 8
are supported by the fact that Head Start programs,
conducted in the 4 to 6 year period, are generally
less successful than programs conducted during either
the earlier or later period. Extrapolating these
results to the middle school years, and recognizing
the need for further study, the argument is made for
reinforcement of existing cognitive skills, and reinforcement of psychomotor, affective, and self-concept
development. Concentration in these areas would
better prepare the transescent child for the next
spurt in brain growth and cognitive growth potential.

1309.   Touton, F. C. and Struthers, A. B. Junior High
School Procedures. Boston: Ginn and Co., 1926.

The junior high is assigned the task of acquainting
the pupil with an ever-broadening environment, thus
enriching his life.

1310.   Trump, J. L. and Baynham, H. D. Focus on Change:
A Guide to Better Schools. Chicago: Rand, McNally
and Co., 1961.

Summarizes innovations in secondary schools: team
teaching, instructional methods, technological aids,
and school buildings. The author criticizes rigid
curriculum, recommends steps for designing curricula
to meet individual variability, presents staff projects, reports on a new kind of junior and senior
high education, and offers ideas for changes in
elementary schools.

1311.   Trump, J. L. "The junior high school: curriculum
changes for the '60s." Bulletin of the National
Association of Secondary School Principals, February
1963:16.

Suggests that the best arrangement might be 5-5-5
(K-4, 5-9, and 10-14) thus extending free public
education through the first two years of college.

1312.   Trump, J. L. "Junior high versus middle school."
Bulletin of the National Association of Secondary
School Principals, 40,6(1967):71-73.

Article discusses the National Association of Secondary School Principals' Committee on Junior High
School Education and its recommended grades or years
in the junior high or middle school. Careful studies
are needed to discover whether different organizations of secondary education produce better conditions for student learning and better conditions for
teachers' professional development. Whatever the

name--junior high, intermediate, or middle school--
the institution is not a primary or elementary
school, nor is it a senior high. Although its program is basically of a secondary level, the school in
the middle should provide a smooth transition from
the elementary school so that a continuum of education results. The article contrasts books by M. Dale
Baughman and Neal C. Nickerson, Jr. Nickerson
(Junior High Schools Are On The Way Out)   concludes
that the junior high school is finished and sees a
promising new vehicle for helping better educate
young adolescents, the middle school. Baughman
(Administration of the Junior High School)   suggests
ways to make junior high schools better. He focuses
on such administrative details as staffing patterns
for schools of different sizes, and how principals
delegate certain responsibilities.

1313.   Trump, J. L. A School for Everyone: Design for a
Middle, Junior, or Senior High School that Combines
the Old and the New. Reston, Va.: National Association of Secondary School Principals, 1977.

A model school project emphasizes alternatives that
creative educators can use to improve schools. Major
statements by the National Association of Secondary
School Principals are issued as guidelines for
improving schools into a workable model. The school
must develop the maximum potential of each student,
teacher, and supervisor. Unconventional methods for
evaluating individual productivity are presented as
are ideas to improve the quality of school programs.
Chapters cover the rationale, a description of the
people involved, the program description, priorities
and procedures for making change in schools, and a
total plan overview.

1314.   University of the State of New York. "A Design
for Early Secondary Education in New York State: An
Abstract." Bulletin 1426. Albany, December, 1953.

Presents a design for early secondary education,
based on the best thinking of lay and professional
groups, which New York State used as a guide to
improve their educational programs for grades 7, 8,
and 9. The abstract contains sections on: local and
state responsibility for the program, the need for
reexamining early secondary education, the task of
early secondary education, the society served, the
pupils served, the task defined, some considerations
in fulfilling the task, a program for the task, subject areas, extra-class activities, pupil personnel
services, the library services, sustaining the program, getting on with the task, leadership, fostering
security and confidence, use of democratic group

procedures, working groups, need for adequate communication, securing broad participation, the organization for program improvement, facilities needed,
professional materials, services of consultants, and
time for planning. The task of early secondary education can be broadly defined as follows: 1) to
develop orientation toward other people necessary for
American citizenship, 2) to provide for pupil health
in personal adjustment, 3) to help pupils become more
independent, 4) to give a breadth of exploratory
experiences, 5) to help pupils appraise themselves
realistically, 6) to make basic skills and knowledge
functional, 7) to prepare pupils for the experiences
of later adolescence.   All pupils do not need the
same things to the same extent, nor do all pupils
need the same things at the same time, yet at any
given time some needs of a pupil may be so urgent
that they require immediate attention.

1315.   Urell, K.   "What do they want out of life?"
Teachers College Record, 61(1960):329-330.

Since there are notable differences in the social
aspirations of the students from two school neighborhoods, the programs of education must be varied to
accommodate the needs in each. This is supported by
results from the following study.   In a research
project on the aspirations of students in grades 8
and 9, 398 students in an experimental school (which
reported a high rate of delinquency) and 232 students
in a control school (which claimed average or above
average behavior) were asked among other questions:
If you could become any kind of person you wanted to,
what kind would you choose to be?   In the experimental school 16.6 percent of the students and 44.8
percent in the control group aspired to professional
careers; 11.1 percent of the students in the experimental school wanted to be nurses as compared to 2.6
percent of those in the control group.   In the experimental group 25.9 percent and in the control group
only 10.3 percent identified as desirable the personal traits of obedience, respect, and orderliness.
To become a good family person and have a happy home
appealed to only 4.8 percent of the students in the
experimental school compared with 12.5 percent of the
students in the control school.   Another study
reported on 345 experimental school students in
grades 8 and 9 from a neighborhood of high delinquency and 215 control school students in an average
or slightly above average neighborhood, who were
asked: Who is the most successful person that you
know?   Parents and other relatives were most often
considered more successful than any other person by
37.1 percent of the experimental school students and
24.7 percent of the control group.   One third of the
students in both schools designated a wide range of

persons indicating a broad social acquaintance and admiration. Entertainers were more popular with the less privileged students in the experimental school than with those in the control school. In the author's view, some of the goals and values identified by adolescents through their aspirations and perceptions of successful persons are important in planning an effective program of socialization and pre-vocational training in the junior high school.

1316.   Van Hoose, J. "Attending proactively to psychological and social concerns." Transescence, 8,1 (1980):26-30.

The author contends that one of the most glaring flaws in middle schools is that educators handle developmental concerns reactively instead of proactively. Psychological and social concerns are dealt with when a problem occurs, instead of anticipating transescent concerns and designing ways to address them. This article assesses the current posture regarding psychological and social concerns and outlines some specific ways for middle school educators to change from being reactive to proactive regarding student concerns. Sections cover these topics: the current middle school posture, examples of typical middle school effort, assuming a proactive posture, sharing heros, visual strength bombardment, social skills training, use of open-ended simulation, parent education and parent involvement.

1317.   Van Til, W. "Junior high school or middle school?" Contemporary Education, 41,5(1970):222-231.

Will the junior high or the middle school be the form of school organization used in the years ahead? We must examine how the junior high school came into being and how the middle school is developing. We must also look at the difficult and possibly unanswerable problem of the degree of success experienced or to be experienced by these forms of organization. Only then will we be in a position to make intelligent decisions rather than be at the mercy of the shifting winds of education. The chapter titles are: Genesis of the Junior High School, Social Influences, Psychological Influences, Reorganization Influences, Institutionalization of the Junior High School, Successes and Failures, Social Influences, Emergence of the Middle School, Psychological Influences, and The Road Ahead. Eminent researchers predict the future of middle years education. Will these predictions come true? It depends on the power of the forces fostering middle school organization and the power of the forces still supporting junior high school organization. But it depends also on what supporters of junior high school education actually do in their own schools and in state and university relationships. The success or failures of junior high school teachers and administrators in developing a distinctive junior high school program of education will contribute to choosing the road ahead--junior high school or middle school. New forms of organization grow out of the power of new forces. New forms of organization also grow out of the failure of old forces.

1318.   Van Til, W. and Lounsbury, J. H.   "Meet junior." National Education Association Journal, 46(1957): 594-596.

A biographical sketch of the junior high school with an historical background of the junior high school and an evaluation of its status.

1319.   Vars, G. F.   "Change--and the junior high." Educational Leadership, 23,3(1965):187-189.

An institution that would truly serve the young adolescent in contemporary society will combine the elementary school's traditional concern for the whole child with the secondary school's stress on scholarship and intellectual development. It will seek intellectual development through learning experiences in part organized around broad problems that are meaningful to students and in part through study in some depth of the recognized disciplines. Crucial to the success of such a combined approach is the development of middle school teachers whose preparation is a judicious blending of elementary and secondary, with specific attention to teaching in the middle school. Neither changing the institution's name, nor moving its grade level bracket up or down a notch will necessarily affect the character of the education it provides. Instead, educators at all levels must seize the opportunity represented by the present state of flux to try once again to make the intermediate unit a truly unique institution for the age group it embraces. Block-time is an antidote for extreme departmentalization and enables the teacher to know each student as a person, the first step toward effective guidance. Interdisciplinary team teaching program, school-within-a-school organization, and carefully developed homeroom guidance programs have all been used to make sure that the young junior high school student is not lost in the shuffle. Reading instruction, so crucial for academic success, is carried through grades 7, 8, and 9.

1320.   Vars, G. F.   "What do we believe about junior high education?"   Bulletin of the National Association of Secondary School Principals, 50(1966):140-143.

Fundamental questions were raised and answers not found. To what extent should the junior high or middle school be a separate and distinct institution? What grade or age level should it include? What patterns of curricular organization, both horizontal and vertical are most appropriate for intermediate institutions? How should students be grouped? What types of staff organization are most appropriate at the junior high school level? What certification will obtain for us the best possible teachers?

1321.   Vars, G. F. (Ed.) Guidelines for Junior High and Middle School Education, a Summary of Positions. Washington, D.C.:   National Association of Secondary School Principals, 1966.

A three-year junior high or middle school provides a desirable and separate learning environment for young adolescents. The school program provides courses that interest and benefit students age 11 to 15. A three-year institution provides time for the young person to establish identity with the school as well as furnishes program continuity needed to help students develop leadership abilities and social skills. A two-year school requires the pupils to grow from their position as a follower to that of the leader in a few short months. Separate identity for the junior high or middle school gives clear cut status to the students and enables the faculty to devote full attention to youngsters passing through puberty. Housing the junior high in separate buildings has the added advantage of segregating young adolescents from smaller children and from the more sophisticated senior high students. These possibilities establish a pattern of discipline appropriate to this age level when it is housed separately. Because of earlier physical maturation, some 11-year-old students are better served in a junior high or a middle school than in the conventional elementary school. Similarly, some 15-year-old students, whose maturity and interests merit more advanced courses and facilities than those typically available in the junior high school, are better served in the senior high school. Whether, as a matter of general policy, the intermediate school should include all fifth and/or sixth graders as opposed to ninth graders is still debated. Nongrading also is likely to affect decisions on the desirable ages or levels to include in an intermediate school.

1322.   Walton, R. E.   "Middle school in Bloomington: catastrophe turned to opportunity." Hoosier Schoolmaster, 7,4(1967):24-29.

To decide which grade organization pattern would be better in the Bloomington schools, educators studied

the following ideas: 1) an increasing concern over
the effectiveness of the traditional junior high
school program, 2) a reexamination of the organization and function of the comprehensive high school,
3) recognition of forces bringing about change in
education, 4) what teachers know about teachers, 5)
techniques of organization and instruction, and 6)
trends in school construction.

1323.   Wattenberg, W. W. "Preadolescents and the junior
high school." Educational Leadership, 14(1957):
473-477.

Indicates possible gains by having an administrative
unit devoted to meeting the needs of student groups.
While an administrative arrangement would undoubtedly
make it easier to serve the group well, it is by no
means a guarantee that this will happen. Above all,
the psychological needs of the students require that
the junior high school have a flexible curriculum and
educational procedures which nurture individual
differences. Regardless of the structure--an 8-4, a
6-3-3, or a 6-4-4 plan--the significant educational
objective should be to create a setting where groups
mixed as to developmental phase may work together on
problems which are vital to the individual. The
argument should begin at that point rather than
assume that the structure will determine the program.

1324.   Wattenberg, W. W. "Today's junior high student."
Educational Leadership, 23,3(1965):190-193.

Young adolescents differ from those of previous
generations: they mature earlier, they have greater
intellectual sophistication, but they are more
divided. Article is concerned with this dichotomy
and its possible educational implication. Current
procedures in junior high school may not be reaching
significant numbers of students. The solution, then,
calls for retention and improvement of practices that
benefit some and find ways to meet the needs of those
who are being alienated. How can this be done? One
possibility is for teachers to individualize instruction or subgroup classes so that different processes
can be geared to the psychological needs of young
people. Let the self-propelling pupils work in their
own ways to reach long-range goals; give the self-
doubters the security of definite assignments. The
second possibility is to group together the alienated
youth and have teachers work with them intensively to
develop appropriate approaches. We can no longer
afford to deal with educational problems by swings of
the pendulum. Any approach if applied to all children alike will be bad for some. There is no solution but to deal with each boy or girl in terms of
his or her characteristics. This is especially the

case of the junior high level, where individual differences are most visible.

1325.   Wattenberg, W. W. "The junior high school: a psychologist's view."   Bulletin of the National Association of Secondary School Principals, 49(1965): 34-44.

The junior high school is a paradox. Its clientele is composed of so bewildering an assortment of young people at crucial turning points in their lives as to defy description. Second, colleges of education make believe that there is no such institution: schools are considered either elementary or secondary; young people are either children or adolescents. Young people do not develop in accordance with timetables. Junior high school populations are heterogeneous not only in ability and all the usual variables, but also in developmental stage. Youngsters may make sharp changes in the course of intellectual growth, emotional adjustment, and social goals. Our knowledge of what forces cause the changes is fragmentary at best. By gradual steps, young people drift into a contrasting stage which is called early adolescence or transescence. Here three major shifts take place. The young people react very strongly to their age mates: some become utterly dependent on their peers; an equally normal but puzzling minority court relative solitude. There is considerable vacillation in attitudes toward adults, strong revolt against childishness, and sporatic displays of hostility toward parents and teachers. While all this is happening, the young people are quite conscious of their own sex roles. Physically, rapid growth and puberty are on the agenda. The first and most important fact about the junior high school is that its classes are unstable and constantly changing. Too little has been done to use the junior high school to cope with these situations.

1326.   Wattenberg, W. W. "The middle school as one psychologist sees it."   High School Journal, 53(1969): 164-171.

Expresses skepticism and raises questions regarding grade level juggling in creating middle schools. Unless a new administrative arrangement gives rise to new programs, it is wasted effort. There is no evidence that young people who come to a 6-3-3 plan differ in any degree from those who come to an 8-4 plan. A number of popular beliefs influence early teenagers: 1) The basic ability and the basic behavior pattern of young people represent a relentless unfolding of genetic traits. If we accept this idea, we should base our middle schools on programs that find out each young person's level, and then

train him to operate at that level. 2) Translated
into educational strategies, the sequential development pattern carries three inconsistent implications:
a) Since the formative years are so important, there
should be a concentration of effort at the preschool
levels. b) Special mental health services should be
available in the community or through the school. c)
Middle school programs should be established to
enable students to work on the developmental patterns
associated either with late childhood or early
adolescence. These tasks include the establishment
of heterosexuality, the firming up of ego identity,
and the practice of adult roles.

1327.   Weber, E. (Ed.) Intermediate Education: Changing
Dimensions. Washington, D.C.: Association for
Childhood Education International, 1965.

This curriculum booklet promotes strong personal
development of each pupil and gives examples of
guidelines for program development with special
application to the middle school grades and later
years.

1328.   Wiley, R. B. "The Middle School--A New Plan."
Paper presented at the National School Board Association Convention, Minneapolis, Minn., April 25, 1966.

In noticing that in the past the 7-9 plan has been an
experimental force in curriculum planning, author
concludes junior high schools have not stood by their
convictions and have allowed, even encouraged, the
Carnegie Unit, which so constrains high school cur-
riculums, to expand its influence to the 7-9
curriculum.

1329.   Williams, E. "Transescence and identity crisis."
Transescence: The Journal of Emerging Adolescent
Education, 3(1975):13-17.

During the brief period of transescence, children
experience major changes in their physical, social,
intellectual, and emotional selves. Middle school
teachers need to have several intellectual models to
meet demands of young people during this sometimes
turbulent, frequently frustrating, and potentially
rewarding period. By far the most widely used model
is the developmental task concept which postulates
certain tasks to be achieved for successful progress
through the major developmental stages of infancy,
childhood, transescence, and adolescence. Another
interesting framework for thinking about development
is provided by Erik Erikson in his book, Identity:
Youth and Crisis, Norton and Co., 1968. This article
is not a review of Erikson's book, but an attempt is
made to consider some of the general propositions

about the identity crises construct which may give
teachers another view of transescence. Erikson uses
crisis, not to imply impending disaster, but rather
to mark a turning point when development must move
one way or another. Transescence is filled with high
potential and great vitality, but it is also fraught
with hazards--a period of extreme vulnerability. In
his search for identity, a youth may find a negative
identity. Teachers of transescents are familiar with
the list of trait characteristics of this age group.
The typical list includes such characteristics as:
turbulent, moody, restless, lethargic, other-
directed, inward-looking, concerned with opinions of
peers, rejecting standards of adults. Several implications for middle school programs are clear. First,
neuroses of transescents are only temporary. Behavior that may seem defiant or delinquent or deviant
may be only exploratory behavior in the transescent's
identity search. The second point stressed by
Erikson is that crises tasks of transescents are
epigenetic. That is, they exist in some form in
younger children--these are not new crises. Epigene-
sis means that everything that grows has a ground
plan which comes into fruition at a future time. How
is this concept helpful to middle school teachers?
Differences among elementary school children, middle
school youngsters, and high school youth are differences in degree, not in kind.

1330.   Williams, E. L. "What about the junior high and
middle school?" Bulletin of the National Association
of Secondary School Principals, 52(1968):126-134.

From a national perspective the author sees the
middle school on the threshhold of greater growth.
Although no single pattern has dominated, many of the
features of the middle school relate directly to
special characteristics of preadolescents; some of
the common features are related to the innovative
character of our times. The middle school is a very
flexible school, and this fondness for change makes
it difficult to establish precise research measurement. The middle school movement is an exciting
development accompanied by the excitement of creativity. All this interest generated by the middle
school movement is good for the junior high because
it causes us to analyze programs in the light of
present realities and future possibilities. The
middle school is actually a reformed junior high
school.

1331.   Williams, E. L. "Questions about the middle
school." Junior High School Newsletter, 7,3(1969):1.

The author proposes answers to the following questions: What are the appropriate grades? What is the

difference between a junior high school and a middle
school? Will the middle school work? He is comfortable with middle schools which encompass grades 5-8,
5-9, 6-8 or 7-9. The middle school is merely an
idea, and organizations and structures never work,
only people work.

1332.   Williams, S. W. Educational Administration in
Secondary Schools: Task and Challenge.   New York:
Holt, Rhinehart and Winston, 1964.

A chapter in this book focuses on the function of the
junior high school in secondary education. Topics
covered in relation to the junior high include a
presentation of early reports, appearance in the
United States, the 6-3-3 vs. 6-6 vs. some other plan,
research, the developmental task concept of adolescents, strengths and weaknesses, the James Conant
report, guidelines for junior high education, the
junior high school of today, the junior high school
that is needed, special characteristics, the program
of study, a discussion of articulation, exploration,
integration, differentiation, socialization, personnel, scheduling, guidance, student activities, and
administration.

1333.   Wilson, M. T. and Popper, S. H.   "What about the
middle school?" Education Digest, 35,5(1970):16-18.

Two viewpoints by leading educators: Mildred T.
Wilson believes the middle school is tailored to the
individual, and she discusses the ungraded Conwell
Middle School in Philadelphia. The staff is of
primary importance, and teachers and teams are
specialists in the basics, social studies, math,
science, and communicating skills. The school where
she is principal focuses on six major areas of development: personal responsibility, learning strategy,
critical thinking, creative thinking, effective
social behavior, and effective communication. Samuel
H. Popper, on the other hand, feels that the middle
school is an institutional corruption. Middle school
advocates who claim adolescence comes sooner for
children are not necessarily right. The junior high
school is not fulfilling its mission to protect young
adolescents. The crux of the problem is the lack of
special preparation programs for those who will teach
early adolescents.

1334.   Wilson, W. E. "The Junior High School." Indiana
Association of Junior and Senior High School Princi-
pals, Bulletin 246. Indianapolis: State of Indiana
Department of Public Instruction, 1961.

The study makes recommendations for the curriculum
and implications for teacher training in the

following chapters: 1) Introduction. 2) Character-
istics of Adolescents--Developmental Tasks of
Adolescents, Relationship to Work. 3) Organizational
Patterns for the Junior High School--Background of
the Junior High Movement, Related Research Findings,
Organizational Patterns of the Junior High School in
Indiana. 4) The Role of the Junior High School. 5)
Organization of the Junior High School Curriculum--
Areas of Concern, Guideposts for Curriculum Organiza-
tion in the Modern Junior High School, Modern Trends
in Specific Patterns of Curriculum Organization in
the Junior High School. 6) The Core Program. 7)
Language Arts in the Junior High School. 8) Social
Studies. 9) Mathematics. 10) Science. 11) Foreign
Languages. 12) Fine Arts. 13) Health Education.
14) Physical Education. 15) Music. 16) Practical
Arts. 17) The Physical Plant. 18) The Junior High
School Library as an Instructional Materials Center.
19) Guidance in the Junior High School. 20) The
Exceptional Child. 21) Extra-Class Activities. 22)
Junior High School Teacher Certification. Areas of
learning and programs offered by teacher education
institutions which would strengthen the junior high
school staffs in the Indiana Public Schools are
listed: 1) the physical, mental, emotional, and
social characteristics and needs of early adolescents, 2) the nature of the learning experience to be
provided for direction and learning of the early
adolescent, 3) organization of the junior high school
curriculum, and 4) organizational patterns which best
meet the needs of early adolescents (block-time
classes or core programs).

1335. Wolf, R. E. "Variations in personality growth
during adolescence." Journal of Pediatrics, 59
(1961):743-746.

An attempt is made to outline normal adolescent
development and to emphasize the normal variations
during this growth period. Whether one refers to
physical, intellectual, social, or emotional growth,
the emphasis is on the positive, healthy aspects of
growth between the ages of 12 and 22. This makes
adolescence "the age of the final establishment of a
dominant ego identity," as Erikson puts it, and "it
is then that a future within reach becomes part of
the conscious life plan." To look to the future
implies standing in the present, having traveled from
the past, whether remembered or not, the "before"
cannot help but affect the "now" and the "to be." If
the adolescent would ask his own questions, they
would probably be something like this: "Who and what
do they think I am?" "What do I feel I am?" "What
should I become?" An analogy can be drawn between
the development of America, as a nation, and the
development of each American adolescent. Just as

America is a melting pot made up of people from differing backgrounds, the adolescent personality is made up of identifications of multiple sources in his background. An American today grows out of what he has come from, been exposed to, and wants to become. An adolescent is what he is, based on what he has come from, his parents, and what he has been exposed to, to which he adds his ideas of what he is to become. Just as America tries to establish a dominant identity from all the identities of her constituent immigrants, so, too, does the adolescent need to be able to sink his roots in established tradition and institutions, but still have within him the frontiersman's urge to venture beyond, to find the new, the unestablished, and thereby push the culture a little farther. Piaget said, "The adolescent is committed to possibilities." The hope for him is that he has good ones from which to choose, that he has the self-assertion to create something new, and that the adults, his parents, are willing for him to have greater success than they.

1336.   Woodring, P.   "The new intermediate school." Saturday Review, October 16, 1965.

In light of New York City's return to four-year high schools, the newly created intermediate school, because it is not bound by college entrance requirements, offers opportunities for experimentation. New staffing patterns, including varieties of team teaching and dual progress plans, are particularly appropriate at this level. There are opportunities for the use of programmed learning and for new course concepts, including an early approach to foreign language. The social life can be geared to children within the prepubescent age range rather than to adolescents. The emerging intermediate school creates a demand for teacher education distinctly different from the preparation for either primary or high school teachers. If this demand is met in time, and if those schools show imagination and courage, the new school organization can contribute to the improvement of educational quality.

1337.   Wynn, R.   Organization of Public Schools.   Washington, D.C.:   Center for Applied Research in Education, 1964.

The book contains a chart showing organizational patterns of secondary schools. The traditional four-year high school has declined sharply. More than four fifths of the seventh and eighth grade students in 1964 were attending some form of junior high school or combined junior/senior high school. The most common form of junior/senior high school combination was the 6-3-3 plan followed by the 6-6 plan.

1338.   Yale-Fairfield Study of Elementary Teaching. "What about school grades?" Understanding the Child, 6(1957):44.

Most research assumes that a grade or progress for all students in each school year is both fixed and desirable. In the light of the history of school organization and growing knowledge of child growth and development, is it not possible that this organization is seriously outmoded? It is possible that undesirable school problems are motivated by the rigid year-grade scheme, for example, promotion and nonpromotion, subjects of study chopped up and organized in textbooks for individual grades, certification to teach in primary or intermediate or upper grades. Would there not be a better opportunity and more freedom to provide for the needs of children if schools were organized by stages of growth or levels of achievement rather than by grades? As a first step in the study of reorganization, experimentation might be conducted with the unit of organization expanded to include several grades: a primary unit covering kindergarten and the first three grades, an intermediate unit covering the span of grades 4-6. Within these larger units of continuous progress of pupils, it is likely that the greater freedom would make it possible for teachers to solve problems.

1339.   Young, I. F. "What are the most significant functions of the six-year school?" Bulletin of the National Association of Secondary School Principals, 36(1952):304-311.

Compares the advantages of economy of operation, administration, and educational opportunities of the six-year school to separate junior and senior units in systems with small enrollments.

1340.   Zachry, C. B. Emotion and Conduct in Adolescence. New York: Appleton-Century-Crofts, 1940.

Chapter 7--"Education and Changing Attitudes to the Self"--focuses on growth, sex, and character, to explain the factors influencing a youngster's sense of self.

1341.   Zdanowicz, P. Middle School Advantages. Circular 3. Bridgewater, Mass.: Research Service, May 1965.

Advantages to the middle school over the junior high: 1) Special facilities for home economics, shop areas, and a fully equipped gymnasium are available for the first time to fifth and sixth graders. 2) Special programs such as guidance, health, speech therapy, remedial reading, and the service of a helping teacher are also available to fifth and sixth

graders. 3) A four-year span gives ample opportunity
for teachers to get to know and understand youngsters. 4) The limitation of the Carnegie Unit is not
a factor. 5) The newness of the organization will
encourage creativity in developing new techniques in
both administration and teaching. 6) More adequate
and modern equipment is available than could be
provided economically in the neighborhood school. 7)
Seventh and eighth grade subject area teachers are
available to work with fifth and sixth graders.
These teachers can challenge the more able fifth and
sixth grade children in a greater number of subjects,
thereby reducing the size of classes for some subjects. 8) Teacher morale is boosted because innovations are put into operation gradually, after careful
planning, in-service meeting, and support of the
staff.

2

Prescriptions for and Descriptions
of Middle Schools

2001.   Alexander, W. M.   "A Survey of Organizational
    Patterns of Reorganized Middle Schools. Final
    Report."   University of Florida at Gainsville.
    Washington, D.C.:   Office of Education, Bureau of
    Research, 1968.

    This project collected data on the current status of
    middle schools in the United States.   State Depart-
    ments of Education identified middle schools, and a
    survey secured detailed data from a ten percent ran-
    dom sample of 110 schools.   The survey covered 1)
    number of schools, location by region, grades
    included, enrollment, housing, and plans for articu-
    lation with lower and upper schools, 2) establishment
    of schools (dates, reasons, preparation), 3) curric-
    ulum plans, 4) instructional organization, 5)
    arrangements for individualizing instruction, and 6)
    reactions of students, staff, parents and the general
    public to the middle schools.   Report concludes that
    middle school organizations generally have failed to
    provide a program and instructional organization dif-
    fering very much from those in the predecessor
    schools.

2002.   Alexander, W. M.   "The new school in the middle."
    Phi Delta Kappan, 50(1969):355-357.

    The emergent middle school serves a range of older
    children, preadolescents, and early adolescents.   It
    builds on the elementary school program for earlier
    childhood and in turn is built upon by the high
    school program for adolescents.   It is different from
    the childhood and adolescent schools and bridges the

two.   The article offers suggestions to help districts that are moving toward or have recently
changed to middle schools: 1) Build program and
organization, staffing, and building plans on the
basis of careful, extended study of the transescent
population by the staff concerned. 2) Defer visiting
other middle schools and program planning until step
1 has been taken and build whatever plans are made
from the ground up--working with the elementary
school staffs concerned, evaluating existing programs
rigorously, and inviting staff members, children,
parents, and any other interested people to get their
suggestions into the screening-planning process.   3)
Wherever possible, introduce new programs and practices experimentally, with controls of some type to
yield comparative data that will give more than
guesses as to what works and what does not work.   4)
Avoid too early publicity, visitation, external
evaluation, and any other dangers that will cause
innovative teachers either to draw back to escape
unfavorable criticism or to go beyond the ground of
prudence to receive recognition. 5) Most important,
budget for the extra costs of advance planning,
including the costs of releasing the principal and
some staff months in advance of the school's opening
and costs for experimentation with evaluation,
including the appointment of some person specifically
qualified to lead in the experimentation process.

2003.   American Federation of Teachers.   "A National
Design for the Middle School."   Washington, D.C.,
ERIC Doc. ED 083 199, 1973.

Presents guidelines for the operation and general
structure of the middle school. A general outline
for school personnel includes staff such as homeroom
teachers, paraprofessional school aides, administrative personnel, and grade mentors. Report also
covers curriculum planning, teacher training, marks,
alternate schools, and student government. See ERIC
Abstract #ED083199.

2004.   Anderson, W. G.   An Instrument for the Self-
evaluation of Junior High Schools.   Urbana, Ill.:
W. G. Anderson (2507 E. Main Street), 1959.

This instrument helps professional groups evaluate
and improve their education programs. Evaluation
covers eight categories: philosophy, staff, student
population, the setting (the school within the community), curriculum (general orientation and nature),
cocurriculum, and student services. Each of these
categories is viewed in three phases: 1) Inventory.
What is the nature of the educational program? What
is being accomplished?   2) Self-evaluation of the
school program by the staff. How does the program

and its accomplishments compare with the stated aims, objectives, and philosophy of the school? 3) Action Program. Considering pupil, community, and world needs, what shall be done on the basis of experience, the professional literature, and research findings to move forward? What should be undertaken first? Who shall initiate and maintain the improvements? How may the improvements be evaluated?

2005.   Arizona Teacher magazine. "Casa grande plans a middle school." Arizona Teacher, 55(1967):8-20.

In 1967 the diversity in ethnic background in Casa Grande Middle School youngsters is reflected in their diverse cultures, economic status, and social patterns. Many students in the district are bilingual, with English as their second language, and Casa Grande is moving from an agricultural to an industrial economy, causing economic and social mobility in the community. The district school board and administrative leaders are concerned that the schools are not meeting the needs of many children from these diverse backgrounds. Evaluators who studied the district's testing program results noted serious deficiencies in the elementary and junior high programs. Research into the current literature suggested that two-year junior high schools did not suit the growth patterns of the children involved and that many junior high schools have become watered-down senior high schools with stress on interscholastic competition and an advanced social life. A more natural division based on child growth and development would seem to be the fourth and fifth grades. The function of the school with respect to the middle years should be to help each child move in a gradual, orderly progression through this transitional period of life. Research confirms that a child's educational growth is based on his unique characteristics. Development of his unique potential seems to be a worthier goal, for him and for society, than the present and past attention to commonality. The increasing rate of change throughout society and the tremendous technological strides anticipated in the near future demand fully functioning, self-confident individuals. No matter how comprehensive subject content may be, there is a need for the child to know who he is, what he can do, and where he is going. Through self-discipline and motivation he can create his own order in the midst of bewildering change. This article includes a description of a model middle school in the Casa Grande School District.

2006.   Association for Childhood Education International. "The Transitional Years--Middle School 'Portfolio.'" 3615 Wisconsin Ave. N.W., Washington, D.C. 20016, 1968.

Contains the following leaflets dealing with middle
school students: 1) "In Between" by Gordon Vars. 2.
"Pre-adolescent: Misunderstood" by Edward Bantel.
3) "Bases for Grouping Within the Class" by E. T.
McSwain. 4) "Current Organizational Patterns" by
Madeline Hunter. 5) "Creativity in Learning" by
Kaoru Yamamota. 6) "Acquiring Power in Reading" by
Althea Beery and Lenore Wirthlin. 7) "Creative
Writing" by Naomi C. Chase. 8) "Science: Middle
School Years" by Charles K. Arey. 9) "Outdoor
Education" by Reynold E. Carlson. 10) "Language in
the Middle Grades" by Ruth G. Strickland. 11)
"Social Studies: Process of Inquiry" by Edna
Ambrose. 12) "Perspectives on Evaluation" by Vynce
A. Hines. 13) "New Concepts of Learning:
Multi-media" by Margery Snyder.

2007.   Association for Supervision and Curriculum Development. "The Middle School We Need." Washington,
D.C., 1975.

Report prepared by the Working Group on the Emerging
Adolescent Learner discusses the purposes and
rationale of the American middle school and suggests
what its curricular, instructional, and organiza-
tional-administrative programs should be.

2008.   Association for Supervision and Curriculum
Development. "Designing a Middle School for Early
Adolescents." 1701 K St. N.W., Suite 1100, Wash-
ington, D.C. 20036, 1979.

This videotape for staff development features seven
well-known educators. It is available in 3/4" video
cassettes or 1/2" reel to reel.

2009.   Association for Supervision and Curriculum Development. "Profiles of a Middle School." Washington,
D.C. (No year given.)

This 16 mm film and/or videotape takes an inside look
at the operations of an actual middle school program.
Teachers, administrators, and students speak about
the middle school experience and the various elements
of its program. Viewers observe parts of a team
meeting, a teacher advisory session, an interdisciplinary unit, exploratory classes, and a reading lab.
The role of the administration and staff in the
school is highlighted.

2010.   Baldwin, G. H. "Middle school: fantasy, fad, or
fact?" Educational Leadership, 31,3(1973):242-244.

What is needed for the child of 11 to 14 is not a
renamed administrative unit but a middle school that

will allow for his total development, both intellectual and social. Failure to develop a commitment
to the ideas behind the middle school leads to failure in the transition to this new kind of school.
This transition cannot be a patchwork addition of
extras to the program with no basic change within the
structure of the curriculum and the organization of
the school. From retraining comes commitment, and
from commitment comes a middle school.

2011.   Barnes, D. E.   "Your middle school must have a
revised program."   Educational Leadership, 31,
3(1973):230-232.

The name "middle school" means nothing without a
thorough program. The R & D Center at the University
of Wisconsin, Madison, provided a model for McFarland
Community Schools based on seven components: 1) an
organization for instructon, 2) a model for instructional programming, 3) a model for developing measurement tools and evaluation procedures, 4) curriculum materials, related statements of objectives, and
criterion-referenced tests and observation schedules,
5) a program for home and school communication, 6)
facilitative environments in the school building, 7)
continuing research and development to generate
knowledge and to produce test materials and procedures.

2012.   Barrington Middle School. "Barrington Middle
School: A Report." Barrington, Ill., 1966.

Barrington Middle School represents concepts of
education that are fluid and in motion: team
teaching, a flexible building, an exploratory
curriculum, imaginative administration, an eclectic
approach to education. These thoughts obliquely
suggest a definition. But what kind of team
teaching?   What type of building? What is an
exploratory curriculum? Article discusses the sixth,
seventh, and eighth grade offerings, variable pupil
grouping, modular scheduling, a typical modular
schedule, imaginative guidance practices, guide
teachers, the nongrading system, the team of administrators, the planetarium and other areas, and the
middle school building. It seeks to answer the
following questions: why modular scheduling, why
team teaching, why team administration? What about
sound in academic learning spaces? How often do you
plan to move the demountable and operable walls? Why
weren't demountable walls used in the home economics
and other areas? What is the optimum pupil capacity
of this school? Why the use of carpeting? Isn't the
learning center too wide open for quiet study? Is
the building design suitable for a traditional
program? Did the Barrington Middle School require

preplanning with the teaching staff? Why no halls? In the Barrington Grade School System, K-5 provides students with the basic building blocks of the educational process. The middle school, 6-8, serves as a catalyst, helping the students use these building blocks in new ways and in new combinations to solve problems; in short, to plumb the possibilities of their own minds and talents. Preadolescents and young teens are restless and curious and possess extreme differences, with uneven physical, mental, emotional, and social growth patterns. With this in mind, team teaching is used to meet individual student needs in greater depth.

2013.   Beane, J. A. and Lipka, R. P. "Enhancing self-concept/esteem in the middle school." Middle School Journal, August 1979:4.

In early adolescence, self-perceptions appear to undergo dramatic change along with changes in physical, social, and intellectual development. For this reason, middle school programs must pay the same kind of attention to self-concept and self-esteem that it pays to the other areas of development. This article discusses school climate, grouping, curriculum organization, peer and other interactions, academic achievement, and home-school relations as they affect self-development. To the extent that middle schools engage in the suggested strategies, they may expect constructive growth in the area of the transescent's view of self. To ignore or avoid such strategies is likewise to limit the potential for real transescent education in the middle school.

2014.   Billings, R. L. "Musts for a middle school." Clearinghouse, 49,8(1976):377-379.

Discusses the philosophy, objectives, organization, administration, guidance, and curriculum of the middle school. In a bona fide middle school, it is not simple logistical expediency that dictates a course of planning and action. The middle school philosophy must be based on the needs of preadolescent and early adolescent youth and so must separate those students from the younger elementary children and older high school adolescents. The middle school must expose its students to a wide range of educational experiences rather than specialized training, and it must provide for comprehensive socialization in group work, structured social activities, and informal situations. The widened range of middle school education must also provide earlier experiences in sharing and accepting responsibilities. While the controversy over middle school versus junior high school continues, it is now clear that a bona fide middle school philosophy does exist. If that philosophy gets those in traditional junior high schools to consider more child-centered, humanistic education for their students, then the middle school movement will have done more than survive a turbulent early adolescence. It will be well on its way to becoming an educational unit.

2015.   Bondi, J. "Guidelines for Developing and Sustaining Good Middle School Programs." Paper presented at the Annual Conference of the National Middle School Association, Denver, ERIC Doc. ED 150 745, November, 1977.

One of the most important guidelines for developing and sustaining good middle school programs is to involve many people in the planning process. Setting up objectives and a timetable to accomplish objectives and providing continuous in-service training is also very important. Competent principals are necessary to sustain good programs, and a staff that is willing to continue its in-service training is vital. Effective communication programs with parents, the community, and colleagues in other schools within a district is also important. See ERIC Abstract #ED 150 745.

2016.   Bough, M., McClure, J., and Sinks, T. "The middle school: a five state survey." Clearinghouse, 47,3(1972):162-166.

Less than one fourth of the middle schools in the Midwest include the fifth grade in middle schools, despite the human growth rationale of middle school organization.

2017.   Brod, P. "The middle school: trends toward its adoption." Clearinghouse, 40(1966):331-333.

Advantages to the middle school over the junior high are: 1) It gives the unit a status of its own rather than a junior classificaton. 2) It facilitates the introduction in grades 5 and 6 of some specialization. 3) It facilitates the reorganization of teacher education, which is sorely needed to provide teachers competent for the middle school, since neither elementary nor secondary school training programs suffice. 4) Developmentally, children in grades 6-8 are probably more alike than children in grade 7-9. 5) Since they are undergoing the common experience of adolescence, sixth to eighth graders should have special attention, special teachers, and special programs. 6) The middle school provides an opportunity for gradual change from the self-contained classroom to complete departmentalization. 7) Additional facilities and specialists are available to all children one year earlier. 8) It permits

curriculum which continues and enriches the basics.
9) It makes it easier to extend guidance services
into elementary grades.   10) It helps to slow down
the growing process from K-8, because the oldest
group is removed from each level.   11) It puts
children from the entire district together one year
earlier.   12) Physical unification of grades 9-12
permits better coordination of courses for the senior
high school.   13) It eliminates the possibility of
some students and parents not being aware of the
importance of the ninth grade as part of the senior
high school record, particularly in terms of college
admission.   14) It eliminates the need for special
programs and facilities for the ninth grade and
eliminates problems created by the fact that the
ninth grade is functionally part of the senior high
school.   15) It reduces duplication of expensive
equipment and facilities for ninth grade. The funds
can be spent on facilities beneficial to all grades.
16) It provides both present and future flexibility
in building planning, particularly important for a
changing school population.

2018.   Cambridge Independent School District 911,
Cambridge Junior High School.   "Student Evaluation/
Parent Report."   Cambridge, Minn., ERIC Doc. ED 079
355, 1973.

Discusses the Cambridge Junior High School reporting
system which is based on one hundred total points
divided into categories.   The system stresses the
student's academic and social progress and has these
benefits: 1) It has eliminated the archaic A-B-C-D-F
method of grading.   2) It has maintained incentives
for achieving good grades in tests and daily work.
3) Low ability students are able to preserve their
personal esteem by scoring well in areas not measured
by academic ability, thus enhancing self-concept. 4)
Each student is evaluated as an individual. Teachers
say that the new system brings instructors into
closer contact with all students.   Report includes a
sample of the student evaluation/parent report.

2019. Charles, A. D. "Achieving articulation of subject
matter." School and Community, 54(1968):16.

Describes articulation through curriculum from the
middle school to the upper schools and from the
elementary school to the middle school.

2020.   Chop, W. C. "The School in the Middle." Bridgeport, Conn.: Board of Education, September, 1969.

The implications of student developmental characteristics for the middle school program have led to a
rejection of standardized curriculum, grouping

practices, and instructional methods. The most recent developments (as of 1969) have emphasized a program of exploratory experience centered in a flexible curriculum. By providing experiences of two kinds--those common to all students and those that are highly individualized and diverse--the middle school emphasizes the continued development of fundamental skills and the beginning of specialization. It also limits the societal pressures commonly placed upon boys and girls and helps them develop fully as children rather than forcing them into early adult roles too rapidly. In general, the proponents of the middle school envisage a school adapted to a range of children who, rampant individuals though they are, seem to have more in common with each other than with the elementary children as a group or high schoolers as a group. The school would assume, in general, that its population has some mastery of the tools of learning but is not ready for the academic specialization of high school and its attendant college preparation pressures. This school should concentrate, then, on provisions for individual differences, a goal long touted but little effected by American education, taking particular account of the increased sophistication and knowledge of today's 10 or 11-to-14-year-olds over previous generations. The design of the new middle school introduces sixth graders gradually to specialization and provides many physical means to realize individual differences on the one hand and to encourage group activities large and small on the other.

2021.   Compton, C. "Getting two middle schools started: what we learn." National Elementary Principal, 51, 3(1971):50-54.

Describes the establishment of two middle schools in Alachua County, Florida, and provides an abbreviated case study in middle school development. In order to approach the task of curriculum planning systematically, the supervisor of research and evaluation developed a model, and the first year's work concentrated on three events from the model: 1) an analysis of the student population, 2) research on middle school concepts, and 3) identifying the scope of curriculum offerings.   The Institute for the Development of Educational Activities (an affiliate of the Charles S. Kettering Foundation) developed a managment system for individually guided education in the middle schools.   The schools were divided into instructional teams, with six of the teams having a strength (elementary) or major (secondary) in math, science, social studies and language arts. Approximately 120 students with a two-to-four-year age difference were assigned to each of these teams.

2022.   Compton, M. F.   "After the middle school...?"
Michigan Journal of Secondary Education, Summer 1971:
28-36.

Compton presents sections on the what and why of
middle school, the middle school graduate, greater
knowledge about subject areas, independent learning,
personal and social adjustment, creative thinking,
articulation, changes in today's high schools, the
high school in the big picture, disappearance of the
track system, flexibility in grouping and scheduling,
the "non-extra" curriculum, and evaluation of pupil
progress.

2023.   Compton, M. F.   "The middle school: a status
report."   Middle School Journal, 7,2(1976):3-5.

Contains data on the growth of middle schools. Tables
present 1968, 1970, and 1974 surveys, including the
number of middle schools by state, organization of
middle schools, the states by rank order of population compared to rank order in number of middle
schools, and the regional accrediting association by
population, number of member states, number of middle
schools in the region, and percentage of the national
total.   The increase in the number of middle schools
has been dramatic, from 1,101 in 1968 to 3,723 in
1974, nationwide, and since 1974 hundreds have been
organized.   Grade organization patterns have remained
relatively the same since 1968, with the 6-8 plan
still accounting for sixty percent of the schools.
The percentage with grades 5-8 and 4-8 decreased
slightly, while the 5-7 and 6-9 patterns increased
slightly.   The ten most populated states have the
greatest number of middle schools.   Likewise the ten
least populated states have the fewest number of
these schools.   There is great diversity, however,
among states which would be classified as the middle
thirty in population.   The states are grouped in
regions by the several accrediting associations.   The
North Central U.S. Association region, which accounts
for 33.5 percent of the U.S. population had slightly
fewer middle schools than the Southern Association
region, which includes only 25.2 percent of the
population.

2024.   Compton, M. F.   "Elementary-middle school relationships."   Michigan Middle School Journal, 6,2
(1976):5-7.

The number of middle schools continues to increase in
this country.   In a recent study, the authors counted
about 3800.   This burgeoning has been accompanied by
a growing level of anxiety among educators at other
school levels, partly because they do not understand
the philosophy and purposes of the middle school

movement.   Elementary educators may point to the
depth of content preparation of middle school teachers and label the school as an extension downward of
secondary education.   High school teachers may view
the middle school's concern for the student as an
absence of content and label it "a glorified elementary school."   But with understanding, they may see
that the middle school is neither elementary nor
secondary but draws its strength from the best of
both levels.   It is as unique as the students it is
designed to serve.   Its success depends largely on an
open, positive, cooperative relationship with the
schools its children come from and those they later
go to--in short, a partnership.   The thesis here is
that middle school and elementary school partnership
is natural and that it will follow when educators
take the trouble to make clear what the middle school
is and how middle school educators welcome elementary
educators in partnership.

2025.   Connecticut State Department of Education.   "A
Guide to the Writing of Educational Specification in
the Planning of Middle School Programs."   Hartford,
Conn. 1972.

Discusses how to identify the needs of middle school
students, purposes and functions of the middle
school, planning the learning environment, the
program, resources, organization, services, and
spaces, and how to test the adequacy of planning.
Includes a summary and selected references.

2026.   Coppock, N.   Middle Schools. School Leadership
Digest Series, no. 2.   Arlington, Va.:   National
Association of Elementary School Principals, 1974.

Along with increasing numbers of middle schools, the
past decade has seen the emergence of a middle school
philosophy which takes into account the wide range of
physical, intellectual, and emotional differences
among pupils who are between childhood and adolescence.   Among the labels applied to these pupils are
transescents and emerging adolescents.   While no
attempt to categorize them is wholly satisfactory,
these students are generally identified as those in
grades 5 or 6 to 8, or as 10-to-14-year-olds.   This
book covers middle school historical roots and present trends, philosophy, ideal program characteristics, and staff.   Recurrent themes include individual attention and continuous progress up the
school ladder.   Various transitional and exploratory
functions of the middle school institution are
examined.   A substantial bibliography is provided.

2027.   Croft Educational Services. "Administration: New England's first middle school, a success." Education Summary, 14(June 12, 1962):2.

The principal of the first middle school in New England cites three major advantages of the middle school over junior high school or separate elementary facilities for grades 5 and 6:   1) Facilities: science labs, typing room, gym, and industrial arts shop were built for high school use.   Now younger students can get an earlier start.   2) Four-year instead of two- or three-year program: a junior high school staff does not get to know the youngsters in only two or three years, and this is an age when pupil-teacher relations are still more important than teacher-subject relations.   3) Special programs: guidance begins in earnest at the fifth grade level, and health, remedial reading, and industrial arts programs are available.   For further information, write Paul J. Zdanowicz, Bridgewater Middle School, Bridgewater, Massachusetts.

2028.   Cuff, W. A. "Middle schools on the march." Bulletin of the National Association of Secondary School Principals, 50,316(1967):82-86.

A national survey of middle schools stated as major problems the certification of teachers, need for in-service training, and quality of teacher preparation courses.   The most common forms of middle schools reported were 5-3-4 (55 percent) and 4-4-4 (30 percent).   The 3-5-4 organization was found in 9 percent of the middle schools surveyed. For purposes of the survey, middle schools included grades 6 and 7 and did not extend below grade 4 or above grade 8. Author found that the number of middle schools was increasing, accompanied by a decrease in the number of high schools.   Examination of the literature and a sample of the middle schools showed that eighth graders usually follow the departmental plan commonly associated with high schools.   For seventh graders, departmentalization is sometimes found with only two pairs of subjects.   Sixth graders most often operate in a one room, one teacher comprehensive plan common in elementary schools.   Fifth and fourth graders generally have comprehensive instruction except in nonacademic subjects which are departmental at all levels.   Middle school offerings showed a general uniformity.   English, social studies, mathematics, science, physical education, art, and music were standard in all grades.   Sixty years ago four-year high schools and eight year elementary schools were standard in the United States.   Since then the junior high school movement has presented several alternatives to housing grades 7, 8, and 9, but no consensus has been reached on the best way to do it.   Now, just under half of these students are in the 6-6 or 6-3-3 school system, and about one third remain in the traditional 8-4 set-up. The rest attend two-year junior high schools or middle schools.

2029.   Cuff, W. A.   "Can middle schools cure a national disgrace?"   American School Board Journal, 157,5 (1969):38-39.

Author states the curriculum for grades 5 through 8 must complement complex changes within students and differences in their rate of growth.   Courses of study in middle schools should include: 1) group activities that bring pupils into direct contact with their steadily expanding natural and social environments and that provide opportunities for pupils to influence these environments as well as comprehend and cope with them, 2) independent inquiry into the natural, technological, and social phenomena that interest the pupil, 3) experiences with suitable literary and artistic works and opportunities to relate these to pupils' own lives, 4) creative participation in a variety of fine arts, literature, and domestic and manual crafts, 5) frequent appropriate individual and group activities as well as practice and principles of sound physical and mental health, 6) regulated guidance for exercising the options that become increasingly available to pupils as they move from grade 5 through grade 8.   This stable level of organization, the middle school, can correct many shortcomings of the junior high school and can provide recognition, conduct research, and demand a fair share of resources for the "15 million boys and girls and their half million teachers now in the intermediate grades--grades 5 through 8."

2030.   Curtis, T. E.   "The Middle School."   Paper presented at a Curriculum Conference at State University of New York, Albany, Center for Curriculum Research and Services, 1966.

Conference concentrated on three objectives: 1) to gain insight into the principles of early adolescent education, 2) to become aware of the strengths of the various theoretical approaches to educating the adolescent, and 3) to examine the pragmatic problems of applying the theories.   Emphasized throughout eighteen addresses was the responsibility of academic transition assumed by the middle school.   At the elementary level, the emphasis is on developing basic skills in a self-contained classroom; in the high school the emphasis is on specialization in a subject-oriented program.   Middle schools fit into this picture by building self-awareness in the student--thus aiding in the process of social adjustment--and by providing exploratory intellectual experiences in subjects that are studied more intensely at the high school level. Paper covers administration, curriculum design, architectural design, and instructional techniques and includes a selected bibliography of sixty-eight citations.

2031.   Curtis, T. E. "Rationale for the middle school." Impact on Instructional Improvement, Winter 1967-68: 6-10.

A major emphasis of the middle school movement is a conscious attempt to redefine general education--academic and social--for emerging adolescents. This article develops a rationale for the middle school: 1) The middle school is a transitional school concerned with the personal and educational needs of early adolescents. 2) Earlier physical maturation of pupils has caused a need for change in school age groupings. Research indicates that children achieved puberty on the average 1.3 years earlier in 1965 than in 1915, when junior high school grouping was determined. 3) Changing social expectations of American school children also have caused a need for different age groupings. Speedier transportation, more efficient communication, and greater affluence among the middle class require earlier recognition of broader horizons. 4) A major emphasis of the middle school should be the encouragement of social activities most appropriate for youngsters passing through early adolescence. 5) The primary intellectual purposes of the middle school should be the teaching of basic learning skills, with an emphasis on opportunities for exploring areas of individual pupil interest. 6) In order to realize the transitional function of the middle school most truly, responsibility for the pupils' learning should move progressively away from dependence upon the teacher and toward independence of the individual pupil.

2032.   Curtis, T. E. and Bidwell, W. W. "Rationale for instruction in the middle school." Educational Leadership, 27(1970):578-579.

The distinctive purposes of middle school education derive from the personal developmental needs of early adolescents. Many rationales for the middle school place considerable stress on purposes unique to the middle school while accepting some purposes of both elementary and secondary schools. Authors discuss instructional imperatives and suggest the primary emphasis in the middle school should be on personalizing the program for individual pupils.

2033.   Cutler, M. H. "It took time and tenacity to make Thurston outstanding." American School Board Journal, 156(1968):16-20.

Marie Thurston Intermediate School in Laguna Beach,
California, is ahead of its time, academically and
architecturally. It blends grace and good looks with
a curriculum unhindered by the academic status
quo--an example of architectual talent supported by a
board, administration, faculty, and community that
believe beauty belongs where students study. Hub of
the complex is the octagonal learning center. Here
students use audiovisual materials and carrels,
browse through the stacks, or confer with teachers.
All activities occur under one roof but in semi-
separate locations. Adjoining the library is a
courtyard where youngsters also study, meet with
teachers informally, or hold discussions. Thurston's
nongraded program demands flexibility from students,
faculty, and facilities. The task of determining the
day's program rests with students and teachers. This
necessitates rearranging class sizes and locations
rapidly. Major subject areas are taught by teams,
putting even greater demand on the facilities. Each
academic building includes special areas where
teachers may study, counsel students, and prepare for
classes or where teaching teams meet to discuss plans
and problems.

2034. DeVita, J. C., Pumerantz, P., and Wilklow, L. B.
The Effective Middle School. West Nyack, N. Y.:
Parker Publishing Co., 1970.

This book presents practical and successful strategies to help teachers, administrators, and boards of
education develop their own middle school programs
and organizations or make changes in the ones they
have. It also offers many stimulating discussions
and illustrations to help middle school teachers deal
more effectively with their students despite conventional settings and/or rather limited resources.
Chapters are: 1) How Middle School Meets the Needs
of Today's Youth (historical perspective, failure of
the junior high school). 2) The Middle School--A New
Approach to Educating Pre-and Early Adolescents
(status, rationale, other aspects of the middle
school, the challenge to old approaches). 3) Understanding the Middle School Pupil (developmental characteristics, gathering information about student
needs and interests in the lower socioeconomic
school, results, perceptions of middle school
pupils). 4) Developing the Middle School Curriculum
(touchstones in curriculur design, developing the
curriculum, curriculum content). 5) Effective
Guidance in the Middle School (orientation program,
beginning the new school year). 6) Schedules and
Staffing for the Middle School (types of schedules,
special scheduling practices, staffing patterns,
administrative support). 7) Securing Teachers for
the Middle School (the most effective teachers,

administration of the staff, in-service training).
8) Supportive Programs for Middle School Students
(orientation for entering pupils, extended curricular
activities, social and interest activities, orientation for the high school).   9) Effective Middle
School Classroom Instruction (teaching techniques,
team teaching, individualized instruction, planning
for instruction).   10) Designing the New Middle
School (imperatives of planning, the environment, the
learning center). Appendices include a sample middle
school lesson plan and unit plan. A selected bibliography is included.

2035.   Dettre, J. R. "The middle school: a separate and
equal entity." Clearinghouse, 48(1973):19-23.

The middle school frequently finds itself in the same
predicament as the middle child--bullied by the older
and coerced by the younger.   What it needs is a
distinct identity and parity with the elementary and
secondary school levels.   Until the middle level
achieves this parity legally and within the profession, all the curricular and instructional ideas
regarding youngsters in the middle years will go for
naught.   Until rhetoric is replaced with certification requirements for teachers for the middle years,
curriculum standards, fiscal support as reflected in
foundation programs, a separate and equal treatment
within the school system, and the creation of a
national force championing the cause of the middle
level in and for itself, education for youth in the
middle years will remain subordinate in the public
school system.   Middle school advocates need to
understand that legal and professional parity brings
clout, and clout produces results.

2036.   DiVirgilio, J. "The administrative role in developing a middle school." Clearinghouse, 43(1968):
103-105.

Released from Carnegie Unit hour requirements and
prompted by some startling developments in schools
all over the United States, the new middle school
movement has experimented with a flexibility that can
meet the everchanging needs of transescents.   This
article by the Supervisor of Middle Schools for
Howard County in Clarksville, Maryland, reports on
the successful experience of the five middle schools
under his jurisdiction.   "The exciting part is the
freedom to attempt new ideas free from the controls
which operated in the junior high."   One problem
encountered by middle schools is the extreme diversity of the student body.   Another problem is developing a curriculum which incorporates the immediate
concerns of children who are in the sensitive transescent period of development and who are in the

active process of reacting, counterreacting, or
rebelling against growing up in today's world.
Finally, uncertainty about what type of social life
is desirable for middle school students is a problem
in middle schools, where educators are trying to
develop a unique institution that is neither secondary nor elementary in nature.   Flexible scheduling,
program learning, independent study, variable grouping, dio-access systems, educational television, and
new electronic discoveries, give the middle school an
advantage that other innovative schools and programs
in previous years did not have.   What is needed today
is a middle school administrator who is knowledgeable
about the latest developments in education, one who
is creative and has an intense feeling of purpose for
a cause.

2037.   Education, U.S.A. magazine.   "Middle school takes
shape as research poses questions."   Education,
U.S.A., February 22, 1971:133.

The middle school seems to have arrived as a permanent fixture on the educational scene with more
than two thousand now in existence across the United
States.   But the new movement is still a little
unsure of where it is going and how to get there.
The number of middle schools has been growing faster
than carefully developed theory and research.   But
William Alexander sees hope and improvement in middle
schools since he surveyed them in 1967-68 and found
that most were just warmed-over junior high schools.
Now most middle school educators are insisting that
this innovation should be not just a grade reorganization (usually grades 5-8 or 6-8) but a carefully
planned program to serve the needs of those between
childhood and adolescence. Several common characteristics are now appearing in middle schools: individualized instruction, interdisciplinary team
teaching which involves real cooperative planning,
flexible scheduling, student-planned activities, and
a home base and teacher for every student to provide
continuing observation and guidance.   Middle schools
are also giving balanced attention to three major
purposes of schooling--not only the use of organized
knowledge, usually the dominant goal in secondary
schools, but also skills of continued learning and
personal development.   If middle school educators are
still confused, it is because they lack professional
identity and support.   Accreditation standards are
forcing the middle school to be both elementary and
secondary, an outcome which either refutes the basic
concept of the middle school or makes the principal
lie about what he would really like to boast about.
Certification standards and teacher education programs are also a problem. Middle school principals
have to take elementary and high school trained

people and convert them to the middle school.   In
attempting to develop teacher education for the
middle school years, Alexander says, "We run squarely
into the vested interests of elementary and secondary
education departments."   As for administrative control, school districts are having trouble deciding
who should be responsible for middle school--the
director of elementary education or the director of
secondary education or both or neither?   A united
approach is needed to solve these problems.

2038.   Educational Equipment and Materials.   "Model
Proposal for a Middle School Program: Across the
Editor's Desk."   Educational Equipment and Materials,
a Communication Services Publication, no. 3, 1970.

The Newport-Mesa Unified School District south of Los
Angeles has put considerable time and effort into
studying a proposed middle school program.   A
preliminary report prepared by Dr. William
Cunningham, Superintendent, and others contained a
concise and thorough statement of the rationale for
the middle school concept and the steps to be taken
in building a middle school system from scratch.   The
traditional two-year junior high school does not
typically provide the needed transition between the
security of pupil-oriented elementary programs and
the demands of departmentalized subject-oriented high
school program.   On the contrary, the junior high
school is closely modeled on the high school, emphasizing sophistication, uniformity, and college or
vocational performance goals.   A redesigned three-
year middle school would allow better program continuity at the middle level.   Perhaps more than at
any other age group, middle level youngsters need
exploratory programs to discover interest and
abilities before plunging into the specialized,
factual high school curriculum.   The middle school
concept emphasizes this need for personalization
while introducing students to many of the specialized
subjects they will be expected to choose from upon
entering high school.   The five main points of the
proposal are: 1) The transitional phase between
elementary and high school programs must be expanded.
2) Middle schools should deemphasize memorizing facts
in favor of using them.   3) The homeroom teacher's
job should include personal guidance, team teaching,
and concentrated and extended study groupings.   4)
Some courses should be packaged so students can
complete them at their own rate.   5) The middle
school should be planned spatially as a group of
subschools.

2039.   Educational Facilities Laboratories.   "Two Middle
Schools, Saginaw Township, Michigan."   New York,
1960.

Twin middle schools (one compact, one campus plan) were conceived and planned by a superintendent who left the district before the buildings were completed. The schools opened with a staff generally committed to the self-contained classroom and conventional instruction, but since then the staff has made great strides in developing new ways of teaching and grouping children.

2040.   Educational Facilities Laboratories. "Middle School: A Report of Two Conferences in Mt. Kisco on the Definition of Its Purpose, Its Spirit, and Its Shape." New York, 1962.

Presents an overview of the middle school with a summary from leading middle grade educators and theorists.

2041.   Educational Leadership magazine. "The middle school: a selected bibliography of introduction." Educational Leadership, 23(1965):217-223.

Some advantages of the middle school: 1) It provides an identity for the pupil. 2) It introduces specialization and team teaching in grades 5 and 6. 3) It allows reorganization of teacher education in order to provide teachers competent for the middle school. 4) Developmentally, children in grades 6 through 8 are probably more alike than children in grades 7 through 9. 5) It provides for planned, gradual change from the self-contained classroom to complete departmentalization. 6) It helps to extend the guidance services into the elementary school. Article reviews two books, The American Middle School: An Organizational Analysis by Samuel Popper and Perspectives on the Middle School by M. Ann Grooms. It also presents a selected bibliography on middle schools.

2042.   Educational Leadership Institute. "Middle School Curriculum: Let's Talk Reality." Paper presented to the Educational Leadership Institute, Box 354, Hartford, Conn. 06101. (No year given.)

Paper discusses the middle school curriculum, the present status of middle schools, the 1969 middle school project of the Richmond Public Schools, New York's Middle Island Central School District no. 12, and the middle schools in Upper Saint Clair, Pennsylvania, and Howard County, Maryland. It asks, "Can the middle school educator move beyond the argument of which grade should be in the middle-junior high school? Can emerging adolescent educators develop curricular designs which meet the unique needs of middle school youngsters? Can middle school educators create an effective alliance with high school

education, state departments of education, and professional associations? Will the middle school
accept in practice the theory of uniqueness?"
Article discusses the future of the middle school.

2043.   Educational Leadership Institute. Selected Middle
School Bibliography, Box 354, Hartford, Conn. 06101.

Selective bibliography includes books, pamphlets,
journal articles, and general bibliographic materials
on middle schools.

2044.   Egnatuck, T., et al. "The Middle School: A Position Paper." East Lansing: Michigan Association of
Middle School Educators, 1975.

Many educators feel the traditional junior high
school is failing to answer the needs of transescents. A middle school can provide the best
opportunities in educational programs for children
who are undergoing rapid physical, mental, emotional,
and social growth. Authors outline the elements of
an effective middle school program, including grade
organization, school administration and staffing,
curriculum, and team teaching.

2045.   Eichhorn, D. H.   The Middle School.   New York:
Center for Applied Research in Education, 1966.

Research shows that physical maturation is occurring
at an earlier age in our culture, which means that
transescents with similar physical characteristics
are now being educated in two separate organizational
levels established in earlier years --the sixth
grade, considered elementary, and the seventh and
eighth grade, associated with the junior high school.
Although the current 6-3-3 grade organization effectively met the needs of youngsters in the earlier
decades of this century, it no longer relates realistically to physical characteristics of transescents.
Research also consistently shows a significant correlation between physical maturation and social interest and peer involvement patterns, so transescents
also develop earlier social peer interaction patterns. Author's findings suggest that present grade
groupings are incompatible with the diverse characteristics of transescence. Youngsters develop
toward maturity irrespective of grade level or age--
there is no stereotype for levels of human
development.

2046.   Eichhorn, D. H. "New Knowledge of 10-to-13-Year-
Olds." Paper presented at the Conference of the
Middle School Idea, College of Education, University
of Toledo, Toledo, Ohio, November 11, 1967.

The middle school concept, based on early adolescents' dramatic growth and their interaction with society, may emerge into a successful type of school organization, but only if educators develop programs designed specifically for the characteristics of 10-to-13-year-olds.

2047.   Eichhorn, D. H.   "Middle school organization: a new dimension."   Theory Into Practice,   June 1968: 111-113.

Transescence begins prior to the onset of puberty and extends through early adolescence. Since puberty does not occur at precisely the same age in humans, the term transescent refers to a state that begins with the many physical, social, emotional, and intellectual changes that appear prior to puberty and extends to the time when the body gains a practical degree of stabilization over these complex stages.   Transescence, with its complex set of social and emotional characteristics, must be treated in a different manner than the stages of childhood or adolescence, and changes in school program are clearly indicated.   Traditional programs cannot cope with the dynamic personal needs of middle school youngsters.   Educators need to analyze the purposes of long established courses in light of the needs of trancescents.   Several components of a revitalized curriculum are suggested by the nature of transescence.   First, there needs to be an analytical facet, including the traditional areas of mathematics, science, social studies, and language characterized by logical, sequential, and cognitive learning.   Second, evidence suggests the need for an innovative component involving personal dynamics, and characterized by the concept "know thyself," because transescents have a substantial need to understand their growth changes.   A third curriculum component, closely related to personal dynamics but differing in emphasis, is self-expression.   Revised educational programs for the middle school suggest the need for different patterns of grouping students for instruction.   The guidance function in the middle school also needs consideration.

2048.   Eichhorn, D. H.   "Planning Programs for Transescents."   Paper presented at the University of New York at Buffalo, October, 1968.

Transescents (the prefix "trans" meaning "to go across" and the suffix "escent" meaning "to become something") are young people in transition from childhood to adolescence.   Middle schools provide educational processes uniquely suited to students of this age group.   Transescents are in transition physically, mentally, and socially, each developing to his own timetable. Because transescents mature at different rates, they have different interests and attitudes. Irregular social and emotional patterns are common. This paper presents programs for transescents and emphasizes the importance of curriculum, grouping techniques, and guidance.

2049.   Eichhorn, D. H. "Middle school in the making." Educational Leadership, 31,3(1973):195-197.

The middle school has 1) prompted a reconsideration of the purpose of programs for the transescent learner, 2) provided our society with a means to adjust to the pluralistic needs of its citizenry, 3) enabled teachers to emphasize learners rather than structure, 4) pioneered organization and learning strategies, 5) caused state departments of education, universities, and the public to reassess basic positions, 6) reaffirmed that a unique level of education exists between the elementary and high school levels, 7) provided a catalyst for change and articulation of the total K-12 program, 8) established a convenient vehicle for the employment of promising instructional concepts such as open education, continuous learner progress, and nongrading, 9) created opportunities for educational alternatives within the public school system, and 10) provided potential for future growth and development. If the middle school movement is to achieve its great potential, all groups within the educational establishment must support it. It is time for the leadership of the great associations, such as the National Association of Secondary School Principals, the Association for Supervision and Curriculum Development, the National Association of Elementary School Principals, and all agencies with concern for middle level education to create an interdisciplinary team. Also, teacher education institutions must develop a preparation component that emphasizes emerging adolescent education. These institutions must join in a coalition with community, school personnel, and students to produce a trained group of professionals dedicated to improving middle unit education. This cooperation is essential if education is to continue to develop sensibly as a continuum of learning experiences rather than a fragmented division between elementary and secondary schools.

2050.   Eve, A. W. "The Emerging Middle School." Address presented at the Workshop on the Middle School, Miami University, Oxford, Ohio, June 19, 1967.

Discusses the history of junior high schools, the forces influencing nationally emerging middle schools, and the educational roots of the Washington Township Middle Schools in Centerville, Ohio.

Considers current knowledge about learners at this
age, the changing role of teachers, curriculum
reform, new methods of organization and instruction,
and school construction changes.

2051.   Finley, R.   "An Illinois middle school."   In The
Middle School: A Symposium, p. 33.   London: School
Master Publishing Co., 1967.

A middle school principal says the middle school is
based on a knowledge of child development, especially
a knowledge of the preadolescent.   It is a school
devoted to the education of the 10-to-14-year-old
child.

2052.   Flinker, E. and Pianko, N.   "The emerging middle
school."   Clearinghouse, 46,2(1971):67-72.

If it is to provide the educational advantages
claimed for it, the middle school must have a valid
philosophy, unique courses of study, capable
teachers, and an appropriate plant in which all of
these ingredients can be properly mixed.   Ideally,
the middle school with an optimum number of twelve
hundred students would have between seventy and
eighty professional workers recruited, interviewed,
selected, and trained by the principal and the
supervisory staff.   The curriculum of the emerging
middle school would help the child prepare to meet
the demands of his future world and would recognize
the needs of each child through flexible grouping,
independent study, occasional large group instruction
by teachers, visiting lecturers and performers,
multitrack classes, individual acceleration, and
remedial courses.   Team teaching enables teachers to
pay more attention to problems of children through
large and small group instruction and through
frequent planning conferences.   Teachers work in
cooperating units to integrate subjects.   Each child
passes through a four-year transition from a self-
contained classroom to complete departmentalization.
Each subject is supervised by a chairman who is a
specialist in the field, and teams of teachers are
guided by grade leaders.   A rich extracurricular
program of literacy, athletic, and social activities
as well as talent class instruction requires an
extended day.   For total effectiveness in this middle
school, an appropriate physical plant must be
designed.   The first item of importance is the oval
shape of the school building.   This shape has been
chosen as one way of reinforcing the idea that education is a constantly moving, never-ending process.

2053.   Florida State Department of Education.   "The Exceptional Child in the Open Middle School." Tallahassee, Fla., 1971.

Book discusses why an open-spaced school is particularly suitable for the middle years. It is flexible for grouping, scheduling, and instruction. It brings together youngsters who vary greatly in development but who share many interests and abilities. It provides the best of two worlds--being part of a large group and being treated as an individual. Teachers can work cooperatively to plan a program suited to the youngster rather than one which is predetermined by textbook, curriculum guides, or accreditation bodies. Working in groups of varying sizes or on their own, youngsters can become more self-directed, taking increasing responsibility for their own learning now and in the years to come. The book includes the following chapters: 1) Rationale. 2) Characteristics of Pre- and Early Adolescents. 3) Characteristics of the Middle School Program and Staffing Pattern. 4) Open Space and the Exceptional Child (space characteristics of the open middle school, the mini-matrix, the need for follow-up activity, observation check sheet, conclusions about organization, and space needs for exceptional children). 5) The Exceptional Child in the Open Middle School. 6) Summary and Appendix with speeches by middle school experts.

2054.   Florida State Department of Education, Special State Committee on the Middle School. "The Development of Middle Schools in Florida." Tallahassee, Fla. (No year given.)

Middle schools have been used to eliminate de facto segregation, alleviate population and building problems, be fashionable, build upon the changed elementary school, respond to dissatisfaction with the typical junior high school, facilitate educational change, respond to earlier physical, emotional, social, and intellectual maturation of children, and provide a program to meet the needs of the 10-to-14-year-old child. Manual includes an excellent list of resources and contains the following sections: 1) Defining the Middle School: Rationale. 2) Moving to the Middle School Plan. 3) Organizing for Instruction. 4) The Program of the Middle School. 5) Development of the Curriculum. 6) Staffing the Middle School. 7) Staff Development in the Middle School. 8) The Physical Plant. 9) Evaluating and Reporting of Pupil Progress. 10) Evaluation of the Middle School. 11) Relating the Middle School to Elementary and Senior High Schools.

2055.   Fox, D. J. Expansion of the More Effective School
Programs. New York: Center for Urban Education,
1967.

Describes several model junior high and middle school
programs that school systems can adapt.

2056.   Fraser, D., et al.   "Middle School Overview."
Seattle: Seattle Public Schools, Washington
Southeast Educational Center, 1969.

Discusses the planned middle school facilities of the
Washington Southeast Educational Center, where students will move at their own pace in an individualized program. The center proposes to develop a
school system in which professional educators,
involved citizens, and community agencies jointly
educate students to solve problems in their social,
psychological, and physical environments. The
program, which will study the effects of individualized instruction on students, will have a low
teacher-counselor ratio with emphasis on teacher-
counselor functions, curriculum writing and organization, student grouping, special education and
accelerated learner needs, and building planning.

2057.   Furlong, C. B.   "Priorities for the Middle
School."   Arizona State University at Tempe.
Dissertation Abstracts International, 28, 1235, 1967.

Priorities for the middle school include 1) using
ideas from different disciplines, 2) providing for
the exploration of values, the pursuit of personal
interests, and the development of independence,
leadership potential, and a sense of social
responsibility, 3) helping students develop a healthy
self concept, 4) helping them use the tools of
independent learning, 5) providing special correction
programs and facilities in language arts and math, 6)
providing a special program of student activities, 7)
offering increased choice of classes and increased
independent study, 8) making vertical organizational
patterns nongraded, 9) using team teaching to make
horizontal assignment of students, 10) having
flexible schedules that allow for varied time
patterns.

2058.   Gallina, M. N. and Miller, C. S.   "Middle
schools: an alternative for the transescent."
Adolescence, 12(1977):511-522.

An effective transition to middle school requires
recognition that it is a unique educational institution appropriate for youngsters who are at the
onset of adolescence, and it therefore has objectives
different from high school, elementary, or even

junior high school. Authors define the middle school
as a school according to the idea of Robert Finley
(see entry 2051) based on a knowledge of child
development, especially a knowledge of the preadolescent. "The developmental growth patterns of
this group demand an environment that is free from
tension...and enhancing to the sensitive emotional
and social behavior of children." (DiVirgilio,
James. "Switching from Junior High to Middle
School?" Clearinghouse, 44(December 1969):224-226.)
Article includes sections on the transitional age
youngster, staffing patterns, facility, educational
program, feasibility, and it cites many authorities
on the emergence of the middle school. Authors
discuss three considerations a school district must
take into account prior to a commitment to the middle
school: 1) "A change in organizational pattern does
not seem feasible unless it has a reasonable chance
of acceptance by the people most concerned. Specifically, it is questionable whether any change in
pattern should be attempted without some prior
involvement and general approval by an adequate
representation of the parents and faculties concerned. If involvement has been negligible, or if
the reaction is negative or even just lukewarm,
reorganization would seem practical." (In Alexander,
William M., The Emergent Middle School, Second ed.,
p. 152. New York: Holt, Rhinehart and Winston,
1969.) 2) Adequate preparation must be made for
reorganization of a middle school. This would
involve planning pre-service and in-service training.
3) Teachers must be given time to plan and develop
curriculum cooperatively.

2059.   Garvelink, R. H. "The anatomy of a good middle
school." Clearinghouse, 48(1973):2.

Discusses the Abbott Middle School of the West
Bloomfield Schools in Orchard Lake, Michigan.

2060.   Garvelink, R. H. "Creating a good middle school:
through revolution or evolution?" Clearinghouse, 49,
4(1975):185-186.

Discusses an administrator's eight steps to building
a good middle school: 1) Begin by asking, "Why do we
want middle schools?" 2) Assess your present program, but not in the familiar way. Ask each staff
member to list and then talk about things they do
right. 3) Examine the nature of effervescent youth.
Recognize the middle school student as a unique human
being. 4) Now you are ready for a commitment to the
philosophy of education. 5) Touch base with your
board of education. 6) Get rid of some of the traditional activities or methodology in your school.
That is, kill some sacred cows. 7) With all the

sacred cows dealt with, you will have lost certain teachers. 8) Build new traditions. Take a new look at all of the teaming possibilities. Look at all the innovative things that are going on in schools.

2061.   Gatewood, T. E.   "The Middle School We Need." Report from the ASCD Working Group on the Emerging Adolescent Learner. Washington, D.C.: Association for Supervision and Curriculum Development, 1975.

This position paper presents the purposes and rationale of the middle school, outlines what the middle school program should be (including curriculum, instruction, organization, and administration), and discusses leadership implications. If educators understand the causes of transescent behavior, they can deal more rationally and sanely with it. Discusses transescent physical, intellectual, and mental and personality growth and bases specific recommendations to improve teaching and learning on these characteristics. Paper considers program implications of the recommendations and various program alternatives.

2062.   George, P. S.   "The middle school in Florida: where are we now?"   Educational Leadership, 31,3 (1973):217-220.

Describes Florida's middle schools, which are testing the vitality of this new movement. Discusses the certification now offered through the Florida State Department of Education, changes in instruction, team teaching, and some things that still remain to be done. The middle school movement in Florida is dynamic and exciting. Almost everyone who is participating in the improvement of education for emerging adolescents in Florida seems caught up in an enthusiasm which has been missing from this part of schooling for a long time. If this momentum continues to grow, great progress will be made in education for the middle school years.

2063.   George, P. S.   The Middle School: A Look Ahead. Fairborn, Ohio: National Middle School Association, 1977.

In March 1976, three hundred educators at the National Middle School Leadership Seminar in Gainesville, Florida, identified the most significant issues in the field of middle school education: 1) To what degree should competition be encouraged in the middle school? 2) What are the characteristics of an effective middle school teacher? 3) Are many functioning middle schools really much different than junior high school? 4) What needs to be done regarding teacher certification for middle schools? 5) What special curriculum areas should be the focus for the future in middle schools? 6) Can the philosophy of a middle school be implemented in a researchable form? 7) Can universities be expected to fulfill their responsibilities in middle school education? 8) Are there enough educators to meet the challenge of developing and maintaining good middle schools in large numbers? Fourteen contributors recognized for their national stature as middle school educators responded to these issues in the following sections of this book: 1) The Middle School--Present and Future: A Collage (optimism, pessimism and the Future, issues and answers). 2) Renewing the Middle School Movement: Individual Perceptives (the people in the school, curriculum and instruction). 3) A Look Ahead.

2064.   Georgiady, N. P. and Romano, L. G. "Do you have a middle school?" Educational Leadership, 3(1973): 238-241.

Article suggests evaluating programs according to the characteristics of the pupils, the nature of knowledge, and the needs of the society: 1) Is continuous progress provided for?   2) Is it a multimaterial approach to use? 3) Are the class schedules flexible? 4) Are appropriate social experiences provided for? 5) Is there an appropriate program of physical experiences and intramural activities? 6) Is team teaching used?   7) Is planned gradualism provided for?   8) Are exploratory and enrichment studies provided for? 9) Are there adequate and appropriate guidance services? 10) Is there provision for independent study?   11) Is there provision for basic skill repair and extension? 12) Are there activities for creative experiences?   13) Is there full provision for evaluation?   14) Does the program emphasize community relations?   15) Are there adequate provisions for student services?   16) Is there sufficient attention to auxiliary staffing?

2065.   Georgiady, N. P., Riegle, J. D., and Romano, L. G. "What are the characteristics of the middle school?" In The Middle School: Selected Readings on an Emerging School Program, pp. 73-84. Chicago: Nelson-Hall, 1973.

Discusses characteristics of the middle school: 1) continuous progress, 2) multimaterial approach, 3) flexible schedules, 4) social experiences, 5) physical experiences and intramural activities, 6) team teaching, 7) planned gradualism, 8) exploratory and enrichment studies, 9) guidance service, 10) independent study, 11) basic skill repair and extension, 12) creative experiences, 13) security, 14) evaluation, 15) community relations, 16) student services, and 17) auxiliary staffing. Article also discusses problems with the junior high school, including its failure to recognize and provide for the early adolescent or transescent child as he is today and its serious lack of relevance to the true nature of the society in which these transescents must live. "Transescence is defined as that period in an individual's development beginning prior to the onset of puberty and continuing on through early adolescence. It is characterized by changes in physical development, social interaction, and intellectual function."

2066.   Grooms, M. A.   "Perspectives on the Middle School." Section 4 in Middle School Program Aspects. Columbus, Ohio: Charles E. Merrill Publishing Co., 1967.

The main objective of a middle school is to further student self-development in academic disciplines, study skills, problem analysis, and problem solving. Curriculum and program should be determined by students and teachers, with emphasis on individual growth and academic work in social science, science, mathematics, and language arts. The following things should be unacceptable for middle schools: self-contained classrooms, the use of professionals to teach one or two subjects, disregard for individual student interests, grades as motivators, and inter-scholastic athletics. Author presents four examples of middle school program structure and organization and describes a Midwest middle school's historical development. A reading list is included. See ERIC Abstract #ED 027 602.

2067.   Hansen, J. H. and Hearn, A. C. The Middle School Program. Chicago: Rand-McNally and Co., 1971.

Book surveys current thoughts about the subjects of the middle school program and draws parallels between the histories of the middle school and the junior high school.   Around 1900-1915, in reaction to supposed evils of the 8-4 administrative organization, a middle school which became known as a junior high school was formed without an educational philosophy for a base. In the mid-1960s, in reaction to supposed evils of the existing 6-3-3 administrative organization, a middle school which was called a middle or intermediate school was formed for the same expedient reasons--building problems, desegregation, rapid pupil expansion--used fifty years earlier. Authors contend that the generic term "middle school" needs to be accepted as "an education program designed to meet the needs of early adolescents" and that school design, curricular offerings, grade groupings, and staffing are local problems that demand local decisions. The book contains the following sections: 1) The People and the Place (overview, history, function and definition of the institution, the adolescent, the teacher). 2) The Rationale of the Program (overview, thoughts concerning curriculum, organization for instruction, learning activity packages). 3) Instructional Program (overview, English language arts, social studies, mathematics, science). 4) Instructional Program (overview, exploration courses, health and physical education, library, instructional materials center). 5) Support Programs (overview, student activities, guidance, organization and administration, evaluation).

2068.   Hines, V. A. "Perspectives on Evaluation." Middle School Portfolio, Leaflet 13. Association for Childhood Education International, 3615 Wisconsin Ave. N.W., Washington, D.C. 20016, 1968.

Discusses the importance of evaluation for middle grade youngsters and addresses the questions, What is evaluation? Why evaluate the middle school? What is evaluated? How evaluate?

2069.   Holliston Public Schools. "Holliston's Project Model Middle School." Bulletin 4. Holliston, Mass., October, 1967.

Sections are: 1) The Middle School Movement. 2) Why a Middle School in Holliston, Massachusetts? 3) Some Philosophic Consideratons. 4) The Pre- and Early Adolescent Student of the Middle School. 5) The Teacher of the Pre- and Early Adolescent. 6) General Characteristics of the Holliston Curriculum. 7) Independent Study. 8) Data Storage and Retrieval System. 9) Matching of Teacher, Pupil, and Learning Material Characteristics. 10) Unified Arts Program. 11) Extracurricular Program. 12) Intramural Athletic Program. 13) Some Organizational Characteristics of the Middle School, Including Team Teaching, House Plan, and Learning Centers. 14) General Guidelines for the Middle School Program. 15) Scheduling of Pupils' Time.

2070.   Hood, C. E. "Teaching as a career." Clearinghouse, 40(1965):228.

Discusses characteristics of the middle school: 1) The middle school is adapted to a wide range of children who are extreme individualists but have more in common with each other than with children in grades above or below. 2) It operates on the belief that the students have some mastery of the skill of learning but are not ready for the academic specialization of the senior high school. 3) It concentrates on provisions for individual differences without losing sight of the increased sophistication and knowledge of the 10-to-14-year-old over previous generations. 4) The middle school introduces fifth or sixth graders gradually to specialization. It provides many physical means to realize individual differences on one hand and to encourage group activities, large and small, on the other.

2071.   Huber, J. D. "Reincarnation of the one-room schoolhouse: the American middle school." Clearinghouse, 49(1975):103-105.

One-room schoolhouses have not disappeared; they have just been reincarnated in the form of American middle schools. Almost all the things we call innovations today were commonplace, in many cases because of necessity, in the old one-room schools. If the contemporary middle school planner emulates these traditional patterns and especially emphasizes key attitudes of openness, child-centeredness, and humanness, these middle schools will have a long and productive life expectancy.

2072.   Johnston, R. J. and Casmey, H. B. "Golden Valley confirms middle school philosophy." Minnesota Journal of Education, 47(1966):16-17.

Individual autonomy of local boards of education, enabling each school district to meet the needs of its students as it deems best, has been and is a vital cornerstone of American education. The exercise of such autonomy made possible the creation of a middle school in Golden Valley. Basically, a transitional school that bridges the upper elementary and lower secondary grades, this middle school's 4-4-4 pattern makes possible new and realistic age and grade groupings. A transitional experience between the elementary and secondary schools extends the best child growth and development concepts of the elementary classroom upward into grades 7 and 8 while incorporating into grades 5 and 6 the best aspects of departmentalized, specialized instruction. It was believed that if a reasonable balance of the best features of these approaches could be achieved, this four-year transitional period could provide middle school students with an educational experience eminently less precipitous than that which marks the usual movement from the relative security of the self-contained classroom into the Carnegie Unit.

2073.   Jones, C. K. "Dynamics of transescence in the middle school setting." Urban Review, 11,1(1979): 37-43.

Defines the middle school, discusses its growth characteristics and teaching implications, and describes the Detroit middle schools. Middle schools

should have: 1) a span of at least three grades
between 5 and 8 to allow for the gradual transition
from elementary to high school instruction practices,
2) emerging departmental structure in each higher
grade for a gradual transition from the self-
contained classroom to the departmentalized high
school, 3) flexible approaches to instruction--team
teaching,   flexible   scheduling,   individualized
instruction, independent study, tutorial programs,
and other approaches aimed at stimulating children to
learn how to learn, 4) required special courses,
taught in departmental form and frequently with an
interdisciplinary or multidisciplinary approach, 5)
guidance program as a distinct entity to fill the
special needs of this age group, 6) faculty with both
elementary and secondary certification or some
teachers with each type, 7) limited attention to
interschool sports and school activities.

2074.   Jones, D. R.   "A Descriptive Study of the Organization, Curriculum, and Personnel Structure of
Selected Middle Schools in the Southern States Association of Colleges and Secondary Schools Region."
Ed.D. Dissertation, George Washington University,
1977.

Findings from a survey of 110 randomly selected
middle schools show: 1) Half the middle schools
surveyed had a 6-7-8 grade pattern.   2) This 6-7-8
pattern dominated every enrollment classification.
3) Less than 30 percent had self-contained classrooms, tutorial programs, closed-circuit television,
interdisciplinary teams, and programmed instruction.
4) There was no predominant preference between
heterogeneous and homogeneous grouping.   5) Total
departmentalization was extensive in grades 7 and 8.
6) Individual instruction and coeducational programs
were represented in over 50 percent of the schools.
7) The building presently occupied was usually not
originally intended for use as a middle school.   8)
Elementary certificates were more common among fifth
and sixth grade teachers, while secondary school
certificates predominated among seventh and eighth
grade teachers.   9) A majority of the schools had at
least one media specialist and one guidance
counselor.

2075.   Kunzweiler, C. E.   "Learning for behaviorally dis-
oriented children in regular classrooms in middle
schools."   Journal of Instructional Psychology, 1,3
(1974):11-15.

Discusses mainstreaming children with behavioral
problems in open-concept middle schools that have
built-in flexibility in the normal classroom environment.   Teachers of special education help with the

regular classes by incorporating methods and materials previously found in self-contained special classes. Article covers rationale, procedure, implementation, role of the exceptional education teacher, and evaluation. Article also includes an open-area construction model which contains spaces for a lounge, shop or projects, social studies (project and process), science (project and process), communication skills resources and semiquiet activity, a special education teacher, minimal L.B.D. resources and counseling, and math resource and quiet activities.

2076.   Leeper, R. R. (Ed.) <u>Middle School in the Making:</u> <u>Readings from Educational Leadership.</u>   Washington, D.C.:   Association for Supervision and Curriculum Development, 1974.

The thirty-two articles in this volume suggest many ideas to consider in planning a middle school. The traditional junior high school organization and program have for some years caused much concern. This level of schooling has seemed to some to be too much influenced by the high school curriculum. Observations suggest that sixth graders are more compatible with seventh and eighth graders than with other elementary students and that ninth graders are more compatible with high school students. Five sections consider the rationale for the middle school, its definition, its pupils and teachers, its curriculum, and some examples of middle schools in action. The articles present guidelines for establishing goals and for planning and staffing middle schools.

2077.   Lounsbury, J. H. and Vars, G. F.   <u>A Curriculum</u> <u>for the Middle School Years</u>. New York: Harper and Row, 1978.

This new (1978) text on junior high and middle school years contains the following sections: 1) The Teacher in the Middle School (the changing nature of teaching, the special importance of middle school teaching, tools for self improvement).   2) Schools for the Transitional Years (the junior high school, the middle school, the organizational issue, some points of view and perspectives).   3) Curriculum Accommodations (the transescent learner and how he learns, the social and cultural milieu, organized knowledge, implications for the curriculum, purposes of education).   4) Curriculum Organization (a recommended curriculum organization and alternative curriculum organizations.   5) The Core Component (rationale of core, two types of core, varied role of the core teacher, strengths and limitations, some admonitions).   6) The continuous Progress Component (single, multiple, variable, and multiunit sequence approaches and recommendations). 7) The Variable Component: Exploration and Activities (health and physical education, required exploratory courses, electives, interest-centered enrichment courses, independent study, student activities, guidelines for a middle school activity program, scheduling and staffing, evaluation). 8) Reporting Student Progress (evaluation and reporting). 9) Curriculum Leadership (basic principles of curriculum change, group roles and curriculum improvement, in-service education and curriculum improvement, implementing the curriculum proposed in this book). 10) Resources for Middle School Educators. Authors are neither doctrinaire defenders of the traditional junior high school nor eager champions of the new middle school. Both patterns are quite defensible yet inherently vulnerable. Authors are strong believers in intermediate or early adolescent education. Generally they question the wisdom of placing fifth grade in the intermediate institution, as recommended by some middle school advocates, but under certain circumstances this is a very acceptable practice. Similarly, they find a two-year school acceptable but a three-year school more desirable. They believe that the focal point of any intermediate institution, no matter what its label or grade composition, is diversity. Arguments over the purported advantage of one organizational arrangement over another are not intellectually resolvable and often draw attention away from important matters such as curriculum or staffing.

2078.   Lynch, J. J.   "A Primer on a Current Trend: The Middle School."   ERIC Doc. ED 168 183, 1979.

Discusses the philosophy and history of the middle school from its beginnings in 1893 and compares middle schools and junior high schools. Also discusses psychological theories underlying the middle school, including the theory of the period of transescence between childhood and adolescence. Presents practical considerations involved in instituting a middle school, including decisions about objectives, grade span, public relations, staff selection, curriculum, facilities, and long-range planning. Special teacher training is stressed. Offers guiding principles for a middle school regarding grading, student involvement in decision making, learning objectives, encouragement of creativity and diversity, and interdisciplinary experiences. See ERIC Abstract #ED 168 183.

2079.   Madon, C. A.   "Middle school: philosophy and purpose."   Clearinghouse, 40(1966):329-330.

The middle school is a new approach to providing for the needs of the early adolescent. It is not patterned after the high school but builds its curriculum around the child, recognizing that he is going through a period of transition accompanied by marked physical, intellectual, social, and emotional changes. The middle school has been receiving considerable attention in recent years, spurred by the declared intention of the mammouth New York City School System to disband all of its 138 junior high schools and to begin operating a 5-3-4 plan in 1973. At least forty-five of the fifty states now have one or more middle schools in operation. However, the majority of these schools are concentrated in about eighteen states. Leaders in the area are: East--New York and Massachusetts; North--Ohio; West--Washington; and South--Kansas. In Texas, ninety-two of 201 schools responding to educational research surveys are operating a 5-3-4 or 4-4-4 plan.

2080.   McCarthy, R. J.   "Why an ungraded middle school." Chapter 1 in Successful School Administration Series. Englewood Cliffs, N.J.:   Prentice-Hall, 1967.

Discusses an ungraded, team teaching system dependent on curriculum reform and flexible scheduling in the Liverpool Middle School, Liverpool, New York. Author presents a rationale for ungraded middle schools. Today's youth are maturing earlier, are more sophisticated, and are capable of greater accomplishment. A traditional grade 7-9 arrangement does not meet the needs of ninth grade students, while elementary schools cannot meet the needs of sixth grade students. The article supports the idea that grouping students by grades 6, 7, and 8 in the middle school helps solve the problem of the earlier maturing transescent. Grouping students of several ages to study each subject and recognizing students' unique qualities and individual capabilities are features of a true middle school.

2081.   McCarthy, R. J.   "A nongraded middle school." National Elementary School Principal, 47,3(1968): 15-21.

Interdisciplinary teams, their flexibility, and the responsibility given to staff to develop and evaluate individualized student programs exist for one major purpose in the Liverpool Middle School: to seek continually for better methods to help each youngster progress according to his own ability, interests, talent, and drive.

2082.   McDonald, W. and Tierno, M. J. "From junior high to middle school: the story of one conversion." Middle School Journal, 10,1(1979):20-22.

A new middle school usually replaces an established
junior high school. Such a transformation should
involve much more than exchanging a ninth grade for a
sixth grade. This case study of the Falk School,
laboratory school for the University of Pittsburgh,
suggests guidelines for the change: 1) Faculty and
staff should be involved in the planning. 2) Preliminary planning should emanate from the developmental needs of the students. 3) Opportunity for
parent input should occur prior to finalization of
plans.   4) Adaptive educational organization often
requires curricular additions. 5) The transescent
deserves special attention. 6) Faculty teams must
agree on structure and process. A faculty needs time
to meet and assess the design of the student schedule, student involvement in decision making, and
student/parent/teacher planning and reporting. Perhaps the most significant consideration which has
evolved through this complex process is the fact that
middle school program development, even if initiated
for the wrong reasons, can succeed if administration,
faculty, students, and parents work together to construct a meaningful program, allow time for piloting,
incorporate evaluation, and attend to the real needs
of the students involved.

2083.   McGee, J. C. and   Blackburn, J. E.   "Administration of the middle school program."   Theory Into
Practice, 18,1(1979):39-44.

Discusses the administrative advantages of a middle
school compared to a traditional junior high school
because of a unified social and academic atmosphere.
Sections of this article are: Accreditation. State
Department Handbooks. Nonsexist Staff.   The Prin-
cipal as Instructional Leader. Capital Expenditure
Savings.   Certification Flexibility.   Sharing of
Equipment/Materials. Expanded Opportunities in the
Subschool.   Improved Student Behavior.   Related/
Unified Arts Program. Exploratory Program.   Pro-
fessional Identification and Support.   Master
Schedule. Increased Noise Level. Potential Teacher
Personality Conflicts. Cost of Operation. Dimin-
ished Textbook Orientation. Differences Between Team
Programs. Conflicts with Band and Athletics. Dele-
gation of Responsibility. The Exploratory Program as
Another Preparation. Increased Paperwork and Time
Requirements. The Burden of the Traditional Build-
ing.   Support Areas Too Small or Poorly Placed.
Community Involvement. Feeder/Receiver Schools.
Lack of Adequate Storage Space. Liability. Lack of
Staff. School Level In-service.

2084.   McHugh, E. A.   "The middle school that evolved."
Impact on Instructional Improvement, Winter 1967-68:
27-30.

The principal of a junior high school of Central
School District East Patchogue, Long Island, discusses the junior high and middle school patterns in
his district under these headings: 1) Overall Plan
for a Middle School.   2) Basic Program of General
Studies.   3) A Program for Student Exploration.   4)
Independent Study and Emphasis on Learning Skills.
5) Teacher Aides.   6) Scheduling.   7) Evaluation.
The most important thing is not what the school is
called or what organization it uses but what goes on
between teachers and students. Good schools are made
by good teachers.   The middle school offers a new
opportunity for those interested in the education of
youngsters of this age.   Author hopes that some day
administrative organization will be determined on
educational grounds rather than for such reasons as
building efficiency, economy, or racial balance.

2085.   Mellinger, M. and   Rackauskas, J. A.   Quest for
Identity: National Survey of the Middle School,
1969-70. Chicago: Chicago State College, 1970.

Survey of 1,988 middle schools, 275 elementary
schools, and 91 high school reports on the characteristics of the middle school.   Tables show: 1)
location by region, grades included, and enrollment
in various types of schools, 2) ratios of pupils to
counselors, teachers, and administrators by grade and
enrollment, 3) types of class schedules and study
provisions, kinds of programs and activities, and
discipline responsibility by grade organization.
Less than half the respondents believed their schools
were fully putting into practice a true middle school
philosophy. A bibliography is included.

2086.   Midjaas, C. L.   "Avoiding the Pitfalls of Middle
School Planning."   Address to the National School
Board Association Convention, San Francisco, April
13, 1970.

The middle school has struck a responsive cord for
many educators and concerned laymen.   First, it
reflects the growing realization that our priorities
and educational expenditures have been woefully mis-
placed. Second, the middle school concept makes some
valid points regarding the unique nature of transescent learners.   Third, the middle school can
reduce crowding in upper elementary schools, junior
high schools, and senior high schools. Fourth, the
middle school can be a useful tool in meeting the
challenge of racial and social integration.   Fifth,
the middle school idea serves other political ends by
allowing some districts to achieve instant innovation
without much planning or educational commitment.
Author discusses the many pitfalls in planning and
creating a middle school in a new district.

2087.   Mindess, D.   "What to do with your old high
        school."   American School Board Journal, 156(1968):
        21-22.

        Discusses the main advantages of the Ashland middle
        school in its first two years.   School officials
        foresaw some of them--others were a surprise: 1)
        Purchasing duplication reduced.   Under a specialized
        curriculum, materials can be kept in specific areas
        and fewer identical materials are needed.   Maps, for
        example, are housed in the social studies complex
        instead of being spread through several fifth and
        sixth grade classrooms.   The approach also allows
        purchase of a greater variety of materials.   2)
        Discipline problems diminished.   The opposite was
        anticipated: namely, that children, especially fifth
        and sixth graders, would misuse their freedom under
        the flexible scheduling arrangement. One explanation
        for the reverse occurring is that pupils use plenty
        of energy changing from one classroom to another and
        during physical education classes.   Pupils also seem
        more interested in their work, and teachers report
        fewer personality clashes--probably because they
        specialize and teach their favorite subjects.   3)
        Extracurricular activities were coordinated.   Activ-
        ities used to be fragmented when children were
        divided up by school.   Now the extracurricular pro-
        gram has cohesion, with pupils participating as a
        larger, unified group in student council, band, and
        athletics.   4) Lower grades benefited.   After grades
        5 and 6 were consolidated, grades 1-4 wound up with
        more space in their respective schools, a lower
        pupil-teacher ratio, and greater grouping flexi-
        bility.   5.   Teacher morale improved.   Each middle
        school teacher has one unscheduled period per day in
        which to plan, confer with people offering specific
        services, talk with parents, or work with individual
        children.   This free time and the latitude teachers
        have in pursuing their specialized areas of instruc-
        tion have generated enthusiasm and decidedly improved
        Ashland's curriculum.

2088.   Moore, J. and   Stephens, W.   "Analysis of the
        Middle School Educational Programs." Seattle, Wash.:
        Seattle   Public   Schools,   Washington   Southeast
        Educational Center, 1969.

        Discusses the continuous progress plan of the
        proposed Seattle Southeast Middle School. This plan
        is an integrated organization of professional educa-
        tors, curriculum, instructional modes and media,
        facilities, and administrative management.   Students
        are arranged in grades 5 through 8 with programs
        which focus on small groups and independent study.
        The student has an advisor and confidant in his
        teacher-counselor, who is directly responsible for

his education. The program has a twelve-month school
year, and a student may start and stop as he needs
to.   The plan is based on an enrollment of fifteen
hundred students aged 9-to-14.   There will be eight
sections, each one a home base for 188 to 190 students in a nongraded organization. Prepared curriculum materials and the freedom of the student to
develop his own materials are features of this plan.

2089.   Morrison, W.   "Good Schools for Middle Grade
Youngsters: Characteristics, Practices, and Recom-
mendations."   Series edited by Robert Malinka,
National Middle School Resource Center, National
Middle School Association, P. O. Box 968, Fairborn,
Ohio 45324, 1978.

Section 1 presents characteristics of a good middle
school.   It does not explain or defend these characteristics.   Section 2 discusses district, administration, physical environment, personal environment,
guidance, scheduling, grouping, instruction, team
teaching, interdisciplinary units, general curriculum, subject curriculum (art, foreign language,
health, home ec, industrial arts, math, music,
physical education, science, and reading), independent study, career education, outdoor education,
student involvement, library, clubs, activities,
mini-courses, reporting to parents, articulation,
in-service education, staffing, and state and federal
funding.   Section 3 discusses recommendations for:
State Department of Education, local school district,
building level, organization, citizenship, instruction, independent study, reporting to parents, administration and supervision, teachers, curriculum,
guidance, library. Section 4 is a conclusion.
Section 5 is an appendix listing the schools visited
by the writer for this report.

2090.   Moss, T.   Middle School. New York: Houghton-
Mifflin Co., 1969.

Book contains the following chapters: 1) Evolution
of the Middle School (the junior high school movement, the middle school, phase 2 of the reorganization movement, summary).   2) The Middle School
Student and His Curriculum (the literature on
preadolescence, characteristics of middle school
students, middle school curriculum overview).   3)
Middle School Curriculum: Skills (the individual
approach, reading, listening, handwriting, spelling,
language structure, computation, typing, library).
4) Curriculum Area II (English, social studies,
mathematics, science, and foreign languages).   5)
Curriculum Area III (Art, music, drama, industrial
arts).   6) Curriculum Area IV (health, recreation,

physical fitness). 7) Organization and Administration in the Middle School (grouping, scheduling the program, area coordinators, skill area resource teachers, paraprofessionals, middle school administration). 8) Guidance in the Middle School (guidance and the core curriculum, role of the guidance teacher, noncore teachers and guidance, additional guidance opportunities for all teachers). 9) Teachers for the Middle School (pre-service preparation and in-service education for middle school teachers). 10) Buildings and Facilities for the Middle School (new, existing, and old buildings). Book concludes with sixteen recommendations.

2091.   Murphy, J.   Middle Schools: Profiles of Significant Schools.   New York: Educational Facilities Laboratories, 1966.

Contains articles on exemplary middle schools across the United States, including ones in Amory, Mississippi, Barrington, Illinois, Mount Kisco, New York, in Plainview, Long Island, Sarasota, Florida, Pleasant Hills, Pennsylvania, Little Rock, Arkansas, Natick, Massachusetts, Los Altos, California, Rowland Heights, California, and Tiburon, California. These schools share a sense of freshness, innovation, and adaptibility, a sense of coming a bit closer than past efforts to matching institutions to the needs and potential of children from 10 to 14. All are housed in new buildings designed to serve new purposes. Within this broad consensus, the schools show all kinds of variation, some are wholly committed to innovation, from team teaching to completely nongraded organization, but others follow fairly conventional classroom patterns. Diversity is the keynote. Least important is the precise scheme of grades. The schools themselves support the strict believers in the 4-4-4 system no more than they do the junior high traditionalists. Research may never catch up with the complex nature of the student for whom the middle school is designed. Among many moot questions are these: Are fifth graders better off in an elementary school or with their elders? Are ninth graders better grouped with high school students or below? What are the best ages to group together between elementary and high school? A host of unresolved questions underscores not only the necessity but the virtue of keeping prescriptions for the middle school fluid and eclectic and hedging middle school design against the unknown and perhaps the unknowable. Most middle schools are born for reasons primarily economic, social or political. While it is possible to devise a detailed and convincing rationale for the middle school on purely educational grounds, any such formula lays itself open to the charge of being ex post facto and, more to the point, inflexible and unrealistic. The middle school can proceed best without generating a new orthodoxy.

2092.   Nation's Schools magazine. "School of the month: Shelburne Middle School." Nation's Schools, 85 (1970):96-97.

Presents discussion, blueprint, and construction statistics for a model school with innovative acoustics and the freedom to make an open plan work. The grade 5-8 school allows its students to roam about the four-winged building almost at will. The approach stems from a philosophy that the way to help children to be responsible is to give them responsibility and keep regimentation to a minimum.

2093.   Nation's Schools magazine. "Middle school dilemma: still searching for identity." Nation's Schools, 86, 6(1970):62-63.

A new study by Dr. Morris Mellinger and John A. Rackauskas of Chicago State College reveals that most middle schools cover students in grades 4-8 and have a grade span of two to five grades, including either grades 6-7 or 7-8.   It points to widespread confusion on the part of school administrators about which grades to include in a middle school classification.   While the number of such schools is increasing rapidly, there is still a significant gap between the ideal middle school program as outlined by theorists in the movement and actual programs now underway. Specifically, the survey sought information regarding the number of middle schools now operating in the country, their state and regional distribution, enrollment, staff-pupil ratios, scheduling patterns, and exploratory courses.   The research also attempted to determine whether institutions calling themselves middle schools actually embraced the middle school philosophy or had simply adopted the name.   Questionnaires were mailed to all schools with a 5-8 grade span, to all self-styled middle schools regardless of grade, and to schools with a variety of names, such as senior elementary school or intermediate school, that suggested nonconventional organization.   Questionnaires were also sent to a stratified random sampling of elementary and junior high schools.   The total number of middle schools identified by the study is 1696.   Leading the nation in density are the midwestern states--Illinois, Indiana, Michigan, Ohio, and Wisconsin--containing 433 middle schools or 25.5 percent of United States middle schools.   The Pacific states occupy second place, and California accounts for more than 80 percent of all the region's middle schools.   In the Midwest, Illinois, Michigan, and Ohio each have more than a hundred middle schools. The Middle Atlantic states occupy third place. Two thirds of all middle schools have enrollments of between two hundred and eight hundred. The average number of students per school is somewhat larger than previous studies have indicated, with 63 percent reporting enrollment combinations of grades 5-7 or 6-8. Only 11 of 350 self-styled middle schools included grade 9, and only 12 had grade 4. If current practice is any guide, all but a handful of school organizations subscribe to the notion that neither grade 4 nor grade 9 properly belong in the middle school movement.

2094.   Nation's Schools magazine.   "School of the month: Beloit-Turner Middle School."   Nation's Schools, 85 (1970):114-116.

Article describes a school that is open seven days a week, and it provides a blueprint of this model middle school. The school planners think their program is innovative in that it is based on "the society, values, and institutions as related to the subculture, characteristics, and developmental patterns of the early adolescent, rather than revolving upon the organized discipline and subjects." The program involves a commitment to interdisciplinary team teaching. Students spend about half their day in social studies-language arts pods, one quarter of their day in the creative interest areas, and one quarter in the math-science pod. In addition to a full-time teaching staff of twenty-five, the school has a guidance director, audiovisual director, instructional materials center director, part-time nurse, and part-time psychologist. Twenty-five paraprofessionals serve as teacher aides. Students of high school and junior high age were included in the central planning committee.

2095.   New Jersey State Department of Education, Task Force on Intermediate Education. "The Middle School: An Idea Whose Time Has Come." Trenton, N.J. (No year given.)

Despite the fact that the middle school has frequently come into being for noneducational reasons, many educators maintain that if a new school system could be organized from scratch with nothing but educational desiderata to guide its creators, the middle school would be the foundation of this system. Included in this portrait of the middle school are data concerning its organizational designs and schedules, the distinctive traits and needs of its pupils, and its purposes, characteristics, salient features, potentialities, instructional needs and styles, and building services.

2096.   Olson, N. G.   "A middle school: no easy way."
Educational Leadership, 3(1973):206-210.

Discusses guidelines for making middle schools
responsive to the needs of students, teachers, and
parents. For the student the main goal is to accept
each student as unique and help him develop his own
potential: 1) Work toward individualizing instruction.   2) Encourage students to become more self-
directed learners.   3) Build instructional areas for
large and small groups.   4) Arrange for adequate
library and resource facilities for self-directed
learning.   5) Consider the whole child by providing
for his emotional and physical needs. 6) Abolish the
traditional grading system.   The learner becomes
responsible for his own progress toward a goal which
he has helped to set.   For the teacher: 1) Provide
the time and organization for teachers to work and
plan together so that their talents might be used as
fully as possible.   2) Encourage teachers to become
planners and implementers rather than lecturers. For
the parent, foster closer cooperation between home
and school: 1) Bring the child into the reporting
procedure. 2) Provide a way for parents and teachers
to communicate.   3) Keep the parents informed of
goals, policies, and curriculum.   4) Encourage
participation of parents through a parent council.

2097.   Omaha Public Schools.   "Middle school patterns
being explored."   Superintendent's Bulletin of the
Omaha Public Schools, 58,15(1968):2.

In developing a rationale for the middle school, one
basic question must be answered: are the needs of
the early adolescent the same in the 1960s as they
were in 1910 when the junior high system was inaugurated?   The most recent medical research indicates
that puberty is occurring an average of 1.3 years
earlier today than in 1915.   If the movement could
develop a valid 7-9 grade rationale for the personal
and educational needs of that period, then the 6-8
grade middle school can develop a rationale for early
adolescents today.   Keeping the physiological maturation and broader experiences of the early adolescent in mind, the middle school has the following
advantages: 1) It provides the opportunity to
advance children academically and intellectually
while slowing them down socially.   2) Developmentally, children in grades 5-8 are probably more
alike than children in grades 7-9.   3) The unit has a
status of its own rather than a "junior" classification.   4) Grades 5 and 6 are introduced to some
specialization and still retain block-of-time
advantages.   5) It provides for a stronger program in
physical education, music, and art, using the services of trained teachers in these areas.   6) It

helps extend more formal guidance services into the
elementary grades. 7) Since the students involved
are undergoing the common experience of early
adolescence, they should have the special attention,
special teachers, and special programs that the
middle school permits. 8) It provides for a more
gradual change from the self-contained classroom to
complete departmentalization. 9) It reduces the
duplication of expensive equipment and facilities,
allowing funds to be spent on facilities beneficial
to more students. 10) It permits emphasis on a
continuation and enrichment of basic education in the
fundamentals. 11) Physical unification of grades
9-12 may occur, permitting better coordination of
courses for senior high school.

2098.   Overly, D. E., Kinghorn, J. R. and Preston, R. L.
Middle School: Humanizing Education for Youth.
Worthington, Ohio: Charles A. Jones Publishing Co.,
1972.

Book contains the following sections: 1) Rationale
for the Middle School (humanizing aspects, history of
the middle school movement). 2) The Learning
Environment (behavioral objectives, assessment and
evaluation, team teaching, inquiry grouping, independent study and open laboratories, continuous progress, schoolwide curriculum committee, diversified
learning activities, time allocations). 3) Staff
Allocations (differentiating teaching staff, teacher
aides, parent volunteers, and student teachers, staff
development for facilitating change). 4) Student
Outcomes (learning how to learn independence and
self-reliance, student involvement). 5) Facilities
(procedures for initiating change in school facility
design, middle school site selection, design and
spatial requirements).

2099.   Overview magazine. "Planning and operating the
middle school." Overview, 14,3(1963):52-55.

Article describes the Bedford Public Schools, Mount
Kisco, New York, which have these philosphies and
characteristics: 1) Children aged 11 or 12 to 14 or
15 are undergoing basic physiological and psychological changes that have an educational import only
recently appreciated. 2) Limits to the Bedford
School were set at a thousand-student capacity,
grades 6-8. 3) All Bedford schools aim at the development of self-educating, inquiring, individuals. 4)
All instructional programs become more and more
individualized, with emphasis on small groups, seminars, independent study, and project work. 5) More
learning goes on in the schools, involving the community's adults as well as its youth. 6) Not only
are the middle school's interior spaces conducive to

quick and easy rearrangement, but its outward shape is also capable of change and reorganization. 7) A thousand-pupil school needs to be broken down into more intimate, manageable units. The house plan is used at Bedford. 8) The middle school becomes ungraded as rapidly as possible. 9) The schoolhouse has many attributes of the home. 10) The environment creates an atmosphere for quiet but intensive activity. 11) It is the individual student who counts today: his program, his activities, his environment. 12) The article presents the time allotments for the middle school groupings. 13) The home and industrial arts programs are combined with art, music, and theater into a unified arts program. 14) Physical education means something quite different today than in the past, with facilities freed from the domination of a basketball-type gymnasium. 15) A central library serves the middle school best. 16) Teaching spaces ideally make possible interchange with easy mobility of students and teachers. 17) The middle school is organized around teaching teams. 18) The buildings are quite different, with students quartered in three distinct houses.

2100.   Pennsylvania State Department of Education. "The Middle School." Harrisburg, Pa., 1971.

Brochure contains information on the philosophy and general objectives of a middle school, physiological characteristic and needs of middle school children, a program for a middle school, a suggestion for organizing and staffing a middle school, special features of a middle school, evaluation of middle school programs, educational advantages of the middle school, general directions for applying for reapproval, specific directions for completing forms on middle schools and a bibliography. For further information, write to Bureau of Curriculum Development and Evaluation, Box 911, Harrisburg, Pennsylvania 17126.

2101.   Pennsylvania School Study Council.   The Middle School: A Selected Bibliography.   University Park, Pa., 1967.

Bibliography contains 110 entries on middle schools, 48 entries on related innovations, and 32 entries (some annotated) on middle school and junior high organization.

2102.   Perry, I. L. (Comp.) "The Middle School: Postsession Report." Tallahassee: Florida State Department of Education, Division of Curriculum and Instruction, ERIC Doc. ED 043 128, May 27, 1969.

Booklet contains four addresses from the Florida State Division of Curriculum and Instruction staff session on middle school years. The purpose of the seminar was to review the theory of the middle school, its status in the educational organization, its student population characteristics, and its special requirements with respect to teacher education programs. The addresses are: 1) "Background of the Middle School Movement" by Dr. William Alexander. 2) "Characteristics and Desired Behaviors of the Middle School Child" by Dr. Mary F. Compton. 3) "The Middle School Teacher" by Dr. Ronald Kealy. 4) "Teacher Education Advisory Council Task Force on the Middle School" by Jack Gant. A middle school selected bibliography is also included.

2103.   Piele, P.   Selected Bibliography of Journal Articles on the Middle School. Eugene: University of Oregon, ERIC Clearinghouse on Educational Administration, 1967.

Five books, one bibliography, thirty-five journal articles and twenty-one reports on the middle school are included in this bibliography.

2104.   Popper, S. H.   "The middle school of tomorrow." Chapter 15 in The American Middle School: Organizational Analysis. Waltham, Mass.: Blaisdell Publishing Co., 1967.

The future of the middle school depends on its continued commitment to a differentiated early adolescent education and its use of innovations that integrate its values with a changing society. Flexibility of programs and developing the self-concept of adolescents are key middle school responsibilities. In the socialization process for this age group, doctors, social workers, psychologists, guidance counselors, and nurses are needed to perform auxiliary functions. Similarly, the use of core technology and the humanization of education are important in the middle school's success. Of all public school units, the middle school is best equipped to accommodate built-in flexibility in curriculum design. Many designs of plants for future middle schools already exist; it is important that these designs be considered, for the middle school houses youth at the age where proper guidance could keep them from a life of delinquency.

2105.   Pumerantz, P.   "State recognition of the middle school." Bulletin of the National Association of Secondary School Principals, 53(1969):14-19.

A 1968 survey showed that Connecticut was the only state with legislation defining the middle school. Only five state departments of education, without benefit of legislation, recommended or endorsed

middle schools. Forty-four other states had not
defined the middle school concept through law;
neither had their state education agencies recommended or endorsed the middle school plan. The
author believes that because of the growing interest
in many school districts in innovations of all kinds,
especially the middle school, state departments of
education ought to play a more active role, especially in doing research to determine the potential
of the middle school concept. People and resources
at the state level could help districts planning
middle schools as well as those with middle schools
in operation and could help solve the problem of
rising costs and enrollments, teacher preparation,
and certification standards for the middle grades.

2106.   Pumerantz, P. and Galano, R. W.   Establishing
Interdisciplinary Programs in the Middle School.
West Nyack, N.Y.:   Parker Publishing Co., 1972.

Interdisciplinary learning in the middle school
allows pupils to develop better understandings of
themselves and to work out areas of weakness without
harm to their self-images, to proceed at a pace commensurate with their interests, skills, and experiences, to reinforce and improve skills, to pursue
special interests, to see present social interrelationships and focus on past and present cultures,
and to develop individual responsibilities.   The
interdisciplinary approach accomplishes these goals
through 1) multiple instructional groups and independent study, which help teachers focus on the
individual, 2) better communication among teachers,
among students, and between teachers and students, 3)
more effective use of innovation in instructional
media and technology, 4) development of independent
study which can provide retreats from the often
excessive competition, 5) better use of staff
talents, interests, and expertise, and 6) more
effective use of team teaching and large and small
group instruction to release some staff for more
preparations and research or for work with cluster
groups or individuals. The book develops these ideas
in the following chapters: 1) Building Realistic
Interdisciplinary Programs for Grade 6 or Level I.
2) The Level II or Seventh and Eighth Grade Programs.
3) Determining the Most Effective Use of the Plant
(designing a new plant, developing individualized
learning environments in existing schools).   4) How
to Interest and Involve the Staff.   5) How to
Schedule Interdisciplinary Programs. 6) The Role of
the Teacher in Interdisciplinary Programs.   7)
Teaching Strategies in the Interdisciplinary Program.
8) Guidance in Interdisciplinary Programs.

2107.   Putney, E.   "Open spaces, teams, and unified learning." Learning Today, 6,1(1973):24-31.

Describes Florida's Plantation Middle School, which is developing a new kind of learning through use of the generic book. The school emphasizes team effort, learner-centered activity, use of the media center, and innovative materials. Key ideas of the program are: 1) It should assist the student to become a creative, responsible, and productive citizen. 2) Learning is primarily an individual matter. 3) Skill in continuous learning is important. 4) To be effective, continuous learning must develop stability in the student. 5) The development of responsible human values must underlie all aspects of the program.

2108.   Richardson, J. A.   "The Middle School: Pitfalls and Possibilities."   Paper presented at American Association of School Administrators Annual Convention, Atlantic City, N. J., ERIC Doc. ED 064 756, February 12, 1972.

A middle school campus in Winnetka, Illinois, consists of two schools and provides a continuous four-year program that recognizes the differences in development during the middle school years. Fifth and sixth graders are housed in one school, while the second school contains the seventh and eighth grade students. The following areas are coordinated for services: PTA, teaching forces, administration, and student government. Article discusses the middle school campus, the Washburne School, and the many functions of the school.

2109.   Riegle, J. "Middle schools: ghosts of the truth." Michigan Journal of Secondary Education, Summer 1971: 46-47.

A study of one hundred Michigan schools which house grades above 4 but below 9, suggests that certain problems are typical of middle school education in Michigan and elsewhere in 1971. Total agreement exists in the literature about the need for guidance services in middle school education. Transescent youth obviously need guidance programs led by skilled counselors and teachers who recognize their roles as guidance people as well as instructional leaders. In spite of this emphasis, very few of the middle schools in Michigan at this time had guidance programs for their youngsters. The middle school literature also deals amply with the problems of the Carnegie Unit and the fixed grade level organization, and educational publications frequently suggest patterns for eliminating these roadblocks to learning. Yet the survey questions about continuous progress programs, flexible scheduling techniques, and teaching revealed only a large number of programs labeled as pilot programs, experimental programs, or trial programs. Truly flexible schedules were nonexistent, continuous progress programs were never fully implemented and team teaching, frequently reported, usually comprised only a very limited part of the program. Author suggests that schools suffer from a lack of informed leadership. The middle schools of Michigan need administrators who have read the great quantity of available material about middle school education and the nature of transescent youth and who have the leadership skills to put into practice what they learn from the literature.

2110.   Romano, L. G., Georgiady, N. P., and Heald, J. E. The Middle School: Selected Readings on an Emerging School Program. Professional Technical Series, Chicago: Nelson-Hall, 1973.

Contains articles on the middle school movement in five sections: 1) Introducing the Middle School. 2) This is the Transescent. 3) Curriculum Strategy for the Middle School. 4) The Middle School Multi-Purpose Plant. 5) Questions Facing the Middle School.

2111.   Schein, B. and Schein, M. P. Open Classrooms in the Middle School. West Nyack, N.Y.: Parker Publishing Co., 1975.

Adapting and applying the principles of open education to the middle school stimulates dynamic change in students, teachers, and parents. For all three groups, school becomes exciting and more rewarding. While releasing the natural but often hidden eagerness of middle school children to learn, open education enhances their self-awareness, self-reliance, knowledge, and use of skills. This book concentrates on successful techniques to change traditional middle schools to open ones. Based on actual events, the book contains practical material that can be quickly and smoothly adapted to any middle or junior high school. What is happening in our most sophisticated middle schools or junior high schools may be innovative, but flexible, modular scheduling, mini-courses, and the types of programmed instruction that characterize these schools does not necessarily add up to open education. Openness is, instead, children controlling time and learning episodically--not according to a rigid, predetermined course or sequence. The book is designed for those who want to help children learn more while achieving greater personal satisfaction than is possible in traditional schools. Sections of the book are: 1) Providing Choices: Transition to an Open Classroom. 2) Discovering

Student Interest in the Open Classroom. 3) How to Know When Children are Learning: Ways to Let Parents Know. 4) Scheduling in the Open Middle School. 5) Developing the Supervisory Role. 6) Discipline in the Open School. 7) Making a Big School Smaller Promotes Student Involvement. 8) Involving the Community: A Two-Pronged Dilemma. 9) What Open Education Is--And What It Is Not.

2112.   School Management magazine. "Why one district is building a 'middle school.'" School Management, 7, 5(1963):86-88.

Amory, Mississippi firmly believes that a 4-4-4 administrative plan with a strong middle unit is far superior to a conventional junior high school in converting eager children into studious teenagers. A middle school can provide children with a four-year transitional period between the self-contained class-room concept of elementary school and the departmen-talized, specialized instruction found in secondary schools. The middle school of four years also pro-vides ample opportunity for children to pass through the awkward stage of maturation--it is in effect a school for growing up. Amory looks to the example of Saginaw, Michigan, where two middle schools for grades 5-8 operate on the following basis. In the fifth grade children are taught in a self-contained home situation with a single teacher. In the sixth grade,there is some movement between classrooms with a team teaching arrangement. This is the neighbor-hood situation. In the seventh and eighth grade there is a great deal of movement between classes for specialized instruction. "The middle school gives the district a lot more flexibility in planning," states Jonathan King, Secretary/Treasurer of Educa-tional Facilities Laboratory. Says Amory superin-tendent C. E. Hayman, "We believe that children in the fifth to eighth grades should be separated both physically and intellectually from older children. An eighth grader has more in common with sixth graders than with high school juniors and seniors who are smoking, dating, and using cosmetics." Children at these ages have much in common with each other. In terms of social development, they are all at the awkward stage. Not yet independent, they need more personal attention. Hayman says, "We want to handle these youngsters as a separate educational unit. We are developing a special four-year sequential curric-ulum, special school facilities, special guidance and teaching for them to carry them through the middle years." Educators also justify the middle school by noting that colleges are increasingly demanding a four-year sequence of courses for admission, and a 4-4-4 plan makes it easier to satisfy their requests. In this article an excellent physical plant description presents a blueprint for an ideal middle school and a curricular model with a complete description of all facilities by the architect.

2113.   Skill Development Council. "Focus on the Middle School." Prepared by the research staff of Skill Development Council, a division of Kelly-Mead and Co., Rochester, N. Y. 14605. (No year given.)

Included among the claims made for the junior high school or the middle school are: 1) The curriculum is more comprehensive. 2) The curriculum is more flexible. 3) Activities are more available to the students. 4) Teachers are trained to teach junior high or middle school. 5) Better guidance opportunities are available. 6) Exploratory opportunities are more available. 7) Costs are more reasonable. 8) Discipline problems and school violence are reduced. 9) Middle schools provide a laboratory for interpersonal and intercultural relations. 10) Students in the early adolescent period have unique physical, social, emotional, and intellectual needs which distinguish them from high school students. That some of the claimed advantages are significant cannot be denied. There is, however, no manual or script which will be appropriate for every community considering school reorganization. Each community must consider its own needs.

2114.   Spring Branch Independent School District. "The Junior High School Program, Grades 6-8." Houston, Tex., 1966.

Bulletin reviews the reasons for adopting the middle school, evaluates its success (stating that there are fewer discipne problems in 6-9), and describes the courses given.

2115.   Stemnock, S. K. Middle Schools in Action. Educational Research Circular 2, American Association of School Administrators. Washington, D.C.: National Education Association, March, 1969.

What is the difference between a middle school and a junior high school? A middle school program is designed to recognize the uniqueness of the growth stage spanning the transition from childhood to adolescence. The junior high has evolved into exactly what the name implies--junior high school. This book helps establish just what middle schools do in practice around the country as of 1969. In 1965 queries sent by the Educational Research Service to 461 school systems identified only 63 middle schools concentrated in 20 systems. Only 13 of these 20 systems enrolled more than 12,000 pupils. When size was again polled at the opening of the 1968-69 school year, 70 systems reported 235 middle schools. The growth in these four years prompted this detailed 1969 report on the characteristics of each school, including: 1) identification of the school system and the name of the school, 2) first year operated, 3) grades included, 4) number of students, 5) number of staff positions, 6) ability grouping, 7) instructional practices, 8) subjects taught by teams, 9) special subjects--both required and elective, and 10) activities. Book also includes special comments by principals of middle schools, an index to school systems with middle schools, a bibliography of books, pamphlets, and articles and a sample questionnaire.

2116. Stier, S. "Middle Schools in Perspective." Seattle, Wash.: Seattle Public Schools, 1973.

This report is divided into five major components. Part I contains a brief description of middle schools as they have developed throughout the United States since the beginning of the century. Part II reviews the history of middle schools in the Seattle School District. Emphasis is placed on the role of the district's mandatory and voluntary desegregation program and on the introduction of commercialized learning units as part of an individualized curricular approach. In Part III Seattle's original planning for the middle schools is described in terms of a "Prototype Middle School Model" that discusses "student progress, curriculum development, staff development, and internal and external organization" and provides a conceptual framework for analyzing 1971-72 and the 1972-73 middle school evaluation results. Part IV includes the goals agreed on for evaluating middle schools through the 1971-72 school year and the results obtained from this evaluation. Part V does the same for 1972-73. Report includes thirteen appendices containing supporting data.

2117. Stradley, W. E. A Practical Guide to the Middle School. Library for Education Series. New York: Center for Applied Research in Education, 75th Ave., 1971.

Written for the experienced administrator, this book discusses curriculum structure, staffing, organization and student programing. It also discusses teaching in the middle school, with practical information on teacher preparation, the changing role of the teacher, increasing teaching/learning effectiveness in the middle school structure, and how and why the uniqueness of the true middle school program demands different approaches by the teaching staff. The middle school must concern itself with the following educational functions: 1) Build the curriculum from the elementary school program and continue to offer a general program of education. 2) Provide students with exploratory opportunities to meet the challenge of their widening range of interest and to serve as guides to vocational pursuits. 3) Prepare students for the more specialized program of the senior high school. 4) Promote, develop, and nurture individual differences and provide an educational structure to meet these individual social and scholastic needs. Some other areas with which the middle schools must be concerned and which broaden the function of the school are development and maintenance of sound concepts for the middle school as the unique educational unit, limited vocational guidance, student adjustment and social development, terminal courses, human relations, and potential dropouts.

2118.   Stradley, W. E.   The Transitional Years.   Middle School Portfolio 4.   Association for Childhood Education International, 3615 Wisconsin Ave. N.W., Washington, D.C. 20016.   (No year given.)

This portfolio is a collection of fourteen leaflets on topics concerning the pupil and programs of the middle school.

2119.   Task Force on Intermediate Education. "The Middle School, An Idea Whose Time Has Come."   Trenton, N.J., 1972.

This excellent publication includes: Forward: An Innovation with Possibilities.   Introduction: An Opportunity for Imaginative Approaches.   Chapter 1) The Schools in the Middle, An Historical Approach. 2) The Pupils of the Middle School, A Profile View. 3) The Program of the Middle School, A Comprehensive View.   4) The Middle School Staff, The Essential Element.   5) Housing the Middle School, A Facilitative View. 6) The Middle School Studies Itself, An Evaluative Self-Study.   7) The Middle School, Issues and Conclusions. Appendix A) A Capsulated End View, Characteristic Comments Concerning the Middle School. B) A Middle School Bibliography, Books for Professional Study.   C) A Middle School Glossary, Definition of Pertinent Terms.   D) Creating a Philosophy: A Sample.

2120.   Teacher Education Resources.   "The Modern Middle School."   2001 N.W. 58th Terrace, Jamesville, Fla. (No year given.)

This is a series of four film strip cassette programs.

2121.   Pittsburgh Public Schools.   "What is a Pittsburgh middle school?   Bridging program between elementary, high schools."   The News, 30,1(1975):2.

Presents many views of an exemplary middle school. Discusses the school's organization, administrative staffing, teacher preparation and selection, scheduling, and central supervisory services. The purpose and functions of a middle school must be based on an understanding of the special physical, social, emotional, and intellectual characteristics and needs of the preadolescent. In order to meet these needs an urban middle school program must emphasize the continued acquisition of basic reading and mathematical skills, provide continuing assistance to the preadolescent in making decisions about special needs and learning opportunities, and help preadolescents learn to solve problems and become independent learners. In order to realize these three major goals, the following requirements are essential: 1) a major emphasis on guidance, which means changing the traditional role of the counselor, 2) consideration of the needs of the whole child, 3) a school organization based on the house concept, which maximizes the possibility of student adjustment to the expanded pupil population of the middle school, 4) an interdisciplinary teaching team organization, which delegates to the teacher more responsibility for the pupil's total learning experience. In the mid-1970s preadolescents are more sophisticated than those of a generation ago. They read more widely, they are better informed through television, radio, and newspapers, their vocabulary is more extensive--at least when they want it to be--and they remain in school longer. They are more interested in school than their peers of the past, and though their interests are stronger in the active studies (physical education, music, art), they also are more interested in the academic disciplines, especially in those where new instructional methods are employed. The chief educational advantages of middle schools are better libraries, better study facilities, better health and physical education courses, opportunities for more individualized teaching, and interdisciplinary teaming, a wider range of academic subjects, a rich introduction into the realities of the world of work, and a broadened range of friends.

2122.   Thibadeau, G. and Lagana, J. F. "Opening up the middle school: a case study."   Catalyst for Change, 5,1(1975):16-19.

Discusses how a school in the North Allegheny School District changed from a traditional to an open interdisciplinary approach to teaching and learning. Sections cover the planning of the open school, the program, the key decisions, the final stage, and collaboration.

2123.   Thompson, L. J.   "Benchmarks for the middle school." Theory Into Practice, 15,2(1976):153-155.

A middle school program which is related to the developmental stages of the student has the following characteristics: 1) There is a proper ratio between active experiences and quiet experiences. 2) There is a balance between concrete experiences and abstract experiences. 3) Whatever the demands of the program, there is consistency. 4) The relationships between students and adults are open, humane, and honest. 5) The program provides for experience in clarifying values. 6) Attention is given to learning basic skills and concepts. 7) The program provides the opportunity to make choices. This kind of school is distinctly different from the junior high school. Educators must see the middle school as appropriate for early adolescents because it deliberately attempts to match the educational program to the characteristics of the students.

2124.   Tobin, M. F. "Purpose and function precede middle school planning."   Educational Leadership 3(1973): 200-205.

Article discusses the physical, emotional, and intellectual needs and characteristics of middle school students. Tobin discusses the purposes and functions of a middle school. He notes that the middle school building should reflect the flexibility of the program, the rapidly changing child, the motivating atmosphere. It must in itself be a dynamic force. The main focus of the article is on planning for learning, including a chart titled "Is your Middle School Relevant?" Planning organizationally to accommodate your instructional program to the learning needs and progress of your students involves the following questions: 1) In what specific ways will an individual student's schedule differ from that in a conventional junior high school? 2) What alternative approaches to instruction are to be provided? 3) What provision has been made for growth and independent study skills? 4) In what ways does the school program coordinate the subject fields? In what ways is instruction in any subject linked to other activities? 5) What is your plan for evaluating program effectiveness on a year-by-year basis? What baseline data will you employ? How many aspects of growth will be surveyed? How will these studies help you modify your program for individuals and groups? 6) How will you adapt your building for changes in program from year to year? 7) What factors in the middle school program indicate that the emphasis is on the child and his opportunities for success? 8) What provisions are being made to assure that the background, experience, training, and attitudes of the staff members are commensurate with child-centered rather than subject-centered approaches to working with middle school students? 9) What in the middle school program will promote student and staff communication and enhance the scope and quality of relationships? How can you eliminate factors that might inhibit communication and relationships? 10) What chances do students have for orientation and exploration beyond academic subjects? What chances do they have to become familiar with work and leisure? 11) What provisions have been made for use of the middle school in the immediate and larger community as a learning laboratory?

2125.   Today's Education.   "Picture if you will: Far-quhar Middle School." Today's Education, 61,6(1972): 34-36.

The Farquhar Middle School is based on individualization of instruction, a team approach, flexible scheduling, nongraded organization, and an environment that fosters student independence and self-direction. Article describes the team as the basic unit of activity at Farquhar. It presents pictures of students and staff at this new school and discusses the Institute for the Development of Educational Activities, which is developing multimedia packages of in-service training materials for this middle school.

2126.   Todd, S. M.   "Creativity and the middle school years." In Thornburg, H. (Ed.), Preadolescent Development, pp. 129-136. Tucson: University of Arizona Press, 1974.

An environment that is conducive to creativity requires creative teacher-student relationships. Good teachers help students communicate their ideas and evaluate possible results. They provide thinking time for their students as part of scheduled activities. They arrange stimulating lessons for the whole class and for small special-interest groups as well as individual conferences with students to motivate further work, diagnose problems, and express satisfaction with work well done. To nurture the fullest creativity, greater emphasis should be placed on seeking the implications, deeper meaning, and possibilities inherent in the student's ideas. This is a matter of pursuing ideas in depth and in scope, not of criticizing and rejecting the idea, which is easy to do and which is so crippling to creativity. Creative solutions to problems are not achieved unless their consequences are tested in application and revised and extended. Teachers influence creativity in young people by establishing the atmosphere for learning that the students in their classes will experience. They decide which qualities they wish to develop in their students, and they must consider whether they are prepared to accept the problems that creative people make. Teachers must teach children a balance between creativity, self-discipline, and cooperation. Article discusses several relevant aspects of the creative process which are worth testing.

2127.   Toepfer, C. F., Jr. "Challenge to middle school education: preventing regression to the mean." Middle School Journal, 7,3(1976):3.

Presents eight characteristics of nationally recognized, outstanding middle schools as benchmarks that all middle schools might use in examining their programs. See ERIC Abstract #EJ 146 424.

2128.   Trauschke, E. M. and   Mooney, P. F.   "Middle school accountability."   Educational Leadership, 30,2(1972):171-174.

The following characteristics describe a middle school organization: 1) A middle school takes full cognizance of the dynamic physical, social, and intellectual changes occurring in young people during the 10-to-14-year-old age span and provides a program that helps the transescent understand himself and the changes that are occurring within and around him. 2) Middle schools generally locate the ninth grade, with the awesome influence of the Carnegie Unit, in senior high school settings because ninth graders are more like tenth, eleventh, and twelfth grade students than seventh and eighth grade students. 3) Middle schools provide opportunities for innovations like team teaching, individualized instruction, flexible scheduling, and some form of continuous progress. Flexible rearrangements of time, space, materials, and people are valuable features of the true middle school. 4) Middle schools deemphasize the sophisticated activities that are commonly found in the junior high school, such as marching band, interscholastic athletics, and sophisticated dances. The program of activities permits each child to participate and is based on the personal development of the student rather than enhancement of the school's prestige. 5) Middle schools provide opportunities for exploratory study and enrichment activities earlier than conventional elementary schools do. 6) Middle school instructional staffs combine talents usually developed by teachers trained in the elementary school with the ability to specialize in a given

field, so often a characteristic of a secondary
teacher. Authors investigate the achievement of
middle school students in grades 5, 6, 7, and 8 when
compared with that of students in grades 5 and 6 in
elementary school and 7 and 8 in junior high, using
the same control and experimental groups.

2129.   Treacy, J. P.   "What is the middle school?"
Catholic School Journal, 68(1968):56-58.

Article is divided into these sections: 1) Defining
the Middle School.   2) How Prevalent are Middle
Schools?   3) Middle Schools, Pros and Cons.   4)
Advantages of the Middle Schools for Pupils: a) the
middle school adapts education to the developmental
stage of children in those grades, usually the preadolescent and early adolescent ages; b) children are
maturing earlier--physically, socially, personally,
emotionally, and intellectually, and the middle
school accelerates their socialization at the same
time that it acts as a damper on a tendency for some
students in grades 7-9 to grow up and become sophisticated too early; c) the middle school makes it
possible to bring to children certain services
usually identified with high schools.   5) Advantages
for the Teaching Staff: a) the middle school can
have a status of its own, rather than having a
"junior" classification without a definite identity;
b) departmentalization makes possible greater
specialization of teachers; c) middle school organization makes possible more experimentation with
educational innovations; d) middle school helps to
adjust education to the diversity of needs found in
the upper grades;   e) middle school organization
makes possible greater professionalization of
teachers in grades 6-8; f) some writers claim that
discipline in the upper grades is easier without
ninth graders present.   6) Advantages for Administration: a) the middle school improves coordination
of effort in grades 9-12; b) the middle school makes
possible a gradual change from the self-contained
classroom to complete departmentalization in the high
school;   c) the middle school can be used as one
means of facilitating desegregation;   7) What Grades
Should be Included?   8) Are Junior High Schools
Passe?   9) Questions, Issues, Problems.   10) Some
Observations.

2130.   Turnbaugh, R. C.   "The middle school: a different
name or a new concept?"   Clearinghouse, 43(1968):
86-88.

The middle school offers these benefits to pupils:
1) It emphasizes intellectual development with
opportunities for special staff, facilities, and
programs.   2) It cultivates an atmosphere free from

pressure--social, academic, athletic, or other. 3) It relieves anxieties by providing wholesome and appropriate outlets that grow out of the natural social, intellectual, and physical needs of the children. 4) It reduces isolation of racial, socio-economic, age, sex, or other groups. It seems clear that many of the new developments in education in the next decade will be associated with middle schools.

2131.   Tyrrell, R., Johns, F., and McNally, M. "Are open middle schools really open?" _Elementary School Journal_, 76,1(1975):2-8.

Presents the educational programs of fifteen open plan middle schools in Ohio. These schools were studied for evidence of innovative use of facilities, the teaching-learning environment, the psychosocial environment, and the curriculum. Inappropriate use of space was a major problem, and very few innovations were going on. The principal is the key to an effective support system. Decision-making groups should be formed within the faculties to help make change occur, and a support system from a university could be helpful in assisting teachers and students.

2132.   Tyrrell, R. W. "The open middle school: a model for change." _Bulletin of the National Association of Secondary School Principals_, 58,381(1974):62-66.

Several changes made at one time in Ohio's Beachwood Middle School allowed it to make progress in providing successful innovative programs. Author discusses hopes for the middle school, the fact that changes must occur simultaneously, the question "change to what end?," guidelines for decision making, and the great strides made at this school. It is an open-space school enhanced by many groupings and teaching styles. Teachers were organized into interdisciplinary teams which initiated a rethinking of traditional junior high school experiences. A major question asked was, "What kind of experiences should be designed for emerging adolescents?" Teaming assisted in bringing enthusiasm to new teaching strategies. Staff participation in decision making was necessary to ensure commitment to the direction of the new school. This staff is definitely making a contribution to the improvement of schooling for the emerging adolescent.

2133.   University of Oregon at Eugene. _The Changing Middle School_. The Best of ERIC Series, no. 13. Washington, D.C.: National Institute of Education, ERIC Clearinghouse on Educational Management, ERIC Doc. ED 114 905, November, 1975.

This booklet is a bibliography including fourteen publications on the topic of middle schools. Practicing educators may use it to gain easy access to information available through the Education Resource Information Center (ERIC). Articles are: 1) "The Sixth Grade: Elementary or Middle School?" by F. W. Ball. 2) "The Principalship: Junior High and Middle School" by J. Bobroff, J. Howard, and A. Howard. 3) "The Nature of the Transescent as it Affects Middle School Program Evaluation" by T. Bondi and T. Tocco. 4) "Bibliographies in Education No. 50" by Canadian Teachers Federation, Junior High and Middle Schools. 5) "Middle Schools" by N. Coppock. 6) "The Middle School Should be a Separate and Equal Entity" by J. Dettre. 7) "Summary of Research on Middle Schools: Research Brief" by H. Doob. 8) "The Middle School Period, An Institution in Search of an Identity" by D. Friesen. 9) "The Anatomy of a Good Middle School" by R. H. Garvelink. 10) "A Conception of Early Adolescence" by J. Kagan. 11) "Middle School in the Making, Readings from Educational Leadership" ed. by R. Leeper. 12) "The Middle School: Whence? What? Whither?" (Fastback Series No. 22) by M. McGlasson. 13) "The Middle School: A Monograph" by D. Mullen. 14) "The Middle School: Pitfalls and Possibilities" by J. Richardson.

2134.   Vars, G. F. "New Knowledge of the Learner and His Cultural Milieu: Implications for Schooling in the Middle Years." Paper presented at the Conference of the Middle School Idea, College of Education, University of Toledo, Toledo, Ohio, November 11, 1967.

Paper discusses the learner in the middle school years, the social and cultural milieu, knowledge of transescents, implications for schooling, and it presents a model program. How feasible is the program? All of its elements already exist in some form in the schools today. In fact, the plan may appear to be nothing more than something old and new combined. Yet the best curriculum for the middle school may represent a marriage of the best features of the elementary school with the best from the high school. The most promising curriculum offspring of this union might well embody these three concepts: core, nongrading, and flexibility.

2135.   Vars, G. F. "In Between." Middle School Portfolio. Washington, D.C.: Association for Childhood Education International, 1968.

Discusses the in-between student, in-between school, and in-between curriculum of the middle school. A school that would truly serve youngsters during their in-between years must combine the elementary school's concern for the whole child with the secondary school stress on scholarship and intellectual development. This balance may best be provided through a program that includes a block-time or core class for guidance and problem-centered learning paralleled by more specialized courses, sometimes nongraded in organization, in such fields as mathematics, science, foreign languages, art, and music.

2136.   Wiles, J.   Planning Guidelines for Middle School Education. Dubuque, Iowa: Kendall-Hunt Publishing Co., 1976.

Book contains the following chapters: 1) The Emergence of the Middle School.   2) A Program Designed for Middle School Education.   3) Planning Considerations in the Development of Middle Schools.   4) Instruction in the Middle School.   5) The Evaluation of Middle School Programs.

2137.   Wilson, M. A.   "The self-appraisal program in the Philadelphia Junior High School."   Educational and Psychological Measurement, 6(1946):81-92.

Presents a successful guidance program for junior high school youngsters.

2138.   Wilson, M. T.   The Middle School Defined Now: Freedom to Behave.   Dissemination Services on the Middle Grades, vol. 5, no. 9.   Springfield, Mass.: Educational Leadership Institute, 1974.

The middle school years should be a special experience for each student according to his own requirements.   To this end, educators must provide opportunities in many divergent fields in order to find that entry point where learning takes on meaning. Hence, many activities are available and a flexible, personalized program makes participation in them possible. Underlying this broad approach is the very real responsibility of the staff to make sure that the skills of learning are mastered to the degree that each student is able.   All the student's experiences should contribute to the development of self-discipline and strong personal values and to the gradual assuming of responsibility for his own learning--now and in future years. Author describes the program at the Conwell Middle Magnet School, Philadelphia, based on the concept "freedom to behave."

2139.   Zdanowicz, P. J.   "The Middle School: A Reading List."   Bridgewater, Mass.:   Meredith G. Williams Middle School, November, 1965.

This is a bibliography of references on the middle school.

3

Prescriptions for and Descriptions of Junior High Schools

3001.   Andreen, E. P. (Ed.) "Symposium: the challenge facing the junior high school." California Journal of Secondary Education, 29(1954):263-301.

Statements mainly by principals and other school staff members describe policies and practices in California junior high schools, including the importance of junior high school, characteristics of the adolescent, teachers, sixth grade orientation, the homeroom, etc.

3002.   Association for Supervision and Curriculum Development. "Developing Programs for Young Adolescents." Washington, D.C.:   National Education Association, 1954.

Presents eight principles guiding the development of the junior high school program.

3003.   Baughman, M. D. "Organization and administration of the modern junior high school." Teachers College Journal, 34,2(1962):51-54.

Discusses grade organization, organization for administration, staffing, curriculum organization, and scope of the guidance program. Covers major aspects of administration, including planning, controlling, directing, evaluating, and decision making.

3004.   Beals, L.   "The junior high school: past and present."   Bulletin of the National Association of Secondary School Principals, 36(1952):15-24.

Summarizes trends in junior high school education, reviews main functions, and suggests ways to achieve them.

3005.   Bossing, N. L. and Cramer, R. V. The Junior High School. Boston: Houghton-Mifflin Co., 1965.

This textbook has the following: 1) Development of the Junior High School. 2) Philosophy, Purposes, and Functions. 3) The Nature of Early Adolescence. 4) Influence of Learning Theories on the Curriculum. 5) Development of the Curriculum. 6) Block-Time Class Organization. 7) The Core Curriculum. 8) The Personal Interest Program. 9) Health and Physical Fitness. 10) Student Activities. 11) Guidance and Counseling. 12)) Evaluating and Reporting Student Progress. 13) Staffing Problems. 14) Housing the Junior High School. 15) Problems of Articulation. 16) Evaluation of the Program.

3006.   Brackett, R. D. "What curriculum changes are needed in the junior high school?" Bulletin of the National Association of Secondary School Principals, 38(1954):160-164.

Answers the question in the title.

3007.   Brimm, R. P. The Junior High School. Washington, D.C.: Center for Applied Research in Education, 1963.

Monograph chapters are: 1) The Junior High School in the American Educational System (the junior high school yesterday and today, administrative organization, the unique functions of the junior high school). 2) The Psychological Basis for the Junior High School. 3) The Instructional Program. 4) The Extra-Class Program. 5) Social Services (the principal's office, the library, audiovisual services, guidance services, health services, clinical services, auxiliary services, Public Relations). 6) Evaluating and Reporting Pupil Progress (evaluation vs. marking, the parent-teacher conference, the use of test results, the report card). 7) Staffing the Junior High School (teacher education, in-service training, selecting teachers). 8) Forward-looking Practices (educational television, out-of-doors education, programmed instruction, flexible time schedules, team teaching, the ungraded junior high school, the learning laboratory, other innovations). 9) Issues in Junior High School Education (vertical vs. horizontal enrichment, ability grouping, administrative organization, interscholastic athletics, regional accreditation, merit pay, homework). 10) Evaluation of the Junior High School (standardized tests, follow-up studies, self-evaluation). 11) The Junior High School Today and Tomorrow.

3008.   Brinkopf, J. W. "Transition from sixth to seventh grade made easy at Cherry Creek (1960)." Bulletin of the National Association of Secondary School Principals, 46(1962):70-73.

This plan makes the transition from elementary school to junior high a pleasant experience for new seventh graders.

3009.   Buell, C. E. "Position Papers for the Junior High School." National Association of Secondary School Principals, October, 1963.

These position papers are almost all by junior high school principals, with a few by professors of education. Titles and authors are: 1) "Interscholastic Athletics: Yes or No in Junior High Schools?" by Earl R. Hatcher and W. B. Unruh. 2) "What Are the Unique Features of the Junior High School Today?" by Donald G. Gill and W. Lloyd Johns. 3) "Acceleration vs. Enrichment in the Junior High School Years" by I. Paul Handwerk and E. W. Nieman. 4) "What About Regional and National Accreditation of Junior High Schools?" by Mark C. Lloyd and Joe J. Rousseau. 5) "Junior High School Homework: More, Less, or Different?" by G. Derwood Baker and Robert F. Eberle. 6) "What Do We Believe Is a Desirable Degree of Subject Departmentalization in the Junior High School?" by Leonard H. Clark and Clifton Alice. 7) "What Do We Believe about the Junior High School Nonathletic Activities Program?" by Everett V. Samuelson and Emerson Slacum. 8) "Negative Approach with Positive Implications: What Should the Junior High School Not Try to Accomplish?" by Edith C. Smith and Gordon F. Vars. 9) "How Should Junior High Schools Exercise Responsibility to Early School Leaders?" by Carl Gastwirth and Carey M. Pace, Jr.

3010.   Bulletin of the National Association of Secondary School Principals, November 1960:Whole Issue.

Issue is devoted to the junior high school.

3011.   Bureau of Field Studies and Surveys. "St. Paul Junior High School Study: A Progress Report and Preliminary Tabular Findings." Report 25. University of Minnesota, College of Education, September, 1962.

The St. Paul Public School system requested that the University of Minnesota's Bureau of Field Studies and Surveys evaluate the St. Paul junior high schools. This report focuses on the functions of the junior high school and findings about St. Paul student achievement, curriculum, teaching practices and school service, student activities, school relationships, and the survey experience.

3012.   Bush, P. I.   "The junior high school student 1944-1964." Bulletin of the National Association of Secondary School Principals, 49,300(1965):50-55.

Compares 1947, 1957, and 1964 studies of junior high schools in small communities, where students were asked to rank their needs and interests. The ranking seems to give greater priority in 1964 to vocational preparation, family relationship, leisure, and cooperative living values. A lower ranking is given to rational thinking, appreciation of the arts, health, and science. The biggest increase is in the need for both study and activity dealing with the problem of searching for self. Adolescents expressed this need in terms of becoming used to themselves as individuals and developing independence from adults, especially authority figures such as parents and teachers. They are beginning to reach decisions about their potential in the vocational field. Apparently the community is meeting the needs expressed in the 1947 study.   The importance of search for self is based upon fear of failure in the rapidly shifting society.   An observation highly relevant to the purposes of the junior high school is the following: The adolescent has had no childhood during which freedom to explore his physical world would have provided a cognitive mass for future learning.

3013.   Byers, R. S.   "Articulation in the junior high school (1955)." Bulletin of the National Association of Secondary School Principals, 46(1962):416-418.

Describes how articulation can better be realized from elementary to junior high and from junior high to senior high.   Includes helpful hints for school administrators.

3014.   California Association of Secondary School Principals.   "Procedures for Appraising the Modern Junior High School." Burlingame, Calif., 1960.

This is a self-evaluation instrument for use in the junior high schools.

3015.   California Journal of Secondary Education, May 1956 and October 1957:Whole Issues.

These issues are devoted to the junior high school.

3016.   Campanale, E. H.   "An Appraisal of Elementary and
Junior High School Articulation in the Bloomington,
Indiana, Schools."   Ed.D. Dissertation, School of
Education, Indiana University, 1961.

Author compiled from the literature a list of articulation practices in junior high schools.   The list
was submitted to five junior high school principals,
who identified the practices they considered desirable, and then these were evaluated by a group of
students and teachers at the Indiana University
Laboratory School.   A final inventory of twenty-six
desirable articulation practices was obtained,
classified, and submitted to two hundred pupils and
their parents and forty-two seventh grade junior high
school teachers.   In each group 75 percent of the
respondents said that thirteen articulation practices
were applied and considered helpful: club membership, student council representatives, giving information to incoming seventh grade pupils, visits by
6th grade pupils to the junior high school, relationship in subject matter content, pupil-organized
activities, aid to seventh grade pupils early in
their careers, a continuous orientation program,
parents' visit to the junior high school, opportunities for leadership, teachers for more than one
period (block-time classes), social activities, and
parent-teacher conferences.

3017.   Chalender, R. E.   "What the junior high school
should not do."   Bulletin of the National Association
of Secondary School Principals, 47,285(1963):23-25.

1) The junior high school should not ignore the early
adolescent's burgeoning of intellectual power--
relatively uncluttered by distractions at this
age--but should make the most of it.   2) The junior
high school should not be a training ground for
senior high school teachers, counselors, and administrators.   Teachers should not be assigned to the
junior high school while awaiting transfer to the
senior high school.   A single salary schedule is
recommended for both junior and senior high school.
3) The junior high school should not attempt to be a
little senior high school.   The most frequently
stated functions of the junior high school are
exploration, integration, individualization, socialization, and guidance.   4) The junior high school
should not be a training ground for senior high
school athletic programs.   However, a well-developed
intramural program is desirable for junior high
school.   5) The junior high school should not be a
training ground for senior high school programs.
Social activities in the junior high school should be
planned for early adolescents.   6) The junior high

school should not yield to uninformed pressures. 7) The junior high school should not be required to use worn-out buildings and equipment. 8) The junior high school should not necessarily exclude grade 6. Sociological factors plus the accelerating maturity of youth mean that sixth graders may belong in a school with older rather than younger students. 9) The junior high school should not fail to take advantage of experimental programs. Too much of our work has been aimless. We must experiment, get involved with research, and keep pace with the times. 10) The junior high school should not become highly departmentalized. 11) The junior high school should not base decisions for grouping, promotion, and retention on commercial tests. Such tests should be used only as one criterion for making decisions. Teacher evaluation must not be overlooked.

3018.   Clearinghouse, October 1956:Whole Issue.

This issue is devoted to the junior high school.

3019.   Commission on Secondary Schools and Commission on Research and Service. "The Junior High School Program." Atlanta, Ga.: Southern Association of Colleges and Schools, 1958.

Although general agreement has never been reached on the most desirable size for a junior high school, most educators suggest that an optimum staff is most feasible in schools with an enrollment of 600 to 900 students. The Southern Association of Colleges and Schools recommends an average daily membership of 720 students in the junior high school, with 25 to 30 students per class in grades 7, 8, and 9 and block-time classes or core programs which include language arts, social studies, guidance, mathematics, physical education, and exploratory courses. Specialized subjects should be introduced in the ninth grade.

3020.   Commission on Secondary Schools and Commission on Research and Service. "The Junior High School Program." Atlanta, Ga.: Southern Association of Colleges and Schools, 1962.

Four basic assumptions should underlie the programs of all junior high schools: 1) The junior high school is an established and essential unit in public education. 2) The curriculum of the junior high school should be different from that of the senior high school or the elementary school. 3) The program should emphasize general education. 4) The program should be geared specifically to the problems, concerns, and interests of preadolescents and early adolescents and the impact of the society upon their lives. Paper includes sections on 1) The Growth and

Development in Boys and Girls of Junior High School
Age (physical, social, emotional, and mental development, developmental tasks). 2) Functions of the
Junior High School. 3) The Instructional Program in
the Junior High School (providing for the needs of
early adolescents, general education as the main
function of the curriculum, block-of-time instruction, required subjects, exploratory experiences,
elective courses, the cocurricular program, planning
for program improvement). 4) Organization and Administration of the Junior High School Program (personnel, core program, other administrative and organizational responsibilities). 5) Facilities for the
Junior High School (site, plant, guide for planning,
educational specifications). 6) Staffing the Junior
High School (competencies, certification, professional growth, working conditions, the principalship). 7) Evaluation in the Junior High School
(meaning and purpose of evaluation, steps in evaluation, techniques and procedures, approaches to
evaluation, criteria for evaluating the total school
program).

3021.   Commission on Secondary Schools and Commission on
Research and Service. "The Junior High School Pro-
gram." Atlanta, Ga.: Southern Association of
Colleges and Schools, 1964.

Monograph revises and updates the 1962 report (entry
3020). In Chapter 2, information is provided about
the developmental growth of preadolescents and early
adolescents with some implications for the school
program. Chapter 3 has drawn on the best thinking
regarding the basic functions of the junior high
school, and some of the unique purposes are highlighted. In Chapter 4 a design for the curriculum is
explored in some detail with specific suggestions for
the various aspects of the program. Chapter 5 provides pointed suggestions on how the program can be
organized and administered with some consideration of
the responsibilities of the principal as an instructional leader. Chapter 6 stresses the need to plan
the program first and then the facilities to house
this program. The problems involved in staffing a
junior high school are discussed in Chapter 7. Matters relating to total school evaluation and the
appraisal of growth toward objectives in the classroom are given consideration in Chapter 8. Specific
suggestions for evaluation are included.

3022.   Connecticut State Department of Education. "An
Assessment Guide for Use in Junior High Schools."
Hartford: Connecticut State Department of Education,
June, 1960.

This self-evaluation instrument is concerned with articulation, exploration, integration, differentiation, and socialization. 1) Articulation: both elementary and junior high school staffs should plan jointly for the change from one level to the next. Programs of study should be known at both levels, teachers should visit back and forth, and guidance counselors at both schools should be in constant touch with each other. At least one teacher should provide a home base for seventh grade student, with departmentalization and specialization introduced gradually, as the pupil progresses. Transition into the senior high school should have similar arrangements: interlevel planning, teacher intervisitations, counselor conferences, pupil orientation meetings and visitation, and parent orientation. 2) Exploration should be cultural, vocational, avocational, and civic. Exploratory courses should be required in grades 7 and 8 and elective in grade 9. 3) Integration: the curriculum should continue to develop skills, attitudes, ideals, and understanding established in the elementary school and broaden them for senior high school. Provisions should be made for cooperative teacher planning in the school, for relating the various subject areas, and for teacher intervisitation. 4) Differentiation: programs should be based on individual differences, intelligence, physical maturity and health, scholarly achievement, work habits, and attitudes. Teacher judgment and recommendations should be used in program planning. Classes should be planned for individual differences, transfers should be made easily when warranted, and provision should be made for challenging rapid learners, assisting those with an academic deficiency, and scheduling corrective activities for those with a physical deficiency. 5) Socialization: human relationships and human values should be stressed, and the pupil should be helped to understand himself as a person as well as his role in the school and community.

3023.   Council on Junior High School Administration. "Ten tenets of junior high school administration." Clearinghouse, 38(1964):329-333.

The ten tenets are: 1) The school must be organized for the benefit of all pupils who are able to profit from this type of education. 2) It is widely recognized that pupils of this age should have a broad program of general education. 3) Recognizing the differences among pupils of junior high school age, teachers should provide a wide variety of methods and materials for dealing with this range of differences. 4) All who come in contact with pupils of junior high school age should recognize the variations in these students' development and should provide varying

standards of accomplishment.   5) Adequate administrative staffing can be justified in many ways.   The
cost of adequate staffing may be high.   6) Exploration continues throughout life.   The junior high
school age is an especially fruitful time for
exploration, and provision should be made in the
junior high school for this type of experience.   7) A
vital guidance program should be provided to help
each pupil fulfill his potential; lip service is not
a substitute for a good guidance program.   8) Personnel services for all ages are important in organized
modern life.   The need is urgent at the junior high
school age, and adequate services should be provided.
9) A good junior high school cannot exist without a
competent staff. Our society can and should provide
such a staff.   10) Finally, everything attempted in
the junior high school should be subjected to constant and careful evaluation.   Testing in business
and industry often prevents waste and spoilage, and
in education adequate evaluation will prevent a perpetuation of ill-conceived and ineffective procedures.   The article breaks each of the ten points
down into specific goals and objectives.

3024.   Daniels, L. M. and Robinson, A. A.   "Refuting the
sterotype: academic achievement at Northwestern
Junior High School."   Negro Educational Review, 30,1
(1979):17-20.

Evaluates a project to reform Northwestern Junior
High School in Jacksonville, Florida.   Discusses
improved scores on standardized tests, less teacher
absenteeism, and strategies which effected these
improvements.   See ERIC Abstract #EJ 197 338.

3025.   Denton, W. D.   "An experiment with selected junior
high school orientation techniques."   Bulletin of the
National Association of Secondary School Principals,
46(1962):324-325.

Author studied orientation techniques used in experimental teaching with seventh grade junior high school
students.   Major findings were: 1) Guided tours and
floor plan charts are effective ways to orient new
students to the school plant.   2) The homeroom program helps orient new seventh grade students to the
routine of the junior high school.   3) The upper
class committee is not effective in orienting new
seventh grade students to the increased self-
discipline and self-direction required by the junior
high school.   4) Having students in a guidance class
report on interviews with teachers is effective in
orienting new students to departmentalized instruction.   5) Group guidance, using photographs, helps
orient new students to the larger faculty of the
junior high school.   Orientation can have long-range

implications, since oriented pupils received significantly higher ratings by teachers.

3026.   Douglass, H. R.   "Junior high schools evaluated and accredited."   Bulletin of the National Association of Secondary School Principals,   February 1963: 126.

Author writes: "Among the agencies which might be considered for carrying on accreditation are the following: 1) the regional accrediting association, 2) state departments of education, 3) state groups of secondary school principals, 4) state groups of junior high school principals, 5) a national board made up largely, if not entirely, of junior high school principals. Although evaluation by the regional accrediting association would no doubt be very helpful, it seems rather clear that a national board would most likely lead to the attainment of values and objectives for evaluations of junior high schools.   The membership of such a board should be made up largely of junior high school educators, probably appointed by the president of the National Association of Secondary School Principals, but it should also include at least one senior high school principal, one superintendent of schools, one elementary school principal, and one outstanding leader in junior high school education among professors of education."

3027.   Douglass, H. R.   "Evaluating and accrediting junior high school."   Teachers College Journal, 34, 2(1963):69-71.

Author presents purposes of accreditation as seen by junior high school principals throughout the United States.   He discusses values of accreditation, procedures in evaluation, follow-up, and financial matters.

3028.   Educational Leadership, May 1957:Whole Issue.

This special issue is devoted to the junior high school.

3029.   Educational Research Council of Greater Cleveland. "Junior High School Leadership Conference, 1960:   A Summary Report." Cleveland, Ohio, 1960.

Discusses the status and future of middle school education, with emphasis on the leadership role of principals and teachers.

3030.   Elicker, P. E.   The Administration of Junior and Senior High Schools.   Englewood Cliffs, N. J.: Prentice-Hall, 1964.

Considers the total program through schedule building in the junior high years.

3031.   Ellis, J. R.   "Momentum in the junior high school movement." Teachers College Journal, 34,2(1962):43.

An American organizational innovation only a little more than fifty years old, the junior high school has experienced phenomenal growth in size and to a lesser extent in form and function as an educational program based on the uniqueness of the age group being served.   Spending much of its time in the shadow of schools serving students of other ages, less bound by custom and tradition and often freer than they of uninformed criticism by people little qualified to control the educational process, the junior high school has stimulated the development of many excellent practices and now holds the promise of becoming the leader and the locale for many of the professional and creative advances needed in education today.

3032.   Everhart, R. B. "The fabric of meaning in a junior high school." Theory Into Practice, 18,3(1979):152-157.

In this holistic study of a junior high school environment, author sees a disparity between student and teacher cultures as well as widely differing views between students and teachers about the role and importance of instruction in the school day. See ERIC Abstract #EJ 215 119.

3033.   George, P.   "The Roosevelt Program: Changing Patterns in Education at Roosevelt Junior High School." Oregon School Study Council Bulletin, vol. 16, no. 6. Eugene: Oregon School Study Council, University of Oregon, Field Training and Service Bureau, ERIC Doc. ED 075 901, February, 1973.

Chronicles the first years of an experimental program: its background, history, philosophy, goals, and evaluation.

3034.   Grambs, J. D., Noyce, C. G., Patterson, F., and Robertson, J. C.   "The Junior High School We Need." Washington, D.C.:   Association for Supervision and Curriculum Development, Commission on Secondary Curriculum, 1961.

Chapters are: 1) Current Interests in the Junior High School.   2) The Adolescent of Today and Tomorrow.   3) The Junior High School: Its Development. 4) The Junior High School Today.   5) The Junior High School of the Future.   6) Moving toward the Junior High School We Need.   Monograph states that a good junior high school should: 1) be of moderate size, 2) have a well-stocked library staffed by a profes- sional librarian, 3) provide ample guidance services, 4) offer block-of-time instruction each year for the three years so that one teacher will have a group of children for a substantial period, 5) maintain flexi- bility of scheduling, 6) be staffed with teachers prepared for junior high school teaching and devoted to junior high school aged students, 7) provide help for teachers by principals, supervisory staff, and clerical personnel, 8) provide a modern instructional program in subject areas, 9) have adequate physical education programs, 10) have ample laboratory and workshop facilities, and 11) have an established, reasonable teacher load. The junior high of the future should: 1) continue to recognize the develop- ment of democratic values as its central commitment, 2) experiment with new instructional ideas, 3) seek continually to improve time arrangements for effec- tive learning and teaching, 4) plan instruction specifically for the junior high school years, 5) be ungraded, 6) incorporate routines that encourage civility in living, 7) use varying instructional procedures, 8) provide many means for the student to see himself as a significant individual in a larger world setting, and 9) extend the school year to provide a richer and more effective educational program.

3035.   Gruhn, W. T. and   Douglass, H. R.   The Modern Junior High School. New York: Ronald Press, 1947.

The authors give an adequate statement of the his- tory, philosophy, and functions of the junior high school, discuss prevailing nationwide educational practices in the junior high school, and suggest and describe improved programs and procedures not yet common in the typical school.

3036.   Hamm, R. L. "Junior high school: the uniquely American institution." Junior High School Newsletter, 4,1(1966):1.

The junior high school is an expression of the both/and rationale of John Dewey: it strives for a balance between skills of a specific kind and general understandings. In stressing both general education and special education without favoring either, the junior high school is a synthesis--a compromise, a transition--for clientele that is both adult and youngster at this stage of growth. The functions of the junior high school are consistent with pragmatic philosophy: in contrast to the proliferation of courses offered in the comprehensive high school, the junior high school emphasizes integration of learning experiences. In the junior high school years, a student is given opportunity to explore, to discover specialized interests, aptitudes, and abilities-- vocationally, socially, and culturally. Some of the major aims of junior high school are definite expressions of the pragmatic orientation: 1) to promote the physical well-being of students through a well-balanced physical education and health program, 2) to provide a climate for students to understand themselves--their emotions, their body, their think- ing and the society in which they live, 3) to explore the wide range of vocational and avocational alterna- tives, both in the local community and in the large community, 4) to provide opportunity for students to be involved in decision making and to encourage open-mindedness and tentativeness in thinking, 5) to continue work in the fundamental processes begun in the elementary school and to capitalize on individual specialties and skills.   In summary, the junior high school is the best representative in American educa- tion of pragmatic philosophy, not only in terms of when and where it evolved but in terms of its philo- sophical background, its aims, and its functions.

3037.   Harrington, H. L. "Detroit expands its junior high school program."   Bulletin of the National Associa- tion of Secondary School Principals,   February 1962: 36-38.

The first assistant superintendent of the Detroit Public Schools describes how very large junior high schools with complete departmental programs were modified in building and population size.

3038.   High School Journal, December 1956 and January 1960:Whole Issues.

These issues are devoted to the junior high school.

3039.   Hughes, D. E., et al.   "Seventh Grade Expanded Program at Northeast Junior High, 1970-71."   Minnea- polis Public Schools, Minnesota Department of Research and Evaluation, May, 1972.

Discusses an expanded seventh grade program developed from a proposal of the guidance department.   The idea was to change the role of the counselor to emphasize program coordination and the teacher-counselor work- ing relationship, to organize the program into smaller units based on more interstaff planning, and to provide students with more input into program development.   A one-week summer workshop was provided for educators in this program as well as an addi- tional counselor.   Increased teacher-counselor and teacher-teacher communication during the school year produced a number of objectives and activities,

including a new report grading system, student elective units, circle meetings in the classrooms, coordination of instruction between subject areas, less
objective testing, and greater use of discussion/
inquiry teaching methods. At the end of the year 81
percent of the teachers rated the counselors in this
school as very helpful.

3040.   Johnson, M., Jr. "The dynamic junior high school."
Bulletin of the National Association of Secondary
School Principals, 48(1964):119-128.

Gives useful suggestions for principals to improve
their junior high programs and curriculum.

3041.   Koos, L. B. Junior High School Trends. New York:
Harper and Bros., 1955.

This book is concerned with reorganizing education
for early adolescents and includes sections on the
growth, status, and purposes of reorganization, grade
grouping, curriculum, retreat from departmentalization, extra-class activities, guidance, differentiation, and prospects of further reorganization. It
contains a description of the core curriculum, block-
time scheduling, athletics in the junior high grades,
gifted pupils, needs of slow learners and other
exceptional groups, ability grouping, and remedial
instruction. While a variety of grade groupings can
serve the purposes of reorganization, three ideas
seem preeminent. First, the reorganized secondary
school, whatever the pattern of grades, should reach
down to the beginning of adolescence, which is about
the twelfth year of age, although boys are known to
lag behind girls on this criterion. Second, reorganization should span the early adolescent years.
This means that the grade grouping should include
three-year or four-year junior high schools or six-
year secondary schools on a 3-3 or undivided basis.
This criterion discredits the 6-2-4 plan, although it
must be admitted that reorganization can be accomplished under this arrangement, which is at least
preferable to the 8-4 pattern. Third, whatever the
grade grouping, provisions should be made to serve
the needs of early adolescents. There is no reason
why these provisions should differ in extent or
nature in the different patterns.

3042.   Lee, F.   "Opening up a junior high school."
Education Canada, 13,3(1973):28-32.

Discusses the flexible plant and program of the
MacDonald Drive Junior High School in St. Johns,
Newfoundland, which was built in 1969 to house students in grades 7-8-9 together. The school placed
great emphasis on providing the basic facilities in a

flexible environment so that the principal and staff would have freedom to develop a program that could respond to changing educational ideas and needs. The school is designed to carry out a philosophy of continuous progress with an emphasis on learning rather than teaching and on the individual process of discovery rather than rote memorization.

3043.   Liederman, E.   "The function of today's junior high schools."   Bulletin of the National Association of Secondary School Principals, 35(1951):151-158.

Discusses certain developments in junior high schools of New York City, namely, a project in character training, work in shops and creative expression, and curriculum changes for integrated learning.

3044.   Long, F. E.   "Trends in junior high school education."   Bulletin of the National Association of Secondary School Principals, 35(1951):143-151.

Summarizes trends in guidance, curriculum, marking and reporting, athletics, and other aspects of the junior high school program.

3045.   Lounsbury, J. H.   "What keeps junior from growing up?"   Clearinghouse, 34(1960):301-303.

Considers five major conditions which hamper the full development of the present junior high school.

3046.   Lounsbury, J. H.   "So far, so good: the junior high school."   Teachers College Journal, 34,2(1966): 44-46.

The junior high school story now covers well over half the century, yet it is by no means finished. As a matter of fact, it lies more in the future than in the past. But the story of the American junior high school is already a success story very much in keeping with the traditions of this country. To refer to the "American junior high school" is perhaps redundant, for the junior high school is an "all-American" institution.   Unlike other school types, it was developed in America by Americans for educational situations that were particularly related to our own culture. And though it no longer remains exclusively an American school unit, the junior high school is still predominantly located in this country. Now that a renaissance of junior high school education is well under way, it behooves all educators to review the junior high school story. The article goes on to present the philosophy and purposes of junior high school education. A good junior high school curriculum ought to 1) continue and extend the general education program of the elementary schools, 2) provide for a transition between the organization and approach of the elementary school and the senior high school, 3) provide for continued development in the basic skills, 4) introduce new subject areas and additional specialization within basic areas, 5) provide opportunities to discover and pursue pupils' special interests and aptitudes, 6) provide experiences to guide the rapid physical development characteristics of early adolescence, 7) provide experiences that develop the social competence needed for young manhood and womanhood, 8) provide experiences that help students develop values and build their philosophies of life, 9) provide ample opportunities for self-management and the development of leadership under supervision.

3047.   Malm, M. "The junior high school period: time for a unique educational program." Teachers College Journal, 34,2(1962):46-50.

The junior high school years make more demands on the school than perhaps any other student age period does. Rapid change, both physical and psychological, bring such a diversity of new interests, possibilities, and problems that it takes unusual insight to understand them and genuine creativity to devise educational procedures that will best fit them. Author discusses physical change, the peer culture, independence, and heterosexual behavior and says the most important point to remember about the junior high school boy or girl is this: basic to all that we should do for him is that we understand him. All adults, adolescents, and children want to be understood. That is, they want others to see life, for the moment at least, through their eyes. At the same time, it is also essential that we try to achieve insight into the true causes and relationships affecting the personality of the young adolescent boy or girl. Either kind of understanding is difficult for the adult. Students of 12, 13 and 14 are at a stage of life where they definitely disagree with much adult behavior toward them, and the resultant friction interferes with mutual understanding. In addition, they have many characteristics that make it difficult to get close to them or to penetrate the mask of their outward behavior. They are inconsistent, secretive, touchy, swayed by feelings not understood, defensive, eager to put on a good front, seemingly self-centered. It is essential, nonetheless, that more than a casual effort be made by teachers and schools to comprehend the viewpoints of this age and to look below the surface of the youngster's conduct. There should be careful observation, faculty study both of the period and of their

individual students, and a genuine effort to understand an age group far enough away in years and in
reactions to be something of a mystery.

3048.   Manlove, D. C. and McGlasson, M. A. "Principles
and Standards for Junior High School Evaluation."
Bulletin of the School of Education. Bloomington:
Indiana University, Division of Research and Field
Service, 1965.

Bulletin discusses 1) a policy statement on junior
high school accreditation, 2) organizations for
junior high school education, 3) a junior high school
philosophy, 4) the needs of the individual as a guide
to developing a junior high school program, and 7)
principles and standards for school community, curriculum, staff, instructional media center, guidance
services, student activities, the physical plant,
administration, and recommended criteria development.

3049.   McGlasson, M. "Let's think through proposals for
junior high school accreditation." Bulletin of the
National Association for Secondary School Principals,
48(1964):69-75.

Presents the rationale behind various components of
junior high accreditation.

3050.   Mortimore, D. E., et al. "The Emergence and
Development of a Radically Innovative Junior High
School Program." Salem: Oregon Association for
Supervision and Curriculum Development, ERIC Doc. ED
083 669, October, 1973.

This discussion of the first three years of an innovative program at Theodore Roosevelt Junior High
School in Eugene, Oregon includes 1) background, 2)
formal and informal development of the program, 3)
implementation of the program, 4) the first year of
operation, and 5) problems and solutions. An evaluation is included with conclusions reached in the
workshops and a short bibliography. See ERIC
Abstract #ED 083 669.

3051.   Nation's Schools magazine. "Don't copy the senior
high's mistakes." Nation's Schools, 75(1965):33.

Discusses many differences between the junior high
and the senior high in Riverton, Wyoming.

3052.   National Association of Secondary School Principals. "Evaluation in the secondary school." Bulletin of the National Association of Secondary School
Principals, 32(1948):154.

Of special interest to junior high school teachers, this is a useful statement about how evaluating criteria are used.

3053.   Office of Secondary and Vocational Education, St. Paul, Minn. "The organization and curriculum of the new junior high schools in St. Paul." The Schools, Fall 1958:8-9.

Junior high school leaders in St. Paul have displayed imagination and flexibility in providing for exploration in the curriculum. All regular classes are scheduled four days a week in order to make it possible to broaden the program. A special interest activity is included for one hour a week in part of the free time. Students select three activities in each of the three years in junior high school, giving them a total of nine exploration activities in the junior high school years. More than fifty offerings are organized in five areas: 1) Exploring Career Opportunities. 2) Exploring Recreational Opportunities in the Home. 3) Exploring Recreational Activities in the School. 4) Exploring Useful Hobbies. 5) Exploring Opportunities for Better Human Relationships. The plan combines English and social studies into core classes under one teacher who meets fewer pupils and therefore has time for three to four guidance periods per week for parent and pupil conferences in addition to preparation periods. Core teachers perform counseling duties at a level just below that of a trained counselor for all students in their core classes.

3054.   Osmon, R. V. "Junior high schools at the crossroads." School and Community, 54(1967):14-15.

What type of school should the junior high school be? Research in adolescent psychology and school administration has not given clearcut, concise answers. Article includes opinions from experts in this area, including Margaret Mead, W. W. Wattenberg, James Conant, and William Alexander. Author stresses that a complete teacher must have a good working knowledge of 1) the principles of growth and development of the early adolescent years, 2) the nature and functions of the junior high as a separate school, 3) the guidance program and how it affects the junior high pupil, 4) the teaching of reading in the upper elementary levels, 5) the teaching of study skills to slow learners, and 6) the preventive and constructive approach to classroom discipline. The single greatest problem that remains is an effective evaluation and the development of certain accepted understandings concerning what we believe about junior high school programs.

3055.   Phi Delta Kappan magazine. "Are role models better live than dead?"   Phi Delta Kappan, 60,1(1978):
58-59.

Discusses the Steve Garvey Junior High School,
including the controversy over changing the name from
Lincoln Junior High and the innovative programming of
the principal, Dr. Robert Edwards.

3056.   Remmers, H. H. and   Bauernfeind, R. H.   Junior
Inventory--Form S.   Rev. ed. Chicago: Science
Research Associates, 1957.

This is a problem checklist designed for use with
children in grades 4 to 8. It is similar in purpose
to the Mooney Problem Checklist designed for the
junior-senior high school level.

3057.   Reynolds, L. J. and Van Noy, F. "A Description
of Educational Change within a Selected Junior High
School. A Working Paper."   Reprints and Occasional
Papers Series. Eugene: University of Oregon, Center
for Advanced Study of Educational Administration,
ERIC Doc. ED 057 444, October, 1970.

This report is part of a broader project--the formulation of a conceptual language for the study of
educational innovation. Authors discuss a big-city
junior high school where an attempt at institution-
wide changes stemmed from a basic philosophical
position adopted by the school administration and
staff. The program was charged with helping each
student become his own agent, become personally
involved in his learning, develop confidence in
himself and others, and find true satisfaction in
learning. Report discusses scheduling changes, the
house, class organization and content, program continuity, grade reports, personnel utilization,
teacher role change, student-initiated classes, and
time and energy demands on the staff.

3058.   Rogers, H. J. "The best type of schools for young
adolescents." California Journal of Secondary Education, 30(1957):20-23.

Discusses junior high school pupils, teachers, curriculum, design, and implementing the curriculum.
The three-year junior high school has successfully
withstood the test of forty years and has become an
accepted part of the standard school district organization throughout the nation. It is the best type of
school to meet the needs of young adolescents. A
good junior high school program is possible in a
school with as few as five hundred. The optimum size
for a junior high school depends on factors such as
size of the area served by the school, the type of

student body, whether students are promoted annually or semiannually, and efficient utilization of the school plant. Article stresses the belief that the junior high school is a distinct and essential element of secondary education.

3059.   Rosser, M. A.   "Junior high school program in Raleigh."   Bulletin of the National Association of Secondary School Principals, 43(1959):157-162.

Describes practices in Raleigh junior high schools.

3060.   Samuelson, E. V.   "The accreditation of junior high schools by the North Central Association of Colleges and Secondary Schools."   North Central Association Quarterly, 37(1963):233-236.

Describes means by which junior high schools are accredited.

3061.   Swenson, G. A.   "The Brookhurst junior high school program."   In Beggs, D. W., III, and Buffie, E. G. (Eds.), Independent Study: Bold New Venture.   Bloomington: Indiana University Press, 1965.

Chapter 6 deals with the Brookhurst Junior High School Program in Anaheim, California.   Junior high school leaders must recognize and accept the needs and characteristics of the junior high school aged pupil and design a program to eliminate the present evils of a system that is organized on the following assumptions: 1) All subjects in the junior high school should be given equal time regardless of the value placed upon them by society.   2) All students are the same in abilities, needs, and interests.   The concept behind the time schedule of the traditional school is that every child needs exactly the same number of minutes of instruction in each subject as every other child even though a pupil with third grade reading ability may be the same age as another reading at the tenth grade level.   3) Students grow uniformly, so a new master schedule is not necessary.   4) Administrators know best and should dole out time, number of students, facilities, and methodology to the teacher regardless of his or her professional training and ability.   5) All teachers possess with equal efficiency and effectiveness those abilities necessary for a quality instructional program.   6) Junior high school age youngsters are not mature enough to make decisions regarding the use they will make of their time during the school day.   The article goes on to attack these assumptions by showing how an independent study program worked at this junior high.

3062.   Teachers College Record, May 1956:Whole Issue.

Issue is devoted to the junior high school.

3063.   Texas Study of Secondary Education.   "Characteristics of Junior High School Pupils." Research Study
21. Austin: University of Texas, 1954.

The junior high school pupil 1) is much concerned
about his relationship with other people (article
discusses ways in which these characteristics are
revealed and some ways schools meet these situations), 2) shows increased curiosity about himself in
his environment, 3) has to adjust to rapid and pro-
found body changes, 4) tries to achieve independence
and at the same time maintain security, 5) strives
for personal values in his social setting, 6) desires
many outlets for expressing his ideas and feelings,
7) needs to acquire knowledge and skills sufficient
to permit him to proceed on his own, and 8) wants to
participate as a responsible member in larger social
groups. The Texas Study of Secondary Education is
the first comprehensive list of evaluative criteria
for junior high schools.

3064.   Texas Study of Secondary Education.   "Criteria for
Evaluating Junior High Schools." Research Study 37.
Austin: University of Texas, 1963.

This is a self-evaluation instrument for use in the
junior high school.

3065.   Thayer, L. Y. "What educational program is needed
in the junior high school?" Bulletin of the National
Association of Secondary School Principals, 41(1957):
94-98.

Describes various educational programs used in junior
high schools.

3066.   Tompkins, E. and   Roe, V.   "The two-year junior
high school." Bulletin of the National Association
of Secondary School Principals, September 1957:27-43.

At the time this article was printed (1957), more
than 21 percent of all junior high schools in the
United States were two-year schools, and the Committee on Junior High School Education of the
National Association of Secondary School Principals
developed this report on such junior high schools. A
letter requesting information on status, organization, and principal's preference for type of organization was sent to all two-year junior high schools
known to be in existence in 1952. Responses provided
data on the number of two-year junior high schools
responding (by grades and by size of enrollment in

each state), number of years a two-year junior high
school has been in existence, grades for which present two-year junior high school building was constructed (by state), reasons for adoption of two-year
junior high school organization, number of two-year
junior high schools contemplating change to another
type of junior high organization (by state), and
preference for junior high school organization
expressed by principals of two-year junior high
schools (by state).

3067.   Trump, J. L. "New directions to quality education
in the junior high school." Bulletin of the National
Association of Secondary School Principals, September
1961:25-30.

In this 1961 article author predicted the junior high
school of the future would 1) pay better attention to
individual differences among students, 2) organize
teaching teams to recognize individual differences
among teachers and improve use of professional staff
competences, 3) make fuller use of modern technological aids to instruction, and 4) break the lockstep of
rigid organization of time, content, and space
through more flexible scheduling. The ideas presented in this article are discussed more in detail
in the following three National Association of
Secondary School Principal publications: 1) "Images
of the Future: A New Approach to the Secondary
School." 2) "New Directions to Quality Education:
The Secondary School Tomorrow." 3) "Focus on Change:
Guide to Better Schools."

3068.   Trump, J. L. "Developing a more dynamic junior
high school program." Educational Forum, 28(1964):
129-143.

Emphasizes that criteria different from those typically used in today's evaluation scheme can stimulate
a more dynamic junior high school program. Qualitative standards of evaluation need to supplement quantitative data. Author suggests ten essentially qualitative criteria that arise from different applications of quantifiable data. Above all, they are
flexible and developmental rather than static, and
they emphasize constant searching for better ways of
doing things than basing excellence on average performances in large numbers of schools. These criteria are open-ended rather than closed. They
suggest that a given school compare itself with its
past performance rather than mainly with the current
performance of other schools. Author discusses the
individual criteria of a dynamic junior high program:
1) Some oft-repeated goals that are hard for students
to achieve in today's schools are taken seriously and
present practices are changed to help students

develop more personal responsibility for learning, to
recognize individual differences among students, to
improve students' communication, problem-solving, and
critical thinking skills, and to develop better
interpersonal relations among students.   2) The
curriculum furnishes essential content in all areas
of human knowledge, keeps students continuously in
contact with all the areas, stimulates student interests and talents, encourages creativity, and provides
opportunities for studies in depth.   3) Extra-class
activities are integrated with the curriculum.   4)
The program takes advantage of and recognizes the
limitations of technical devices that can aid the
teaching/learning process.   5) Educational facilities
are systematically reexamined to obtain maximum
contributions to the teaching/learning process.   6)
Decisions on reducing expenditures in some areas
while increasing them in others are based on logic
and research about the effects of these financial
changes on education.   7) The program creates an
improved image of teaching as a profession through
such activities as separating what professional
teachers must do and what may be done by clerks,
instruction assistants, and general aides, providing
teachers with technical devices and showing them how
to use such devices, giving teachers time for activities like keeping up to date, conferring with
colleagues, preparing materials, and improving
techniques of instruction and evaluation.

3069.   Van Til, W., Vars, G. F., and Lounsbury, J. H.
Modern Education for the Junior High School Years.
New York: Bobbs-Merrill Co., 1961.

Textbook on junior high schools has these chapters on
1) The Birth and Background of the Junior High
School.   2) The Original and Changing Functions of
the Junior High School.   3.) Programs, Policies, and
Practices in the Junior High School of the 1950s.   4)
The Growth of the Junior High School Movement.   5)
Organizing the Curriculum for Instruction.   6) Influence of Social Realities on the Program.   7) Influ-
ence of the Personal and Social Needs of Early
Adolescents on the Program.   8) Influence of Demo-
cratic Values on the Program.   9) Core in Action.
10) Preplanning for Core Teaching.   11) Problem-
centered Teaching.   12) Developing Basic Skills in a
Core Program.   13) Literature and Creative Writing in
the Arts in a Core Program.   14) Science and
Mathematics.   15) Exploration through Industrial
Arts, Homemaking, Arts and Crafts, and Music.   16)
Physical Education, Foreign Languages, and Business
Education.   17) Providing for Guidance in Exceptional
Children.   18) Developing the Cocurricular and
Activity Program.   19) Obtaining and Evaluating
Instructional Materials.   20) Organizing and Using

Instructional Materials. 21) Evaluation and Reporting. 22) A Junior High School Program for the 1960s.

3070.   Wagner, G. "What schools are doing: junior high
trends." Education, 86(1965):57-61.

Describes exemplary middle grades programs in various
areas of the United States.

3071.   Whyte, W. "Markles Flats Junior High School: A
Project of the Ithaca School System and the Human
Affairs Program of Cornell University." Ithaca,
N.Y.: Ithaca Public Schools, New York, ERIC Doc. ED
069 575, 1971.

Discusses the rationale, objectives, description,
evaluation, and plans of an alternative school, a
joint effort of the Ithaca Public School System and
the Human Affairs Program of Cornell University. The
aim is for the school's eighty-five students to grow
individually and in relation to fellow human beings.
The school classroom is both the community and the
world at large. Article discusses student goals,
evaluation, the student body, selection of teaching
assistants, separate location, financing, Cornell
academic credit, and plans for continuation of the
school. The first year is discussed in sections on
organization and leadership, drifting versus
learning, disciplinary problems, and community
relations.

4

Guidance Programs

4001. Abramowitz, M. W. "Values clarification in junior high school." Educational Leadership, 29(1972):621-626.

Discusses values clarification exercises for junior high school students, including: 1) "I love to do..." 2) alternative search, 3) values voting, 4) the continuum, and 5) rank order.

4002. Alessi, S. J. and Toepfer, C. F. Guidance in the Middle School: the Teacher-Counselor Team. Dissemination Services on the Middle Grades, vol. 2, no. 7. Springfield, Mass.: Educational Leadership Institute, 1971.

The lack of objectives, preplanning, and definition of role which often characterize a school district's reorganization to a middle school structure become of critical importance when one considers the function of guidance. A successful counseling program cannot be established unless time is taken to identify the educational and developmental needs of youngsters. And even if such identification is accomplished, it is meaningless unless time is available for cooperative planning between teachers and guidance counselors. Only then might a preventive guidance program be devised, one which removes the minor administrative duties from the counselor's job and which carefully considers the needs of the middle school student. An effective way to implement such a program is to take the responsibility for first level and entry guidance functions from the counselor and place it with the teacher. Ideally, a period of guidance activities conducted by a classroom teacher will be a part of each student's daily schedule. The period will be designated the home base, the teacher a home-base teacher. It is this teacher, one who meets his students daily, who will assume the responsibility for first level guidance functions. The home-base teacher provides a logical interface between the self-contained classroom teacher of the elementary school and the predominantly administrative homeroom teacher of the senior high school. Possibilities for individual and group activities within the home-base setting are limitless. In fact, the situation seems ideal for the practice of student-teacher planning and planning for emerging needs. Initial activities might involve orientation and development of expectations. Later activities might include: 1) planning developmental and remedial sequences for individuals and small groups with similar needs, 2) planning student programs, 3) teaching study and learning skills, 4) class discussions and explorations of personal concerns common to emerging adolescents (distress over physical awkwardness and delayed early pubescence; curiosity about emerging drives, feelings, and biological capacities; disillusionment over lost childhood values and institutions; disappointment over newly perceived adult foibles and inconsistencies; boy-girl relationships; uncertainties about future adolescent and adult roles), 5) class discussions and activities to help students develop a personal value system.

4003.   Association for Supervision and Curriculum Development. Fostering Mental Health. Washington, D.C., 1950.

Book contains a section on guidance for junior high youth.

4004.   Baruth, L. G. and Phillips, M. W. "Bibliotherapy and the school counselor." School Counselor, 23,3 (1976):191-199.

Discusses how a counselor can use written materials for a therapeutic purpose and gives the example of a young adolescent reading books about children whose parents are getting divorced when that student is in the same situation. "Books can provide a source of psychological relief from the various pressures and concerns that stem from the things that happen to children." Bibliotheraphy can be used to solve problems and help a child make a satisfactory adjustment to some trying future situation. The author suggests books to be read by children involved in: delinquency, divorce, being handicapped, being orphaned, death or sickness, family relationships, and peer relationships.

4005.   Beals, L. M. "The guidance program in Colin Kelly
Junior High School." Bulletin of the National Association of Secondary School Principals, 34(1950):
248-257.

A principal's description of the guidance program in
a five-hundred-student junior high school in Eugene,
Oregon.

4006.   Beavers, W. S. "Effect of Two Counseling Treat-
ments upon the Task-Oriented Behavior of Seventh
Grade Students." Illinois State University, Normal.
Paper presented at American Personnel and Guidance
Association Convention, Atlantic City, N.J., April,
1971.

Author studied insight/relationship counseling as
practiced by two experienced school counselors and
systematic counseling by two counselors who had
participated in an in-service training program using
teaching/learning units, flow charts, and videotapes
developed at the Michigan State University School
Counselor Training Program. Behavioral objectives
were emphasized throughout the training in systematic
counseling. Subjects for the experiment were randomly selected and assigned to these four counselors
and to another counselor who had a control group that
received no direct counseling. The students participated in eight counseling sessions over ten weeks.
The students had been identified by teachers as
having little interest in task-oriented behaviors; in
the counseling, each was assigned a task. The subjects were videotaped in English and social studies
classes and evaluated on a five-point scale. 1) High
Task Orientation: the pupil reads, writes, figures,
seeks assistance and information, and engages in
other activities to complete tasks assigned by the
teacher. 2) Task Orientation: the pupil prepares
for work by getting out materials and arranging
materials. 3) Neutral Behavior: too few cues to
permit a decision. 4) Nontask Orientation: pupils
sit quietly, look into space, play with objects,
stare at other pupils, and rock back and forth in
chair. 5) Low Task Orientation: pupils engage in
horseplay or talking to other pupils. The study
showed no significant differences between the systematic counseling and insight/relationship counseling
treatment on any of the measures. However, a significant difference, favoring the systematic counseling
group, was found in the task-oriented behavior rating
between the systematic counseling group and the no-
contact control group. Authors conclude that the
most important finding is that systematic counseling
is an effective approach for helping students improve
task-oriented behaviors, and it is in the field of

in-service training that the results of this study
could have the most far-reaching implications.

4007.   Bergmann, S. P. "Designing and Implementing a
Drama-Guidance Model to Enhance the Self-concepts of
Transescents." Kent State University, Kent, Ohio,
1976.

This model, tested in a middle school in northeast
Ohio, includes preparation for two dramatic performances as well as guidance sessions following each
day's work. The goals of the model were based on the
needs of the transescent, including the building of a
group rapport among the cast and crew. The study
includes case studies of eight transescents involved
in the drama class. The most significant finding is
that the model is practical and usable for middle
school teachers.

4008.   Bohlinger, T. "Implementing a comprehensive
guidance program in the middle school." Bulletin of
the National Association of Secondary School Principals, 61,410(1977):65-73.

Establishing an appropriate guidance program for the
middle school is at best a difficult task. This
article takes a look at the components necessary that
principals can use to implement the comprehensive
model proposed. Author discusses the discrepancy
between guidance as described in the literature and
practiced in middle schools on the one hand and the
comprehensive guidance model on the other. The
counselor component is vital in this middle school
model, as the counselor contributes guidance and
counseling expertise. Other components include the
advisor, teacher-student interaction, peer counseling, and the exploratory program. Author presents
stages to implement the model: 1) the search stage:
awareness of the new idea, 2) feasibility stage:
make preliminary decision to initiate change, 3) seek
additional information, 4) analyze population of
faculty and students, 5) do preliminary cost benefits
analysis, 6) sample community reaction, 7) discuss
program with supervisors, 8) the unfreezing stage:
sensitize faculty, 9) present specific proposed
guidance program to faculty, 10) appoint task groups,
11) discuss task group recommendations, 12) develop
budget and order material, 13) hold in-service
training, 14) inform community, 15) pilot stage:
begin pilot operation, and 16) evaluate pilot
project.

4009.   Boy, A. and Pine, G. Client Centered Counseling in
the Secondary School. Boston: Houghton-Mifflin Co.,
1963.

Describes details of organizing and carrying out a complete guidance program in a junior high school as a part of a districtwide program of pupil personnel services.

4010.   Brod, P. "Guidance Services in the Functioning Middle School." Paper presented at American Personnel and Guidance Association Convention, Detroit, Mich., April 7-11. Washington, D.C.: American Personnel and Guidance Association, ERIC Doc. ED 022 231, 1968.

This study concerns not only guidance but the general functioning of middle schools. Author sent question-naires to more than a thousand middle schools throughout the country and received five hundred responses. Of these, 385 schools consisted of grades 5-8 or 6-8. Author states the following conclusions: 1) The middle school is an overwhelming success in operation. 2) Because of the age grouping and release of secondary school pressure, the philosophy of a transitional school has been translated effec-tively into practice. 3) The age grouping and edu-cational philosophy requires a different focus for guidance counselor's activities and training. 4) Guidelines for preparation of middle school coun-selors are needed. Author states that until the time of her study (1968), most discussions of the middle school were based either on theoretical speculations or the practical experiences of one school or school system. She feels this study offers factual data about the functioning of middle schools throughout the country and has a wide range of applicability.

4011.   Brough, J. R. "A profile of junior high school counseling." School Counselor, 17,1(1969):67-72.

As a counselor in a three-year junior high school in an affluent suburb of Minneapolis, the writer was responsible for 450 seventh grade students and remained with them through grades 7, 8, and 9. This study was based on the routine procedure of writing case notes for each interview with each student, resulting in a three-year longitudinal description of counseling interview content. Cumulative case conference notes for 154 girls and 163 boys were analyzed in terms of frequency and type of interview content. Study suggests that counselors at this level ought to expect to have counseling contacts with almost all of the students, to have extended or continuing reviews with many, and to be involved in a full spectrum of normal adolescent conflicts. The frequency of interviews was higher for girls than for boys at all grade levels, and twice as many girls as boys had more than six interviews over the three-year period. The three major interview areas were educational/vocational planning, general achievement, and personal social development.

4012.   Casteel, J. D., Corbett, L. H., Corbett, W. T., Jr., and Stahl, R. J. "Valuing Exercises for the Middle School." Resource Monograph 11. Gainesville: University of Florida, College of Education, Research and Development, P. K. Yonge Laboratory School, March, 1974.

Value sheets are carefully planned and written activities designed to elicit from students writing that clarifies their values. The value sheets may be written in the standard format, forced choice format, affirmative format, rank-order format, classification format, and criterion format. This monograph describes the elements of the value sheet and four interrogative models (empirical, relational, valuing, and feeling). It includes samples of the six formats. Authors stress that values clarification lends itself to logical systematic thought, and they present samples of the valuing exercises in social studies units focusing on the bill of rights, the topic of justice, and the concept of due process. Included also are questions to start discussion and guides for the student.

4013.   Castore, G. F.   Action Language in Junior High Groups. New York: Vantage Press, 1977.

Book describes a program for interactive groups of junior high school aged students. Author calls the program a major step toward the integration of human personality. It begins with nonverbal communication and adds increasing amounts of verbal communication, a process that can change human behavior. Book chapters are: 1) The Student in Junior High School. 2) Action Language. 3) Views and Attitudes. 4) Organizing a Group. 5) The Role of the Group Counselor. 6) Evaluation. 7) Rationale. 8) Effects Upon Individual School Staff Members. 9) Broader Effects of Groups on the School as a Unit. 10) Summary.

4014.   Center for Early Adolescence. "Young Adolescents as Peer Counselors: A Resource List." Chapel Hill: Center for Early Adolescence, University of North Carolina at Chapel Hill, Suite 223, Carr Mill Mall, Carrboro, N.C. 27510, 1979.

Resource list describes the following programs: 1) Adolescents as Peer Counselors (Pasadena Planned Parenthood, Pasadena, California). 2) Discovery: Peer Program (Wake County Public School System, Raleigh, North Carolina). 3) Models for Group Counseling in the Middle School (Gwinnet County School System, Snellville, Georgia). 4) The Palo

Alto Peer Counseling Program (Palo Alto Unified School District, Palo Alto, California). 5) Peer Counseling (Indian Hill High School, Cincinnati, Ohio). 6) Peer Counselor Training Model (University of Northern Colorado Laboratory School, Greeley, Colorado). 7) Peer Education (Planned Parenthood of Metropolitan Washington, D.C.). 8) Peer Helping: Students Helping Students (National Conference of Christians and Jews, Memphis, Tennessee). 9) Project Healthy Babies: Chance or Choice? (March of Dimes, White Plains, New York). 10) Project P.R.O.M.I.S.E. (Baltimore, Maryland). 11) The Teenage Health Consultants Program (Peer Education Health Resources, St. Paul, Minnesota). A list of books and articles is also included.

4015.   Clark, L. H., Klein, R. L., and Burks, J. B. The American Secondary School Curriculum. New York: Macmillan, 1965.

The following list of guidance concerns indicates the expansion of the guidance program at the junior high level: 1) admission and school placement, 2) orientation at successive educational levels, 3) assisting in self-understanding, in understanding environmental opportunities and demands, and in making life plans and adjustments, 4) vocational guidance, 5) educational guidance, 6) planning an educational program, 7) extracurricular programs, 8) students as junior citizens, 9) housing, 10) achieving physical and mental fitness, 11) guidance in learning to learn and in developing a value system and self-discipline, 12) identification and treatment of the exceptional, 13) placement and follow-up.

4016.   Costar, J. W. "Questions school board members ask about middle school guidance programs." MASB Journal, September 1972:26-29.

Includes brief responses to some common questions about middle school guidance and counseling asked by school board members and school administrators: What are middle school pupils like? What is the purpose of the school guidance program? How are the functions of the guidance program carried out? What does a school counselor do? What special qualifications does a middle school counselor need? What do middle school pupils talk to counselors about? Do teachers provide guidance services to children? What about the child's parents? Who is responsible for directing the guidance program? Why do guidance programs seem to vary from one school system to another? What is the difference between guidance services and pupil personnel services? How much should a middle school guidance program cost?

4017.   Cottingham, H. F. and Hopke, W. E. Guidance in the Junior High School. Bloomington, Ill: McKnight and McKnight, 1961.

Guidance is the process of helping a person to develop and accept an integrated picture of himself and his role in the world of everyday living, to test his concept against reality, and to convert it into a reality with satisfaction to himself and benefit to society. The guidance process should result in the student being more capable of self-understanding and self-direction in obtaining his needs in a democratic society.

4018.   Creamer, R. C. and Creamer, J. K. "Values clarification in the middle school classroom." Contemporary Education, 49,2(1978):110-112.

Describes how students can be aided in self-fulfillment and growth through the values clarification process. See ERIC Abstract #EJ 182 409.

4019.   Detjen, M. E. F. and Detjen, E. W. Homeroom Guidance Programs for the Junior High School Years. New York: Houghton-Mifflin Co., 1940.

The homeroom is to the school what the home is to society. It is the unit around which all the activities of the school are centered. In the home-room, members who have common interests meet in an informal and intimate relationship. Here junior high school pupils are given guidance and training which cannot be obtained from books and lessons. Educators agree that the junior high school must endeavor to develop character, teach citizenship, discover interests and aptitudes, and aid pupils in successful living. In schools where no provision is made for regular guidance classes, these fundamentals of guidance must come from the homeroom teacher. This series of programs covers a different phase of guidance for each of the six terms of junior high school. The apportionment of definite topics to each group eliminates much of the unnecessary duplication and overlapping which naturally occur from year to year when each teacher independently plans his home-room activity. The selection of subjects has been made on the basis of the age, the interests, and the needs of the child in each grade. The sections are: 1) orientation program, 2) social, moral and ethical guidance, 3) recreational and cultural guidance, 4) general educational guidance, 5) vocational guidance, and 6) educational guidance. This book, though dating back to 1940, is still a valuable source of detailed suggestions, outlined in units.

4020.   Dougherty, A. M.   "Helping adolescents encounter an important developmental task."   Humanist Educator, 16,3(1978):127-132.

Describes how a counselor can help junior high students develop heterosexual relationships by helping them achieve self-awareness and a sense of being normal.   Author gives a step-by-step description of this counseling process, which is a form of group dynamics, and includes a student questionnaire used in this technique.   Drawbacks are described as well as follow-ups to the counseling.   Students will find this technique effective, enjoyable, and interesting.

4021.   Edgerly, R. F.   "Parent counseling in Norwell Junior High."   Journal of Education, 154,1(1971): 54-59.

This study showed that more than sixty percent of children whose parents were counseled achieved higher grades.   Article describes Norwell Junior High, the selection of parents and families participating in the program, the counseling sessions, results, siblings' grades, and conclusions.   Author feels that junior high school officials would be well advised to develop a full-time program in parent counseling.

4022.   Ference, C.   "Participant Observers: A Low Threat Approach to Junior High Counseling."   Paper presented at American Personnel and Guidance Association Convention, New York, March 23-26, 1975.

Describes an experimental counseling procedure in which junior high school students were required to interact with preschool youngsters as well as with each other.   Twice-weekly group counseling sessions were conducted for a nine-week period to discuss the interpersonal behavior of the preschoolers and to have the junior high students relate these to their own behaviors.   The purpose of the procedure was increased self-understanding and understanding of others as expressed by improved interpersonal relations with persons both younger and older than the student as well as his peers.   Twenty-four students in an experimental junior high school and twelve students from a neighboring traditional school took part in this study.   The Title III ESEA model school had three hundred students.   The program uses the natural affinity young people have for small children in a laboratory experiment that benefits both of them.   Article discusses the program schedule, selection of students, responsibilties of students, role of the director, focus of learning concepts, research setting, and results.   A pretest and posttest using the California Psychological Inventory showed the program had a significant effect on self-acceptance, sense of well-being, self-control, good impression, and flexibility.

4023.   Flanders, J. N.   "Guidance and the Cultural Arts: School Enrichment Programs--A Model for America." Livingston, Tenn.:   Overton County Board of Education, ERIC Doc. ED 033 422, 1969.

This demonstration guidance program dealing with disadvantaged and minority groups improved student behavior, capacity for creative thinking, and attitudes toward self, school, and community.   The program provided instruction in music, art, and drama and gave children and adults opportunities for creative expression.   Results show a positive attitude toward the program by pupils, parents, and educators. Changes in attitude, while positive, did not result in attitudes significantly different from those of subjects in the control school.   See ERIC Abstract #ED 033 422.

4024.   Fletcher, B. J.   "Middle/junior high school counselors' corner."   Elementary School Guidance and Counseling, 10,3(1976):210-213.

In order to promote a positive image for the guidance department and to assure parents that counselors are involved with children even before trouble arises, parental contact should be made before children enter the middle or junior high school.   Orientation programs, parent discussion groups, parent conferences, and career guidance could strengthen parent involvement.   Author stresses that parents are a very important element in the guidance program.

4025.   Grant, W. R., Sr. "A functional junior high school guidance program."   Journal of Secondary Education, October 1966:255-259.

Discusses orientation, inventory services, information services, counseling, and follow-up.

4026.   Hall, H. L. and Bowden, W.   "Found: a way to wean seventh graders."   School Management, March 1969:50.

Convinced that the seventh grade is the most significant and difficult period of adjustment for students, Kirkwood, Missouri, school staff members designed a program that combines a core curriculum with a comprehensive system of counseling: each core teacher is the guidance counselor for his/her class. The aim of the core curriculum is to unify subject matter. This means incorporating guidance into the subject matter of seventh grade English and social studies. In English, teachers emphasize short stories and books that deal with adolescence, and each class discusses the problems of growing up, responsibility, and self-discipline. Core pupils visit elementary students to prepare them for junior high school, and specialized guidance counselors talk with sixth grade teachers about the coming fall's seventh graders. The day before school opens in the fall, core teachers meet with their students for a special orientation. Core teachers use their counseling time during the school year, for conferences with students and parents, for preparing and reviewing student progress reports, which are sent to parents throughout the year, for studying student records on a day-to-day basis, for plannng and coordinating new group projects with other staff members, and for discussing particular problems with district guidance specialists.   Says Kirkwood Superintendent W. A. Shannon, "Many schools use the core approach, but few coordinate English and social studies with guidance. By doing so, we place greater emphasis on the youngster's personal need, without sacrificing the time that should be devoted to learning."

4027.   Haller, C. E. "The Child, the School, the Guidance Counselor in the Middle School (Grades 6, 7, and 8)." Washington, D.C.: U. S. Department of Health, Education and Welfare, ERIC Doc. ED 056 319, 1971.

Author describes his personal philosophy of guidance as a personal feeling, a way of thinking and a way of life. He then discusses his approach and goals as a counselor at the Norseman School. Next he considers the distribution of the counselor's time, techniques used, counseling in general, group work, and working with teachers. Case studies are included. A final section evaluates the Norseman guidance program of 1969-1970 and includes interviews with the principal, teachers, and students. Finally, the author suggests possible changes. An example of the author's work week is included, with time set aside for teaching guidance classes, counseling, group work, and teacher collaboration.

4028.   Hanson, J. W. "Guidance in an atmosphere of crisis." Educational Leadership, 9(1951):115-118.

Describes a guidance counselor's role in the junior high school.

4029.   Heller, R. W. and Hansen, J. C. "The middle school and implications for the guidance program." Peabody Journal of Education, March 1969:291-297.

Presents a rationale for counselors in the middle school, where a strong guidance program increases the recognition of individual abilities and problems and gives students a more direct individual contact with teachers and guidance personnel. The counselor can help the teacher understand pupils and place them in programs that meet individual needs. It is vital that enough efficient and well-prepared guidance counselors be available to help develop each pupil's program. To really help this age group, everyone on the pupil personnel services staff must know the assets and disabilities of each child and must work with the classroom teacher in developing the student's total program, including academic work, social activities, and guidance for psychological problems. The master classroom teacher and the efficient pupil guidance program are the keys to the success of the middle school program. Working together with the administration, they can avoid the problems which doomed the junior high school.

4030.   Hicks, J. A. and Hayes, M. "Study of the characteristics of 250 junior high school children." Child Development, 9,2(1938):219-243.

Study used interviews, controlled observations, objective tests, ratings, and other data obtained by the school to put together a fairly comprehensive picture of the development of a large group of emerging adolescents. A more specific purpose was to compare the development of the best adjusted and intellectually promising children with the development of the other children in their classes, in a search for clues to locating potential leaders. Finally, all information was to be used in developing the guidance program of the school, so that the educational, vocational, and personal needs of children might be met more adequately.

4031.   Human Development Training Institute. "I Gotta Be Me..., You Gotta Be You: A Moderately Challenging Awareness Unit." Junior High Interchange 11. La Mesa, Calif: Human Development Training Institute, ERIC Doc. ED 151 454, 1977.

This awareness unit develops self-concept and self-esteem in junior high school students. Introduction discusses aspects of self-awareness. Students are encouraged to examine their feelings and behavior. Publication includes guides for teachers of the unit, teaching methods and objectives, and discussion of materials and class time. See ERIC Abstract #ED 151 454.

4032.   Jennings, H. H. Sociometry in Group Relations. 2nd ed. Washington, D.C.: American Council on Education, 1959.

Book contains a section on guidance in the junior high school.

4033.   Johnson, E. G., et al. <u>The Role of the Teacher in
Guidance</u>.   Englewood Cliffs, N.J.:   Prentice-Hall,
1959.

Book contains a section on guidance in the junior
high school.

4034.   Johnson, L. "Reorganized Junior High Program: An
Evaluation of 1971-72.   A Title III ESEA Project."
Minneapolis: Minneapolis Public Schools, Department
of Research and Evaluation, ERIC Doc. ED 083 288,
September, 1972.

Evaluates the first year of this reorganized junior
high program at Jordan and Marshall University Junior
High Schools.   The objectives of the program were:
1) increased counselor effectiveness, 2) positive
student attitude towards teachers, counselors, and
schools, and 3) increased parent and student involvement in school.   Activities to the objectives were
workshops, classroom visits, coordination of support
services, meetings between counselors and teachers,
and publicizing program activities.   The teachers
evaluated the counselors and the program, and students evaluated the school, and teachers.   Parents
were also involved in the program. See ERIC Abstract
#ED 083 288. (For an evaluation of the third year of
the program, see bibliography entry 4050 and ERIC
Abstract #ED 115 685.)

4035.   Johnson, M., Jr., Busaker, W. E., and Bowman, F.
H., Jr.   <u>Junior High School Guidance</u>.   New York:
Harper and Bros., 1961.

This book is based on the premise that neither
academically inclined students nor others can excel
in their studies or realize their full potential
later unless at the junior high level they: 1)
attain a fairly realistic understanding of themselves, 2) make decisions about their high school
programs on bases other than misinformation, personal
whim, or the choices of friends, 3) are spared the
experience of floundering aimlessly for lack of
thought regarding even tentative vocational goals, 4)
are minimally distracted by problems of growth and
development or handicapped by physical or emotional
difficulties, 5) negotiate effectively the change to
secondary school procedures, particularly in regard
to independent study, 6) have ample opportunity to
discover and nourish worthwhile interests, 7) come in
contact with teachers who know enough about them to
provide the kind of educational experiences they
need, 8) encounter adults who are able to furnish
them with reliable information about educational and
vocational opportunities available to them.   The book
contains the following sections: 1) The Place of

Guidance in the Junior High School. 2) Adjustment
Problems of Junior High School Pupils. 3) The
Orientation Program. 4) Guidance in the Homeroom,
Classroom, and Student Activities. 5) Improving
Adjustment through Counseling. 6) Guidance and
Discipline. 7) Exploration and Self-appraisal. 8)
The Testing Program. 9) Educational and Vocational
Decisions. 10) Providing Information about Opportu-
nities. 11) Guidance of Exceptional Children. 12)
Coordination of the Guidance Program. Book also
contains selected materials for the junior high
school homeroom, fifty-seven varieties of study
suggestions, addresses of publishers of tests listed
in text, and a calendar of typical procedures for the
junior high school counselor.

4036.   Keck, M. B. "We get to know Joe in double period
program, Folwell Junior High School, Minneapolis."
National Education Association Journal, 41(1952):561-
563.

Describes an effective student-teacher interaction
model in a block-time junior high setting.

4037.   Kenny, F. X. "The Comparative Effect of Three
Guidance Practices on Middle School Students." Ed.D.
Dissertation, Lehigh University.   Dissertation
Abstracts International, 34 (4-A) 1617-1618. Order
no. 73-23,804, 1973.

Author studied the counselor as a consultant to the
classroom teacher and the counselor in direct contact
with students. The study was conducted in a middle
class suburban community for twelve weeks with 120
randomly selected students, 40 in each of the three
grades (sixth, seventh, and eighth). The junior/
senior High School Personality Questionnaire (HSPQ)
was completed by all students. Results showed that
counseling and prescribed teacher behavior, alone and
in combination, had no significant effect on the personality factor of social interaction or on achievement in selected developmental tasks, as measured by
the HSPQ. Grade level of the subjects did have a
highly significant effect on two of the three developmental tasks tested: developing conscience,
morality, and a scale of values and achieving emotional independence of parents and adults. The
teacher treatment and the group counseling treatment
had a significantly stronger effect than the combination treatment in helping students develop emotional
independence, but the two treatments were not significantly different in effect from each other or from
the nontreatment of the control group.

4038.   Kesner, P. M. "A Comparison of Guidance Needs
Expressed by Preadolescent and Early Adolescent
Students."   Ed.D. Dissertation, Northern Illinois
University, 1977.

Guidance needs expressed by 1518 students, as shown
by the Guidance Needs Assessment Inventory, were: 1)
academic skills development, 2) educational and vocational development, 3) interpersonal relationships,
4) intrapersonal understanding, and 5) career
development. Size of school district and number of
school districts attended did not affect the
statement of needs by preadolescents. However, for
significantly early adolescents, sex, size of school
district, and number of school districts attended all
yielded significant differences in one or more of the
guidance needs. Size of school district, in particular, affected all five guidance needs for early
adolescents.

4039.   Ketron, S. R. "Guidance: junior high school."
Teachers College Journal, 34,2(1963):59-61.

The nature and size of the bulging school population
has forced administrators to broaden curriculum in an
effort to meet the needs of all young people. The
preadolescent and the early adolescent seem to have
enough needs peculiar to their group to warrant a
school structure in which these needs could be effectively met. Curriculum for this age group must
provide for: 1) integration of previously learned
skills and attitudes with new basic knowledge, 2)
exploration of specialized interests and abilities,
3) variety in subject matter and activities to meet
the needs of different groups of young people, so
that each student may develop a sense of personal
worth, 4) socialization: the opportunity to learn
how to participate in a changing social order. The
basic concepts underlying the junior high school idea
are: 1) better provision for the needs of young
adolescents, 2) better provision for exploration of
interests and abilities, 3) better individualization
in the instructional program, and 4) better articulation between elementary and secondary education.

4040.   Knudsen, G. "Considerations for middle school
guidance." School Counselor, 19,2(1971):77-79.

Specific guidance needs of junior high and middle
school pupils have not been thoroughly considered.
Present counselor roles are based on secondary (and
to some degree elementary) school training and
experience, and middle school guidance unfortunately
is likely to be based on counselor orientation rather
than on the student's preadolescent phase of development. The author, a counselor, stresses the

importance of parent consultation, orientation programs, testing, peer relationships, group counseling,
and individual visits.   She stresses that a long-
range view is essential in middle school planning as
well as a careful examination of the role of the
counselor who works with this age group.

4041.   Lazzaro, E. and Stevic, R. "Counselor initiated
counseling: can it be of benefit to clients?"
Journal of Counseling Services, 2,3(1978):6-13.

Study evaluates the effect of a counselor-initiated
and sustained humanistic intervention paradigm upon
personal and social problems of nonreferred black
junior high school students.   Study also measures the
influence of counselors' sex and race on the treatment.   Previous research has substantiated the effectiveness of facilitative counselor behavior in the
helping relationship. In this study, nonfacilitative
counselors were able to influence positively the
behavior patterns of black junior high school
students.   Results suggest that the counselor,
regardless of race or sex, can initiate counseling
with the expectation that client change will occur.
Moreover, the counselor can assume a more active role
in seeking out clients who may benefit from counseling.   This more active stance makes sense in the
current milieu of school counseling, where students
may not realize the counselor can help with their
social and psychological problems.

4042.   Lee, J.   "Groups as a Method of Counseling and
Staff Development."   Paper presented at the Annual
Meeting of the Canadian Guidance and Counseling
Association, Vancouver, British Columbia, ERIC Doc.
ED 122 177, June 4-6, 1975.

Junior high school youth, who are obliged to remain
in school regardless of their suitability for that
environment, often cause problems.   This paper
describes groups designed to help some of these
students adjust better in school and in society and
to get along better with their families.   The group
experiences are meant to increase the members' self-
esteem and sense of self-direction.   The groups are
characterized by the presence of many unruly, poorly
disciplined, impulsive, talkative youngsters who have
the potential for very honest and meaningful conver-
sation with each other.   Honesty, self-awareness, and
acceptance plus the capacity to discipline a small
group are essential qualities for the group leader in
this program.   See ERIC Abstract #ED 122 177.

4043.   Lerrigo, M. O., Southard, H. S., and Senn, M. J.
E. "Finding Yourself."   Chicago: American Medical
Association, ERIC Doc. ED 035 914, 1968.

This pamphlet intended to help students through changes in adolescence is specifically recommended for junior high school children. Chapters are: 1) Find Yourself Here. 2) More about the New Look. 3) Steps toward Womanhood. 4) Steps toward Manhood. 5) Looking toward Parenthood. 6) Boy-Girl Friendships.

4044.   Lewis, J., Simpson, D., and Miles, D.   "Student Needs Assessment Guide."   Vale School District 15, Oregon.   Salem: Oregon State Board of Education, Division of Community Colleges and Career Education, July, 1974.

Completion of the Student Needs Assessment Guide is a major component of the Career Exploration Program at Vale Middle School.   The guide helps students 1) discover their own interests, abilities, aptitudes, potentials, and values in relation to the world of work, 2) discover the importance of communication skills, academic skills, and decision making skills in relation to their role as adults, 3) discover the world of work through real and contrived experiences, 4) accurately associate their inner assets with the requirements of good citizenship, family responsibilities, use of leisure time, and economic proficiency. Booklet discusses the format of the guide, activities, films, film strips, kits, and goals and includes charts of objectives, goals, activities, and resources.   Included also are rating sheets, self-concept/personality checklists, interest data sheets, evaluation checklists, profiles, and self-analysis questionnaires.

4045.   Lincoln Public Schools. "Lincoln Career Education Project: Final Report. Book 4:   Junior High Career Guidance Sequence." Lincoln, Nebr., ERIC Doc. ED 136 066, August, 1976.

This guide includes materials and activities a teacher can use to help students in a teacher-advisor group get oriented to a new school year, get to know themselves and others, and begin exploring the world of work in the course of twelve sessions.   Each activities unit is organized according to title, size of class, purpose, time required, materials needed, and directions. See ERIC Abstract #ED 136 066.

4046.   Lloyd-Jones, E. "Goals and roles in the guidance program." Teachers College Record, 54(1951):1-8.

Describes a guidance program in a junior high school.

4047.   Miller, L. P. "What kind of guidance and counseling programs in the junior high school?" Bulletin of the National Association of Secondary School Principals, 25(1951):157-162.

Describes a guidance program to help pupils adjust to the present and plan for the future.

4048.   National Study of Secondary School Evaluation. Evaluative Criteria for Junior High Schools. Washington, D.C., 1963.

Book includes a section on guidance services. The complexity, multiplicity, and depth of the personal, social, emotional, and physical problems that early adolescents face make it necessary for all adults working with them to become actively engaged in the guidance function. Teachers and parents provide professionally trained counselors with much of the information needed to complete the student inventory. Counselors, in turn, provide teachers with information and help them use it to fulfill the guidance responsibilities teachers must assume.

4049.   Nelson, B. H. (Ed.) Personnel Services in Education. 58th Yearbook, Part II. Chicago: National Society for the Study of Education, 1959.

Contains a section on guidance in the junior high school.

4050.   Nesset, B. C. "Reorganized Junior High School Program: Third Year Evaluation 1973-74. A Title III ESEA Project." Minneapolis: Minneapolis Public Schools, Minnesota Department of Research and Evaluation, ERIC Doc. ED 115 685, August, 1974.

Discusses the third year of a reorganized junior high school program. The major objective was that the counselor would change from a traditional resource person to more of a team member, program coordinator, and facilitator in creating a positive, student-centered program. Objectives were increased counselor effectiveness, positive student attitudes toward school, and increased parent and student involvement. Questionnaires were administered to teachers, administrative and resource personnel, students, and parents at both schools. Counselors had more contact with students in each of the three years of the project than in the year prior. Parents were generally aware of the program options available, could identify and describe the problems, and felt well informed. See ERIC Abstract #ED 115 685. (For an evaluation of the first year of this program see bibliography entry 4034 and ERIC Abstract #ED 083 288.)

4051.   O'Dell, F. L. "Where the Challenge Is Met: A Handbook for Guidance in Grades Seven, Eight, and Nine." Columbus: Ohio State Department of Education, Division of Guidance and Testing, August, 1968.

Handbook chapters cover 1) definition of guidance, the need for guidance, objectives of the junior high guidance program, developing the junior high school guidance program, and the team approach, 2) orientation, the need for orientation, objectives and content of an orientation program, and evaluation of an orientation program, 3) tests and the unique nature of early adolescence, basic elements of a junior high school testing program, special use of tests in junior high schools, and evaluation of the testing program, 4) information services such as educational opportunities, career information, placement information, sources of information, personal-social information, additional informational sources, getting the information to students, and evaluation of the information service, 5) what group guidance contributes to the guidance program, objectives of a group guidance instruction program, organization of group guidance, parent guidance in groups, and evaluation of the group guidance program, 6) the counseling process, time for counseling, goals for counseling, and types of counseling sessions, 7) evaluation, 8) working with students who have special problems: the chronic attendance problem, the nonacademically inclined, the limited sphere of interest, the minor discipline problem, the maturation problem, the clique oriented, the child with poor peer relations, the nonparticipant, unrealistic self typing, the child from a one-parent family, and cautions, 9) calendar for junior high school guidance.

4052. Ohio School Counselors Association. "Report of the Ninth Annual All-Ohio Junior High Guidance Conference, 'Up, Up With People: Through a Galaxy of Services for the Individual.'" Reprint from the Conference, Toledo, May 7, 1971. Columbus: Ohio State Department of Education, Division of Guidance and Testing, 1971.

Three hundred school counselors, other educators and guests took part in this conference, and eighteen workshop sessions are summarized in the report: 1) Integrating Sex Education into the Health Curriculum. 2) Social Work Services in the Inner City. 3) Instructional Resource Material Center. 4) Help for the Learning Disabled Child. 5) Career Orientation. 6) Sheltered Training Experience Project. 7) Family Life Education. 8) Drug Intervention Center. 9) Student Rights, Student Unrest. 10) Behavior Modification. 11) Teaching the Unteachables. 12) Adapting Materials to the EMR Child. 13) The Dilemmas of Planning a Group Testing Program. 14) A Negotiating Problem: Counselor's Salaries. 15) Staff Development: The Concept and the Process. 16) The Hillcrest Project: On-the-Job Training. 17) Regional Pupil Personnel Centers: The Team Approach. 18)

ASCA Issues Related to Middle and Junior High Schools.

4053.   Redl, F. and Wattenberg, W.   <u>Mental Hygiene in Teaching</u>. New York: Harcourt, Brace and Co., 1951.

Contains information on guidance in the junior high schools.

4054.   Reese, W. M.   "Redskin Images: Roy Junior High School." ERIC Doc. ED 177 111, 1978.

A self-improvement program at Roy Junior High School involved 1) developing a way for students to evaluate their own performance, 2) a daily fifteen-minute reading session, 3) a dance and movement education program using visiting artists, 4) developing a one-on-one method of improving the self-esteem of less self-confident students, 5) an adopt-a-grandparent program, and 6) a revision of class period structuring and community achievement activities. This paper also discusses management by objectives, Redskin images of potentiality, Redskin staff self-esteem, Redskin trails, class self-selection, positive phone calls or letters to the home, A-B week, and TORSCA: Trophy of Redskin School/Community Achievement.

4055.   Robinson, L. S. (Comp.)   <u>The Middle School Recipe Book</u>. Columbia: South Carolina State Department of Education, ERIC Doc. ED 153 139, 1977.

Provides activities, forms, and information to help middle school counselors improve services and programs and to help newly employed counselors set up programs. The discussion on guidance is divided into twelve subsections: Orientation, Analysis of the Individual, Curriculum Input, Classroom Behavior Management, Consultation, Public Relations, Information, Counseling, Group Guidance, Interschool Relations, Follow-up and Feedback, and Professional Growth. See ERIC Abstract #ED 153 139.

4056.   Rowe, F. A. "Foundation for a Seventh Grade Guidance Unit: An Analysis of the Developmental Level of the Seventh Grade Student and Nationally Current Occupational Guidance Classes." Salt Lake City: Utah State Department of Public Instruction, ERIC Doc. ED 052 492, May, 1970.

Reviews the literature and current practices in vocational guidance at the seventh grade level and discusses implications for curriculum. Author considers the choice process, vocational development, choice factors, independence, active-passive involvement, means-ends cognizance, time projection, daydreaming and fantasy, self-knowledge, job knowledge, and self and work. One large section deals with developmental tasks (especially vocational developmental tasks) and characteristics of seventh graders (vocational, emotional, social, and intellectual).

4057.   Royal Oak City School District. "Career Development via Counselor/Teacher Teams: Guide for Implementation." Royal Oak, Mich., ERIC Doc. ED 112 055, 1975.

During 1973-74, counselors from four junior high schools took part in a state-funded career education project that combined the expertise of both teachers and guidance counselors. Guidance components within the project include: 1) "Me": students develop a profile of their own characteristics, interests, achievements, and attitudes. 2) "Recognize Me": students recognize self-development as a lifelong process. 3) "It's O.K. to Be Me": students identify their own emotional, intellectual, and physical strengths. 4) "What Makes Me Tick?": students realize that who they are influences what kinds of work will be satisfying to them. 5) "Myself, My Time, My Friends (Getting It Together)": students initiate creative activities involving interpersonal relationships. 6) "What Career For Me?": students identify a high-interest area and occupational exploration experiences related to that area. 7) "Decisions, Decisions, Decisions": students know and are able to apply the decision-making process. 8) "Investigating Careers": students increase their awareness of careers through language arts objectives. Article presents an overview of the project, background, rationale, goals and subgoals, the process, orientation/objective selection, team development, module development, implementation/evaluation, time involved, resources provided, and a project evaluation.

4058.   Ryan, M. K. "Middle school/junior high school counselor's corner." Elementary School Guidance and Counseling, 6,2(1971):121-123.

This is the first "Counselor's Corner" column, and it describes the purpose of the middle school/junior high section of the journal Elementary School Guidance and Counseling. Article discusses the framework of counseling for junior high and middle school and the need of a common definition for the middle school.

4059.   Ryan, M. K. "Middle school/junior high school counselor's corner." Elementary School Guidance and Counseling, 6,3(1972):195-197.

Author discusses the American School Counselors'
Association and the role of middle school and junior
high counselors in this group. She sees the need for
a role statement for middle/junior high school
counselors, suggestions for college and university
counselor training programs for this work setting,
and a review of appropriate curriculum, teacher-
counselor relationships, counselor-administrator
relationships, and counselor-parent relationships.

4060.   Ryan, M. K. and Fletcher, B. J.   "Middle/junior
high school counselor's corner." Elementary School
Guidance and Counseling, 10,3(1976):210-213.

Discusses parental involvement in the guidance program, orientation for new students and their parents,
parent discussion groups, parent conferences, and
career guidance. Author stresses the importance of
parents in the guidance program and the fact that
parents work in many different careers and thus
become one of the main resources for career education
programs.

4061.   Silbergeld, S. and Mandersheid, R. W. "Comparative
assessment of a coping model for school adolescents."
Journal of School Psychology, 14,4(1976):261-273.

Coping courses for early adolescent students were
conducted in junior high schools for two classes of
twenty-four students who regularly used school
guidance personnel and another nineteen students who
did not. Authors conclude that students' interpersonal coping skills were improved from the coping
courses. See ERIC Abstract #EJ 150 036.

4062.   Smith, C. W. and Wilson, H. L. "The Development
and Evaluation of Needs Appraisal Instruments for
Determining Priorities for Guidance and Counseling
Services for Elementary, Junior High, and Secondary
Schools. A Research Report." Baton Rouge: Louisiana
State University, Department of Vocational Agricul-
tural Education, ERIC Doc. ED 147 543, August, 1976.

Study identified the counseling and guidance needs of
students as expressed by students, teachers, and
administrators. The project was conducted to develop
and field test a set of needs appraisal instruments
which would effectively determine the counseling and
guidance needs for junior high schools, secondary
schools, and elementary schools in Louisiana.
Development of the instruments involved research on
instruments used in other states, format and item
selection, consultation with a jury of counseling and
guidance experts, field testing, and revision. A
list of priorities was produced for each participating school. Authors concluded: 1) The instrument

developed can be used to assess the student counseling and guidance needs on an individual school basis.
2) The instrument can identify unmet needs that stem
from students' sexual and racial differences.   3)
Students and teachers tend not to agree about the
guidance and counseling needs of students, while
students and parents tend to agree.   See ERIC
Abstract #ED 147 543.

4063.   Stalnaker, E. M.   "A study of several psychometric
tests as a basis for guidance at the junior high
school level."   Journal of Experimental Education,
20(1951):41-66.

Presents testing procedures which have been found
useful in junior high school guidance.

4064.   Stanton, W. W.   "Middle school years and career
development."   Clearinghouse, 44(1970):531-533.

The author stresses the need for vocational education
in the middle school years.   Education for citizenship is a concern of middle schools, and the life
skills needed for citizenship are based on development of cognitive, interactive, creative, and
vocational skills.   Early recognition of the
student's vocational and avocational needs has too
often been lost.   The student must know academic
requirements for different fields in case the student
might need them for college entrance.

4065.   Thomas, J. K.   "Adolescent endocrinology for counselors of adolesents."   Adolescence, 8(1973):395-406.

Outlines a program that can easily become part of a
guidance program in a middle or junior high school.
The program informs students of the extent, type, and
variation in the physiological changes of early
adolescence in order to relieve any anxiety related
to these changes and to augment self-acceptance.
Article describes the program structure and general
content and reviews specific studies to give counselors background knowledge.

4066.   Thomasson, A. L.   "How may guidance be effective
in junior high school?"   Bulletin of the National
Association of Secondary School Principals, 36(1952):
235-242.

Principal explains the steps taken to develop a
guidance program in the Champaign, Illinois, junior
high school.

4067.   Van Riper, B. W.   "Student perception: the counselor is what he does."   School Counselor, 19,1(1971):
53-56.

Counselors are identified by the functions they emphasize, and changes in emphasis can bring about changes in image. The work of counselors is not always well defined, and this fact often prevents them from attaining a separate identity in the school. See ERIC Abstract #EJ 045 176.

4068.   Vannote, V. G. "A practical approach to behavior modification programs." School Counselor, 21(1974): 350-354.

Describes a project that is conducted by a school counselor and that incorporates principles of behavior modification in dealing with classroom misbehavior in a traditional public junior high school. See ERIC Abstract #EJ 097 634.

4069.   Vogel, F. X. "Guidance in the junior high school." Bulletin of the National Association of Secondary School Principals, 46(1962):93-97.

In many junior high schools the homeroom teacher is considered to have a major role in the guidance program.   He has four major guidance duties: to counsel individual students, to conduct group guidance sessions for the homeroom, to serve as a contact between the student and the special subject teacher, and to serve as a liaison between the school and home.

4070.   Volpe, R. "Assertiveness in early adolescence." School Guidance Worker, 30,6(1975):11-14.

Helping early adolescents to become more effective in expressing themselves is an appropriate and worth-while educational undertaking. To be assertive is to be open and express feelings directly. The counselor can contribute to the well-being of adolescents by providing them with competence-enhancing information that may lead to new and more effective ways of deal-ing with themselves and others. A major section of the article deals with school counseling and assert-iveness training. The author discusses the following techniques: feeling talk, facial talk, expressing contradictory feelings, using "I," spontaneous response, agreeing when complimented.   Schools for early adolescents spend a great deal of time teaching subjects and little time teaching how to share thoughts and feelings.

5

Design and Renovation of Schools
for Middle Years Education

5001.   American School Board Journal.   "New Providence came through its break with tradition in fine shape." American School Board Journal, 156(1968):17-20.

To accommodate team teaching, multiple grouping (small, large, individual), and flexible scheduling, the architect for the New Providence Junior High School in Clarksville, Tennessee, divided the school into two parts. One contains academic and administrative areas, the other physical education, music, drama, home economics, and vocational education. The article presents a floor plan based on unobstructed openness. Four open auxiliary libraries are positioned in relation to the academic emphasis in nearby classrooms. Three common areas with a capacity of 150 people each are important features. Banks of individual study carrels cut swaths through open spaces. Classrooms take on more individualized character when storage cabinets mounted on casters are moved about to create semiseclusion within a room. Subtle refinements that refresh the eye include a folded concrete plate roof over academic and administrative areas. Giving the exterior a bright, lively look that contrasts with walls of gray brick, this roof treatment provides interiors with interest, especially above unbroken stretches of open space.

5002.   American School Board Journal.   "Berger was built to blaze trails--and it has."   American School Board Journal, 156(1969):15-18.

For West Fargo, North Dakota, Berger Middle School represents a significant shift in educational philosophy, bringing changes that were eyed skeptically at

first but are backed solidly today. The superintendent of schools (who has held the post since 1935)
states that the board of education had confidence in
the administration and enough conviction in the
future of education to permit selection of an imaginative architect with unusual ideas. Absence of
permanent walls, no long corridors with classrooms on
each side, the use of carpet, having a large instructional materials center--all are structural changes
unfamiliar to some architects, many teachers, and
most of the public. No school district should move
into a building of this type without first retraining
the teaching staff. The teacher who is used to the
traditional cubicle cannot function effectively in
this strange new setting without training in how to
use it. The constant visibility that a teacher
experiences in a team teaching situation can be
nothing less than traumatic to the unoriented.
Because of its notable design for middle schools,
Berger was included in the exhibition of school
architecture at the March 1969 annual meeting of the
American Association of School Administrators in
Atlantic City.

5003.   American School Board Journal. "At MacDonald, it's
anything but middle of the road." American School
Board Journal, 156(1969):22-26.

Two-level flexibility is found at the center and
entrances of MacDonald Middle School in East Lansing,
Michigan. Article presents architectural plans,
photographs, and statistical data on the building.
The two-tiered library/learning center is the hub of
academic activity: Twenty-nine classrooms on the
first and second floors are grouped in a circle
within a ninety-foot range of the library.

5004.   American School Board Journal. "28 ways to build
mistakes out of your middle school." American School
Board Journal, 158,1(1970):17-24.

The Warren Holmes Company, a group of architects and
engineers, discussed twenty-eight ways to help districts avoid errors in middle school design: 1) Put
counselors where the action is. 2) Provide dining
environments where food is fun. 3) Do not let a
problem site deter you from creative educational and
architectural solutions. 4) Be realistic about folding doors. 5) Consider ceiling grids for art and
other special areas. 6) Tailor the shape of the
building to the site. 7) Give students a place to be
themselves. 8) Consider privacy. 9) Encourage
independent study through the territory concept. 10)
Do not be locked in by lockers. 11) Make the
learning center a legitimate learning center. 12)
Use windows wisely. 13) Zone vehicles within the

campus.   14) Plan a small assembly area for the
middle school.   15) Keep shop areas open and free.
16) Try a variable theater.   17) Give visitors a
firsthand look at the school in action.   18) Turn
kids on from inside.   19) Make the home economics
space more than a cooking/sewing area.   20) Don't
overfurnish.   21) Plan with sex in mind.   22) Sound-
condition your open-plan spaces.   23) If you're
unsure about instructional technology, provide the
support facilities.   24) Provide multiuse storage and
preparation schemes.   25) Provide staff offices that
improve interdepartmental communication and cooperation.   26) Consider use of integral furniture-wall
systems.   27) Avoid linear corridors.   28) Provide a
large heated slab for outdoor activities.

5005.   American School Board Journal.   "East Naples, a
'systems' middle school, went from plans to reality
in just seven months."   American School Board Journal, 159,1(1971):26-27.

Presents a plan and pictures of the East Naples,
Florida, Middle School, which uses a School Construction Systems Development component.   This type of
system was the prime mover in developing school
building performance specifications and a guaranteed
market that encouraged manufacturers to develop component subsystems.

5006.   American School and University magazine. "A middle
school above par."   American School and University,
38,8(1966):68-69.

Helen Keller Middle School, Easton, Connecticut,
houses preadolescent children in grades 5-8.   Completed in 1965, the school was designed by architects
to provide this age group with a fuller and more
flexible educational experience than was possible
under the school system's old K-6, 7-12 organization.
This school also meets longstanding community needs
for a recreational and cultural center.   The school
staff presented the architects with the following
specific requirements: careful adaptation to a
steeply sloping site, opportunity for major future
expansion, flexible interior spaces for a changing
educational program, economical construction, and low
maintenance costs.   Article includes a plan of the
building.

5007.   American School and University magazine.   "Three
buildings: two junior high schools and an elementary
school."   American School and University, 45,7(1973):
30-31.

Thomas Jefferson Junior High School and Community
Center in Arlington, Virginia, hopes to meet the

developmental, intellectual, and physical needs of a community. Article includes illustrations of the building, the instructional program, the controlled environment facility, and the auditorium. The Stanwood Junior High School is the first systems-built school building erected in Pennsylvania. Article includes pictures of the school, considers costs and specifications, discusses the gymnasium and other interesting features. The new Dalhart, Texas, elementary school is also pictured. Article discusses its five metal building systems.

5008.   American School and University magazine. "Harverford: a lesson in energy conservation." American School and University, 52,4(1979):28-29.

Article discusses a renovation which cost 2.3 million dollars and concentrated mainly on mechanical systems and windows that helped cut fuel consumption 30 percent at a Pennsylvania junior high school. A major objective was the creation of three separate mini-schools for the three grades assigned to the facility. Pictures of this renovation are included. See ERIC Abstract #EJ 212 386.

5009.   Bick, L. W. "New Concepts in Design of Middle Schools." ERIC Doc. ED 109 798, July 14, 1975.

This annotated bibliography covers seventeen articles and books dealing with the design of middle school buildings. The introduction discusses recent trends and changes, open-plan buildings, and adaptation for after-school use by community groups. Articles include: 1) Attractive, Functional School at a Surprisingly Low Cost. 2) Intermediate, Open, and Carpeted: Bandford's a School that Could Give Ideas. 3) New Middle School Did More than Retread a Small Town District. 4) Forecast: Fair Weather in Budget Building Ideas. 5) Planning Educational Facilities: The New Environment. 6) Henry B. DuPont Middle School. 7) Coan Sets Its Sights on an Entire Community. 8) Middle School Butterfly Design Has Roof with Cable Supports. 9) Needed: Playground and Park. Solution: Go to the Roof! 10) One-room Schoolhouse 1972 Style. 11) Planning School for Intermediate Students. 12) Model Middle Schools. 13) Twenty-eight Ways to Build Mistakes Out of Your Middle Schools. 14) A Plan for Middle Schools, Buffalo, New York. 15) Teaching-loft Concepts Solve Open-plan Problems. 16) The New Importance of Renovation. 17) The Open Middle School: A Model for Change.

5010.   Bloomington Metropolitan School District. "Bloomington, Indiana, Metropolitan School Study, 1967-68." Bloomington, Indiana, 1968.

A search of the literature reveals twenty-five characteristic features of a middle school: 1) a new
building, 2) effective use of school plant, 3) home
economics and industrial arts shops, 4) use of television, 5) foreign language instruction, 6) language
laboratories, 7) divisible auditorium, 8) large and
small group activities, 9) air conditioning, 10) movable walls, 11) carpets, 12) imaginative architectural design, 13) plans for the future, 14) instructional swimming pool, 15) library carrels, 16) audiovisual materials, 17) programmed learning, 18) team
teaching, 19) specialization and departmentalization,
20) individualization, 21) flexible schedules, 22)
nongradedness, 23) a program based on twenty-minute
or thirty-minute modules, 24) a program based on
fifty-five-minute units, and 25) a program based on
units of one and a half or two hours.

5011.   Bothwell, K. H. "An Investigation of Personal and
Social Effects of Two Diverse Spatial Environments
Designed for Education." Ed.D. Dissertation, Univer-
sity of Georgia, 1974.

In this study of how space arrangements affect students, author randomly selected eighty-four eighth
grade students from an open-space and a closed-space
school.   Findings were as follows: 1) Students in
the open-space school were statistically more likely
to select a closer seat, indicating a desire for
interaction.   2) Students in the open-space school
were statistically more likely to respond cooperatively.   A study of students who had enrolled in an
open-space school for an extended number of years
provided a test of other hypotheses.   Educators must
realize that a given environment possesses varying
potential for different children.

5012.   Building Design and Construction magazine.   "A
busted baby boom teaches school builders new tricks."
Building Design and Construction, 14,10(1973):46-48.

The birth rate plunge has inspired a resourceful
building team to shift to conversions, renovations,
and the design of new, flexibe schools called human
resource centers.   Article describes programs and
includes plans of Thomas Jefferson Junior High in
Arlington, Virginia, the Witman Center in Pontiac,
Michigan, and the John F. Kennedy School and Community Center in Atlanta, Georgia.   Article also
discusses the magnet school, savings and popularity,
and an architect's warning.   (For more on Thomas
Jefferson Junior High see bibliography entries 5018
and 5066.)

5013.   CEFP Journal.   "Needed: playground and park.
Solution: go to the roof." CEFP Journal, 11,2(1973):
12-13.

Article presents photographs, specifications, and a
plan of New Jersey's East Orange Middle School, which
is both a school and a community activity center.
The focal point is the roof, which becomes both a
school playground and a community park.   Eight
hundred pupils attend the school in grades 6 through
8 in family groups of three hundred each.   Six open
loft spaces grouped in pairs offer maximum adaptability to various educational and community programs.   Service facilities grouped in adjacent towers
produce uninterrupted spaces.   The "street" is an
underground passage which connects all the major
elements.

5014.   Clinchy, E.   "Two Middle Schools, Saginaw Town-
ship, Michigan.   Profiles of Significant Schools."
New York: Educational Facilities Laboratories, ERIC
Doc. ED 031 871, September, 1960.

Paper profiles two middle schools designed to improve
the transition of elementary pupils to a high school
program featuring individualized, self-directed study
and research.   One school uses a cluster plan, the
other a compact design.   The description emphasizes
why and how the schools were designed and built as
they were.   See ERIC Abstract #ED 031 871.

5015.   Cutler, M. H.   "A new middle school did more than
retread a small-town district."   American School
Board Journal, 157,11(1970):32-34.

Discusses the Templeton Middle School, which brings
together children from six Wisconsin villages in the
Hamilton Joint School District, grades 6 through 8.
This model middle school plan features a cluster
concept with four classrooms constituting a cluster
that becomes one wide open space when movable partitions are folded back.   At the heart of the school is
the library or the materials production center, which
is surrounded by the clusters, carrels, and conference rooms.

5016.   Cutler, M. H.   "If zoos and junior highs have
things in common, then Hinsdale's new junior high is
no junior high." American School Board Journal, 163,
9(1976):26.

Parents, merchants, politicians, students, and
teachers all helped design this new junior high
school.   The ground level of the building contains a
large central mall with "feel and do" spaces for
music, drama, home economics, etc.   The building is

designed to combine fresh teaching techniques with conventional philosophies of learning. The second floor includes a loft devoted mainly to academic disciplines and a spacious library. Certain sections consist of self-contained classrooms, whereas others are unhindered by walls and partitions. The arrangement of the building allows for flexibility within the program, giving teachers numerous options in their instructional approaches. Small resource centers are used for testing, group projects, and lectures.

5017.   Cutler, M. H. "Intermediate, open, and carpeted, Branford's a school that could give you ideas." American School Board Journal, 160,5(1973):48-49.

Discusses the school design that won the 1972 honor award from the Connecticut chapter of the American Institute of Architects. It is a school for students 10 to 13 years old and includes an extensive carpet installation, a supersized swimming pool, a roomy gym, and many other nonacademic areas that are used many hours during the day. Public use of school facilities has increased considerably since the new building opened.

5018.   Dean, A. O. "Evaluation: a suburban junior high designed for double duty as a 'community living room.'" AIA Journal, 65,11(1976):62-66.

Discusses the Thomas Jefferson Junior High School and Community Center in Arlington County, Virginia. Article includes pictures and design specifications and discusses the origin of the idea for this two-purpose building. Author describes the library, the openness of space, the gymnasium or controlled environment facility, and the reactions of both students and staff. (For more on this school see bibliography entries 5012 and 5066.)

5019.   Drake, J. C. "Everything's new but the walls." National Education Association Journal, 56(1968):16.

Describes a middle school's model physical facilities.

5020.   Duran, L. A. Middle School Architecture: Tomorrow's Schools with Yesterday's Facilities--Guidelines for Adaptation. Dissemination Services on the Middle Grades, vol. 2, no. 5. Springfield, Mass.: Educational Leadership Institute, 1971.

Contains plans and descriptions of exemplary middle schools: Drew Junior High School in Miami, Florida, based on the loft plan; the Rockaway Junior High School in Miami, Florida, based on the divisible

auditorium; the Washburn Middle School, Winnetka,
Illinois, based on the houses and the hub feature;
and the New Salt Junior High School, Spring Valley,
New York, based on a divisible-area theater.   The
major physical implications of individualized learning programs for middle grade youngsters appear to
be: 1) greater variety of group sizes, 2) more and
smaller groups with individual or personal emphasis,
3) greater variety of activities, 4) varied degrees
of formality in structure of groups, 5) variety in
flow (sequence) of activities, with an emphasis on
the transition and interaction of groups, and 6)
emphasis on education through all experiences and the
whole physical environment.

5021.   Educational Facilities Laboratories. Profiles of
Significant Schools: Schools for Team Teaching.   New
York: Educational Facilities Laboratories, 1960.

Gives examples of junior high schools designed to
house team teaching programs.

5022.   Ernst, L.   "Hinsdale Junior High: a three-level
building tuned to environment."   School Business
Affairs, 44,6(1978):183-185.

Describes a colorful, fully carpeted, multipurpose
building for grades 7 and 8 with commons and minimum
use of fixed equipment.   New arrangements, such as
interdisciplinary programs, may be formed with ease.
Article covers building and site, first floor,
mezzanine and second level, a plan and photographs,
third floor, and utility touches.

5023.   Florida State Department of Education.   "Florida
School Facilities Conference Report."   Tallahassee,
Fla., 1956.

Booklet describes a model junior high school plant.

5024.   Fresno County Schools. "Buildings for Tomorrow's
Educational Programs." Fresno, Calif., ERIC Doc. ED
041 473, May, 1969.

A compilation of seven papers from a symposium on
planning school buildings sponsored by the Fresno
County Regional Planning and Evaluation Center.
Papers discuss changes in educational philosophy and
technology, educational finance, educational specifications, and innovative programs in relation to
middle schools and open schools.

5025.   Gross, R. and Murphy, J. "The middle school." In
Educational Change and Architectural Consequences,
pp. 56-67. New York: Educational Facilities Laboratories, 1969.

Authors present drawings of a model middle school plant, including the library, humanities forum, languages forum, typing center, communications area, arts barn, and science-math barn. The drawings suggest in broad strokes an environment designed to meet the diverse needs and capacities of intermediate age children. It offers a marked change of pace and sophistication from primary school yet is radically different from the rigid departmentalization of the conventional junior high. The school introduces the child to departmentalization by grouping together the facilities for related disciplines in large, open, barn-like areas. Central to the whole design, in fact and in spirit, is the library, where each child may be assigned a carrel and a storage space. The middle schooler, as his powers and confidence increase, makes greater and greater independent use of the library and its resources.

5026.   Herrick, J. H., McLeary, R. D., Clapp, F. W., and Bogner, W. F.   From School Program to School Plant. New York: Henry Holt and Co., 1956.

Contains a section on facilities which will greatly enhance the junior high philosophy and program.

5027.   Hoffman, J. and Stranik, E. "Spotlight on innovative middle schools: Rhodes Middle School, Philadelphia." Middle School Journal, 7,2(1976):20-22.

Rhodes Middle School houses sixteen hundred students in grades 5-8. It is divided into four identical building components, called houses, and an elective wing. Each house is multiage and multigrade. Thus each house is a "school within a school" consisting of four hundred students, fifteen teachers, a counselor, a nonteaching paraprofessional, and a House Director responsible for the supervision of all students and teachers in the house. Essentially the principal envisioned his original planning task as one of developing a unique middle school which would be characterized by a pleasant, purposeful environment for pupils. He focused on 1) adapting the instructional program to the inherent physical attributes of the building (for example, the original building construction plans fostered the development of a true school-within-a-school idea), 2) developing a model of educational excellence (he decided to use and adapt various programs from different school levels), 3) avoiding the built-in defects of junior and senior high schools, especially a) fragmented roster, b) a large, unmanageable lunchroom, c) inordinate preoccupation with remediation, d) tracking, e) focus on subject rather than kids, f) bells and changes of class each period, g) floating teachers, h) detention rooms, and i) study halls. The faculty at Rhodes is optimistic that the humanistic approach of the house type of organization can offer students in large inner-city schools the sense of family togetherness that is needed before any educational program can work. The faculty feels this ellusive yet important purpose is being realized at Rhodes.

5028.   Instructor magazine. "Middle school: Goshen, New York." Instructor, 79(1969):35-39.

In the forefront of the middle school movement is the teacher-planned, child-oriented Goshen Middle School. Article describes two large group instruction areas for use by any grade or by cross-grade groups and discusses band practice areas, cafeteria services, and the library and curriculum center for seventh and eighth grade students.

5029.   Justus, J. E. (Ed.) "Athens Junior High School, Athens, Tennessee. Profile of a Significant School." Knoxville: University of Tennessee, School Planning Laboratory, ERIC Doc. ED 037 014, 1965.

Describes the process leading to the design of an innovative school building: 1) The Athens School Board determined the need for a new school. 2) The School Planning Laboratory was employed. 3) Athens personnel and the School Planning Laboratory personnel developed educational specifications: a) objectives were determined, b) enrollments were anticipated, c) space needs were determined, d) space relationships were developed, and e) environmental control factors of color, acoustics, visual needs, and equipment were delineated. 4) The architect developed preliminary plans for the building. 5) Plans were approved by the Board. This article includes a floor plan and discusses the design of the building, the instructional materials center, communications, teacher work centers, auditorium, team teaching, independent study, the core, the learning environment, and construction specifications, size and cost. The integration of the parts of the building into a complete learning environment reflects the core curriculum concept that commonly integrates subjects in junior high schools.

5030.   Klein, I. R. and Associates, Architects/Planners. "Second Guess: A New Concept in School Planning." Houston, Tex., ERIC Doc. ED 036 139, 1969.

Describes the design of the Kirkwood Middle School, which has these special features: 1) open-plan design, 2) movable walls, 3) ramp system for vertical circulation, and 4) built-in planning for future growth. A floor plan is included. "In a time of rapid change in education, school design needs a system which will permit the inevitable mistakes. The conventional secondary school with its egg-crate design, its double loaded corridors and its permanent classroom partitions is no longer an adequate solution. Thus, after extensive research by the architects listed, the built-in 'second guess' concept has evolved in Kirkwood. Research has included inspection trips to other facilities, an open mind, and close contact with the Educational Facilities Laboratories of New York, which is part of the Ford Foundation."

5031. Leggett, S. "Trends in educational spaces in junior high school." In American School and University, 1954-1955, pp. 219-228. New York: American School Publishing Corp., 1955.

Describes various junior high school plants and the philosophies behind them.

5032. Lutes and Amundson, Architects and Community Planners. "Design Development Plans for Altamont Junior High School, Klamath Falls, Oregon." Klamath Falls, Oreg.: Klamath County School District, ERIC Doc. ED 128 893, September, 1971.

The design of this new school was based on the ideas of the architect, teaching staff, administration, students, and community. Paper describes the students and faculty, site, educational program, design concept, building facilities program, houses, resource center, mathematics, science, home living, arts and crafts, music, vocational arts, the forum, food service, physical education, administration, physical plant and services, the design development plan, construction methods and materials, mechanical and electrical systems, and life safety and fire control. Organizational diagrams show the desirable interrelationship of the spaces and functions.

5033. MacConnell, J. D. Planning for School Buildings. Englewood Cliffs, N.J.: Prentice-Hall, 1957.

Describes an innovative approach to school facilities with examples of effective junior high school plants.

5034. Magid, M. K. "A community designs its school." Clearinghouse, 49,4(1975):157-159.

Discusses the new Woodrow Wilson School in Oakland, California, which was designed with the assistance of members and advisors of the school's building site committee. Describes the steps taken by the planning committee with the architect and discusses the requests of parent and neighborhood members of the site committee. Many innovations accommodate the changing interests of students in the junior high grades.   A floor plan of the model school is included.

5035.   Maguire, H. P. "How to prevent excess power consumption in all-electric schools." Modern Schools,
September 1971:3-5.

Shows how designing and operating school electric
comfort systems for economy helps cut unnecessary
costs. Includes sections on ventilation and setback,
night setback thermostats, humidigraph, calculating
pickup time, graphic meters, and controls. The
school discussed in the article is a total electric
junior high school which provides an optimum environment for learning.

5036.   McClurkin, W. D. School Building Planning. New
York: Macmillan, 1964.

Describes evolution in school plants, the planning
process, the development of educational policy,
educational planning, architectural and construction
services, costs and economies, and contains an
excellent bibliography. Useful for decision makers
as they consider cost and other economic factors.

5037.   Midjaas, C. L. "The middle school: what's in a
name?" Michigan Journal of Secondary Education, 12,4
(1971):55-61.

Educators who want to plan meaningful middle school
facilities must: 1) evaluate learning program criteria carefully, 2) establish priorities for those
criteria, and 3) insist that both program criteria
and priorities be adhered to in the physical design
of the middle school facility. Well-designed middle
school facilities which reflect well-planned programs
are far more than neutral vessels for the curriculum.
They cause positive behavior changes among students
and staff, and promote the integration of instructional effort and the establishment of learning programs more meaningful to middle school students. The
article describes what a middle school facility
should be.

5038.   Midjaas, C. L. and Millu, M. J. "School triples
capacity by adding 'towers.'" American School and
University, 47,6(1975):66.

Describes how the Grand Rapids School System changed
a seven-year-old junior high for 750 students to a
3000-student senior high school. Towers became the
answer. The staff and administration imposed these
additional requirements: 1) Provide within the
recycled facility an unconventional learning environment avoiding both the standard classroom and the

totally open-plan space while supporting individualized learning and group instruction.   2) Create a
setting which allows students to maintain a strong
sense of personal identity and group cohesion and
which promotes a feeling of closeness between
teachers and students.   3) Develop new and expanded
facilities including an auditorium, a natatorium, and
a special "school within a school" for the physically
handicapped.   Article presents a floor plan for the
addition of the towers and charts a critical path
schedule to complete the project.

5039.   Mills, G. E.   "The how and why of the middle
schools." Nation's Schools, 68(1961):43-54.

The Edsel Ford Foundation Curriculum Study in Dearborn, Michigan, concluded that the four-year high
school should be under one roof, thus promoting the
cause for the middle school.   Author strongly supports the concept of the middle school, citing the
success of the Saginaw, Michigan, middle schools,
which had opened two buildings when the article was
published.   Author describes the tremendous amount of
leadership and understanding that go into creating a
new organizational structure.   Being dissatisfied
with the downward movement of high school activities,
athletic programs, and instructional progress in the
junior highs, he set out to design something more
satisfactory.   First he studied 320 physical, mental,
emotional, and social growth characteristics of boys
and girls and their teaching implications.   From this
data he found the most prominent similarities to be
grouped in the primary school grades K-4, middle
school grades 5-8, and high school 9-12.   The
faculties in Saginaw studied adolescent psychology,
theories of learning, and needs of youth in their
community and school and designed a curriculum for
their middle schools.   From the curriculum requirements, two types of buildings were designed and built
to be compared in their accommodation of the educational program.   One of the buildings has no classroom "cells."   All rooms are only three sided, the
fourth side opening onto a mall which is a resource
center and equipment area.

5040.   Modern Schools magazine.   "Brooklyn builds a
school with a planned-in expansion." Modern Schools,
May 1971:3-6.

Describes a modern, totally electric educational
facility designed to provide an atmosphere of functional beauty where students and teachers engage in
stimulating and creative work.   Includes pictures of
the building and describes its many features, including a spacious cafeteria-dining area, a well-equipped

all-electric food service, fluorescent lighting, and provisions for audiovisual equipment.

5041.   Modern Schools magazine. "The most for your money: a case in point." Modern Schools, May 1973:6-8.

Describes the McKinley Junior High School in South Holland, Illinois. This school has won awards for its design as an all-electric school which was constructed using the problem-solving approach and which has cost-effective individual room temperature control. Article includes pictures.

5042.   Modern Schools magazine. "School solutions: window wall/windowless." Modern Schools, February 1975:9-11.

These two unique designs--window walls and windowless help to solve special problems while creating aesthetically pleasing buildings. Article discusses the glass curtain walls at George Gund Hall housing Harvard University's Graduate School of Design, the windowless classrooms at a junior high school next to Chicago's O'Hare Airport, and the Iroquois Junior High. Includes pictures of this building.

5043.   Modern Schools magazine. "Relighting reduces operating costs." Modern Schools, April 1976:12.

Twin beam luminaries that control ceiling reflections provide better visibility with one-third the wattage of the previous lighting in the Charles Brewer Middle School in Clark, New Jersey. Includes pictures.

5044.   Modern Schools magazine. "All-electric school profile: Gilford Middle High." Modern Schools, September 1976:8-9.

A high school and a middle school share core facilities in a building equipped with all-electric heating and cooling systems. This school in Gilford, New Hampshire, combines a unique design with the latest in electrical equipment. Article includes pictures and a floor plan.

5045.   Modern Schools magazine. "School colors enhance learning process." Modern Schools, December 1976: 12-13.

The Greenhill Middle School in Dallas, Texas, with its dramatic use of bold interior colors, stimulates student interest and enthusiasm. It won the 1975 Burlington Award for innovative design. Includes pictures.

5046.   Modern Schools magazine.   "Sam Houston Junior
         High: an example of excellence."   Modern Schools,
         February 1977:8-9.

         This junior high school has won several awards for
         innovative concept and design.   The school is located
         on a heavily wooded site with low profile mesquite
         trees and is designed to flow with the site's ter-
         rain.   Situated on a crest of a low hill, the floor
         levels work down the slope in both directions.
         Includes pictures.

5047.   Modern Schools magazine.   "Junior high gets energy
         efficient VAV system."   Modern Schools, May 1977:7.

         The Isanti Junior High school in Minnesota, with its
         energy efficient Variable Air Volume system, has an
         innovative design selected for display at the 1977
         Exhibition of School Architecture in Las Vegas.
         Article discusses its many features and the design
         goals, which were: a pleasant and supportive place
         in which students and teachers could work, an econom-
         ical building for the community to own and operate, a
         simple, straightforward building system for heating
         and ventilation, adaptability for future change, and
         flexibility for immediate needs.

5048.   Modern Schools magazine.   "School renovation wins
         award."   Modern Schools, September 1977:7.

         The design for the Cambridge Junior High School in
         metropolitan Minneapolis was selected for display at
         the 1977 Exhibition of School Architecture in Las
         Vegas.   Article describes the buildings, including
         open classrooms, a multipurpose lecture hall which
         also serves as an assembly space for both day and
         evening uses, a new gymnasium and a new art class
         area.

5049.   Modern Schools magazine.   "What's new in modern
         schools."   Modern Schools, October 1977:12-13.

         Describes the Dunbar High School in Washington, D.C.,
         and the Old West End Junior High School in Toledo,
         Ohio, which use a device that converts an incan-
         descent fixture to fluorescent light.   Includes
         pictures.

5050.   Mullen, D. J.   "The Middle School Period: A
         Monograph."   Georgia Association of Elementary School
         Principals and University of Georgia at Athens,
         Bureau of Educational Studies and Field Service,
         1972.

         Contains articles on the middle school movement by
         Mary Compton, Donald Nesbitt, D. J. Mullen, O. Paul

Roaden, and C. McGuffey. Roaden presents alternatives to consider in construction of middle school
buildings, and McGuffey discusses useful guidelines
for planning a middle school plant.

5051.   Nation's Schools magazine. "How award-winning
schools compare. A special report." Nation's
Schools, 75,1(1965):Whole Issue.

Describes twelve high schools, seven junior high
schools, and twelve elementary schools of distinguished design, including pictures, plans, and
commentary as well as construction data. Report
shows what is happening in new school design as
compared with--and occasionally as opposed to--what
consultants, architects, and educators think should
be happening. See ERIC Abstract #ED 023 278.

5052.   Nation's Schools magazine. "School of the month:
Barrington Middle School, Barrington, Illinois."
Nation's Schools, 76,5(1965):61-68.

Architect Spencer Cone of Cone and Dornbusch,
Chicago, responded to the need for middle school
flexibility by using the system of components that
emerged from the School Construction Systems Development Project. Sponsored by Educational Facilities
Laboratories, the project has been heralded as the
basis for a new tradition of American school architecture. The four SCSD components are: 1) structural system, 2) ceiling lighting system, 3) air
conditioning system, and 4) movable and operable
partitions. They are compatible and can be easily
divided by maintenance staff into rectangular chunks
of almost any size. Includes floor plan of this new
system especially designed for a middle school plant.

5053.   Nation's Schools magazine. "School of the month:
Hubert Olson Elementary and Junior High School,
Blooming, Minnesota." Nation's Schools, 83,1(1969):
84-86.

This school features an audiovisual and dial access
information retrieval system in the junior high
resource center, closed circuit television system, a
physical education plant which includes an eight-lane
indoor-outdoor swimming pool, a central kitchen and
heating plant, two lunchrooms, and a beautiful,
sprawling fifty-acre site. Article includes pictures. It also explains how schools of the month are
selected.

5054.   Nation's Schools magazine. "School of the month:
L. E. Berger Middle School, West Fargo, North
Dakota." Nation's Schools, 83,3(1969):108-109.

This model middle school has folding walls, movable cabinetwork, and portable chalkboards. Flexibility is the key. A major feature is the multipurpose gymnasium which is also used as an auditorium and theater. Teacher work areas are included and the entire building is based on the educational philosophy that the middle school should take students from the single-teacher classroom and gradually introduce them to specialization and the departmentalized environment.

5055.   Nation's Schools magazine. "How 18 award-winning schools compare." Nation's Schools, 85,1(1970):49-66.

Presents photographs, design plans, and sketches of eighteen schools which have received the citation for design excellence by a special architectural jury of the American Association of School Administrators. The three middle schools discussed are Big Walnut School in Sunbury, Ohio, the Sammye E. Coan School in Atlanta, Georgia, and the Patapsco School in Ellicott City, Maryland. The Coan Middle School is almost windowless, with reinforced concrete columns. The Big Walnut Middle School is in a Midwest rural setting and includes curved corners and even-faced brick blend. Article compares the schools by general statistics, cost statistics, area statistics, typical classroom characteristics, equipment characteristics, learning resource centers, and teaching area.

5056.   Nation's Schools magazine. "Freedom, partitions, and native stone: School of the Month--Chief Peguis Junior High, Winnipeg, Manitoba, Canada." Nation's Schools, 88,4(1971):92-93.

This building was planned by an architect, administrators, and teachers of all subjects. It looks like a square donut with a materials resource center as the hole. The building has many sliding and folding doors, an auditorium theater seating 320 people, a projection room and an instructional TV studio. One interesting feature is a crawl space with a quarter-mile running track. Includes pictures and floor plan.

5057.   National Council on Schoolhouse Construction. Guide for Planning School Plants. Nashville, Tenn.: Peabody College, 1953.

Booklet has useful ideas for constructing a school which can best meet needs of junior high school students.

5058.   Overly, D. E. "School of the month: Hithergreen
School, Centerville, Ohio." Nation's Schools, August
1967:53-57.

Instead of using separate classrooms, the interior of
this grade 6-8 school is entirely open. The architect divided the main space--functionally, not
physically--into three learning centers plus a practical arts area and an administration area. In the
center is a circular commons with a curved arch at
one end. Flexible partitions running along the arch
of the circle close off the commons for large classes
and band rehearsals. A circular gym curves into the
commons, while its brick exterior wall continues as
an interior separation. Includes pictures and floor
plan.

5059.   Philadelphia School District. "Education Specifications: New Middle School."   Philadelphia, ERIC
Doc. ED 032 726, 1968.

Describes the desired educational program and the
spaces necessary to carry it out. Booklet sections
are: 1) Introduction. 2) The Present Situation. 3)
The Educational Program. 4) Design Requirements. 5)
Space Allocations and General Area Relationships.
6) Facilities Specifications. 7) Administration Cen-
ter. 8) Grade Center.   9) Instructional Materials
Center.   10) Humanities Center.   11) Mathematics
Center. 12) Science Center. 13) Fine and Performing
Arts.   14) Practical Arts Center.   15) Dining/
Activities Center. 16) Physical Education Center.
17) Maintenance and Operations Center.

5060.   Philadelphia School District.   "Report on Task
Force Division of School Facilities, School District
of Philadelphia: Commission to Investigate Relation-
ships Between Educational Performance and Size of
Student Body."   Philadelphia, ERIC Doc. ED 046 101,
August 1, 1970.

Consultants objected to the design of the Eastwick/
Pepper Educational Complex because of the prohibi-
tively large numbers of children the school would
serve, the overly broad age span of the students, and
the inadequate outside space. However, the task
force concluded that the design of the proposed
school complex was adequate enough to override the
objections of experts in education, psychology, urban
planning, and architecture. (See also bibliography
entry 5061 on this school.)

5061.   Progressive Architecture magazine.   "Award:
Caudill, Rowlett, Scott and Bower and Fradley. Proj-
ect: Eastwick High School and George Pepper Middle
School." Progressive Architecture, 52,1(1971):62-63.

The second half of this article deals with a model
middle school which is separated from a high school
by a spine of common facilities. The school houses
five thousand students and staff. Economic advantages led to merging the common facilities of the two
schools in one structure while maintaining the integrity, functional separation, and autonomy of each
school. Includes pictures and floor plan. (See also
bibliography entry 5060 on this school.)

5062.   Progressive Architecture magazine. "By the people:
schools."   Progressive Architecture, 53,2(1972):88-
95.

The architects established community action as an
integral part of the design process for the East
Orange School Design Center, which operates in a
rented storefront in East Orange, New Jersey.
Article includes a floor plan and discusses the
planning stages for this innovative middle school.
The physical plant is composed of three blocks, each
containing a house. A central space contains all
shared facilities, and houses are connected by a
street with a variety of configurations and spatial
events along the way.

5063.   Progressive Architecture magazine. "A light touch
to learning: Jackie Robinson Middle School, New
Haven, Connecticut." Progressive Architecture, 60,2
(1979):68-72.

The architecture of this building minimizes the
school size by siting it to reveal only one level at
its entrance. Extensive use of transparent and
translucent materials projects openness and light.
Article includes a site plan, the school's three
houses, which are identified by separate entrances
and stair towers, the translucent exterior walls and
roofs, plan for each of the levels, and pictures
which show the unique functions of this building.

5064.   Reid, J. L., et al. "A special kind of middle
school." Nation's Schools, 83,5(1969):76-79.

Authors feel this proposed school for ninth graders
only provides a year close to their teachers, a year
of challenge surrounded with reassurance, competition
set among friends who are in the same boat, and a
chance for students to open doors for themselves and
others. Article includes a site plan, a plan of
instructional space, a departmental floor plan, a
description of core and teacher stations, and a
description of an individual study space and common
area. The building permits students to take stock of
themselves and work in an environment conducive to
learning about subject matter and themselves before

going on to high school. Architects stress that it
provides the greatest variation in achievement levels
by enabling a variety of groupings, that it encourages individual study, and that above all it stresses
teacher and pupil relationships.

5065.   Richter, M. G.   "Open spaces can open minds."
Teacher, 95,8(1978):70-72.

A teacher discusses her experiences in an open-space
classroom at Argyle Junior High in Montgomery County,
Maryland. The school houses nine hundred students in
grades 7-9.   Article sections are: 1) A Typical
Class Period.   2) Organization.   3) You Can't Hide.
4) Floor Plan.   5) What Works.   6) Learning Centers.
7) Coteaching.   8) We've Got Each Other.

5066.   Ringers, J., Jr. "The Arlington, Virginia, Story."
Paper presented at Southeastern Regional Conference
Workshop of the Council of Educational Facility
Planners, Knoxville, Tenn., ERIC Doc. ED 049 556,
April 20, 1971.

Discusses the Thomas Jefferson Junior High School and
Community Center, which accommodates combined services while conserving lands and funds.   The objective was "to create a community growth center to be
primarily an educational plant with focus on the
middle years of youth as well as providing a school
for people with interests for all ages."   County
agencies and school systems joined forces to acquaint
the public with the community center concept.
Article discusses the background of the Thomas
Jefferson Project, the mechanics of cooperative planning, the county manager representative, the general
planning committee, and the responsibilities and
composition of the staff planning committee.   (For
more on this school see bibliography entries 5012 and
5018.)

5067.   Schipper, J. F.   "Truly a middle school."   MASB
Journal, July 1967:15-22.

From the organizational point of view, Zeeland's new
school is a middle school because it is designed to
house grades 6, 7, and 8, though a fifth grade could
easily be included if the need arose.   The school was
planned to be a "transition" school for growing up,
where the individual boy or girl can move from one
class group with a single teacher to many groups with
an increasing number of teachers.   Another reason for
calling it a middle school was suggested in a March
1966 editorial in Nation's Schools magazine, which
recommended that "new schools start with a learning
materials center as the core and loveliest part of a
new building, then let carrels and teaching stations

work themselves out around the perimeters." Zeeland
school has such a plan. Article discusses classroom
wings, learning materials center, faculty sessions,
and arts and crafts centers and it includes a discussion by students about their feelings toward the
school. Another section includes teacher comments,
custodian remarks, and construction statistics. The
main thrust of the article concerns the physical
plant. Quality materials have been used throughout.
The school has no movable walls; they were sacrificed
for additional size and economy in classroom construction. Rooms have been provided with adequate
artificial lighting. Attractive colors, the soft
feeling of natural wood, furniture comfortable for
students of this age, and the extensive use of carpet
has made this school a home away from home.

5068.   School Management magazine.   "Five superintendents
plan a junior high school."   School Management, 4
(1960):88.

Describes what administrators feel should be included
in a junior high school building.

5069.   School Management magazine.   "Middle school for
tomorrow: successor to the junior high school."
School Management, 4,11(1960):101-107.

Describes the middle school house concept, organization, design components, homeroom area, seminar and
classroom space, work space, large group meeting
room, and team teaching center. Also describes the
machine in the house plan, the barn, and how the
design would function in a suburban middle school, in
a multifloor urban school, and in an exurban middle
school. Following the White Plains Conference of
School Superintendents in 1960, architect Brubaker
and consultant Leggett drew up their idea of a middle
school. The article contains sketches of their
ideas. Plans for this model school were sent to five
superintendents, who were asked whether the design
would fit the needs of their community and what
changes they would want to make. Article gives
responses by the superintendents.

5070.   School Management magazine.   "Remodel or build?
How one district decided."   School Management,
October 1964:71-75.

The Evert, Washington, school district decided to
remodel a school into a new middle school. The
article presents photographs of the remodeling, plans
showing the alterations, and a timetable. The
remodeled school had these advantages: 1) The new
classrooms and laboratories were comparable to the
best model facilities.   2) Planners departmentalized

the classrooms that were not scattered around the
building. 3) They provided facilities which did not
exist in the old building: counseling offices,
faculty lounges, and adequate student activity
spaces. 4) The new building will be easier to
maintain.

5071.   School Management magazine. "Teachers designed
this school." School Management, August 1968:30.

Teachers had the major responsibility for developing
the specs for the Goshen, New York, Middle School.
It was designed to serve as a bridge between the
primary school's concentration on basic learning
skills and the secondary school's relative specialization; between self-contained classrooms and
departmentalized instruction; between the relative
simplicity of childhood and the complexity of
adolescence. Teachers decided on six main ideas for
the building: 1) separate schools within a school
for the different grades, 2) a central core of
facilities with the focus on the library-curriculum
center, 3) regular classrooms, 4) wings (including a
science wing, an independent study wing, and an art,
home ec, and industrial arts wing), 5) an auditorium
which may be subdivided into three large-group
teaching stations or joined to the cafeteria for
large assemblies and meetings, and 6) a gymnasium
which divides into three smaller gymnasiums.

5072.   School Management magazine. "One-room schoolhouse
1972 style." School Management, 15,4(1971):17-20.

Describes an open-plan middle school with split-level
classroom areas. Article presents pictures of the
central area of this school, in the Middle Island
School District on Long Island as well as a model
showing the split-level classroom area, a floor plan,
and a site plan showing parking and playing areas.
An important philosophy of the school was that movement of children from one learning group to another
would be expected rather than unusual and the size of
learning groups would vary from hour to hour and day
to day, providing a healthy balance between group
interests and individual needs. The middle school
educational program was based on the philosophy of
multilevel learning with recognition of the differences among children of the same age. The program
would include multiage grouping, special emphasis on
the individual, and maximum flexibility of learning
activities. The school was divided physically into
three sections: the academic, the unified arts, and
the physical education area. Four student house
clusters functioned as small schools within the full
educational plan.

5073.   School Management magazine. "Five remodeling projects and the ideas they offer." School Management,
17,7(1973):18-23.

Tells how the Shoreline School District outside of
Seattle responded to a decrease in elementary and
junior high population and an increase in high school
age population by converting old lower level schools
into high schools. The architects employed several
methods to gain the spatial relationships and the
quality of space needed for the new program.

5074.   School Management magazine. "Modernization gives
a fresh face and new uses to three already existing
schools." School Management, 18,7(1974):22-25.

One of the three schools in this article is the
Marcus Kiley Junior High School in Springfield,
Massachusetts. Article discusses how a building with
too many children was remodeled to provide room for
the continually rising number of students. Pictures
are included. The basic decision favored building a
dramatically larger media center supplemented by full
support spaces, including a language laboratory, and
subdividing the original library into conventional
teachers' stations. Also added were two new science
rooms, preparation areas, storage areas, and an
olympic-sized swimming pool.

5075.   Sumption, M. R. and Landes, J. L. Planning Functional School Buildings. New York: Harper and Bros.,
1957.

Describes a model junior high facility.

5076.   Tenoschok, M. "After-hours community school programs." Journal of Physical Education and Recreation,
48,9(1977):38.

Describes the Dodgen Middle School in Marietta,
Georgia, an open-classroom facility for grades 6-8.
Each grade has its own cluster area which is broken
down into three pods. Much flexibility is found in
the building, and at the end of the school day the
building continues to provide many opportunities for
interested individuals through the community school
program. This program operates in conjunction with
eleven middle schools in Cobb County and provides
thirty-eight classes in subjects such as yoga,
macrame, real estate, and computer data pocessing.
Article discusses the physical layout of the building
and includes pictures.

5077.   Texas Education Agency. "Planning for Tweeners."
Bulletin 571, Austin, Tex., 1955.

This bulletin is primarily concerned with plant design for schools for teens. Discussion is organized according to eight pupil traits.

5078. Truesdell, W. H. "The new importance of renovation." School Management, 17,7(1973):12-15.

This article on the dramatic and economical remodeling of an old school building is useful for school boards which have old buildings that need renovation. The administrative office complex was remodeled and expanded, and the small gymnasium became an auditorium and large-group instruction area. Four standard lecture/lab facilities were built into a large open area, and new acoustical ceilings were installed throughout. New stairwells and an elevator were installed, a boiler was replaced, and modern lighting was added.

5079. West, G. "Why even the best prepared voters rebel at educational innovations." American School Board Journal, 160,1(1973):53-55.

Discusses the problems that arose when the Polk County, Florida, Board of Education decided to build an open-space junior high school based on the individualized instruction concept. Author makes seven suggestions for other principals who are planning innovative schools: 1) Take stock of the character and attitude of the community. 2) Make contingency plans that establish procedures to follow in routine and emergency situations, including potential discipline problems. 3) Select the best-qualified principal available and do so at the earliest possible moment in the planning of the school. 4) Employ qualified, highly motivated teachers. 5) Conduct a formal public relations campaign if your budget permits. 6) When trouble erupts, respond with open meetings. 7) Early and continuing communication between parents and educators is the single most important ingredient in the introduction of a new educational concept to any community.

5080. Whiteside, Moeckel, and Carbonell, Architects. "Henry B. duPont Middle School, Alexis I. duPont School District." Wilmington, Del., ERIC Doc. ED 035 255, 1966.

This new middle school is designed for individualized instruction, team teaching for large and small groups, and independent study. Sections of this paper cover the middle school concept, the vertical team approach, the horizontal team approach, a typical pupil schedule, a typical teacher schedule, a floor plan of team offices, a floor plan of the main level, a data sheet, and diagrams of the functional relationships of the basic program elements.

5081. Wilson, R. E. and Bennett, H. K. "Junior high school built to meet community specifications." Nation's Schools, 51(1953):66-73.

Describes the planning and establishing of a junior high school following a study of the Dearborn, Michigan, community. Includes illustrations of plant and facilities.

5082. Wohlers, A. E. "Planning middle school facilities." The Administrator, 2(1972):23-26.

Any educational facility must be planned on the basis of qualitative and quantitative needs on the one hand, and available resources on the other. Qualitative needs are the needs of the educational program and include the school's philosophy, curriculum, and instructional and learning modes. Quantitative needs concern enrollment figures. Available resources include people and existing facilities as well as dollars. Article discusses the characteristics and needs of middle school students and their implications for planning. Sections of the article are: 1) Planning on the Basis of Needs. 2) Middle School Youth. 3) Variety and Flexibility. 4) Instructional and Learning Modes. Many middle schools throughout the country exemplify the desirable qualities mentioned in this article, including the Andrew Jackson School in Kanawha County, Charleston, West Virginia. Article describes its program, large-group activities, small-group and independent activities, specialized activities, other program elements, and support facilities.

5083. Wolin, R. B. "School features divisible theatre-in-the-round." American School Board Journal, 153 (1966):8-11.

Discusses a school plant suitable for junior high students.

6

Internal Organization of Schools
for Early Adolescents:
Team Teaching, Departmentalization,
and Related Concepts

6001.   American Federation of Teachers.   "Tomorrow's middle school." American Teacher, 58,6(1974):16-17.

The American Federation of Teachers advocates an enrollment of 750 to 800 pupils for a middle school with units of four classes (20 students each) and three units per grade level.

6002.   Anderson, R. H.   "Organizational character of education: staff utilization and deployment." Review of Educational Research, 34(1964):455-469.

Author concludes that "recent research upon which policy of staff utilization and deployment must be based, at least temporarily, is woefully inadequate. Existing arrangements do not seem to satisfy some criteria for a school organization and a program consistent with psychological and physiological needs of pupils."

6003.   Anderson, R., Hagstrum, A. A., and Robinson, W. M. "Team teaching in an elementary school." School Review, 68(1960):71-84.

Describes the organization of Franklin School, Lexington, Massachusetts, where the delta plan for fifth and sixth grade teachers has a team leader in charge assisted by a senior teacher.

6004.   Association for Supervision and Curriculum Development.   A Look at Continuity in the School Program.   1958 Yearbook. Washington, D.C., 1958.

A section discusses the problems students have with the abrupt change from elementary self-contained classrooms to the departmentalized junior high school. A core program that gives students two or more periods with one teacher can help because that teacher gets to know better the strengths and weaknesses of each student. Author discusses ways one school system scheduled the seventh, eighth, and ninth grades to provide for the transition from the self-contained classroom to the departmentalized program. He also discusses the procedures used in one junior high school to orient students to the senior high school they will attend. A section on orientation to new school levels based on systemwide responsibility is included.

6005. Association for Supervision and Curriculum Development. "The Self-contained Classroom." Washington, D.C., 1960.

Bulletin describes self-contained classrooms at the elementary and junior high school level. It supports the idea of the self-contained classroom and the junior high school core program.

6006. Association for Supervision and Curriculum Development, 1964 Yearbook Committee, Doll., R. C. (Ed.) Individualizing Instruction. Washington, D.C., 1964.

Chapter 5 deals with the effect of environment on individualized instruction. The book is especially helpful for a middle school or junior high school in its discussions on the criteria for a setting conducive to personal fulfillment of the learner, the climate for learning, and establishing a climate for release of potential. A section on the teacher as a catalyst notes that the classroom atmosphere is a reflection of the teacher, who builds respect for learning and helps each child to achieve new perceptions. A chapter on the school setting, facilities, and furnishings stresses that they should be flexible, should encourage interaction, and should promote a variety of ways to learn. There are sections on space, time and timing, resources for learning, types of resources, human resources, exploratory and experimental materials, materials and opportunities for self-expression, printed materials, audiovisual materials, and newer learning media. A section on guidelines for selection and use of learning resources points out that the selection of resources should be based on definite criteria, that certain conditions facilitate classroom use of resources, and that the ultimate test of resources is their usefulness to the individual learner. The book discusses how learning can be individualized in an institution originally organized to deal with masses of learners.

6007.   Bahner, J. M. "Grouping within a school." Childhood Education, 36(1960):354-356.

Describes 5-6, 4-5, and 4-6 groupings of students
and has a section on team teaching.

6008.   Bair, M. and Woodward, R. G. Team Teaching in
Action. Boston: Houghton-Mifflin Co., 1964.

Covers five years of team teaching in the Lexington,
Massachusetts, school system, including examples in
several junior high schools.

6009.   Baker, J. A. "Interdisciplinary grade level
teams: from jargon to reality." Middle School
Journal, 7,1(1976):10-11.

Discusses the background of the teaching concept,
team composition, sociology of the team, minimum
expectations for the team, the possibilities of teaming, and this message: "A house grade level team at
Jamesville-DeWitt Middle School is comprised of six
or more educational specialists whose primary, joint
concern is fulfilling the scholastic needs of the
approximately 120 individual students for whom they
share responsibility. The extent to which it accomplishes this awesome task determines, in significant
measure, the success of the school."

6010.   Baker, V. K. "Big friend, a tutorial program."
Educational Leadership, 30,8(1973):733-735.

The most effective teachers for some children, some
of the time, are other children. Time, space, and
personnel can make it possible for two children to
work together as a team in a one-to-one relationship.
An older student, 9 to 13 years of age, teams with a
younger student, 5 to 8 years of age, in order to
meet the needs of one or both. Article discusses the
peer and big friend tutorial program at Holmes School
in Mesa, Arizona.

6011.   Barrett, R. E. "Nongraded learning units revamp
junior high school." Bulletin of the National
Association for Secondary School Principals, 57,
370(1973):85-91.

A nongraded learning approach described in this
article resulted in improvement on standardized
tests, fewer discipline problems, less school
vandalism, and better student-teacher relationships.
Article contains sections on the program organization
of this nongraded learning approach, the unit placement, the scheduling, a sample schedule, record
keeping, and early evaluative data.

6012.   Beane, J. A.   Options for Interdisciplinary Teams.
Dissemination Services on the Middle Grades, vol. 7,
no. 5, pp. 1-4.   Springfield, Mass.:   Educational
Leadership Institute, 1976.

Presents the interdisciplinary team concept, with
ideas on how to integrate teaming into various areas
of the curriculum.

6013.   Bishop, D. W.   "The role of the local administrator in reorganizing elementary schools to test a
semi-departmentalized plan."   Journal of Educational
Sociology, 34(1961):344-348.

Describes the administrator's role in a core concept
upper elementary school.

6014.   Brown, E. D.   "New Approaches to Flexible Scheduling at Harwood Junior High School."   Paper presented at the Annual Meeting of the National Association of Secondary School Principals, Las Vegas,
ERIC Doc. ED 101 460, February, 1975.

Describes a trimester program that divides the
regular school year into three equal sixty-day
periods.   The option of a summer quarter can be
added.   Periods of seventy minutes in the junior high
school are divided into smaller blocks of time to
better accommodate new teaching methods.   The school
uses team teaching, open-space classrooms, and
resource labs.   This plan enables students to concentrate on fewer courses at a given time and have more
school resources available.   Students who do not make
adequate progress have an opportunity to catch up
within the school year without losing normal course
offerings.   Teachers have longer planning periods,
can teach more in their fields of interest, and have
increased student contact.   See ERIC Abstract #ED 101
460.

6015.   Buffie, E. G.   "Potentials for team teaching in
the junior high school."   In Beggs, D. W. (Ed.),
Team Teaching, pp. 73-74.   Bold New Venture Series.
Bloomington: Indiana University Press, 1964.

If the junior high school is to serve as a transition
between the self-contained elementary classroom and
the departmentalized arrangement of senior high
school, then a junior high program which combines the
strengths of both is a must.   As team teaching
becomes a strong, vigorous element on the educational
scene in junior high schools, one can expect to see
significant curricular changes taking place.   Schools
will move in the direction of a nongraded curriculum
with complete emphasis on continuous education for
all students.

6016.   Bulletin of the National Association of Secondary
         School Principals.   "The daily schedule in junior
         high schools."   Bulletin of the National Association
         of Secondary School Principals, 40(1956):176-221.

         Studies indicate that some form of block-time organi-
         zation (combining two, three, or four class periods
         in a single class under one teacher) is used in over
         40 percent of junior high schools having an enroll-
         ment of less than three hundred pupils and in over 50
         percent of schools with more than three hundred
         pupils.   According to a study of large junior high
         schools, 57.3 percent of 1170 responding schools used
         some block-time classes, and in schools enrolling
         over a thousand pupils, 72.5 percent used block-time
         classes.

6017.   Byhre, E. B.   "Bloomington's flexible modular
         scheduling: an enabling act."   Minnesota Journal of
         Education, September 1968:11-13.

         Discusses the hypothetical case of Joe Smith entering
         a junior high school with flexible modular sched-
         uling.   Describes the structured and unstructured
         mods, increased participation of students, and the
         use of free time.   Presents a student schedule with
         descriptions of curriculum in English, United States
         history, mathematics, and life science.   Also dis-
         cusses the schedules of teachers and paraprofes-
         sionals.

6018.   Claremont Graduate School.   "The Claremont Teach-
         ing Team Program." Claremont, Calif., 1961.

         Describes the school-within-a-school concept and
         explains how it works in various situations,
         including junior high schools.   (Another source
         describing the Claremont plan is given in bibliog-
         raphy entry 6023.)

6019.   Clinchy, E.   "Profiles of Significant Schools:
         Schools for Team Teaching."   New York: Educational
         Facilities Laboratories, 1961.

         Gives ten examples of recent and planned elementary
         and junior high schools designed to house team
         teaching programs.   Team teaching is defined and
         discussed, and a section is included on the demand it
         places on school construction and organization.
         Article suggests ways buildings can make team group-
         ing and movement natural and easy.

6020.   Committee for Economic Development, Research and
         Policy Committee.   "Innovation in Education: New
         Directions for the American School."   A Statement on
         National Policy, New York, July, 1968.

In Chapter 3, Parts I and II on curriculum and individualized instruction pertain to middle schools and junior high schools. They discuss how flexible student groups can provide more meaningful contact with teachers and student peers, and can permit maximum independence for those who are capable of pursuing their studies on an individual basis. This is especially important where teachers use the new media. The traditional grouping of students simply by age or years in school ignores the importance of treating every person in accordance with his individual needs and talents. The committee recommends continued and more extensive experimentation in school organization to eliminate the regimentation of students that results from the conventional class units and lockstep method of advancement. "We believe that the combination of differentiated staffs, team teaching, and variable student groups, together with the use of instructional television and other audiovisual media, has much promise for individualizing instruction."

6021.   Council for Administrative Leadership.   "The Administrative Organization of Modern Junior High Schools." Albany, N. Y., 1959.

This study of junior high schools in New York State revealed: 1) There is no distinct pattern for the performance of administrative functions on the junior high level.   2) Administrative functions are not being delegated to subordinates. 3) The junior high school staffs were inadequate numerically. 4) No single pattern staffing is best for all junior highs. The study suggested the following guides for the administration of junior high schools: 1) greater organizational flexibility than is necessary at the high school level, but at the same time greater adherence to basic rules and regulations than is necessary in the self-contained classroom of the elementary school, 2) a truly gradual transition from relative informality to a more complex and necessarily rigid operation, 3) extended use of the specialist or teacher with special talent within the organizational structure, 4) provision for maintaining close contact with the child as he moves away from the atmosphere of the self-contained classroom, an organization which recognizes that children will err and which creates an atmosphere in which young adolescents can test their emerging self-concept. Study also provides an organizational chart with an optimum staffing pattern for a junior high school of seven hundred to a thousand students.

6022.   Davis,   H.   S.   Team Teaching Bibliography. Cleveland: Educational Research Council of Greater Cleveland, 1964.

This is a comprehensive bibliography containing an annotated books and pamphlets section. All articles are cataloged according to teaching level, and sub-divided by topic.

6023.   Davis, H. S.   How to Organize an Effective Team Teaching Program.   Successful School Management Series.   Englewood Cliffs, N. J.: Prentice-Hall, 1966.

Answers the question "What is team teaching?" Discusses hierarchic teams and synergetic teams, and describes team teaching in schools throughout the United States, including the Claremont school-within-a-school plan used in many middle schools. Includes chapters on implementing a team teaching program, planning for large-group instruction, small-group discussion, independent study, and evaluating the results of team teaching. (For another source on the Claremont plan, see bibliography entry 6018.)

6024.   Delavan, F. E. and Hartwig, K. E.   "A Partial Assessment of the Will C. Wood Junior High School Nongraded Plan of Organization."   Sacramento, Calif.: Sacramento City Unified School District, ERIC Doc. ED 011 408, February 28, 1967.

Using standardized tests and teacher opinions, the nongraded plan of school organization at Wood Junior High School in 1964 was evaluated and compared with graded programs at other schools. In the nongraded plan skills and concepts in reading and arithmetic are divided into convenient, logical, and sequential units of work called phases. Each phase is a continuum of work with a varying time element. The population in this study consisted of three pupil groups: 212 seventh graders in a nongraded organization, 223 eighth graders in a nongraded organization, and pupils in graded junior high schools who were matched with the second experimental group. Student achievement and attendance were measured. The academic status of the first two groups remained virtually the same under the nongraded plan. The gains made by the graded pupils in the matched pair group exceeded those made by the nongraded pupils. Attendance did not decrease as a result of non-gradedness, and teachers generally agreed with the theory of the nongraded plan.

6025.   DiVirgilio, J.   "Guidelines for effective interdisciplinary teams."   Clearinghouse, 47,4(1972): 209-211.

Interdisciplinary teams hold meetings to become professionally effective in working with children, in selecting and using various teaching strategies, and

in planning the curriculum. Article presents good
ideas for interdisciplinary teams. The team should
be aware that the curriculum has two objectives: one
is concerned with student behavior and growth, and
the other is concerned with knowledge of academic
subjects. Teaching methods vary depending on which
of these objectives is foremost, and the ability of a
team to recognize and clearly delineate the two will
affect the quality of discussion about children as
well as decisions about how to help them.

6026.   Docking, R. and Hogan, D. "Breaking grade barriers." Michigan Educational Journal, 42(1965):
16-17.

Discusses the effect of a school change to
ungradedness, elimination of study halls and heterogeneous groups, individualized programs, and flexible
schedules, with ramifications for middle grades and
junior high schools.

6027.   Dougherty, J.H., Gorman, F.H., and Phillips, C.A.
Elementary School Organization and Management.   New
York: Macmillan, 1936.

Some of the advantages claimed for departmental
organization are: 1) It provides for more efficient
instruction. 2) It offers an enriched curriculum.
3) It attracts more highly trained teachers. 4) It
allows for concentration of equipment. 5) It allows
pupils to be promoted by subject instead of grade.
6) It allows pupils to have contact with more teaching personalities. 7) It is favored by both teachers
and children in schools with departmentalization.
The arguments against departmentalization are: 1) It
overemphasizes the subject matter. 2) Teachers are
only narrow specialists. 3) Behavior problems are
more difficult to handle. 4) It destroys the unity
of school life for the pupil. 5) It prevents integration of subject matter. 6) The plan has been
borrowed from secondary school practice.

6028.   Douglass, M. P.   "Team teaching: fundamental
change or passing fancy?" California Teachers
Association Journal, 59(1963):26-29.

Tells teachers how to begin a team teaching approach
in an elementary or junior high school.

6029.   Drummond, H. D. "Team teaching: an assessment."
Educational Leadership, 19(1961):160-165.

Describes the various types of team teaching,
including a hierarchy of teaching assignments,
coordinate or coteaching, and team teaching across
departmental lines.

6030.   Dunn, S. V.   "The Educational Park: The Middle School."   A report on material on file in the Berkeley Unified School District Research Office and some additional sources from the Berkeley Schools Professional Library. September, 1966.

Educational parks have from 10,000 to 25,000 students, a central location, administrative centralization, and decentralized school design. Advantages include: 1) providing a partial solution to de facto segregation, 2) reducing the cost and complexity of educational facilities, and 3) better accommodation of location population shifts.   Disadvantages include: 1) large size, 2) impersonal atmosphere, 3) tighter administrative control, and 4) cost of transporting students.   Middle school benefits include: 1) improved transition from elementary to high school, 2) a specially designed program to fit the needs of preadolescents, and 3) promotion of integration by drawing students from a larger attendance area.   An annotated bibliography is included.

6031.   Edling, J. V.   "Programmed instruction in a continuous progress school."   In Four Cases of Programmed Instruction.   New York: Fund for the Advancement of Education, 1964.

Brigham Young University Laboratory School in Provo, Utah, is intensively using various forms of programmed material in grades K-12 as part of a continuous progress curriculum.   They have found in the junior high school that there is some student complaint about boredom, dullness, and taking too much time.   They have also concluded that the use of programmed materials is difficult in a conventional junior high classroom; this requires a greatly changed approach by the teacher.   Their conclusions are: 1) Programmed instruction is effective and worth continuing.   2) This requires a comprehensive knowledge of the subject by the teacher, since in any given class young adolescents will exhibit an extreme range of performance.   3) Programmed instruction requires more, not less, work from the teacher since he must be prepared to work with many students, few if any of whom are at the same place.   4) Young adolescents are so variable that it is difficult to write a single program that fits every student.   5) Discipine problems are reduced.   6) Effective learning cannot be expected from all students who use programmed materials.   7) Class participation and contribution of other students are reduced and may be eliminated.

6032.   English, J. J. and Canady, R. L.   "Building the middle school schedule."   Middle School Journal, 6,4(1975):59-62.

Article shows how parallel scheduling can reduce pupil-to-teacher/adult ratios. It is a modification of a basic block scheduling practice employed in many elementary schools. A second type of modular scheduling helps make skill groups flexible and reduces their size by using an extension center along with parallel scheduling. These approaches have been designed to provide differentiated instruction and to help readers design schedules for their own situations.

6033.   Farran, D. C. and Yanofsky, S. M.   "Change in Junior High Schools: Two Case Studies." Philadelphia: Pennsylvania Advancement School, ERIC Doc. ED 169 165, April, 1972.

Discusses background information and history of two mini-schools and the development of relationships between their administrative teams. Topics include the instructional programs, team functioning, effects of the mini-school on each student, general junior high school problems such as discipline, and teaching approaches. See ERIC Abstract #ED 169 165.

6034.   Fazzaro, C. J. "The nongraded junior high school: a place for the young adolescent to grow." North Central Association Quarterly, 49,4(1975):380-386.

Making intelligent decisions about a nongraded program for junior high and middle schools requires a substantial conceptual framework based on the nature of the nongraded school concept, the young adolescent, and the teaching staff. Article discusses the traditional junior high school, the traditional American concept of school organization, the definition of a nongraded school, the young adolescent, the junior high school teacher, and the advantages of the nongraded school for early adolescents.

6035.   Finley, R. "The Middle School and Flexible Scheduling."   Paper presented at the Minnesota School Facilities Council Conference, Minneapolis, 1968.

Author sees more possibility for flexible scheduling in a middle school of grades 5-8 than in a junior high setting where the scheduling is actually a miniature of the high school program.

6036.   Fisher, D. L.   "When students choose and use independent study time." Educational Leadership, 31,3(1973):267-270.

Students develop confidence and poise through a Detroit middle school's built-in plan for decision making.

6037.   Fleming, R. F., Hurley, B., Keliher, A. B., and
Manolakes, G. "Reactions to the dual progress plan."
Educational Leadership, 18(1960):92-95.

Discusses problems in implementing the dual progress
plan and the need for further evaluation of this
organizational pattern for upper elementary students.

6038.   Fogg, W. F. and Diamond, H. J. "Two versions of
the 'house' plan." Nation's Schools, 48(1961):65-69.

Describes a vertical house plan for grades 6, 7, and
8 and a horizontal house plan for grade 6 only in a
school serving grades 6, 7, and 8. The schools are
in Scarsdale and Niskayuna, New York. Both districts
report benefit from the house plan in increased
attention to individual pupils without loss of large-
school facilities. The article answers these questions: How is the school organized?   Is there any
grouping? How do the teachers function? What about
administration? How are classes scheduled? What are
the advantages of the house plan? What are the special problems? Is the house plan expensive? Keys to
this concept are: 1) Most important in creating and
maintaining the elementary school atmosphere has been
the establishment of heterogeneous homeroom groups.
2) Team teachers plan their activities and schedules
together.   3) The dual approach to teaching assures
balanced instruction.   While the heterogeneous homeroom group and the homeroom teacher assure warmth and
security for the individual child, the homogeneous
reading, mathematics, and science classes provide
special stimulation and challenge.   4) Important in
the program is the activity.   5) School people have
seen in this new junior high house program, including
the new kind of sixth grade, answers to two pressing
needs: higher quality of education and adequate
school housing for a rapidly growing school population.

6039.   Garner, A. E.   "Interdisciplinary team teaching:
is your middle school ready?" Bulletin of the
National Association of Secondary School Principals,
60,403(1976):98-102.

Author suggests analyzing the curriculum to improve
use of equipment, resources, facilities, and the
skills and talents of the teaching staff. Analysis
and planning involve the following steps: identify
the content and objective of the instruction unit,
develop a tentative time schedule, select materials,
determine who should teach, and plan the grouping
arrangements. To determine if your interdisciplinary
teaching system is viable, answer the following questions: 1) Do we have specific reasons for implementing interdisciplinary team teaching?   2) Does our

schedule provide time for adequate team planning? 3) Will team members adapt better to a hierarchical or rotating team leader approach? 4) Are leadership attributes evident in the team leaders? 5) Do we have adequate facilities to house large-group, small-group and independent instruction? 6) Are proper instructional materials available? 7) Are the resources and time available for in-service preparation of team teachers? 8) Do we have adequate testing programs to provide continuous feedback on pupil progress? 9) Is our grading system properly correlated with the instructional objectives of team teaching? 10) Will the grouping patterns be flexible to provide for transferring students between groups? 11) What instruments do we have for identifying and capitalizing on the strengths of each team member? Article also discusses some problems of team teaching: 1) Faculty members may not have internalized the philosophy upon which the concept is based. 2) Team members may be unprepared to develop an interdisciplinary instructional unit. 3) There may be inadequate provision of resources and space. 4) Team members may be unable to schedule student activities to accomplish the learning objectives. 5) Some team members may be incompatible.

6040.   George, P. S.   "Ten years of open-space schools: a review of the research."   Florida Educational Research and Development Council at Gainesville, Research Bulletin, 9,3(1975). ERIC Doc. ED 110 431.

This ninety-page report reviews the past ten years of research on open-space schools. Report discusses open space and teachers, open space and students' achievement and behavior, critiquing the research on open-space schools, conclusions and recommendations, and references. Author concludes: 1) Both teachers and students in open-space schools believe that noise level is a problem. 2) Neither the open-space school nor the conventional school has demonstrated academic superiority. 3) Open-space schools seem to provide greater opportunities for alternative learning. 4) Open-space schools seem to help students develop a more positive self-concept. Sections are included on definitions, historical development, overview, the Stanford studies on open-space schools and teaching, interaction and visibility, visibility and evaluation, teacher influence in open-space schools, job satisfaction, ambition in open-space schools, other studies of teacher behavior in open-space schools, verbal interaction and use of time, preparing teachers, teacher opinion about open-space schools, teaching style, effects of in-service education, student achievement, student attitudes and quasi-academic behavior, the open-space school and student affect, the open-space school and organizational climate.

6041.   Glancy, P. B.   "Brookside Junior High School, Sarasota, Florida, strives for quality education." Bulletin of the National Association of Secondary School Principals, 46(1962):157-160.

In this team teaching program in English, American history, physics, algebra, and general science, student groupings were sometimes made on an ability basis, sometimes not, depending upon the purposes and nature of instruction.   Students met in large groups once or twice weekly and in regular classrooms other days.

6042.   Glenn, E. E.   "Plan ahead for team teaching." American School Board Journal, 154(1967):34-37.

The MacArthur School Plan for Team Teaching emphasizes flexible scheduling, nongraded study, individualized instruction, independent study featuring the student's responsibility for his own learning, and critical and creative thinking.   The MacArthur School was organized with the following personnel: 1) a school principal to serve as the instructional leader and coordinator and consultant for the teacher teams, 2) team leaders to call, organize, and preside at teacher team meetings, 3) teachers who plan the instructional program cooperatively, 4) clerical aid and school secretary/clerks. The article contains information concerning the selection of staff, preparation of parents, flexible scheduling, and parent, teacher, and student reaction to the MacArthur plan of team teaching.

6043.   Goodlad, J. I. and Anderson, R. H.   The Nongraded Elementary School.   Rev. ed.   New York: Harcourt, Brace and World, 1963.

Authors propose reorganizing the elementary school in part to accommodate a curriculum organized vertically around fundamental concepts, principles, and modes of inquiry.   The plan is appropriate to the middle grades.

6044.   Goodlad, J. I. and Rehage, K.   "Unscrambling the vocabulary of school organization."   National Education Association Journal, 51(1962):34-36.

Discusses horizontal school organization, vertical school organization, team teaching, and the school's overall organizational pattern.

6045.   Green, D. R. and Riley, H. W.   "Interclass grouping for reading instruction in the middle grades." Journal of Experimental Education, 31(1963):273-278.

In four Atlanta elementary schools the Jocklin Plan of Interclass Grouping by Reading Ability or Reading Instruction was tried. Typically, students in grades 4-5 and 6-7 or grades 4-6 met daily for forty-five minutes in groups made as homogeneous as possible with respect to reading skills. The study implies criticism of the self-contained classroom for middle grade students.

6046. Heathers, G. "Dual progress plan." Educational Leadership, 18(1960):89-91.

Describes the dual progress plan of learning with special emphasis on individualized learning.

6047. Heathers, G. Organizing Schools Through the Dual Progress Plan: Tryouts of a New Plan for Elementary and Middle Schools. Danville, Ill.: Interstate Printers and Publishers, 1967.

Book discusses a demonstration test of the dual progress plan in grades 7 and 8 of junior high schools in New York. The plan includes nongraded curricular sequences, employment of full-time specialist teachers, and the rejection of self-contained general purpose classrooms. Objectives include mastery of communication skills and knowledge of United States tradition and background. One half of the day students are with other students of the same age and a core teacher. It was concluded that the dual progress plan does not accomplish major improvement and instructional quality and that ability grouping was harmful in some areas. Chapters are: 1) A New Approach to Organizing Instruction. 2) Planning the Cooperative Study of the Dual Progress Plan. 3) Installing the Dual Progress Plan. 4) Building Curricular Sequences for the Plan. 5) In-service Education for Specialist Teachers in the Plan. 6) A Master's Degree Program for Elementary Specialist Teachers. 7) Problems in Implementing the Dual Progress Plan. 8) Assessing the Implementation of the Dual Progress Plan. 9) Student Achievement in the Dual Progress Plan. 10) Attitudes and Adjustment of the Participants in the Plan. 11) Disseminating the Plan through Affiliated School Systems. 12) Summary Assessment of the Dual Progress Plan.

6048. Heathers, G. Grouping. Philadelphia, Pa.: Research for Better Schools, 1967.

In the junior high school, core programs provide a compromise between the self-contained classroom and the fully departmentalized programs of most secondary schools. In the core approach as described by Wright and Della-Dora (1960), English and social studies are taught as one integrated curriculum in one time

block by one teacher. Similarly, in many core programs, mathematics and science are taught together by
one teacher. Core programs are meant to offer a more
secure setting than regular departmental programs and
to correlate instruction in related subjects better.
Research studies reviewed by Michelson (1957) did not
demonstrate any major effects of core programs on
students' achievements or their adjustment at school.
In a pilot study of the dual progress plan (see
bibliography entry 6047), an attempt was made to
implement the plan in grades 7 and 8 of junior high
school, but it proved impossible to find teachers who
were prepared and willing to teach both English and
social studies.

6049.   Henry, N. B. (Ed.)   Individualizing Instruction.
61st Yearbook of the National Society for the Study
of Education, Part I.   Chicago: University of
Chicago Press, 1962.

Chapter 8 by Harold E. Jones and Mary Cover Jones
deals with individual differences in early adolescence, including physical development, cognitive
functioning, the peer culture, and the independence-
dependence dilemma. Chapter 12 by John T. Goodlad
deals with individual differences and vertical
organization of the school and discusses school function and organizational form, modifying grade structure in the search for continuous progress plans, and
nongraded plans.

6050.   Hoffmann, E. B. "The Brookhurst plan." National
Education Association Journal, 54(1965):50-52.

Brookhurst Junior High School in Anaheim, California,
experimented with a pilot program for ninth graders.
The Brookhurst Plan is based on a schedule which
changes daily according to teaching team requests for
time and students.   Teachers may request a single
student or as many as 350 for lengths of time which
vary from twenty minutes to a full day. The article
answers these questions about the plan: 1) Who
determines the amount of time, the facilities needed,
the size of the group, and the time of day for a particular activity?   2) How are priorities assigned?
3) Who determines what classes a student will attend
each day?   4) What are the mechanics of the scheduling process? 5) How long does it take a student to
fill out his schedule? 6) How does the office handle
the problem of providing a class role? 7) Has flexible scheduling affected academic achievement?

6051.   Howard, E. R. and Bardwell, R. W.   How to Organize
a Nongraded School.   Successful School Management
Series.   Englewood Cliffs, N. J.:   Prentice-Hall,
1966.

Discusses nongradedness as an approach to flexibility, with sections on how nongradedness is used in
some elementary schools and secondary schools,
including some promising practices in the junior high
schools.   Monograph surveys nongradedness in math,
science, English, and history and discusses in detail
the nongraded schools of Melbourne and Redgewood.
Facilities for large-group instruction, seminars,
learning laboratories, and the library are considered, and suggestions are given for establishing a
nongraded program.

6052.   Hyland, A.   "First round draft choice for middle
school teaching team."   Middle School Journal,
7,2(1976):14-15.

The middle school resource center specialist organizes materials and can work with teachers in curriculum teams or in planned conferences to 1) identify
topics, concepts, and skills to be introduced, reinforced, and extended, 2) identify teaching and learning experiences which require support media, 3)
determine student usage patterns necessary for knowledge building, 4) design resource usage sequences to
reinforce learning needs and experiences, and 5)
preplan for class, group, and individual student use
of resources.   Preplanning will allow the resource
center person to 1) locate presently owned materials
and borrow or purchase others which match specific
topics, concepts, and skills, 2) introduce students
to new tools, techniques, or related skills necessary
to use specific resources effectively, and 3) guide
student use toward interpretation, extension, and
evaluation of information.   Cooperatively, the
resource center person and teacher evaluate how
students use the resource center and decide how to
modify the program.

6053.   Institute for Development of Educational Activities.   "A Report of the National Seminar: Models
for Nongraded Schools."   Institute for Development of
Educational Activities, 5335 Far Hills, Dayton, Ohio
45429, 1970.

Monograph brings together knowledgeable theoreticians
and practitioners to examine the status of the
nongraded school in the United States and establish
guidelines for teachers and administrators based on
the ways nongrading and continuous progress work in
actual practice.   It presents a conceptual model of
the nongraded school including school function,
curriculum, instruction, evaluation, organization,
and role of the learner and describes the nongraded
school concept for the preadolescent.

6054.   Instructor magazine.   "A critical look at team
        teaching." Instructor, 71(1961):39-42.

        Discusses advantages and disadvantages of various
        team teaching concepts.

6055.   Kennedy Junior High School. "Pupil Placement and
        Subject Organization in the Kennedy Junior High
        School." Natick, Mass., September, 1966.

        This school grouped students into four instructional
        levels   with   differentiated   placements   for
        English/social studies and mathematics/science.

6056.   Krug, E. A., Liddle, C., and Schenk, Q. "Multiple
        period curricular organization in Wisconsin secondary
        schools." Bulletin, University of Wisconsin, School
        of Education, 1952.

        This report on Wisconsin's experience with block
        scheduling (multiple period programs) includes
        data on the years the programs were introduced, the
        grade location of the programs, courses included,
        purposes, and teaching procedures used.

6057.   Landman, J. "Who needs human relations?" Educa-
        tional Leadership, 3(1973):236-237.

        The middle school goes beyond traditional basic
        skills. One school in the Bronx tries to give human
        relations equal status with subject matter in hetero-
        geneous groupings.

6058.   Lawhead, V. B. "Guidelines for evaluating core
        programs." Educational Leadership, 18(1960):187-189.

        Presents useful suggestions for evaluating a core
        curriculum in a junior high school.

6059.   Leigh, T. G. "Big opportunities in small schools
        through flexible, modular scheduling." Journal of
        Secondary Education, 42(1967):175-187.

        Describes modular scheduling in Julien Junior High
        School in San Diego County, California.

6060.   Lovetere, J. P. "Instructional team: an approach
        to a more effective junior high school organization."
        Clearinghouse, 41(1967):301-303.

        Describes a model middle grades program.

6061.   Lowe, A. D.   "Three schools within a school."
        Bulletin of the National Association of Secondary
        School Principals, 46(1962):47-51.

Outlines the administrative structure of the school-within-a-school concept in a junior high school, suggesting responsibilities for the various members of the administrative team.

6062.   LuPold, H. G.   "Defense of the block-of-time." Clearinghouse, 39(1965):538.

Presents the rationale behind the block-time arrangement in junior high scheduling.

6063.   Marion County Board of Public Instruction.   "A Team Teaching Approach for Middle School EMR Students."   Ocala, Fla.:   Marion County Board of Public Instruction and Tallahassee: Florida State Department of Education, Education for Exceptional Children Section, ERIC Doc. ED 085 935, July, 1973.

Describes a program based on team teaching for forty-five educable mentally retarded 10-to-14-year-old students. The main focus of the program was to meet individual needs of the students.   Article describes physical facilities, qualifications of team members, student population, and curriculum development. Goals and objectives are presented in the areas of self-concept, social relations, and academics.   The students improved in reading and arithmetic in this special project, and positive behavioral changes were observed.   Article sections are: Project Rationale, Project Description, Goals and Objectives, Evaluation of the Program, Results of the Evaluation, Teaming: The Instructional Process, and Appendix.   Included are recommendations for personnel selection, class-room management, curriculum, and physical space.

6064.   McCarthy, R. J.   How to Organize and Operate an Ungraded Middle School.   Successful School Management Series.   Englewood Cliffs, N. J.:   Prentice-Hall, 1967.

Tells in detail how the Liverpool Middle School staff altered traditional attitudes and behavior to combine a whole-child approach, drawn from the elementary schools, with an emphasis on achievement in subject areas, as found in the high schools.   This was done through ungraded learning, interdisciplinary teaming of teachers and students, and establishing support systems for teaching and learning.   Monograph discusses changes in maturation of youth, staffing the ungraded middle school, organizing the staff, grouping students, coordinating teams, teacher-student relations, the role of team coordinators, the instructional consultant, a typical daily schedule, and promoting independent study.   An appendix includes evaluation sheets, progress report, model forms, and research proposals.

6065.   Merenbloom, E. Y.   "Interdisciplinary team teaching: a successful approach." Middle School Journal, 10(1979):10-11.

The faculty of the Woodlawn Middle School in Baltimore County, Maryland, has chosen to use interdisciplinary team teaching as well as other forms of team teaching at the three grade levels of their middle school. The faculty maintains that interdisciplinary team teaching is the key to the program for these reasons: 1) Students have subject matter specialists for each subject area, but there is coordination of the total program. 2) The teams can provide special units and activities beyond the regular curriculum to meet the needs of pupils. 3) Teachers can better focus on the needs of pupils through a team effort. 4) Content and skills are readily correlated. 5) A skills program is best implemented when it is integrated throughout all disciplines. 6) A personal development program is best implemented when it is integrated throughout all subject areas and among all teachers. 7) Planning periods can be used for pupil and parent conferences as well as for coordinating the instructional program. 8) A discipline code for the entire team can be established, communicated, and implemented cooperatively. 9) The use of contiguous classrooms reduces problems in the hallways; students may change classes at times decided by team members. Article sections are: 1) Faculty Chooses Interdisciplinary Model. 2) Curriculum Implemented by Team. 3) Teachers Form Their Teams. 4) Planning Period Essential for Team Success. 5) Facilitating Team Effectiveness.   6) Teachers Create Schedule. Though the number of middle schools that use team teaching is still very small (15 to 21 percent depending on the grade), the faculty of Woodlawn Middle School has demonstrated that a viable middle school program using interdisciplinary team teaching can be developed through a comprehensive staff development program. The success of the middle school concept is closely related to the ability of teachers to work together in teams to design flexible programs for meeting the needs of early adolescents.

6066.   Nanuet Public Schools.   "Grouping Policies." Nanuet, N. Y., 1966.

Suggests the following criteria for grouping: 1) general mental ability, 2) measured achievement, particularly in the basic areas of reading and arithmetic, 3) scholastic performance as measured by course grades, 4) teacher recommendation, and 5) the educational and vocational goals of the student and parent.

6067.   National Education Association. Planning and
Organizing for Teaching. Washington, D.C., 1963.

Report by the NEA project on the instructional
program of the public schools includes several
recommendations regarding team teaching in the junior
high school.

6068.   National Education Association, Department of
Classroom Teachers, Time to Teach Project. Innovations for Time to Teach. Washington, D.C., 1966.

Describes reorganization in support of good teaching,
including flexible grouping, cooperative teaching,
flexible scheduling, nongraded programs, reorganization of instruction, effective use of learning
resources, essential teaching functions, and effective pupil evaluating and reporting programs. Especially useful for middle and junior high school
teachers.

6069.   New Jersey State Department of Education. "Block-
of-Time Programs in Junior High Schools and Six-Year
High Schools in New Jersey." Secondary School
Bulletin 2. Trenton, N.J., 1960.

Describes block-time scheduling in junior high
schools.

6070.   Nickerson, N. C., Jr. "Regroup for another try."
Minnesota Journal of Education, 47(1966):14-15.

It has been said that the very name "junior high
school" is part of the reason junior high people have
been castigated for running miniature high schools.
We have given the junior high school a fifty-year
trial and seem to be faced now with vociferous complaints about it. So let's fall back and regroup for
another try. We can make a fresh start at educating
these wonderful and challenging and changing early
adolescents by reorganizing our forces around the
middle school concept.

6071.   Noall, M. F. and Jensen, L. "Team Teaching at
Roosevelt Junior High School, Duchesne County, Utah."
Bulletin of the National Association of Secondary
School Principals, 44(1960):156-163.

Authors describe and evaluate the staff utilization
studies of the National Association of Secondary
School Principals. Article is very much in favor of
team teaching.

6072.   O'Connell, W. I. "Clustering: A Means of Assist-
ing Boston Junior High School Administrators and
Staff Members to Structure a New Organizational
Pattern at the Building Level." Ed.D. Dissertation,
Harvard University, 1974.

A new pattern of organization was tested in 1970 at
the Solomon Lewensburg Junior High School in Boston.
It was designed in response to troubles which had
been besetting the school for more than a year.
Clustering staff and pupils has proven effective, and
four other junior high schools have since adopted
this organization. Paper examines the changes from
three perspectives: historical, present, and
theoretical.

6073.   Office of the County Superintendent of Schools.
"A Policy Guide for Junior High Schools in Gloucester
County." Clayton, N. J. (No year given.)

To facilitate ability grouping within the heterogeneous classroom, pupils with special needs or
problems are identified and distributed equally so
that no teacher receives too many of these pupils in
one group. The junior high school policy for
Gloucester suggests planning an enriched instructional program and increased participation in
cocurricular activities for the gifted pupil. Generally, such treatment is socially and emotionally
better for gifted pupils than acceleration by extra
promotion.

6074.   Office of Public Instruction. "Block-of-Time
Scheduling Practices in Illinois Junior High
Schools." Springfield, Ill., 1960.

Describes block-time programs in junior high schools
in Illinois.

6075.   Olsen, F. "Programmed learning in the nongraded
school." In Calvin, A. D. (Ed.), Programmed Instruction, pp. 181-192.   Bold New Venture Series.
Bloomington: Indiana University Press, 1969.

Programmed instruction can be used within a traditional bell schedule, can be a part of team teaching,
is most compatible with nongraded schools, and is
distinctly a part of independent study. Students may
progress at their own speed, and if the program is
carefully constructed an enormous number of students
can come into contact with one expert. Programmed
instruction gives each student individual attention.

6076.   Oregon Consolidated Schools, Wis. "So You Want to Team Teach in a Junior High School." Washington, D.C.: U. S. Department of Health, Education and Welfare, National Institute of Education, ERIC Doc. ED 141 348, 1977.

Sections are: 1) So You Want to Team Teach in a Junior High School. 2) We May Be Small but We Are Mighty. 3) Watch Out for the First Step! 4) Later On, You Can Get into Deeper Water. 5) The Building Has to Be Changed a Little. 6) Teaming Really Let Us Get Our Act Together. 7) There are Other Benefits Too. 8) Making Teams Is Not the End of It Though. 9) Not Everyone Thinks It Is Such a Hot Idea. 10) Shared Decision Making Gave Us a Piece of the Action. 11) The Cabinet Sounds Like a Good Idea, but It Won't Replace the Light Bulb. 12) The Cabinet Has to be Kept in Its Place. 13) All this Shared Decision Making Can Be a Drag. 14) Block Schedules Really Let Us Individualize Our Program. 15) Block Scheduling Loads Up Your Work for Half the Day, but It Doesn't Let Off the Other Half Either. 16) There are Some Limitations to Teaming in a Junior High School. 17) Goal Setting Gave Us Something to Shoot For. 18) Eventually the Curriculum Will Need a Careful Review. 19) We Took Advantage of Teaming to Produce Interdisciplinary Curriculum Units. 20) For Us, Teaming Is More Than Just Organizational. 21) So You Want to Team Teach in a Junior High School.

6077.   Patrick, J. J. "The political learning of junior high school students." Indiana Social Studies Quarterly, 24,2(1971):13-20.

Questions considered in this article are: 1) What are the model political beliefs and attitudes of junior high school students? 2) What are their capabilities for political learning? 3) What suggestions for improving instruction can be derived from studies of their political learning? See ERIC Abstract #EJ 049 602.

6078.   Pence, W. R., Jr. "A Study of Student Personality as a Function of Open vs. Traditional School Plans, Educational Climate, and Teacher Personality." Ed.D. Dissertation, University of Houston, 1976.

Author randomly selected 289 seventh and eighth grade students from five junior high schools to respond to the High School Personality Questionnaire. The faculty members of the schools responded to the Sixteen Personality Factor Instrument and the Occupational Climate Description Questionnaire. Results indicated that students seem to relate to teachers with similar traits, and certain student and teacher personality traits tend to be related to certain types of school

plans and organizational climates. The type of
school plan and teacher personality do account for
almost one fifth of the variance in student personality. The finding that educational climate showed
very little effect on student personality may have
been a function of the measure used. Further
research needs to be done using multiple measures to
gauge the effect of school climate on student personality in conjunction with school plan and teacher
personality.

6079.   Pint, R. F.   "Staff and Student Attitudes toward
Innovative Programs at the Middle School Level."
Ph.D. Dissertation, Walden University, ERIC Doc. ED
102 109, 1973.

The entire Bettendorf, Iowa Middle School staff and
student body responded to questionnaires about
Bettendorf's four-year experience with innovative use
of space, team teaching, continuous progress, independent study, standards and expectations, and
expressed philosophy. Staff and student attitudes
were equally positive toward some of the innovations,
differed significantly on some, and were equally
uncertain or negative about others. See ERIC
Abstract #ED 102 109.

6080.   Powell, W.   "The Joplin plan: an evaluation."
Elementary School Journal, April 1964:387-392.

This plan groups children in intermediate grades
homogeneously on an interclass basis by measuring the
achievement and needs of the children, organizing the
children into relatively homogeneous groups independent of their grade classification, scheduling reading classes at the same hour during the day, and dis-
persing pupils to reading classes with instructions
that adapt to their needs. A study showed no significant difference in the reading achievement of intermediate grade pupils who were taught this way and
those who were taught in a self-contained classroom.

6081.   Raymer, J.   "Kids and teachers: the why of team
teaching in the middle school." MASB Journal,
19,7(1972):17-19.

The middle school of the 1970s will find it difficult, if not impossible, to succeed without team
teaching. Team teaching should help teachers meet
the personal needs of the students through a variety
of teaching and learning techniques in a secure and
professional atmosphere where teachers have the
freedom to innovate. When administrators and
teachers work together in a happy and secure middle
school program, the same satisfaction and security is
passed on to the most important team member, the
student.

6082.   Richardson, J. A. and Cawelti, D. G. "Junior high
program lets fast and slow students take time for
independent study." Nation's Schools, 79(1967):
74-77.

Describes an independent study program at a Winnetka,
Illinois, junior high school. Sections of the arti-
cle are: 1) Including All Students. 2) Fitting
Program to Pupils. 3) Establishing a Right Environ-
ment. 4) Including Academic Consultants. 5)
Releasing Students in Three Ways. 6) Pinpointing
Progress. 7) How a Learning Lab Director Spends His
Time. 8) How a Learning Lab Student Spends His Time.

6083.   Romano, L. "A revolution in middle school education: individually guided education." Michigan
Journal of Secondary Education, Summer 1971:7-15.

Research by the Kettering Foundation's Institute for
the Development of Educational Activities supported
the concept of Individually Guided Education (IGE).
This program is designed to meet the learning needs
of the individual on the basis of an assessment of
his achievement, aptitude, and overall learning personality as these are related to his learning objective. An IGE program is a school within a school
that is designed for children rather than forcing
children to fit the school. Article describes the
organizational improvement council and in-service
training of an IGE school. Teachers must learn to 1)
plan in a team situation, 2) define objectives behaviorally, 3) use preassessment and postassessment
tools, 4) critique the work of the teaching team, 5)
ungrade the skills taught in reading, mathematics,
and spelling, and 6) develop a unit of study based
upon present ideas. In an IGE school many of the
traditional modes of operation are gone. Flexibility
in grouping, scheduling, planning, and any other
activity related to teaching and learning is the key.

6084.   Scherer, J. and Slawski, E. J. "Desegregation and
school space." Integrated Education, 16,6(1978):
38-44.

After a background of violence, an emphasis on control accompanied desegregration of this open-space
school. Unfortunately, desegregation became an end
in itself and not a step leading to more effective
learning or some form of psychological integration.
Article is divided into sections on school desegregation, the history of Pawnee West High School, soft
walls and the problem of control, and closing open
spaces (reducing openness, avoidance, reducing
permeability, and not using facilities). Another
section is on ambiguity and the use of space.

6085.   Shaplin, J. T. and Olds, H. F. (Eds.)   Team
Teaching. New York: Harper and Row, 1964.

A comprehensive treatment of the theory and practice
of team teaching, based primarily on the experiences
of faculty members at Harvard's Graduate School of
Education with cooperating schools in the region,
including many middle and junior high schools.

6086.   Simney, L. "A teacher looks at the double period
program." California Journal of Secondary Education,
27(1953):146-147.

This teacher supports block-time scheduling in junior
high school.

6087.   Sinks, T. A. "How Individualized Instruction in
Junior High School Science, Mathematics, Language
Arts, and Social Studies Affects Student Achieve-
ment." Ph. D. Dissertation, University of Illinois,
ERIC Doc. ED 058 024, 1968.

Study analyzed the effects of changing the educational environment in every way possible to achieve
an individually prescribed curriculum in social
studies, language arts, science, and math for 108
seventh grade students in four homerooms. The
Sequential Tests of Educational Progress in social
studies, writing, science, and mathematics were used
to evaluate differences in achievement between
experimental and control subjects. Results suggest
that the experimental treatment accounted for
increased gains in achievement scores on the STEP
tests in the four subject areas. See ERIC Abstract
#ED 055 158.

6088.   Springfield, C. A.   "Learning centers/station/
places." Educational Leadership, 30,8(1973):736-737.

Learning stations are successful with some students,
while other students are turned off, so the stations
should be used in connection with other techniques.
Both teachers and students may find in skill building, exploratory, or reinforcing learning stations
opportunities for more help and more individualization in an atmosphere of fun.

6089.   State Committee on Core and General Education.
"The Status of Block-Time Programs in Michigan
Secondary Schools." Bulletin 426. Lansing, Mich.:
State Superintendent of Public Instruction, 1960.

As of 1960, a majority of organized junior high
schools teach general education within blocks of two
or more periods.

6090.   Stelle, A. and Wallace, H.   "Meeting learning
         needs of the young adolescent."   Thrust for
         Educational Leadership, $\underline{8}$,3(1979):25-27.

Article describes a middle school program designed to
facilitate transition from the elementary grades.
Students may choose from self-contained, multiage, or
team teaching classrooms.   Many join the self-
contained basic education program, which moves into
departmentalized teaching in grades 7 and 8. Article
discusses how the Poway district organizes its middle
grade schools, good planning procedures, philosophy
underlying the middle school organization, and trends
in California. See ERIC Abstract #EJ 207 510.

6091.   Stepanovich, M. M.   "McKeesport Junior High
         School: School C."   Resources in Education, December
         1973:29.

Reorganization plan divides a 1600-student junior
high school into three schools within a school, each
with its own faculty team that can focus on the
individual student.   Document discusses program
rationale, advantages of having three subschools,
organizational pattern of a typical subschool,
seventh, eighth, and ninth grade curriculum, team
teaching, inductive learning, the inquiry method,
roles of the teacher and counselor, ideas for
scheduling, organizations and activities, student
involvement,   community   involvement,   program
orientation, student discipline, and evaluation of
the program, curriculum, students, and faculty.

6092.   Stoddard, G. D.   The Dual Progress Plan: New
         Philosophy and Program in Elementary Education.   New
         York: Harper and Bros., 1961.

In the dual progress plan a home teacher is in charge
of two rooms, spending a half-day in each. For each
homeroom she is responsible for doing registration
and counseling as well as teaching reading and social
studies.   In the other half-day the students have
special teachers for math and science, music, arts
and crafts, recreation and health, and--beginning
with grade 5--an optional sequence in foreign language.   The special teachers in each subject or a
cluster of subjects offer the work straight through
the elementary grades or, in a combined school,
through the twelfth grade. Thus the special teachers
as a team are in a good position to judge the quality
of special aptitudes and their growth throughout the
child's school life by observation as well as test
scores, profiles, ratings, and sample items from a
continuous comprehensive record.   A pupil's grade
standing will be determined by his home teacher, but
he will be free to pursue avidly a specialty

according to his aptitude. The specialists offer
their work as a basic education for all and as an
opportunity for the gifted. The home teacher is
concerned with pupil organization, knowing the
pupils, the families, and the neighborhoods, and
linking this knowledge to the work in social studies.
It may be predicted with confidence that the redesigning of textbooks, methods, and testing procedures
in all fields will yield dramatic results if they are
based on a knowledge of the discipline through to its
advanced levels, a knowledge of the psychology of
learning, and a knowledge of new methods of teaching.
The dual progress plan involves 1) the concept of
cultural imperatives versus cultural electives, 2)
the dual progress of pupils (advancement through the
grades being based on language arts and social
studies), 3) a reorganization of the curriculum, and
4) a new design for teacher preparation. Chapter 4
critiques the common scheme of elementary school
organization, the self-contained classroom. Chapter
5 describes a demonstration study in cooperating
school systems.

6093.   Stone, W. J. "Communities of learning in a large
junior high school." Bulletin of the National
Association of Secondary School Principals, February
1962:53-54.

At each grade level in this junior high, each half of
the students are assigned to half the teachers to
form two small schools for the grade, or six for the
total school. Each has its own student body, faculty, counselors, instructional coordinators, and
administrators. The small school organization aids
in the transition from elementary to junior high
school by decreasing the number of teacher-student
contacts. The student has the same teacher for two
periods and is with the same group of students for at
least four periods of the school day. Each small
school has a counselor: a regular teacher who is
released half time for guidance activities. Counselors have the same preparation as the other
teachers and discuss with them the total guidance
program as well as problems of individual students.
The counselor handles all of the major guidance and
discipline referrals of the students in his small
school and follows through on each case with the
student, the referring teacher, the counseling
teacher (block-time teacher), and in many cases the
parent.

6094.   Summers, A. A. and Wolfe, B. L. "Which school
resources help learning? Efficiency and equity in
Philadelphia public schools." Federal Reserve Bank
of Philadelphia Business Review, 1975:4-21.

The research department of the Federal Reserve Bank
of Philadelphia found in a study of Philadelphia
public school students in elementary, junior, and
senior high schools that school inputs (such as class
size and teacher experience) do help student achievement and can compensate for the disadvantages of
poverty, racial discrimination, and low ability.
Moreover, some inputs have a larger impact on students' performance than others. Small classes, for
example, help low achievers but are of no special
benefit to average and high achievers. Further, some
characteristics of staff inputs--extra educational
credits of teachers, for example--do not appear to
boost learning. Results of this study that are particularly relevant to junior high students include:
1) Residential moves: coming from a family that
moves more frequently has an adverse effect on the
achievement of junior high students. In contrast,
frequent family moves appear to show little or no
effect on elementary or senior high school students.
2) Size of school: in smaller schools increased
learning at the elementary and senior high levels
seem to take place. Black students seem particularly
to benefit from being in small elementary schools,
and low achievers benefit from being in smaller
senior high schools. At the junior high level,
school size seems inconsequential over the range
examined. 3) It seems much more beneficial for
eighth graders to be in an elementary school than to
be in one that is not. 4) Teacher experience: in
junior high, an experienced English teacher appears
to be particularly effective with high ability students, but teacher experience of ten or more years
helps all students. Among mathematics teachers,
however, those with three to nine years of experience
are particularly effective, but those with more than
ten years reduce the rate of learning mathematics.

6095.   Taormina, F. R.   "Team Teaching in the middle
school." New York State Education, 56(1969):22.

Explains how team teaching can be used effectively in
a middle school.

6096.   Taylor, H. A. and Cook, R. F.   "Schools within a
school: teaching team organized for junior high
school." High School Journal, 48(1965):289-295.

Describes a successful team teaching approach in a
junior high school.

6097.   Teachers College Journal. "Ability grouping: an
issue at the junior high school level." Teachers
College Journal, 34,2(1962):64-67.

Contains two statements: "Arguments Favoring Ability Grouping: Grouping for More Effective Teaching-- Emphasis upon Needs of Gifted Children" by M. C. McDaniel and "Arguments Opposing Ability Grouping: Why Not Group by Ability" by R. C. Faunce.

6098.   Tompkins, E. "The daily schedule in junior high school." Bulletin of the National Association of Secondary School Principals, 40,220(1956):178.

This study in 1955 of 1250 junior high schools showed that a majority used block-time classes, and in schools with more than 1,000 students the percentage was 72.5. Author predicted, "As time goes on, fewer and fewer junior high schools will retain the single period practice for general education classes."

6099. Vars, G. F. "Can team teaching save the core curriculum?" Phi Delta Kappan, 47(1966):258-262.

Defines and discusses team teaching, interdisciplinary teams, and drawbacks in team teaching. Concludes that team teaching seems at first glance to be eminently suited to a core program, when the latter is defined in the older sense of block time. Incompatibilities begin to appear, however, when core is defined more precisely as a curriculum organization with primary focus upon the personal and social problems of the learner. The staff time absorbed in just keeping a complex team in operation, the limitations of teacher-student planning imposed by the team schedule, the difficulties of establishing close teacher-student rapport, and above all the staff specialization that seems inevitable in a team, all militate against successful core teaching. "Far from being the salvation of core, team teaching may prove to be the devil in disguise."

6100.   Waldrep, R. "Core teaching has plenty of room for grammar." English Journal, 42(1953):24-28.

Discusses the teaching of grammer in a core program.

6101.   Webb, R. "Mini-schools: McMurray Junior High, Nashville, Tennessee." ERIC Doc. ED 081 060, 1972.

Describes a mini-school program that is designed to provide a smooth transition from elementary school to the independent discipline approach of high school. Students spend two thirds of each school day in a mini-school where they learn language arts, math, health, science, and social studies. Mini-schools have teachers for each of the four subject areas. During four class periods students are in the mini-school. Report describes how the schools operate, tells how to schedule mini-schools, and outlines some

of the advantages of mini-schools over traditional
methods of schooling. See ERIC Abstract #ED 081 060.

6102.   Whiting, R., et al. "NOVA: A Brief." Fort
Lauderdale, Fla.: Broward County Schools, ERIC Doc.
ED 002 325, 1965.

A six-year junior/senior high school program called
NOVA is described in this article. Features of the
program include the trimester program, the continuous
progress curriculum, team teaching, a unique class
schedule, data processing equipment useage, and
modern instructional aids. Several individual buildings, as on a college campus, are devoted to language
arts, science, and mathematics. A multipurpose patio
area is a central feature of the design. Each center
house includes materials pertinent to the subject
area taught in its building. Article includes statistics concerning student enrollment, number and type
of faculty, and a cost analysis.

6103.   Whitley, A. C. "Student Scheduling in a Year-round
Middle School. A Simulation Notebook." Paper pre-
sented at National Seminar on Year-round Education,
Chicago, ERIC Doc. ED 090 641.

Presents a model of a successful student scheduling
pattern for a year-round middle school (grades 6-8).
The model allows 100 percent of resource lab teaching
time to be used for the student population in attendance during each session. The plan uses a house
design, and a team teaching structure facilitates
smooth scheduling of groups of students. Article
suggests ideas for persons involved in student scheduling. Designing a schedule involves determining the
amount of time to be allotted weekly to each subject,
determining amount of planning time desired, facilitating flexible scheduling, slotting students into
the pattern, and charting an entire school year in
advance to discover patterns and methods of rotation
that best implement the school philosophy. See ERIC
Abstract #ED 090 641.

6104.   Wiles, J. W. "Developmental staging: in pursuit
of comprehensive curriculum plans." Middle School
Journal, 6,1(1975):5-10.

If substantial and lasting curriculum change is to
occur in schools, the planning of such change must be
both comprehensive and coordinated. The literature
on change and the experience of practitioners in the
field suggest that change in school environment is
both complex and difficult to control. Curricular or
programmatic changes are rarely isolates and comprise, intentionally or otherwise, a series of interrelated and interdependent events. The challenge of

curriculum planning lies in the development of a comprehensive monitoring device to observe and, where
possible, direct ongoing changes. Developmental
staging is basically a way of analyzing discrepancies
between the ideal and the real and consists of outlining anticipated change steps between what actually
exists and what is desired. In this way developmental staging attempts to break down the sometimes
enormous gaps between the real and ideal while at the
same time displaying the comprehensive nature of the
change being planned. The utility of the staging
concept to promote desired curricular change is
dependent upon several essential conditions. First,
it is assumed that some sort of philosophical con-
census is present among those engaged in the change
process so that terminal goals can be described and
progress toward those goals accurately assessed.
Second, it is mandatory that the staging plans toward
desired goals begin with an accurate portrait of
present realities. A staff must use its best
judgment to distinguish between educational intentions and day-to-day practices. Often the only
accurate means of testing potential discrepancies is
to view the condition or practice thorugh the eyes of
a single randomly selected student. Finally, the use
of developmental staging should be preceded by an
acceptance of the fact that lasting change of a
curricular nature is almost always a tedious process.

6105. Wilson, L. S. "Can an open-space middle school
meet the educational needs of minority youngsters?"
Journal of Negro Education, 44,3(1975):368-376.

The Hempstead, New York, School District added a new
open-space instructional wing to its middle school in
1973. Article discusses how the open space is working, views of students and staff, and preparation of
staff through in-service programs. A floor plan is
included. A crucial element to the success of this
middle school program was the extensive attention
given to in-service training, which is described in
depth. Article also gives firsthand accounts by
teachers and students of the benefits of an open-
space middle school. The historical background of
the school as well as the design of the school and
community reaction to it are included.

6106. Wolfson, B. J. "Individualizing instruction."
National Education Association Journal, 55(1966):
31-33.

Presents an individualized instruction plan which can
be used in a junior high school.

7

Development and Implementation
of Curriculum

7001.   Abramowitz, M. W. and Macari, C. C. "The camelot
program."   Educational Leadership,   30,2(1972):
144-148.

The Camelot Program at Niles Junior High School in
the Bronx, New York, is an experimental program
designed to meet the needs of forty-five potential
dropouts. As a classroom without walls and with its
own curriculum, it is essentially independent of the
mainstream of the school. The purposes are to give
boys and girls a flexible program which will allow
them to 1) explore, free of customary curricular
restraints, areas of study in which they are interested, 2) progress at their own rate of speed, 3)
develop innate talents, 4) relate to one another as
human beings, and 5) assume responsibility for their
actions.   The taste of success, which has been an
elusive thing for the past nine years for these students, is the psychological key to their future. The
program has provided success for the first time for
many of them during this first experimental year at
the school.

7002.   Adams, L.   "Family living in the junior high
school."   California Journal of Secondary Education,
26(1951):220-221.

A family living program used in grades 7 and 8 in
Moline, Illinois, consists of courses in homemaking,
experiences in personal and group relationships, and
experiences in the sharing of home and family duties.
The article briefly describes units on family life.
Program emphasis is on experience and activities.

7003.   Aldrich, J. C. Social Studies for the Junior High School. Washington, D.C.: National Council for the Social Studies, 1956.

Presents a model curriculum and teacher's guide for social studies in grades 7, 8, and 9.

7004.   Allegheny Intermediate Unit. "Consumer in the Marketplace. An Interdisciplinary Approach to Consumer Education." Developed for Grades 5-8. Pittsburgh, Pa.: Allegheny Intermediate Unit, ERIC Doc. ED 164 388, 1978.

Manual identifies activities and resources for combining consumer education with English, social studies, science, mathematics, and home economics courses in grades 5-8. The purpose is to help students recognize the rights and responsibilities of consumers and to teach them how to make intelligent decisions in light of personal and economic value systems. Four concepts are stressed: 1) basic economics of the marketplace, 2) legal rights, redress, and consumer law, 3) major purchases of products and services, and 4) special problems such as advertising and product safety. Consumer education competencies are listed for each of the four concept areas. See ERIC Abstract #ED 164 388.

7005.   Allen, F. B. "Mathematics tomorrow." National Education Association Journal, May 1957:310.

The junior high mathematics program must move away from emphasis on terminal learnings to content that is an integral part of the twelve-grade sequence. Increased demand for technically trained manpower plus new developments in the field of pure mathematics have caused a critical reexamination of school mathematics programs. Seventh and eighth grade mathematics often are the weakest links. Too often they review ideas which have been presented earlier. This means that many pupils who are able to learn easily at this stage not only fail to learn anything new but are repelled by the stultifying repetition and the constant emphasis on manipulative skills.

7006.   Allen, R. E. and Holyoak, O. J. "Evaluation of the conceptual approach to teaching health education: a second look." Journal of School Health, 43,5 (1973):293-294.

This conceptual approach to teaching health education had no positive effects on the reported health behavior pattern of junior high school students but produced senior high school students who were knowledgeable regarding positive health behavior. See ERIC Abstract #EJ 079 269.

7007. Almen, R. E. "The Evaluation of a Vocational Program for Dropout-Prone Junior High School Students." Ph.D. Dissertation, University of Minnesota, University Microfilms, Ann Arbor, Mich., ERIC Doc. ED 056 191, 1971.

The Work Opportunity Center, a vocational facility in a nonschool setting, was designed to meet the special needs of disadvantaged, inner-city youth. The program served two hundred junior high school students who attended a half-day program of vocational and related training. Small classes, individualized instruction, and the development of positive attitudes toward work, school, and self were encouraged. An experimental study designed to compare this center with a regular school program collected data from school records and pretest/posttest measures. The Vocational Development Inventory, the Attitude Scale, the Self-Esteem Inventory, and the School Attitude Inventory were all given to students. Author concluded that the Center program was more effective in developing vocational maturity, increasing general self-esteem, increasing school esteem, and producing positive school attitudes. Author highly recommends that career exploration laboratories with well-developed prevocational programs be made accessible to more students. See ERIC Abstract #ED 056 191.

7008. Alpren, M. and Cammarota, G. "Social studies curriculum." In The Subject Curriculum: Grades K-12. Columbus, Ohio: Merrill, 1967.

Authors suggested this social studies plan for grades 7, 8, and 9: One year studying various areas throughout the world in light of their geography, history, government, economic conditions, how people live, and education; one semester each of geography and medical science; and one year of U. S. history to 1900.

7009. American Association for the Advancement of Science. The New School Science. Washington, D.C.: 1963.

Papers discuss the new science curricula, including those for students in the middle years. The papers were prepared for a series of nine regional conferences of school administrators.

7010. American Association of School Administrators. Curriculum Handbook for School Administrators. Washington, D.C., 1967.

This program for junior high school mathematics is designed for three ability levels: 1) Accelerated: students' seventh grade work will include much of the usual eighth grade program. By the end of grade 8 they will have completed first-year algebra, and by the end of grade 9 they will have completed plain and solid geometry. 2) Regular level: arithmetic in grade 7, introduction to algebra and geometry in grade 8, and elementary algebra in grade 9. 3) Slow: in grades 7 and 8 students will complete a modern, slow-paced version of some of the content for these grades. In grade 9, some of these students will be ready for pre-algebra and will move into algebra in grade 10.

7011. American Council of Learned Societies and National Council for the Social Studies. The Social Studies and the Social Sciences. New York: Harcourt, Brace and World, 1962.

Discusses social studies concepts, knowledge, and techniques that students should acquire in junior and senior high school.

7012. American Industrial Arts Association. "Industrial Arts in the Middle School." 1201 16th St., N.W., Washington, D.C., ERIC Doc. ED 098 377, 1971.

These guidelines were compiled after a series of sessions held by the American Council of Industrial Arts Supervisors. The middle school philosophy in this program is child centered and uses an individual study approach to meet the unique needs of early adolescents. The industrial arts program is concerned with 1) common learning needed by all persons to function effectively in our industrial-technological society, 2) the development of attitudes, interests, abilities, and skills, and 3) occupational information. Suggestions are offered for both unified and traditional patterns of operations. See ERIC Abstract #ED 098 377.

7013. American School Board Journal. "Flexible design matches curriculum." American School Board Journal, 155(1968):55-58.

This is a description of the physical plant and curriculum in the new Jefferson Junior High School in Decatur, Illinois. It discusses team teaching, flexible grouping, flexible scheduling, teachers, teaching aids, and construction statistics. The physical facilities are based on flexible design to integrate a middle grade's curricular program.

7014. Anderson, H. S. "A key to the science interests of junior high schools." Science Teacher, 21(1954): 227-230.

Describes a questionnaire which can be useful in ascertaining the science interests of junior high school pupils.

7015.   Arey, C. "Science: Middle School Years." Middle School Portfolio, Leaflet 8. Washington, D.C.: Association for Childhood Education International, 1968.

Includes sections on cultivating scientific thought processes, the importance of mathematics, earlier basic concepts, and experiences: structured and unstructured.

7016.   Arnspiger, R. H., et al. "Reading and Writing in Junior High School Unified Studies (English-Social Studies)." Paper presented at the Annual meeting of the Association for Supervision and Curriculum Development, Washington, D.C., ERIC Doc. ED 167 997, March, 1978.

Deliberate instruction and intensive classroom practice can help students interrelate the processes of reading, writing, and thinking. A skills extension project was devised to aid in this instruction. Paper describes specific project activities and in-service training sessions for teachers and includes lesson materials. See ERIC Abstract #ED 167 997.

7017.   Arth, A. A. and Olsen, M. "How to assign homework to a middle school student." Middle School Journal, 11,1(1980):4-5.

Because the middle school is a unique program for educating young adolescents, the homework assignments given in such a school should be different from those given in other segments of the school system. This article discusses nine categories of homework assignments that appear to be specifically appropriate to the needs of the young adolescent student. 1) Parent-student homework is initiated by the student but completed at home with the assistance of the parent or guardian. 2) Group homework is assigned to a group of students, sometimes peers, groups of three to five, or the entire class. 3) Differentiated homework allows student choice and encourages students to be responsible by having them identify their own errors. 4) For roulette homework the student spins a pointer on a paper plate where the night's homework tasks are listed by number. The student does the problem indicated by the pointer plus the one preceding and the one following that number. 5) Mix and match homework helps to correlate the academic areas. The student is allowed to substitute homework from another discipline if he can justify the exchange. 6) "Write and tell" the homework

assignment is a method rather than a type of homework.   7) Television-related homework assignments
permit the school to take advantage of the vast
amount of time during which the adolescent is influenced by this electric medium.   8) For student-
generated homework, the students write questions for
other students to answer.   To do this adequately,
students must read the topic covered and look for the
main points.   9) Teacher-student homework is the
culmination of the effort to encourage students to
learn.   It is a joint effort between students and
teachers to explore a question to which neither knows
the answer.

7018.   Baillie, J. H. "Laboratory experiences for disadvantaged youth in the middle school." School Science
and Mathematics, November 1970:704-706.

Shows how "hands on" activities within a science
curriculum can be of advantage to middle grade
disadvantaged students.

7019.   Ballinger, T. O. "Some problems and issues in art
education with special consideration of the junior
high school level." Education, 75(1955):379-382.

Discusses the weaknesses of the junior high school
art program, with particular reference to the
attitudes of administrators, the training of
teachers, and the philosophy of art teachers.

7020.   Bates, P. and Bannen, J. "Grade seven science-
social studies interdisciplinary on the scientific
method." Journal of Open Education, 2,2(1974):112-
122.

Describes activities for junior high school science
and social studies units on teaching the scientific
method and interrelationships between the scientist
and the social scientist.   See ERIC Abstract EJ 095
372.

7021.   Beard, E. M. L. and Cunningham, G. S. (Eds.)
"Middle School Mathematics Curriculum. A Report of
the Orono Conference." University of Maine at Orono.
Washington, D.C.: National Science Foundation, July,
1973.

Four position papers were presented at this mathematics curriculum conference: 1) Attention to Com-
putational Skills. 2) Relevance in Mathematics
Education to Meet Societal Needs. 3) Development of
Students' Mathematical Maturity. 4) Establishment of
a Definite Philosophy of Mathematics Education.
Fernard Prevost presented a paper entitled "Mathematics in the Middle School: Muddling the Mind or

Minding the Muddle?" His main premise was that the
more complicated parts of the long division algorithm
should be shifted to the middle school and that the
responsibility for multiplication and division of
rational numbers should be given to middle schools.
He then discusses the content of the middle school
mathematics program. Donovan Johnson presented the
paper "What Should Be Introduced into the Middle
School Mathematics Curriculum?" George Baird presented the paper "How to Make a Curriculum Operational." A conference summary by Preston C. Hammer
is included.

7022.   Bell, E.   "Some things to try in junior high.
"Music Educators Journal, 37(1952):38-40.

Points out some of the difficulties of teaching music
in the junior high school and suggests music activities which are particularly suitable for the junior
high.

7023.   Bender, L. W. and Sharpe, W. C.   "A junior high
school course for disadvantaged students." Bulletin
of the National Association of Secondary School Principals, March 1963:129-130.

To help disadvantaged students in the Washington
Irving Junior High School in Tarrytown, New York,
guidance and shop classes were incorporated into one
specially designed "discovery course," composed of
boys and girls under the direction of a teacher with
training in both guidance and industrial arts.
Block-of-time double class periods were scheduled in
the afternoon for the disadvantaged students. Such
scheduling permitted the completion of projects or
field trips without conflicting with other school
activities. The principal and guidance director
explain how they used real life situations in the
community for the class.

7024.   Benson, P. and Estrada, R. J.   "Exploration of
Home Economics Occupations: Home and Family Education." Miami, Fla.: Dade County Public Schools,
1973.

Describes a series of junior high school career
exploration courses in home economics. They are part
of the Quinmester Program.   Article covers course
titles and descriptions, goals, specific block objectives, resources, pretest and posttest, and a curriculum guide. Also included are sections on homemaking, personal development for careers, child care,
guidance services, institutional and home management
in supportive services, home furnishings, equipment
and services, clothing management, food management,
and production services. Students should be able to

identify job titles, job descriptions, and applications of homemaking roles in the work world through these courses. Students learn about personal characteristics and attitudes of the successful employee and participate in experiences designed to develop these qualities. They also learn about procedures involved in getting a job.

7025.   Bettelheim, B.   "The social studies teacher and the emotional needs of adolescents." School Review, 56(1948):585-592.

The greatest service the social studies junior high school teacher can render to adolescent students is to educate them to a critical understanding of themselves and their society. Every teacher, in addition to the unique contribution of the subject he teaches, has two general responsibilities: to demonstrate true, satisfying interpersonal relations and to set an example of continuous critical examination and intellectual mastery of emotional and intellectual problems.   It helps the adolescent to master a problem intellectually, even though he is not able to solve it in action.

7026.   Bienenstok, T.   "Strains in junior high teaching." Education Digest, 29(1964):34-35.

Fifth graders are natural intellectuals and can enjoy choosing a set of algebraic axioms and developing a variety of algebraic theorems from them. This topic is normally encountered in the latter grades of college or in graduate school. By contrast, seventh and eighth graders are more like engineers at heart. The usual school regime of sitting at desks, reading, writing, and reciting seems to ignore the basic nature of children at this age; they want to move around physically, to do things, to explore, to take chances, to build things. Educators are asking themselves if mathematics, social studies, and other subjects need to be sedentary at this grade level.

7027.   Birkmaier, E. M. and Hallman, C. L.   "Foreign language education."   In Conner and Ellena (Eds.), Curriculum Handbook for School Administrators, p. 77. Washington, D.C.: American Association of School Administrators, 1967.

Benefits of language in the junior high school curriculum are: 1) the undeniably increased need for our citizens to communicate with foreign speakers, both within and without the United States, 2) increased understanding of the culture, problems, and thought processes of citizens of other countries, 3) increased information available to those who can read

foreign journals, 4) widening of aesthetic boundaries, 5) enhanced occupational and professional
opportunities, 6) the very real sense of achievement
and gratification in mastering another language, and
7) recognition that language is the verbal manifesta-
tion of a culture.

7028.   Blanc, S. S.   "Science interests of junior high
school pupils."   School Science and Mathematics, 51
(1951):745-752.

Author reports the results of a questionnaire study
of the science interests of 486 pupils in the Denver
junior high schools.

7029.   Bocolo, J. M.   "Foreign language program in the
junior high school."   Clearinghouse, 42(1968):358-
362.

Discusses the status, problems, and scheduling of
foreign language study in the junior high school and
makes recommendations for improving foreign language
programs.   Article stresses that all junior high
school students, not just the intellectually
advanced, should have the opportunity to take a
foreign language.   Studies have shown that IQ,
achievement, reading level in English, success in
other school subjects, and results of prognostic
tests are all poor predictors of success in a foreign
language.   The only reasonable way to determine if an
individual will succeed is to give him an experience
in the foreign language.   In terms of the stated
purposes of the junior high school, the nature of the
tasks as revealed by research and experience, and the
needs of contemporary society and the learner, there
is no basis for continuing a program that is based on
false assumptions about who should study languages.
Indeed, the junior high school may offer the last
opportunity for large masses of pupils to have an
experience in a foreign language as part of their
general education.

7030.   Booth, N.   "Science in the middle years."
Education, 6,2(1978):37-41.

Discusses methods and content of science instruction
in the middle years and considers teacher qualifications and pupil differences.   See ERIC Abstract #EJ
199 014.

7031.   Bortner, D. M.   "Experience core curriculum."
Clearinghouse, 33(1958):237-240.

Describes math and science courses which may be
taught jointly through the core concept.

7032.   Bossing, N. L.   "What is core?"   School Review, 63(1955):212-213.

Characteristics of the core curriculum are: 1) It is based on the fundamental psychological principle that learning involves change in behavior which is brought about through experience, and that the curriculum should foster those types of learning experiences most likely to produce desirable behavior change. 2) It is organized around personal and social problems that are common to all youth in a democratic society. 3) It draws on a wide range of resources and activities. 4) It uses problem-solving techniques in personal and social problem situations. 5) It provides for much teacher cooperation. The core curriculum activities must be planned for as a whole and by all teachers as a group as well as individually. 6) Pupils and teachers plan jointly for the solution of vital problems. 7) The core makes individual and group guidance an integral part of teaching. The core teacher accepts as his basic responsibility many of the major functions now assumed by guidance specialists and counselors in the more traditionally organized schools. In the core curriculum, teaching and guidance become largely synonymous. 8) The curriculum is divided into two highly interrelated parts, one devoted to the types of problems common to all early adolescents and the competencies all must possess to function successfully in our society, and another devoted to helping students explore and develop their individual concerns, interests, and abilities. Both divisions are based on the same principles of learning, teaching, and organization. 9) The daily schedule is divided into large blocks of time to facilitate guidance, the maximum use of problem-solving processes, and the use of community resources. 10) The core idea provides for longer association between core teachers and pupils so teachers may know the pupils better--their backgrounds, interests, abilities, and learning development.

7033.   Bossing, N. L.   "Trends in block-time classes in junior high school." Bulletin of the National Association of Secondary School Principals, 43(1959):34.

Discusses scope, trends, and problems in core curriculum in Alabama.

7034.   Bossing, N. L. and Kaufman, J. F.   "Block-time or core practices in Minnesota secondary schools." Clearinghouse, 32(1958):532-539.

Describes the 1950s core curriculum in Minnesota schools.

7035.   Bouvier, J., et al. "Curriculum Guide for Junior High School English (Grades 7, 8, and 9). Revised Draft." Darien, Conn.: Darien Public Schools, ERIC Doc. ED 161 076, 1978.

Part I discusses developing skills in written composition, grammar and usage, spelling, vocabulary, speech, and library skills. A section provides numerous suggestions on written composition, with sample assignments and activities and examples of effective writing. Skills sections provide such aids as lists of grammar objectives and requirements, basic spelling and vocabulary lists, and suggestions for speech making activities and library reference work. Part II discusses the reading of short stories and novels, mythology and the Bible, drama and poetry. Numerous literary works are recommended for each genre and specific activities, composition topics, and approaches to the works are suggested. See ERIC Abstract #ED 161 076.

7036.   Brandwein, P. F. "Building Curricular Structures for Science with Special Reference to the Junior High School." Washington, D.C.: National Science Teachers Association, ERIC Doc. ED 015 134, 1967.

Articles in this booklet are: 1) The Meaningful World: The Problem in Broad Strokes. 2) Diversity with Constancy: The Junior High School Child and the Time-binding Nature of the School. 3) Curricular Structure: Corrective and Adaptive. Sections of this article discusses the variety and richness of science, science teaching, a vertical development in the conceptual structure bridge, a flexible network, learning through inquiry, and apprentice investigation. 4) Science as Democracy. Included at the end is a list of other NSTA publications for the junior high school. Author stresses that the science curriculum must enrich impoverished experience and must adapt to a variety of abilities. The program should reflect the nature of science as an enterprise of intelligence and should use the methods of intelligence. The purposes of the science teacher must be in harmony with those of scientists.

7037.   Broward County School Board. "Broward County Home Economics Curriculum Development Project, July 1, 1967, to July 1, 1970. Final Report." Fort Lauderdale, Fla.: Broward County School Board, ERIC Doc. ED 055 158, 1970.

This three-year curriculum development project was conducted in a senior and three junior high schools to test an innovative homemaking program which would: 1) achieve the broad home economics objectives, 2) improve attitudes toward home ec, 3) assist in the development of critical thinking and independent study habits, 4) develop proficiency in the skills needed for food preparation and clothing construction, 5) promote transfer of learning from the classroom to the home, and 6) create more interest in and understanding of the concepts of homemaking. Two groups were selected, including a control group electing a comprehensive homemaking course and an experimental group electing a skill development course emphasizing a semester each of clothing and foods. The experimental group showed significant gains in attitude toward home ec and skill development. There were no significant differences in study habits, general knowledge, development of critical thinking, or transfer of learning. See ERIC Abstract #ED 055 158.

7038.   Brown, B. F. The Appropriate Placement School: A Sophisticated Nongraded Curriculum.   West Nyack, N.Y.: Parker Publishing Co., 1965.

Proposes a nongraded curriculum with specific suggestions for both middle schools and junior high schools. The book is a report on the dialogues of the Massachusetts Institute of Technology Conference held in May 1963 and the subsequent discovery of a new strategy for nongrading schools.

7039.   Brown, F. "Three slants on parents and curriculum." Integrated Education, 13,5(1975):30-32.

Survey of students, parents, and teachers at four schools in a large northern school district focuses on their opinions about what should be taught and how much parent involvement in school matters seems desirable. The survey was conducted as part of a community policy board's feasibility study of ways to govern a junior high school. Strong evidence from the study suggests that black students and parents desire a school curriculum that includes the teaching of basic skills: reading, writing, spelling, speech, mathematics, and social sciences. Vocational education received a low rating from the students, as did art and music.

7040.   Brown, J. "The middle school learner: instructional planning for a transitional stage." History and Social Science Teacher, 13,3(1978):157-162.

Report examines Piaget's concrete and formal operational stages of intellectual development in relation to the middle school learner. Author describes teaching strategies which require the learner to use concrete and formal operational forms of thought in dealing with social studies. See ERIC Abstract EJ 178 551.

7041.   Brueckner, L. J., et al. Developing Mathematical
Understanding in the Upper Grades. Philadelphia:
Winston, 1957.

This book contains many helpful teaching methods for
junior high grades, with emphasis upon the meaning of
mathematics.

7042.   Bryan, J. N. "Science in the Junior High School."
Washington: National Science Teachers Association,
1959.

California, Washington, and Oregon teachers present
many aspects of a junior high school science program.

7043.   Budke, W. E. and Woodin, R. J.   "Guidelines for
the Development of Prevocational Education Programs
at the Junior High School Level." Research Series in
Agricultural Education.   Columbus: Ohio State University, Department of Agricultural Education, ERIC
Doc. ED 047 129, October, 1970.

Study developed guidelines for organizing, operating,
and administering junior high prevocational programs.
Seventy questionnaires returned by directors of local
occupational orientation and exploratory programs
resulted in guidelines that cover 1) program objectives, 2) program design, 3) instructional staff
selection, 4) grade level of student involvement, 5)
staff training, 6) program financing, 7) curriculum
and activities, 8) community involvement, 9) student
selection, 10) facilities and equipment, 11) guidance
and counseling services, 12) administration and
supervision, and 13) program evaluation.   The study
was undertaken for the following reasons: 1) a
growing acceptance of the need for continuous vocational education from early childhood throughout
life, 2) an expanding program of vocational education
in the secondary schools, 3) the increasing importance of and difficulty in making a rational career
choice, 4) federal funding of prevocational education, 5) unsatisfactory present methods that provide
no clear pattern, 6) some promising pilot and demonstration programs which have been established in prevocational education.   Purposes of the study were:
1) to identify important characteristics of existing
prevocational education programs, 2) to identify
different approaches to such programs, 4) to synthesize tentative guidelines which merit wide application for junior high school prevocational education, and 5) to select and refine the tentative
guidelines with the assistance of a jury of experts.

7044.   Burkhart, P.   "Planning for Career Education:
Grades 7-9."   Pocatello, Idaho: Pocatello School
District 25, ERIC Doc. ED 136 061.

Sections are: 1) Introduction. 2) Teacher Training. 3) Career Resource Information Bank. 4) Field Trips. 5) Positive Action. 6) Evaluation. 7) Teaching Units. See ERIC Abstract #ED 136 061.

7045.   Burnett, L. W. "Core programs in Washington State junior high schools." School Review, 59(1951):97-100.

Article reports on a study of the core program and block-time arrangements in junior high schools, with opinions by the principals.

7046.   Burton, D. L. "English in no man's land: some suggestions for the middle years." English Journal, 60,1(1971):23-30.

Discusses the role of the English department and curriculum in middle schools and junior high schools. See ERIC Abstract #EJ 033 003.

7047.   Butler, C. H. and Wren, F. L. The Teaching of Secondary Mathematics. 3rd ed. New York: McGraw-Hill, 1960.

Several chapters are devoted to mathematics in the junior high school years.

7048.   Capehart, et al. "Evaluating the core curriculum: a further look." School Review, October 1953:406-412.

In Oak Ridge, Tennessee, a study of individuals and matched groups showed that students in core programs learn language skills and study skills as well as, and frequently better than, students in more conventional courses. (Extends the analysis described in entry 7049.)

7049.   Capehart, Bertis, E., Hodges, A., and Berdan, N. "An objective evaluation of a core program." School Review, 60(1952):84-89.

This is an experimental inquiry, using matching pairs of students, of a core program in the Oak Ridge, Tennessee, Junior High School. (See entry 7048.)

7050.   Carlson, R. E. "Outdoor Education." Middle School Portfolio, Leaflet 9. Washington, D.C.: Association for Childhood Education International, 1968.

Discusses outdoor education specifically geared for the middle grade youngster. Contains sections on the need for conservation of energy, guidance for the teacher, the experiences children may learn from, and a bibliography on outdoor education.

7051.   Carson, M., et al. (Eds.) "The Years of Uncertainty: Eighth Grade Family Life Education." Cedar Rapids, Iowa: Cedar Rapids Community School District, ERIC Doc. ED 098 364, September, 1972.

Contains a family life sex education unit with daily lesson plans for twenty-nine one-hour class sessions. Topics covered are: problem solving, knowledge and attitudes, male and female reproductive systems, conception, pregnancy, birth, birth defects, venereal disease, dating, peer group influence, emotions, values clarification, and decision making. Teaching aids are included in these materials. See ERIC Abstract #ED 098 364.

7052.   Case, T. N. "Curricular changes in junior high schools."   Bulletin of the National Association of Secondary School Principals, 47,285(1963):49-54.

The Committee on Research Studies of the Los Angeles City Schools and the California Association of Secondary School Administrators sponsored a study designed to determine 1) the curricular changes made from 1956 to 1963 in three California junior high schools, 2) the influences which brought about these changes, 3) what changes the principals considered valuable and why, and 4) what changes in general are rated most valuable by junior high school specialists and other educators. A survey of 293 principals of three-year public junior high schools in California yielded findings reported here on curricular organization, organization of instruction, program scheduling, staff utilization, curricular requirements, facilities, equipment, and materials.

7053.   Center School District 58. "Language Arts Curriculum for the Junior High School." Kansas City, Mo., ERIC Doc. ED 102 600, 1973.

This student-centered curriculum guide stresses learning activities. Part I offers a brief course description of the seventh, eighth, and ninth grade language arts programs. Part II describes in detail objectives and activities for written communication, oral communication, grammar, spelling, vocabulary, reading, literature, and study evaluation. Appendices include communication activities, composition topics, and book lists. See ERIC Abstract #ED 102 600.

7054.   Chiara, C. R. "The Core." Series 3, no. 2, Kalamazoo, Mich.: School of Graduate Studies, Faculty Contributions, August, 1956.

Booklet discusses a definition of the core curriculum, how to initiate a program, working with a core class, materials needed, evaluation, and qualifications needed by core teachers.

7055.   Cook, P.   "How's Your Plumbing? Aids to Individualize the Teaching of Science, Mini-Course Unit for Grades 7, 8, and 9."   Frederick, Md.:   Frederick County Board of Education, 115 E. Church St., Frederick, Md. 21701, ERIC Doc. ED 130 900, 1973.

This unit introduces students to the study of human health, the human cardiovascular system, and diseases.   Subjects and activities are designed to supplement a basic curriculum or to form a total curriculum built around practical, process-oriented science instruction rather than theory or module building.   A student section includes performance objectives and science activities for individuals or the class as a whole.   A teacher's section contains notes on science activities, a resource list, and references. See ERIC Abstract #ED 130 900.

7056.   Costantino, R. and LaRue, C. J.   "Middle school science: teams of teachers and students make it possible."   Science Teacher, 41,5(1974):47-49.

Discusses organization for learning, the scope and sequence of a science program in the middle school, individualization of instruction, and the middle school today.

7057.   Council for Basic Education. "A core curriculum." Bulletin of the Council for Basic Education, February 1961.

Describes the core curriculum.

7058.   Craig, M. L. and Everett, F. U.   "Developing health potentialities."   Teachers College Record, 61 (1960):429-430.

Health education in the junior high is often viewed as total fitness for living--man in a state of physical, emotional, social, and spiritual well-being.   Authors see four major teaching and guidance tasks for junior high school health education: 1) maintenance of a healthful and safe school environment, 2) provision of adequate school health services, 3) provision of meaningful and functional health and safety instruction, and 4) use of home and community resources in health education.

7059.   Cramer, R. V.   "Common learnings program in the junior high school."   Bulletin of the National Association of Secondary School Principals, 35(1951): 158-166.

Describes the early stages, schedules, subjects, and positive results of five years' experience in a common learnings program in West Junior High School, Kansas City, Missouri.

7060.   Crosby, H. H. "Beatles to Bernstein: the teenage progression of taste." Journal of Education, 148 (1965):57-62.

Presents a good music curriculum.

7061.   Curtis, T. E. (Ed.) The Middle School. Albany, N.Y.: Center for Curriculum Research and Services, State University of New York at Albany, 1968.

Contains addresses and reactions from a middle school curriculum conference in the summer of 1966 at SUNY, Albany, New York. Well-known curriculum specialists Gruhn, Vars, Beggs, Bossing, Clute, and Zdanowicz contributed.

7062.   Curtis, T. E. and Bidwell, W. W. Curriculum and Instruction for Emerging Adolescents. Reading, Mass.: Addison-Wesley, 1977.

Graduate students, in-service teachers, administrators, and knowledgeable lay persons should find the pragmatic approach of this book and its reference to basic principles useful. It should give direction to those who are concerned with providing a broadly based education for emerging adolescents. A commitment to personalization is the major premise upon which a middle school program should be built. The question of whether to retain a traditional 7-9 pattern or to change to a 5-8 or 6-8 organization may hinge upon other issues or problems unique to each district, and no major defense is tendered here for any particular pattern of grades. The focus is upon curriculum and instruction rather than upon organizational structure, except as structure within a school relates to program. The guidelines and principles presented in this book can be applied within any grade pattern devoted to emerging adolescent education. The first chapter enunciates the middle school concept with definitions, purposes, and corollaries. The first unit presents the unique characteristics of the emerging adolescent in the middle school and stresses the phases of his or her growth and development--the physical, the socioemotional, and the intellectual. The second unit considers the antecedents of public education, the culture which surrounds the school, and learning theory relevant to education for the emerging adolescent. The curriculum guidelines for middle schools are in the third unit and are supported by a strong argument for balancing the acquisition of learning skills with

intensified exploration in a wide range of equivalent
but alternative content. The fourth unit is devoted
to instructional procedures which support this
balance for individual pupils. This makes imperative
an increase in flexibility and alternatives in both
curriculum and instruction so that individual needs
can be met. Chapter 14 analyzes the most common
curricular organizations in terms of how well they
serve the differing purposes of individual pupils
during emerging adolescence.

7063.   Cyphert, F. R.   "A Survey of the Core Curriculum
Program of Penn Junior High School."   Pittsburgh:
Penn Township School District, 1954.

Comparative studies in Penn Township revealed that
students in core programs learned language and study
skills as well as, and frequently better than, students in more conventional courses.

7064.   Cyphert, F. R.   "The junior high school library
develops investigative skills."   Clearinghouse, 33
(1958):107-109.

To maximize their effectiveness in developing junior
high students' library skills, teachers and librarians should consider these questions: 1) Are faculty
members convinced of the need for having children
develop these skills and abilities?   2) Have these
skills and understandings been spelled out?   3) Do
teachers direct their efforts toward student growth,
independence, and responsibility rather than a dependence upon teacher thinking and ingenuity?   4) Have
channels of communication among teachers and between
teachers and librarians been cleared so that each
knows what the other is doing?   5) Do teachers and
librarians have some time and place during the day to
work together?   6) Are library materials selected by
librarians after an analysis of teacher and pupil
needs and objectives?   7) Is the schedule of the
library flexible enough for students to visit it as
needed?   8) Do both librarian and teachers approach
the teaching of investigative skills by beginning
with concrete situations?   9) Do we arrange for
pupils to deal with problems and develop profi-
ciencies commensurate with their abilities?

7065.   Cyphert, F. R.   "How core affects the junior high
school library."   Library Journal, 84(1959):7-9.

Discusses how the junior high school library fits
into the core philosophy.

7066.   Dade County Public Schools.   "A Guide for Industrial Arts."   Curriculum Bulletin 12.   230 S.W. 22nd
Ave., Miami, Fla. (No year given.)

This junior high school industrial arts program includes general graphics in seventh and ninth grade and general shop in eighth and ninth grade.

7067.   Davey, E. J. "Provide the tools: a basic program for the nonacademic pupil." Clearinghouse, 39(1965): 351-352.

A core program centered around the industrial arts with special emphasis on automobile and electrical appliance repairs was introduced at the Seaford Junior High School in New York in 1963. The program was designed for the nonacademic male pupil by a small group of teachers. At this junior high the critical year for school dropouts occurred during the ninth grade for nonacademic boys, so the teachers concentrated their efforts toward identifying, screening, and selecting boys in the eighth grade who might profit educationally if placed in this experimental program. The goals of the course were: 1) to teach boys elementary work disciplines: punctuality, ability to take orders from a boss, ability to work cooperatively with others in a team, responsibility on the job, 2) to adapt to the interests and ability of the group, 3) to lead directly into stable, adult jobs, 4) to be organized so that a work study program could be planned in the eleventh and twelfth grade, and 5) to encourage boys to remain in school and graduate. At this school they believe the junior high slow learner has a place, and it is the duty of the school to help him find it.

7068.   Davis, H. S. (Comp.) The Instructional Materials Center: An Annotated Bibliography. Cleveland, Ohio: Educational Research Council of Greater Cleveland, 1965.

Bibliography is for administrators and librarians interested in staffing and operating an Instructional Materials Center. Includes useful hints for librarians in middle and junior high schools.

7069.   DeFrancesco, I. Art Education: Its Means and Ends. New York: Harper and Bros., 1958.

Junior high school art activities should 1) provide for the continuous development of each individual pupil, 2) develop assurance, pride, and confidence in each pupil, 3) encourage each pupil to search for the techniques that will facilitate expression, 4) stimulate each pupil to solve creative and aesthetic problems, and 5) use the personal endowment and experiences of pupils, their widened interests, and their desire for a larger sphere of activity in many aspects of living.

7070.   Deaton, J. C., Sr. "A core organized school in action." California Journal of Secondary Education, 27(1952):133-138.

Explains and evaluates a core program in Yosemite Junior High School, Fresno, Calfornia.

7071.   Delaware Valley School District. "Long-Range Plan: Curriculum Addendum for Middle School." Delaware Valley, Del. (No year given.)

The broad skill areas which should be incorporated in a middle school curriculum are: 1) personal respon- sibility, 2) learning strategy, 3) critical thinking, 4) creative thinking, 5) effective social behavior, and 6) effective communication. The Delaware Valley Middle School based its curriculum on the following priciples: 1) The curriculum is related to the reality around the student. 2) It reflects the stresses and strains of the student's world. 3) It humanizes the student by building a human relation- ship and insight, skills, and information. 4) It helps students confront each other honestly and respectfully as human persons and not as enemies. 5) It is involved in the art and science of becoming a more human person and living decently with one's fellow human beings. 6) It is run by a staff that respects all students regardless of background and believes in the students and their capacities to succeed and learn. 7) It helps students to meet contemporary problems head on with courage and con- fidence and emphasizes emotional as well as intellec- tual development and understanding. Goals of the school's new approaches to learning, curriculum, and teaching are: 1) Identify potential dropouts and provide them with an educational program that will help them stay in school. 2) Institute educational changes and establish new methods of teaching and learning. 3) Develop a sense of human worth in the individual. 4) Change teacher attitudes and methods to meet the needs of all children. 5) Implement a truly individualized approach to instruction which allows each middle grade youngster to progress at his own rate. 6) Develop educational programs that stem from interests of students. 7) Enrich student interest in the curriculum by relating it to first- hand contact with everyday life. 8) Allow reading, writing, and academic inquiry to facilitate the process of developing humanness. These goals are based on a general middle school philosophy with four main tenets: 1) The middle school should be child centered and concerned with the special problems of transescent children. 2) The instructional emphasis should be on overall education and development of the child rather than primarily on academic specialties. 3) The middle school should promote an atmosphere in

which a child can make a gradual and comfortable
transition from elementary school dependence to
secondary independence. 4) The middle school should
help its students develop their natural instincts for
inquiry.

7072.   Deller, D. K. and Wright, J. E.   "An associate
faculty program incorporates community resources."
Middle School Journal, 8,3(1977):11.

One of the most essential ingredients for an effective instructional program is participation by adult
members of the school's community.   At Westchester
Middle School a program identifies and recognizes
those members of the community who voluntarily contribute time and effort to the school's program.
Recognition as "Associate Faculty Members" helps
participants develop a closer, more personal involvement and attachment to the school.   Although there
are numerous ways in which a community member may
serve as a resource to the school program, Westchester uses two: assistance in career education and
assistance in the general instructional program.   The
entire Associate Faculty Program can be an excellent
method of providing for 1) better communication with
parents and community participants and greater
insight on their part into the school's program, 2)
an added dimension for the instructional program, 3)
expanded resources for the school staff, 4) direct
assistance by qualified personnel in career education, and 5) more effective public relations in
general.

7073.   Denman, T. "Yes, he can add."   Instructor, 83,10
(1974):28.

A math consultant discusses a program for junior high
school students who are weak in the fundamental
operations of arithmetic. See ERIC Abstract #EJ 097
261.

7074.   DiVirgilio, J.   "Reflections on curriculum needs
for middle schools."   Education, 92,4(1972):78-79.

The curriculum needs to be made more relevant to the
interests and needs of preadolescents. The middle
school is a total experience in which the curriculum
is used to develop all aspects of the human being--
social, emotional, physical, mental. The affective
domain is as important as the cognitive domain.
Author's guidelines for a new curriculum: 1) It
should not be in a straightjacket but should differ
in content from school to school and from situation
to situation within a school. It should be in tune
with the psychosocial developmental stage of the
learner.   2) It should be developed on a K-12

continuum, but such a continuum may not be linear for this age level.   It must be broad in its possibilities and based on developmental levels.   3) It should enable teachers to plug in where needed after a student is diagnosed.   Therefore, structure is needed. 4) It recognizes that content is the vehicle through which the learner develops his skills.   Content also serves the purpose of transmitting knowledge considered important by society, the society which invests in school and education.

7075.   DiVirgilio, J.   "Why the middle school curriculum vacuum?"   Educational Leadership, 31,3(1973):225-227.

Will supporters of the middle school be able to create a new instructional program congenial to today's preadolescents?   Some efforts in this direction are noted.   The article discusses local school efforts and national curriculum projects.   The middle school curriculum, like the middle school organization, will use the best of two worlds, a combination of disciplinary and interdisciplinary relationships.

7076.   Dippo, J. (Ed.)   "Steps Toward Healthy Growth: Health Education Curriculum Guide, Grades 7-9." Homer, N.Y.:   Cortland-Madison Board of Cooperative Educational Services, and Bouckville, N.Y.:   Madison County Board of Cooperative Educational Services, ERIC Doc. ED 107 663, 1975.

Curriculum guide covers health education, nutrition, sensory perception, dental health, disease prevention and control, smoking and health, alcohol education, chemical substances, human sexuality, environmental health, consumer health, safety, and first aid.   Each chapter includes an overview, list of objectives, a list of major concepts, and a content outline. Learning and evaluative activities are included as well as a list of resources.   See ERIC Abstract #ED 107 663.

7077.   Dravatz, B. and Soroka, D. J.   "Inquiry in the middle grades."   Social Education, May 1969:540-542.

This social studies program stresses inquiry skills.

7078.   Duffy, G. G. (Ed.)   Reading in the Middle School. Perspectives in Reading, no. 18.   Newark, N.J.: International Reading Association, 800 Barksdale Road, Newark, N. J. 19711, ERIC Doc. ED 098 556, 1974.

Book has the following sections: Part I.   A Frame of Reference.   1) Current Themes and Problems in Middle School Reading.   2) The Middle School: A Historical

Frame of Reference. 3) The Middle School Student and the Reading Program. Part II. Organizing a Middle School Reading Program. 4) The Reading Coordinator: Key to an Effective Program. 5) Roles of the Reading Teacher. 6) Assessing Reading Progress. 7) Involving Content Teachers in the Reading Program. 8) Selecting Materials for a Middle School Reading Program. 9) Organizing a Reading Laboratory Program. Part III. Teaching Reading in the Middle School. 10) Problems and Principles in Teaching Middle School Reading. 11) Helping the Disabled Reader. 12) A Technique for Teaching Word Identification in the Content Areas. 13) Improving Achievement through Differentiated Instruction. 14) Techniques for Improving Comprehension in English. 15) Techniques for Improving Comprehension in Social Studies. 16) Techniques for Improving Comprehension in Mathematics. 17) Techniques for Improving Comprehension in Science. 18) Techniques for Developing Study Skills. 19) Techniques for Developing Reading Interests and Attitudes. Part IV. The Future. 20) Middle School Reading Programs in the Future.

7079.   Dupuis, M. M. and Askov, E. N. "The Content Area Reading Project: An In-service Education Program for Junior High School Teachers and Teachers of Adults. Appendix C, Model Teaching Materials. Final Report." University Park: Pennsylvania State University, College of Education, ERIC Doc. ED 155 668, 1977.

Section 1 contains group informal reading inventories and discusses teaching English in nine concept areas. Tests for the content areas are included. Section 2 includes plans for grouping students according to informal reading inventory scores. Section 3 groups reading skill exercises into three categories: vocabulary, comprehension, and study skills. The concluding section includes guidelines to help teachers develop the types of materials featured. See ERIC Abstract #ED 155 668.

7080.   Edgmon, A. W. "Alexandria City Public Schools: The Middle Schools--Curriculum Development." Position paper. Alexandria, Va.: Alexandria City Public Schools, 1968.

The director of middle school education in Alexandria discusses responsibilities of staff in planning for the city's middle schools. The most important feature of the curriculum is its unified approach: the entire staff of the middle school is assumed to have some degree of responsibility for the entire instructional program. A corollary is that priorities must be established, compromise must be an acceptable procedure, and continuing inquiry into the successes and failures of the school program must be

the prevailing climate in each middle school. Each
staff member needs to accept responsibility for
keeping informed on specific areas and on general
school topics.

7081.   Educational Products Information Exchange Insti-
tute. "Selector's Guide for Junior High School
Science Programs." Report 89M. Box 620, Stony
Brook, N. Y. 11790, ERIC Doc. ED 178 365, 1979.

Describes in common language twenty-six life,
physical, and earth science offerings for junior high
schools from nine commercial publishers. Information
is presented in the following headings: 1) Intents.
2) Contents. 3) Methods and Activities. 4) Tests
and Assessments. 5) Learner Verification and
Revision. See ERIC Abstract #ED 178 365.

7082.   Ellis, J. R. "The junior high school curriculum:
a general point of view." Teachers College Journal,
34,2(1962):55-56.

Presents curriculum in relation to the culture, the
school, guidance and exploration, and the teacher.
Author concludes that the ultimate--although perhaps
unmeasurable--criterion of the good school and the
good teacher is how effectively they serve the persistent needs of the individual and the community.

7083.   Erie County Board of Education. "Curriculum:
Part IV. Junior High Grades, 6-8." Sandusky, Ohio,
1966.

This is a detailed summary of the curriculum objectives at each grade level, including texts used.

7084.   Faunce, R. C. and Bossing, N. L. Developing the
Core Curriculum. Englewood Cliffs, N.J.: Prentice-
Hall, 1958.

This is a practical guide for incorporating the core
curriculum concept in a junior high school.

7085.   Flanigan, M. C. "Modernizing English instruction." Clearinghouse, 39(1965):167-169.

In 1963 the federal government granted $47,000 to
Euclid Central Junior High School at Western Reserve
University to demonstrate improved methods of English
instruction. As a result the Project English Demonstration Center, the only organization of its kind in
the country, was created to give teachers and administrators the chance to observe new methods and
materials in English being used in a typical junior
high school.

7086.   Ford Foundation. "Eagle Program." New York, ERIC
         Doc. ED 001 018. (No year given.)

The philosophy of the Wanamaker Junior High School in
Philadelphia is that human behavior can be modified
and cultural enrichment of disadvantaged children can
change their aspiration, achievement, and adjustment.
The purpose of this program is to provide educational, cultural, and social experiences for pupils
and their parents and to strive constantly for
improvement in pupil achievement. Report discusses
school organization, personnel, services, parents,
pupils, community organizations, emphases in school
programs, coordination, and evaluation of school
programs. Conclusions consider physical, service,
and program needs.

7087.   Fox, L. H. and Stanley, J. C. "Educational Facil-
         itation for Mathematically and Scientifically Preco-
         cious Youth." Paper presented at meeting of the
         American Educational Research Association, New
         Orleans, ERIC Doc. ED 075 969, December, 1972.

A program was designed to facilitate instruction for
mathematically and scientifically gifted junior high
school students. Nine educational alternatives for
the gifted (e.g., homogeneous grouping, early admission to college) were compared in terms of educational goals such as allowing for individual differences. No obvious difference in college class participation between college students and the junior high
school students were found and no grade of less than
B was reportedly received by a student taking a
college course. Mathematics knowledge appeared to
derive from independent study or from working math
puzzles. Also noted was a Saturday class in algebra,
geometry, and trigonometry for a group of twenty-two
mathematically gifted sixth graders. Schools were
encouraged to identify advanced students to stimulate
the highly talented, provide additional testing and
counseling, and allow flexible scheduling and program
planning. See ERIC Abstract #ED 075 969.

7088.   Fraser, D. M. "Current Curriculum Studies in
         Academic Subjects." Report for the Project on
         Instruction. Washington, D.C.: National Education
         Association, 1962.

Describes curriculum projects in the junior high and
senior high, with some guidelines for use.

7089.   Friedman, R. M., et al. "Teacher Training in
         PREP: Toward a More Idiosyncratic Model." Paper
         presented at the Annual Meeting of the American
         Educational Research Association, San Francisco,
         April, 1976. Silver Spring, Md.: Institute for
         Behavioral Research, ERIC Doc. ED 124 521.

PREP (Preparation through Responsive Educational Programs) was a teacher training model and part of a
research project which was in its fifth year when
these materials were published. Washington, D.C.
area junior high schools took part in the program,
which was designed to help academically or socially
deficient junior high school students improve their
school achievement and increase constructive out-of-
school behavior. It was a multifaceted program involving intensive academic skill training, individualized instructional procedures, and social skill
training, with specially developed curriculum,
training, and liaison work with parents, special
reinforcement procedures, and training of teachers.
This paper describes past changes and the present
model for PREP teacher training. See ERIC Abstract
#ED 124 521.

7090.   Gabor, G. M. "Teaching methods and incentives in
relation to junior high mathematics achievement.
"California Journal of Educational Research, 23,2
(1972):56-70.

Author discusses an experiment to promote growth in
classroom mathematics learning at the junior high
level. See ERIC Abstract #EJ 056 853.

7091.   Gardner, G. A. "Conflicting Concepts of the Core
Program."   Ph.D. Dissertation, University of Washington.   Summary in College of Education Record, 25
(1959):33-39.

Although not necessarily limited to the following
statements, purposes for a core program should
include helping youth to 1) acquire basic citizenship
skills, understandings, and behaviors through a more
effective curriculum than is found in the conventional junior high school, 2) deal with significant
personal and social problems that involve learnings
of common concern to all youth, 3) understand their
own behavior and the behavior of other persons, 4)
live democratically--thinking critically, working
cooperatively with others, respecting the work of
other people, and 5) deal with guidance problems.

7092.   Garstens, H. L. "Experimental mathematics in the
junior high school." National Education Association
Journal, 48,5(1959):42-44.

Describes the University of Maryland Mathematics
Project for junior high school students.

7093.   Gee, T. "Language Arts 'B' Option."   ERIC Doc. ED
149 340, 1977.

Suggests a complete junior high school language arts curriculum and presents in detail two courses, creative writing and literary appreciation. Rationales are discussed, along with objectives, scope, and sequence. Units contain several sample lesson plans, various teaching techniques, and suggested methods of evaluation. Bibliographies of sources used in each unit are included. See ERIC Abstract #ED 149 340.

7094.   Georgia State Department of Education.   "Industrial Arts for the Middle Grades." Atlanta, 1960.

Pamphlet presents an industrial arts model for use in A middle school.

7095.   Georgiady, N. P. and Romano, L. G. "Growth characteristics of middle school children: curriculum implications." Middle School Journal, 8(1977):1.

A basic principle of education stresses the importance of providing different kinds of education for different maturity levels.   It is essential that educators consider the ways that transescents are different from younger and older children and examine the kinds of educational programs called for by transescent characteristics.   It is because the traditional junior high school did not recognize the unique nature of the students it sought to serve that it continued to offer a program that was both irrelevant and inadequate.   The task of the middle school, therefore, becomes quite apparent.   It is to be an educational unit with a philosophy, structure, and program which will realistically and appropriately deal with 11-to-14-year-olds as they indeed are and behave.   The article discusses transescent physical growth and emotional characteristics and their implications for the curriculum.   Middle school administrators and teachers need to gain a thorough understanding of the growth characteristics of the preadolescent.   Without this knowledge, teachers do not have an adequate basis for defining the types of teaching-learning experiences needed.   This lack of knowledge made the junior high school a copy of the senior high school.   The middle school movement provides an opportunity to develop schools truly designed for preadolescents.

7096.   Gibbs, J. "Not why, but how." California Journal of Secondary Education, 28(1953):186-188.

Gibbs emphasizes the importance of maintaining a free, spontaneous, and creative approach in the art education program in the junior high school.   He suggests that pupils should not be made to stress the end result, but rather should concentrate on "the sheer thrill of the experience of doing."

7097.   Godbold, J. V. and Fournet, G. P. "An Evaluation
of the Impact of an Inquiry Curriculum in Social
Studies on Pupil Growth in Selected Cognitive Func-
tions." Paper presented at the Annual Meeting of the
American Educational Research Association, New York,
ERIC Doc. ED 138 629, April, 1977.

A study to evaluate a social studies curriculum based
upon inquiry methods surveyed 308 eighth grade students. Results indicated no significant changes in
creative thinking, attitude toward power, understanding of power concepts, and problem-solving skills as
a result of experience with the inquiry curriculum.
However, there was significant improvement in information mastery. See ERIC Abstract #ED 138 629.

7098.   Golub, L. S. "Reading in the Middle School Using
an IGE/Teacher Corps Instructional Model." Paper
presented at the Annual Meeting of the International
Reading Association, Houston, ERIC Doc. ED 158 229,
May, 1978.

Presents seven goals for middle school teachers who
use the Teacher Corps and Individually Guided Education programs. Goals are: 1) Teachers will learn to
conduct a needs assessment. 2) Teachers will involve
parents and the community. 3) Teachers will use
multicultural considerations in the reading program.
4) Teachers will use individualized diagnostic/
prescriptive instructional approaches. 5) Teachers
will work collaboratively with school staff, parents,
and faculty. 6) Teacher interns, student teachers,
students, teachers, and parents will evaluate
students' progress toward learning objectives. 7)
Teachers performance will be observed and critiqued
for continuous improvement of the reading program.
See ERIC Abstract #ED 158 229.

7099.   Grossnickle, F. E. "Teaching arithmetic in the
junior high school." Mathematics Teacher, 47(1954):
520-527.

Factors which influence the teaching of arithmetic in
the junior high school include 1) acceptance of a
theory of learning which emphasizes meaning and
understanding, 2) continuous promotion, and 3)
Gradual deferment of certain topics to higher grades.

7100.   Gruhn, W. T. "Curriculum changes in the junior
high school." High School Journal, 50(1966):122-128.

The junior high school is concerned with youth as
part of a young adolescent society, youth as they
approach the older teenage society, and youth as they
prepare for their place in the adult world. In any
study of the junior high school curriculum, it is

important to begin with a study of young adolescents. Gruhn discusses the many individual differences among young adolescents due to the mobility of our population and diversity in background of pupils. He discusses the problems caused by the concentration in our cities of large numbers of families with low incomes: young adolescents in the cities are not kept busy with useful activities as they had been in the rural areas, and as families move to the cities they often leave behind relatives, friends, church affiliations, and community interests which provide stability to children and youth. Disadvantaged youth present a particularly serious problem in the junior high school because after this age their educational, cultural, and family limitations show up more sharply. The junior high school has introduced more new programs to meet the diversity in background and ability of individual pupils in recent years than during any other period in its history. They include programs for the more able pupils, the mentally retarded, the disadvantaged, and the potential drop-out. Most schools have honors classes to provide enrichment for the more able pupil, but there are problems with these honors programs, including increased pressure for academic achievement, lack of a satisfactory policy for marking pupil achievement, and pressure from parents to have their children admitted to such classes even when the students are not qualified. Honors classes should be limited to pupils with the motivation, ability, and health which such classes demand.

7101.   Gruhn, W. and Douglass, H. R.   "The junior high school program."   Atlanta, Southern Association of Colleges and Schools, 1964.

Article discusses emerging junior high school trends: 1) closer interrelation between the various subjects through organization into broad fields, fusion of subjects, correlated courses, integrated or core courses, and the experience curriculum, 2) greater participation by pupils in planning learning activities, 3) the organization of course material and learning activities into large units, 4) the use of resource units in place of or as a supplement to the typical conventional courses of study, 5) less dependence upon the textbook and greater flexibility in its use, 6) correlation of the curriculum with real-life activities outside the school, 7) preparation for intelligent consumership and effective home life, 8) more adequate preparation for intelligent citizenship, 9) postponement of college-preparatory and vocational studies, 10) less differentiated curriculum and fewer courses, 11) emphasis on general education and the common needs of youngsters rather than elective subjects in fields of special interest.

7102.   Hackett, D.   "Communications course for junior high school."   Industrial Arts and Vocational Education, 55(1966):20-22.

This communications course is intended to develop concepts, attitudes, skills, and knowledge that give junior high school children a realistic picture of the world today. Some of the concepts are: 1) Man is a tool maker and tool user. 2) Man civilized himself through technology. 3) Communications enable man to civilize himself more rapidly. 4) Man communicates in many ways. 5) Social and economic problems result from changes in communications technology. 6) All industries are interdependent and therefore dependent upon communications.

7103.   Hamm, R. L.   "Core curriculum at the crossroads." Teachers College Journal, 39(1967):62-64.

Discusses the characteristics of the core curriculum that are most viable and suggests other ways for teachers to make the core curriculum work effectively.

7104.   Hantula, J.   "Junior High School Student Understanding of Modern Society."   Paper presented at Annual Meeting of the National Council for the Social Studies, Washington, D.C., ERIC Doc. ED 152 636, November 4, 1976.

Author used a pretest and posttest to measure junior high school student attitudes and images of modern society before and after instruction. Subjects were students in seventh and eighth grade social studies classes. One method used a textbook while the other method used investigator-devised case studies. Findings show that different patterns of teaching make a difference in the development of student understanding of modern society. See ERIC Abstract #ED 152 636.

7105.   Harmer, E. W.   "A new program in junior high school: a school staff attempts to develop an integrated program."   Educational Leadership, 17 (1960):509-511.

Through a series of curriculum workshops, the staff at the Stewart Junior High School, University of Utah, developed a curriculum which moved beyond the usual core-plus-conventional-subjects for grades 7, 8, and 9: 1) The grade levels would remain intact. A large block of time would be available for work. The core would fuse English and social studies. The general method would continue to be unit teaching. 2) All of the special interests areas of the curriculum--music, art, home ec, industrial arts, clubs--would consist of six-week and twelve-week predetermined units of work in a block of two class periods. Students would have a variety of choices and be able to cross over into other grades. 3) The science and mathematics programs would consist of predetermined units, and students would not observe grade lines. 4) Units in physical education and health would be required of all students. The school staff indicated clearly their stand on such fundamental questions as the social context, the nature of learners, and the learning process. The staff members believed they knew what they were trying to do, how they were trying to do it, and that the results would be worthwhile.

7106.   Harnett, A. L.   "The scope of health education." Bulletin of the National Association of Secondary School Principals, 44(1960):29-33.

Adequate health services in junior high schools should include 1) health appraisal (the determination of health status by observation, by screening tests of vision and hearing, by medical, dental, and psychological examination, and by measurement of height, weight, and posture), 2) health counseling and follow through (guidance to pupils and parents in securing medical, dental, and other necessary care), 3) safety and emergency care procedures (provision for protection from injury and for care in case of accident or sudden illness), 4) adjustment to individual pupil needs (a challenging, flexible school program aided by discerning, understanding teachers), and 5) communicable disease control and sanitation (emphasis on immunization, exclusion and readmittance, attendance at school, and close observation).   A program of junior high health education is usually composed of incidental health teaching, correlated health teaching, units of health offered in other courses, and direct teaching in specific health courses.

7107.   Harries, E.   "Curriculum continuity in the social studies." Education, 6,2(1978):46-50.

Suggests a framework of social studies concepts and inquiry processes to be developed in the middle years. See ERIC Abstract #EJ 199 016.

7108.   Harvell, H.   "The core curriculum." Social Education, 14,4(1950):158-160.

Describes the core curriculum and its effectiveness for teaching social studies.

7109.   Haueter, L. R.   "A Comparative Study of the Salt
Lake City Junior High School Mathematics Program
1959-60." Masters Thesis, University of Utah, 1960.

Eleven western school districts reported that ability
grouping was common in their math programs, algebra
was usually offered to eighth grade students, and
accelerated ninth graders on the whole took geometry.
Many school districts were conducting in-service
training programs for their junior high school
teachers.

7110.   Hawke, S.   "Individualized Elective Program."
Profiles of Promise 27.   ERIC Clearinghouse for
Social Studies/Social Science Education.   Boulder,
Colo.:   Social Science Education Consortium, ERIC
Doc. ED 091 284, 1974.

The Parcells Middle School allows social studies
students in grades 7 and 8 to select six-week courses
from forty classes available in geography and United
States history. The curriculum is based on a philosophy that values 1) an open-ended, self-renewing curriculum, 2) the rights of youth in education, 3) the
legitimacy of different learning techniques for different children, 4) the importance of making learned
skills adaptive, 5) the responsibility of schools in
attitude formation, 6) relieving teachers of the
burden of having all the answers, and 7) nongraded
education. This program allows for the selection of
a particular course or an independent study as well
as a particular learning plan consisting of a variety
within the course.   Making this approach work
requires new uses of old space as well as a flexibility of programming which allows teachers to work
alone, in teams, or as resource teachers. See ERIC
Abstract #ED 091 284.

7111.   Hawke, S.   "Women's Studies in the Junior High
School." Profiles of Promise 42. ERIC Clearinghouse
for Social Studies/Social Science Education. Boulder,
Colo.: Social Science Education Consortium, 1975.

A middle school in Colorado offers a social studies
mini-course entitled "Women's Studies." This nine-
week course examines ideals, sex roles, sex stereotyping, the historical development of women, and
social issues relating to women. The main impact of
the course is on personal development and increased
student awareness. Teacher neutrality permits students to develop their own views. Activities include
keeping a journal, providing opportunity for students
to reflect on the personal meaning of being female,
and role playing.   The article outlines the course
and discusses introducing women's studies in the

curriculum, growing and awareness, and women's studies, present and future.

7112.   Hearn, A. C. (Ed.) Mathematics in the Junior High. Curriculum Bulletin 176. Eugene: School of Education, University of Oregon, June 10, 1957.

Discusses objectives, scope, and sequence for seventh and eighth grade mathematics, ninth grade general mathematics, and the first year of algebra.

7113.   Henrich, M. and Nelson, C. "The Classroom Teacher and the Reading Consultant: Cooperation at the Junior High Level." Paper presented at the Annual Meeting of the International Reading Association, Houston, ERIC Doc. ED 163 398, May, 1978.

Fifty-two guidelines for establishing junior high school content area reading programs were developed from a program in Columbia, Missouri. One set of guidelines concerns developing effective qualities and attitudes and dealing successfully with faculty and administration. Organizational guidelines deal with establishing the need and purposes of a content area reading program, writing program objectives, developing materials, integrating the program into the school curriculum, and promoting communication among teachers. Guidelines for in-service programs concern assessment of students and materials, vocabulary teaching and reinforcement, reading comprehension, and study skills. An appendix lists publications, cassette tapes, and films useful in developing a content area reading program. See ERIC Abstract #ED 163.

7114.   Hergebroth, E. H. "Art curriculum." In Alpern, M. (Ed.), The Subject Curriculum, K-12. Columbus, Ohio: Merrill, 1967.

A three-year junior high art curriculum should promote 1) an understanding of the principles and elements of art through use of design elements, decorative design, crafts, applied design principles, and an emphasis upon function design, 2) cultivation of initiative, flexibility, and fluency, 3) an understanding of cultural and historical contributions, 4) development of skills and techniques through exposure to a variety of materials, media, and methods from silk-screening to mechanical drawing and photography, 5) critical comparison of art forms and an understanding of the necessity for variety, 6) identification of special student talents, interests, and abilities, 7) opportunities for personal communication and expression in designing such items as signs, posters, and displays, 8) increasing abilities to become discerning creators and consumers through

examination and analysis of consumer products, advertising, painting, sculpture, architecture, and other
art forms, 9) work that supplements other learnings
in the school, and 10) exploring art as a possible
vocation.

7115.   Hickerson, J. and Wild, P. H.   "The City: Two
Interdisciplinary Units for Junior High or Middle
School Classes."   ERIC Doc. ED 137 179, 1972.

This resource unit in urban studies is designed to be
used by suburban social studies teachers in grades
7-9 and aims at developing a positive attitude in
suburban students toward the central city.   Students
are introduced to the social dynamics and cultural
resources unique in large urban centers.   See ERIC
Abstract #ED 137 179.

7116.   Highline Public Schools.   "Occupational Versatility.   Final Report for the Three-Year Period July
1969 to June 1972."   Seattle, Wash., ERIC Doc. ED 079
540, 1972.

Occupational versatility, an innovative approach to
the teaching of industrial arts, began in the fall of
1969 in three pilot schools, two junior high schools
and one middle school.   The major components are a
multiexperience general shop facility, team teaching,
student management, a self-instructional system for
learning, career guidance opportunities, and a nongraded approach to reporting student performance.
Evaluations of the program are included in this
report.   Reactions of teachers, parents, and students
were most positive.   Shop area layouts and forms used
in the program are appended.   See ERIC Abstract #ED
079 540.

7117.   Hiles, D., Kaspert, J., Lifton, E., and Parkin, D.
"Social Studies: Teenage Living--Home and Family
Education."   Miami, Fla.:   Dade County Public
Schools, ERIC Doc. ED 062 247, 1971.

Article describes a grade 7-9 quinmester course
focusing on factors influencing the young teenager's
attitudes, behavior, and relationship with others.
The major objective is for the teenager to examine
values and behaviors of himself and his peers in
order to prepare himself for the changes and challenges that will confront him and to set goals that
will help him get the most from his teen years.   The
nine sections of this course are: 1) basic human
needs, 2) personality development, 3) character
growth, 4) rules and self-discipline, 5) unique
challenges of today's society, 6) social relationships, 7) boy-girl relationships, 8) family relationships, and 9) self-assessment.   The rationale of the

course is that students entering junior high school are in a position to make many of their own decisions for the first time. They have problems unique to their age group. They are also able to make contributions to their school, family, and community. A guidance/human relations approach would make the course relevant to studies, and if it is offered early in the junior high years it can acquaint the student with his guidance counselors through informal discussions and question-and-answer sessions.

7118.   Hinrichs, R. S. (Comp.)   Experiencing the Free Enterprise System Through Industrial Arts.   Industrial Arts Series 10,000.   Mississippi Research Coordinating Unit for Vocatonal-Technical Education, State College.   Jackson: Mississippi State Department   of   Education,   Division   of   Vocational   and Technical Education, ERIC Doc. ED 099 643, 1974.

This manual provides guidelines for helping junior high school students develop an understanding of industry. The first section discusses industry and the free enterprise system. The second section is an instruction unit to be used as a guide in setting up and operating a small student industry.   See ERIC Abstract #ED 099 643.

7119.   Hoffman, A. J. and Hoffman, N. L.   "Using Research Methods   in   Elementary   and   Middle   School   Social Studies   Classes."   Paper   presented   at   the   Annual Conference   of   the   National   Council   for   the   Social Studies,   Houston,   ERIC   Doc.   ED   161   815,   November, 1978.

Describes how to use social science research methodologies to teach social studies. The goal is to help children develop independent thinking and problem-solving skills. Authors describe historical, experimental, descriptive, and survey research methods and give examples of how each methodology can be applied in the classroom.   See ERIC Abstract #ED 161 815.

7120.   Hoppe, A.   "Curriculum developments: junior high school   years."   Educational Leadership,   December 1960.

Describes innovations in various areas of the junior high curriculum.

7121.   Hott,   L.   and   Sonstegard,   M.   "Relating   self-conceptions   to   curriculum   development."   Journal of Educational Research, 58,8(1965):348-351.

Authors studied student self-attitudes through a simple group-administered projective device.   The subjects were sixty-one seventh and eighth grade Iowa

public school students in a 1960 summer seminar in
mathematics and science at the University of Northern
Iowa, Cedar Falls. Each student ranked in about the
ninetieth percentile in performance on skills tests.
Findings showed a tendency for students to exhaust
their consensual remarks before they resorted to sub-
consensual statements. Not a single response could
be interpreted to mean interest in, concern for, or
identity with social studies experiences. Very few
references were made to patriotic and ecological
identities, religion, political conviction, and
concern for peer groups. Possibly not nearly enough
is being done in school administration in conjunction
with counseling and guidance to relate curriculum to
students' self-conceptions. Junior high school
social studies teachers should give serious attention
to the question, "How functional is the traditional
social studies curriculum in promoting desirable
self-conceptions in students?"

7122.   Houston, L. "Articulating junior high mathematics
with elementary arithmetic." School Science and
Mathematics, 51(1951):117-121.

Junior high articulation with the elementary school
might be improved by 1) a gradual shift from the work
of the elementary school, 2) an understanding of the
content of the elementary school program, and 3) an
emphasis on meanings and understandings.

7123.   Howard, A. "Industrial arts in the junior high
school." Chapter in Stoumbis, G. (Ed.), Schools for
the Middle Years: Readings. Scranton, Pa.: International Textbook, 1969.

Especially for the junior high school student, industrial arts should emphasize the exploratory function
and work toward relating industrial arts to other
fields. It is possible and desirable, for example,
for the science and industrial arts teachers to
coordinate their instruction to permit students to
develop projects and studies which use the facilities
of both laboratories. The required junior high
school program should emphasize breadth, not depth,
and should provide electives in such areas as graphic
arts, drafting, metal, wood, plastics, and power
mechanics. Students need to develop manipulative
abilities and skills and to learn the proper use of
hand tools. Industrial arts should be accepted as a
necessary part of the junior high school comprehensive program.

7124.   Howard, A. W. "Physical education in the junior
high school." Chapter in Stoumbis, G. (Ed.), Schools
for the Middle Years: Readings. Scranton, Pa.:
International Textbook, 1969.

A sound physical education program for junior high school boys and girls will take into account several considerations: 1) There is a definite need in our mechanized age for a regular, sequential, planned developmental curriculum in physical education which builds bodies, promotes physical fitness, and encourages a carryover and long-time interests in sports and physical activities suitable for out-of-school youth. 2) The physically educated student develops a range of basic skills in running, walking, jumping, throwing, and controlling his or her body. 3) The physically educated junior high school boy and girl learn team sports, the need for team action, the necessity for learning the rules of the game and abiding by them, and the desirability of good sportsmanship. There is too little emphasis upon character and sportsmanship and too much stress upon winning and upon proselytizing for varsity teams which have but dubious value, if any, in junior high school. 4) Physical education instructors in the junior high school should not have coaching assignments. 5) There is a place for some academic work in physical education, but there is no justification for the avalanche of paper work which sometimes proliferates in physical education classes. 6) A good physical education program in the junior high school teaches a wide knowledge of games and sports. Students know the rules and background of many games, which permits them to derive more pleasure as participants and spectators. 7) A basic physical education program includes instruction and participation in games, sports, athletics, play activities, gymnastic self-testing activities, rhythmical activities, and physical fitness and developmental activities. 8) Physical education should be a required course which meets daily for one period for all three years of junior high school. 9) There must be adequate funds, facilities, equipment, and personnel for the required program. 10) Physical education classes should develop citizenship, respect for the rights of others, recognition of the worth of the individual, and the habit of courtesy and good manners. 11) Body contact sports should be avoided, if not eliminated, in junior high school. 12) There should be a diversified, well-staffed intramural program which is adequately funded, encourages widespread participation, and is scheduled to permit maximum student involvement. A good physical education program in the junior high school does not stress team nor varsity sports at the expense of individual or dual activities.

7125.   Howard, A. W. "Home economics in the junior high school." Chapter in Stoumbis, G. (Ed.), Schools for the Middle Years: Readings. Scranton, Pa.: International Textbook, 1969.

Home economics in the junior high should 1) be required for all girls for at least one year and probably two, 2) probably be required for all boys for at least one semester, 3) recognize that there are several levels of economic status and adjust the program accordingly, 4) recognize that in these times of rising prices and inflation it becomes essential that boys and girls learn about consumer education, budgeting, buying wisely, and the hazards and problems of installment buying, sales, and discounts, 5) relate homemaking courses to the everyday life of the student with an immediate or imminent application in nutrition, money management, personal grooming, child care, home furnishing, and the possibilities of creative expression in home decorating and art, 6) refuse to let the high school determine content, scope, and sequence of the junior high school curriculum in home economics, and 7) give potential dropouts a program which is of real interest to them, excites their curiosity, creates a desire to learn more, and includes content of relevance to their situation. The seventh grade curriculum should include clothing selection and construction, foods, textiles, personal finances, and nutrition. In the eighth grade, course offerings commonly include more clothing and foods, purchasing food and clothing, and home management. Offerings in the ninth grade are generally consumer education, clothing and foods, home management, child care and development, health and home nursing, personal grooming, and home decorating.

7126.   Howard County Board of Education. "Howard County Public Schools Social Studies Curriculum Unit: Middle School Human Relations." Clarksville, Md., ERIC Doc. ED 061 115, 1970.

The rationale for this course is that learning to cope with everyday social interaction is of utmost importance to the individual. Since a major premise of the middle school is the process of socialization, it is important that a curriculum be responsive to that idea. Students must become aware of the importance of the dignity of every other individual. The objectives of this course are that the student will 1) better understand and accept himself as an individual and as a member of a group, 2) be better prepared for the conflicts and problems of preadolescence, and 3) learn by example and discussion that knowledge should result in action. The course stresses that students will follow written directions, identify purposes of a group, identify roles in a group, and participate in sociodrama. Each section contains objectives, large-group activities, small-group activities, student handouts, and a think-discuss-write question.

7127.   Hughes, W. O.   "Planning educative experiences in junior high school general music."   Music Educators Journal, 52(1966):76-78.

Describes music activities for middle school and junior high youth.

7128.   Hurd, P. D.   New Curriculum Perspectives for Junior High School Science.   Belmont, Calif.:   Wadsworth Publishing Co., ERIC Doc. ED 047 949, 1970.

Examines the purposes and subject matter of the conventional junior high school science curriculum and describes more than twenty experimental instructional practices. Author discusses the controversies surrounding organizational proposals for junior high school, the diversity in student population, and innovative curriculum models. See ERIC Abstract #ED 047 949.

7129.   Hurd, P. D. (Ed.)   Final Report of the National Science Foundation Early Adolescence Panel. Washington, D.C.:   National Science Foundation Directorate for Science Education, Office of Program Integration, 1978.

The panel reviewed the current education of early adolescents in science, social studies, and mathematics, and explored ways to improve their education in both formal and informal out-of-school contexts. The first section of this report deals with the early adolescent as a person, while the second section deals with the types of research, development, and action programs needed for this age range. Appendix B contains position papers by the eight panel members. The final appendix by Geneva Haertel contains a review of the literature on early adolescence and implications for programming.

7130.   Illinois Teacher of Home Economics magazine. "OVT (occupational, vocational, and technical) students explore the world of work." Illinois Teacher of Home Economics, 18,1(1974):14-18.

Describes a middle school program designed to provide boys and girls together with a career-oriented experience in what have traditionally been called home economics, industrial arts, and business education. It is a student-centered, open classroom program with an experimental approach. See ERIC Abstract #EJ 105 413.

7131.   Instructional Objectives Exchange. "Sex Education: Grades K-12."   P.O. Box 24095, Los Angeles, Calif. 90024, ERIC Doc. ED 169 084, 1975.

This booklet contains fifty objectives, related sample items, and directions for administering and scoring tests in the sex education course. Sections include growth and development, animal and human biology, social and emotional growth, sexual development, and clarifying values. Each section is divided into levels for elementary, junior high, and senior high school students. See ERIC Abstract #169084.

7132.   James, S. M. "Mini Media Centers and the Middle School English Teacher." Paper presented at the Annual Meeting of the Conference on English Education, Colorado Springs, Colo., ERIC Doc. ED 103 877, March 20, 1975.

Proposes a mini media center for middle school English programs. Students help plan and create the materials and learn to prepare visuals, charts, audio and visual tapes, slides, games, books, movies, and radio shows. See ERIC Abstract #ED 103 877.

7133.   Jennings, W. "What is a core program?" Clearinghouse, 40(1965):223-225.

Describes a model core program.

7134.   Jennings, W. B. "What is the Effectiveness of the Core Program?" Master's Thesis, University of Minnesota, Minneapolis, 1961.

A complete survey of core evaluations in the literature up to 1961.

7135.   Junior High School Association of Illinois. Challenging Talented Junior High School Youth. Urbana, Ill.: Interstate Printers and Publishers, 1959.

Describes Illinois junior high school programs for academically talented pupils.

7136.   Jurjevich, J. C., Jr. "Methods and results in a junior high school core class." Educational Leadership, 14(1957):483-487.

Describes a core curriculum in practice and research findings about it.

7137.   Kaiser, D. W., et al. "A Junior High School Industrial Technology Demonstration Program: The World of Construction, 1969-1970. Final Report." Pontiac City, Michigan, School District. Lansing: Michigan State Department of Education, ERIC Doc. Ed 075 661, 1970.

Authors studied a demonstration program in fifteen junior high school classes in 1969-70. The curriculum on the world of construction was developed by the Industrial Arts Curriculum Project of the Ohio State University. Comparisons of experimental and control group test results revealed that the experimental students achieved significantly higher scores at the seventh and eighth grade levels, but there was no difference at the ninth grade level. Included in this publication are questionnaire results plus a supervisor report and budget information. See ERIC Abstract #ED 075 661.

7138.   Kalamazoo Public Schools.   "How Much Did They Grow? An Evaluation Study of the Junior High Schools Unified Study Program."   Bulletin 164.   Kalamazoo, Mich., 1952.

A unified studies core program in Kalamazoo increased pupil participation in learning activities. Achievement, according to standardized tests, remained as good as or better than could be expected for the ability range of the students. Accomplishments in art, music, athletics and dramatics were usually above average. The effectiveness of student participation in administration and control (student council) was evidenced in emerging group controls, quiet corridors, clean and orderly lunchrooms, purposeful activity in the absence of a teacher, and a good experience in assemblies. Core effectiveness in skill development can be evaluated by comparing results of standardized tests with test norms or national averages. A large-scale comparison of test results in Kalamazoo found that core students usually make normal or average progress in language and study skills.

7139.   Keedy, M. L.   "Mathematics in junior high school."   Educational Leadership, 17(1959):157-161.

Stresses the need for a more precise mathematical language for junior high school students. Present vocabulary and habits of usage have accumulated over thousands of years of mathematical activity, and one easily finds vague and contradictory notions as well as a lack of words with which to express today's mathematical ideas clearly and briefly.

7140.   Kibblewhite, S.   "Teaching design."   Education 3-13, 5,1(1977):47-51.

The head of the art department at Dingleside Middle School discusses teaching context, past approaches, and present objectives of the art program: 1) to establish a new image of design as a means of expression which is a satisfying and enjoyable experience

for all concerned, 2) to encourage more acute observation of the environment by using language as an
initial form of communication which becomes secondary
as the products of creative design emerge, 3) to
boost children's self-confidence until they are able
to organize their own individual work and apply to it
their own standards and values, 4) To help children
experience continuity of design from the initial
observation through the combining of techniques and
media to the final result, 5) to choose work that can
extend the experience of the most able children and
can offer a genuine opportunity of successful
achievement for the least able, and 6) to encourage
children to experience a wide range of techniques and
media.   Article also discusses objectives in action,
evaluation, and implications for other schools.

7141.   Kindred, Wolotkiewicz, Mickelson, Coplein, and
Dyson.   Middle School Curriculum: A Practitioner's
Handbook. Boston: Allyn and Bacon, 1976.

Book gives an overview of the curriculum-building
process and describes new avenues of learning.   It
discusses ways of using personnel to meet school
objectives, the place of student activities in the
curriculum, and evaluation of the student performance.   The book should be useful for students who
are taking courses in elementary or secondary school
curriculum, curriculum development, the junior high
school, or the middle school.   It is useful also for
in-service preparation of teachers for the middle
school.   It is an important reference for conferences, workshops, and study committees concerned with
the improvement of middle school education.   Chapters
are: 1) The Rationale (growth of the middle school,
characteristics of a middle school).   2) The Child 10
to 14 (self-concept, factors influencing growth,
growth patterns, growth and the curriculum, the
teacher's role).   3) Learning and Intellectual Development (theories and their implications for the
middle school).   4) Curriculum Design (purposes and
objectives, content, strategy, putting it all
together, evaluation).   5) Middle School Organization
and Programs (aspects of curriculum, selected middle
school programs).   6) Individualizing Instruction
(developing strategies, the learning environment,
grouping practices, nongraded instruction).   7)
Technology in the Middle School (learning packets,
differentiated learning paths, instructional systems,
programmed materials, computers for middle schools,
language laboratories, science laboratories, television and films, instructional material media centers,
contributions of regional laboratories).   8) The
Activity Program (background, types of activity
programs, organizing an activities program, student

governance, practical policies). 9) Staff Organization and Utilization (team teaching, using specialists and aides, qualifications of staff, staffing
schedules, organization of middle schools, communication).   10) Evaluating Performance (rationale,
diagnosing student performance, evaluating instruments, marking student performance, reporting student
performance, curriculum evaluation). The book contains a selected bibliography.

7142.   King, D. C. "Missing the point." Intercommuni-
cations, 88(1978):17-19.

Describes activities that help junior high school
students understand that common barriers to communication are cultural differences, ethnocentrism,
prejudice, and misinterpretation. See ERIC Abstract
#EJ 178 547.

7143.   Knopp, M. A. "Learning Module: The Self Theory
and the Transescent." ERIC Doc. ED 142 512, 1974.

A learning module prepares teachers to foster in
transescents a positive self-image and improve their
academic achievement and ability to cope with life's
situations. Includes many self-evaluation tests and
perception tests and a bibliography.

7144.   Kohlmann, E. L. and Ericksen, J. K. "Home economics in transition in the middle/junior high
school." Illinois Teacher of Home Economics, 20,2
(1976):81-84.

Authors draw on research to develop a sixth grade
home economics curriculum. They also explore
teaching-learning strategies and program organization
in light of middle school philosophy. The curriculum
is child-centered and exploratory. See ERIC Abstract
#EJ 150 992.

7145.   Kokomo Consolidated School Corp. "Guide for
Health and Safety in the Middle School, 6, 7, 8."
Kokomo, Ind., ERIC Doc. ED 048 008, 1970.

Guide for the health educator presents units on
personal, physical, community, and social health for
grades 6, 7, and 8. Individual units outline goals,
subject matter, learning experiences, resource
material, and length of time to complete the unit.
See ERIC Abstract #ED 048 008.

7146.   Konicek, R. and Tinsley, T. "They need to know:
a sex education program in junior high." Science
Teacher, 34(1967):48-50.

A sex education curriculum for seventh, eighth, and ninth graders.

7147.   Krevolin, N. "New approach to exploration in the junior high school." Journal of Secondary Education, 42(1967):32-33.

New ideas for an exploratory junior high curriculum.

7148.   Kroenke, R. G. "Individualizing Reading Instruction at the Junior High Level." Paper presented at the International Reading Association Meetings, Atlantic City, N.J., ERIC Doc. ED 051 971, April 19-23, 1971.

Individualized reading can take many forms in junior high school. Article discusses the concept of individualized reading instruction, the need for individualized instruction at the junior high level, class organization with emphasis on individualized reading, total group reading, skill development in smaller groups, interest groups, and applications to all subjects. Included is a chart showing class organization for reading: 1) total class, 2) small groups at different reading achievement levels, 3) interest groups, and 4) individualized reading. Each approach has its place in the classroom and can be used in all content areas. Teacher, administrative, and evaluative planning are the keys to a successful program.

7149.   Kurth, R. J. and Moseley, P. A. "Using Research on Readability to Enhance Middle School Curriculum Materials." Paper presented at the Annual Meeting of the National Reading Conference, New Orleans, ERIC Doc. ED 149 294, December, 1977.

Offers seven guidelines to help middle school teachers select and present reading materials that enhance learning by minimizing insecurity. The guidelines are: 1) Provide as much independent reading as possible. 2) Structure choices for independent reading. 3) Analyze reading materials according to sentence length and complexity, vocabularly, and concept density. 4) Provide materials on subjects that are familiar to the students. 5) Use reading materials that have egocentric content, reflecting a learner's interest. 6) Emphasize content organization as a means of improving reading comprehension. 7) Value convergent thinking which will stimulate learning while it provides security. See ERIC Abstract #ED 149 294.

7150.   Kurtz, V. R. Metrics for Elementary and Middle Schools. Curriculum Series. Washington, D.C.: National Education Association, ERIC Doc. ED 159 066, 1978.

Mathematics teachers will find this book useful. Part I is a primer of information designed to help a teacher in answering many questions that children and parents will ask. Part II consists of ideas and activities that teachers in the nonmathematics curriculum may incorporate into their lessons. Part III deals with classroom activities that teachers of math may use. A special section uses only nonstandard measurement activities. See ERIC Abstract #ED 159 066.

7151. LaRoe, M. E. "Social Studies: The Florida Story." Miami, Fla.: Dade County Public Schools, ERIC Doc. ED 062 249, 1971.

Describes a grade 7-9 social studies course based on the quinmester year. The course covers Florida's history, population centers, economy, government, current problems, ethnic groups, and future aspirations. The primary goal is to give students the background they need to understand contemporary issues and problems in Florida. The course focuses on the concept of growth and on some central developments that almost everyone agrees typify Florida and have molded the state.

7152. Lauchner, A. H. "How can the junior high school curriculum be improved?" Bulletin of the National Association of Secondary School Principals, 35(1951): 296-304.

Discussion uses examples from schools in many cities.

7153. Lavender, J. "Get the kid to the content." School Shop, 36,8(1977):78-81.

Project Occupational Versatility is a self-instructional industrial arts shop program in which junior high school students select, manage, and evaluate their own projects. Article discusses student procedures, facilitation, and teacher procedures and includes a school shop floor plan. See ERIC Abstract #EJ 158 262.

7154. Lawhead, V. B. "A block of time for general education." Educational Leadership, December 1960: 148-152.

Two essential characteristics of the core curriculum are: 1) It is concerned with general or liberal education in contrast to special or technical education, which is also necessary but is organized for differences in talents and interests. 2) Instead of short, separate periods for isolated subjects, the core embraces a larger block of time for a unified organization of experiences cutting across the major disciplines. These comprehensive and integrating characteristics foster other values in a core program, including four that are especially relevant to the junior high school: 1) The core program encourages students to establish relationships between and among fields of knowledge. 2) The core program facilitates guidance and counseling of students. 3) The core program connects the curriculum content more directly to the needs of students and demands of society. 4) The core offers additional opportunities for improving instruction. With educators at all levels decrying the rigidity of curriculum based on narrow specialization, it seems crucial in the junior high school to consider a program which asserts the unity of human knowledge but recognizes the need to extend individual talents toward diverse competencies.

7155.   Leeds, W. L. "Core classes in action." Education, 73(1953):273-296.

Describes in detail the core classes in grades 8 and 9 in a midwestern junior high school.

7156.   Leonard, J. P.   Developing the Secondary School Curriculum.   Rev. ed.   New York: Rhinehart, 1953.

The major job of the core curriculum is developing in all youth the competence and personal and social responsibility necessary for participation in a democratic society.

7157.   Lowry, A.   "The turbulent years."   Journal of Health, Physical Education and Recreation, 32(1961): 16-17.

The purposes of physical fitness programs for boys and girls during their junior high school years are different in many ways from those for later adolescents in senior high schools. A junior high school program should offer 1) a basic program of physical fitness, including special activities for students not physically able to participate in the regular program, and 2) intramurals and recreational programs.

7158.   Lum, S.   "Meeting mathematical needs in the middle grades."   Arithmetic Teacher, 24,3(1977):233-237.

A seventh grade teacher discusses her dual approach in which students, with the cooperation of parents, decide on either large-group instruction or individualized programs in their mathematics classes. Article includes the letter she sends to parents concerning the mathematical program and describes the classroom alternative, the individualized program, the contract, the materials for the individualized program, and the record keeping system.

7159.   Lumpkin, D. "Strengthening Reading at the Secondary Level." Paper presented at the Annual Convention of the International Reading Association, Detroit, ERIC Doc. ED 063 586, May, 1972.

Author visited twenty-five middle schools, junior highs, and senior high schools in Arizona, California, Illinois, Indiana, Michigan, Pennsylvania, and Wisconsin to identify reading programs that hold promise. These observations were made: 1) More than half maintain a reading center or lab. 2) A number of schools use modular scheduling and team teaching. 3) Commercial contracts, behavior modification strategies, and differentiated staffing are incorporated to some extent in most programs. 4) All programs value and attempt to provide a variety of types and levels of instructional materials. 5) Reading personnel attempt to involve subject matter teachers in strengthening students reading skills. Sections of this paper include: 1) The Need for Secondary Reading Instruction. 2) The Status of Secondary Reading. 3) Current Reading Programs. 4) Facilities. 5) Organizational Patterns. 6) Instructional Strategies. 7) Materials. 8) Reading in Content Areas. 9) Goals for Secondary Reading. 10) Learning to Read to Learn. 11) References. An ideal reading program at the secondary level is discussed at the conclusion of this paper. Author includes teenagers' comments taken from school discussions on the importance of reading and learning to read.

7160.   Lurry, L. P. and Alberty, E. J. Developing a Core Program. New York: Macmillan, 1957.

A review of the literature and judgments of thirty curricular workers suggest sixteen issues that should be addressed in a core curriculum: 1) school living, 2) self-understanding, 3) finding values by which we live, 4) social relationships, 5) employment and vocation, 6) using and conserving natural resources, 7) education in a democracy, 8) constructive use of leisure time, 9) family living, 10) communication, 11) democratic government, 12) community and personal health, 13) economic relationships in a democracy, 14) achieving world peace in the atomic age, 15) intercultural relationships, and 16) critical thinking.

7161.   Machek, K. and Cockfield, D. "Functional creativity in the junior high school." School Arts, 51 (1952):226-227.

Art can play a part in all areas of the junior high
school curriculum. Authors describe some of the
integrative activities carried on in Rockford Junior
High School, Rockford, Illinois.

7162. Man/Society/Technology magazine. "Industrial arts
in the middle school." Man/Society/Technology, 31,1
(1971):18.

Discussion of an industrial arts program for transescents covers curriculum planning, equipment, and
facility requirements. See ERIC Abstract #ED 046
570.

7163. Mazza, P. "Social studies in the second generation." Indiana Social Studies Quarterly, 24,2(1971):
32-35.

Discusses how the middle school can meet the special
needs of preadolescent and early adolescent students
and how "Man: A Course of Study" is applicable to
the middle school. See ERIC Abstract #EJ 049 604.

7164. McTeer, J. H. "Student Interest in Social Studies
Content and Methodology." ERIC Doc. ED 139 712,
1976.

Study measures attitudes of 391 seventh and eighth
graders toward certain subjects and teaching methods
in social studies. Responses to an open-ended questionnaire showed that in terms of content, students
prefer social geography, social history, current
events, and culturally oriented areas of social
studies. In terms of methodology, students prefer
discussion classes, films and filmstrips, interesting
and readable texts, and no homework. See ERIC
Abstract #ED 139 712.

7165. Meister, R. W. "What about 'unified arts' in the
middle school?" Educational Leadership, 3(1973):233-
235.

Unified arts in the Madison, Wisconsin, middle
schools are learner oriented. Goals include:
1) exploration geared to interest and ability, 2)
proficiency and skills, 3) developing confidence as a
consumer, 4) selecting approaches to careers, and 5)
deciding about the use of leisure time.

7166. Merritt, D. L. "Middle school: organization for
learning (LAGs, LAPs, and CAPs)." Middle School
Journal, 10,5(1974):55-59.

Middle school philosophy suggests that we provide a
wide variety of learning activities, but too often
students are burdened with ineffectual, banal texts.

The curriculum may be conceived of in terms of relationships among Learning Activity Guides (LAGs),
Learning Activity Packages (LAPs), and Contract
Activity Packages (CAPs). The LAG primarily serves
as an organizational, planning, and evaluation tool
for teachers. The LAP and CAP are both for students,
and the latter involves student input. Students may
learn to manage themselves as they pursue learning
through this program, which is readily adaptable to a
continuous progress program and is especially suited
to the middle school philosophy. The key to success
is proper in-service training for the teachers who
must organize and use the program.

7167.   Mickelson, J. M.   "What does research say about
the effectiveness of the core curriculum?"   School
Review, 65(1957):144-160.

Cites various studies which attest to the effectiveness of the core curriculum model.

7168.   Miles, L. C.   "Adolescent explorer finds what he
needs."   National Education Association Journal,   42
(1953):557-558.

Describes exploratory activities in the junior high
school in Cedar City, Utah.

7169.   Minkler, M.   "Sex education in the junior high: a
comprehensive approach."   Journal of School Health,
42,8(1972):487-490.

Describes how a sex education program was developed
and carried out in a local junior high school, the
obstacles which were faced and overcome, and the
lessons to be learned by such a demonstration
project. See ERIC Abstract #EJ 066 204.

7170.   Minnesota Instructional Materials Center.   "Middle
School/Junior High Coeducational Mini-units in Home
Economics Units 8 to 13."   White Bear Lake: Minne-
sota Instructional Materials Center, University of
Minnesota, St. Paul, Division of Home Economics Edu-
cation, ERIC Doc. ED 133 535, 1976.

Six self-contained mini-units on personal development
are part of a set of twenty-one home economics units
for middle school/junior high boys and girls.
Designed to be free of sex-role stereotyping, the
units are: 1) Grooming and You.   2) Becoming a
Person: a Lifelong Process.   3) Making the Most of
Your Resources.   4) Understanding Yourself and Human
Sexuality.   5) Together: You and Your Family.   6)
Learning to Care for Children.   Each unit contains 1)
an introductory page that describes the focus,
rationale, and objectives of the unit, 2) the content

of the unit, and 3) support material.   See ERIC
Abstract #ED 133 535.

7171.   Mitchell, W. E.   "The adolescent and his time."
Educational Leadership, 23,4(1966):290-292.

The curriculum for the adolescent should provide each
student with opportunities to identify, develop, and
express his individual personality and it should help
the student develop satisfying relationships with
others.   Certain personal skills in human relationships that are necessary for successful living in a
democracy cannot be learned by writing essays, by
memorization, or by studying in a science lab. Young
people learn to be kind only by working with other
people.   They learn to be tolerant only in human
relationships.   They learn to influence the conduct
of others by working with people whose rights are
equal to but not necessarily the same as theirs.
Every personal contact within the school is part of
this process.

7172.   Mott, K.   "Language arts: social studies fusion
in the junior high school block."   Bulletin of the
National Association of Secondary School Principals,
March 1960:124-131.

When students become aware of the fact that language
arts embraces all that they do in writing, reading,
speaking, and even thinking and that they must not
think of English as only grammar which is divorced
completely from other subjects, then the idea of
language arts/social studies becomes meaningful and
workable.   The author has been a supervising teacher
for social studies work within the framework of the
language arts program and feels that fusion on the
junior high school level is workable and productive.
This is substantiated by the fact that a large
majority of the students who have gone through the
program outlined in this article are generally
performing better than those students who were taught
otherwise in these schools.   Methods without meaning
are sterile.   Fusion, according to the procedure
explained, gives real meaning to the language arts
methods which are currently used.   This procedure
will produce good results in any junior high school
block period in which the language arts/social
studies combination is taught.

7173.   Murwin, S. and Murray, M.   "First Year Progress
Report on Project Open, Ona Junior High School,
Cabell County, West Virginia, 1977-78 Project Year."
Charleston: West Virginia State Department of
Education, ERIC Doc. ED 167 722, 1978.

This unified curriculum combines art, home ec, music, and industrial arts. Each student takes nine weeks of one subject and then rotates to another. Describes components of the curriculum. See ERIC Abstract #ED 167 722.

7174.   Nampa School District 133. "Communication Skills Improvement Center." Idaho, ERIC Doc. ED 106 827, April, 1974.

This program to increase reading proficiency serves eight hundred students and faculty of a junior high school. It concentrates on three approaches. The first approach, in-service training, emphasizes diagnosis and remediation and consists of sessions for volunteers in the entire faculty. It includes a preschool workshop for language arts teachers, mini-workshops, demonstrations for small teacher groups, and faculty visits to other schools and projects. The second approach involves students with severe reading problems. The third approach involves all students and is aimed at increasing interest in reading. See ERIC Abstract #ED 106 827.

7175.   Nardelli, W. "Business education in the middle school." Balance Sheet, 48(1967):307-309.

Great curriculum changes will take place in the middle school in the near future. All students should be oriented to the demands of the American economy through a study of their business and industrial community. All phases of economics will be the vanguard of business education, because business today is so much affected by the economic influences and demands of the local, community, state, and federal governments. Free enterprise is American and the sooner Americans begin to understand the term, the better for the general health of the country. Business education in the middle school should cover community industries, service businesses, recreational businesses, home products, organizations that bring in new businesses and industries, economics of nonprofit organization, image building, and the community's share of new businesses, new families, new schools, new fire and police protection programs, new water and sewerage problems, etc.

7176.   Nashville-Davidson County Metropolitan Public Schools. "Language Arts in the Junior High Years: Exploration--Stimulation--Preparation. A Language Arts Resource Prepared for Grades 7 through 9." Nashville, Tenn., ERIC Doc. ED 088 071, 1973.

This guide suggests a competency-based language arts program with minimal performance expectations. Sections of the book include 1) Language (listening, reading, word study, semantics, language structure, and speaking). 2) Literature (fiction and nonfiction). 3) Composition (expository writing and creative writing). Each section discusses teacher objectives, student objectives, performance expectations, and suggested activities and ideas. See ERIC Abstract ED 088 071.

7177.   National Association of Secondary School Principals. "Planning for American Youth." Washington, D.C., 1944.

This noteworthy early publication prompted a study of adolescent needs and resulted in an exemplary curriculum covering vocational preparations, health, citizenship, family relationship, consumer education, science, appreciation of the arts, leisure, cooperative living values, and rational thinking.

7178.   National Association of Secondary School Principals. Bulletin of the National Association of Secondary School Principals, 47,280(1963):Whole Issue.

Part I assesses The Junior High School--Needs for the '60s: 1) "Needs for the '60s" by Mauritz Johnson, Jr. 2) "Curriculum Changes for the '60s" by J. Lloyd Trump. 3) "The Teachers We Need" by Christian W. Jung. 4) "The Principal's Role in Change" by Eugene S. Thomas. 5) "Judging the Effectiveness of the Program" by Roland C. Faunce. 6) "Friend, Why Are You Here?" by Gene F. Berkley. Part II discusses Improvement of Instruction in the Junior High School: 1) "New Developments in Instruction." 2) "Junior High School Personnel." 3) "Functions of the Junior High School." 4) "The Junior High School Principal." Part III includes "Junior High Schools Evaluated and Accredited" by Harl R. Douglass.

7179.   National Association of State Directors of Teacher Education and Certification and American Association for the Advancement of Science. "Guidelines for Science and Mathematics in the Preparation Program of Upper Elementary School Teachers." Washington, D.C.: American Association for the Advancement of Science, 1963.

Booklet sets forth objectives of science and math teaching in the upper elementary grades and discusses science and math teacher education programs.

7180.   National Council of Teachers of Mathematics. "The Revolution in School Mathematics." Washington, D.C., 1961.

The Council discusses proceedings of eight regional conferences designed to help school administrators and mathematics supervisors with leadership problems in establishing new and improved mathematics programs.

7181.   National Education Association. "Social Science for the Contemporary Classroom: Description of Teacher In-service Education Materials." Washington, D.C.: National Education Association, Project on Utilization of In-service Education R & D Outcomes, ERIC Doc. ED 173 297, 1973.

This course is intended for junior high school pre-service and in-service training and helps to update teaching in social studies. Activities, resources, and modules are included. See ERIC Abstract #ED 173 297.

7182.   National Education Association, Department of Superintendents. The Junior High School Curriculum. Fifth Yearbook. Washington, D.C., 1927.

In thought and in experience, no part of the whole school system has proven so rich in musical possibilities and performances as the junior high school. Innumerable problems of time allotment and scheduling must be solved by junior high school principals and teachers before "the rich vein of ore that runs through the junior high school can be tapped and its wealth be brought to the surface. But we may not doubt that the wealth is there, and that it is our duty to devise the machinery and direct the operation which will bring it into the world."

7183.   National Education Association, Educational Policies Commission. "Education for All American Youth." Washington, D. C., 1944.

This Common Learnings course consists of learning experiences which everyone needs to have regardless of what occupation he may expect to follow or where he may expect to live. The distinctive purposes of the course are to help all young people grow in six areas: 1) civic responsibility and competence, 2) understanding of the operation of the economic system and of the human relations involved therein, 3) understanding of family relations, 4) intelligent action as consumers, 5) appreciation of beauty, and 6) proficiency in the use of language.

7184.   National Education Association, Project on the Instructional Program of the Public Schools. "Planning and Organizing for Teaching." Washington, D.C., 1963.

Pamphlet examines and defends alternative proposals for organizing school, curriculum, classroom, and instructional resources in American education.

7185.   National Education Association Journal.   "What makes a good junior high art program?"   National Education Association Journal, 56(1967):14-17.

This article describes the junior high art program in Kansas City, Missouri.   According to a visiting art consultant, much of the work students are doing shows genuine artistic skill and emotional depth for junior high students.   The curriculum guides in Kansas City set goals but leave room for each teacher to meet them in the context of his particular students and teaching situation. The junior high program builds on a good elementary program and toward a good senior high program.   Principals respect and support the art program.   Teachers are unusually well qualified. Students respond favorably to the program.

7186.   National Elementary Principal, 43, September 1963: Whole Issue.

This issue is a collection of articles on changes in mathematics, science, social studies, language arts, and foreign languages in elementary schools, with supporting papers on the roles of innovation, the allotment of time, and technological changes.   It is appropriate to the upper grades of elementary school or early middle school years.

7187.   Neill, S. B.   "Making math tracks at Franklin." American Education, 14,2(1978):21-26.

Article describes a successful Long Beach, California, junior high school program for mathematics students who are far below grade level.   Article considers how and why the program works, how outsiders react to the program, and further questions. Many of the students are transient with a minority background, and many are from welfare families. Studies have shown that students who have been as much as two grades or more behind did better in high school math than many students who had been in a regular mathematics program.

7188.   Nesbitt, D. R. and Bingham, N. E.   "Science for the transition years."   Science Education, 57,3 (1973):365-375.

Article reports on the 1969-71 studies of a subcommittee of the AAAS Cooperative Committee on the teaching of science and math.   The committee chose to 1) develop from the literature a philosophical and psychological perspective on transescence and the middle school, 2) identify desired characteristics of a science program for the transition years, 3) visit a limited number of middle schools to see if their programs harmonize with the philosophical and psychological perspective and to get the reactions of principals and science teachers to the list of science program characteristics developed by the subcommittee, and 4) report recommendations to the Cooperative Committee. This article discusses each of these portions of the committee's responsibilities. Included are two reports on school visitations and an abridged section on transescence and the middle school.

7189.   New York City Board of Education. "Developing a Core Curriculum in the Junior High School Program." New York, N.Y., 1958.

Presents a practical plan for initiating a core curriculum schedule and philosophy in a junior high school.

7190.   New York State Education Department. "Homemaking/ Family Living: Curriculum Planning Guidelines, Level 1 and 2, Middle School (Grades 5-8)." Albany: New York State Education Department, Bureau of Secondary Curriculum Development, 1974.

Guidelines supplement the New York State Syllabus for a comprehensive program for home economics education. Includes decisions of homemaking/family living curriculum, development of the course, developing a module for local use. Level 1 and level 2 have their own sections on scopes of learning, framework, human development modules, housing, furnishing and equipment modules, food and nutrition modules, and clothing and textiles modules. Appendix includes analysis of student needs, needs analysis chart, glossary of terms, mini-guide for writing measurable objectives, a list of words for writing behavioral objectives, module effectiveness forms, and sample forms. These guidelines are unique in that they reorganize programs for grades 5 and 6 into four basic subject areas and six content emphases. The four subject areas are 1) human development, 2) housing, furnishing, and equipment, 3) food and nutrition, and 4) clothing and textiles. The content emphases in each subject area are management, buymanship, leisure, careers, health and safety, and relationships.

7191.   New York State Education Department, Bureau of General Education Curriculum Developent.   "Toward Civic Responsibility." Albany, ERIC Doc. ED 161 808 (Not available through EDRS), 1978.

Junior high social studies teachers can use these guidelines for units on local, state, and national government to help students understand governmental structure and functions and develop skills in evaluating government activities. See ERIC Abstract #ED 161 808.

7192.   Nickols, B. S.   "A Study of Reading Programs in the Middle Schools of Pennsylvania."   Ed. D. Dissertation, University of Florida.   University Microfilms, Ann Arbor, Mich., ERIC Doc. ED 138 946, 1976.

Author studied current practices in teaching reading in twenty-one middle schools of Pennsylvania. Report makes recommendations for structured reading programs based on the characteristics of middle school students. Questionnaires were also sent to fifty-four selected middle schools, with 76 percent responding. All the schools had some sort of organized reading instruction in grades 6, 7, and 8. Three-fifths of the schools had every student participating in a formal reading program. A limited number of school districts employed full-time reading supervisors, and schools with professionally trained reading staff and special reading departments reported the highest percentage of organized reading program activity. See ERIC Abstract #ED 138 946.

7193.   Noall, M. F. and Winget, L.   "The core curriculum project."   Bulletin of the National Association of Secondary School Principals, 43(1959):196-203.

Describes the "Core Curriculum Project" with useful suggestions for junior high principals.

7194.   North Dakota State Board for Vocational Education at Bismarck. "Insights into Industry and Technology. Curriculum Guide."   Bismarck, ERIC Doc. ED 147 648, 1978.

This curriculum guide for industrial arts concentrates on industry and technology.   Emphasis is on the discipline of industrial technology in relation to the role of industry materials.   Units are: 1) Introduction to Industry and Technology. 2) Elements of Producing a Product.   3) Processes of Industry. 4) Resources.   5) Organization of Industry.   6) Mass Production.   7) Marketing.   8) Sociological and Environmental Impacts of Industry and Technology. See ERIC Abstract ED 147 648.

7195.   Olson, A. T. and Freeman, E.   "The objectives for teaching mathematics in the junior high school as perceived by parents, students, teachers, and professional educators."   Alberta Journal of Educational Research, 22,1(1976):52-58.

Fifteen objectives for teaching junior high school mathematics were drawn from the literature by the authors and were ranked in importance by selected groups of teachers, parents, students, and professional educators. See ERIC Abstract #EJ 144 133.

7196.   Orloff, J. H. (Ed.)   "Realizing Their Potential." Falls Church, Va.:   Proceedings of the Northern Virginia Council for Gifted/Talented Education, Manassas, Va., March 3-4, 1978.

Contains a summary of the workshops at the Third Annual Northern Virginia Conference on Gifted and Talented Education.   Papers included are: 1) Realizing Your Potential.   2) Developing the Gifts of All Children.   3) What Is Leadership Training for the Gifted?   4) Theoretic Foundations of Differential Education for the Gifted.   5) Developing Defensible Programs for the Gifted and Talented.   6) Counseling the Gifted: An Interpersonal Relations Approach.   7) Measuring the Progress and Achievement of the Gifted Child.   8) Simulations: Bringing Real Life to the Classroom.   9) Project Improve: A System for Identifying Gifted and Talented Students.   10) Adding a Gifted and Talented Program: Working Out the Change Process.   11) Future Studies: Exploring and Creating.   12) Evaluating Programs for the Gifted: Some Problems and Procedures.   13) Middle School Centers for the Gifted/Talented: A Place to Be.   14) Choices for Children: The Gifted Child in the Regular Classroom.   15) Motivating the Gifted to Want to Learn. 16) Evaluating Values Clarification.

7197.   Otto, A. C.   New Designs in Homemaking Programs in Junior High School.   New York: Bureau of Publications, Teachers College, Columbia University, 1958.

The objectives of the junior high school homemaking program are: 1) development of personal attitudes, values, and habits that make one successful in a social situation, 2) understanding and accepting the responsibilities of successful family life, 3) development of skills and techniques necessary to the efficient operation of the home.   Includes examples of many of the new trends in junior high homemaker education.

7198.   Overton, H.   "The rise and fall of the core curriculum."   Clearinghouse, 40(1966):532-537.

Discusses how the core curriculum idea grew and why it failed: 1) failure to achieve a common definition, 2) exhortation vs. experimentation, 3) the return to dormancy, and 4) cult to crisis to collapse.

7199.   Ovsiew, L.   "Making the Core Work."   New York: Metropolitan School Study Council, 1951.

The author presents techniques for core teaching from experiences in the Elizabeth, New Jersey, School System.

7200.   Page, W. R.   "Instructional Systems for Students with Learning Disabilities: Junior High School Program." St. Ann, Mo.: Central Midwestern Regional Educational Lab, ERIC Doc. ED 035 138, September, 1968.

This pilot program was for seventh and eighth graders who had learning disabilities and who were one year or more below grade level in reading and arithmetic. The remedial and developmental program included physical education, music, art, industrial arts, homemaking, English, math, social studies, and science in a six-hour day. There were no structured time periods for the lessons. Children helped each other, made their own worksheets and tests, charted their own progress, tutored others, and did independent projects. The children developed better attitudes and enjoyed school more, improved their social skills, and learned to progress by their own efforts. Objectives of this course included: 1) strengthening self-concept and self-image, 2) individual programs with completely individualized teaching, 3) shifting responsibility for learning to the child so that the teacher serves as a resource person, 4) raising academic skills to the appropriate age level by using appropriate materials and attitudes, 5) changing the attitudes in teachers, administrators, pupils, parents, and the public toward disabled learners, 6) training teachers in theory and procedures for working with the disabled learners, 7) remediating perceptual deficits, 8) determining the implications of teaching the disabled learner for traditional classroom teaching and integrating perceptual activities into regular instruction, 9) developing diagnostic devices for dealing with disabled learners and for recognizing potential problems in regular classrooms, and 10) adapting and originating materials at various levels.

7201.   Palminteri, P.   "Foreign language articulation from the junior high school viewpoint." Highpoints, 34(1952):36-40.

Makes the case for introducing junior high students to a foreign language.

7202.   Paradis, E. E. and Arth, A. A.   "Reading: Vanguard of junior high/middle school curriculum." Elementary English, 52,3(1975):329-334.

Discusses the stress on reading in the middle school curriculum. See ERIC Abstract #EJ 117 446.

7203.   Peetoom, A.   "Our children, your students." English Quarterly, 10,1(1977):13-19.

Describes a parent's view of his children's junior high experience. He believes there should be fewer subjects taught in longer periods and there should be fewer teachers for each child, thus promoting more stable relationships. See ERIC Abstract #EJ 165 774.

7204.   Pennsylvania State Department of Education, Bureau of Curriculum Services. "Guidelines for the Junior High School Reading Curriculum Regulation." Harrisburg, Pa., ERIC Doc. ED 170 704, 1978.

These guidelines were developed in response to a Pennsylvania State Board of Education mandate that all junior high school students should take one planned course that incorporates improved reading instruction, promotes student reading achievement, and advances positive attitudes toward reading. Report covers minimum requirements, three suggested course models (separate, integrated, and innovative), assessment, grouping, peer tutoring, school volunteers, in-service training, and information resources. See ERIC Abstract #ED 170 704.

7205.   Philadelphia Public Schools. "Core Curriculum in Philadelphia: An Analysis of Principles and Practices." Philadelphia, 1949.

A 1949 comparison of standardized test scores by Philadelphia students with test norms or national averages showed that students using the core curriculum usually made normal or average progress in language and study skills.

7206.   Philadelphia School District, Office of Curriculum and Instruction. "Ada H. H. Lewis Middle School Curriculum Guide." Philadelphia, ERIC Doc. ED 138 989, 1975.

This school is based on a house arrangement which accommodates students from all grade levels in an open-classroom structure. The curriculum guide covers philosophy, goals, team structure, conversion scale for student ranking, roster and schedule, alternative program, special education, and curriculum development in reading, communications, science, mathematics, social studies, Latin, typing, art, visual communications, industrial arts, industrial materials, home economics, music, health and physical education. A summary is included.

7207.   Pingry, R. W. "For a better mathematics program in the junior high school." Mathematics Teacher, 49 (1956):112-120.

These junior high mathematics curricula are geared for twelve different ability and achievement levels.

7208.   Ploghoft, R. E. "Developing a junior high school instructional materials center." Midland Schools, 81 (1967):11-12.

Describes a model Instructional Materials Center in Brody Junior High School in Des Moines, Iowa. Why an IMC? Many educators believe that locating various kinds of learning media in one central place and making them easily accessible to faculty and students increases the opportunity to develop to the fullest each child's potential learning capacity.

7209.   Politzer, R. L. "The foreign language curriculum: background and problems." Journal of Secondary Education, 40(1965):156-163.

Examines the forces which are helping to shape the foreign language curriculum in the junior high and senior high years: 1) public attitudes and public pressure, 2) views held by language specialists, and 3) current knowledge about the psychology of learning. The new language curriculum shaped by these forces has certain characteristics: 1) It is a long curriculum to assure mastery in the skill and an early beginning. 2) It emphasises audial techniques. 3) The teaching of grammar is deeply influenced by linguistic science. 4) There is heavy reliance on SR (Stimulus-Response) through repetition and imitation. Correct responses are reinforced by being performed and rewarded in language laboratory exercises. 5) A very slow and gradual progression leads from very strict control of the pupil's responses to a more loose structuring and finally to self-expression. The article describes articulation problems between the junior high and senior high foreign language programs.

7210.   Pontiac City School District. "The World of Manufacturing, 1970-71. A Junior High School Industrial Technology Exemplary Program.   Final   Report." Pontiac, Mich., ERIC Doc. ED 068 690, 1971.

This industrial arts curriculum project acquainted junior high students with the manufacturing industry. In-service training was provided for teachers prior to the beginning of the two-semester course for three hundred seventh, eighth, and ninth graders. Pretest and posttest results showed significant gains for seventh and eighth graders but loss or lack of gain for ninth graders. Student reaction to the program and reports on the budget and dissemination activities are included. See ERIC Abstract #ED 068 690.

7211.   Portland Public Schools. "Family Living and Sex Education. Curriculum Guide." Portland, Maine, ERIC Doc. ED 054 117. (No year given.)

Guide for program in grades 5-9 contains these units and lessons: Unit I, Discovering Yourself. Lesson 1) Orientation. 2) Reproduction. 3) The Changing Boy: Understanding Physical Changes. 4) The Changing Boy: Understanding Emotional Changes. 5) The Changing Girl: Understanding Physical Changes. 6) The Changing Girl: Understanding Menstruation. 7) The Changing Girl: Understanding Emotional Changes. 8 and 9) Fertilization and Birth. 10) Human Relationships: Large Group Discussion. 11) Human Relationships: Small Group Discussion. Unit II, Growing Up in Relationship with Others. Lesson 1) Introduction. 2) Male Anatomy. 3) Female Anatomy. 4) Femine and Masculine Hygiene. 5) The Endoctrine System. 6) Endoctrine System: Questions and Answers. 7) Fertilization, Pregnancy, and Birth. 8) Heredity. 9) Understanding Your Emotions. 10) Family Relationships. 11) Developing Social Relationships. 12) Summary. Unit III, Adolescent Development. Lesson 1) Orientation and Sexual Maturation. 2) Male Reproductive System. 3) Female Reproductive System. 4) Fertilization, Pregnancy, Childbirth, and Lactation. 5) Question and Answer Period. 6) Maturation. 7) Problems of Human Sexuality. 8) Peers and Personality. 9) Boy-Girl Relationships. 10) Family. 11) Social Values. 12) Summary. Unit IV, Understanding Maturity. Lesson 1) Orientation. 2 and 3) Anatomical and Emotional Review. 4) Human Reproduction. 5 and 6) Problems of Human Sexuality. 7) Masculinity and Femininity. 8 and 9) Dating. 10) Sexual Responsibility. 11) Family Conflicts. 12) Summary. Objectives and activities are included with each unit as well as instructional materials and a student assessment.

7212.   Powell, A. and Todd, S. The Middle School: Factors Which Distinguish. Dissemination Services on the Middle Grades, vol. 8, no. 1. Springfield, Mass.: Educational Leadership Institute, 1976.

The University of Virginia School of Education with the assistance of the Educational Leadership Institute conducted a national survey in 1974 of middle schools to examine grade levels, populations, curriculum designs, exploratory programs, athletic organizations, certification/staffing, and in-service. The last question was: Are there any factors not previously mentioned which distinguish

your school as a middle school? Several schools had
some very interesting additional programs. The
Worcester East Middle School in Worcester, Massachusetts had an alternative program called Project
Extend for habitual truants and students with
diagnosed school problems. The PACE program (Project
of Alternatives in Community Education) was begun in
this school system, as was the Satellite Program,
which was limited to girls. Teachers in the
Louisville Middle School in Colorado use "Good News
Memos" for positive reinforcement with students who
have not been doing well but have shown a great deal
of improvement either in attitude or academic
progress. These memos are sent home to parents in
the mail as a note of congratulations from the
teacher. A differentiated flexibility program was
found in Henderson Middle School, Richmond, Virginia,
where "responsible movers" who demonstrate the
ability to govern their behavior and have a serious
attitude toward education can schedule their own work
during a two-week period. Another program at
Portland Middle School in Oregon was based on differentiated staffing. At the J. T. Henley Middle
School, Albemarle County, Virginia, the following
activities promoted good community relations: 1)
written communication, 2) wire communication, 3)
verbal communication, 4) school-community programs,
and 5) programs to the community through the child.
The Howard Middle School, Ocala, Florida offers
"small-group guidance and instruction." And
Nisavally Middle School, Olympia, Washington, has an
exploratory mini-course program.

7213.   Powers, L. S. "The correlation of science and
mathematics in the junior high school." School
Science and Mathematics, 54(1954):571-573.

Junior high mathematics may be correlated with
science units on weather, birds, insects, and
measurement of time.

7214.   Rankin, S. "Forging a junior high general music
program." Music Educators Journal, 53(1966):31-32.

Music is important for general education, especially
in the junior high school years, which are an excellent time for exploration. The best kinds of
exploration highlight the essence of music and are
devised intentionally to teach basic understandings
of music. Music educators must do the same job that
is being done in mathematics, science, social
studies, and English: they must take a long look at
the structure of music itself in order to build a
curriculum which will provide a richer and more
meaningful life in music.

7215.   Rash, A. M. and Grimm, R. L.   "Individualized
         instruction in mathematics in an open junior high
         school."   Journal of Personalized Instruction, 1,1
         (1976):23-27.

         The Boyertown Area School District opened a new open-
         space junior high school in 1971.   Self-directed
         learning was stressed.   In-service training for
         teaching mathematics in large, open areas was pro-
         vided, with team planning experience part of the
         program.   The mathematics team consists of six
         teachers who meet daily to plan personalized instruc-
         tional activities for students.   Learning activity
         packages are also a major part of this program.
         Article discusses selecting teachers for open educa-
         tion, the math department in operation, the program's
         uniqueness and effectiveness, and success in the
         future.

7216.   Ray, W. E.   "Conceptualization of a Practical Arts
         Program Component for Junior High/Middle School
         Youth."   Columbus: Ohio State University Research
         Foundation, ERIC Doc. ED 155 356, 1978.

         School programs are not designed to assist youth to
         cope effectively with life problems and usually exist
         merely to prepare for more schooling.   School should
         be reorganized to include a large segment of prac-
         tical arts experiences that are broadening and
         humanizing at the same time that they help students
         become more self-sufficient, intelligent, and produc-
         tive citizens in a highly complex, technological
         society.   This program establishes a rationale for a
         practical arts component for the junior high/middle
         school curriculum and outlines a school program of
         the practical arts in agriculture, home and family
         living, health, industry, and business.   The report
         describes the problem, objectives, activities,
         techniques of evaluation, contribution to education,
         personnel, facilities, and project expenditures.
         References are listed.   The report is intended to
         provide a blueprint for major redesign of schooling
         in the United States.

7217.   Reed, C. Early Adolescent Art Education. Peoria,
         Ill.: Charles A. Dennett Co., 1957.

         Text deals with the art program in relation to the
         early adolescent.

7218.   Research for Better Schools, Inc.   "An Introduc-
         tion to Skills for Ethical Action."   Washington,
         D.C.: National Institute of Education, Basic Skills
         Group, 1976.

These junior high instructional materials are used in the field of morals, values, and ethical education. Monograph describes several theoretical positions on moral education and explains the uniqueness of the "Skills for Ethical Action" package. The program helps students internalize a process for acting ethically so that they consciously use it in their daily lives. Training emphasizes component skills and behavioral outcomes. The introduction provides an overview of the skills for ethical action, instructional materials, and information about the learner outcomes which may be anticipated. The main steps in the SEA program are: 1) Identify the value program. 2) Think up action ideas. 3) Consider self and others. 4) Judge. 5) Act. 6) Evaluate. Unit I: Ethical Action--What, Why, and How. Unit II: Using the Strategy with Pete, Diane, Andrea, and Jack. Unit III: Using the Strategy with Your Own Value Problem. Unit IV: Using the Strategy to Help You Act on Your Values. Instructional considerations include reading level, remedial activities, absentees, individual lessons, time, and unit tests. Different approaches to the program are the component skills approach, the case study approach, and the curriculum planning approach. Suggested readings are included.

7219.   Ritz, J. M. "A unified arts program for the middle grades." Man/Society/Technology, 35,7(1976):203-206.

Describes an interdisciplinary approach to the teaching of industrial arts, home ec, and art at Cox Landing Junior High School, Huntington, West Virginia. The needs of the early adolescent are emphasized. See ERIC Abstract #EJ 137 495.

7220.   Robinson, M. "Career Education English: Units for Career Exploration in Sixth, Seventh, or Eighth Grade." Stillwater: Oklahoma State Department of Vocational and Technical Education, Curriculum and Instructional Materials Center, and Washington, D.C.: U. S. Office of Education, ERIC Doc. ED 118 736, 1976.

Includes six English instructional units concerned with career exploration. Components of each unit are: content outline, lists of suggested activities for instructor and student, reference list, assignment sheets, job sheets, and unit tests. See ERIC Abstract #ED 118 736.

7221.   Roehler, L. R. "Teaching Comprehension Skills in the Middle Schools." Paper presented at the Annual Meeting of the International Reading Association, New Orleans, ERIC Doc. ED 089 225, 1974.

Suggests techniques for teaching reading comprehension in a logical sequence of skills (understanding word meaning, understanding structure, literal and inferential thinking, and critical reading). The strategy uses a spiraling hierarchy in which students master prerequisites before learning new skills. See ERIC Abstract #ED 089 225.

7222.   Roman, R. J.   "Change can be dynamic."   Clearinghouse, February 1970:343-346.

At McTigue Junior High School the curriculum, which was once very limited and traditional, has been expanded to offer a comprehensive program to all students--college bound, prevocational, or undecided. A goal of the school is to give all students every opportunity to explore as many facets of the academic program as they can at their own rate and level. Author describes the advanced mathematics program, a new science program, improvement in the foreign language department, a new humanities course, a pilot course in communicative skills, a new industrial arts plan, and prevocational training specifically for girls. A new innovation is the trimester plan and three-phase grouping. The major premise of this grouping is to schedule students into academic subjects commensurate with their ability, achievement, and interest in each subject. The school also has a new program in career exploration with the following goals: 1) arranging for students to communicate with working people as they do their jobs, 2) getting students interested in becoming a part of the world of work, and 3) helping student become productive citizens who want to make a contribution to their community. The author outlines some positive effects of the change process experienced in this junior high school.

7223.   Rosenfeld, G., et al.   "A Study of the New York University Clinic for Learning Project: Whitelaw Reid Junior High School."   New York: Center for Urban Education, ERIC Doc. ED 109 636, September, 1970.

The Clinic for Learning was a demonstration and training center at a junior high school in Brooklyn. New York University used the center to introduce its faculty and students to the public school setting in an attempt to relate theory to the realities of junior high school teaching. New York City school personnel were involved in trying to effect positive change within a classroom and between school and community. Community people from the school neighborhood were trained to help teachers. The Clinic for Learning was found lacking by officials and by the clinic. The purpose of this evaluation was to

assess the cause for failure. See ERIC Abstract #ED
092 636.

7224.   Ryan, F. L. The Social Studies Sourcebook: Ideas
for Teaching in the Elementary and Middle School.
Boston: Allyn and Bacon, 1980.

Book described 477 classroom activities for elementary and middle schools. The activities teach social
studies skills, concepts, and current issues. Some
of the activities are particularly concerned with
developing self-esteem and self-awareness.

7225.   San Diego Unified School District. "San Diego
Right to Read." San Diego, Calif., ERIC Doc. ED 108
140, 1974.

This is one of twelve exemplary programs summarized
in the Introduction to Right to Read's "Effective
Reading Programs: Summaries of 222 Selected Programs." This program serves the students of an
inner-city junior high school and has as its main
thrust training teachers in a diagnostic-prescriptive
approach to teaching reading. Teacher assistants and
ninth grade tutors help teachers in carrying out
individual student reading programs. See ERIC
Abstract #ED 108 140.

7226.   Sanders, S. G., et al. (Eds.) "Project Order:
Reorganizing a Middle School for Responsibility,
Dependability, Education, and Reality." Houston:
North Forrest Independent School District, 1977.

Project Order involved the reorganization of a school
in a low-income, predominantly black neighborhood.
Prior to Project Order, the school experienced a
fairly high incidence of disorderly student behavior
and disruption, which has since diminished. The
paper describes the reorganized administration and
instructional staff, its curriculum and extracurricular activities, its changes in facilities and in
student body organization, and its actions to improve
school-community relations. Evaluation of the program shows clear evidence of success. Students'
attitudes toward school are more positive, student
behavior has improved, and attendance is up.

7227.   Savannah-Chatham Public Schools. "A Language Arts
Program for the Middle School: Reading, Language,
Composition and Literature." Savannah, Ga., December,
1976.

Curriculum guide covers content flexibility,
materials, developmental reading, corrective reading,
reading and literature, and language. Included are
suggested teaching objectives for a middle school

language arts program, and a developmental reading program for middle school students in grades 7 and 8, with sections on placement of students, adjusting the program to individual needs, considerations in selecting a basic program, and skills and understanding. For each grade the guide has a scope and sequence chart in language composition and literature, with sections on objectives, knowledge and activities. The curriculum guide also includes introductions to print journalism, speech, and drama.

7228.   Scannella, A. and Rabuck, J. "Planning and teaching for the middle school/junior high schools: teaching ideas." English Journal, 66,4(1977):55-56.

Article describes a middle school program on world cultures taught jointly by English and social studies teachers. See ERIC Document EJ 162 028.

7229.   Schaller, G. W. "A Study of Opinions Concerning the Effectiveness of Block-Time Classes in the Junior High School in Ohio." Thesis, University of Michigan, 1962.

Presents research favoring block-time classes in junior high schools.

7230.   School Science Review. "Middle school science notes." School Science Review, 58,205(1977):742-753.

Discusses science activities and laboratory techniques for use in the middle school. See ERIC Abstract #EJ 164 924.

7231.   Schubert, D. G. "Why gifted junior high school students read." School and Society, April 11, 1959: 171-172.

Gifted pupils become increasingly interested in reading at an early age, read a considerable amount of material, and show intensified reading interests up to and beyond the age of 17. What is responsible for this intense interest in reading among the gifted? With the help of college students who were enrolled in the author's reading courses during the spring and fall semesters of 1957, the writer was able to accumulate 104 responses from gifted junior high school students. The query to which they responded was "Why do you like to read?" The responses, grouped in order of their frequency, were: 1) knowledge and information, 2) occupy time, 3) escape, and 4) vocabulary development. Since reading constitutes about 85 percent of the ability to study, it was gratifying to the researchers to learn that gifted children, one of our nation's most valuable resources, found the process enjoyable.

7232.   Schuncke, G. M. and Bloom, J. R.   "Cooperative groups: from theory to practice." Social Studies, 68,5(1977):208-210.

Explains how social studies teachers can teach cooperative behavior to junior high school students. Three factors are critical: length of time student groups have worked together, interdependence of goals attached to the task, and interdependence of means to accomplish the tasks. See ERIC Abstract EJ 170 578.

7233.   Schwartz, B. "Investigation of the effects of the seventh and eighth grade core program." Journal of Educational Research, 53(1959):149-152.

In Yardley Junior High in Pennsylvania, individual and matched group studies show that students in core programs learn language skills and study skills as well as, and frequently better than, students in more conventional courses.

7234.   Scott, F. C.   "Curriculum made interesting for the adolescent in the middle school." Middle School Journal, 7,3(1976):15.

Describes a pilot program of exploratory science and language arts mini-courses. Changing to a mini-course curriculum makes content more challenging to teachers and students and meets individual needs more adequately by giving the students an opportunity to succeed and to make decisions. The faculty at the test school believed that the mini-course concept should not be restricted to exploratory courses and works well in basic and general education.

7235.   Seefeldt, V. "Middle schools: issues and future directions in physical education." Journal of Health, Physical Education and Recreation, 45,2(1974):32-34.

Discusses the future of physical education for transescents. See ERIC Abstract #EJ 092 046.

7236.   Shaw, R. A.   "Pendulum swings back in junior high/middle school math." Bulletin of the National Association of Secondary School Principals,   58,384 (1974):90-95.

Describes an organizational scheme based on an instructional process model of goals, objectives, methods, materials and evaluation. See ERIC Abstract #EJ 103 485.

7237.   Shawnee Mission Public Schools. "Junior High Unified: Sequencing and Keying of Unified Studies, Test Specifications for Criterion-Referenced Testing, Achievement-Awareness Record for Language Arts." ERIC Doc. ED 116 193, 1975.

This language arts curriculum guide for grades 7-9
describes how the Shawnee Mission Unified Studies
Curriculum synthesizes language arts skills with
social studies concepts. The guide discusses composition, study of language, listening and viewing,
literature and reading, and speaking. Each area is
sequenced according to objectives. The curriculum
teaches skills such as 1) recognizing and using the
four types of sentences, 2) evaluating appropriate
composition elements, 3) recognizing and using communication words, phrases, and clauses, 4) recognizing figurative language, and 5) recognizing tone.
Also included are methods of evaluation. See ERIC
Abstract #ED 116 193.

7238.   Shockley, R. E.   "Curriculum articulation: what
does it mean to the middle school?"   Transescence:
The Journal of Emerging Adolescent Education, 8,1
(1980):13-17.

Districtwide curriculum articulation (interrelation
of curriculum at different school levels) is an
extremely relevant concept for the middle school
because one of the primary purposes of the school in
the middle is to bridge the gap between 1) the
learner-centered elementary school and the content-
centered high school, 2) the childhood of the elementary school and the adult patterns of behavior
expected in high school, and 3) learner dependence in
the elementary school and independence in the high
school. Author discusses ways to articulate programs
at different levels and stresses the following
points: 1) Teachers should participate in district
and schoolwide curriculum planning committees.   2)
Time should be made available for teacher visitations.   3) Interdisciplinary team planning should be
part of any middle school.   4) Multiage grouping
patterns in the middle school can be an effective
method of meeting the diverse needs of learners
during this age range and also a method for fostering
cooperative planning by staff.   5) The middle school
should include gradual transitions in grouping,
instructional, and organizational patterns.   6)
School district personnel should involve teachers and
principals in the evaluation and accreditation
process within the school system.   7) The elementary
school, middle school, and high school should use
consistent testing methods, diagnostic procedures,
and student information forms.

7239.   Sigurdson, S. E.   "Mathematizing motion geometry."
Elements: Translating Theory into Practice,   5,7
(1974):2-5.

Junior high school students can profitably study
transformational geometry. See ERIC Abstract #EJ 093
951.

7240.   Singer, H. "Preparation of Reading Content Specialists for the Junior High School: Teaching Reading in the Content Areas at the Junior High School Level--Strategies for Meeting a Wide Range of Individual Differences." University of California at Riverside, Riverside Unified School District, and San Bernardino City Unified School District, California, Eric Doc. ED 088 003, 1973.

The premise of this project was that teachers who were committed and trained to teach reading in junior high content areas could improve the reading performance of all their students, particularly blacks and Mexican-Americans. Booklet stresses program accomplishments. It summarizes the program, reviews research done prior to the study, describes the teaching materials found to be beneficial, discusses instructional processes and strategies for teaching reading in the content areas, describes the consulting role of the specialist, and contains reading specialist evaluations. See ERIC Abstract ED 088 003.

7241.   Slater, R. D. and Strehle, J. "Anything but average." Bulletin of the National Association of Secondary School Principals, 53(1969):54-61.

Describes a model curriculum in a junior high school.

7242.   Slimak, P. "They're reading more and enjoying it more." American Education, 8,3(1972):4-9.

Describes in detail the new and exciting reading program at the Keokuk Community School District and Junior High School in Iowa, where interdisciplinary teaching teams coordinate their projects to put reading theory into practice. Article describes the science curriculum which is based on reading, the flexible scheduling plan used to enhance reading, and Keokuk's use of the school-within-a-school concept.

7243.   Smitherman, B. J., et al. "Impact: vocational home economics for junior high school students." Journal of Home Economics, 70,2(1978):20-23.

A home economics program called "Impact" is designed for inner-city junior high school students in Ohio. The content varies according to individual student needs, and emphasis is on helping students who have problems develop a positive self-image. See ERIC Abstract #EJ 180 838.

7244.   Sneed, L. C. "Implementation of a Middle School Basic Competencies Reading Program." Paper presented at the Annual Meeting of the International Reading Association, Houston, ERIC Doc. ED 157 044, May, 1978.

In the Gary, Indiana, middle schools a test of twenty reading skills is given to all seventh grade students. Those who do not score well are placed in remedial reading classes which focus on developing decoding skills. As they improve, students are transferred into a corrective reading class to pinpoint and correct specific reading deficiencies. Students may move from corrective to developmental reading upon passing a checkpoint examination. Two to four basic skills reading teachers work with regular subject teachers, and special in-service training sessions are held each year. See ERIC Abstract #ED 157 044.

7245.   Snooks, L. and Long, D.   "Project BACSTOP, ESEA, Title III. Evaluative Report, 1975-1976." Battle Creek, Mich.: Battle Creek Public Schools, August 9, 1976.

BACSTOP, which stands for Better Acquisition of Cognitive Skills Through Outdoor Programming, was implemented to help with the racially troubled atmosphere of the Northwestern Junior High School in Battle Creek, Michigan. Goals included: 1) Create a mechanism that would stop and reverse the racial separatism and isolation that began to develop among new seventh graders. 2) Improve the educational performance of seventh graders in basic skills by refocusing students, faculty, and administrative attention on the school's cognitive responsibilities. Activities that were useful in this situation include rope courses, backpacking, cross-country skiing, and winter camping. Students were encouraged to attend a five-day expedition in an isolated area in northern Michigan. At the end of the 1975-76 school year human relations at the school had much improved because of this program. This curriculum guide describes the project and discusses needs assessment, the community, the school, general goals and activities, the evaluation design, and the evaluation result. Also included are judgments of worth, parent letters, and activity descriptions.

7246.   Snow, R. and Reid, M.   "Home economics in the middle years." Education 3-13, 6,2(1978):42-46.

Five key concepts in home and family education are nutrition, management, interdependence, development, and protection. The teaching of each concept is geared to the developmental stages of students aged 8-13. See ERIC Abstract #EJ 199 015.

7247.   Snyder, R. A.   "The scope of physical education." Bulletin of the National Association of Secondary School Principals, 44(1960):53.

The physical fitness program in the junior high
school should teach all boys and girls to function
skillfully and efficiently without undue fatigue. It
should afford multiple experiences in thirty or more
sports and in various exercises that teach students
to conduct themselves in a socially approved manner,
respect individual differences, cope with victory and
defeat in a sportsmanlike way, and practice appropriate self-control during periods of emotional
stress.

7248.   Spokane School District 81. "Social Studies
Program Guide, 6-9." Spokane Public Schools, 825
Spokane Falls Boulevard, Spokane, Wash. 99201, ERIC
Doc. ED 152 620, 1977.

This curriculum guide suggests social studies
materials, resources, and activities for grades 7-9.
Included also are sixth grade activities. Guide
outlines lessons on all social science disciplines,
with particular emphasis on economics, geography,
environment, and political science. The major
objective is to help students become responsible
citizens. See ERIC Abstract #ED 152 620.

7249.   Stafford, E. "Middle schools: status of physical
education programs." Journal of Health, Physical
Education and Recreation, 45,2(1974):25-28.

Author discusses physical education programs in
middle schools around the United States. See ERIC
Abstract #EJ 092 044.

7250.   State University of New York. "Career Education
Instructional Guide." Oswego, N.Y.: State
University of New York, College at Oswego, Department
of Industrial Arts and Technology, ERIC Doc. ED 106
501, 1974.

This guide for middle school industrial arts teachers
presents lessons and activities that balance career
information, technical information, and hands on
experience. Lessons cover topics such as The World
of Work, Knowing Yourself, and Manufacturing and YOU.
The guide also contains suggested materials for
evaluating the project, twelve transparency masters,
procedures for writing of public relations news
releases, sample news releases, and an eight-page
bibliography. See ERIC Abstract #ED 106 501.

7251.   Steinmann, A. and Jurich, A. P. "The effects of a
sex education course on the sex role perceptions of
junior high school students." Family Coordinator,
24,1(1975):27-31.

A major goal of junior high school sex education courses is to present information about the sex roles of both sexes, balancing the orientation between self and family. Implications for teaching are discussed. See ERIC Abstract #EJ 113 874.

7252.   Stewart, H. and Alberty, H. B. Improving Reading in the Junior High School: A Librarian and a Core Teacher Work Together. New York: Appleton-Century-Crofts, 1957.

Describes a successful reading program in a junior high school.

7253.   Stillwater Junior High School. "Progress Report." Stillwater, Okla. (No year given.)

Discusses Stillwater Junior High teaching innovations and experimental programs: 1) In the mathematics program students may take courses that fit their ability. 2) Social studies and English classes are blocked together during two periods in the seventh grade. 3) Introductory physical science is taught in the ninth grade. 4) Ninth grade social studies teachers have experimented with team teaching and teaching interns. 5) An in-service program was established to determine what the junior high school must do to fit the needs of young adolescents. 6) Teachers visited other schools to study curriculum and programming. 7) A social studies research center has been established. 8) There is a social worker-counselor-teacher program. 9) Time for health and physical education has increased. 10) There is a remedial program in speech and reading. 11) The program of exploratory courses was extended. 12) All students participate in an active activity program held daily for forty-five minutes. The staff has concentrated on exploring the needs of young adolescents in this school system, the curriculum for the early adolescent, the role of the teacher in new educational programs, and various scheduling devices to permit flexibility.

7254.   Stockhaus, S. (Ed.) Selected Social Studies Skills: 88 Reinforcement Lessons for Secondary Students. ERIC Clearinghouse for Social Studies/ Social Science Education. Boulder, Colo.: Social Science Education Consortium, ERIC Doc. ED 170 188, 1979.

These lessons reinforce junior high school social studies skills, including 1) use of reference aids, 2) understanding tables, graphs, and cartoons, 3) developing graphic skills, and 4) evaluating information. See ERIC Abstract #ED 170 188.

7255.   Stoddard, G. D.   "The dual progress plan."   School and Society, 86(1958):351-352.

The dual progress organization divides the curriculum into two basic areas. One is the required core program of language arts and social studies within the traditional graded structure. Advancement from grade to grade depends upon the mastery of the subject matter. Ability grouping is used when forming the classes at each grade level. The other half of the day consists of instruction in the electives of mathematics, science, art, and music taught to ability groups in a nongraded approach. Advancement in these areas is based on personal ability and interest.

7256.   Strickland, R. G.   "Language in the Middle Grades." Middle School Portfolio, Leaflet 10. Washington, D.C.:   Association for Childhood Education International, 1968.

An important trend in the middle grades is helping boys and girls understand the significance of the English language and recognizing some of what is happening to it today.   Knowing something of the spread of English in our time to all continents could be a starting point. The article discusses language backgrounds of students, dialects of English, what persons do with and to words, and the importance of writing. A language program for middle grade boys and girls can be an exciting program based on real uses of language in the real world of human interaction. It should start with attention to language in the world outside the school. Trends in the language arts are clearly pointed toward making the study of language in school as exciting as children obviously find language outside of school.

7257.   Strickland, V. E.   "Scheduling music in junior high school." Nation's Schools, 48(1951):43-44.

Presents ways to schedule music into a junior high school curriculum.

7258.   Suess, A. R. "The industrial arts curriculum for the early adolescent." In American Council on Industrial Arts Teacher Education Yearbook, pp. 114-146. Bloomington, Ill.: McKnight and McKnight, 1972.

Discusses ten goals set by the Pennsylvania State Education Department for quality education in the middle grades and the implications of each goal for an industrial arts program. See ERIC Abstract #EJ 061 560.

7259.   Sur, W. R. and Schuller, C. F.   Music Education for Teenagers. New York: Harper and Bros., 1958.

Helpful information for junior high music teachers.

7260.   Tannebaum, A. J.   "Curriculum Development and Teacher Training for Disadvantaged Pupils in Special Classes (Career Guidance) in Regular Junior High School." New York: Center for Urban Education, ERIC Doc. ED 011 022, 1968.

Author reports on evaluation of a career guidance program for eighth and ninth grade students in New York City. The program was designed to reduce the number of ninth grade dropouts and provide students with marketable skills. Author describes the program, the plan of the evaluation, the June Teacher-Supervisor Training Program, the objectives of the training program, objectives of the evaluative study, and the interview/questionnaire/observation methodology employed in the study. Evaluation concludes: 1) In-service teaching should be given at the beginning of the school year using actual proposed material. 2) Teachers should be prepared in specialized subjects and trained by those involved in preparing the new curricula. 3) More time should be given to in-service training. Included also are sections on application, role differentials, research team evaluation, curriculum development, objectives and design of a curriculum writing project, objectives of an evaluative study, and conclusions.

7261.   Thompson, M. "The junior high program." National Education Association Journal, 50,9(1961):22-24.

In a vertically coordinated program, the foreign language courses in the junior high school should be devoted to 1) continued imitation of models and repetition, 2) continued planned presentation of structure with a greater variety of types and drills than students find in elementary school, 3) planned presentation of basic sound-letter correspondences with drills and exercises, and 4) an orderly development of reading and writing skills in conjunction with listening comprehension, speaking, and the presentation of grammar.

7262.   Toepfer, C. F., Jr. "Curriculum planning priorities for the middle school." In Leeper, R. (Ed.), Middle School in the Making, Readings from Educational Leadership. Washington, D.C.: Association for Supervision and Curriculum Development, 1974.

In the early 1960s mounting dissatisfaction with the discontinuity of elementary and secondary schools along with widespread criticism of schooling in general and the search for innovations and alternatives created a receptive climate for middle school curriculum proposals and reorganizations.

7263.   Tripp, R. L. "Self-directed study: a junior high school pilot program." Clearinghouse, 43,6(1969): 344-348.

Within SEDS students study topics of their own choosing, under their own guidance, and on school time. This method is more far-reaching than independent study.   The primary stress of SEDS is not on the particular project or how well the student does but on work for its own value and the opportunity to confront genuine conflicts of time and interest. This self-directed study program and project REMIDY had both teachers and students making education more relevant and interesting for all students.   Six teachers worked in this study.   The committee laid down guidelines for the pilot program: 1) Students may choose any topic.   2) Students must select a teacher-consultant.   3) They may take off from any class without prior approval to work on an SEDS project.   4) They may sign out each morning before school starts, indicating which period they will take off for SEDS.   5) They must keep up with their work in any classes missed.   6) They must secure parental approval to participate.   7) They must keep a diary of the progress and write a self-evaluation of their experiences.   8) They may self-direct themselves out of SEDS at any time prior to the end of the seven-week pilot period.   Article includes a dialogue between students on the value of SEDS to them.   The students clearly demonstrated through this study that the experience was valuable and important to them and one on which they could build.   They also demonstrated the degree to which they were affected by conventional norms and assumptions of traditional American education.   The fifteen students in the pilot program demonstrated that junior high school students can be ready and willing to take on individual work and the format of such a program.

7264.   Tritzkaw, P. T.   "Curriculum trends in the junior high school."   High School Journal, December 1966: 137-146.

Educators tend to confine their thinking about the junior high schools to questions of organization rather than questions about the experience of inquiry.   They may unwittingly support systems that alienate youth simply because the questions they ask aren't basic enough.   Consider: Does regrouping of children into a so-called middle school constitute another form of organizational "band-wagonitis"? Might the flurry of rearrangements keep people from

recognizing how young people naturally pursue knowledge? Does putting youth into age and grade groups
resign us to making them fit into society without
encouraging us or them to question the absurdities of
this condition? Do junior high schools reward completion rather than the pursuit of knowledge?   In
other words, do they unwittingly promote the death
image rather than the life image of the pupil?   Can
block scheduling, core classes, and other arrangements become systems which obscure the issues of
alienation and identity which youth must confront?
These are questions that bring us back to what is
real and help us develop openness to true dialogue.

7265.   Trowbridge, L. W.   "Trends and innovations in
junior high school science teaching in the United
States." Science Teacher, 41,4(1974):12-15.

Describes the development and philosophy of science
teaching in the middle grades and discusses the
direction of science education in the next decade.
See ERIC Abstract #EJ 098 450.

7266.   Trump, J. L. and Miller, D. Secondary School Curriculum Improvement. Boston: Allyn and Bacon, 1968.

Authors report three approaches suggested by an ad
hoc curriculum committee for social studies within
the National Association of Secondary School Principals: 1) Grades 7 and 8: American history to 1870,
government, and U.S. geography.   Grades 9 and 10:
World history and world geography presented by
culture areas. 2) Grade 7 and semester 1 of grade 8:
broad field, geographic center, socioeconomic units
on key and representative nations and regions of the
world.   Grade 8, semester 2:   the citizen and his
government.   Grade 9, semester 1:   introduction to
understanding of people and their institutions.
Grade 9, semester 2, and grade 10: world history and
problems.   3) Grade 7:   history of the people of
Africa and EurAsia. Grade 8: U.S. history to 1876.
Grade 9: state history and American government.

7267.   Tucker, B. Teaching English in the Middle Years.
Ward Lock Educational, 116 Baker Street, London WIM
2BB, England, ERIC Doc. ED 116 204 (Document not
available from EDRS), 1973.

Discusses a theoretical framework and an indication
of where to begin and how to proceed with the teaching of English.   Chapters on poetry, fiction,
creative writing, drama, listening, and talking discuss why these subjects should be taught, how they
may be introduced, what the teacher might hope to
achieve, and the type of work which will meet the
different needs of the child at each stage of the

middle years. The final chapter on "Organization and Resources" deals with coordinating activities, integrating English with other aspects of the curriculum, planning the work for the year, and the use of audiovisuals. See ERIC Abstract #ED 116 204.

7268.   Tullock, B. (Ed.), et al. "Solar Energy Project, Activities: Junior High Science." State University of New York, Atmospheric Science Research Center, Bureau of Science Education. Albany: New York State Education Department, and Washington, D.C.: Department of Energy, ERIC Doc. ED 173 159, 1979.

This science guide contains lesson plans and outlines of activities for teaching junior high school students concepts of solar energy. See ERIC Abstract #ED 173 159.

7269.   Tyler, R. W. "The core curriculum." National Education Association Journal, 42(1953):563-565.

Discusses characteristics of the core curriculum, the influences which stimulated its invention, the extent of its use, objective appraisals that have been made, and the problems of putting it into effective operation.

7270.   Tyrrell, R. W. "Personalizing educational activities: an approach to student-directed learning." Middle School Journal, Spring 1973:7-11.

The Beachwood Board of Education in Cleveland, Ohio, promoted the "open-space" school, hoping that it would significantly improve education by fostering change, encouraging flexibility, and creating an open and informal psychosocial environment. The Board also planned that an open architectural design would help the staff to depart from past and current middle school/junior high school practices and to develop a program specifically designed to suit the educational and social requirements of emerging adolescents. To bring about a significant difference, the middle school was organized into six interdisciplinary teams. Each team comprised a hundred students, four teachers, and two or three associate teachers. These teaching teams were given the responsibility and the resources to initiate, plan, implement, and evaluate the courses for their students. This organizational structure allowed the faculty to take advantage of a variety of teacher talents and skills, thus greatly expanding the range of educational experiences offered by the school. Students developed their own "personalized educational activities," and in the process of planning and carrying out personal educational goals they expanded their participation in real world experiences. This article presents a model of the personalized educational experiences, including expectations of teacher and student, the process (including student decision making), and the output (including the conference, critique, written report, oral defense, and demonstration or visual display).

7271.   U. S. Office of Education.   "Block-Time Classes and the Core Program in the High School."   Washington, D.C., 1958.

Pamphlet presents statistics concerning use of block-time and core curriculum in junior high schools in the United States.

7272.   University of the State of New York, State Education Department.   "A Design for Improving Early Secondary Education in New York State."   Albany, N. Y., 1954.

Bulletin focuses on the value of physical education in providing opportunities for leadership and for putting moral values into practice.   For the young adolescent who is becoming oriented toward other persons, no better opportunity exists for learning how a person's behavior affects others and what sportsmanship means.   He also gains a clearer realization of people's roles as leaders and fol- lowers and furthers his self-appraisal through a better understanding of his body and what it can do. At a time when rapid growth has made him awkward, he learns anew how to use his muscles and coordinate his body.   Physical education activities give many adolescents a feeling of exhilaration and a means of expression.   These activities bring the satisfaction of achievement to many who do not derive it from academic pursuits.

7273.   Vars, G. "We'll Paint You a Picture: Core Today-- Rationale and Implications."   Kent, Ohio: National Association for Core Curriculum, Kent State Univer- sity. (No year given.)

Introduces and describes the core concept and the assumptions and beliefs upon which core is based: 1) Interests, concerns, and needs expressed by pupils provide a valid basis for curriculum content and are central to the learning process.   2) Learning involves changes in behavior which are brought about through experience.   3) A democratic society values the worth and dignity of the individual.   4) A democratic society requires citizens who are skilled in decision making. 5) Higher priority must be given to the development of learning skills and the clarification of values than to the acquisition of specific information in subject matter areas.   6)

Learning experiences are enhanced when the learner is helped to draw upon all appropriate sources of information.   7) The extent and nature of classroom activity should determine the allocation of time.   8) The teacher's primary roles should be those of advisor, facilitator, friend, and fellow learner.   9) Teaching and many aspects of guidance are complementary functions of the teacher.   10) To bring about continuous improvement in learning, all concerned parties should be involved in evaluation.   The article discusses the implications of each of these points for the core program and the core teacher.

7274.   Vars, G. F.   "Core or correlated?"   National Education Association Journal, October 1951:464-465.

The problem solving emphasis in core classes is a "natural" for developing scientific attitudes and methods.   Students learn fundamentally sound methods of problem solving without tying them up exclusively with the field of science.   Scientific methods may be applied even to minor problems of group living.

7275.   Vars, G. F.   Bibliography of Research on the Effectiveness of Block-Time Programs.   Kent, Ohio: Department of Secondary Education, Kent State University, 1967.

Partial listing of research on the effectiveness of block-time and core programs includes thirty-nine comparative studies, fifteen normative studies, and six major summaries of research.

7276.   Vars, G. F.   "Core curriculum in the middle school."   Ideas Educational, 5(1967):25-28.

Examples of team approaches to the core curriculum include a team program in Northern Hills Junior High School, North Topeka, Kansas, and interdisciplinary team programs at Niskayuna, New York; Santa Barbara, California; Arvada, Colorado; Park Ridge, Illinois; and Dearborn, Michigan.   Interdisciplinary team programs, often under the rubric of humanities, are gaining increasing acceptance at the junior high school level.

7277.   Vars, G. F. "The core curriculum: lively corpse." Clearinghouse, 42,9(1968):515-519.

Three kinds of evidence demonstrate that the core curriculum is far from dead. First, a sizable number of schools continue to use block-time in their efforts to approach the core ideal. Second, concepts long associated with the core curriculum are manifest in other contemporary programs such as interdisciplinary team teaching, humanities courses, certain independent study and nongraded programs, modified self-contained classes in middle schools, and special programs for the culturally disadvantaged. Third, there appears to be a perceptible swing away from extreme concern with subject matter mastery toward a more human, personal, problem-centered approach to education. The core curriculum idea will undoubtedly continue to have an important place in American education as long as there are human problems that do not fall neatly within the boundaries of conventional subjects, as long as education is viewed as essentially a human and humanizing encounter between youth and adults, and as long as educators keep in mind that young people learn best when they are actively involved in wrestling with problems that have personal meaning to them.

7278.   Washington Evening Star. "Catholic schools to pair math with science." Washington Evening Star, Washington, D.C., July 13, 1960.

Catholic schools in the archdiocese of Washington, D.C., experimented with unification of mathematics and science in grades 4-8. An evaluation report issued in July 1960 indicated that students who received the integrated instruction learned considerably more mathematics in conjunction with science than those taking the subject separately.

7279.   Washington State Coordinating Council for Occupational Education, Vocational Education, and Home and Family Life Section. "Developing Curriculum for Middle and Junior High School: Personal, Home, and Family Education Programs." Olympia, Wash., 1974.

This bulletin is a guide for making administrative decisions and planning curriculum for personal, home, and family education programs for 10- to 13-year-old boys and girls. General information for organizing programs is directed to superintendents, principals, curriculum and vocational directors, supervisors, and teachers who are planning to establish new programs or evaluate existing programs. Curriculum recommendations directed to the teacher include suggestions for planning and outlines of content concepts. A resource section gives examples of appropriate behavioral objectives and learning experiences for concepts.

7280.   Watson, G. E. "Guides to Curriculum Building: Junior High Level." Pamphlet authorized by the Curriculum Guiding Committee of the Wisconsin Cooperative Educational Planning Program, 1950.

Book is arranged in three parts: 1) characteristics and behavior related to early adolescent growth, 2) developmental and social tasks the pupils face, and 3) what the school can do to help them with these tasks. In building a curriculum based on problems rather than subjects, the curriculum committee addressed these questions: 1) What happens to the traditional time schedule if a problems approach is substituted for a pattern of subjects? What happens to textbooks? Will it be appropriate or helpful for the same book to be in the hands of each pupil in a given class group? Will the approach increase or limit the need for reference material? 2) How can we be reasonably sure we are not neglecting basic skills in a problems approach? Can we assure for each pupil maximum opportunity to grow in reading, writing, spelling, computing? Does such an approach rule out the possibility of group or individual work in basic skills? 3) Does this approach deny boys and girls the opportunity to pursue special interests? 4) What effect would the problems approach have on teaching security? 5) What is the role of the specialist? 6) What effect does the problems approach have on school-community relations? 7) By what gradual steps might a school introduce the problems approach? 8) What effect does the problems approach have on patterns of pre-service professional education? 9) What about guidance? Does the core teacher play a more or less significant role as the teacher-counselor? Are the facilities, time schedules, and pupil loads better or worse for youth?

7281. Waukegan Community Unit School District 60. "Developmental Reading Instruction." Waukegan, Ill., ERIC Doc. ED 106 836, 1974.

This program serves 2400 junior high school students from middle and low income families. It provides one hour a day of remedial instruction in reading in addition to a period of language arts. Students' skill deficiencies are diagnosed at the beginning of the year, and the teacher prescribes and teaches according to the results of the diagnostic testing. Objectives focus on skills in word recognition, comprehension, rate, critical reading, and appreciation. Reading matter is correlated with curriculum content. See ERIC Abstract #ED 106 836.

7282. Weaver, J. F., et al. "Calculator Explorations with Seventh Grade Students: Some Calculator-Inspired Instructional Materials, Observations, and Investigations." Technical Report 497. Washington, D.C.: U. S. Department of Health, Education and Welfare, National Institute of Education, ERIC Doc. ED 177 019, 1979.

Contains materials developed from 1976 to 1978. Describes student performance with number sentences and calculator notation and tasks and includes examples. See ERIC Abstract #ED 177 019.

7283.   Whitley, T. W.   "The effects of individualized instruction on the attitudes of middle school pupils."   Journal of Educational Research, 72,4 (1979):188-193.

Study showed that individualized instruction had a favorable impact on attitudes of fifth, sixth, and seventh grade pupils toward teachers, learning processes, language arts, and arithmetic/mathematics. Instruments were administered to a treatment group and a comparison group of pupils at the start and end of a school year in which the pupils in the treatment group were exposed to individualized instruction in language arts and mathematics. The results contradict reports that individualized instruction has resulted in less favorable pupil attitudes than other modes of classroom organization or that individualized instruction has had no statistically significant impact on pupil attitudes.

7284.   Williams, E. L.   "A transactional curriculum for the transescent learner."   Paper presented at the Annual Convention of the National Council of Teachers of English, Atlanta, November 27, 1971.   English Journal, 60,5(1971):599-602.

Curriculum is based on the needs of transescent students. See ERIC Abstract #EJ 036 184.

7285.   Williams, G. "A Curriculum Guide for Occupational Orientation and Exploration in Junior High School Home Economics and Industrial Arts." Memphis, Tenn.: Memphis City School System, ERIC Doc. ED 107 940, 1971.

Curriculum guide for industrial arts and home economic teachers provides information to make students aware of job opportunities so the students can select courses that will prepare them to work in these areas. The program organization, general objectives, and various teaching methods are described. The guide presents twelve teaching units plus case studies, additional instructional materials, students' self-evaluation tests, learning activities, resources, and a bibliography. See ERIC Abstract #ED 107 940.

7286.   Willson, M. F. and Schneyer, J. W. Developmental Reading in the Junior High School. Educational Service Bureau, South Penn School Study Council, University of Pennsylvania.   Danville, Ill.:   Interstate Printers and Publishers, 1959.

One of the most crucial problems facing secondary education is that of organizing developmental reading programs which meet the needs of all students. This is particularly true at the junior high school level. Before the advent of the junior high school, reading was generally taught in each of the elementary entry grades, 1-8. With the development of the junior high school, formal instruction in reading generally ceased at the end of grade 6. While it was expected that emphasis would continue to be placed upon reading, in all too many cases this did not happen, for several reasons. First, because of departmental organization, emphasis was generally placed upon the teaching of subject content rather than skills. And because junior high school teachers are often certified by subjects, many are not prepared to teach reading. This study explored the problems and suggested solutions for a developmental reading program for grades 1-12.

7287.   Wisconsin Cooperative Planning Program, Superintendent of Public Instruction. "Guides to Curriculum Building: The Junior High School Level." Madison, Wis., 1950.

This is one of the most useful documents available for those who work on the junior high school curriculum. It charts systematically the characteristics of young adolescents and lists the tasks the pupils face and what the school can do to serve youth.

7288.   Wixson, E. A. and Evans, R. C. "A Teacher's Handbook of Middle School or Junior High School Physical Education Activities Emphasizing Metrics." Guide prepared through the Northeastern States Metric Education Consortium. Washington, D. C.: U. S. Office of Education, ERIC Doc. ED 177 188, 1977.

Describes activities involving applications of physical skills or principles of health to measuring in the metric system or knowledge of metric measure. See ERIC Abstract #ED 177 118.

7289.   Wright, B. "A global approach to middle school social studies." History and Social Science Teacher, 13,4(1978):237-242.

The Indiana University Global Studies Project is an experimental alternative to world geography or world studies for junior high school students. Approaches taken are global, topical, contemporary/futuristic, and activity oriented. The packet of materials also contains sample lessons. See ERIC Abstract EJ 180 288.

7290.   Wright, G. "Core Curriculum." Bulletin 5. Washington, D.C.:   U.S. Office of Education, Federal
Security Agency, 1952.

A list of colleges that prepare teachers for teaching
a junior high school core curriculum.

7291.   Wright, G. S., Jr. "Towards a curriculum for
understanding: junior high school." Art Education,
January 1963:4-7.

Since art in the average high school is an elective
subject and participated in by relatively few, the
junior high school course can be considered terminal
for most students. This curriculum is based on the
fact that man has been creating art for tens of
thousands of years. Every society in history has
produced its artistic expression. An understanding
of man is incomplete without an understanding of his
art, and an understanding of his art leads to a
deeper understanding of man. It is this understanding which is the goal of this junior high course of
study. If understanding begins in the preteenage
mind through a curriculum designed for this age
group, it stands a good chance of lasting for a
lifetime. These suggestions are based on the reality
of the junior high classroom, not on the idealistic,
often unrealistic atmosphere of the scholar's library
or educator's seminar.

7292.   Yager, R. E. "Innovations in junior high science."
Midland Schools, 81(1967):28-32.

In October 1966 seven junior high schools in Iowa
began instruction with a completely new approach and
new materials for their science program. Article
describes the test center, features of the project,
the energy unit in the seventh grade, courses in the
eighth and ninth grades, emphasis on the scientific
approach, individual effort and attention, and the
skill-developing process. Specific process skills
incorporated into the three-year program are: 1)
recognition of significant problems in science, 2)
delimiting and defining of broad problems in science
to levels which allow attack by empirical means, 3)
the ability to state testable hypotheses upon which
critical experiments may be designed, 4) the design
and conduct of experiments which yield data that test
hypotheses, 5) interpretation of data obtained from
experiments and other measurements of nature, using
simple statistical techniques, 6) drawing conclusions
from a relevant set of data and ordering such conclusions into generalizations, 7) testing the general
applicability of conclusions drawn from the limited

data, and 8) building scientific models (with particular emphasis on the advantages in scientific investigation and their tentative nature).

7293. Zupfer, J., et al. "Career Related Science Units. Teacher Edition." Roseville, Minn., Area School District 623. St. Paul: Minnesota State Department of Education, Division of Vocational and Technical Education, ERIC Doc. ED 120 348, 1973.

Presents ninety-one career-related modules for individualized science programs. Integrated with the presentation of scientific theory, knowledge, and skills is information on applications in work settings and on employment opportunities in science and other fields. See ERIC Abstract #ED 120 348.

8

Development and Implementation of Cocurricular and Extracurricular Activities

8001. Alley, L. E. "Guides for conducting junior high school athletics." School Activities, 33(1961):81-85.

In 1952 a joint committee of representatives from five major educational organizations published a statement that "interscholastic competition of varsity pattern and similarly organized competition under the auspices of other community agencies are definitely disapproved for children below the ninth grade." The organizations were the National Education Association and two NEA departments (the Department of Elementary School Principals and the American Association of Health, Physical Education and Recreation), the National Council of State Consultants in Elementary Education, and the Society of State Directors of Health, Physical Education and Recreation.

8002. Anderson, L. D. "The activity-based middle school." Man/Society/Technology: A Journal of Industrial Arts Education, 31,1(1971):10-12.

Discusses activity-based learning in the middle school, especially in the industrial or unified arts. Receptivity by curriculum specialists, administrators, and industrial arts teachers has helped make industrial arts activities an integral part of an activity-centered program.

8003. Association of Wisconsin School Administrators. "JAM Commission Athletic Position Paper and Statewide Survey Data." Available from Association of Wisconsin School Administrators, 1310 Mendota St., Madison, Wis. 53714, ERIC Doc. 168 980, February, 1979.

Position paper reviews middle school and junior high school athletic program guidelines concerning opportunities that should be offered to all students, health and safety of participants, equal opportunities for boys and girls, athletic resources, and control of athletics sponsored by school districts. Paper also discusses a statewide survey of student participation in intramural sports, team and individual. Paper includes suggestions for improving interscholastic athletic programs at the junior high school level. See ERIC Abstract #ED 168 980.

8004.   Barnes, D. G.   "The Organization and Administration of Student Government in Selected Junior High Schools in Southern California."   Ed.D. Dissertation, University of Southern California.   Dissertation Abstracts International, 40 (09) 4813-A, 1980.

Author reviewed the literature on student government and examined constitutions of selected student governments in an effort to establish the ideal way to organize and administer a junior high school student government.   He surveyed five principals, eleven faculty sponsors and 219 students at fifteen junior high schools.   Responses showed that these groups considered student councils to be an important part of the educational program.   Principals, faculty sponsors, and students were not completely satisfied with the types of student government now in use, though many felt their participation in such a school government was worthwhile.   Many of the elements of the student government constitutions did not differ significantly from the ideal elements proposed in the literature.   Many of the faculty sponsors thought it was very important to have a student government.   The author recommends a model constitution that could help faculty sponsors and students organize and administer student government and also recommends that members of the student government meet daily as a class with a faculty sponsor.

8005.   Baxter, B.   "Student body organizations and functioning."   Bulletin of the National Association of Secondary School Principals, 35(1951):117-119.

The principal of a junior high school in Los Angeles presents certain principles for operating a student body organization.

8006.   Bossing, N. L.   Principles of Secondary Education. 2d ed. Englewood Cliffs, N, J.: Prentice-Hall, 1955.

Presents guidelines for developing constructive student activity in junior high schools: 1) Student activities should be an integral part of the total school curriculum.   2) All activities should be

scheduled on school time.   3) As far as possible a
specific place on the school schedule should be set
aside for student activities.   4) Participants should
be free of financial obligations for all basic costs
of an activity.   5) Student participation in activities should be encouraged, and minimal participation
should be required.   6) Students should be free under
guidance to participate in the activities of their
choice.   7) The administration of admission and participation requirements should be democratic.   8)
Each activity should be evaluated annually to consider its continuance in the program.   9) Credit for
participation in student activities should be awarded
on the same principles that govern other curriculum
offerings.   10) Sponsors should be limited to the
school staff.   11) The function of the sponsor should
be advisory and guiding in nature.   12) Student
activities should be financed by regular budgetary
provision of the Board of Education on the same basis
as other curricular activities.

8007.   Botts, R. E.   "Lakewood's special interest club
program." California Journal of Secondary Education,
27(1952):153-157.

Among the most desirable activities for junior high
schools are those in which pupils make things and
have opportunities to express themselves creatively.
In Lakewood's school, for example, the clubs have
been replaced by Special Interest Groups. They are
organized only when a number of students ask for
them and remain in operation only so long as the need
for them exists. They may meet at times when other
children are attending regular classes or after
school, according to the flexibility of the program.

8008.   Braham, R. V.   "What role for student activities
in   the   new   emphasis   on   quality   in   secondary
education?"   Bulletin of the National Association of
Secondary School Principals, 44(1960):111.

Student activities are both meaningful and desired by
youth attending junior high school. To deemphasize
them in an effort to insure quality of learning would
be as foolish as requiring every pupil in the junior
high school to take accelerated mathematics, science,
and modern foreign language.

8009.   Brown, I. S.   "Group development in a junior high
school   student   council." Educational Leadership, 9
(1952):496-501.

Author reports on an educational psychology graduate
class research project concerning student councils in
junior high school.

8010.   Clute, M.   "Student activities for early adolescents." Teachers College Journal, 34,2(1962):62-63.

Describes the personal social adjustment of adolescents, the development and expansion of intellectual
interest through student activities, and the necessity of special interests, hobbies, and social service for preadolescents. A good student activities
program for a junior high school should 1) further
the student's personal social adjustment with peers
and with adults, 2) promote learning the skills and
concepts of democracy through actual practice, 3)
offer an opportunity for students to pursue a wide
variety of interests and adjust readily to changes in
interests, 4) provide for discovery and development
of abilities, 5) provide an outlet for the altruism
and idealism of junior high school youth.

8011.   Coleman, J. S.   "The adolescent subculture and
academic achievement."   American Journal of Sociology, 65,4(1960):337-347.

An adolescent social system that values academic
achievement encourages young people of high intelligence to concentrate on academic work, while an
adolescent social system that values other pursuits
more highly encourages intelligent young people to
direct their energies to these pursuits. Author
studied this hypothesis about the effect of adolescent value system on education in ten schools with
differing value systems.   He also discusses the
source of these value systems and presents evidence
suggesting an apparently powerful effect on education
of interscholastic athletics.   This result raises
questions about the general effect of interscholastic
competition of other sorts on the adolescent value
system of a school.

8012.   Collins, D. "Providing recognition for the seldom
recognized." School Activities, 40(1969):17.

Presents useful ideas for providing positive
reinforcement to junior high students who show low
academic achievement.

8013.   Conant, J. B.   "Some problems of the junior high
school." Bulletin of the National Association of
Secondary School Principals, 44(1960):310-322.

A joint committee on athletic competition for
children of elementary and junior high school age,
representing four national organizations, condemned
highly organized competition for children of elementary and junior high school age.

8014.   Cronin, R. L.   "Are junior high school PTAs, student council cold?" School Activities, 32(1961): 135.

Presents a code of behavior for parents and students: "We, the students of Hastings Junior High School and our parents, in a spirit of cooperation and with a sense of responsibility to each other, our home, our school, and our community, recognize that our characters and reputations depend upon good behavior at all times. Our common purpose is to make the social activities of the junior high school years as happy and as pleasurable as possible to all concerned, and to this end we adopt this code of conduct and pledge ourselves to its year-round observance. In so doing, we recognize that parents' authority is at all times the final authority."

8015.   Dukelow, D. A. and Hein, F. V.   "Junior high athletic leads." Today's Health, 29(1951):13.

An editorial on the controversy over grade school and junior high school participation in highly organized interschool athletic events.

8016.   Eash, M. J. "The school program: nonclass experience." Review of Educational Research, 30(1960):62.

Several research studies on student activities in junior high schools, analyzed by Rennicke and Hearn and edited by Eash, indicated certain trends: 1) a conscious effort to relate objectives of nonclass activities to the general objectives of education, 2) increased attention to the problems of overparticipation and underparticipation, 3) attempts to solve problems of imbalance, whereby some activities are overemphasized to the detriment of the remainder of the program, 4) broadened student participation in school government and more shared responsibility between students and school management, 5) viewing nonclass activities as part of the teacher's regular load and not as an adjunct of the formal curriculum, 6) linking nonclass activities to projects sponsored by local community and civic clubs.

8017.   Evans, C. L.   "Student Questionnaire." Fort Worth, Tex.:   Fort Worth Independent School District, 1970. ERIC Doc. ED 057 092. (Document not available from EDRS.)

This questionnaire assesses the educational and social growth of students in middle schools of grades 6-9.   Students answer eleven questions individually and anonymously by marking the response they feel is correct or writing their own response.   See ERIC Abstract #ED 057 092.

8018.   Frank, J., Jr.   Complete Guide to Cocurricular
Programs and Activities for the Middle Grades.   West
Nyack, N. Y.:   Parker Publishing Co., 1976.

Sections of this book are: 1) Highlighting the
Middle Grades Cocurricular Activities Concept (why
expanded cocurricular activities programs are necessary, developing potential activity programs by
categorizing, a new approach to elective programs,
activity periods, developing flexibility with mini-
course activities, creating a viable schoolwide
activity program, adapting programs to meet local
needs).   2) Updating Middle Grade Elective Programs
(reviewing traditional elective programs, adding new
activities to the program, establishing individual
electives, a reservoir of successful elective activities for the educator).   3) Successful Ways to
Develop Schoolwide Activities (getting teachers and
others to help, developing a checklist of possible
schoolwide activities, establishing a yearly calendar
of activities, how to encourage greater student participation, recommended schoolwide activities, looking ahead to a new year).   4) Building a Viable
Middle Grade Activity Program (what type of activities to use, when to conduct the activity period
program, constructing useful activity descriptions, a
collection of popular activities).   5) Mini-courses:
A Positive Activity Program Approach (establishing
the mini-course program, how many mini-courses,
determining teacher-student interests, sample interest survey sheet, preparing mini-course descriptions,
a resource bank of mini-course activities for
teachers and administrators, developing a descriptive
program handbook for student selection).   6) A
Special Activity Program for Fifth Grade (why create
a separate program for the fifth grade, schoolwide
activities for the fifth grade, a sample fifth grade
schoolwide calendar, introduction to the activity
program through clubs, conducting a miniature
multiphase activity program).   7) Utilizing the Best
of Each Cocurricular Activity Program.   8) Organizing
and Operating a Complete Middle Grade Activity
Program.   9) How to Schedule Middle Grade Activity
Programs.   10) Evaluating Middle Grade Cocurricular
Activity Programs.

8019.   Frederick, R. W.   The Third Curriculum: Student
Activities in American Education. New York: Appleton-
Century-Crofts, 1960.

Describes student activity programs in junior highs
and middle schools.

8020.   Fryklund, V.   "Interscholastic competition: is
junior high school too soon?"   Minnesota Journal of
Education, 46(1966):15-16.

Author states that the junior high school should not
be like a senior high school in interscholastic competitive activities.

8021.   Fuller, K. A. "Finance--an area for junior high
school participation." Bulletin of the National Association of Secondary School Principals,   37(1953):57-
73.

Presents the purposes and basic principles of pupil
participation in financing extra-class activities and
describes a plan used in one junior high school.

8022.   Gerard, G. K., et al. "Focus on Physical Educa-
tion, Intramurals, and Interscholastics."   Michigan
Association of Middle School Educators, East Lansing,
ERIC Doc. ED 157 872, 1978.

Includes a brief analysis of the problems involved in
physical education at the middle school level and a
position paper on physical education, intramurals,
and interscholastics emphasizing that intramural
sports should be the central objective in middle
school physical education. Paper discusses the
middle school learner, generalizations from the
literature on this subject, and the identification of
key program components. See ERIC Abstract #ED 157
872.

8023.   Grady, J. B.   "Middle school activities--more
meaningful with more." Bulletin of the National Association of Secondary School Principals, 61,413(1977):
74-78.

Author stresses the need to involve more students in
acitivities of middle schools. See ERIC Abstract #EJ
169 770.

8024.   Graham, G.   Improving Student Participation.
Washington, D.C.:   National Association of Secondary
School Principals, 1966.

The characteristics of the preadolescent and early
adolescent make a good junior high school program of
activities a necessary part of the school. Ninth
graders, whether in a junior high school or high
school, can especially profit from a carefully
planned and developed student activity program.
Author makes the following generalizations about
early adolescence: 1) Adolescents need to be
recognized and praised, to belong; and to have peer
companionship.   2) The adolescent peer group is a
distinct factor in shaping the personality of its
members.   3) Adolescents perform better in both
academics and social activities when they feel
secure. 4) Higher morale results when adolescents

form a cohesive group. 5) Through peer association, adolescents learn and develop many of the skills of cooperative endeavor. 6) Learning to be adult is easier for adolescents when they associate with adults. 7) Adolescents learn to accept responsibility by being given responsibility. 8) Learning to make sound decisions results from practice in decision making. Generalization about student activities are: 1) Student activities more nearly approximate the kinds of learnings to be found in peer groups than do regular class activities. 2) Counseling and guidance receive substantial contributions from student activities. 3) The need to belong can be met by student activities, especially for an adolescent who is not a member of a peer group. 4) The recognition and rewards for achievement provided by student activities are satisfying psychologically. 5) The teacher, changing his role from that of a director of instruction, becomes an advisor who assists adolescents to improve their personal relationships, develop democratic behavior, and increase achievement. 6) The school atmosphere is enhanced when faculty and administration work cooperatively with pupils in class and extra-class activities. 7) It is probable that adolescents will learn more about some kinds of human relationships and democratic behaviors in extra-class than class activities. 8) The activities program provides opportunities for students to learn to apply skills acquired in classes and to explore various knowledges in depth.

8025.   Hatch, M. "A Newspaper for the Middle School." Paper presented at the Annual Meeting of the Secondary School English Conference, Boston, ERIC Doc. ED 120 777, April, 1976.

Author describes experiences as the faculty advisor for a monthly student newspaper in a secondary school. Lead stories included editorial opinion concerning controversial issues in the school, club news, interviews with new teachers, reviews of television programs and movies, sports coverage, etc. Author stresses the role of faculty advisor as motivator and director of student output and views the experience of writing and publishing a paper as an important exercise in written and spoken communication. See ERIC Abstract #ED 120 777.

8026.   Herring, L. H. "Provisions and Procedures for the Rapid Learner in Selected Texas Junior High Schools." Texas Study of Secondary Education, 417 Sutton Hall, University of Texas, Austin, Tex. 78701, ERIC Doc. ED 021 351, 1962.

Author surveyed principals of forty junior high schools concerning their administrative provisions for rapid learners, procedures for discovering rapid learners, and provisions for special instruction for rapid learners in English, social studies, mathematics, science, home economics, and industrial arts. Author contends that all junior high schools should have a well-developed plan for locating the rapid learner and provide an organized program of learning experiences which present a real challenge to pupils with special abilities. Enrichment can be provided in a special curriculum taught to gifted children in groups, special adaptations of the instructional program in regular classes, and special activities and responsibilities in the homeroom. Instructional methods which work well with rapid learners include pupil participation in planning learning activities, pupil leadership in carrying on learning activities, creative work, freedom, a variety of instructional material, problems and projects which demand abstract and critical thinking, individual and group oral activities, a minimum of repetitive drill teachers and students enjoying a freedom from unnecessary administrative restrictions, and pupil leadership and responsibility in organizing the class.

8027.   Hoover, N. R. "An Inventory of Cocurricular Drama Programs in the Secondary Schools of Jefferson County, Kentucky." Masters Thesis, University of Louisville, ERIC Doc. ED 124 991, May, 1976.

In order to compile an inventory of secondary school cocurricular dramatics programs in the Jefferson County, Kentucky, public schools, author surveyed eleven principals, eighteen teachers, and eighty students randomly selected from thirteen high schools, five junior high schools, and five middle schools. Questionnaire responses revealed that dramatics programs were rated as fair, that principals and teachers placed dramatics third in importance in activities programs while students placed dramatics first, that all respondents rated dramatics as relevant to other experiences, and that students attended movies more frequently than school plays and live theater. See ERIC Abstract #ED 124 991.

8028.   Johnston, E. G. "Critical problems in the administration of student activities." Bulletin of the National Association of Secondary School Principals, 36(1952):1-12.

Discusses student activities in the junior high school.

8029.   Jordon, J. W. "Nonathletic activities program in the junior high school: position papers and practices." Bulletin of the National Association of Secondary School Principals, 47,285(1963).

The idea of a nonathletic activities program is educationally sound, but the program must be developed to meet the needs of the adolescent and must be suited to the facilities of the school.

8030. Junior High School Association of Illinois. "Extra-class Activities in the Junior High School Grades." Urbana, Ill., 1957.

Presents samples of problems and practices for extra-class activities.

8031. Katzer, W. D. "A Study of the Organization and Administration of Student Activity Programs in Michigan Middle Schools." Ed.D. Dissertation, Wayne State University, 1974.

Study concludes: 1) The most common grade structure in Michigan middle schools is 5-8 and 6-8. 2) Student activity programs are established in 79.1 percent of the surveyed schools. 3) Student activities in Michigan middle schools are viewed primarily as cocurricular. 4) The primary organizational structure in the middle school is the seven-period day designed to accommodate an activity period. 5) Little emphasis is given to evaluating student activities, with formal evaluation being virtually nonexistent. 6) In-service training to prepare staff for the sponsorship of activities is virtually an untapped resource for improving programs.

8032. Lowe, J. Y. "What kind of activities program for students in junior high school?" Bulletin of the National Association of Secondary School Principals, 43(1959):254.

The principal of the Beverly Hills Junior High School, Huntington, West Virginia, surveyed the principals of twenty-five consolidated and city junior high schools with enrollments of fifteen hundred in West Virginia. All but one the principals endorsed the value of the student activities programs because it gives students a chance to experience new activities, arouse latent interest and abilities, try out new subject areas, learn to do new things, and thus be properly fitted for the gradual transition from preadolescent education to the specialization that suits the needs of older adolescents.

8033. Ludden, W. "How extensive an activities program in the junior high school?" Bulletin of the National Association of Secondary School Principals, 36(1952): 257-262.

A principal describes the activity program in the junior high school at Rome, New York.

8034.   MacKenzie, W. J. and Elwell, W. C.   "A Case Study
of Student Government in a Middle School." ERIC Doc.
ED 114 388, 1975.

Examines a student government's role in decision
making at a New York junior high school. The student
body, faculty, and administration response to a questionnaire showed that a majority believed that
students were not involved in the decision-making
process. Students were disenchanted with the performance of the student council, did not feel that the
council solicited their opinions, and did not think
the council served as a link between the students and
the administration. See ERIC Abstract #ED 114 338.

8035.   Massachusetts Association for Health, Physical
Education and Recreation, Research in Education Commission. "Physical Education, Secondary Schools
Facilities, and Basic Equipment." ERIC Doc. ED 021
397, January, 1965.

According to this commission, the junior and senior
high school gymnasium should be located away from
classrooms and near outdoor play areas. Junior high
school gymnasiums should be a minimum of 84' x 98' x
22'. Areas should be divisible. Provisions should
be made for basketball, volleyball, badminton, seating, and teaching areas. Gymnastics and wrestling
and a simulated outdoor area should also be provided.
Outdoor facilities should provide twenty acres plus
an additional acre per hundred pupils for junior high
pupils. Also included are outdoor and indoor equipment lists and a bibliography. See ERIC Abstract #ED
021 397.

8036.   Massialas, B. G. and Simone, M. W.   "Decision
Making in the School: A Participatory Model." Paper
presented at Annual Meeting of the American Educational Research Association, New York, April, 1977.

This model program helps middle school students
understand how political decisions are made by having
the students apply basic participatory concepts and
skills to school decisions that affect them. This
program is meant to increase students' political
efficacy, interest, trust, and social integration. A
three-year study of three schools, two experimental
and one control, evaluated the program through a
survey of students, teachers, administrators and
parents through paper and pencil instruments, structured interviews, and observation. Article contains
sections on the schools' political effect on youth,
methodological issues, a proposed participatory
model, research findings from a literature survey,
and a model describing the school as a political
system that involves group decision making and

individual self-realization. It also includes
materials on the cognitive, affective, evaluative,
normative, and participatory aspects of decision
making, as well as definitions and activities for
political proposing, mobilizing, organizing, cost
benefit analysis, bargaining, establishing roles, and
rule making. Article defines objectivity, political
interest, political efficacy, political trust, and
social integration. Appendix includes pencil and
paper instruments, structured interviews, attitude
surveys, teacher model evaluation forms, and other
methods for collecting data.

8037.   McEachen, H. D. "Status and Trends in Organization of Selected Junior High Schools." Ed.D. Dissertation, University of Kansas, 1955.

In a study of the organization and curriculum in 155
junior high schools, author found that club activities for all students have become an integral part of
the curriculum in all the schools surveyed.

8038.   Means, L. E. The Organization and Administration
of Intramural Sports. St. Louis: C. V. Mossby Co.,
1949.

Describes intramural and interscholastic sports in a
junior high school setting.

8039.   Meehan, M. L. "Career exploration in middle/
junior high schools." Man/Society/Technology:
Journal of Industrial Arts Education, 34,4(1975):
114-116.

Discusses the various meanings of career exploration,
the middle school role, and exploration as problem
solving. Career exploration is a term used to
describe a life stage, processes, programs, outcomes,
goals, or any combination of these. The middle/
junior high school years are a good place for career
exploration activities which allow preadolescent
learners to systematically assess their interests,
aptitudes, and skills.

8040.   Merenbloom, E. Y. "A model for teaching reading
in the middle school." Middle School Journal, 11,2
(1980):21-23.

Considers the rationale for teaching reading as
determined at the Woodlawn Middle School in
Baltimore, Maryland, which has a formal reading
program, teaches reading through the content areas,
and has individualized programs. Sections of this
article consider each of these approaches to teaching
reading. Also included are sections on scheduling

considerations and a section on key steps in implementing the model.

8041.   Mitchell, E. D. "The case against interscholastic activities in the junior high school." Education Digest, 17(1952):46-48.

Author questions the development of teams and the big interscholastic game schedules in junior high school. Points of controversy include: centering too much time, energy, and money on a few children at the expense of the many, too early specialization, the hidden cost of a junior high education whose program is undemocratic because many children cannot afford even to attend the games, and pressures exerted on students to buy tickets, often causing resentment and hostility.

8042.   National Association of Secondary School Principals. "The Student Council in the Secondary School." Washington, D. C., 1950.

Pamphlet describes the role of a student council in a junior high school.

8043.   National Education Association, Educational Policies Commission.   "School Athletics: Problems and Policies."   Washington, D.C.:   National Education Association and American Association of School Administrators, 1954.

When 220 physicians were asked to express opinions on the suitability of eleven sports for interscholastic competition for boys 12 to 15 years of age, a substantial majority rejected each of the sports. The ratio against football was 9 to 1 and against basketball 4 to 1. The Educational Policies Commission of the National Education Association and the American Association of School Administrators recommended that "no junior high school should have a school team that competes with school teams of other junior high schools in organized leagues and tournaments. Varsity-type athletics and interscholastics for junior high boys and girls should not be permitted."

8044.   Oakley, J. P. "A middle school student council." Clearinghouse, 50,7(1977):296-297.

Discusses the Fred S. Engle Middle School in West Grove, Pennsylvania, which serves 835 students in grades 5-8. The council in each grade consisting of fourteen to eighteen representatives has these responsibilities: 1) to plan activities for that grade, 2) to discuss school policies and procedures, 3) to advise teachers and administrators of problems and concerns of students, and 4) to coordinate activities with the other grades. A coordinating council consisting of two representatives from each grade council has these responsibilities: 1) to coordinate school activities across grade levels, 2) to plan and carry out schoolwide activities, 3) to advise administrators and teachers on school policies and programs, and 4) to approve expenditures from the Student Council treasury. This type of council structure has a lot of built-in flexibility and is adaptable to schools with team organization or school-within-a-school plans as well as grade level plans. It also has the advantage of broader representation from diverse groups.

8045.   Pitkin, V. E. "What kind of activities programs for students in junior high school?" Bulletin of the National Association of Secondary School Principals, April 1959:255-256.

In a survey of a limited number of junior high schools, a consultant in citizenship education in the State Department of Education, Hartford, Connecticut, requested students to respond to the question, "What is the most important honor you ever had?" The student answers were classified into two groups according to whether these experiences occurred in or out of school. Honors in school included the honor roll, president of the class, student council, singing a solo in an assembly, and art work in the art club exhibit. Author concluded that student activities are both meaningful to and desired by youth attending junior high school.

8046.   Plumley, D. L. and Dunn, J. A. Teacher's Guide to Career Education: Middle School Grades. Career Education Series, vol. 8. Palo Alto, Calif.: American Institutes for Research in the Behavioral Sciences, ERIC Doc. ED 101 210, September, 1974.

The purpose of this manual is to serve as a curriculum guide and resource handbook to assist teachers in the introduction of career education into their classrooms. Three main questions are answered: 1) What is career education? 2) How can teachers use career education materials in the classroom? 3) How can teachers develop their own career education materials? Book contains the following chapters: 1) Introduction to Career Education. 2) Career Education Curriculum. 3) Infusing Career Education into the Academic Program. 4) Teaching Career Education Units. 5) How to Use Supplementary Resources. 6) Selecting Instructional Objectives. 7) Learning Processes and Career Education. 8) Developing an Instructional Unit. 9) Method of Assessment.

8047.   Reichert, J. L.   "Competitive athletics for preteenage children."   Journal of the American Medical
Association, 156(1958):1701-1707.

Researcher maintains that preadolescent and adolescent children are at a physically disadvantaged age
for athletics.   Bone growth is occurring at a more
rapid rate than is muscular development, resulting in
a lack of protection for the bone by the covering
muscles and supporting tendons.   Furthermore, stren-
uous athletics can alter bone position, causing added
stress and even possible physical damage.   The transescent is caught in a dilemma caused by the expectation of strength which he may or may not be able to
meet, depending on his personal capabilities.

8048.   Reum, E. "Of Love and Magic: The Junior High/
Middle School Student Council Adviser."   National
Association of Secondary School Principals, Dulles
International Airport, P. O. Box 17430, Washington,
D.C. 20041, ERIC Doc. ED 075 756, 1973.   (Document
not available from EDRS.)

Author discusses the role he played as student council adviser in a junior high school.   He discusses
the characteristics of students in sixth through
ninth grade and the characteristics of student
leaders.   He stresses the need for a student council
adviser to like junior high school students and
relate well with them.   He discusses role conflicts
for the adviser.   Author provides helpful suggestions
for conducting meetings, organizing meetings, handling finances, planning activities, managing public
relations and publicity, and evaluating projects.
See ERIC Abstract #ED 075 756.

8049.   Riegle, J. D.   Motivating, Organizing and Conducting Exploratory Activities.   Dissemination Services
on the Middle Grades, vol. 5, no. 6.   Springfield,
Mass.:   Educational Leadership Institute, 1974.

Most educators have accepted the concept of a broad
and generalized curriculum for the middle school,
including an exploratory program.   It is usually safe
to assume that what motivates one child strongly
enough for him to seek further information will also
motivate several other students.   Therefore, the
exploratory activity curriculum is not individualized
but more accurately is an "ad hocracy" of small
groups working on a diversity of topics.   Each group
draws its genesis from pupil interest.   Teachers must
1) help the student successfully undertake the projected plan, 2) serve as a resource and help students
find other resources, 3) highlight for students the
educationally significant items they have achieved or

discovered, 4) refine the students' efforts without
becoming critical or negative, 5) evaluate and
remotivate daily on a group and individual basis.
The article presents ways of motivating teachers and
implementing the exploratory program, with a concrete
example of how these methods are carried out.

8050.   Rizzo, M. E.   "An active activities program."
Clearinghouse, November 1969:182-184.

Ingelmar Middle School in the North Allegheny School
District of suburban Pittsburgh strives for maximum
student involvement in cocurricular activities.   The
activity program operates one day per week during a
regularly scheduled period at the end of the day.
The comprehensive student activities program is based
on six objectives: 1) to help students experience
the responsibilities of living in a democratic
society, 2) to help students develop appreciation and
skills in physical, instructional, and recreational
activities, 3) to help students develop initiative
and self-directions in accordance with the maturity
of early adolescents, 4) to complement and supplement
regular classroom activities, 5) to meet the needs
and interests of early adolescents, 6) to encourage
maximum student involvement in cocurricular activities.   The key factor is developing responsibility,
which involves stressing the responsibility of the
staff as well.   The program is successful because the
school administration supports it, the staff continually strives to keep it dynamic, and perhaps most
important, the students accept the many responsibilities associated with the program.

8051.   Rowe, F. A.   "Should the junior high school have
organized, competitive athletics?" School Activities,
22(1950):96-99.

Presents pros and cons of the junior high athletics
controversy.

8052.   Schreiber, D.   "What Can Be Done to Reduce
Academic Retardation in Minority Group Children."
Washington, D.C.:   Office of Education, ERIC Doc. ED
014 516, April 29, 1962.

Describes the Higher Horizons Program, a New York
City junior high school course that identified and
stimulated able disadvantaged children.   The goal was
to encourage higher aspiration levels, achievement,
and an image of being college bound. Individual counseling, group guidance, stress on college and
careers, and cultural enrichment opportunities were
included.   Parent involvement and cooperation was
stressed.   Students who took part in this program

showed gains in the number of courses they passed, academic averages, high school class rank, IQ scores, behavior, and attendance. Sixty-five New York City schools as well as schools from other cities adopted the Higher Horizons Program.

8053.   Society of State Directors of Health, Physical Education, and Recreation. "A Statement on Junior High School Athletics." Springfield, Ill., 1951. Distributed by State Superintendent of Public Instruction, 1961.

National educational organizations and prominent educators describe here their athletic policies for 12-to-15-year-old boys and girls. The Society of State Directors of Health, Physical Education and Recreation vigorously emphasizes the danger of a highly organized athletic program as becoming the tail that wags the dog. Stressing the importance of protecting the health and welfare of the relatively immature students in junior high school athletic programs, it states that competitive athletic activities must be appropriate to the age level of 12 to 15 years.

8054.   Toepfer, C. F., Jr. Intramural and Interscholastic Athletics: Priorities for the Middle Grades. Dissemination Services on the Middle Grades, vol. 4, no. 8. Springfield, Mass.: Educational Leadership Institute, 1973.

Discusses the athletic program within a middle school philosophy.

8055.   University of Michigan, Survey Research Center. "Adolescent Girls: A Nationwide Study of Girls Between 11 and 18 Years of Age." Ann Arbor, Mich., 1957.

This study done for Girl Scouts of the United States of America presents sections on the hopes and fears girls live with, future plans and aspirations, the family setting, friendship and dating patterns, activities and interests, group membership, non-members, and some contrasts between boys and girls. It could be of help in planning middle school and junior high curriculum and activities for girls of this age.

8056.   Watkins, J. H. "Intramurals in the junior high school." American Association of Health, Physical Education and Recreation Journal, 21(1950):28-82.

Stresses that intramural rather than interscholastic sports should be part of a junior high school program and that intramurals should be part of the school day for boys and girls.

8057.   Williamson, E. G. "The extra curriculum in general education." In General Education, 51st Yearbook of the National Society for the Study of Education, Part I, p. 241. Chicago: University of Chicago Press, 1952.

Teachers and other school leaders typically have taken the position that the goal of extracurricular activities is the student's personal development as a human being in a democratic society. Author suggests that like the curriculum, extracurricular activities have not only a personal value but a social value as well.

8058.   Yinger, J. M., Ikeda, K., Laycock, F., and Cutler, S. J. Middle Start--An Experiment in the Educational Enrichment of Young Adolescents. Cambridge: Cambridge University Press, 1977.

This book discusses an experimental program designed to discover whether a summer of intensive academic work in recreation on a college campus would help the educational performance of economically disadvantaged 13-year-olds. For three summers, sixty-five children in the experimental group and sixty-five in the control group were selected randomly from schools in three small towns and two large communities. These two groups were carefully matched, and they were supported by a follow-up program during their high school years. The results were assessed in six areas: persistence in school, junior high school grades, senior high school grades, achievement test scores, assignment to a special school track, and attendance at academic or other special schools. On these six measures, the performance of experimental pupils was judged superior to that of their matched control partners. Many such experimental programs in the past have dealt with preschool and early grade school children. The results of Middle Start indicate that even in the middle years of schooling, inner-city children, both minorities and whites, can be helped significantly by skillful educational intervention. The book explores this theme in the following chapters: 1) The Sources of Academic Achievement: Theoretical Perspective (approaches to the study of human behavior, literature on education intervention). 2) Methods of the Middle Start Program (origins of the Overland College Special Opportunity Program, selection procedures, research design, the role of matching and sociological experiments, measures of initial and long-term impact, summary of procedures). 3) Background of the Middle Starters (the experimental group). 4) Testing a

Hypothesis by Matched Pairs (estimation of missing information, effect of the program on academic achievement, multiple classification analysis).   5) Toward educational enrichment (summary of empirical findings, lessons from the Middle Start program).

9

Policy Analyses Concerning Schools for Early Adolescents

9001.   Adcock, D. and Cooper, C. "Junior High Task Force Report--A Critique of the Junior High Program including Curriculum, Organization, and Staffing." School District 4J, 200 N. Monroe St., Eugene, Oreg. 97402, January 25, 1980.

Despite handicaps created by an incomplete district-required curriculum, the presence of two sets of clients (seventh and eighth grades who are not under graduation requirements and ninth graders who are), a restrictive traditional structure based on the Carnegie Unit of credit, and the difficult nature of the transescent learner, individual schools already have on their own initiative implemented many of the recommendations in this booklet.   Sections of the booklet are: 1) The Charge.   2) The Process.   3) The Unique Client.   4) Program Implications/Curriculum Design Components.   5) Present Junior High Program. 6) Recommendations.   7) Budgets.   8) District Norms and Appeals.   The study critiques the district junior high school program, including organization and staffing.

9002.   Berkeley Unified School District, Calif. Integrated Quality Education: A Study of Educational Parks and Other Alternatives for Urban Needs. Washington, D.C.: Office of Education, Bureau of Elementary and Secondary Education, ERIC Doc. ED 024 127, July, 1968.

Describes the Berkeley search for a permanent solution to the problem of maintaining racial heterogeneity and educational quality in its school system.   Sections in this report include: 1) Historical Background and Characteristics.   2) Elementary School Integration.

3) The Plan for Integration. 4) The Long-Range Planning. 5) Present Plan. 6) Conclusions. The book describes the long-range planning of an educational park complex and a prototype model of the middle school, grades 4-8, as part of that complex.

9003.   Booth, W., Ham, I., Hill, R., Johnson, H., Matthews, L., and Pierce, L.   "School Organization Patterns: The Educational Park. The Middle School-- Project Design."   Interagency Planning for Urban Educational Needs, no. 33. Fresno, Calif.: Fresno City Unified School District, ERIC Doc. ED 038 771, June, 1969.

This study was part of a two-year project to develop a long-range master plan of education for the Fresno City Unified School District in California. Year one focused on assessing current and projected needs in the urban area served by the Fresno City Schools. Year two focused on generating and evaluating practical alternate solutions and designing short-term, intermediate, and long-range recommendations. The research reported here concerns the educational park and the middle school concepts. The study suggests that the use of the educational park facilitates racial integration, improves efficiency and productivity, and increases facility utilization. It also recommends that the Fresno schools seriously consider adopting an organizational pattern containing middle schools. Many of the recent innovative trends in Fresno would be further facilitated if the district would adopt the middle school concept. Sections of the study include: 1) Educational Park--a Debatable Definition. 2) The Educational Park--Why? 3) The Educational Park Feasibility for Fresno. 4) Bibliography of the Educational Park. 5) The Middle School --Some Questions. 6) The History of Educational Organizational Patterns. 7) Middle Schools--A Definition. 8) Rationale for the Middle School. A current middle school, according to the study, had a number of innovations including team teaching, flexible scheduling, individualized instruction, independent study, and open-space facilities. The middle school had these advantages: 1) greater ability to cope with the variability of the in-between age groups, 2) ability to use different curricular approaches unrestricted by ninth grade scheduling or rigid departmentalization, 3) newness, which encourages experimentation with a variety of approaches to instruction, 4) a greater variety of facilities, services, teachers, and activities because of the nonrestrictive curriculum, and 5) a blending of elementary and secondary practices and teacher attitudes.

9004.   Buchmiller, A. A. and Teitel, M. "A Working Paper
on Problems of Racial Imbalance in Schools." Washington, D.C.:   Office of Education, ERIC Doc. ED 016 696,
May, 1966.

This analysis of northern de facto school segregation
and racial imbalance reviews the legal issues and
court decisions germane to desegregation efforts.   Six
basic plans to alleviate racial imbalance are rezon-
ing, open enrollment, busing, controlled balance
involving a specified racial percentage, site selection, and school reorganization.   An example of a
school reorganization plan is the 4-4-4 proposal
recommended in the Allen Report in New York state.
Often within this new grade reorganization scheme,
scholastic remediation and cultural enrichment is
needed.

9005.   Burt, C. W. "High school just for freshmen reduces
discipline problems." Nation's Schools, July 1965:27.

Discusses a district which is very pleased with the
8-1-3 organization.

9006.   Calvert County Board of Education. "Middle Schools
of Calvert County, Maryland: Programs and Options."
Dares Beach Rd., Prince Frederick, Md. 20678,
November, 1979.

Booklet has sections on the middle school, sixth grade
program, seventh grade program, eighth grade program,
revision in middle school programs, and guidance and
testing.   Subsections cover developmental reading,
social studies, mathematics, science, foreign language, physical education and health, general music,
instrumental music, industrial arts/home arts, special
reading instruction, outdoor education, and special
education.

9007.   Commonwealth of Virginia, Department of Education,
Middle School Advisory Committee. "Guidelines for
Middle Schools in Virginia." Working Committee Fourth
Tentative Draft.   P. O. Box 60, Richmond, Va. 23216,
February, 1980.

The Virginia Department of Education appointed a
statewide advisory committee to develop guidelines for
middle schools, setting forth program goals and
activities for early adolescents.   Report includes
sections on rationale, goals and objectives, organizational patterns, educational program, student
services, program, health, library and media, special
education, gifted and talented, staffing, evaluation,
and a selected bibliography.

9008.   Dearborn Public Schools, Mich., Division of Instructional Services. "Report of the Committee to Study the Four-Year High School." Dearborn, Mich., June, 1979.

Booklet includes an appendix containing the Middle School Research Committee report reviewing advantages, disadvantages and concerns, research, and guidelines for the middle school. The report discusses sixteen characteristics of the middle schools: continuous progress, multimaterial approach, flexible schedules, social experiences, physical experiences and intramural activities, team teaching, planned gradualism, exploratory and enrichment studies, guidance services, independent study, basic skill repair and extension, creative experiences, evaluation, community relations, student services, and auxiliary staffing. The committee concluded that it would be possible to adopt a middle school program in Dearborn and recommended guidelines for 1) sixth, seventh, and eighth grade required subjects, 2) elective classes, 3) grouping and teaming, 4) extracurricular activities, and 5) one counselor.

9009.   Division of Instructional Learning Systems, West Virginia Department of Education. "Standards for Middle Childhood Educational Programs in West Virginia." Charleston, W. Va., 1978.

Booklet has sections on a rationale for middle childhood educational programs, a needs assessment, curriculum, instruction, staffing, program management, evaluation, communication, facilities, and funding.

9010.   Donovan, B. "Action for Excellence." New York: New York City Public Schools, 1966.

Contains recommendations of the Superintendent of Schools to the Board of Education on grade level reorganization of the New York schools.

9011.   Fairfield Public Schools. "Report and Recommendations of the Junior High School Task Force to the Board of Education." Fairfield, Conn., May 17, 1977.

This task force identified thirteen needs of the preadolescent: 1) to develop the basic skills and knowledge necessary for academic and career success, 2) to understand and accept their physique and rate of development, 3) to constructively direct the high degree of energy typical of this age group, 4) to develop close cooperative relationships among peers, staff, and parents, 5) to cope with peer pressure and the need for peer approval, 6) to develop a system of values and clarify values, 7) to develop decision-making skills, 8) to achieve recognition, 9) to develop leadership skills, 10) to express feelings in an accepting environment, 11) to understand and value, 12) to learn how to accept rights and responsibilities, 13) to learn in an environment where they may progress at their own rate. Recommendations of the task force included: 1) Institute significant staff development programs both within the school day through release time and at other nonschool times. 2) Develop the team concept of instruction. 3) Expand the electives program to stimulate student interest. 4) Investigate the possibility of creating more opportunities for students to channel their high energy levels. 5) Arrange for late bus programs for the junior highs. 6) Initiate a well-organized, well-coordinated parent volunteer program. 7) Employ an adult to direct after-school recreation programs. Long-range recommendations were: 1) Change from junior highs to middle schools of grades 6-8. 2) Implement the cluster concept and provide planning time for cluster teachers. 3) Attempt to improve the opportunities for students to achieve meaningful one-to-one relationships with adults. 4) Provide alternative programs to meet the needs of youngsters with varying abilities, interests, and learning styles. 5) Expand physical facilities. 6) Alter staffing and scheduling practices to provide after-school programs. Document also includes subcommittee reports on preadolescent physical growth and development, social emotional development, and intellectual development. Journal articles are cited.

9012.   Georgia State Department of Education, Division of Curriculum Services, Office of Instructional Services. "The Middle Grades in Georgia: A Position Paper." Atlanta, 1979.

Position paper has sections on a rationale for schools for the middle grades, the learner, community in the middle grades, staff, program, objectives, content and strategies, resources, evaluations, management, support services, guidance and counseling, school psychological services, social services, health services, school facilities, school food services, school transportation, media center, special education, and paraprofessionals and aides. Paper stresses that the middle grades build on the needs and interests of young people ranging in age from 10 through 14; the child, not just the program, is important, and opportunities to succeed are ensured for all students. The middle grades should also facilitate personal development and self-actualization and provide for general education with emphasis on developing a sense of inquiry, curiosity, critical thinking, and commitment to learning.

9013.   Harrison County Continuing Education Council and Teacher Education Center. "Harrison County Middle Childhood Education Training Program." Submitted to West Virginia Department of Education, 1980.

Chapter 1 includes a rationale for the beginning of middle schools in Harrison County, a state plan for out-of-level authorization, and documentation of the need for middle schools. Chapter 2 contains an overview of learner needs of 10-to-14-year-olds in Harrison County, educator needs in the county, philosophy, and educational goals. Chapter 3 discusses the needs assessment process. Chapter 4 lists objectives for middle childhood education. Chapter 5 concerns competencies to be obtained under each objective, and Chapter 6 presents six target areas of training needs. A description of the training level is included in Chapter 7, with awareness level activities, basic skill components, curriculum content components, and a rationale for the middle school. Chapter 9 deals with remediation plans, 10 with monitoring procedures, 11 with evaluation procedures, and 12 with record keeping.

9014.   Hinkley, G. "Middle school key to Shorewood vote." Milwaukee Journal, June 5, 1967.

Describes the economic necessity to build a middle school in a suburban school district and the middle school's practical and educational advantages over a junior high.

9015.   Imhof, H. E. "Declining Enrollment--A Blessing." ERIC Doc. ED 120 913, 1974.

Declining enrollment in the New York elementary schools, an innovative plan for reorganizing the schools, voter approval for some renovations, and a small addition to one building made it possible to eliminate junior high double sessions in the East Norwich Central School District. Article describes several alternative propositions presented to voters by the Board of Education. A key factor in the voters' decision was a concerted effort by the Board of Education and the District Administration to win support for the plan among staff members, students, and the community. The plan involved closing one of the three elementary schools and converting the building into a middle school, thereby freeing the former high school/junior high building for full-time use as a high school.

9016.   Larson, C. O. and Kramer, L. "A Proposal for the Sixth Grade--Ralston Middle School." Ralston, Nebr.: Ralston Board of Education, 1970.

In 1968-69, the Ralston Public School System changed
its organizational structure from K-6, 3-year junior
high, 3-year senior high to K-5, 3-year middle school,
and 4-year high school.   Paper describes the Ralston
middle school program in terms of its objectives,
organizational structure, curriculum, reasoning, and
evaluation.   It also explains the blocking and time
sequence for students.

9017.   Larson, J. C. "Middle School Evaluation--Year 1
Progress Report." Rockville, Md.:   Montgomery County
Public Schools, Department of Educational Accountabil-
ity, March, 1980.

This report evaluates program implementation in the
county's middle schools, compared to implementation in
non-middle schools, including interdisciplinary teams,
broader school programs, interdisciplinary resource
teachers, guidance and counseling, and teacher
advisory programs.   It also examines the effects on
students of the middle school program compared to the
effects of elementary and junior high programs,
including relationship with teachers and principals,
school programs and activities, opinions on grade
placements, peer social environment, and program
costs.   The report includes a middle school evaluation
design, a middle school policy statement, and a cost
analysis of middle schools compared to alternative
organizations.

9018.   Little Rock Public Schools, Jim R. Newell, President, Board of Directors.   "Reorganization of the
Little Rock Public Schools." Little Rock, Ark., May,
1978.

Pamphlet includes sections on plans for reorganization.   The school system is structured as follows:
primary schools K-3, intermediate schools 4-6, junior
high schools 7-9, and senior high schools 10-12.
Sections include advantages to students, the Board's
commitment to the community, and maps of the attendance areas.

9019.   McGuffey, C. W. (Ed.) "Educational Facilities
Survey: Atlanta Public Schools, 1971-81."   Atlanta:
Atlanta Public Schools and Athens College of Educa-
tion, ERIC Doc. ED 081 077, 1972.

This study showed that developing a middle school
program in Atlanta would have significant effect on
the city's elementary and secondary school programs
and facilities.   The study determined the need for
middle school facilities throughout the school system
and recommended ways to house the middle school
program.   It also recommended changes necessary for

schools at other levels. The report produced a long-range plan that can help other school systems make effective decisions about educational facilities.

9020.   National Education Association. "De facto segregation in New York: A proposed remedy." Education USA, May 21 (1964):153-154.

Middle schools serving grades 5-8 have been suggested as a means of helping to alleviate the problems caused by segregation in New York City.

9021.   National Education Association. "New Jersey City Plans Educational Park." Education USA, November 19, (1964):45-46.

A middle school serving grades 5-8 is planned as the first step in the construction of an educational plaza in East Orange, New Jersey, to better meet the needs of preadolescents.

9022.   National School Board Association. "Pride, and how a school brought it back to a neighborhood." American School Board Journal, 157,5(1969):33-37.

In Atlanta the Board of Education constructed the city's first nongraded school for 12-to-14-year-olds (grades 6, 7, and 8) in the midst of a ghetto district. It is a well-organized, thoughtfully developed middle school that serves as a focal point for the surrounding community. It includes efficient, pleasant spaces for learning and has vandal-resistant qualities without the usual appearance of institutional indestructibility. The article presents a blueprint of this building. The school is of the community and the community owns the school. Parents, children, visitors, and friends move freely through the school with the pride that can only result from a feeling of genuine belonging. The name of the school is Coan.

9023.   New Mexico State Department of Education. "Instructional Reports: The Status of Education at the Junior High School/Middle School Level." Sante Fe, 1978.

Pamphlet describes the history and educational program of schools for early adolescents, with sections on interscholastic sports, community pressure for competitive sports, lack of alternatives, exploratory courses, individualized instruction, and preparation of staff. Report concludes: 1) Middle schools are more alike than they are different. 2) Since the beginning of the middle school movement, little progress has been made toward defining a program that better meets student needs. 3) Educators should be placing primary emphasis on programs consistent with the developmental needs of K-12 students rather than on organizational structures and labels.

9024.   New York City Board of Education.   "Action Toward Quality Integrated Education."   Brooklyn, N.Y., ERIC Doc. ED 011 539, May 8, 1964.

Solutions to the problem of segregation in the New York schools have included: 1) transferring eighth graders in ten junior high schools to more integrated high schools, 2) shifting sixth graders to the ten junior high schools, 3) pairing elementary schools under community zones, 4) changing feeder patterns, 5) instituting some district-developed rather than community zoning plans, 6) continuing free choice transfers, and 7) closing one high school and redesigning others as comprehensive high schools.   Appendices explain junior high school patterns, elementary school patterns, data sheets for community zoning, junior high school feeder pattern changes and district plans. Paper includes sections on better ethnic distribution and quality education and discusses additional services which will be supplied to primary and junior high schools.

9025.   New York City Board of Education.   "Toward Quality Integrated Education--Blueprint for Further Action. Proposals for Discussion."   Brooklyn, N.Y., ERIC Doc. ED 001 944, March 22, 1965.

After nine months of intensive study and planning beginning in May 1964, this report includes recommendations for school reorganization and quality integrated education.   It synthesizes the current New York City educational program with planned improvements and discusses the reports and studies of many committees.   A summary of the junior high school committee report's major recommendations includes the following points on school reorganization for the middle school years: 1) For reasons of logistics, create new middle schools as grade 6, 7, 8 junior high schools.   2) Try at least one 4-4 organization.   3) Maintain flexibility to adapt to needs of children and space requirements.   4) Build new junior high schools to serve Negro and Puerto Rican pupils outside their immediate areas but convenient to travel.   5) Maintain junior high schools with high concentrations of minority group pupils only to the extent that parents indicate clearly that they wish their children to attend these schools.

9026.   Nield, J. B., Ward, D. E., Duffy, S. and Napier, G. "Making the Most of the Middle School Years." Topeka: Kansas State Department of Education. (No year given.)

Handbook contains the following articles: The Objectives Most Families have in Common. The Courage to be Imperfect. Cooperation: What is it? Education for Freedom. Thoughts on Education. Basic Propositions of Individual Psychology. Meaningful Quotations Gleaned Primarily from the Writings of Rudolph Driekurs. Identifying the Goals of Children's Misbehavior. Goal Disclosure Techniques. Goals of the Vertically Oriented. The Mistaken Goals of Adults with Children. How to Recognize and Correct Teenage Misbehavior. Mistaken Goal Worksheet. But Punishment Works. Why Not Praise. Natural and Logical Consequences. Some Differences Between Logical Consequences and Punishment. Encouragement--Key to Success With Children. Understanding Encouragement. Specific Techniques for the Encouragement of Children. Roosevelt-O-Gram. What Else Can a Teacher Do To Encourage a Child. How We Can Encourage Children. The Encouragement Council. General Guidelines for Class Meetings. Models for Initial Class Meeting. Responsibilities in a School Setting. The Characteristics of the Family Constellation. Parent-Student-Teacher Conferencing. Priorities: Stages. Personal Priorities Chart.

9027.   Nolan, M. "Portland Public Schools 1950-1977." Portland, Oreg.: Portland Bureau of Planning, April, 1978.

Reviews various aspects of public education in Portland since 1950, including past enrollment trends, the current decline in enrollment, and the demographic distribution of that decline. Describes the number and physical condition of public schools in the district and cooperative programs between the city and the district. Discusses the outcome of a reorganization plan drawn up by the school board in 1970 to strengthen educational policy in the upper grades and shift to middle schools for adolescent students.

9028.   Odell, W. "Philadelphia Public Schools Educational Survey." Philadelphia: Board of Public Education, 1965.

Mixed feelings about the success of the K-6-3-3 school organization, coupled with interest in promoting racial integration, prompted consideration of a K-4-4-4 arrangement in Philadelphia. This plan represents a return to the elementary school, splitting these eight years into two schools of four years each. The first four years would generally be in a smaller neighborhood school much like a present elementary school. The second four years would be in a larger school serving more than one immediate neighborhood, using more specialization in teaching, and bringing together a more heterogeneous population of pupils.

The K-4-4-4 plan received support in a report of the special committee on nondiscrimination of the Board of Education. The committee recommended exploring the effects of the K-4-4-4 organization on pupil progress and on racial integration in connection with proposals to establish an educational park in a strategic location in the city. Conviction about the superiority of one type of organizational arrangement over others is difficult to sustain with empirical data and tends to rest on rhetoric rather than systematic research. In order to evaluate the K-4-4-4 organizational plan, the intentions and anticipated consequences should be clearly stipulated at the outset, and comparable data should be collected on achievements from both the new middle schools, grades 5-8, and existing intermediate units, grades 7-9.

9029.   Olson, J. C. "Making Desegregation Work." Pittsburgh: Pittsburgh Public Schools. Paper presented at the Annual Meeting of the American Association of School Administrators, Atlantic City, N.J., ERIC Doc. ED 126 190, February 23, 1976.

Article discusses Pittsburgh's routes to school desegregation: constructing new buildings and renovating old ones, restructuring school attendance patterns, developing innovative programs, drawing on community resources and support, and being willing to devote a lot of time and effort to a frequently unpopular cause. The report recommendes: 1) Continued open enrollment with free transportation, 2) busing students from overcrowded schools to under-enrolled schools, 3) redrawing attendance district boundaries where this would enhance racial balance, 4) pairing schools to ensure racial balance, 5) creating racially balanced attendance districts for all middle schools and all new schools, 6) racially integrating the staff in all schools and in central administration, and 7) moving rapidly toward building the great high schools. Article discusses the newly constructed, well-equipped Reizenstein Middle School as a racially balanced facility. It also describes an exploratory occupational, vocational, and technical education program which introduces students to several areas of study. The report also discusses a mental health and intergroup relations project that exemplifies cooperation and support from community organizations.

9030.   Olympia Public Schools. "The School in the Middle-- A Description of The Olympia School District's Middle School Program." Olympia, Wash., 1975.

Summarizes ideas about the education of sixth, seventh, and eighth graders. It covers suggestions from concerned citizens and interested parents, recent research from many sections of the country, and the writing of educators who deal with students of this age group. Sections describing these students discuss sixth graders, seventh graders, eighth graders, physical characteristics (size, coordination, activity, sexual maturity, and appearance), intellectual capacity (formalized thinking, basic skills, memory, creativity, and persistence), and social and emotional characteristics (acceptance and approval by peers, resentment of authority, insecurity, instability of interests, emotional reactions, and instability of values). Sections describing schools cover "the school in the middle," goals, the block program, electives, the advisory program, middle school activities programs, intramural sports, extramural sports, and interscholastic sports.

9031.   Paxson, W. M. "The Middle School Plan of the Bellevue Public Schools." Bellevue, Nebr.: Bellevue Public Schools, Office of the Superindendent, August 25, 1966.

Arguments for a change in the Bellevue Public School System to middle school are: 1) Junior high schools have copied the senior high school program rather than developing their own. 2) Ninth grade pupils, now being more advanced mentally and physically, should be in a high school program. 3) Upper elementary pupils are now advanced to the point that they are ready for some departmentalization and specialized teaching, which is more easily offered in the middle school. This type of organization would also provide a way to reduce classroom size at the elementary level in Bellevue and it would ease building requirements at that level for a year or two. Feasibility will be studied through the following committees: 1) Certification and Personnel, 2) Enrollment and Space Utilization, 3) Philosophy of the Middle School, 4) Curriculum, 5) Cocurricular Activities, 6) Maturity of Middle School Students, and 7) Transportation. The report contains a personnel opinion inventory to determine if teachers are prepared for and receptive to working in a middle school.

9032.   Pennsbury School Board. "Grade Reorganization Steering Committee Report to the Pennsbury School Board." Fallsington, Pa.: Queale & Lynch, Professional Planners, 20 N. Pennsylvania Ave., Morrisville, Pa., June 2, 1980.

Booklet discusses the report of the Steering Committee for Grade Reorganization and includes sections on background information, enrollment trends, enrollment projections, and new construction. Appendices include

Function and Scope, Building Facilities Report, Curriculum Report, Four-Day School Week Report, Enroll-
ment-Impact Report, In-service Costs, Projected Sixth
Grade Students, Transportation Report, Staffing Needs,
and Financial Report.

9033.   Philadelphia Urban League.   "Integrating Philadelphia Public Schools, A Proposal."   Philadelphia, ERIC
Doc. ED 001 047, August, 1967.

Booklet proposes ways to improve integration in the
Philadelphia Public Schools.   One idea is to
reorganize the grade systems into a primary school
(K-4), a middle school (5-8), and senior grades
(9-12).   Educational clusters would be used with three
or more schools under one administrator.   Intensive
remedial instruction and a consideration of teacher
attitudes would be important under the new system.
Educational research must be coordinated and intensified, and blacks should be considered fairly for
promotion.   Faculty should be provided with in-service
training in intergroup relations and teaching skills.
Booklet has a section on Philosophy and Goals and
separate sections on nine proposals: 1) Organizational Change, 2) Educational Clusters (including
Consolidation or Merging of School Populations, Other
Use of Existing Facilities, Capital Budgeting, Administration, Within-School Organization, and Target
Dates).   3) Educational Campus, 4) Curriculum and
Teaching Innovations (including Educational Improvement Program, Teaching Innovations, and Curriculum),
5) Instructional Supplies and Equipment (including
Libraries), 6) Educational Research, 7) Staff Placement and Promotion Policies, 8) In-service Training
and Intergroup Relations, and 9) Involving School
Personnel.

9034.   Pittsfield Public Schools. "Middle School Committee
Report." 269 First St., Pittsfield, Mass. 01201, May
1, 1980.

Report on Pittsfield middle schools discusses historical development of middle schools, local history,
rationale, goals, philosophy, organization for
instruction, team teaching, interdisciplinary curriculum, administrative organization, house/subject
reader, program of studies, provision for varying
abilities, student services, pupil behavior, pupil
reporting, extracurricular activities, and implementation procedures. The rationale of this report is that
the middle school is different from yet related to
both the elementary and the high school and should
reflect the unique nature of pre- and early adolescents.   The term "transescents" has been coined to
identify these students in transition from childhood
to adolescence.   The physical, intellectual, and

social/emotional characteristics of transescents have
been well established, but perhaps the most important
characteristic of this age group is great variation in
rate of maturation. In view of this fact, individualization is an essential prerequisite to a successful
middle school program and is a key element in this
report.

9035.   Pray, H. E. and McNamara, J. A.   "Transition to
middle school." Clearinghouse, March 1967:407-409.

Describes the change in the Van Antwerp Junior High,
Niskayuna, New York, from a 6-8 to a 5-8 organization.
Conclusions will be helpful for others moving to a
middle school arrangement: 1) A change in organization must reflect a change in functions. 2) Teachers
in grades 5 and 6 need to be specialists in subject
disciplines. 3) While competence in subject disciplines is important, one must not lose sight of the
child centered philosophy. 4) The primary task is to
meet students' individual needs for self-instruction,
self-expression, and growth. Report presents a
pattern which melds the two philosophies of junior
high school departmental, vertical organization and
elementary school horizontal organization. A graph
pictures these educational patterns. The junior high
in the article moves into the horizontal, team organization, which has these advantages: 1) Teachers tend
to know each other better. 2) Teachers know students
better. 3) A guidance counselor sits with a teaching
team during planning sessions. 4) During study pool
periods each teacher may draw out the pupils he wants
for individual or small group teaching. 5) All kinds
of flexibility in scheduling are possible. 6) Ordinarily, house plans try to break large enrollments
into more manageable groups. A transition to middle
school is more effectively accomplished when it is
understood that middle school objectives and methods
of implementation do not resemble those of high
school, elementary, or even junior high school,
because the middle school is a unique institution
appropriate for youngsters at this age and maturity.

9036.   Ramsey, M. "Declining Student Enrollment--Five Year
Plan of Action and Basic Materials Developed to Offset
the Financial Impact Due to the Decline in Student
Enrollment." Clinton, Iowa: Clinton Community
Schools, January, 1978.

One section of booklet reports on a proposed middle
school curriculum and activities program. The curriculum proposal grew out of a review of current
procedures in both the sixth grade and the junior high
school. The goals of the middle school in this community were: 1) to facilitate self-development and
self-actualization, 2) to provide general education,

including opportunities for the development of a sense of inquiry, curiosity, and commitment to learning, 3) to provide opportunities for exploration, 4) to provide individualization of instruction, 5) to improve articulation with elementary and high school programs. Sections cover an activities proposal, student government, journalism, performing arts, interscholastic activities, intramurals, cheerleading, special interest clubs and activities, summary of a proposed activity program for middle schools, and a listing of grades involved.

9037.   Rist, F. H. (Supv.) "Guidelines and Procedures for Junior High/Middle Schools." Boise: State of Idaho, Department of Education, Accreditation and Educational Audits, 1972.

Booklet contains sections on the premise of junior highs and middle schools, needs of students, responsibilities of the school, guidance and counseling, school health, special education, and other services. Guideline 1 discusses the philosophy, goals and objectives. Guideline 2 discusses educational programs. Guideline 3 concerns learning media center and records. Guideline 4 covers staffing--preparation of professional personnel, administration, counselors, teacher loads, and examples of discount formulas. Facilities are discussed in Guideline 5 and quality and improvement of educational programs in Guideline 6. Evaluation and reporting is the topic of Guideline 7.

9038.   Springfield Public Schools, Middle School Study Committee. "Proposal for the Adoption of the Middle School Concept for District 186." Springfield, Ill., March 17, 1980.

In the fall of 1980 the Springfield, Illinois, School System adopted the middle school organization. This earlier adoption proposal discusses middle school background and philosophy, proposed middle school structure, number of periods, block scheduling, team planning, teacher assignments, assignment of students to teams, assignment of noncore teachers to teams, curriculum, seventh grade program, eighth grade program, gifted program, basic skills emphasis, middle school activities programs, interscholastics, intramurals, clubs and organizations, transportation, activity coordinators, guidance and counseling, counselors, consultants, coordinators, team members, and evaluation. The final section discusses implementation of this program, including in-service and staff development, curriculum planning, industrial arts, home economics, foreign language, language arts basics, developmental reading, sustained silent reading, cost factors, and selection of students for special programs.

9039.   <u>Times Educational Supplement</u>.   "Integration in
clusters: efforts of New York City."   <u>Times Educational Supplement, 2557</u> (May 22, 1964):1421.

Early in 1964 New York State Education Commissioner
Dr. James E. Allen, Jr. announced that the New York
schools would go to a K-4-4-4 organization.   Comprehensive four-year high schools outside ethnic ghettos
would be attended by commuting students from all over
the city as well as by local residents.   The 5-8
middle schools would use shuttle buses and would offer
experience in an integrated school.   Primary units,
pre-kindergarten through 4, would be neighborhood
schools.   Two to six primary units clustered around a
middle school would form a complex with a single
administrator.   These complexes should "integrate
educational activities, include distribution of
facilities and resources, and promote communications
between faculties, parents, and students from diverse
ethnic backgrounds."

9040.   Topeka Public Schools.   "Phase III--Middle School
Implementation Task Force Report. Continuing Plans for
the Middle School."   Topeka, Kans.:   Unified School
District 501, May, 1971.

Booklet contains sections on the philosophy of
planning for middle school, goals of middle school
education in Topeka, district-wide middle school
implementation task force, and the task force subcommittees.   Includes reports on middle school
activities, curriculum, art, business education,
foreign language, home economics, industrial arts,
language arts, mathematics, music, physical education,
science, social studies.   Also contains an evaluation
of student progress, and discusses individualization
of student needs, public information, staff development, and staff profile.   Includes building reports on
four junior highs and four middle schools in this
system.   Report lists these goals of middle school
education: 1) an atmosphere and a program different
from those of the elementary and high school and
designed for the special transitional nature of the
student between childhood and adolescence, 2) flexible
scheduling which helps students adjust to the wide
variance from the self-contained elementary school to
the departmentalized high school, 3) instruction to
help each student move from the concrete operations
stage to formal operations stage of mental processes,
4) emphasis on attaining basic survivor skills in
mathematics, reading, language arts, social studies,
science, physical education, and health, and 5)
courses that enable students to explore their own
interests and to enhance their abilities in areas such
as music, art, industrial arts, home economics,
typing, and foreign language.

9041.   Torrance Unified School District.   "The Middle School Report." Torrance, Calif., 1973.

Report covers organizational goals assessment and current concerns of the middle school, such as financial implications, staffing needs, and physical needs.   A 1974 addendum includes procedures for developing a middle school course of study, the use of data processing, procedures for textbook accounting, and recommendations for resource centers, teacher-counselor programs, and minimum science facilities in middle schools.

9042.   Vredevoe, L. E.   "Let's reorganize our school system." Bulletin of the National Association of Secondary School Principals, 42,238(1958):40-44.

The author made a plea for consideration of a K-5 and 3-3-3 organization for schools in California.   His proposal offered a possible solution for the separate elementary and secondary districts prevalent in that state, thus providing more opportunities for all types of learners in both presecondary and postsecondary schools.

9043.   Wichita Public Schools.   "Final Report of the Middle School Ad Hoc Committee." Prepared by Members of the Middle School Ad Hoc Committee, Unified School District 259, Wichita, Kans., April, 1977.

This report was designed to help the Board of Education determine appropriate policies for middle years education.   It discusses objectives of the middle school, research on middle school years, use of facilities, transportation, elementary school programs, certification and staff assignments, training, vocational education, home ec, special education, pupil services, and supportive services.

9044.   Wolff, M. and Stein, A. A Plan for Middle Schools, Buffalo, New York. A Study of Sites, Organization and Program, Part III, Component 4. Final Report.   New York: Center for Urban Education, ERIC Doc. ED 085 902, March, 19.

Study attempts to plan locations, attendance areas, and organizations for middle schools to make it feasible for the Board of Education in Buffalo to eliminate racial imbalance progressively, at least from the fifth grade on. Describes ways to meet this goal, given the plant obsolescence problem and the urgent need to improve the quality of schooling at every grade level for every pupil. Sections of the book are: 1) A New Middle School Program (considerations in planning middle schools, criteria for choosing sites, metropolitan educational parks). 2) Urgent

Problem of the Buffalo Public Schools (old buildings
and new construction, old-fashioned education and new
needs, map: location of K-8 schools, keeping a good
staff).   3) De Facto School Segregation in Buffalo
(map: ethnic composition of Buffalo Public Schools).
4) The Plan: A Design for a Middle School Complex for
the City of Buffalo (structure of the middle school
complex, program design, implementing the program,
course offerings). 5) The Plan: New Middle School
Complexes for Buffalo (size and character of the
complexes, sites proposed and feeder patterns, map:
planned middle school complexes and their feeder
patterns, effect of the plan on existing middle and
junior high schools, effect on high schools, effect on
elementary schools). 6) Fillmore Middle School Complex: An Architectural Study (educational specifications, costs and transportation, map: public transportation serving Fillmore Middle School Complex,
design: the complex as a whole and detail drawing).
7) Priorities, Transportation, and Cost Considerations. 8) Conclusions.

9045.   Zdanowicz, P. J. "The Meredith G. Williams Middle
School." Educational Horizons, 41,2(1962):45-52.

Describes a middle school planned for creative teaching and learning. The organizational and curricular
changes were made in a democratic manner which provided an effective, creative experience for administration and teachers alike. Article describes the
philosphy and function of the Williams Middle School,
programs for grades 5 and 6, programs for grades 7 and
8, activity programs, articulation, and special
features of the Williams Middle School. The middle
school has these advantages: 1) Special features such
as home economics suite, shop areas, and a fully
equipped gymnasium are available for the first time to
fifth and sixth graders. 2) Special programs such as
guidance, health, speech therapy, remedial reading,
and the service of a helping teacher are also available to all children. 3) A four-year span is ample
opportunity to get to know and understand youngsters.
4) The Carnegie Unit does not limit the program. A
corollary is that electives are not as much of a
problem as they may be in a school serving pupils in
grade 9. 5) The newness of the organization encourages creativity in developing new techniques in both
administration and teaching. 6) More adequate and
modern equipment is available than could be provided
economically in neighborhood schools. 7) Seventh and
eighth grade subject matter teachers are available to
work with fifth and sixth graders. 8) Teacher morale
is excellent because teachers are not standing pat and
because innovations are put into operation gradually.

10

Research on Organizational Patterns and the Effects of Schools on Early Adolescents

10001.   Adams, C. W. "The Relationship Between the Level of Authoritarianism of Teachers and Their Perceptions of the Degree of Bureaucratic Structure of Selected Junior High Schools." Ed.D Dissertation, Mississippi State University. Dissertation Abstracts International, Order no. 7814854, 1978.

Ten public junior high schools in the state of Mississippi were used in the study, and 240 teachers participated. Results indicated a positive correlation between the level of teacher authoritarianism and the total test score and three of the six subscales of the Organizational Inventory, Part Two. The three subscales that were found significant were: 1) Hierarchy of Authority, 2) Procedural Specifications, and 3) Impersonality. The level of teacher authoritarianism was compared with the variables of teacher sex, age, and length of service in the schools. The variables were not found to be statistically significant.

10002.   Albert, N. and Beck, A. T. "Incidence of depression in early adolescence: a preliminary study." Journal of Youth and Adolescence, 4,4(1975):301-307.

Questionnaires were administered to seventh and eighth grade students in a parochial elementary school (K-8). The findings indicated that 33.3 percent of the school population was experiencing moderate to severe depression and 35 percent of the sample acknowledged current suicidal thoughts. A comparison of mean scores showed a trend toward more depressive symptoms in the eighth grade, possibly

indicating a critical developmental period. A correlation of individual scores and teacher ratings
suggests that teacher evaluation may have some direct
effect on the student's emotional health. The
authors make specific suggestions for promoting
improved mental health in a school setting.

10003.   Alexander, W. M.   "The middle school movement."
Theory Into Practice, 7(1968):114-117.

A U.S. Office of Education project determined that
there were 1,101 middle schools in the United States.
The middle school was defined as a school which combines into one organization and facility certain
school years (usually 5-8 or 6-8) which had in the
past usually been separated into elementary and
secondary schools under such plans as 6-3-3, 6-2-4,
and 6-6. The survey sought to discover: what grades
are included, recency of establishment, reasons for
the reorganization, extent of reorganization, and
implications. School districts contemplating changes
in their instructional ladder should relate the programs and organizations of new schools to educational
purposes and pupil populations. If care is not taken
now, the middle school movement soon may be like the
junior high--simply another instance of moving down
an organization developed for an older population.
With proper planning and programs designed for training rather than transplanting personnel, the middle
school movement can be made an effective step in
educational improvement, but this study indicates
that it may already be too late to seek and attain
this result.

10004.   Anderson, J. G.   "Strategies of control and their
effects on instruction." Journal of Research and
Development in Education, 9,1(1975):115-122.

Organizational control strategies used in the schools
studied were found to directly affect the teacher's
instructional role. A random sample of 170 teachers
in ten junior high schools in an eastern metropolitan
school district was analyzed by questionnaire.
Teachers responded to increased control over the
performance of their instructional duties by spending
less time with individual students and by making less
of an attempt to adapt instructional practices to
individual students. They also did not use a variety
of approaches in the classroom or try new techniques
for teaching. The research also determined that as
the school grows in size, bureaucratic control inten-
sifies, and the composition of the student body also
affects the school's internal structure and the
teacher's instructional role. School administrators
should be aware of the unintended negative effects

that result from the imposition of bureaucratic instructional rules.

10005.   Andriette, W. R.   "Differences in Retention Between Populations of Seventh Grade Science Students Taught by Two Methods of Instruction: Small Group Laboratory and Teacher Demonstration."   Ph.D. Dissertation, Syracuse University. University Microfilms, Ann Arbor, Mich., and ERIC Doc. ED 084 078, 1970.

The study compared two methods: 1) teacher demonstration where the students observed all science activities, and 2) student laboratory where individually or in small groups the students helped plan and carry out science activities.   The Taxonomy of Educational Objectives (Cognitive Domain) was used as the basis for developing and measuring the techniques used with 133 above average seventh grade students. Students were given pretests and unannounced posttests.   Comprehension learning was significantly greater for the teacher demonstration group, yet no significant differences between methods were found in a specific unit on light in the science classes.   The percentage of comprehension learning retained was found to be significantly greater than the knowledge learning retained.   See ERIC Abstract #ED 084 078.

10006.   Arends, R. H. and Ford, P. M.   "Acceleration and Enrichment in the Junior High School.   A Follow-up Study."   Olympia: Washington Office of the State Superintendent of Public Instruction, ERIC Doc. ED 001 220, July, 1964.

Students in the program of acceleration and enrichment performed in a manner consistently superior to their peers on standardized tests.   The program was especially strong in mathematics and weakest in science.   Such a program of acceleration and enrichment for the academically talented student did not produce a beneficial atmosphere for the average student.   Problems considered were: 1) What conclusions could be obtained concerning the positive effects of acceleration and enrichment for the academically talented student?   2) Did such a program produce a school atmosphere beneficial to average students?   3) What difference was there from one school district to another regarding the performance of academically gifted students, or do the attitudes of students in a school with a program of acceleration and enrichment differ from those in any other school?   The California Test of Mental Maturity was given and questionnaires were used with teachers and students in two studies--1962-63 and 1963-64.

10007.   Arlin, M.   "The interaction of locus of control, classroom structure, and pupil satisfaction."   Psychology in the Schools, 12,3(1975):279-286.

The study compared pupil attitudes in open and structured classrooms and sought to answer these questions: "What kinds of pupils enjoy open environments, and what kinds of pupils enjoy structured environments?"   Six hundred and sixty-six students in grades 4, 6, and 8 in open and traditional classrooms were subjects.   Locus of control as measured by the Intellectual Achievement Responsibility Scale (IAR) appeared to offer promise as a psychological trait that mediates pupil satisfaction and educational environment.   Females profiting more from open education is an example of main effect (sex) obscuring a significant interaction effect, namely the special attitude pattern revealed by internal males.   The research offered an excellent example of a situation in which the main effects of two competing kinds of educational treatment, open and structured, were obscured, or possibly overlooked entirely, without considering the function of a psychological variable.

10008.   Athey, I. J. and Holmes, J. A.   "Reading Success and Personality Value-Systems Syndrome: A Thirty-Year Then and Now Study at the Junior High School Level.   Final Report."   Washington, D.C.:   U. S. Department of Health, Education and Welfare, ERIC Doc. ED 026 547, 1967.

Combining Erikson's theory on the development of a healthy personality and Holmes' theory of reading, the authors contributed specified personality characteristics to reading success and validated their findings.   Three phases were used in the study: the construction of new skills composed of personality items which significantly differentiated good and poor readers at the ninth grade level in 1936, a longitudinal application of these skills to the same sample of students when they were seventh and eighth and ninth graders in 1933 and 1934, and a cross-sectional replication thirty years later.   Specific personality characteristics suggested from the integrated Erikson-Holmes theory were consistently related to reading in the seventh, eighth, and ninth grades.

10009.   Backer, R., et al.   "Individual Development Program.   A Humanizing Ungraded Program for Alienated Youth."   Greenwich, Conn.:   Greenwich Public Schools, ERIC Doc. ED 001 528, July, 1964.

A flexible program was initiated to deal with academic and human deterioration of students. Individual development students were compared with a matched control group from regular cases. The control group did not improve and often showed further deterioration. The underachieving program students of high and low ability and of low motivation showed achievement, both individually and as a group. The program was designed so that over a period of time the quality of material presented would produce meaningful results in human development and achievement. Cooperative teaching was used as an interdisciplinary approach to give continuity and meaning to the program. Students chose reading which was of interest to them and served as a basis for meaningful discussions. Intellectual nourishment was aimed primarily at fact or skill acquisition. This booklet contains sections on the fundamental concepts and program development, learning, processes of instruction, pupil reporting, selection and placement, characteristics of the students, the idea of the program, goals, plans, curriculum, pupil reporting and records, total school involvement, outcomes of the program, use of test information, student and parent reaction, teacher evaluation, program development, recommendations, improving evaluation, improving communications, contrast in individualized instruction, semi-program materials, experimental English activity units, cultural enrichment, scheduling for an individual development program, and discussion of the national problem.

10010.   Baker, L. G. "A Study of Selected Variables in a Change From a Junior High Organization to a Middle School Organization." Ph.D. Dissertation, Syracuse University, 1972.

A suburban school system in New York was reorganized from a K-6, 7-9, 10-12 to K-5, 6-8, 9-12. Children in grades 6, 7, and 8 and certificated staff members directly involved in their instruction were studied prior to reorganization and immediately thereafter. The Science Research Associates Achievement Test was administered to pupils. Differences in pupil intelligence were measured by the Lorge-Thorndike Intelligence Test. Pupils in the middle school organization appeared to have better mental health, an improved attitude toward school, themselves, and others, and higher academic achievement. Pupil intelligence remained constant with no significant change in IQ scores. The results of the study also provided evidence of improved attitudes of teachers.

10011.   Barrow, L. H. "A study of seventh graders' comprehensions of human reproduction concepts." Journal of School Health, 47,2(1977):119-121.

This study in an Iowa junior high school revealed that 1) knowledge levels of seventh grade pupils were raised after studying human reproduction, and 2) pupils thought that human reproduction should be included in life science classes. See ERIC Abstract #EJ 165 014.

10012.   Baruchin, F. "A Comparative Study of Transitional Grades with Middle and Traditional School Types in Upstate New York." Dissertation, State University of New York, Buffalo, 1971.

The study attempted to answer the following questions: 1) What reasons do school districts in New York give when asked why they had adopted the middle school? 2) What are the organizational characteristics, instructional programs, administrative practices, and staffing factors of New York middle schools? 3) How do the programs and practices of middle schools compare with the programs and practices for transitional youngsters (grades 5 to 8) in traditional schools? 4) Are the middle schools more innovative in their educational programs than traditional schools? The data indicated overwhelmingly that middle schools are generally more innovative than traditional units. But most of the differences in favor of middle schools were reported for grades 7 and 8. The differences do not distinctly favor either middle schools or traditional schools at the fifth or sixth grade levels.

10013.   Baur, M. S. "Truancy: An Examination of Social Structural Influences and Traditional Approaches." Ph.D. Dissertation, University of Colorado, Boulder, 1976.

This research tested the basic assumptions of many school and community policies dealing with truancy: truants are social isolates, youngsters from unhappy homes, poor students. To identify other variables related to truancy, and to investigate the effects of school social structure on truancy, a survey questionnaire was given to 941 junior high school students in three schools. The schools were ranked according to the extent to which their social structures helped or hindered truancy. The policies and practices were identified by interviews with school personnel and community youth workers. The school having the social structures most permissive of truancy had significantly higher rates of self-reported truancy than the other schools. Students who strongly agreed that regular attendance at school was important reported more truancy in their school than was reported in the others. Some educators believed that students liked school better if there were open attendance policies. But, at the schools having the most open policies, fewer students liked school in comparison to students at the other schools. Also, students in the more open school were more likely to believe that teachers did not care about students or care whether students attended. Therefore, traditional assumptions about causes of truancy were in general not supported by the data. Truancy was not related to social isolation, and unhappy homes were related to truancy only for students whose parents had been officially notified. A low grade point average was found to be related to frequent truancy.

10014.   Billings, R. G.   "A Comparative Study of the Relationship Between Administrative Organizational Leadership Patterns in Two Middle Schools and the Use of Educational Learning Resources."   Ph.D. Dissertation, Wayne State University.   Dissertation Abstracts International, 36 (5-A), 2520.   Order no. 75-25,224, 1975.

Two middle schools were analyzed: one used management team leadership where the school's administrators shared equally in its operation; the second employed the traditional pattern of a principal and three assistant principals.   Both organizational patterns for leadership in the two middle schools promoted the use of educational learning resources. A management team middle school was more positive toward the use of educational learning resources and promoted consistent use.   The following types of environment are needed to encourage teachers to use educational learning resources: 1) open attitude of middle school administrators, 2) creative atmosphere, 3) flexibility, 4) the need for individualized programs, 5) teachers and administrators working as a team, 6) professionalism, 7) support of independent study by students, 8) support the use of small houses for administrative units, 9) the availability of administrators to teachers, 10) the involvement of teachers in curriculum design, 11) the need for support services such as the media center, and 12) a curriculum which offers freedom of choice for students.

10015.   Bishop, W. J.   "A Study to Determine Alternative Approaches for Administering a Curriculum for Adolescents, Ages 12-14."   Ed.D Dissertation, University of Alabama.   Dissertation Abstracts International, Order no. 7819161, 1978.

Successful programs were identified and classified. Student characteristics were examined and inferences drawn for desirable curriculum planning, school organization, and administrative procedures.   Educators must depart from the textbook to improve understanding of the student, plan innovative approaches

for meeting needs, and build a flexible school program that will nourish personal as well as academic
goals.   A questionnaire allowed 843 students,
teachers, and parents of students in grades 6 though
8 to indicate their curriculum choices for the
Birmingham, Alabama, public schools.   Each of the
three groups chose career education, field trips, and
exploratory courses as three of the five items they
wanted incorporated into the school program.   Students chose the school newspaper and the skill
exchange; parents were more interested in the areas
of leadership and study skills; teachers shared the
interest in study skills along with school volunteers, enrichment courses, and information seminars.

10016.   Blakslee, R. W.   "Research on the Use of a Counselee Problem Classification Plan at the Junior High
Level."   ERIC Doc. ED 011 670, 1967.

A school counselor developed a classification plan
for confidential records to help counselors save time
and to have a useful summary at the end of the year.
The categories consisted of: 1) two major problem
areas--information giving and personal emotion, 2)
six stimulus categories--self-understanding, environmental understanding, self-conflict, others-conflict,
academic difficulties, general, and 3) the referral
categories--self, teacher, administrator, parent,
friend, and counselor.   Two hundred and six
individual counseling sessions were studied at Hood
Memorial Junior High School.   A counselee problem
classification plan can greatly assist the amount of
information that a counselor can acquire relative to
his student population.   The findings of the study
suggest these possibilities: 1) The counselee
problem classification plan can be a useful device
for helping school counselors understand the types of
counseling problems confronting them at the junior
high level.   2) The junior high student experiences
many personal emotional problems which require a
great deal of this type of counseling, indicating a
need for a trained counselor.   3) Students of this
level experience many conflicts with others, such as
teachers, parents and students.   4) The problem of
self-conflicts and the lack of self-understanding are
important concerns of the junior high level. 5) Boys
experience more academic difficulties at this level
than girls.   6) More males seek individual counseling, but more females seek counseling in groups.   7)
The large majority of counselees are self-referrals.
8) A majority of the counseling sessions last less
than 30 minutes.   9) Sessions requiring more than 30
minutes tend to be personal and emotional in nature.
10) Eighth grade students demand more of a counsel-
or's time than seventh grade students because eighth
graders need educational and vocational planning.

10017.   Blyth, D. A.   "Continuities and Discontinuities
During the Transition into Adolescence: A Longitudinal Comparison of Two School Structures."   Ph.D.
Dissertation, University of Minnesota.   Order no.
77-18,958, 1977.

The present study explores the extent to which variations in several social psychological and behavioral
characteristics are a function of the educational
system the student was in.   One system (that of a K-8
school), provides minimal differentiation between
sixth and seventh grade; while the second system
(that of a K-6 school and its associated junior
high), provides two separate types of schools.
Students in the two school systems are compared at
both the sixth and seventh grade level as well as
longitudinally.   The focus is on the student's behaviors, values, self-esteem, and perception of other's
expectations.

Sixth grade students were selected by means of a
stratified random sample of 18 Milwaukee Public
Schools (6 K-8 and 12 K-6).   All sixth graders in the
sampled schools were invited to participate with 924
(82%) doing so.   Eighty-six percent of the sixth
grade participants were followed-up during seventh
grade.   This thesis is based on 329 white students
who were randomly selected to be measured early in
the school year.

The results indicate that those students who went
into the junior highs perceived a high degree of
anonymity, a significant increase in victimization, a
marked decrease in participation in extracurricular
activities, and a continued emphasis on competence.

10018.   Blyth, D. A., Simmons, R. G., and Bush, D.   "The
transition into early adolescence: a longitudinal
comparison of youth in two educational contexts."
Sociology of Education, 51(1978):149-162.

Because many school systems have gone from an 8-4
grade pattern to the more popular 6-3-3 or 6-6
educational system, and because of the increasing
interest in the type of school appropriate for early
adolescents, this study reports results of a longitudinal study of sixth graders.   The research
investigates how two different types of school grade
level organization affect the social and psychological development of youth as they enter adolescence.
In particular, the authors compare the school organization of kindergarten through eighth grade, which
provides minimal differentiation between sixth and
seventh grade, with kindergarten through sixth grade
elementary schools and associated junior high
schools, which provide two separate schools with

radically different age compositions and structures for sixth and seventh graders. Differential changes between sixth and seventh grade in the student's self-esteem, participation in extracurricular activities, dating, anonymity, and victimization experiences are presented and discussed in light of the different seventh-grade environments. Answers to two basic questions are sought: 1) How is the social and psychological development of sixth grade students affected, if at all, by the differences in the grade level organization of the school? 2) Are there differences in the nature or amount of change which students in the two types of school organizations experience as they make the transition into seventh grade? That is, does the type of school structure a student goes through result in differential amounts of change in any of the five areas of social and psychological development selected for study? The transition into seventh grade within two different educational contexts lead to a number of outcomes. First, even in the sixth grade, students in both contexts experienced different types of behavior and had different values. Second, the females going into the junior highs experience a loss in self-esteem while all others gain in self-esteem between sixth and seventh grade. Third, males in the junior highs are much more likely to be victimized. Finally, students in the junior highs experienced a higher degree of anonymity than those in the K-8 schools. This report is the first in a five-year longitudinal study exploring school structure effects.

10019. Blyth, D. A., Thiel, K. S., Bush, D. M., and Simmons, R. G. "Another look at school crime: student as victim." Youth and Society, 11,3(1980): 369-388.

The authors focus on the victimization experiences of seventh grade students in two different types of schools: K-8 elementary schools and 7-9 junior high schools. They explore some social and psychological characteristics of victims and nonvictims. Using only junior high students, the authors assess some of the impacts of victimization experiences and victimizing environments on the attitudes of early adolescents. As part of a larger longitudinal study dealing with transition into early adolescence, data were collected on the victimization experiences of white and black seventh grade students. Information on students' victimization experiences in or around schools was gained by asking students three sets of parallel questions about any instances of threats, thefts, or beatings that they have experienced since the beginning of seventh grade: 1) Since you started seventh grade, has anyone threatened to beat you up or hurt you if you did not give them your money or something else that belonged to you? 2) Since you started seventh grade, has anything that cost more than a dollar been stolen from your desk or locker when you weren't around? 3) Since you started seventh grade, has anyone actually beaten you up or hurt you? Students were then divided into victims and nonvictims based on whether they had experienced incidents of different types. Information was also gained on the students' self-esteem, perception of danger, and perception of anonymity. Over 34 percent of the seventh grade students in the sample of 321 experienced at least one incident of victimization between early September and late November during the school year studied. When the students are separated by school type, the researchers found that the rate of victimization for seventh graders in the K-8 schools was only 24.3 percent compared to 39.3 percent for seventh graders in the junior high schools. The differences between school types was primarily a function of thefts and threats and might be due to the number of older peers existing in these two different types of schools.

10020.   Bondi, J. and Wiles, J. "What do middle school students value?" Middle School Journal, 10(1979): 4-5.

During in-service workshops conducted by the authors, teachers were asked to give a value survey to middle school pupils. The instrument asked students to rank the following values: a comfortable life, equality, family security, self-respect, sense of accomplishment, freedom, happiness, true friendship, exciting life, world at peace, and good education. The survey was administered to over five thousand middle school students (grades 5-8) in Pinellas County, Florida. The first choice of almost every group of students was family security. When middle school teachers were asked to rank the same values, they too listed family security as their first choice. Freedom was ranked second for both groups, and exciting life ranked last among the values rated. The results of this study challenge much of the literature on pre- and emerging adolescent learners which shows movement of youngsters away from adult influence toward a dominant peer influence. Reviewers of such literature have the impression that middle school students have no strong ties to parents or other adults and simply want to follow the whims of their peer group.

10021.   Bondi, J. C. and Tocco, T. S. "The Nature of the Transescent as It Affects Middle School Program Evaluation." Paper presented at the Annual Meeting of the American Educational Research Association, April, 1974.

Transescence is marked not only by disruptive acceleration in physical development and physiological
change, but also by emotional and social pressures
resulting from the transfer of authority from the
family to the peer group. At no time are differences
in the physical, social, emotional, and intellectual
development of youngsters greater than during the
middle years, 10 to 14 years of age. To get an
understanding of the middle school student, this
report looks closely at each area of development.

10022.   Bonekemper, H. G.   "Perceptions of Teaching
Behavior by Middle School Teachers and Pupils in an
Open Education Setting." Dissertation Abstracts
International, 35 (4-A), 1861-1862, 1974.

The purpose of this study was to analyze critical
incidents reported by participating teachers and
requirements for effective teaching in an open
education setting. The critical incident technique
used in the study was developed by John C. Flanagan.
The twenty-four middle school teachers and pupils
reported 398 critical incidents in one middle school.
Critical requirements were found in three major
areas: interaction with the pupil on an individual
basis, preparation of materials for the learning
environment, and facilitation of learning in a group
situation. The largest number of effective and
ineffective behavior incidents reported by teachers
was in the area of interaction with the pupil on an
individual basis. All the assumptions concerning the
task of the teacher in an open setting as a facilitator of learning were confirmed by the findings in
this study. Additional investigation should look
into pre-service and in-service preparations for
teachers in an open setting. Recommendations
included: 1) a detailed understanding by the teacher
of the emotional, intellectual, physical, psychological, and social characteristics of the middle
school pupils, 2) training in tutorial instruction,
3) competency in the use and preparation of audiovisual materials and equipment, 4) ability to use the
local community as a learning resource, 5) active
involvement in small group learning tasks, and 6)
ability to assist the student to relate his individual tasks to the group goal.

10023.   Bonnar, C. F. and Hutson, P. W. "Recognition of
the variation of maturity of pupils in six-year high
schools." Bulletin of the National Association of
Secondary School Principals, 38(1954):108-116.

A tabular analysis of instructional and other provisions in the different grades of six-year schools
discloses frequent neglect of the needs of pupils in
grades 7-9.

10024.   Bosher, W. C., Jr.   "The Effects of Two Methods of
Instruction on the Self-Concept and English/Language
Arts Achievement of Middle School Students."   Ed.D.
Dissertation, University of Virginia.   University
Microfilms, Ann Arbor, Mich., and ERIC Doc. ED 099
869, 1974.

One instructional method did not include the usual
constraints--grades, tests, homogeneous grouping,
grade level grouping, and assigned homework, but the
second method did.   After 150 teaching days, the Self
Social Symbols Tasks and Sequential Tests of Educational Progress were administered to the seventh and
eighth grade students in the study.   The author concluded: 1) Students who functioned without the constraints had significantly greater academic gain.   2)
Neither method of instruction affected self-concept.
3) Males and females were affected equally despite
the method.   4) Black students in an experimental
group gained significantly greater egocentricity, but
a control group of black students had a greater gain
in self-esteem.   5) No significant differences were
found between the gains of heterogeneously grouped
seventh and eighth grade students.   See ERIC Abstract
#ED 099 869.

10025.   Briskin, A. S.   "Developmental Stage Theory and
Drug Abuse Education."   Paper presented at the Annual
Meeting of the American Educational Research Associa-
tion, Washington, D.C., March 30-April 3, 1975.

The planned research was to intervene in the developmental period of transition from concrete to formal
operational thinking (ages 11 and 12) to assist movement to the next stages of psychological development
which should result in the youth choosing in the
future to regulate drug use.   The author gives an
overall view of psychological stage development, a
general review of the literature pertaining to
preventative programs in drug abuse education, a
description of the research design, and a statement
of expected research outcomes.   Within the theoretical discussion of stage theory are sections on the
concept of stage, developing readiness for self-
awareness, preferred modes of interaction, and a
description of stage development.   Also included are
sections on triggering self-awareness, behavioral
patterns indicating achievement of self-awareness,
and the relationship between theory and research.
The curriculum consisted of the following six units:
1) Drugs: Yesterday and Today.   2) Drug Effects on
Body Systems.   3) Psychological and Sociological
Factors Influencing Drug Decisions.   4) Drug Misuse.
5) Legal Implications of Drug Use.   6) Natural, Non-
drug Highs.   Expected research outcomes included: 1)
Students who achieve higher stage development choose

to regulate drug use, avoiding drug abuse. 2) If broad intervention can facilitate stage development, then it will correspondingly have a long-term effect on drug use patterns. 3) There will be no score differences on dependent variables among students who participate in any of the experimental curriculum conditions. 4) There will be no score differences on dependent variables between students participating in four experimental conditions and students participating in a control curriculum. 5) The intervention program will show greater effect on the change in scores on the "Who am I?" survey which rates self-insight development than on the six-stage psychological development scale. 6) Parent involvement in the evening parent program will result in higher student scores on three dependent variable measures.

10026.   Broadhead, F. C. "Pupil adjustment in the semi-departmental elementary school." Elementary School Journal, 60(1960):385-390.

Study indicated pupils adjust well to the semidepartmental upper elementary school.

10027.   Brooks, K. "The middle school, a national survey: part I--establishment and administration." Middle School Journal, February 1978:6-9.

During 1977, a national survey was conducted to determine the status of the middle school movement. A similar project had been directed by William Alexander a decade earlier. This article contains Part I --Establishment and Administration; Part II--Staffing and Curriculum follows in bibliographic entry 10028. The study began with an identification of the middle schools in operation. The definition used for a middle school was that used by Alexander: "a school serving at least three grades, no more than five grades, and including grades 6 and 7." A major difficulty with middle schools from the outset has been a common definition. Each state department provided a listing of schools including the essential information needed to identify those meeting the definition. The precision of the identification process is a function of the quality of state department data. A total of 4,060 middle schools were operating in 1977. The number of schools has grown significantly in every state except Nebraska, and the District of Columbia had none. The more populous states--Texas, Florida, Illinois, Michigan, New York, Ohio, Pennsylvania, and Virginia--account for over half of the middle schools. Middle schools ranged in enrollment from fewer than two hundred pupils to over two thousand. The majority of schools ranged from four hundred to eight hundred with more than half having fewer than seven hundred pupils. The reasons for establishing middle schools included: 1) to bridge the gap from elementary to high school more effectively, 2) to provide a program tailored to the needs of the early adolescent, and 3) to eliminate overcrowding. Middle school principals surveyed were predominantly male, only 6 percent were female. Administrative problem areas were these: 1) teachers resisting change, 2) teachers inadequately oriented to the school philosophy, 3) articulation between middle schools and high schools, 4) lack of finances for this type of program, 5) lack of time for evaluation of changes, 6) articulation between elementary schools and middle schools, 7) lack of materials and supplies needed for individualized instruction, 8) inadequate physical plant, 9) insufficient planning time prior to new programs, 10) development of flexible scheduling, 11) insufficient materials to implement the designed programs, 12) scheduling of individual students.

10028.   Brooks, K. "The middle school, a national survey: part II--staffing and curriculum." Middle School Journal, 9,2(1978):6-7.

Continues the previous bibliographic entry by discussing staffing in the middle school, a teacher profile of the curriculum, the structure and the organization of the middle school, the content areas, and a profile of the typical middle school. The typical middle school enrolls about 650 students in grades 6-8. It has been in operation about seven years with generally a positive reaction. The school was established to provide a program suited to early adolescents, to better bridge the transition from elementary to high school, and to reduce crowding. The principal is male, 40 to 45 years old, with ten to twelve years of experience as a principal. He holds a masters degree and has a secondary education background. It seems his most difficult administrative problem is teacher resistance to change. The support staff, in addition to teachers, includes an assistant principal, counselor, media specialist, and paraprofessionals. The overall teacher/pupil ratio is 1 to 18. The thirty-three person teaching staff is young and has limited experience. There are slightly more females, and more than half are secondary oriented. The program offered is essentially discipline oriented and uses traditionally sized learning groups for the most part. Team teaching is rarely employed. Students are required to take math, language arts, social studies, science, and physical education. A number of electives are available including band, intramural athletics, home economics, industrial arts, foreign language, and student publication. This study of middle schools in 1977 reveals little significant difference from the findings of a similar study in 1967 other than that the number of middle schools has quadrupled. It occurred to the author, as it had to others, that it was hard to tell the difference in programs between the middle school and the junior high school or even from the high school for that matter.

10029.   Bryan, C. and Erikson, E.   "Structural Effects on School Behavior: A Comparison of Middle School and Junior High School Programs."   Grand Rapids, Mich.: Grand Rapids Public Schools, 1970.

This study found a significant difference in the positive attitudes middle school students had toward school compared to their elementary counterparts. The study also found among parents an increase in favorable attitudes toward the middle school program. Responses to questionnaires are extensively analyzed.

10030.   Bryan, K. and Hardcastle, K.   "Middle years and middle schools: an analysis of national policy." Education 3-13, 6,1(1978):5-10.

Authors state that the educational arguments relating to middle schools have been used as a front for economic and political expediency.   They suggest that educators should take a more rigorous look at the achievements and shortcomings of various organizational patterns used to educate children during the middle years.   See ERIC Abstract #EJ 182 799.

10031.   Campbell, R. E., et al.   "Vocational Development of Disadvantaged Junior High School Students.   Final Report."   Research Series 41.   Columbus: Ohio State University, Center for Vocational and Technical Education, ERIC Doc. ED 032 427, August, 1969.

A total of 2,370 students from four different regions of the United States took part in this study which explored the educational and vocational perceptions and expectations of disadvantaged junior high school students.   In each region a school district was chosen which serves primarily disadvantaged students and another which serves nondisadvantaged students. A sample of students who could read at fifth grade level or higher took part in a series of inventories, and additional information was collected regarding their disadvantaged state, personal plans and background, the community and school.   Major findings were: 1) Socioeconomically disadvantaged students are relevant to the community context.   2) The differences between disadvantaged and nondisadvantaged students did not appear as frequently as might have been expected.   3) Educational aspirations of disadvantaged students were generally lower than aspirations of nondisadvantaged students.   4) Disadvantaged students reported giving more thought to school plans and future jobs, viewed teachers in a more favorable light, and reported that school was easier. See ERIC Abstract #ED 032 427.

10032.   Canning, J. A.   "A Comparative Study of Selected Growth Objectives of Sixth Graders in a New Middle School with Sixth Graders in Elementary Self-contained Classrooms."   Ed.D.   Dissertation, University of Florida, 1973.

Author studied gains and losses over time in student achievement, self-concept, attitude toward school, and social acceptance among peers.   Students were compared by 1) school (middle/self-contained), 2) sex (boys/girls), 3) socioeconomic status (high/average/low), 4) subjective teacher rating of achievement (high/average/low), and 5) race (black/white). Students were 115 sixth graders in a middle school (divided into nine subgroups) and 125 sixth graders in an elementary self-contained classroom school (also divided into nine subgroups).   Findings: 1) There was no significant difference between the schools in reading gains, self-acceptance gains, attitudes toward school, boys' acceptance by boys, or girls' acceptance by boys.   2) Student scores in both schools showed significant gains in arithmetic and reading.   3) Elementary students made significantly greater gains in arithmetic, as shown in mean scores for the total group and six subgroups.   4) Teachers rated some middle school subgroups significantly lower in boys' acceptance by boys and girls' accep-tance by girls.

10033.   Carlson, R. E.   "A Career Education Model: Re-search Project in Achievement Motivation for Junior High School Teachers." Washington, D.C.: Metropoli-tan Educational Council for Staff Development, July, 1973.

Ninety-three teachers and counselors participated in an in-service workshop in achievement motivation and career cluster simulations on career decision making skills for junior high school students.   Control and experimental student groups were established at seven schools.   Simulations of careers were used in experi-mental groups while control groups used a visual format.   Students were given pretests and posttests using the Crites Vocational Development Inventory. In five of the seven schools there were significant differences between the two groups.   Teachers partic-ipating in the workshops were able to produce posi-tive changes in student vocational maturity scores. The training manual for the in-service included exer-cises in 1) forced learning and goal setting, 2) decision and career planning, 3) self-assessment and

taking responsibility, 4) working and helping relationships, 5) vocations and self-concepts. Included
in this report is a fifteen-page literature review.

10034.   Carroll, J. L., Harris, J. D., and Bretzing, B.,
II.   "A survey of psychologists serving secondary
schools."   Professional Psychology, 10,5(1979):
766-770.

In a national survey of psychologists serving students in all or in part of grades 7-12, complete
responses were received from 106 school districts
(35%).   The results indicated that a significant
proportion of secondary schools did not provide
psychological services.   In districts where psychologists were employed, the psychologists reported
involvement in a wide range of services with relatively low percentages of time devoted to direct
individual assessment.   Respondents are described in
terms of administrative relationships, level of
training, major areas of training, time spent in
secondary schools, and time spent per week on a
variety of tasks.   Logical extensions of this survey
include descriptions of services provided in districts with low psychologist-student ratios and
identification of skills and knowledge of particular
value to psychologists who provide fulltime services
in secondary schools.

10035.   Case, D. "A Comparative Study of Fifth Graders in
a New Middle School with Fifth Graders in Elementary
Self-Contained Classrooms." Dissertation, University
of Florida, Gainesville, 1970.

Following a year of study at the University of
Florida's Middle School Institute in 1966-67, a group
of educators went to Montgomery County, Maryland, and
helped to open the Farquhar Middle School, grades
5-8.   Pre- and posttest evaluations were made for 131
fifth-grade students in the middle school (the study
group) and for 138 fifth graders from three elementary schools (the control group).   The Stanford
Achievement Test, Gordon's How I See Myself, and The
Ohio Social Acceptance Scale were used.   Did fifth-
grade students in the middle school show more gains
than fifth graders in the elementary school in light
of the following factors: interdisciplinary teams of
teachers, nongrading, individualization, flexible
scheduling, multiage grouping, large and small group
instruction, and a curriculum including the required
subjects of physical education, reading, art, music,
industrial arts, and home economics?   The findings
indicated the following: 1) Both groups gained in
achievement, but students in the study group showed
greater gains particularly in arithmetic.   2) There
was a decrease in self-concept and attitude toward

school for both groups. 3) Social acceptance among peers showed similar results when comparing multi-aged grouping with grouping by same-age peers. 4) It was an advantage for a black student to be in the study group.

10036. Caul, J. L. "A Comparative Study of Student, Teacher, and Principal Perceptions of Organizational Structure Between Middle Schools with High Levels and Those with Low Levels of Middle School Concept Implementation." Ph.D. Dissertation, Michigan State University. Dissertation Abstracts International, 36 (9) Sec. A, 5672, 1975.

The organizational structure of two selected groups of Michigan middle schools was compared, using the Profile of a School Principal Questionnaire, Profile of a School Teacher Questionnaire, Profile of a School Student Short-Form, and Joe Raymer's Questionnaire for Determining Implementation Level of Middle School Concepts. A group of middle school experts identified three middle schools (group 1) which had demonstrated a low level of implementation of middle school characteristics and three middle schools which demonstrated high levels of implementation (group 2). Significant differences were found between student perceptions of leadership, peer team teaching, motivation and attitude toward school in the two groups analyzed. The author concluded: 1) Group 2 middle schools (those with a higher level of implementation of middle school characteristics) have a more participative organizational structure than group 1 schools. 2) Management practices of the principal are reflected in teacher-management practices toward students. 3) Better student and teacher attitudes and motivation result from more participative management styles. 4) Perceptions of students and teachers are more effective indicators of principals' management styles than principal self-perceptions.

10037. Chandler, A. M. "The Effect of Mathematics Curriculum Materials on the Perceived Behavior of Urban Junior High School Teachers of Low Achievers." Ph.D. Dissertation, University of Wisconsin. University Microfilms, Ann Arbor, Mich., Order no. 72-403, and ERIC Doc. ED 071 860, 1971.

This study was designed to assess changes in low achievers' perceptions of classroom climate and junior high teachers' opinions of their teaching practices as a result of introducing a new set of mathematics materials. Participating in the study were nineteen teachers with two classes. Each teacher introduced the new curriculum materials, Experiences in Mathematical Ideas, to one class, while the other class used the regular mathematics program for six weeks. The students felt the EMI materials resulted in less confusion in class activities and goals. The EMI materials did not change the opinions teachers had of their own teaching practices. See ERIC Abstract #ED 071 860.

10038.   Chismar, Sister M. H. "A Study of the Effectiveness of Cross-Level Grouping of Middle School Underachievers for Reading Instruction." Ph.D. Dissertation, Kent State University. University Microfilms, Ann Arbor, Mich., and ERIC Doc. ED 072 410, 1971.

An experimental group using cross-level grouping was studied to see if it made greater gains in reading achievement than a control group using the conventional approach of instruction at one level lower for underachievers. Four hundred students in grades 4 through 8 were randomly assigned to control and experimental groups. Cross-level grouping gave evidence of significant reading achievement: average gains in grades 4 and 7, near significant gains in grade 8 and for the total sample, and nonsignificant gains in grades 5 and 6. It was concluded that cross-level experimentation is safe and worthy of replication--there is more to gain from using it in instructing underachievers than from not using it. See ERIC Abstract #ED 072 410.

10039.   Christenson, G. A. "A study of student morale in a junior high school." National Association of Secondary School Principals Bulletin, 46(1962):314-315.

This study attempted to plan and carry out a program for building student morale in a junior high school and to measure change in morale in specific areas during the 1958-59 school year. One of eleven junior high schools located in a large midwestern city school system with a total enrollment of 912 students was selected as the sample population. The program for building student morale was planned by the administrative committee, composed of the principal, assistant principals, two counselors, visiting teacher, and nurse. The staff carried out the plan democratically under the guise of rebuilding the school academically, socially, emotionally, and in reputation. The entire program was guidance and counseling oriented. The study of student morale revealed that: 1) The morale of junior high school students can be significantly changed. 2) The morale of junior high school students is changed by using indirect methods. 3) There was a significant improvement in the dropout rate, the average daily attendance, the amount of achievement in reading by the students, and in the number of students from the

school who were on probation or parole or in corrective institutions.   4) The democratic form of school
administration was instrumental in bringing about a
positive change in morale.   5) The importance of
guidance and counseling in a program for building
student morale was indicated by the students.   6) No
resentment was expressed by the students for being
placed according to their tested ability and achievement in one of four types of learning groups.   7) The
morale of the students affects their attitudes toward
their teachers, their counselors, the administration,
and their fellow students.   8) Even though there is a
significant improvement in the morale of the students, there will still be specific areas in the
school where morale did not change or became worse.

10040.   Cobain, H. and Ford, P. M.   "Acceleration and
Enrichment in the Junior High School."   Washington,
D.C.:   U.S.   Office   of   Education,   Research   Report
0302, and Olympia: Washington Office of the State
Superintendent of Public Instriction, ERIC Doc. ED
001 315, June, 1963.

A group of educators and citizens in 1959 formed a
committee   to   offer   recommendations   regarding   a
curriculum for the academically talented students in
the Walla Walla School District.   They identified the
academically talented child through 1) teacher observation, 2) school grades, 3) grade placement on standardized tests, 4) grades on intelligence tests, 5)
personality check lists, 6) interest inventories, 7)
parent observations, and 8) individual case studies.
Identification   consisted   of   two   processes: 1)
screening--ranking children from low to high ability
by means of standardized tests and observed performance under standardized conditions--and 2) selection
--determining which of the students observed would be
eligible for the specialized program proposed.   The
committee also determined that educational policy for
the academically talented should provide stimulating
activities and materials beyond the regular classroom
level, promote higher achievement in such areas as
critical thinking, basic skills, citizenship, understanding of environment and world understanding, and
help develop a harmonious personality.   A program for
the talented would consist also of enrichment, acceleration and ability grouping.   Subcommittees were set
up in the content areas, and a report included the
recommendations of these subcommittees.   Content
areas to be stressed were math, science, reading, and
social   studies.   The   research   study   included   a
control and experimental group.   The two problems
investigated were: 1) Does a program of acceleration
and enrichment for the academically talented student
cause him to gain more academically than equally
talented students who are not exposed to such a

program?   2) Does the program of acceleration and
enrichment for the academically talented student
produce a school atmosphere in which the average
student gains more academically than he would otherwise?   Comparing the experimental group of average
students to the control group of average students, it
was found that a program of acceleration and enrichment for the academically talented student produced a
school atmosphere in which the average student gained
more academically than his peers in schools in which
there was no such program.   In all cases of comparison, the experimental groups were superior to the
control groups, and the performance of the experimental group of academically talented students supported the belief that a program of acceleration and
enrichment for the academically talented student
caused him to gain more academically than equally
talented students not exposed to the gifted program.

10041.   Conant, J. B.   "The junior high school years."
Saturday Review, October 15(1960):81-98.

Conant, whose report on the American High School was
an educational best seller in 1959, completed a com-
panion piece on the junior high school entitled
"Recommendations for Education in the Junior High
School Years" (Entry no. 1054).   The report, in the
form of a memorandum to the nation's school boards
published by Educational Testing Service, hasn't had
an important impact on American education.   It is
based on visits to 237 schools in twenty-three
states.   The highlights of the Conant report include:
1) Interscholastic activities and marching bands are
to be condemned in junior high schools.   There is no
sound educational reason for them, and too often they
serve merely as public entertainment.   2) Graduation
ceremonies with diplomas and cap and gown have no
place at the junior high level.   3) The difference
between a good school and a poor school is often the
difference between a good and a poor principal.   4)
Duties of teachers which are peripheral to the main
task of teaching should be minimized and constantly
reevaluated.   No other duty takes precedence over
classroom instruction.   5) The use of uncertified
personnel for nonprofessional duties is one of the
new developments which will be watched with interest.
6) Small classes in shop and home economics, because
of the nature of the facilities, spell very high
costs.   7) One way to improve morale and to stop the
exodus of good teachers from grades 7 and 8 is to
equalize the teaching load of all teachers in grades
7 through 12.   8) Conant considers the lack of what
educators call articulation one of the most serious
problems in many school systems.   Elementary school
teachers seldom meet with junior high school
teachers who, in turn, seldom meet with senior high

school teachers.   9) The gymnasium is more important
in colder regions of the nation than in warm areas
where children can have physical education outside
most of the school year.   One can question whether in
such areas a gymnasium is a necessity for satisfactory instruction.   10) Conant personally recommends
three groups in academic courses with the bulk of the
pupils in a particular grade in a large middle group.
Preferably, the grouping should be accomplished subject by subject.   11) Conant emphasizes the importance of the local school board.   The task that
confronts citizens everywhere is to choose the best
people available for membership on school boards in
thousands of communities across the land.   12) It is
by no means easy to find competent guidance personnel.   13) Instruction in the basic skills begun in
the elementary school should continue as long as
pupils can gain from instruction.

10042.   Costantino, P. S. "A Study of Differences Between
Middle School and Junior High School Curriculum and
Teacher-Pupil Classroom Behavior."   Dissertation,
University of Pittsburgh.   Dissertation Abstracts
International, 30, 614A-615A. University Microfilms,
Ann Arbor, Mich., 1969.

Three Pennsylvania middle schools were compared to
three nearby junior high schools of comparable size
to determine whether the middle schools differed from
the junior high schools in terms of curriculum and
selected dimensions of teacher-pupil classroom behavior.   The curricula of the junior high schools and
the middle schools were predominantly subject-matter
centered and generally similar in all respects.   The
programs of studies included the same subjects at
both seventh and eighth grade levels.   Furthermore,
no significant difference was found between the two
school populations in terms of teacher-pupil classroom behavior.

10043.   Cotterell, J. L. "Expectations and realities: a
study of transition from primary to secondary
school." Australian Journal of Education, 23,1(1979):
21-31.

Students' expectations after a month of secondary
schooling showed improved attitudes toward 'discipline, teachers, school work, and older students.
Considered in the study are variations related to sex
of student and school size.   Students expected
teachers at high school to be strict, school work to
be hard, and older students to be unfriendly and
aggressive.   Follow-up data revealed a uniform trend
toward more favorable views of school, suggesting the
growth-enhancing influences of high school on new
students.   Students from small schools construed

events in the transition more positively than did
those from large schools. Where students interact in
a variety of interpersonal relationships in a number
of central roles, as is generally true in small
schools, they develop more differentiated constructs
and greater ability to anticipate situations. Small
schools are likely to promote adaptability to new
environments. The author stresses that the small
school structure might be designed within larger
schools, creating structures which promote personality development through student participation in a
variety of roles.

10044.   Creek, R. J. "Middle School Rationale: The Sixth
Grade Component." Ed.D. Dissertation, University of
Pittsburgh. University Microfilms, Ann Arbor, Mich.,
1970.

Sought information that supports or denies some
aspects of the rationale for the middle school and
permits informed decisions to be made concerning the
organizational patterns of schools for early
adolescents. An assumption is made that children who
are at a common stage of development can be provided
with a better educational program when they are
included in the same organizational level. Because
children are maturing earlier than they did fifty to
one hundred years ago, one of these stages of development is more likely to include grades 6-8 than it
is to include grades 7-9. The crux of the question
appears to be the placement of the sixth grade. This
dissertation set out to determine whether sixth
graders are more similar to fifth graders or to
seventh graders in characteristics that appear to be
related to school placement. The characteristics
measured were personal adjustment, social adjustment,
social interests, and self-concept. Measuring
instruments were the California Test of Personality,
the Piers-Harris Self-Concept Scale, and the Social
Interest Survey. Two adjacent suburban school
districts which service similar populations were
selected for the study. From one district classes of
fifth graders from elementary schools and sixth and
seventh graders from a large middle school were
tested. From the second district fifth and sixth
graders from elementary schools and seventh graders
from a junior high school were selected. Some
findings of the study are as follows: 1) Certain
personal and social attributes are unrelated to
school placement. Self-concept, self-reliance, a
sense of personal worth, freedom from nervous
symptoms, family relationships, and community
relationships fall into this category for children
who are in the fifth, sixth or seventh grade. Grade
level made no significant difference on these variables. 2) A feeling of belonging, freedom from the

tendency to withdraw, social skills, and total adjustment may be affected by grade placement in school. There are no evident differences between sixth graders and seventh graders nor between sixth graders and fifth graders on these variables.

10045.   Curtis, R. L., Jr.   "Parents and peers: serendipity in a study of shifting reference sources." Social Forces, 52,3(1974):368-375.

This study tested a theory based on the assumption that length of school membership would be systematically related with adolescents' valuation of three significant others: mothers, fathers, and friends. Increasing time in school was predicted to be associated with decreasing valuations of parents and increasing valuations of friends, with the exception in the last school year when anticipated change of settings would reverse these trends. From a secondary analysis of responses from 8966 students in twenty-two schools, the theory in general was not supported. Rather, the effects of school experiences on the valuations of these three significant others occur within the first or second year of membership for junior high school students. An alternative interpretation is that the school may constitute a generalized reference field which takes on increasing importance once the adolescent has been socially incorporated into the school organization. The importance of initial experiences in school or other adolescent settings are identified as important issues for future research. Some anticipated patterns were observed for the middle-and-working students in the 7-8, 7-9, and 7-12 schools, but these differences are unimpressive. In the first year in schools containing grade 7, school size is positively associated with the percentages of students with high valuations of both parents. The differences found to be associated with the two components of school complexity--length of grade ranges and sizes--were relatively small. Because other predictions received no confirmation, these findings are significant in considering what was not found. While the percentages of students with high valuations of mothers and of fathers as reference sources decreased with higher grade levels, these shifts were not associated with any increases in respect for friends as sources of advice and direction. The results of this study strongly suggest that educators turn their attention to the early stages of membership and, more specifically, to the first year to gain an accurate picture of what occurs to adolescents when they move through public schools. Previous studies have been insensitive to the rapid socialization processes.

10046.   Curtis, R. L., Jr.   "The issue of schools as
social systems: socialization effects as inferred
from length of membership."   Sociological Quarterly,
15(1974):277-293.

The problem is approached here as a question of
whether students' orientation vary with lengths of
membership in the same school organization.   Data
were examined for 7954 students in nineteen schools
which contained grade lengths 7-9, 7-12, 9-12, and
10-12.   The analysis indicated that the distinctive-
ness of school normative climate is slightly but
positively associated with length of school membership when school size is controlled.   While schools
can be viewed as relatively distinct systems, they
should also be seen as highly permeable in the midst
of their community and home environments.

10047.   Curtis, T. E.   "Administrators' view of the middle
school."   Highpoints, 40,8(1966):30-35.

In this survey, administrators of middle schools in
New York State supplied either formal statements or
their opinions concerning the effectiveness of the
middle school.   They said: 1) The chief advantage
was the synthesis of elementary and secondary teacher
attitudes.   2) Children are compatible in grades 6,
7, and 8 because they have similar social, emotional,
and physical characteristics.   3) The transition from
the elementary to the secondary curriculum seemed
more effective in the middle school.   4) There was
more freedom to experiment with new programs in the
middle school.   5) One disadvantage was the need of
ninth graders for a year of leadership, since there
would be a tendency for them to be held down in the
senior high school.   6) Eighth grade girls, most of
whom had passed the pubertal stage, were dissatisfied
with the grade 6-8 middle school, since most of the
boys were still physically and emotionally less
mature than they.

10048.   Dacus, W. P.   "Study of the Grade Organizational
Structure of Junior High School as Measured by Social
Maturity, Emotional Maturity, Physical Maturity, and
Opposite Sex Choices."   Ed.D. Dissertation, Univer-
sity of Houston. Dissertation Abstracts International,
24, 1461-62, 1963.

Study was designed to ascertain the most desirable
grade combination for early adolescents.   A random
sample of fifty-five students in grades 5-10 included
students with IQs from 90 to 110.   Boys and girls
were studied separately.   The California Test of
Personality measured social maturity and emotional
maturity.   Physical maturity was indicated by age and
onset of puberty.   A sociometric device measured

students' choices of desirable traits in the opposite sex. A summary analysis of the significant differences between grades for social, emotional, and physical maturity and opposite sex choices provided a picture of the total amount of difference between the grades. The six grades were split into a lower division (grades 5, 6, and 7) and an upper division (grades 8, 9, and 10). In the lower division, there were six significant differences (out of a possible twelve) between grades 5 and 6, whereas grades 6 and 7 registered only one significant difference. In the upper division, there were eight significant differences between grades 8 and 9 as compared to four significant differences between grades 9 and 10. The sixth and seventh grades in the lower division and the ninth and tenth grades in the upper division registered the least amount of difference. Authors concluded that maturity levels indicate a grade pattern allowing sixth and seventh graders to be in the same school and ninth and tenth graders in a different school. The most noticeable feature of the male sample was the marked differences in social and emotional maturity between grades 8 and 9, while there were no observed differences between grades 9 and 10. While the least differences were found between grades 6 and 7 and between grades 9 and 10, the 6-3-3 plan divides the grades precisely between 6 and 7 and between 9 and 10.

10049. Dade County Public Schools, Fla. "South Miami Junior High School Curriculum Project, 1967." Washington, D.C.: U. S. Office of Education, ERIC Doc. ED 023 763, 1967.

Because many disadvantaged students had come into the Dade County School System, in the mid-'60s in-service teacher workshops on desegregation were developed, and an experimental curriculum for black and white disadvantaged seventh graders was initiated. Students took diagnostic tests and received instruction on their grade level. Small groups were formed to improve language arts skills, and student aides from universities provided more individual instruction. The students demonstrated gains from this experimental program and improved attitudes toward school and self. Conclusions from this experimental program include: 1) Group counseling of students with similar problems should be provided to disadvantaged students. 2) A human relations council should be organized to promote better relations between races in such schools. 3) The instructional program must be more individualized, and group work must be with very small groups. Extensive use of teacher aides should be encouraged. 4) There is a great shortage of published materials for culturally deprived students. 5) Although the experimental group showed improvement, they are still substandard and need a continued program with language emphasis. 6) Parents should be involved with school activities. 7) Government grants should be readily accessible to schools. 8) In-service education for teachers of disadvantaged students is essential. 9) An integrated school should have an integrated faculty.

10050.   Dasenbrock, D. H.   "A Comparison of CAI and Non-CAI Student Performance Within Individualized Science Instructional Materials (ISCS) Grade Seven." Ph.D. Dissertation, Florida State University.   University Microfilms, Ann Arbor, Mich., Order no. 71-6992, 1970.

This study tested the usefulness of CAI as a tool for curriculum evaluation.   Grade 7 materials in the 1968 ISCS science curriculum were used.   Twenty students who had used the CAI and forty students who had not used the CAI took part.   The California Test of Mental Maturity and the Metropolitan Achievement Test in Reading were given to subjects.   Process categories were determined in the ISCS materials.   The CAI and Non-CAI student performance was similar using the ISCS materials.

10051.   Davis, E. L.   "A Comparative Study of Middle Schools and Junior High Schools in New York State." Ed.D. Dissertation, University of New Mexico, 1970.

To what extent is the middle school in actual practice doing a better job of meeting the needs of young adolescents than its predecessor, the junior high school.   Thirty-five middle schools and thirty-five junior high schools were paired according to school population, socioeconomic conditions, and geographic location.   Questionnaires were sent to principals. The summaries include the following: 1) The middle schools do permit some departmentalization in grades 5 and 6.   2) In many instances both junior high and middle school administrators recommend the removal of the ninth grade.   3) The middle schools are less likely to have interscholastic sports, cheerleaders, marching bands, night dances, pep assemblies, school annuals, and honor societies.   4) No significant differences were found comparing facilities.   5) Middle schools had significantly more flexible scheduling, team teaching, and independent study than junior high schools.   6) Guidance programs in the paired junior high schools were superior to the programs in the middle schools.   Grade patterns and educational programs are not always the most important considerations in the education of young adolescents.   Rather, it was important to have a carefully designed structure and program suitable to the individual situation, and to implement this program effectively to meet the needs of young adolescents.

10052.   Davis, Houtman, Warren, Roweton, Mari, and
Belcher. "A Program for Training Creative Thinking:
Inner City Evaluation. Report From the Task and
Training Variables in Human Problem Solving and
Creative Thinking Project." Madison: University of
Wisconsin, Research and Development Center for Cogni-
tive Learning, ERIC Doc. ED 070 809, April, 1972.

This development center hopes to contribute to a
better understanding of cognitive learning of youth
and to improve related educational practices. The
strategy for research and development is comprehensive and includes basic research to generate new
knowledge about the conditions and processes of
learning and about the processes of instruction and
the subsequent development of research-based instructional materials. This report, from the Task and
Training Variables in Human Problem Solving and
Creative Thinking Project, investigates creative
problem solving as a trainable, cognitive skill and
develops and tests creative thinking programs following research on basic problem-solving variables in
different situations. The effectiveness of a work
group for training creative thinking called "Thinking
Creatively: A Guide to Training Imagination" was
evaluated with 190 inner-city students. Two sixth
grade classes and two eighth grade classes served as
experimental groups, and four similar classes composed the control groups. All subjects took the
Torrance Test of Creative Thinking. Results determined that most students and teachers felt that the
students had benefited from creative training experiences. The materials sought to teach attitudes which
predisposed an individual to behave more creatively
and offered techniques for producing new combinations
of ideas. It was recommended that teachers allow for
more active participation in classroom problem-
solving activities and that future efforts by
teachers to test creativity in the inner city use a
reading level and cultural experiences common to this
population.

10053.   Dayton University, Office of Educational Services.
"Jefferson Township Schools Study."   Dayton, Ohio,
ERIC Doc. ED 144 188, March, 1977.

This study looked at the possibility of reorganizing
the Jefferson Township (Ohio) Schools from a 7-9/
10-12 grade arrangement to a 7-8/9-12 grade plan.
The junior high school and high school were examined
to determine space availability, use of present
facilities, potential use of facilities with reorganization, general condition of the buildings, enrollment data, demographic information, an examination of
present and potential staffing patterns, present and
potential scheduling patterns, and present junior

high and high school curriculum. Interviews with administrative personnel measured attitudes toward reorganization. Floor plans of the school are included. The study recommended adoption of the proposed reorganization.

10054.   Dearborn Public Schools, Mich. "Project Essay. The Development and Testing of Instructional Materials to Encourage Self-Understanding and Self-Direction in Adolescent Youth. Final Report." Washington, D.C.: U. S. Office of Education, ERIC Doc. ED 048 081, 1971.

A team tried out many learning activities and materials, and the main objective was to develop an informed individual with: 1) a good self-concept with sense of individual worth, 2) a sense of moral judgment, 3) a valid understanding of the nature of race and of the many misconceptions about race, 4) respect of ethnic groups and their achievements, 5) understanding of the nature of conflict as a constant and of socially acceptable ways of resolving it, and 6) understanding of the many roles an individual assumes as a member of society. The end products were two resource guides with cognitive and affective objectives for use by teachers. See ERIC Abstract #ED 048 081.

10055.   Dennis, E. G. "An Exploratory Analysis of School Climates: Factors Affecting Morale in the Schools." Ed.D. Dissertation, Nova University, ERIC Doc. ED 111 109, 1973.

This study investigated the teacher and student morale in two schools, one with and one without obvious problems. The research focused on: 1) staff feelings about coworkers and supervisors, and staff satisfaction with the degree of participation and recognition received from work, 2) student feelings about teachers, student enthusiasm for school, and student self-esteem, and 3) the overall morale in each school. Statistical analysis indicated some significant differences between the schools. See ERIC Abstract #ED 111 109.

10056.   Detjen, N. G. "A Study of Adolescent Self-Concept as Affected by Institution." Ph.D. Dissertation, University of Minnesota. Dissertation Abstracts International, 37 (10) Sec. A, 6170, 1976.

An attempt was made to measure the effects of the school on an adolescent's self-concept to determine: 1) if the self-concept of an adolescent could be enhanced by the phenomenon of self-fulfilling prophecy, 2) if an enhanced self-concept produced higher achievement, and 3) if an enhanced self-concept improved attendance. The principles of the "pygmalion effect" or self-fulfilling prophecy were used to enhance adolescent self-concept and observe and measure the results. The following hypotheses were tested: 1) There is no significant difference on pretest and posttest scores between experimental and control groups as measured by self-esteem inventory. 2) There is no significant difference in achievement between experimental and control groups as measured by grade point average. 3) There is no significant difference in attendance between experimental and control groups as measured by days absent. No significant differences were found in the first two hypotheses, and hypothesis three was not rejected in terms of total mean gain scores for attendance; however, it was noted that there were significant F ratios in some interactions. It was concluded that the pygmalion effect or self-fulfilling prophecy does not obtain clear cut correlations when used to effect change in self-concept and a resultant change in achievement and attendance. The sample consisted of 78 students randomly selected from all students at Fairview Junior High School in Roseville, Minnesota.

10057.   Disinger, J. F.   "Student Development, Teacher Characteristics, and Class Characteristics in Junior High School Science." Ph.D. Dissertation, Ohio State University. University Microfilms, Ann Arbor, Mich., ERIC Doc. ED 107 460, 1971.

Study was an investigation of the development of junior high school science students in specified cognitive and affective areas, as related to teacher characteristics and class characteristics. Variables included: 1) development of understanding of scientific concepts and processes, 2) development of beliefs about science and scientists, 3) development of scientific attitudes, and 4) interest in science as a subject. Tests used include Champlin's Beliefs About and Attitudes toward Science and Scientists Scale, the Remmers' Short Form of Attitude Toward Any School Subject Scale, and a concept-process test. Teachers also provided students with a Science Classroom Activities Checklist. No simple set of teacher and/or class characteristics related to student development. Student interest in science as a classroom subject appeared to be negatively related to student changes in other areas, and positive relationships between the tests and the attitudes scales were generally found throughout the study. See ERIC Abstract #ED 107 460.

10058.   District of Columbia Public Schools, Department of
          Research and Evaluation. "A Comparative Study of
          Seventh and Eighth Grade Programs in the District of
          Columbia Public Schools." Washington, D. C., ERIC
          Doc. ED 157 157, February, 1978.

          Seventh and eighth grade programs located in elemen-
          tary school buildings were compared to seventh and
          eighth grade programs in junior high school build-
          ings. Several studies were designed and conducted to
          gather data. One study surveyed 10 percent of all
          seventh graders in the school system. A second
          approach compared case studies of four different
          seventh and eighth grade programs. Findings
          indicated that seventh graders attending both types
          of schools shared a positive attitude toward the
          academic learning experience in their school and
          toward the family as a source of help with questions
          or problems about sex and family life. See ERIC
          Abstract #ED 157 157.

10059.   Dornseif, A. W., Gross, S., and Sewell, A. F.
          "Multivariate Evaluation of Student Selection Strate-
          gies in Open and Traditional Education. A Prelimi-
          nary Report." Paper presented at the Annual Meeting
          of the American Educational Research Association,
          Chicago, ERIC Doc. ED 093 930, April, 1974.

          Presents preliminary data from a study of open
          education at the junior high level conducted in the
          1973-74 school year. One hundred forty seventh and
          eighth grade students were assigned to a large, newly
          constructed classroom staffed by four teachers and
          two teacher aides. A similar number of students
          randomly chosen were assigned to a traditional
          departmentalized program. The evaluation focused on
          two areas: 1) determining the relative academic and
          socio-emotional values of open education and tradi-
          tional education, and 2) determining which of the two
          types of programs was more appropriate to certain
          student characteristics. Teachers were asked to
          determine the following about each of their students:
          academic underachievement, social introversion, and
          social extroversion. Students were each assigned a
          numerical rating in these areas: attitude, knowl-
          edge, skill, and sociability. The results appeared
          to be a reasonably clear documentation of teacher
          objectives and student perceptions in agreement with
          the idea of open education. Open program teachers
          rated most highly those students who demonstrated
          superior academic achievement and whose personality
          traits could be called quiet and docile. Teachers
          objectives in the open setting did not significantly
          differ from those of teachers in the traditional
          program. Students in the open classroom perceived
          their learning environment as less structured, more

individualized, less tense, and more satisfying than students in the traditional program perceived their environment. The authors conclude that their findings strongly support the belief that openness had not been achieved during the open education program's first year.

10060.   Douglass, H. "What type of organization of schools?" Journal of Secondary Education, 41(1966): 358-364.

Summarizes responses to a checklist sent out to junior high school principals. About 84 percent of them preferred the junior high organization that includes grades 7, 8, and 9. Of principals in 6-7-8 and 7-8 schools, about half said they thought including grades 7, 8, and 9 would be better than 6-7-8 organizations. Douglass concluded that the 6-3-3 organizational pattern would prevail for several decades.

10061.   Downing, L. L. and Bothwell, K. H., Jr. "Open-space schools: anticipation of peer interaction and development of cooperative interdependence." Journal of Educational Psychology, 71,4(1979):478-484.

Eighth graders randomly selected and placed in forty-two same-sex pairs of varied racial composition were studied in two schools, open-space versus closed-space architectural styles. The study concluded that open-space students were more likely to develop cooperative interdependence in a mixed motive game and were more inclined to make proximal seating choices indicative of anticipated peer interaction. The girls of either race learned to cooperate in same-race pairs and to compete in mixed-race pairs. The white boys learned to cooperate, and black boys learned to compete regardless of their partners. The authors concluded that the external locus of control scores were not related to schools, but were higher for blacks than for white students. An open physical environment relates to more anticipation of interaction as assessed by seating choices, and leads to development of more cooperative interdependence.

10062.   Duchi, S. A., Jr. "An Exploratory Study of the Middle School Climate as Perceived by Students, Teachers, and Administrators and the Relationship of These Perceptions with Selected Behavioral Characteristics." Dissertation, University of Pittsburgh. Dissertation Abstracts International, Order no. 7816786, 1978.

The overall purpose of the study was to investigate the middle school climate to provide data and tools for practitioners to understand, assess, and improve

the middle school climate.   This study defined the
term, "middle school climate," and identified the
characteristics of a desirable or positive middle
school climate and the behavioral evidence of an
unhealthy middle school climate.   Student, teacher,
and administrator perceptions of their school climate
in two middle schools were assessed with the rate of
student absenteeism, student tardiness, teacher
absenteeism, and teacher tardiness.   Two data gathering instruments were used: a measurement instrument
called the Middle School Climate Perception Questionnaire and a second questionnaire to measure dependent
variables.   The second questionnaire was to collect
data which served as a check on the accuracy of the
information collected on the first questionnaire.
The following conclusions were drawn from the study:
1) Students' positive perceptions of the school
climate declined from the sixth grade to the eighth
grade.   2) The school climate appears to be perceived
as equally desirable by male and female students,
male and female teachers, new and old students, and
new and old teachers.   3) Academic success appears to
be related to the students' perceptions of the school
climate.   4) The students with good behavior patterns
appear to have higher perceptions of the school climate than students with poor behavior patterns.   5)
The perceptions of the students, teachers, and administrators appear to be accurate for their particular
group and time.   6) The administrators appear to have
higher perceptions of the school climate than do
students and teachers.   7) The students and teachers
with a high rate of tardiness appear to have lower
perceptions of the school climate compared to students and teachers who are seldom tardy.

10063.   Dugan, C. L.   "A Study of Attitude Change and
Achievement in an Innovative Program at the Junior
High School Level."   ERIC Doc. ED 134 480, June,
1973.

A pilot program was assessed in an attempt to develop
a prototype for evaluating innovative educational
programs that delineates the evaluation, design, and
analytic techniques.   Students could elect this
program at Slauson Junior High School in Ann Arbor,
Michigan, as an alternative to traditional education.
It was designed to alter the administrative and
psychological environment of public junior high
schools through flexible modular scheduling and team
teaching.   The study analyzed goals that the teachers
set for themselves: 1) normal student achievement in
reading and mathematics, 2) positive student attitudes toward school, and 3) humane behavior in both
students and teachers.   The control group consisted
of traditional mathematics classes at a junior high
school.   The California Reading Test, California

Arithmetic Test, School Sentiment Index, and an attitude questionnaire were administered, and student and teacher behaviors were observed. The author concluded that the program goals were achieved, but variables such as administrative support, selection bias, team-cluster structure, and program newness confounded the evidence. An evaluation model was not made because of methodological flaws and limitations in the study. See ERIC Abstract #ED 134 480.

10064. Durall, E. P. "A Feasibility Study: Remediation by Computer Within a Computer-Managed Instruction Course in Junior High School Mathematics." Tallahassee: Florida State University, Computer-Assisted Instruction Center, ERIC Doc. ED 074 734, 1972.

Seventy mathematics students in seventh grade worked individually in self-instructional booklets for fifteen weeks. The students were all tested by direct contact with a computer terminal. The two methods of remediation were the same, except that half the students used a computer terminal to get further help. The other group of students was helped by a teacher rather than a computer. There was some indication that low-ability students found teacher remediation more supportive.

10065. Educational Research Services. "Summary of Research on Middle School: A Research Brief." Arlington, Va., 1975.

The research summary includes a rationale for the middle school, the middle school ideal, advantages and disadvantages, pros and cons identified in the literature, student achievement and attendance, student self-concept and attitudes, teacher and parent attitudes, administration, curriculum, staffing, facilities, and a selected bibliography.

10066. Edwards, C. H. "Variable delivery systems for peer associated token reinforcement." Illinois School Research, 12,1(1975):19-28.

Normal junior high school students were analyzed in the natural school environment. The author sought to determine if different token delivery systems would differentially affect the disruptive behavior patterns of students in the normal classrooms. Subjects received special privileges as reinforcement for appropriate behaviors. Teacher and student behaviors were monitored by direct observation and recorded on a special rating scale. Eight of the most disruptive students were chosen from three science classes in the seventh grade. The results indicated that token reinforcement provided a positive reinforcing function in maintaining appropriate classroom behavior

and increasing student productivity for each type of
token delivery system tested. Disruptive behavior
increased when tokens were withdrawn. Some subjects
were differentially affected by different token
delivery systems, while for other subjects no differences were noticed.

10067.   Ehrlich, V. and Murray, K. "New Curriculum Activ-
ities in the Pilot Intermediate Schools of New York
City."   New York: Center   for   Urban   Education,
October, 1969.

Middle school students were compared to similar students in other forms of intermediate education. The
study found no significant differences in student
attitudes toward school, no difference in achievement, and no differences in self-concept and self-
perception.

10068.   Elardo, P. T. and Caldwell, B. M. "The effects of
an experimental social development program on children in the middle childhood period." Psychology in
the Schools, 16,1(1979):93-100.

The study was designed to answer these questions: 1)
Can role taking skills be promoted in the classroom
setting?   2) Can certain social problem solving
skills be increased in a classroom setting? 3) Will
teachers perceive positive changes in classroom
behavior?   The subjects were sixty-eight children
ages 9 and 10.   The thirty-four pairs of children
were matched on the basis of sex, race, age, and
group IQ scores.   Children in the experimental group
gained in respect for others, ability to generate
alternatives to problem situations, creative expression, patience, and self-reliance.

10069.   Elie, M. "A Comparative Study of Middle School and
Junior High School Students in Terms of Social and
Emotional Problems, Self-Concept, Ability to Learn,
Creative Thinking Ability, and Physical Fitness and
Health." Ph.D. Dissertation, Michigan State Univer-
sity, East Lansing, Mich., 1970.

The emerging transescent is characterized by an
increased awareness of himself, his physical, mental,
and socio-emotional idiosyncrasies as he progresses
from childhood to adolescence. He needs a learning
environment conducive to normal and healthy growth
and development.   The trend toward reorganization is
posited on the notion that an educational organization (the middle school) and curriculum designed
especially for this age group can better provide for
their special needs and interests than the junior
high school institution.   To implement this goal,
evaluation of the middle school and its effect on the

behavior of its students is necessary to determine if
it alleviates any of the shortcomings of the junior
high school plan.   This study compared the group
behavior of students attending the middle school and
the junior high school.   The data were collected by
means of four instruments: the Mooney Problem Checklist: Junior High School Form, the Michigan General
Self-Concept of Ability Scale, the Torrence Test of
Creative Thinking Ability, and the AAHPER Youth Fitness Inventory.   A random sample of 108 boys and
girls in grades 7 and 8 was selected for testing.   A
significant difference was found between the middle
school and the junior high school students on the
measures of socio-emotional problems and creative
thinking ability.   No significant differences were
found between the groups on the measures of self-
concept and ability to learn.

10070.   Ellis, J. R. and Peterson, J. L. "Effects of same
sex class organization on junior high school students' academic achievement, self-discipline, self-
concept, sex role identification, and attitudes
toward school." Journal of Educational Research, 64,
10(1971):455-464.

Control and experimental groups of students in grades
7 and 8 were matched in subject areas and took a pretest and posttest in those content areas, such as
English, social studies, math, science, and physical
education.   Differences in academic achievement and
general maturity as measured in this study were consistent with the research about early adolescence in
that the differences favored girls.   Findings failed
to attribute differences to the same sex grouping,
and it was decided that same sex class organization
for seventh and eighth grade students had no effect
on the dependent variables of the study.   Girls
tended to receive higher marks from teachers,
achieved higher scores on achievement tests, reported
more favorable attitudes toward social groups and
institutions, and responded more negatively to the
sex segregated school experience than boys did.

10071.   Emmert, B. A. "An Analysis of the Effectiveness
of Large Group Peer-Helper Training with Pre- and
Early Adolescents in the Middle School."   Ed.D.
Dissertation, University of Northern Colorado.   Dis-
sertation Abstracts International, 38 (8-A), 4581.
Order no. 7730816, 1978.

Fifty-eight students in sixth and eighth grade at the
University of Northern Colorado Laboratory Middle
School were assigned to experimental and control
groups.   Developmental peer training in large groups
using high school students as co-trainers was very

effective in helping middle school students understand and communicate accurate empathy.

10072.   Epstein, J. L. and McPartland, J. M.   "Classroom
Organization and the Quality of School Life."   Report
215.   Baltimore: Johns Hopkins University, Center
for Social Organization of Schools, August, 1976.

The Quality of School Life Scale (QSL) is based on
three dimensions: 1) satisfaction with school is a
measure of general well being in school, 2) the commitment to class work subscale measures the level of
interest in assignments and curricular activities,
and 3) the reactions to teacher subscale concerns the
quality of student-teacher relations.   Previous
research with the QSL shows that the three subscales
relate differently to a number of external criteria.
Survey data from 7200 students in thirty-nine elementary, middle, and high schools which differ significantly on a measure of school openness was gathered
to test the hypotheses that satisfaction with school
should be most responsive to changes in school practices that affect the social structure, commitment to
classwork should relate most to changes in the test
structure, and reactions to teachers should be most
affected by changes in the authority structure of
schools.   This research illustrates how multidimensional subjective indicators can provide information
on the condition of education and on the nature of
structural changes and school organization.   The
results show that openness of the instructional
program has greater positive impact on students'
perceived quality of student-teacher relations than
on other dimensions of the quality of school life.
Openness of the instructional program appears to
involve a basic change of the school authority structure, but may not involve as much change in the
social or task structures of schools.

10073.   Epstein, J. L. and McPartland, J. M.   "Sex Differences in Family and School Influence on Student Outcomes."   Baltimore: Johns Hopkins University, Center
for Social Organization of Schools, September, 1977.

The paper explores three research issues on adolescent development: 1) Is sex a main effect on a
variety of student outcomes?   2) What are the relative influences of family status, family processes,
school processes, and individual ability on academic
and nonacademic behavior of males and females?   3) Do
the same influence processes operate for males and
females, or are there important sex interaction
effects with family or school characteristics?   Data
were gathered from 4,079 white students in ten middle
schools and six high schools in Maryland.   The

schools differed significantly in authority structure. The sample of students from grades 6, 7, and 9
through 12 is diverse in social and family characteristics. Results show: 1) Sex had a significant
effect on five outcomes--self-esteem, college plans,
academic subject preference, adjustment in school,
and report card grades. 2) Clear differences were
found in patterns of influence: family and school
processes are more important for personality and
school coping skills, and family status and individual ability are more important for college plans and
standardized achievement. 3) No consistent significant sex interaction was found.

10074.   Essex, M. W. and Spayde, P. E.   "Junior high
school is here to stay: a study of the first forty
years based on practices in forty cities." Nation's
Schools, 54(1954):31-34.

The data relate to length and number of periods in
the school day, number of pupils per class, curriculum, objectives, guidance programs, and other
practices.

10075.   Evans, C. L. "Short-Term Assessment of the Middle
School Plan." Fort Worth, Tex.: Fort Worth Independent School District, August, 1970.

Twenty-seven hypotheses on middle school operations
were tested.   Using various instruments, data was
obtained from students, teachers, principals, and
central administraters. Most of the major objectives
of a middle school reorganization are being attained.
Considerable progress has been effected in generating
schools for young adolescents which are 1) developing
flexible schedules and innovative curricula, 2)
excluding high school oriented characteristics, 3)
providing enriched experiences for sixth graders, 4)
combining more compatible age groups, and 5) developing staff who tend to nurture, support, and accept
students age 11 to 14. Academic progress of students
has been maintained during this initial adjustment
period.   The data indicate that little progress has
been made toward the goal of providing a "bridge"
between elementary and high schools in terms of easing the transition from modified self-contained to
departmentalized organizations and in terms of
scheduling differentiated opportunities for various
age groups to develop skills and self-direction. The
data also indicate that little progress has been made
toward supplying the substantial amount of individual
guidance recommended for adolescents by proponents of
the middle school philosophy.   Two junior high
schools were matched with two middle schools in terms
of socioeconomic status and academic achievement.
This pairing allowed some comparison between students

and staff at traditional junior high schools with
those at newly organized middle schools. Conferences
were conducted with principals and/or vice principals
to collect information relative to previous, present,
and planned practices. Data were also collected from
appropriate offices in the central administration
building.   Staff and students contributed through
questionnaires. Standardized instruments include the
Minnesota Teacher Attitude Inventory, the California
Test of Personality, and the Iowa Test of Basic
Skills.   Other than questionnaires, two instruments
were developed by the researchers to test teachers'
knowledge of and commitment to the middle school
philosophy and to measure social maturity of
adolescents.

10076.   Evans, C. L.   "Middle School Evaluation: Teacher
Questionnaire."   Fort Worth, Tex.:   Fort Worth
Independent School District, 1970.

The first study by Evans assessed eighth graders in
junior high and in middle school in Fort Worth.   The
California Test of Personality was used.   There was
no significant difference in feelings of self-worth
evidenced by the two groups of eighth graders.
Regarding dating behavior and attitudes, Evans found
that eighth graders in junior high did not date
significantly more often than eighth graders in
middle schools; however, middle school students who
had been in a middle school for two years dated less
than those students in the same grade who had
attended a middle school for one year.   A second
study conducted by Case compared attitudes toward
school and self-concept of fifth graders in middle
school and elementary school.   Gordon's How I See
Myself Scale was used to assess students' self-
concept and attitude toward school.   The Ohio Social
Acceptance Scale was used to evaluate social acceptance among peers.   The test instruments were
administered in September and again the following
May.   Pre- and posttest mean scores were compared,
and data were analyzed by total groups, sex, race,
and socioeconomic and achievement levels.   Over the
school year, both the middle school and the elementary school fifth graders declined in self-concept,
but the study group of middle school students showed
a greater loss in self-concept.   Analysis of the data
from the Ohio Social Acceptance Scale indicated that
there was no significant difference between the two
groups of students regarding acceptance among peers.

10077.   Fallon, J. P.   "A Comparison of Transescent Male
Development in Two Organizational Patterns Centering
on Middle School Grade Reorganization."   Ph.D. Dissertation, Michigan State University, 1969.

The study was posited on the notion that the school as a social setting should have an organizational and curriculum design which fosters interaction, with every experience undertaken by a child intended to help him become aware of his own potential as a human being. The Piers-Harris General Self-Concept Scale and Mooney Problem Checklist Form J were given to sixth and seventh grade boys in two organizational settings: 1) a K-6 and 7, 8, 9 conventional grade setting, and 2) a 6, 7, 8, 9 middle school setting. As the hypotheses suggested, no statistical differences were found among the 277 boys observed in two New York counties.   Setting appeared to have no function.   Health and physical development, peer groups, and self-centered concerns were slightly less of a problem among the sixth grade boys in middle school than among the sixth graders in conventional school. Home and family, money, work, and the future were slightly less a social personal problem among the conventional seventh grade boys than among the middle school seventh grade.   To reorganize middle grade learners to save money or space, or to satisfy a transient population appears to make no difference for the individual or for normal child development. A variety of grade groupings appears to serve a number of reorganizational purposes. The selection of an age-grade arrangement does not necessarily disqualify a school district from having a good middle school program.

10078.   Feld, M., Berns, B., and Radov, C.   "A Report on the Feasibility of a Grade Level Reorganization for the Providence School System, Phase I, May 1, 1979." Providence, R. I.: Providence School System, 1979.

This data collection effort was conducted to provide the initial steps of a comprehensive feasibility study and an implementation stage to be carried out at a later date.   Educators in the Rhode Island School System were concerned that the middle school system was not the optimum structure for delivering quality and cost effective educational services to the student population. Decisions about grade level were to be based on at least three criteria: the learning environment, economic feasibility, and community need.   Data and information were collected in these three categories to document the various consequences of the middle school structure as it existed in Providence.   The researchers strongly suggested that the K-8 grade level reorganization be considered by the school system as the optimum learning environment for the early adolescent and the most cost effective way to deliver this service. Through their research, the authors suggest that grade structure does have an impact on socialization issues which are so significant during the early adolescent phase of development. While data does not clearly support the superiority of one system over another, the authors found K-8 research which seems to indicate some real strength. On the basis of their review of literature and trends, they recommended the K-8 as a heterogeneous, supportive environment for early adolescents at a volatile time of their lives.

10079.   Ferrer, T. The Schools and Urban Renewal: A Case Study from New Haven. New York: Educational Facilities Laboratories, March, 1964.

New Haven has adopted the 4-4-4 plan for reasons that include 1) more effective use of existing plant, 2) a general disposition in favor of the four-year high school, 3) disenchantment with the junior high as currently constituted, and 4) a desire for better racial balance in the schools. The New Haven plan is based on the 1961 report done for the Board of Education by Cyril G. Sargent, Professor of Education at Harvard. This wide-ranging report, which stresses the value of tying school organization and construction into civic redevelopment and neighborhood improvement, advocated a 4-4-4 plan. Sargent believes that the four-year high school facilitates a more sustained and vigorous education program through the high school years, that the small K-4 neighborhood school can be especially effective for the very young, and that the 5-8 middle school can bring to children in these grades improved curriculum and stronger guidance.

10080.   Fisher, L. "Peer judgment of competence in junior high school classrooms." Developmental Psychology, 14,2(1978):187-188.

Junior high school students provided verbatim descriptive statements regarding perceptions of school competence, and a questionnaire using these statements was administered to 203 students. Factor analyses identified the ways junior high school students perceive school competence. See ERIC Abstract #EJ 214 859.

10081.   Forst, C. F. "A Study of Middle Schools in the County School System in the State of Maryland as Compared to Selected Junior High Schools Within the State." Ed.D. Dissertation, George Washington University, 1969.

Author studied junior high and middle school organization, curriculum, personnel, evaluation, and socialization. Analysis of responses to a questionnaire sent to fifty principals of middle and junior high schools suggested these conclusions: 1) There

is no consistency of organization within Maryland
middle schools or junior high schools. 2) The number
of middle schools in Maryland has grown rapidly since
1965, suggesting a new educational movement has
developed in the state. 3) Middle schools had made
little or no significant change from the junior high
school curriculum. 4) Junior high schools seemed to
offer more significant and more varied remedial and
accelerated programs. 5) Socialization was generally
more a part of the middle school day than the junior
high school day. 6) In both the middle school and
the junior high, conferences supplemented report
cards. 7) Better articulation and closer age grouping were deemed the strengths of the middle school.
8) Grades 5 and 9 were not considered appropriate for
either the middle school or the junior high school.

10082.   Fox, D. F.   "A Comparison of Gains in Cognitive
Abilities and Affective Behaviors of Disadvantaged
Black Students in Open and Traditional Middle School
Programs." Ph.D. Dissertation, New York University.
Dissertation Abstracts International, 37 (1-A), 42.
Order no. 76-12,577, July, 1976.

Author determined that the students in the sample
were randomly assigned to traditional and open
education classes, as the school administration had
claimed and that there was no significant difference
in cognitive abilities or affective behaviors between
educational programs, between sexes, or between age
groups. Also, there were no significant differences
between the teaching practices in the traditional and
open classes. The study's random sample, drawn from
the sixth grade population of a middle school consisted of ninety students from traditional classes
and ninety from open classes.

10083.   Frankel, E.   "Grade Reorganization of Middle
Schools in the Public School System."   New York:
Center for Urban Education, September, 1967.

This report evaluates the progress of fourteen pilot
intermediate schools organized in September 1966 into
either a 6-8 or a 5-7 grade structure. Nine of the
schools served children in economically disadvantaged
areas. A specially revised curriculum was introduced
into the pilot schools at the sixth grade level.
Extensive teacher training preceded the program.
Data were gathered assessing 1) the extent of integration in the pilot schools, 2) school personnel and
facilities, 3) school organization and services, 4)
curriculum, 5) reactions of sixth grade pupils and
their parents to the program, and 6) reading achievement of sixth grade pupils in pilot and nonpilot
schools, measured by the metropolitan reading test.
Students in the pilot schools did not read

significantly better than students in nonpilot schools, but the pilot program in general seemed to have some success. The greatest problems were lack of well-trained teachers, high teacher mobility, inadequate school facilities, static ethnic patterns, and high pupil transiency. Test scores and other relevant data are appended. The data included official school records, responses to questionnaires, interviews, and checklists of school administrators, guidance and service personnel, teachers, pupils, and parents. In assessing departmentalization for sixth graders, some assistants to principals indicated that moving children from class to class and adjusting of class periods to meet the shorter attention span of the younger children presented problems. (Among students, nine out of ten preferred departmentalization to the customary elementary school practice.) Concerning inclusion of the sixth grade in the intermediate school, reactions of assistants to principals ranged from enthusiastic acceptance to firm resistance, with several indicating a desire to defer judgment. In itemizing problems met by teachers, the assistants to principals cited the need to adjust expectations and methods to younger children. Some mentioned the large number of pupils each teacher had to relate to because of departmentalization. Several indicated a definite need for more teacher training. General school problems cited by assistants to principals included lack of space, materials, and facilities for many types of activities; the long distances traveled by some pupils; and the need to convince teachers and parents of the advantages of the intermediate school program.

10084. Frankel, E. "Grade Reorganization Preparatory to the Establishment of the Four-Year Comprehensive High School." New York: Center for Urban Education, September, 1967.

This report evaluates a New York City reorganization plan which removed the ninth grade from thirty-nine junior high schools in disadvantaged areas and transferred the students to either academic or vocational high schools. Goals were to achieve quality integrated education and to improve the ethnic balance of the high schools. Evaluations were conducted after the first and second years of operation, using data from questionnaires, interviews, and school visits. This second-year evaluation explores ethnic trends, integration and desegregation, plant utilization, school organization and administration, curriculum modifications, and the reactions of administrators, teachers, and students. Because one purpose of the reorganization was to decrease school leaving and improve academic achievement, findings on student performance are presented in terms of attendance and turnover percentages, academic records, and reading comprehension gains on citywide tests. The major recommendation is for a moratorium on the further transfer of junior high school students until the high schools can absorb and adjust to the present enrollment of disadvantaged students. Also needed is a doubling of funds to better serve the additional students and to provide in-service teacher training and specialized school services. This evaluation marks the end of the second year of the high school grade reorganization plan, a critical period since few educational experiments live beyond this point. The transfer plan has created a favorable ethnic balance in those high schools which previously were partially or fully white. However, in some instances the rate at which disadvantaged minority students were transferred from segregated junior high schools was far greater than the receiving high schools could realistically handle. Since many of these students were educationally retarded, they were placed in general or remedial classes, thus creating segregation within the school setting, the very condition which it was hoped the transfer plan would reduce.

10085.   Frey, S. H. "A Descriptive Study of the Problems and Procedures of Articulation Between the Junior and Senior High Schools Accredited by the North Central Association in Public School Systems Organized on a 6-6 or 6-3-3 Basis." Ph.D. Dissertation, State University of Iowa, 1962.

This study of 206 junior and senior high school principals in 6-3-3 schools and 108 principals in 6-6 systems from nine states explored the articulation problems involved in administrative organization, curriculum, guidance programs, teaching staffs, and extra-class programs. Communication by means of conferences and meetings was a widely used articulation practice. Another widely used practice was having one person responsible for a program or activity from grades 7 through 12. Theory in articulation rests essentially on the idea of good communication between the units concerned. This communication takes place either through direct verbal contact or through the use of sequential curricular materials. The most frequently used articulation practices were those which kept the lines of communication open.

10086.   Frymier, J. and Hawn, H. Curriculum Improvements for Better Schools. Worthington, Ohio: Charles A. Jones Publishing Co., 1970.

Part Two of the book is a study of the problems of transition from elementary to junior high school. Questions explored include how the grade patterns of elementary schools affect the transition, what students think would help them in making the transition, what parents think are the problems confronting their children as they enter the seventh grade, and how teachers feel about these problems. Two questionnaires were completed by 480 students in a Riverside junior high school, another questionnaire was sent to parents, and a third was given to thirty-five students and was supplemented by individual counseling sessions. Students indicated that their elementary schools helped them get ready for junior high school through: 1) discussions in their sixth grade classes, 2) a trip to a junior high school, and 3) departmentalization of the elementary school. Among the seventh graders, 44 percent had some experience in departmentalized schools before entering junior high school, with less than 3 percent indicating they did not like this arrangement. Virtually all the students--97 percent--had a different teacher for each subject in junior high school. Some experience in departmentalization would have been helpful in the upper grades of elementary school, according to 39 percent of the students, and 73 percent of the parents thought limited or complete departmentalization of the sixth grade would be beneficial. Students expressed strong positive feelings for their junior high school. Seventh graders indicated it would have helped their transition if as sixth graders they had: 1) experience in departmentalization, 2) a discussion of rules, regulations, and procedures as stated in the junior high handbook, 3) more homework, 4) more and harder classwork, and 5) teacher explanation about junior high and what would be expected of them. Among parents, 72 percent felt the elementary school was adequately equipped, but only 57 percent felt the junior high was supplied with necessary equipment. The study also explored parents' feelings about the ability grouping of students, the relationship between their child's teacher and themselves and other aspects of their children's school experience.

10087.   Gabel, D. and Herron, J. D.   "The effects of grouping and pacing on learning rate, attitude, and retention in ISCS classrooms."   Journal of Research in Science Teaching, 14,5(1977):385-399.

This study examined the effects of allowing seventh grade students to pace themselves to achieve mastery versus imposing a deadline for completion of materials in the Intermediate Science Curriculum Study (ISCS). Results showed that among the 1,022 subjects, differences in learning rate and retention were related to pacing, mental ability, and grouping. Children of higher ability learned faster, and the rate of learning varied from chapter to chapter. In general, results suggest that students learn more effectively when they are allowed to pace themselves rather than being given deadlines.

10088.   Garbarino, J., Burston, N., Crouter, A., and Kops, P. "Adult Involvement in the Social Maps of Youth: The Transition from Elementary School to Secondary School." Paper presented at the American Psychological Association Convention, Toronto, Ont., ERIC Doc. ED 166 633, 1978.

Researchers studied early adolescent social networks (maps) by interviewing students and mothers in sixth grade and again in eighth grade. Interviews stressed the ages and roles of people in the child's social network, as perceived by the parent and child. Mothers perceived more adults in children's social networks than the children did and both children and parents reported more adult involvement in eighth grade than in sixth grade. Gender, ordinal position in the family, socioeconomic status, family structure, and stage of physical development made relatively few differences in the social maps. The research focused on how the roles of adults in the social maps of children change as the children make the transition from elementary to junior high school and how these changes are affected by maturational, demographic and socioeconomic factors.

10089.   Garcia, G. B. "Junior High School Size." Dissertation, University of Southern California, Los Angeles, 1961.

Study concluded that the optimum junior high school enrollment is 1200 students, with a minimum of 1,000 (with no serious modifications down to 750) and an upper limit of 1400. Under no conditions should there be more than 1800 pupils in a junior high school. Author studied courses, student activities, staff qualifications, and teacher-pupil relationships in twenty junior high schools (grades 7-9) in southern California. He surveyed 2,028 pupils, 894 teachers, and 210 principals.

10090.   Garty, R. H. "The Effect of DRA and SQ3R on the Immediate and Delayed Recall of Seventh Grade Social Studies Material." M.Ed. Thesis, Rutgers University, ERIC Doc. ED 108 125, 1975.

This study of eighty-four seventh graders showed that the Direct Reading Activities (DRA) technique was an effective organizer of seventh grade social studies material for poor readers. See ERIC Abstract #ED 108 125.

10091.   Gatewood, T.   "A Comparative Study of the Functions of Organizational Structure and Instructional
Process of Selected Junior High Schools and Middle
Schools." Dissertation, Indiana University, Bloomington, 1970.

Study compared perceptions of early adolescent
schooling by certified personnel in ten middle
schools and ten junior high schools in Illinois,
Indiana, Kentucky, Michigan, and Ohio.   Questionnaires were sent to the twenty schools, and a visit
was made to each school to interview the principal.
Author had four major hypotheses and 156 subhypotheses.   Findings: 1) Certified personnel in middle
schools and junior high schools differ in their
perceptions of the functions of the middle years of
schooling.   However, middle schools and junior high
schools are more similar than different in actual
organization and instruction.   2) Perceptions of
junior high and middle school teachers differ most on
the functions of vocational preparation, school
government, elective courses, and guidance.   3)
Certified personnel in junior high schools were
predominantly higher in personal acceptance of the
unique functions of early adolescent schooling while
personnel in middle schools perceived a higher degree
of implementation of these functions.   4) In both
kinds of schools, the respondents considered pupil
development through special curriculum and instruction the most important and unique features of their
schools.   5) Middle school organization is established for reasons more administrative than educational.   The opposite is true for the retention of
the grade level organizations of junior high schools.
6) Findings about school functions, organization, and
instruction indicate that in both middle schools and
junior high schools, the middle school concept exists
more as an ideal than a reality.

10092.   Gatewood, T. E.   "What research says about the
junior high versus the middle school." North Central
Association Quarterly, 46,2(1971):264-276.

Conclusions derived from considerable research show:
1) Existing junior high schools and middle schools
are generally more similar than different.   Research
gives no unequivocal answer to which type of
schooling is better. 2) One study does indicate that
grade 5-8 middle schools with five to seven hundred
students develop the most positive self-concepts in
students. 3) In theory and philosophical foundations
the middle school is less oriented to the high school
type of program.   4) Middle schools have been established for reasons more administrative than educational (see bibliography entry 1091).   5) Research
has not given a definitive answer about whether the

middle schools or the junior highs provide a better
grade pattern for grouping emergent adolescents
according to physical, psychological, and social
characteristics. Furthermore, no empirical data are
available to prove or disprove the frequently maintained belief that puberty has been setting in at a
significantly earlier age in recent years. Article
discusses the emergence of the middle school, the
middle school concept, the middle school versus the
junior high, what the research says, research
favoring the junior high school, research favoring
the middle school, and procedures for the study.
Author concludes that a grade 5-8 middle school with
five to seven hundred students is the most appropriate school for transescents.

10093.   Gatewood, T. E.   "What research says about the
middle school."   Educational Leadership, 31,3(1973):
221-224.

Research findings suggest that if some positive
trends continue, middle schools may yet fulfill their
promise of focusing on the period of growth between
childhood and adolescence and providing 1) a home
base and teacher to help every student make almost
daily decisions about special needs and learning
opportunities, 2) balanced attention to personal
development, learning skills, and effective use of
knowledge, 3) emphasis on individual progress, with
many curricular options and with individualized
instruction, 4) interdisciplinary team planning,
instructing, and evaluating, and 5) a wide range of
exploratory activities for the socializing, interest
developing, and leisure enriching purposes of the
bridge school. The phenomenal emergence of new grade
organizations for the middle grades has occurred for
reasons more administrative than educational. Middle
schools have adopted the educational program practices of junior highs, thus not successfully achieving the middle school concept. The most appropriate
grade organization of middle schools cannot be determined from the available research.

10094.   Gatewood, T. E. and Walker, G. H., Jr.   "A Com-
parative Study of Middle Schools and Junior High
Schools in the State of Michigan."   Central Michigan
University. Washington, D.C.:   Educational Resource
Information Center, 1971.

Proportional stratified sampling provided a selection
of 138 junior high schools and 138 middle schools in
Michigan. A survey of the principals showed: 1)
Both school types had programs and instruction similar to those used in the past for early adolescents.
2) The top ranked reason for the establishment of the
grade and age level organization of the middle

schools was "to reduce overcrowded conditions in the
other schools."   3) The top ranked reason for the
retention of the grade and age level organization of
junior high school was "to provide a program designed
for students in the age group served."   4) Slightly
more middle schools than junior high schools used
entire departmentalization with a teacher for each
subject and interdisciplinary team teaching in grades
7 and 8.   5) Slightly more junior high schools used
subject area team teaching and a combination of
either self-contained or block-of-time planned
instruction.   6) Slightly larger numbers of junior
high schools used large-group and small-group
instruction, flexible scheduling, core classes,
ability grouping, tutorial programs, and individually
prescribed instruction.   (The greatest contrast
between junior high and middle schools appeared in
the use of core classes and ability grouping.)   7)
Slightly more middle schools used both small-group
instruction and independent study in the same grade.

10095.   Gaumnitz, W. H.   "Trends in public high school
reorganization."   School Life, 36(1954):77-78.

This statistical report on junior high school reorganization since 1920 shows a rapid increase in all
main patterns of reorganized schools.

10096.   Gauvain, M. T., Roper, S. S., and Nolan, R. R.
"Students' Perceptions of Behavior and Instructional
Practices in Open-Space Schools."   Stanford, Calif.:
Stanford University, Stanford Center for Research and
Development in Teaching, ERIC Doc. ED 143 939, April,
1977.

Study reviews the literature on the effect of open
space on students' academic achievement, self-
concept, and behavior.   Students were asked the following questions: 1) Were you in an open-space elementary school?   2) What are the things you like most
about open space?   3) What are the things you dislike
about open space?   4) Does the noise in the open-
space area bother you?   5) Does anything you see in
the open-space area bother you?   6) Is it easier or
harder for you to concentrate in the open-space area?
7) How often do you use the media center?   8) Do you
get to do more or different things in the open-space
area?   9) If you were a teacher, what would you do to
make open space better?   10) Do you like open space
better than self-contained classrooms?   11) If you
could choose, would you like to be in open space next
year?   12) Is there anything else you would like to
tell me about open space?   Eighty-seven percent of
the students reported they liked open space better
than self-contained classrooms.   Seventy-five percent
interviewed identified noise as the major problem.

Report discusses differences among three schools and implications and makes suggestions for improving use of open space.

10097.   Geisinger, R. W.   "Reasons for Developing Middle Schools in Pennsylvania and the Implemented Characteristics. A Report." Harrisburg: Pennsylvania State Department of Education, Bureau of Educational Research, ERIC Doc. ED 067 737, 1971.

Survey of eighty-eight Pennsylvania school districts showed that the reasons for initiating middle schools were multidimensional and that a concept of a middle school was the most significant single factor. Three fourths of the schools were making attempts to implement a developmental concept of the middle school. Other factors were administrative leadership, a precipitating event such as a study or report, a problem situation, and general predisposing conditions. Respondents felt that there was a lack of adequate teacher preparation for this age group and that such training should emphasize technical skills in instruction and the use of media. See ERIC Abstract #ED 067 737.

10098.   George, P.   "Florida's junior high and middle schools: how do they compare?" Middle School Journal, 23(1977):10-11.

After more than a decade of operation during which time the number of middle schools in Florida has come to exceed the number of junior high schools, it was appropriate to seek answers to several important questions: Is the middle school in Florida really any different from the junior high school in actual curriculum and instruction? Which school organization seems to be implementing the educational programs deemed appropriate for this age group? Has reorganization in grade level and a change in name resulted in important changes in school programs? How does each type of school meet the needs of its students? The sample for this study consisted of 127 junior high schools and 153 middle schools listed in the 1975-76 Florida Education Directory. Findings revealed that the two schools are closely related in many respects, including vertical organization, curricular practices, community service, student activities, organization of pupils, plant design, and counseling. Differences were found in certification patterns for middle school and junior high school teachers, organization of instruction, team teaching, interscholastic sports and social activities.

10099.   Glissmeyer, C. H.   "Which school for the sixth grader, the elementary or the middle school?" <u>California Journal of Educational Research</u>, <u>20</u>(1969): 176-185.

The California Advisory Council on Educational Research, Burlingame, asked sixth grade teachers in both elementary and middle schools to respond to a questionnaire about sixth grade programs. Findings revealed: 1) The middle school and elementary teachers both approved of ability grouping for instruction in arithmetic and reading. 2) The elementary teachers favored much less use of ability grouping in teaching other sixth grade subjects. 3) Ninety-seven percent of the middle school teachers favored ability grouping in the sixth grade, while 71 percent of the elementary school teachers favored such grouping. 4) Eighty-nine percent of the middle school teachers preferred a modified departmentalized classroom with ability grouping for the sixth grader, while 57 percent of the elementary teachers preferred the self-contained classroom. 5) More middle school teachers felt their school program provided a satisfactory educational program for the sixth grade pupil with above average, average, and below average IQ. 6) The middle school teachers generally felt their school provided an adequate counseling program for sixth graders as well as for minorities. Less than 40 percent of the elementary school teachers felt their counseling program was adequate for the sixth graders, and a lesser percentage felt the program was adequate for the minority students. 7) Both the middle school and elementary school teachers expressed little preference between a nongraded or multigraded school, but over 60 percent of both groups expressed a preference for team teaching and flexible scheduling. 8) Ninety-four percent of the middle school teachers and 21 percent of the elementary school teachers felt the middle school offered a better total educational program for the sixth grader. 9) The middle school teachers felt their schools provided a better educational program, better facilities and services, a better social adjustment within and between grades, and better racial and cultural integration.

10100.   Gordon, J., Johnston, J. H., Markle, G., and Strahan, D.   "Priorities for research in middle school education." <u>Middle School Journal</u>, <u>11</u>,2 (1980):15-17.

The purpose of this study was to determine a consensus among people in middle school education on what research is needed. Authors sent three rounds of questionnaire mailings to members of the National Middle School Association. From replies by four

hundred members, authors identified topics of needed
research and the consensus of respondents on the
usefulness of each research topic. Research problems
were classified into five areas: 1) organizing the
middle school (plans, programs, and staff), 2) char-
acterizing middle school students, 3) teaching middle
school students, 4) training middle school teachers,
and 5) obtaining public support for the middle school
concept. A table rates the usefulness of thirty-six
identified research problems. Study concluded that
applied research on specific practices and procedures
is more likely to improve education for middle school
students than is research comparing junior high
schools and middle schools. Theoretical research,
especially on psychological and physiological
development and their impact on learning, would be
helpful.

10101.   Green, R. C. "A Study of the Perceptions of Principals of Michigan Junior High Schools and Middle
Schools on the Degree to Which Their Schools Implement Selected Practices Recommended in Literature on
Intermediate Education." Ph.D. Dissertation, University of Michigan. Dissertation Abstracts International, Order no. 77-26,250, 1977.

Author analyzed responses of 276 middle school and
junior high school principals in Michigan to a survey
asking how much their schools used certain practices
representing quality education in the middle years.
Findings included: 1) In general the selected practices, taken together, were used at a level greater
than that labeled "somewhat implemented." The
highest implementation was in philosophy and staff.
(Principals reported they wanted to use the selected
practices at a level greater than that labeled
"implemented to a high degree," so a substantial disparity appeared between their perceptions of actual
implementation and their desired implementation of
the selected practices.) 2) Principals of grade 5-8
or 6-8 middle schools and grade 7-9 junior high
schools showed no significant differences in their
perceptions of how much their schools implement practices grouped in the areas of philosophy, organization and administration, instructional program,
activity program, staff, and facilities. 3) Using a
school-type definition based on the judgment of the
principals rather than grade organization gives many
more differences between middle schools and junior
high schools, and the differences tend to be more
pronounced.

10102.   Greenfeld, N. and Finkelstein, E. L. "A
comparison of the characteristics of junior high
school students." Journal of Genetic Psychology,
117,1(1970):37-50.

Study showed significant differences in personal and social characteristics between 250 junior high school students who were studied from 1930 to 1935 and a similar sample of students today.   See ERIC Abstract #EJ 026 325.

10103.   Hallinan, M. and Felmlee, D.   "An analysis of intransitivity in sociometric data."   Sociometry, 38,2(1975):195-212.

Analysis of fifty-one sociograms obtained from junior high school classes revealed a very low incidence of intransitivity in friendship choices in every group. Intransitivity refers to relationships in which A chooses B, and B chooses C, but A does not choose C. The intransitive triads which did exist were examined at different choice levels to determine if the intensity of the relationships affected the structure of the triad.   Authors detected patterns in the kinds of intransitive triads that appeared most frequently, and they observed that the number of intransitive triads in which an individual was involved varied with the individual.

10104.   Harper, T.   "Altering the Apathetic Parent-Community Attitudes Toward an Inner-City Secondary Community School."   Ed.D. Dissertation, Nova University, ERIC Doc. ED 113 814, August, 1975.

A support team of nonteaching school personnel and community representatives planned and coordinated efforts at a junior high school to reduce apathy, absenteeism, tardiness, class cutting, vandalism, and failing grades among seventh graders, to help the students become involved in extracurricular activities, and to encourage parent interest and involvement in student affairs.   Report discusses background, support team members, the advisory group, objectives, activities, target population, intervention strategies, evaluation, an attitudinal survey, the communications process, dissemination, and a summary.   Results of the study showed improvement on all student-related objectives but no improvement in parent involvement.

10105.   Harris, D. E.   "A Comparative Study of Selected Middle Schools and Selected Junior High Schools." Dissertation, Ball State University, Muncie, Indiana, 1968.

Study compared the instructional organization, academic programs, teachers' classes and student load, cocurricular activities, and reasons for any changes in selected junior high and middle schools. The middle schools were identified from periodic literature, recently published books, and written correspondence with state and national education organizations. The junior high schools were matched with each of the selected middle schools in size of student body and type of community. Conclusions were: 1) Certain aspects of basic programs were more common in the middle schools, while others were common in the junior high schools, and still others were common in both types of schools. 2) The basic programs of the selected middle schools and junior high schools were more alike than they were different. 3) Each of the selected schools plans to continue its present organizational structure. 4) The selected schools, both as a group and separately, were using very few of the innovative concepts advocated in the review of literature contained in the study.

10106.   Hartman, R. A.   "The Structure of Intellect (SOI) Scores of Gifted Junior High School Students Exposed in Fifth and Sixth Grades to Separate Education Environments."   Ed.D. Dissertation, University of San Francisco. Dissertation Abstracts International, 40 (04), Sec. A, 1961. Order no. 7923017. 1979.

Study correlated Stanford-Binet scores and SRA achievement scores for two groups of gifted students and a third group whose Stanford-Binet score was below 132 IQ. Author also applied Guilford's Structure of Intellect Categories to each Stanford-Binet response. The three groups did show some statistically significant differences in the Guilford's Structure of Intellect scores and their SRA achievement scores. There is firm evidence that the intelligence scores and the Stanford-Binet scores were reasonably well correlated with academic success. There was no evidence that the gifted students could be characterized as convergent or divergent thinkers.

10107.   Hatley, R. V., Holloway, W. H., and Hiebert, R. "Student attitudes toward school: open versus traditional education."   Southern Journal of Educational Research, 11,4(1977):183-196.

Authors administered the Attitude Toward School survey to 160 seventh, eighth, and ninth grade students in an open educational program and 160 similar students in a traditional program. Conclusions: 1) Students in open programs are significantly more positive in their attitudes toward school. 2) These differences hold for seventh, eighth, and ninth grades. 3) Time in an open education program is an important intervening variable. Authors recommend longitudinal research to study the effects of open education, using dependent variables other than student attitudes toward school.

10108.   Hedberg, J. D.   "Pupil Control Ideology of Middle
School Teachers and Its Relationship to Student
Alienation and to Selected Organizational and Teacher
Variables."   Ph.D. Dissertation, Michigan State Uni-
versity.   Dissertation Abstracts International, 34
(3-A), 1024-1025. Order no. 73-20,348, 1973.

A pupil control ideology form was administered to 569
teachers in twenty-three Michigan middle schools
housing grades 6-8 or 7-9.   A tutor-tutee form was
also used.   The data supported previous findings that
the sex of a teacher and the length of his or her
teaching experience are related to pupil control in
ideology.   Teacher certification, age, size of
school, and school organizational patterns were also
related to pupil control ideology of teachers.
Author discusses implications of this study for personnel practices, size and structure of the middle
school, teacher leave policies, teacher training policies, and in-service problem solving.

10109.   Hillyer, J. L.   "A Comparative Study of Maturity
Factors of Elementary and Middle School Pupils with
Implications for School Grade Organization."   Ed.D.
Dissertation, University of Missouri, Columbia, 1972.

Study compared the emotional, intellectual, social,
and interest maturity of students in grades 4-7.   The
students were from five elementary and five middle
schools in six counties of northwestern Illinois.
Twenty-five male and twenty-five female students were
studied in each grade at the ten schools, making a
total of 250 students of each sex.   The middle
schools included grades 4-6, 4-7, or 4-8.   The five
elementary schools had a K-8 grade organization.   The
Otis Quick Scoring Mental Ability Test was used to
measure intellectual ability.   Interest maturity information, including data on which activities were
liked, disliked, avoided, or engaged in, was obtained
through the Interest and Activities section of the
California Test of Personality.   The Personal and
Social sections of this test measured the emotional
and social maturity of the students and included
information on belonging, feeling, sense of worth,
self-reliance, nervous symptoms, withdrawal, family
and community relations, social standards and skills,
and antisocial tendencies.   The data were analyzed
according to type of school, grade level, sex, and
according to the interaction of these three factors.
Findings: 1) In sixteen of seventeen comparisons,
middle school pupils scored higher than elementary
school students, and in one comparison there was no
significant difference.   2) On social and emotional
maturity, middle school fourth graders scored higher
than elementary school fourth graders.   3) On
interest maturity, middle school fifth graders scored

higher than elementary school fifth graders. 4) On intellectual and interest maturity, middle school sixth and seventh graders scored higher than elementary school sixth and seventh graders. 5) Girls scored higher than boys on seven of the sixteen comparisons. 6) In no case did boys score higher than girls on emotional, intellectual, social, or interest maturity.

10110. Holmgren, C. A. "An Assessment of the Possible Relationship of the Practice of Meditation to Increases in Attentiveness to Learning." ERIC Doc. ED 085 608, December, 1972.

Author hypothesizes that meditation, which leads to greater self-awareness, will facilitate greater attentiveness to learning. A pretest and posttest based on simple rote memory showed a significant increase in the number of objects recalled by sixteen experimental subjects, but no significant increase in learning by a control group. A second posttest given at the end of six months showed no significant increases in either group. Study discusses the nature of the adolescent period, coping mechanisms and their relation to low self-esteem, learning as a function of self-exploration, and self-discovery.

10111. Howard, A. W. "The Middle School in Washington and Oregon, 1965-1966." Ed.D. Dissertation, University of Oregon. University Microfilms, Ann Arbor, Mich., 1966.

Study compared the organizational practices, administrative practices, facilities, and programs of twenty-five middle schools and twenty-five grade 7-9 junior high schools paired by enrollment and geographical location in Oregon and Washington. Questionnaire data from the school administrators was hand tabulated, and percentage tables were used for comparisons of items. Author examined the findings in relation to claimed advantages of the middle schools. Claimed advantage 1: The middle school permits some departmentalizing and instruction by specialists in the lower grades of the middle school and at the same time reduces somewhat the fragmentation into which some junior highs have wandered. Finding: These middle schools do permit some departmentalization in grades 5 and 6. They are more apt to be departmentalized in grade 7 than are the paired junior high schools, both in practice and in recommended policies, and so do not appear to reduce fragmentation. Claimed advantage 2: Allows a more logical grouping in terms of social maturity and sophistication. Finding: Better age grouping was most often listed by middle school administrators as an advantage of this form of organization. Claimed

advantage 3:   Permits a reduction in activities and
attitudes which are too mature and reduces over-
emphasis upon interscholastic activities, varsity
sports, and marching band. Finding: The paired
junior high schools indicated definite tendencies
toward operating a larger and more inclusive program
of activities than did the middle schools in
virtually all areas. Claimed advantage 4:   Permits
enrichment of the sixth grade program (and fifth too,
if it is included in the middle school) by introduction of areas such as foreign language, science, and
art. Finding: For the most part middle schools
offer little variety in the way of exploratory and
enriched curriculum. Claimed advantage 5:   Makes
better facilities available to sixth graders. Finding: The middle schools were less likely than the
junior high schools to have the listed facilities.

10112.   Howell, C. E.   "Junior high: How valid are its
original aims?" Clearinghouse, 23(1948):75-78.

More than a hundred junior high school administrators
appraised forty-five original aims of the junior high
school in an early survey reported here.

10113.   Hughes, F. W.   "Self-Concept Development in Inner-
City Seventh Grade Youth as Affected by the Influence
of Community School Counseling on Significant
Others." Ph.D. Dissertation, Catholic University of
America, ERIC Doc. ED 085 613, 1972.

Author studied the effect of parent counseling on
student self-concepts, attitudes, and values after
thirteen weeks. Author also studied the effectiveness of the afternoon and evening community school (3
p.m. to 9 p.m.) in creating a guidance role to
enhance and extend the services of the basic program
(9 a.m. to 3 p.m.). A pretest and posttest and the
California Test of Personality were given to 188
seventh graders in five junior high schools. See
ERIC Abstract #ED 085 613.

10114.   Hunt, J. J., Berg, L. L., and Doyle, D.   "The
continuing trend toward middle school organizational
patterns." Journal of Secondary Education, 45,
4(1970):170-173.

A questionnaire sent to fifty state instruction
offices showed that schools with grades 5-8, 6-8, and
7-8 fit the description of a middle school. Article
ranks states by number of middle schools, lists the
number in each state, and describes the grade
patterns of middle schools in each state. In 1970
there were approximately 6500 junior high schools in
operation in the United States. It was apparent from
three studies identified in the article that a

definite trend from the traditional 7-9 junior high school to some combination of lower grades was underway for the decade of the '70s.

10115.   Jacobs, J. W.   "Leadership, Size, and Wealth as Related to Curricular Innovations in the Junior High School." Ph.D. Dissertation, University of Michigan. Dissertation Abstracts International, 27 (2-A), 354. Order no. 66-6624, 1966.

Findings revealed no significant relationship between the number of curricular innovations and the size and wealth of schools. The hypothesis that the principals who were rated as "high innovative" would display a different type of leadership than the "low innovative" principals was accepted. The "high innovative" principals received higher ratings in 1) initiating structure, 2) predictive accuracy, 3) representation, 4) integration, 5) persuasion, and 6) consideration.   Author surveyed 138 public junior high school principals.

10116.   Jensen, H. L.   "A Descriptive Study of Differences in Social-Psychological Attitudes Between Students in Open and Traditional Middle School Classrooms." Ph.D. Dissertation, Michigan State University. Dissertation Abstracts International, 37 (2-A), 784. Order no. 76-18,636, 1976.

In response to an attitude questionnaire, students in the open classrooms of a Michigan middle school scored consistently higher than students in the school's traditional classrooms on all attitudes except "authoritarian," on which the traditional classroom students scored consistently higher.   No pattern of differences was found in values. Results suggest that either the open classroom experience has a significant influence on social-psychological attitudes of students or that the existence of a priori attitude differences results in success and satisfaction with the open classroom.   There is a lack of definitive information on which to base a judgment about these two possibilities.

10117.   Jester, J. F., Jr.   "A Comparative Study of the Effects of Team Teaching and Departmentalized Teaching on the Scholastic Achievement of Eighth Grade Students in Social Studies and Lanuage Arts." Ed.D. Dissertation, University of Kansas. University Microfilms, Ann Arbor, Mich., ERIC Doc. ED 029 876, 1966.

An experimental group of 197 eighth graders in a team teaching junior high school and a control group of 262 eighth graders in a departmentalized junior high school were tested for mental ability and basic skills in reading comprehension, vocabulary, language skills, and study skills. Study found no statistical difference in social studies achievement between the two groups but concluded that team teaching was significantly more effective than departmental organization in producing achievement in the language arts. See ERIC Abstract #ED 029 876.

10118.   Joans, R. L.   "Student views of special placement in their own special classes: a clarification." Exceptional Children, 41,1(1974):22-29.

Responses of 341 junior high school mental retardates and 717 nonretarded students to Wrightman's School Morale Inventory revealed that retarded students reject the stigma of special placement but hold many positive attitudes toward their own classroom and school experiences. Analysis of responses from 114 suburban mental retardates and 227 inner-city retardates reveals more positive attitudes held by the suburban retarded.

10119.   Johnston, J. H. and McCann, C. K.   "Middle school research: the state of the art." Transescence: The Journal of Emerging Adolescent Education,   8,1(1980): 6-12.

Research has failed to conceptualize the middle school in such a way that educators can identify the practices likely to affect student learning and development.   Instead, educators have tended to develop programs that are well grounded in the theory of human development and then compare schools to see if they have different effects on students.   It would be more profitable to focus research on the nature of the instruction the student encounters.   Researchers should examine only those variables which meet two criteria: 1) They are linked, by theory or by logic, to some anticipated outcome of the treatment provided.   2) They can be mediated, changed, or influenced by the school and its operations.

10120.   Justman, J.   "Academic achievement of intellectually gifted accelerants and non-accelerants in junior high school." School Review, 62(1954):142-150.

This study compares achievement of matched pairs of students in special-progress and normal-progress classes in junior high schools of New York City. Achievement is measured by tests in mathematics, science, social studies, and study skills and by ratings of creative expression in the language arts.

10121.   Kealy, R. P.   "The middle school movement, 1960-1970."   National Elementary Principal,   51,3(1971): 20-25.

Article summarizes national surveys on middle schools through 1970, discusses the present status of middle schools in several states, and draws general conclusions. Author sees a clear trend toward the middle school.

10122.   Kehas, C. D.   "Grouping for instruction and self-definition."   Measurement and Evaluation in Guidance, 2,4(1970):205-213.

Junior high school students were classified into five levels in three subject areas and measured on three subscales of the California Test of Personality--sense of personal worth, feeling of belonging, and school relations.   Results showed self-definition is highly related to ability grouping in science, moderately so in mathematics, and randomly in language arts.   Article includes sections on prior studies, the method used, groupings by content area, and a discussion.   The relation of self-definition to science and mathematics grouping may reflect cultural pressure for achievement in these highly valued fields, making it extremely difficult for students to separate their own feelings of worth from school performance in these areas.

10123.   Khan, M. W.   "A Study of the New Organizational Structure of the Indiana University Junior High School, Bloomington, Indiana."   Ph.D. Dissertation, Indiana University, 1965.

Study discusses a theoretical rationale for one school's new organizational pattern, the administrative processes involved in the change, and the reaction of teachers and students.   Comprehensive change in educational curriculum, methodology, and organization was considered imperative in order to individualize education.   The administrators of five other schools selected on the basis of specific criteria were interviewed.   A questionnaire containing fifty-six items and personal data was distributed to two groups of teachers in the subject school and one group outside the school.   Questions covered employment of school staff, opportunities to attend to the individual needs of students, curriculum reorganization, the effects of variation in class size, needed changes in school plant and physical facilities, use of new technological media, the amount of time available to teachers for planning and preparation, changes in the school's grade organization and evaluation system, goals of the school program, assumptions in support of desired change, teacher responsibility for guidance, and parent-teacher relationships.   The data confirmed the need for organizational change in the school and suggested certain

aspects which should be changed. Conclusions concerned the initiative in administering change, the
extent and process of change, the facilities and
problems involved in change, and the responsibilities
of the school personnel, and human relations within
the school.

10124.   Kidder, F. R.   "An Investigation of 9-, 11-, and
13-Year-Old Children's Comprehension of Euclidean
Transformations."   Paper presented at the Annual
Meeting of the National Council of Teachers of Mathematics, Atlantic City, N. J., ERIC Doc. ED 098 054,
1974.

This study determined middle school children's ability to form a mental image of a planar figure and to
1) mentally flip, turn, or slide this representation
and then construct the resultant image in correct
position ("performing individual motions"), 2) perform two such motions in succession ("composition of
motions"), 3) perform the process in reverse ("inverse motions"), and 4) hold length invariant while
attempting these three operations.   Thirty students
in the upper quartile of ability in grades 4, 6, and
8 were used as subjects.   This study was based on
three major themes from Piaget's research on child
development of space: 1) His major focus in space
development is space representation, not space perception.   2) He believes that these spatial representations are built up through the organization of
mental actions performed on objects in space.   3) He
claims that children's earliest spatial concepts are
topological in nature and that their projective and
Euclidean concepts are extensions of these topological concepts.   A pretest and transformational tests
were given.   The findings did not support the experimental hypothesis that adolescents could perform
Euclidean transformations, compositions of transformations, and inverse transformations at the represen-
tational level.   The findings were not consistent
with the theoretical base of this study, nor were the
results of previous studies.   Author stressed the
importance of the need for further research in the
area of transformational geometry and the content of
the mathematical curriculum for junior high school
students.

10125.   King, M. J.   "A Study of the K-8 School as a Setting for Early Adolescent Education."   Dissertation,
Harvard University, 1978.

Study examined how the eighth graders at one neighborhood K-8 school perceive the school as a setting
for early adolescent education.   The author, who was
an administrative intern at a public suburban middle

class K-8 school, did in-depth interviews of twenty-
one students, fifteen teachers, and the principal.
The K-8 school has been neglected by theorists,
researchers, and practitioners, with the debate over
the best school setting for early adolescents
focusing on specialized, age-segregated institutions.
Author's premise was that the K-8 school should be
reconsidered as a setting for early adolescent
schooling because the broad range of children in a
neighborhood school seems to be more congruent with
basic human needs that are associated with man living
in community, i.e., a sense of history, territory,
and diversity. The premise of his methodology was
that to understand how well a school environment
meets people's needs one must examine how school members relate to, participate in, and orient themselves
toward the environment. The data analysis consisted
primarily of qualitative descriptions of members'
perceptions of the school environment and their conceptions of relevant issues. Author examined what
members said about their experience, assessed their
views through his own perspective as an administrative intern, and analyzed the school's opportunities
and constraints in terms of a framework of human
needs. Four major findings emerged: 1) Students who
have been at the school for as few as three years
speak with much the same sense of cohesiveness and
affiliation as do students who have been there since
kindergarten. This suggests that it helps newer
students develop an attachment to the school if a
nucleus of students has shared a past there. 2) Naturally occurring contacts between younger and older
children at the school are not necessarily positive.
3) The simple staff organization enables staff to
maintain a strong academic focus.

10126.   Knowles, P. L., et al.   "An Evaluation of the
          Operant Method of Teaching Disruptive and Nonlearning
          Students in the Classroom. Final Report to the
          Florida State NDEA Steering Committee." Boca Raton:
          Florida Atlantic University, ERIC Doc. ED 034 711,
          May 1, 1969.

          In this project, behavior modification techniques
          (making some consequence or reward contingent upon
          appropriate behavior of the individual or group) were
          demonstrated at teachers' meetings in a predominantly
          white elementary school, a predominantly black junior
          high, and a special education center. Twenty-four
          teachers volunteered to observe their colleagues' use
          of the techniques, and they recorded data on 367 stu-
          dents. These observers were to count attempted mod-
          ifications of individual behavior and group behavior.
          Data was to have covered three basic observation
          phases: premodification, modification, and postmodi-
          fication. Thirty-seven premodification phases were

not followed by modification; twenty-six behaviors were graphed through modification, and nineteen were completed through the final phase. Results indicate that modification techniques can be applied by teachers, parents, and guidance personnel to produce significant changes in behavior of children. See ERIC Abstract #ED 034 711.

10127. Koepsel, E. A. "The Effectiveness of Individually Guided Education on the Development of Self-Esteem in Middle School Students." Ph.D. Dissertation, Marquette University, 1975.

Individually Guided Education (IGE) is a total system which takes into account the student's previous knowledge, how he goes about learning, how rapidly he learns, and other individual characteristics. Research questions were: 1) Will middle school students enrolled in a multiunit IGE program score significantly higher on a measure of self-esteem than middle school students enrolled in a traditional school? 2) Will middle school boys score significantly higher on this measure of self-esteem than middle school girls regardless of program? 3) Will middle school boys enrolled in a multiunit IGE program score significantly higher on a measure of self-esteem than middle school girls enrolled in the same type of program? 4) Will middle school boys enrolled in a traditional program score significantly higher on a measure of self-esteem than middle school girls enrolled in the same type of program? The results indicated that IGE schools are at least comparable to traditional middle schools in their ability to enhance students' self-esteem and perhaps have the potential to exceed traditional schools in this regard.

10128. Kohut, S., Jr. "The Middle School, a Bridge Between Elementary and Secondary Schools: What Research Says to the Teacher." Washington, D.C.: National Education Association, ERIC Doc. ED 126 054, 1976.

Report contains the following sections: 1) The Middle School (profile of the middle schooler, grade organization). 2) Curriculum and Instruction (individualized instruction, team teaching, smorgasbord of instructional practices). 3) Professional Staff (the teacher, the principal, the guidance counselor). 4) Evaluation. 5) Transition from Junior High to Middle School. 6) Conclusion. 7) Selected Research References. 8) General References. Appendices contain a preliminary planning questionnaire for a middle school action workshop and a general planning outline for a school district.

10129.   Koos, L. B.   "The superiority of the four-year junior high school."   School Review, 51(1943):397-407.

This early research was the first factual description of any considerable number of the four-year (grade 7-10) junior high schools in operation in 6-4-4 plans and the first comparison of four-year and three-year (grade 7-9) junior high schools. Seventeen four-year and thirty-four three-year schools were compared (including all but two of the nineteen four-year schools then operating). Information concerning the four-years was gathered from interviews and an eight-page questionnaire filled out by the principals. Information concerning the three-year schools was obtained from questionnaire schedules only. Visits were made to only a small proportion of the three year schools. The three-year junior high schools selected had enrollments similar to the enrollments in grades 7, 8, and 9 of the four-year schools, so the study could focus on differences that could be attributable to the addition or presence of grade 10 in the schools. The author compared the program of studies, extracurricular activities, schedules, teaching and administrative staff, material facilities, guidance programs, and library. The general conclusion is that the four-year junior high school is a better unit than the three-year school, which in turn is superior to the older 8-4 pattern. Advantages of the four-year junior high include greater enrichment and expanded possibilities of exploration. Extracurricular organizations and activities capitalize on the greater maturity of tenth graders and gives them experience in democratic leadership and participation. Four-year schools encourage a schedule more in keeping with preferred modern theory and practice. They show a trend toward a better prepared instructional staff, more nearly balanced in representation of men and women, and a more nearly adequate administrative staff. The principals report augmentation of the school plant to accommodate the enriched program of instruction and activities.

10130.   Kopp, O. W.   "The school organization syndrome vis-a-vis improved learning."   National Elementary Principal, 48(1969):42-45.

Observations of the middle school, the nongraded elementary school, and the flexibly scheduled school in various parts of the nation indicate some common outcomes. In nearly every case, the following trends seem to be present: 1) Content achievement on an individualized basis tends to be the objective. 2) Teachers tend to be content specialists--for example, a math teacher. 3) Teachers have unscheduled time for planning and independent work with children. 4)

Mobility of children tends to be a feature--for example, movement to different classrooms, resource centers, or laboratory facilities. 5) The principals tend to have a feeling of involvement in this program; usually the organizational pattern is "his baby." 6) Comprehensive information about the total child seems to be lacking. There is a tendency to know him, for example, as a "science" student. 7) Cumulative record data, which should be even more complete and inclusive because of child mobility and multiteacher responsibility, tend to be less comprehensive for this type of operation. Before changing to a new organizational pattern, a faculty might well consider a three-step approach to the problem. (The competent elementary school principal will assume the leadership in steps 1 and 2.) The three steps are: 1) Research. (Carry on a local status study--what are our specific educational objectives? What do we wish to achieve via an organizational pattern? Assess developments and trends found in the literature and compare them with what is being done at the local level). 2) Internalization. (Teachers and principals should become sold on the program they are developing. It should be truly understood and should be thought of as "our program." It should be implemented as a pilot program). 3) Satisfaction in Attainment. (Is there overt evidence that the program is working? Does it attain previously established objectives? No organizational pattern will work unless it is established and evaluated carefully in light of sound and comprehensive but specific objectives and unless the teacher is determined to serve children as individuals and uses the organizational pattern as a means to this end.)

10131. Kruger, J. M. "Interaction Patterns of Industrial Arts Teachers In Laboratory Type Situations at the Junior High School Level." Ed.D. Dissertation, University of Northern Colorado. University Microfilms, Ann Arbor, Mich., ERIC Doc. ED 049 379 (Document not available from EDRS), 1971.

The Industrial Arts Interaction Analysis System was used to study teacher/student behavior in junior high school classes. Twenty industrial arts teachers were observed on three different occasions, and two independent observers recorded the interactions between students and teachers. Findings indicated that during administrative duties, demonstration, and lecture the teachers did nearly all the talking and that the Industrial Arts Interaction Analysis System was capable of providing data. Author concluded that teachers need to know how to use their time more effectively, that student response should be encouraged, and that an important nonverbal link exists between teacher and class members. See ERIC Abstract

#ED 049 379. (See bibliography entry 10142 for a study on the same subject.)

10132.   Lahaderne, H. M. "Adaptation to School Settings: A Study of Children's Attitudes and Classroom Behavior." Research paper, part of a dissertation. University of Chicago, 1967.

Author studied 125 students in six grade and argues that rules of conduct affect their involvement in school, which varies according to their attachment to or detachment from the school. Involvement is demonstrated by their classroom behavior and is reflected in their feelings of personal responsibility and in the amount of information they volunteer about their involvement.

10133.   Lasseigne, M. W. "Assessing attitudes of junior high school students." Contemporary Education, 45,2 (1974):139-141.

In order to develop an instrument for assessing attitudes of students in one junior high school, author asked students in another junior high to list the things they liked and disliked about school. See ERIC Abstract #EJ 097 027.

10134.   Lauchner, A. H. "A study of the trends in junior high school practices in twenty-four states." Bulletin of the National Association of Secondary School Principals, 35(1951):120-125.

Lauchner presents trends observed in personal visits in 1950-51 to seventy-one junior high schools. Observations relate to block-time arrangement, integration in the core, grouping, guidance, physical education and athletics, reports to parents, etc. These schools were engaged in creating modern programs. The most significant thing happening in them was the scheduling of pupils to a single teacher for a long block of time. Some called their classes "common learnings," others called them "core curriculum," and still others referred simply to "unit teaching." Pennsylvania, Utah, California, Michigan, Maryland, West Virginia, California, Denver, St. Paul, Minneapolis, and Arlington, Virginia, had promising core curriculum programs at that time.

10135.   Lawson, A. E. "Combining variables, controlling variables, and proportions: is there a psychological link?" Science Education, 63(1979):67-72.

Discusses using science curriculum materials appropriate to specific Piagetian levels of student intellectual development. Author studied twenty-eight students who were selected from seventh grade mathematics classes in a Lafayette, California, junior high school. Their average age was 12. The subjects were individually administered three tasks, and all interviews were conducted by the same person. The tasks were making chemical combinations, bending rods, and using the balance beam. Task performance ranged widely and the results lend some support to the Piagetian hypothesis of general stages of intellectual development.

10136.   Lesyk, C. K., Katzenmeyer, C. G. and Hynes, M. E. "Student Attitudes Toward Grouping and Their Effects on Self-Concept and School Satisfaction." Kent State University, Ohio, Bureau of Educational Research. Paper presented to the Annual Convention of the American Educational Research Association, New York, ERIC Doc. ED 047 861, February, 1971.

Six hundred students in a rural school system were evaluated, with seventh and eighth graders grouped by ability and other grades included for purposes of comparison. Responses to a twenty-five item questionnaire showed: 1) Students in ability groups expressed positive attitudes toward ability grouping, with those in the highest and lowest groups being more favorable to it.   2) Students perceived their grouping placement with considerable accuracy.   3) The same kinds of attitudes were expressed by both boys and girls.   4) Students who had experienced homogeneous grouping were more favorable toward it than those who had not.   5) No significant relationship existed between course grades and attitudes toward grouping, but a significant relationship existed between achievement test scores and attitudes toward grouping, with higher achievers being more favorable toward grouping. Author also investigated the relationship between students' experience of and attitudes toward grouping, their satisfaction with school, and their self-concepts.

10137.   Lewis, G. M.   Educating children in Grades 7 and 8.   Bulletin 10, pp. 44-81. Washington, D.C.:   U. S. Office of Education, 1954, and U. S. Government Printing Office, 1960.

Part I reports the results of research into common characteristics and needs of children in grades 7 and 8 and projects some characteristics of desirable educational programs for them. Part II reports some of the things schools in this study are doing for children and some of the ways these schools work with parents and the community. The appendix indicates some areas in which the schools need further help. Chapters are: Part I, Chapter 1) Looking at Boys and Girls in Grades 7 and 8. 2) Looking at Some Demands and Hopes Which Society Holds for Children in Grades

7 and 8 and at Some Experiences of Children. 3) Some Commonly Found Qualities of Schools which Are Trying to Meet the Needs of Seventh and Eighth Grade Children. Part II, Chapter 1) How the Schools are Organized. 2) How Schools Provide for Health and Physical Development of Seventh and Eighth Graders. 3) How Schools Provide for the Social and Emotional Development of Eighth Graders. 4) How Schools Help Children in Seventh and Eighth Grade to Become More Independent Individuals and as Group Members. 5) Relationships of Parents, Schools, and Communities.

10138.   Linebarger, D. E.   "A Longitudinal Assessment of the Glendale Junior High School Modular-Flexible Organization for Instruction Focusing on Student Achievement and Morale, 1965-1969." Ed.D. Dissertation, University of Washington, 1971.

This junior high school, the first in the Pacific Northwest to use modular scheduling, team teaching, large-group and small-group instruction, and independent study was based on a philosophy that challenged four basic tenets of traditional junior high schools: 1) Each secondary school subject should be taught daily for a standard number of minutes. 2) Every instructional session should have an equal teacher-student ratio. 3) Every junior high student should be under the direct supervision of a teacher for every instructional activity. 4) Achievement is a function of direct instructional time, so reducing the time students are involved in direct instructional activity would reduce long-term student achievement. The general hypothesis of this assessment study was that in spite of considerable differences in the amount of time students spent on directly supervised instructional activities, Glendale students would do as well or better in achievement and would have higher morale than students from the two most comparable neighboring junior high school districts. The results of the assessment supported the general hypothesis of the fourteen specific hypotheses. All eight concerning junior high school achievement as measured by the SRA Achievement Series were sustained, and all five concerning achievement as measured by high school grades were sustained. However, the hypothesis concerning higher student morale as measured by a revised version of the Hendrickson Student Attitude Survey was not fully sustained.

10139.   Lipsitz, J. Growing Up Forgotten: A Review of Research and Programs Concerning Early Adolescence. Lexington, Va.:   D. C. Heath and Co., Lexington Books, 1977.

Part I: Research on Early Adolescence.   1) Research
Review on Concepts of Adolescence (an overview of
research on early adolescence, biological research,
socioemotional research, cognitive research, federal
funding for research, and research recommendations).
Part II: The Young Adolescent and Social Institutions.   2) Schools and the Young Adolescent (the
purpose of schooling, the historical development of
the junior high school, junior high schools today--
the reformers, schooling for minority youth, emerging
trends, and the abyss).   3) Service Institutions and
the Handicapped Young Adolescent.   4) The Family and
the Young Adolescent (research).   5) Voluntary Youth-
serving Agencies.   6) The Young Adolescent in the
Juvenile Justice System.   From data available in
1976, researchers know that in the school year
1973-74 there were 2,629 middle schools, 58,755
"other elementary schools," 7,462 junior high
schools, 4,445 junior/senior high schools, 2,321 combined elementary-secondary schools, 11,205 senior
high schools, and 1,365 one-teacher schools.   In
1972-73, of the twenty-eight states reporting a division of seventh and eighth grade into elementary and
secondary enrollments, 35.3% of the 7th graders were
in elementary school and 64.7% were in secondary
schools.   For 8th graders, the percentages were 32.2
and 67.8 respectively.   Because of the failure to
research adequately the various and interrelated
changes that occur during early adolescence and
because researchers have failed to conceptualize adequately this time in the life span, we have been
hampered in designing effective educational programs
for young adolescents.   This absence of knowledge and
failure to use the knowledge acquired have had a pro-
found impact on our educational system.   The author
argues that school organization as to grade level
does matter.   The data probably will not support this
argument, partly because the measures in many studies
will be inadequate, partly because content is more
important than form, given the diversity of the
students, and mostly because many of the schools will
be the same crushingly boring and utterly mediocre
environments for young adolescents, whatever the age
organization.

10140.   Livingston, S. A.   "Effects of the Legislative
Simulation Game on the Political Attitudes of Junior
High School Students."   Baltimore, Md.:   Johns
Hopkins University, Center for the Study of Social
Organization of Schools, and Washington, D.C.:   U.S.
Office of Education, ERIC Doc. ED 055 005, 1971.

Two studies investigate the effects of the game
"Democracy" on the political attitudes of eighth and
ninth grade junior high school students.   The
players, assuming the role of congressmen, quickly

discover logrolling to be the most effective way to satisfy their simulated constituencies. Both studies test these hypotheses: 1) Playing "Democracy" will cause students to be less disapproving of congressional logrolling. 2) Playing the game will increase student feelings of political efficacy. 3) Playing "Democracy" will increase the students' interest in politics and the legislative process. 4) Changes in attitude will be positively correlated with understanding of the game. Results supported all hypotheses but the last: attitude change was not positively correlated with understanding of the game. See ERIC Abstract #ED 055 005.

10141.   Livingston, S. A. "Verbal Overload in Achievement Tests." Baltimore, Md.: Johns Hopkins University, Center for the Study of Social Organization of Schools, ERIC Doc. ED 069 700, 1972.

A social studies achievement test made up of items rewritten in simplified language was compared with a test containing the same items in their original form by administering the two tests to the entire eighth grade class of a suburban junior high school near Baltimore. The results showed only slightly higher scores for students taking the simplified tests. Differences among the items in estimated reading difficulty were not associated with differences in actual response difficulty. The findings were interpreted to mean that most students who know enough to answer a test item can also read well enough to understand it. See ERIC Abstract #ED 069 700.

10142.   Loepp, F. L.   "The Development of a System to Analyze Teacher-Student Interaction in Junior High School Industrial Arts Classrooms." Ed.D. Dissertation, University of Northern Colorado. University Microfilms, Ann Arbor, Mich., and ERIC Doc. ED 043 748 (Document not available from EDRS), 1970.

After three of seven observation visits were made to ten different Colorado junior high school industrial arts classes, a system for identifying categories of interaction between students and teachers was developed. Two further observation visits were used to field-test the system, and a jury of six industrial arts educators judged it to describe the categories of interaction accurately. The system was found to be capable of providing data on general patterns of teacher-student interaction and the percentage of classroom time spent in: 1) various responsibilities, 2) all forms of teacher appraisal, 3) direct and indirect teacher talk, 4) student talk divided into categories, 5) silence, and 6) chaos and confusion. See ERIC Abstract #ED 043 748. (See bibliography entry 10131 for a study on the same subject.)

10143.   Logsdon, D. M. and Ewert, B.   "Longitudinal Study
of an Operational Model for Enhancing Central City
Youth's Self-Concept, Academic Achievement, Attitude
Toward School, Participation in School, and Social-
ization/Maturation.   Final Report."   Center for
Community Leadership Development, University of
Wisconsin, Milwaukee University Extension.

Study identified the longitudinal impact of a summer
program and its effects on an arbitrarily selected
group of leadership-prone students.   Report describes
the program's background, history, inputs, changes
over the years, problems and recommendations.   There
were three sets of experimental and control groups.
One set completed three years in the program, another
set two years, and the last set one.   Instruments
were used to measure self-concept and attitudes
toward school, and academic achievement was measured
by the Iowa Test of Basic Skills.   The students completing two years in the program revealed significant
improvements in socialization and maturation, ability
to take care of themselves, and ability to get along
better with others.   The students showed no significant improvement in self-concept, attitude toward
school, participation in school, and academic
achievement.   The authors concluded that a much
broader impact could be achieved if open classrooms
were used year round in public schools.

10144.   Lounsbury, J. H. and Douglass, H. R.   "Recent
trends in junior high school practices, 1954-1964."
Bulletin of the National Association of Secondary
School Principals, 49(1965):92.

Fifty percent of the junior high schools surveyed had
block time classes in 1964, a drop from the 59 percent reported by the same schools in 1954.   Another
researcher (Gruhn) found block time in 46 percent.
These studies suggest that while the incidence of
block time has declined somewhat in recent years,
there has not been a wholesale abandonment of the
idea.

10145.   Lounsbury, J. H. and Douglass, H. R.   "A decade of
changes in junior high practices."   Clearinghouse,
40(1966):456-458.

Although the junior high school is continuing to
develop and change, it has now apparently reached a
level of maturity characterized by a degree of
standardization in practice.   The institution is not
now likely to change by revelation any more than
other types of secondary schools but can be expected
to evolve gradually.   Practices likely to become
common in the future are already clearly in the
making.   In 1966 the authors turned to 251 junior

high schools which Lounsbury had studied in 1954 and found these changes: 1) a 36 percent increase in the number of schools offering special classes for the gifted, 2) a 35 percent increase in the number of schools offering foreign language in grades 7-8, 3) a 33 percent increase in the number of schools offering algebra below the ninth grade, 4) a 30 precent increase in the number of schools with an organized guidance program, 5) an 18 percent increase in the number of schools with ability grouping.

10146.   Lounsbury, J. H. and Marani, J. B.   "The Junior High School We Saw: One Day in the Eighth Grade." Washington, D.C.:   Association for Supervision and Curriculum Development, 1964.

This study sampled the experiences of 102 eighth grade students in 98 schools in 26 states.   Each student was shadowed by a skilled curriculum worker who recorded at ten-minute intervals the situation in which his student was working.   Several generally accepted principles of learning and curriculum which provided points of reference for evaluation of the data were: 1) Learning is most effective when it is timely and when it has worth for the learner.   2) The learning process is highly individualized.   3) Motivation is more effective when it is internal.   4) Learning involves the organization of data into conceptual tools.   5) The progressive independence of the learner is part of the growth process.   6) The creativity of youth represents our richest national resource.   7) The learning environment must show respect for the dynamics of personality formation. The 102 shadow studies, while pointing to much inspired teaching and apparent concern for the best in learning theory, seem more accurately summarized by the closing statement of one observer: "To sum it up, I would not want to be an eighth grader--on such a tight daily schedule, when I was not involved in planning what was to be done and/or how this would be done, where most teachers lectured and treated us as sponges, where my interests and needs were not considered in planning the curriculum, where I could get by very nicely by being quiet, orderly, and following directions, where my learning was bookish, fragmentized, and purposes were not clear, where I had no opportunities for me to grow."   The monograph describes the learning matrix, teachers' roles, pupils' views, priority assessments, the learning environment, the exploratory environment, and the group environment.   It also describes the shadow study technique for possible further research.   (For description of another shadow study, see bibliography entry 10189.)

10147.   Marascuilo, L. A.   "The Effects of Heterogeneous and Homogeneous Groupings on Student Attitudes and Student Performance in Eighth and Ninth Grade Social Studies Classes."   University of California and Berkeley Unified School District, ERIC Doc. ED 039 613, April, 1970.

The report discusses the history of student testing and its import for ability grouping and describes grouping in the Berkeley schools, including its unintended results: 1) de facto racial segregation, 2) intellectual isolation, 3) cultural and economic isolation, 4) lowering of aspiration, and 5) stereotyping of students.   For the study, students were selected from previous tracks and distributed among four experimental classes.   Results showed that student attitudes were not affected by class type, but achievement was: students from lower tracks achieved at a higher level in a heterogeneous grouping than in a homogeneous one.   Teacher activities were similar with both groups.

10148.   Marcus, L.   "Learning style and ability grouping among seventh grade students."   Clearinghouse, 52,8 (1979):377-380.

Students are often grouped because of their learning styles, which are affected by four basic stimuli: environmental, sociological, emotional, and physical. Teacher observation, past achievement, IQ scores, and results of reading comprehension tests placed students in social studies classes which were labeled above average, average, or below average in the school studied.   A learning style inventory was then administered to each of these ability groups in December 1977.   The data revealed numerous differences in the learning styles of the groups tested. The below average group rated itself as needing mobility to a very high degree.   Half of the students in the below average group rated themselves as being relatively unmotivated.   None of the groups monopolized any one element of a learning style.   Results supported the idea that each student is an individual and should be treated as such: to treat all students within an ability group as merely a representative of that group would ignore the crucial importance of individual differences.   The data revealed that teachers were not entirely able to recognize and respond to individual characteristics of their students.   Author suggests ways to improve ability grouping.

10149.   Maring, G. H.   "Maturity in reading for seventh graders."   Journal of Reading, 22,4(1979):325-331.

This study was carried out on the basis of pioneer research by Gray and Rogers. It centered on leisure book reading and assessed the reading maturity of 899 junior high school students in seventh grade English classes. The students completed sections A and B of the reading inventory in September of 1976 and C and D in November. The teachers classified the students in terms of their maturity in reading and profiles of individual students were written. The study validated the assessment procedure and demonstrated its feasibility. Article discusses how to develop maturity in students and includes good reading materials to help teachers of reading and teachers of content areas in junior high schools.

10150.   Marshall, D. L. "A Comparative Study on Instructional Policies of Middle Schools Administered Respectively by Elementary Oriented Principals and Secondary Oriented Principals." Ph.D. Dissertation, Michigan State University, 1970.

Author studied forty-three Michigan middle schools (grades 5-8 or 6-8) which had been in operation for more than one year. An eighty-item questionnaire was used to gather data from principals about teacher teams, flexible scheduling, courses of study, student athletics and other activities, and pupil transition from elementary to secondary school. The principals were classified as elementary oriented or secondary oriented according to the number of years they had served as principal in an elementary or secondary school and their area of original teacher certification. Responses revealed that content areas were often taught in separate courses. Programs aiming to improve the articulation between middle schools and elementary and secondary schools were more commonly reported by elementary oriented principals than by secondary oriented principals.

10151.   Martorana, S. V. "Superintendents view plans of grade organization." School Review, 58(1950): 269-276.

When the dynamics of the junior college movement become more operative, we can be sure that the growth in numbers of the 6-4-4 plan will be resumed. This expectation is based on preference for the plan by superintendents of school systems throughout the country in cities with populations of five thousand or more--cities large enough to justify establishing and maintaining junior colleges. This study surveyed half the superintendents in these cities. Of the 150 superintendents questioned, 13.8 percent preferred the 8-4, 12.2 percent the 6-2-4, 52.2 percent the 6-3-3, and 13.8 percent the 6-6 plan of organization.

10152.   Mason, E. P. "Project Catch-Up, June 1966 to June
1970:   An Educational Program for Socially Disadvantaged 13- and 14-Year-Old Youngsters."   Bellingham:
Western Washington State College, ERIC Doc. ED 056
818, July 1, 1970.

The main premise of Project Catch-Up was that ethnic
and socioeconomic status unfortunately are predictive
of academic success.   Article describes the six-week
summer residence program for junior high aged youth
who come from ethnic minority or poverty backgrounds
and who exhibit high potential but low achievement.
Language arts, art, science, and math are taught.
The program was successful in reducing the number of
school dropouts.   Also described is a fellowship program for experienced teachers of the disadvantaged.
Included in this report are sections on the participants from the 1969 summer program, the staff of the
1969 summer program, the academic program, the cultural, recreational, and counseling activities, and
the results of the program.   (See bibliography entry
10153 for a report on the program's next year, 1970.)

10153.   Mason, E. P. "Project Catch-Up, June 1966 to July
1971:   An Educational Program for Socially Disadvantaged 13- and 14-Year-Old Youngsters."   Bellingham:
Western Washington State College, ERIC Doc. ED 056
819, July 1, 1971.

Progress Report describes Project Catch-Up's 1970
six-week summer residence program of remediation and
cultural enrichment for junior high age youth who are
of ethnic minority status or poverty background and
who show high potential and low achievement.   The
report includes a history of the project and discusses a followup evaluation of participants from the
1966-70 programs.   Test data are included.   The 1968
and 1969 groups improved considerably except in total
arithmetic subskill and female response to the California Mental Maturity Test.   The report also evaluates the potential for change in junior high aged
youth from the American Indian, Mexican, and Anglo
ethnic backgrounds.

10154.   May, D. C. "An Investigation of the Relationship
Between Selected Personality Characteristics of
Eighth Grade Students and Their Achievement in Math-
ematics." Ed.D. Dissertation, University of Florida.
University Microfilms, Ann Arbor, Mich.   Order no.
72-21,080. ERIC Doc. ED 076 372, 1971.

Author studied the relationship between the sensing
and intuitive personality characteristics in 195
eighth grade students.   These students took the
Myers-Briggs Type Indicator, the Stanford Achievement
Tests in mathematics, the Dutton Arithmetic Attitude

Scale, and the California Test of Mental Maturity. Scores on achievement and intelligence measures were significantly higher for students classified as sensing than for those classified as intuitive. Attitude measures did not differ significantly.

10155.   McCaig, T. E.   "The Differential Influence of the Junior High School and Elementary School Organizational Patterns on Academic Achievement and Social Adjustment of Seventh and Eighth Grade Students." Ph.D. Dissertation, Loyola University, February, 1967.

Author studied 360 students in three schools, one from each of three Chicago suburban school systems. Both the junior high and the K-8 schools studied had departmentalized seventh and eighth grade programs. Students from the three schools were matched on the basis of intelligence and achievement scores at the beginning of seventh grade.   Author gathered data from questionnaires, the Stanford Achievement Test, and the Mooney Problem Checklist.   Results showed a significant difference in achievement between the junior high school and the K-8 school in favor of the junior high school.   The matched groups showed no significant differences in grade point averages between the junior high school students and the students in either of the other two schools, but the junior high school helped promote the social adjustment of the early adolescent.   Author also concluded that a seventh and eighth grade junior high school seems better able to provide a quality educational program than the seventh and eighth grades in a K-8 organizational pattern.   The junior high school structure can provide a more flexible schedule, a more adequate program of electives, and an extracurricular program more suited to the needs of the early adolescent.

10156.   McDonald, W. E.   "The Development and Implementation of a Middle School Design Drawn from the Developmental Needs of the Transescent and the Basic Tenets of Middle School Philosophy."   Ph.D. Dissertation, University of Pittsburgh.   Dissertation Abstracts International, 40 (08), Sec. A, 4551. Order no. 8004819, 1979.

This middle school design was developed by the faculty members of the Falk School at the University of Pittsburgh in response to the Falk School Task Force Report.   Rationales for the design were drawn from the literature and research related to middle schools, transescents, and self-concept.   Description of the design development covers: 1) rationale for the development of the middle school, 2) coordination of the middle school philosophy with the existing school philosophy, 3) political, social, and educational issues influencing the design, 4) curricular options, 5) new student grouping patterns, 6) implications for faculty, and 7) differences in the involvement of students in decision making. Author determined that the rationale supported a secure, responsive participatory environment and that coordination of educational objectives throughout the system was a necessity. Planned gradualism provided an opportunity to coordinate the many issues involved in the transition, and student involvement in decision making was important. Major curricular changes included a mini-course in science and social studies, a structured reading program, a library class, and extra opportunities for physical education. The new design used heterogeneous, flexible, and multiaged grouping patterns. Faculty members were very committed to the middle school child and were motivated to undertake further research.

10157.   McGlasson, M. A. and Pace, V. D.   "Junior high school and middle school education: Indiana University research." Viewpoints, 47,6(1971):1-129.

This publication is very complete and summarizes fifty-four doctoral theses in the School of Education at Indiana University. Findings and conclusions are reviewed and analyzed in a form primarily useful to school administrators and teachers. The article contains sections on junior high and middle school functions, administration, curriculum, student achievement in general, student achievement in mathematics, science, and English/language arts, guidance, preparation of teachers, and in-service for teachers.

10158.   McMillan, J. H.   "A Program to Enhance Self-Concept of Junior High Students." Paper presented at the Annual Meeting of the American Educational Research Association, Toronto, Ont., ERIC Doc. ED 156 947, March, 1978.

Author studied eighty students who were considered to have low self-esteem. They took part in an eight-week program to develop skills in personal and social awareness. Pretest and Posttest scores on the Coopersmith Self-Esteem Inventory indicated that students who participated in the program showed a significantly greater gain in self-esteem than students not in the program. See ERIC Abstract #ED 156 947.

10159.   McTeer, J. H. and Beasley, W. M.   "Student Preferences for Social Studies Content and Methodology." ERIC Doc. ED 137 212, 1977.

Three hundred and ninety students indicated on an eighteen-item rating scale their level of agreement with statements explaining why a person might enjoy social studies classes. Girls in junior and senior high school expressed interest in the culturally oriented subjects of sociology and cultural geography. Boys, especially at the junior high level, expressed greater liking for military and political history than did girls. In general, junior high students seemed more favorable than senior high students toward social studies. See ERIC Abstract #ED 137 212.

10160. Meehan, M. L. "The Interrelationships of Pre-adolescents' Student Characteristics Influencing Selection of Career Exploration Courses." Industrial Arts Education Monograph 1. University Park: Pennsylvania State University, Bureau of Vocational, Technical, and Continuing Education, May, 1975.

Study investigated the influence of twenty personal and environmental factors on seventh and eighth graders' selection of career exploration courses. Author studied 496 students out of the 3,479 in the Pennsylvania Public School Occupational, Vocational and Technical Exploratory Program. Seven instruments were administered to these students in groups by their teachers. The personal and environmental factors studied included: 1) achievement test scores in industrial arts, home ec, and business education, 2) age, race, breadwinner's socioeconomic status, and home school (public or parochial), 3) vocational attitude maturity, 4) motivation, 5) occupational values of interest and satisfaction, salary, prestige, and security, 6) attitude scores in industrial arts, home ec, and business ed, and 7) student self-report of influence on course choices by teachers, program, and peers. Conclusions: 1) Exploratory business education courses can successfully be implemented at the middle school level. 2) It is possible to design learning activities that appeal to the wide range of physical growth patterns, religious backgrounds, and socioeconomic status levels represented by the sample. 3) The urban pre-adolescents in the study who were exposed to a year of career exploration activities chose courses for further exploration for a variety of reasons and were influenced by a mix of factors including values, interests, abilities, and socioeconomic variables. 4) Career exploration course selection by preadolescents was only moderately explainable by a combination of the personal and environmental factors included in this study. 5) Sex, race, and occupational security were the most frequently appearing and also the most stable influencing variables on preadolescents' course selections in the career exploration program. 6) Salary did not significantly help predict the selection of any of the career exploration courses, and achievement on tests in industrial arts, business education, and home economics proved to be very weak influencing agents. 7) Students enjoyed the activities of this career exploration program and responded favorably to questions about their attitudes to the program.

10161.   Meister, R. W. "The Relationship of Differentiation of Organizational Structure to the Instructional Program in the Middle School."   Ph.D. Dissertation, University of Wisconsin, 1971.

Study focused on the relationship between middle school curriculum, teaching methods, and organizational structure. Findings showed a statistically significant positive relationship between 1) the quality of the curriculum (based on evaluation of curricular guides) and the teaching structure in middle schools, 2) quality of the curriculum and the management structure, 3) amount of team teaching and management structure, and 4) teachers' perceptions of the teaching structure existing in their school and their conception of an ideal teaching structure. Author found no statistically significant relationship between 1) small-group and large-group instruction and management structure, 2) type of classroom interaction and management structure, 3) instructional materials and management structure, 4) amount of team teaching, small-group instruction, and large-group instruction, 5) teachers' perceptions of existing and ideal management structure, and 6) the ages of teachers and the choice of teaching methods.

10162.   Miller, D. R. "School-Related Attitudes of Inner-City Junior High Students."   Paper presented at the Annual Meeting of the American Educational Research Association, New Orleans, ERIC Doc. ED 076 723, February, 1973.

Author hoped that the revisions of methodology for this survey would avoid the "white psychologist's fallacy." Findings showed that some students felt learning was a pleasurable experience, some students were turned off by the experience, and schools contribute to the turning-off process. See ERIC Abstract #ED 076 723.

10163.   Miller, F. M. "Effects of Small-Group Instruction on Achievement of Technical Information by Ninth Grade Industrial Arts Students."   Ed.D. Dissertation, University of Missouri. University Microfilms, Ann Arbor, Mich., and ERIC Doc. ED 055 178 (Document not available from EDRS), 1971.

Three classroom organizational schemes for presenting technical information in industrial arts were compared: 1) individual achievement in a small-group setting with no teacher interaction, 2) group achievement in a small-group setting with no teacher interaction, and 3) individual achievement in an entire class with no teacher interaction. Forty-eight ninth grade boys enrolled in three industrial arts classes took part in the study. Conclusions: 1) The cognitive understanding attained by students was essentially the same with all three approaches. 2) Students who work in small groups increase their level of enjoyment, consider learning easier, and find it more challenging. All three approaches were found to be an effective means of presenting related information. See ERIC Abstract #ED 055 178.

10164.   Miller, J. F. "The Effects of Four Proxemic Zones on the Performance of Selected Sixth, Seventh, and Eighth Grade Students." Dissertation Abstracts International, 39 (7-A), 3933-3934, 1979.

Study assessed the effects of intimate, personal, social, and public proxemic zones on the performance of sixth, seventh, and eighth grade students from East Tennessee State University Laboratory School. Author randomly selected and assigned 120 subjects to four treatment groups and one control group. The mean posttest score of the students instructed in the four zones were significantly superior to the mean posttest score of the control group. Results did not provide absolute guidelines for distances in which instruction should be provided. There was no evidence of difference in the effectiveness of instruction in the personal, social, and public proxemic zones, but under some conditions instruction might be more effective in one zone than in another. The study did provide evidence that the effectiveness of instruction was greatest when presented in the intimate proxemic zone.

10165.   Minnich, W. K. and Gastright, J. F. "Control of Environment, Acceptance of Responsibility for Choice, and Planning Orientation in Relation to Career Information." Paper presented at the Annual Meeting of the American Educational Research Association, Chicago, April, 1974.

Authors tested the reliability and validity of several instruments with eighty seventh and eighth graders, then administered revised instruments to 122 students. Results showed substantial and apparently stable correlations between students' control of their environment, their acceptance of responsibility for choice, and the amount of career information they acquire in a career education program. Results also

showed that student assessment of the program was not
correlated with various measures of student maturity
or with cognitive success in the program.   The
authors concluded that career development is both a
cognitive and an affective process, and vocational
maturity depends on the relationship between these
two aspects of development.   In this program teachers
were more likely to work on the cognitive aspects of
career education and needed assistance in helping
students develop vocational maturity through planful-
ness and responsibility for choice.   Authors discuss
staff development, noting that in-service training
should begin with an operational definition of
desired changes in noncognitive behavior.

10166. Mooney, P.   "A Comparative Study of Achievement
and Attendance of 10-14-Year-Olds in a Middle School
and Other School Organizations."   Dissertation,
University of Florida, Gainseville, 1970.

Study compared the achievement and attendance of
students in a middle school (grades 5-8) with
students in grades 5 and 6 of a regular elementary
school and grades 7 and 8 of a regular junior high
organization.   Student information and standardized
test results were obtained from the Student Information Records System, a multicounty Title III project in Florida for electronic collection, storage,
and retrieval of student data.   The experimental
middle school operated in a transitional inner-city
neighborhood in a school plant which opened in 1914.
The three hypotheses tested were: 1) Achievement of
middle school pupils on standardized test scores will
equal or exceed that of pupils in elementary and
junior high schools.   (Seven subhypotheses of greater
achievement by middle school pupils were rejected.)
2) Middle school graduates will score as high or
higher on the ninth grade standardized test in the
senior high setting as ninth graders who graduated
from the control junior high school.   (Nine subhypotheses of no significant difference were accepted.
Three subhypotheses of higher achievement by middle
school graduates were rejected.)   3) The average
daily attendance of middle school pupils will be
higher than pupil attendance in elementary and junior
high schools.   (Twenty-seven of the twenty-eight
subhypotheses favoring middle school attendance were
accepted.)   Study concluded that children in the
middle school achieved as well or better on the variables tested and that attendance was significantly
greater in the middle school than in the other
schools.   The major importance of the Miami Edison
Middle School Model is its successful adaptation of a
junior high school to a middle school program in a
physical plant which is outmoded and in need of
replacement.

10167.   Moos, R. H.   "A typology of junior high and high school classrooms."   American Educational Research Journal, 15,1(1978):53-66.

Cluster analysis of nine characteristics of the social environments of two hundred junior high and high school classrooms suggested five types of classrooms: control oriented, innovation oriented, affiliation oriented, task oriented, and competition oriented.   The clusters were associated with systematic differences in student satisfaction, student mood, and teacher satisfaction.   See ERIC Abstract #EJ 187 934.

10168.   Muller, D., Chambliss, J., and Wood, M.   "Relationships between area-specific measures of self-concept, self-esteem, and academic achievement for junior high school students."   Perceptual and Motor Skills, 45(3)part 2(1977):1117-1118.

Study correlated physical maturity, peer relations, academic success, school adaptiveness, self-concept, and self-esteem with reading, language, mathematics, and composite achievement scores for twenty-six boys and forty-eight girls in junior high schools.   Academic self-concept was significantly correlated with each of the achievement measures, and peer relations, self-concept, and self-esteem were correlated with language, math, and composite achievements.   The results supported previous findings of a relationship between self-concept and achievement.   This relationship appears to be area specific, with academic self-concept most directly related to measured academic achievement.   The relationship between self-concept and composite achievement was not weaker than the relationship between self-concept and area-specific achievement.

10169.   Myers, N. K.   "Physical, Intellectual, Emotional, and Social Maturity Levels of Eighth, Ninth, and Tenth Grade Students with Implications for School Grade Organization."   Ed.D. Dissertation, University of Missouri, Columbia, 1970.

The junior high school comprised of grades 7 through 9 was originally organized to meet the special needs of adolescent students.   Current trends and school reorganization favor a middle school comprised of grades 6 through 8, raising the problem of where to place the ninth grade in the school organization. Assuming that ninth graders should be placed with students more nearly resembling themselves, a test was made of the research hypothesis that ninth grade students more nearly resembled tenth grade students than eighth grade students.   From two suburban Missouri school districts, data were gathered relative to the physical, emotional, intellectual, and social maturity levels of eighth, ninth, and tenth grade students. Data analyses showed significant differences between eighth and ninth grade students in physical, intellectual, and emotional maturity. The only significant difference between ninth and tenth grade students was in physical maturity. Results suggest that ninth graders would best be placed in senior high units rather than in junior high or middle school units. A 127-item bibliography is included.

10170.   National Association of Secondary School Principals.   "Let's Look at the Two-Year Junior High Schools."   Spotlight on Junior and Senior High Schools, no. 26, 1957.

In the 1950s the two-year junior high school was the second most common type of junior high school. Over 21 percent of all junior high schools were two-year schools enrolling over 350,000 pupils in forty states. Despite this, the two-year junior high has failed to gain attention in the literature on educational research. This publication contains a twenty-page survey on the two-year junior high school, with findings from 379 schools. Criticism on the two-year school centers mainly on the loss of half the student body each year, making it hard to achieve continuity in guidance and increasing students' feelings of insecurity. One third of the two-year school principals surveyed saw no advantage in this type of school organization; the other two thirds said the two-year school provides a good basis for common learning and interest because the students are similar in age and developent. However, 65 percent said they would prefer to change to a three-year junior high school. The principals reported that 33 percent of all two-year schools were purposely planned; the others were dictated by building needs, overcrowded conditions, or school districting.

10171.   National Education Association. "Trends in city school organization, 1938-1948." National Education Association Research Bulletin, 27,1(1949):10-11.

Survey of 1,372 school systems in 1949 found the following frequencies of different grade patterns: 6-3-3, 35 percent; 8-4, 23 percent; 6-6, 16 percent; 6-2-4, 12 percent; 6-3-3-2, 4 percent; 7-5, 3 percent; 5-3-4, 2 percent; others, 5 percent. The figures show that the 6-3-3 plan was the most popular, but no single pattern of organization for the junior high school had become the clearly dominant type.

10172.   National Education Association.   "The Junior High
School   Today."   National Education Association Research Bulletin, 39(1961):46-51.

Survey of administrative practices in urban school
districts between 1948 and 1958 showed that during
this decade: 1) The percent of districts having
separate junior high schools rose from 40.1 percent
to 53.3 percent.   2) Junior high schools were established for the first time by 15.1 percent of the
school districts and were eliminated by 1.9 percent.
3) The total number of junior high schools in these
districts increased 50.5 percent.   4) In addition to
those having separate junior high schools, 23.3
percent of the districts reported junior-senior high
schools as their typical secondary school pattern.
Article discusses the school grade patterns, size as
a major factor, reasons for expansion, and secondary
school reorganization.

10173.   National Education Association.   "Grade Organization and Nongrading Programs."   National Education
Association Research Bulletin, 45(1967):118-121.

In the sampled systems, the 6-3-3 and 8-4 grade
patterns were about equal in prevalence, with over 21
percent of the systems indicating each organization,
as reported in 1967.

10174.   National   Education   Association   and   American
Association of School Administrators.   "Middle
schools in theory and in fact."   National Education
Association Research Bulletin, 47,2(1969):49-52.

Middle school practices are developing differently in
different schools.   This fact above all stands out in
a survey that profiles 154 middle schools in 51
school systems enrolling over 12,000 pupils.   The
middle school concept, namely to provide an educational program focused on the special needs and
interests of preadolescents and early adolescents,
suggests that certain features must be part of a
middle school: 1) a span of at least three grades
that allows for a gradual transition from elementary
to high school and that includes grades 6 and 7, with
no grade below 5 or above 8, 2) emerging departmental
structure in each higher grade to provide a gradual
transition from the self-contained classroom to the
departmentalized high school, 3) flexible approaches
to instruction--team teaching, flexible scheduling,
individualized instruction, independent study,
tutorial programs--and other approaches aimed at
stimulating children to learn how to learn, 4)
required special courses, taught in departmentalized
form, 5) a guidance program as a distinct entity to
fill the special needs of this age group, 6) faculty

with both elementary and secondary certification or
some teachers with each type, and 7) limited attention to interschool sports and social activities.
The article presents statistics on grade groupings,
gradually increased departmentalization, flexible
approaches to instruction, special subjects taught,
guidance programs, teacher certification, and
deemphasis of social activities.

10175.   National Education Association and American Association of School Administrators.   "Grade Organization Patterns."   Educational Research Service
Reporter.   Washington, D.C., ERIC Doc. ED 032 633,
November, 1968.

Postcard questionnaire sent to 515 school districts
enrolling 12,000 or more pupils yielded 449 responses
showing that the 6-3-3 grade pattern predominates.
This report covers 1968-69 grade organization patterns, middle schools, and a summary.   The charts are
of considerable interest since they indicate grade
patterns in 449 school systems in 1968-69, changes in
grade patterns since 1963-64, and grade pattern
changes under consideration.   Between 1963 and this
report in 1968, the number of 4-4-4 and 5-3-4 middle
school plans increased by 4 percent, and the 6-2-4
plan increased by 6 percent.   (For a report on the
1963 study see bibliography entry 10176.)

10176.   National Education Association.   "Grade Organization."   Educational Research Service Reporter.
November, 1963.

What is the most desirable pattern of grade organization? Should the middle grades be housed in separate
schools?   If so, what grades should be included in
the junior high school?   The information in this report was obtained from a postcard questionnaire sent
in August of 1963 to 366 unified school systems with
pupil enrollments of 12,000 or more.   Of the 344
systems responding, 71 percent had a 6-3-3 plan, 10
percent had an 8-4 plan, and 6 percent had a 6-2-4
plan.   Other patterns included 7-5, 6-6, 5-3-4, and
7-2-3.   Nearly three quarters of the school systems
with 12,000 or more enrollment operated under a 6-3-3
plan, and 67 percent of the eighty-five systems that
had inaugurated their current plan within the past
ten years had chosen the 6-3-3 pattern.   School
administrators generally favored separate junior high
schools.   Chart shows number of years in effect and
size of school system for each grade pattern.   (For a
report on a similar 1968 study, see bibliography
entry 10175.)

10177.   National   Education   Association,   Educational
Research Service.   "Middle Schools."   Circular 3.
Washington, D. C., May, 1965.

This report of a 1965 nationwide survey lists for
each school system, the total enrollment, number of
schools, number of instructional staff members, predominant grade pattern, middle school enrollment,
number of middle schools, middle school instructional
staff, grades in the middle school, year middle
school plan was established, middle school grade
patterns, and middle school organization (including
self-contained grades, partially departmentalized
grades, and totally departmentalized grades).   It
also compares facilities and services offered in
middle and intermediate schools with those in junior
high schools.   The middle school grade patterns found
were 5-3-4, 4-3-5, and 4-4-4.   The circular describes
new organizational schemes in Sarasota County,
Florida; Bay City, Michigan; and El Paso, Texas, with
extensive data on facilities, specialized teachers,
and services and activities.   It also describes
buildings housing middle schools in West Covina,
California; Sarasota County, Florida; Bridgewater,
Massachusetts; Scarsdale, New York; Independence,
Ohio; Swanton, Ohio; and El Paso, Texas.   Grouping
practices are described for Bridgewater, Massachusetts; Independence, Ohio; Spring Branch District
(Houston), Texas; and Palos Verdes, California.
Report includes a questionnaire asking teachers and
staff members about their beliefs concerning middle
schools and a questionnaire on middle school
organizational patterns.

10178.   National Education Association, Research Division.
"Organizational   characteristics   of   elementary
schools."   National Elementary Principal, 38(1958):
52-62.

A trend toward 5-3-4 or 4-4-4 plans suggests that
elementary educators are reluctant to give up any
more of their grades to secondary schools.

10179.   National Education Association, Research Division.
"Teacher opinion poll: the junior high school."
National Education Association Journal,   February
1962:43.

A nationwide representative sample of teachers was
asked: In your opinion, which of the following
methods of organizing elementary and secondary
schools is best for the all-around development of
pupils, considering all age groups: 1) 8 grades
elementary, 4 high school.   2) 6 grades elementary, 3
junior high, 3 senior high.   3) 6 grade elementary, 6
high school.   4) Other, please explain.   The teachers

surveyed in 1962 overwhelmingly endorsed the second option, which included a separate junior high school, with 70 percent being of this opinion, while 21 percent favored the eight-grade elementary and four-grade high school plan. Less than 4 percent favored the six-grade elementary and six-grade high school organization.

10180.   Nebraska State Department of Education.   "Status Report: Middle School Programs USA, 1974-1975." State of Nebraska, Department of Education, 233 S. 10th St., Lincoln, Nebr. 68508. (No year given.)

Report answers to the following questions asked of state departments of education in 1974:   1) How many of your schools are operating middle school programs? 2) If none, is there any move toward this concept? 3) Do you have any universities and/or colleges that currently offer the middle school program as a major area of preparation?   If yes, how many?   4) What grade levels do your middle schools encompass?   5) If a Nebraska graduate with a middle school major makes application for a teaching certificate in your state, what grades would he be certified to teach?   Report notes that ten states offered a special middle school program for future teachers with twenty-six universities and colleges offering a middle school teaching major.

10181.   Neel, R. S. and De Bruler, L.   "The effects of self-management of school attendance by problem adolescents."   Adolescence, 14,53(1979):175-184.

In the Auburn Alternative Junior High School, a public school program for problem children, self-management of attendance and academic performance are requirements for admittance.   A study of seventy-three Auburn students showed that student attendance was significantly improved and that this improvement was maintained throughout the school year.   The results, according to the author, should be interpreted with caution because the strength of the findings rests with the robustness of the dependent measure.   The data were regularly collected by school staffs and continuously displayed providing a running evaluation of the program.   Reviewing attendance over an extended period of time provided a broader context for specific attendance problem days and allowed the staff to distinguish long-term trends from short-term incidents.   The number of program changes was greatly reduced.   More work is needed to identify specific factors that increase attendance and other variables that might affect the remaining students who are frequently absent.

10182.   Nielsen, A. and Gerber, D.   "Psychosocial aspects of truancy in early adolescence." Adolescence, 14,54 (1979):313-326.

Interviews with thirty-three junior high school truants showed that truancy was associated with significant difficulties at home, at school, and with peers.   Two types of truants were delineated: authority defying and peer phobic.   The school environment, including the response to truancy and the transition to the junior high school, played a critical role in creating and aggravating truancy. Truancy is a useful marker for identifying adolescents with significant problems in all areas of social functioning.   Even students truant only once were likely to be experiencing substantial psychological and social difficulties.   A student's being truant should precipitate a thorough assessment of the surrounding circumstances at home, at school, and in the peer group.   Advertising campaigns or lectures from school administrators on the theme "Don't be a Dropout" rest on an assumption of nonexistent subcultural differences and are unlikely to be effective. Career education, work study programs, or in-depth experience with skilled or professional workers might help diminish truancy.   Programs which attempt to diminish the stress of transition to the junior high school should be developed.   Since teacher-student difficulties are often central, school administrators should involve teachers in work to include the situation.

10183.   O'Brien, J. L.   "Articulation in Selected New Jersey Junior and Senior High Schools."   Ed.D. Dissertation, Rutgers University.   Dissertation Abstracts International, 20, p. 3633, and University Microfilms, Ann Arbor, Mich., 1960.

Staff members from twenty-seven New Jersey junior and senior high schools were asked to rate the value of different articulation practices described in the literature.   These schools were selected because of their outstanding articulation practices between the ninth and tenth grades.   (Another twenty schools were selected out of 120 suggested by forty-seven state departments of education and other authorities on articulation in secondary schools.)   The New Jersey respondents considered these articulation practices effective between ninth and tenth grade: student records, course selection, junior high school pupil visitation to the senior high school, joint meetings of junior and senior high school staffs, senior high school counselor and pupil participation in ninth grade orientation program, orientation programs at the opening of school, and parent participation.

10184.   Odetola, T., Erikson, E., Bryan, C., and Walker,
L.   "Organizational structure and student alienation."   Educational Administration Quarterly, 8,1
(1972):15-26.

By use of random sampling methods, 344 seventh and
eighth grade students were selected from one middle
school and one junior high school located in a midwestern city.   Of these students, 108 were assigned
to multidisciplinary teacher teams at the middle
school (150 students per teacher team), while fifty-
three students attending the same school were
instructed according to the traditional one-teacher-
per-class method.   The 183 junior high school
students were also organized on a one-teacher-per-
class basis.   Questionnaire data indicated that
contrary to the expectations of some middle school
supporters, middle school students taught by teacher
teams did not appear to be less alienated than those
students organized in a more conventional manner.
Instead, on a measure of powerlessness, the middle
school pupils taught by teacher teams indicated
having the greatest sense of powerlessness.   These
findings remained unchanged upon further analysis on
the basis of sex, socioeconomic factors, and race.
Differences between the other two groups, traditionally taught junior high and middle school students,
were not consistent.   Middle school pupils organized
on the basis of one teacher per class showed the
greatest sense of pride in and happiness with their
school of the three groups studied, while the middle
school pupils assigned to teacher teams scored lowest
in pride and happiness.

10185.   Olson, C.   "A Comparison Study Involving Achievement and Attitudes of Junior High School Students
from an Open-Concept Elementary School and a Self-
contained Elementary School."   Ed.D. Dissertation,
University of Nebraska at Lincoln.   Dissertation
Abstracts International, 34 (7-A), 3708-3709. Order
no. 74-650, 1974.

Author studied fifty children, half girls and half
boys, in an open and a self-contained elementary
school.   The Nebraska Student Attitude Scale was
administered to all students in May of 1972, and they
took the SRA Achievement Tests twice.   Boys from the
self-contained school scored significantly higher on
all SRA subtests than did boys from the open-concept
school.   Boys from the self-contained school also had
more positive attitudes than boys from the open-
concept school upon entering junior high school.   The
results of the study seemed to indicate that the
open-concept elementary school did not meet the needs
of boys or girls of this age group.

10186.   Onofrio, J. E.   "The Evolving Middle School in
      Connecticut: Principals' Opinions Concerning Unique
      Characteristics and Recommended Trends."   Ph.D. Dis-
      sertation, Fordham University.   University Micro-
      films, Ann Arbor, Mich., 1971.

      A majority of the principals surveyed offered four
      reasons for the establishment of a middle school, in
      the following order of importance: 1) provide a
      program specifically designed for children of this
      age, 2) better bridge the elementary and high school,
      3) eliminate crowded conditions in other schools, and
      4) provide for individualized differences through
      individualized programs.   The principals agreed about
      several characteristics of middle school physical
      facilities, personnel, curriculum, and methods.   Cer-
      tain recommendations were developed: 1) More
      research should be conducted to develop theoretical
      and practical guidelines for the planning and devel-
      opment of middle schools in Connecticut.   2) Non-
      educational motivations for the establishment of
      middle schools should be recognized as secondary con-
      siderations.   3) Efforts should be coordinated among
      principals, superintendents, and boards of education
      for the planning of middle schools or the remodeling
      of other schools to accommodate the middle school
      program.   4) Middle school planners should thoroughly
      investigate and experiment with variations in func-
      tional design and the effects of program innovations
      on design.   5) School systems should formally recruit
      paraprofessional teaching personnel.   6) Efforts
      should be made to fortify as well as diversify all
      elements of the school curriculum.   More exploratory
      courses in the required, elective, or extra-class
      program would help motivate students to learn.   7)
      Efforts to improve articulation practices should
      incorporate better means of direct, personal communi-
      cation among teachers of all subject disciplines and
      levels of instruction.

10187.   Pink, W. T. and Sweeney, M. E.   "Teacher nomina-
      tion, deviant career lines, and the management of
      stigma in the junior high school."   Urban Education,
      13,3(1978):361-380.

      Paper examines how academic tracking operated in one
      school, how it was perceived, and how the stigma
      generated by low-track placement was managed by
      students.   Seventh grade students in a junior high
      school in a large midwestern city were placed in
      tracks labeled academic, general, and practical.   It
      was clear from the study that track placement
      affected performance in the junior high school and
      later in high school.   Questionnaire responses showed
      that while students appeared to understand the
      meaning of differential track assignments, they did

not appear to perceive low placement as a particularly stigmatizing experience. Questionnaire, observation, and interview data showed that track assignment does have a significant impact on seventh grade students, independent of social class, race, sex, type of school, and family size. Authors determined that the student perceptions reported and the operation of the track system were typical of track systems in other schools visited in the country. Seventh grade students were assigned to tracks largely on the recommendation of sixth grade teachers in consultation with the school counselor; grades and test scores played a secondary role. Teachers and students understood both the immediate and long-term implications of track assignments. Low-track assignment signaled lowered expectations by both teachers and students, poor quality work, and a higher incidence of misbehavior. Authors contend that it is the process of schooling that needs examination rather than the outcomes of schooling practices. Educators need to examine the different ways to organize schools so that all students have an equal chance to share in the learning experience and to perform successfully.

10188. Powell, G. J. and Fuller, M. "School Desegregation and Self-Concept: A Pilot Study on the Psychological Impact of School Desegregation on Seventh, Eighth, and Ninth Graders in a Southern City." University of California at Los Angeles, Neuropsychiatric Institute. Paper presented at the 47th Annual Meeting of the American Orthopsychiatric Association, San Francisco, ERIC Doc. ED 048 391. (No year given.)

Study used a self-concept scale and a sociofamilial questionnaire administered to 614 students in segregated and nonsegregated schools. Results showed that black students in segregated or predominantly black schools had significantly higher scores than white students on the self-concept scale. See ERIC Abstract #ED 048 391.

10189. Powell, R. H. and Robertson, W. E. "The junior high 'school world': a shadow study." Bulletin of the National Association of Secondary School Principals, 51,316(1967):77-81.

This study was based on the shadow study described by John Lounsbury and Jean Marani in "The Junior High School We Saw: One Day in the Eighth Grade" (see bibliographic entry 10146). Purposes of the present research were: 1) to observe and describe the behavior of four eighth grade boys as they interacted with their teachers and fellow students, 2) to observe varying classroom climates, 3) to account at least in part for the students' behavior in terms of these climates, 4) to look for examples of teacher integrative and dominative behavior, 5) to bring together a composite picture of what was happening to many students in junior highs in two schools during the routine school day. Results: 1) In the typical classroom someone was talking two thirds of the time, and two thirds of the time the talker was the teacher. 2) Teachers were concerned about what they were attempting to teach but were often unable to reach students with any feeling of real concern for helping them. 3) Student apathy and an atmosphere of boredom were the most observed features of the class-room climate. 4) The school seemed to be a place where students dropped in to fill up on knowledge with little control of the subjects they took or opportunity to cultivate their own interests. 5) Teachers played the role of dispensers of knowledge and authority, keeping student participation at a minimum. 6) The four selected boys in the study and many other students went unnoticed by teachers throughout most of the school day. 7) There was little evidence of a special effort to stimulate or challenge the students of this so-called average group. 8) The schedules of both schools in the study were operated on a rigid "stopwatch" basis. 9) Teacher domination and student adjustment to the group were operative in most of the classes. 10) Boy-girl relationships were much more evident in the school with lower socioeconomic status than in the school with higher status. The study concluded that since the adolescent years are highly active, stu-dents need to test their physical dexterity, mental curiousity, social abilities, and power of critical thinking. If perceptions largely determine a per-son's behavior, educators need to become sensitive to meanings as the learner perceives them.

10190.   Prawat, R. S.   "Mapping the affective domain in young adolescents."   Journal of Educational Psychol-ogy, 68,5(1976):566-572.

Four instruments measuring self-esteem, locus of control, achievement motivation, and moral develop-ment were administered to 885 middle school students in order to obtain a map of the affective domain. Research interest centered on sex differences, developmental trends, relationships between the instruments, and relationship between the affective and cognitive domains, the latter being assessed by achievement test scores. Research showed that sex and age effects varied considerably from trait to trait, but females evidenced greater stability in affective behavior than males. This may be because females have greater emotional maturity than males or because early adolescence is a less stressful time for females than males.

10191.   Rabinowitz, F. M. and Beaton, V. L.   "Delay of
feedback interval, postfeedback interval, distrac-
tion, and high school subjects."   Developmental
Psychology, 5,3(1971):378-388.

The effects of delay of information feedback interval
(0 or 7 seconds), post information feedback interval
(1, 8, or 15 seconds), difficulty (one or three variable irrelevant dimensions), and presence or absence
of a distractor in the post information feedback
interval were investigated in a modified conjunctive
concept-identification task.   Subjects were 240
junior high school children.   As the delay of information feedback interval increased, latencies
increased.   On the positive instance trials, the
7-second delay of information feedback groups
performed better than the 0-second delay of information feedback groups on the easy tasks but not on the
difficult ones.   The 7-second delay groups' performance was impaired while the 0-second delay groups'
performance was facilitated by the presence of the
distractor.   The minimal effects of the post information feedback interval were discrepant with findings reported with adult subjects.   Discrepancies
were explained by prior IQ findings, and a motivational interpretation was offered.

10192.   Rankin, H. J.   "Position Paper on the Middle
School."   Jamesville, N. Y.:   Jamesville-DeWitt
Central School, 1966.

In 1963, the Jamesville-DeWitt Board of Education
ordered the investigation of various school programs
to determine which offered the best opportunity for
student growth.   The investigation concluded that a
middle school organization (5-4-3 grade division)
would most efficiently fulfill student growth needs.
Sixth grade students begin a new adolescent cycle and
require specialized facilities, individualized
programs, and master teachers trained in teaching
methodology and disciplines.   The middle school
places grades 6 and 9 in more natural settings and
allows for easier social adjustment.   Organizational
changes mean little, however, without facility and
curriculum change.   Consequently, a curriculum
council recommended that each middle school consist
of three subschools of approximately 325-350 pupils,
with an organization for dealing with individual
behavior problems.   The middle school curriculum
seeks to avoid the regimentation of grade school and
the pressures of high school and to provide flexibility for individual development.   Master teachers
and efficient guidance programs furnish the key to
academic, social, and emotional student development
in grades 6, 7, and 8.   Included in the document is a
study of the strengths and limitations of 7-8, 7-9,

and 6-8 grade plans in Texas junior high schools. This 1962 report, "A Recent Survey of School Organization" by William J. Yost, revealed that of the schools studied, 54.1 percent had a 7-9 grade plan, 20.6 percent had a 7-8 plan, and 20 percent had a 6-8 plan. The percentages preferring each type of organization were approximately the same: 53.2 percent preferred the 7-9 plan, 18.9 percent preferred the 7-8 plan, and 22.9 percent preferred the 6-8 plan. The administrators of the schools studied were asked the strengths and limitations of the various types of organization. A general summary of the findings appears in the paper.

10193.   Rankin, H. J.   "A Study of the Pre- and Post-Attitudes and Academic Achievements of Students in Grades 5-10 in a Change from a Junior High Organization to a Middle School Organization in a Suburban School System." Dissertation, Syracuse University, Syracuse, N. Y. University Microfilms, Ann Arbor, Mich., 1969.

The district studied changed from a K-6, 7-9, 10-12 arrangement to a K-5, 6-8, 9-12 arrangement in 1967-68. The Science Research Associates Junior Inventory was administered to grades 5 and 6 and the Youth Inventory to grades 7 and 10 in June of 1967 and 1968 (before and after the change), as were a projective incomplete sentence test and the Intellectual Achievement Responsibility Test to all students in grades 5-10. Results demonstrated that student attitudes were healthier under the middle school arrangement of grades 6-8. There were no significant increases in the mean scores on the total number of perceived problems of pupils in the middle school, and sixth grade girls, seventh grade boys and girls, and eighth grade boys had significantly fewer perceived problems. Boys in all grades and sixth, seventh, and eighth grade girls scored significantly more positive responses on the incomplete sentence test after a year of the new arrangement, and total mental health scores were higher for grades five, seven, and nine. Author could draw no conclusions from the Intellectual Achievement Responsibility Test. The results indicated a healthier attitude of students and at least as good, if not better, academic achievement in the change to a middle school arrangement in this New York school district.

10194.   Read, B.   "Grade Level Organization in a School System." Prepared for the Future Schools Study Project, Albuquerque Public Schools, September, 1969.

In recent years, over a thousand middle schools of varying grade patterns have been established in forty-nine states. From an intensive study of materials published between 1961 and 1968 (listed in an appended bibliography), author outlines a basic rationale for the momentum of this trend. The new concept of the middle school (grades 6-8) is viewed as effectively meeting the particular needs of today's youth, who mature physically, emotionally, intellectually, and socially much earlier than did their counterparts at the turn of the century when the junior high school (grade 7-9) was introduced. An ESEA Title III Planning Project led to the recommendation that Albuquerque Public Schools move to a 5-3-4 grade pattern, incorporating a middle school for grades 6-8. Article is divided into sections on physical growth, intellectual development, personality development, and William Alexander's survey in 1967-68 on existing middle schools across the country.

10195.   Reece, J. L. "The three-year junior high school versus the six-year junior/senior high school." Bulletin of the National Association of Secondary School Principals, 46,271(1962):23-33.

Researcher studied a midwestern city school system to compare the 6-3-3 grade pattern and the 6-6 pattern in practice. A thorough review of the literature was made to determine the historical background of three-year and six-year schools, advantages and disadvantages of both types of schools, and previous research which had implications for this study. The summary of findings noted: 1) Neither type is superior in academics or reading achievement of ninth grade pupils. 2) Pupils in both types liked the school they were attending. 3) Parents of both groups of students indicated a preference for a separate junior high school. 4) Students in the junior high school felt they were an important part of their school to a greater extent than did pupils in the junior/senior high schools. 5) Ninth grade pupils in the junior/senior high schools were prouder of their school than were those in the junior high school. 6) Parents and teachers of the junior high school pupils felt teachers in the junior high schools gave more help to pupils than did their counterparts in combined schools. 7) Pupils and parents in both types of schools felt students should have been learning a few things which were not taught in their schools. 8) Pupils, parents, and teachers in both types of schools stated that enough elected subjects were offered. 9) Pupils in both types of schools had about equal access to the school library. 10) A highly significant difference was found in opinions of the students regarding actions of the student council. Pupils in the junior high schools felt their student council was more concerned about their problems than did pupils in the senior high school.

10196.   Riegle, J.   "A Study of Middle School Programs to Determine the Current Level of Implementation of Eighteen Basic Middle School Principles."   Dissertation, Michigan State University, 1971.

Author reviewed the literature on middle schools and compiled a list of principles of middle school education.   The list was sent to five authorities on middle school education.   On the basis of their critique author arrived at a final validated list of eighteen basic middle school principles which focused attention on: continuous progress programs, use of multimedia, flexible scheduling, provisions for students' social experiences, provisions for students' physical experiences, intramural activities, team teaching, programs for planned gradualism, exploratory and enrichment opportunities, guidance services, independent study programs, basic learning skills extension, creative experiences, programs to provide student security, student evaluation practices, community relations, student services, and auxiliary staffing. A survey instrument concerned with application of these eighteen basic middle school principles was sent to all Michigan schools housing grades above 4 and below 9.   The findings were as follows: 1) The rapid increase in the number of schools labeled as middle schools has not been accompanied by a high degree of application of those principles considered by authorities in the field to be basic to middle school education.   2) Author found 46.94 percent application by middle schools in Michigan as compared with 64.9 percent by a national sample measured on the same basis.   3) The number of grades housed in the middle school was not a significant factor in determining application of middle school principles. 4) While a high degree of agreement exists among authorities in the field regarding basic middle school principles, the degree of application of these principles and the wide variation in levels of application provide evidence of a failure by the leadership of the middle schools of Michigan to implement the principles recognized by the authorities.   5) A few middle schools demonstrated application of the basic middle school principles to a degree equal to that level achieved by four selected exemplary schools included in the study.

10197.   Riggs, N. D.   "The Internal Organization of Junior High Schools for Instruction."   Dissertation, University of Utah.   Salt Lake City: Utah State Board of Education, 1968.

An analysis of the internal organization of innovative secondary schools was developed from questionnaire response data supplied by the principals of 121 junior high, intermediate, and middle schools in

thirty-five states.   Criteria for comparison and
evaluation were based primarily on related research
and the literature on organizations. The study found
that the position of department head is the dominant
organizational position and is used extensively by
the principal to upgrade instruction.   Of growing
importance are a number of secondary positions,
including teachers' advisory councils, curriculum
coordinators, and intersubject instructional teams.
Schools with a pupil-teacher ratio of 20 to 1 and
under were more innovative and had more administrative positions than those with a higher ratio.
Supporting data are compared on a percentage basis in
twenty-nine tables.   Findings are illustrated by
organizational charts for fifteen representative
schools and a prototype organizational chart.   A
bibliography of fifty-eight items related to administration, management, and organization is appended.
The researcher posed five questions in anticipation
that the study would provide answers: 1) Is there a
need for the departmental organization in the junior
high schools? 2) If the department head is needed in
the junior high school, what qualifications for
selection are appropriate?   What are the duties of
the department head?   3) If the department is not the
appropriate organizational pattern for junior high
schools, what is?   4) What is an effective administrative span of control in a junior high school
faculty?   5) Can schools be organized so that attention is focused on the total experiences of the
students?   Recommendations: 1) The 7-9 grade organization appeared to be the most popular, but the
number of schools which operated under a different
arrangement suggested that empirical studies should
be done to determine the appropriate grade pattern
for the junior high school adolescent.   2) Since team
teaching was considered the most effective approach
to instructional improvement by the principals in
this study, the position of team leader should be a
part of the organizational makeup.   Team leaders
should have authority just under the department
chairman, because in some schools there will be more
than one team per department.   3) It appeared that
most schools used subject matter workshops and
department study sessions as the vehicles for
improvement of the curriculum.   Author recommended
that study of the student accompany the study of
subject matter.

10198.   Riley, R. D. "Teaching Patterns in Generally Open
and Generally Traditional Classrooms and Their Effect
on Black Urban Middle School Students' Performance on
Selected Measures."   Ed.D. Dissertation, Temple University. Dissertation Abstracts International, 37
(1-A), 252. Order no. 76-15,861, July, 1976.

Author studied open classrooms in a new urban middle school in North Philadelphia in 1972 and selected ten teachers who provided good examples of open or traditional teaching styles. A locally constructed instrument showed distinct differences between the ways open and traditional classrooms were run, but the two types of classrooms did not differ significantly in their effects on student attitudes, creativity, and achievement, though some differences were identified.

10199.   Ringness, T. A. "Nonintellective Variables Related to Academic Achievement of Bright Junior High Boys." Madison: University of Wisconsin, ERIC Doc. ED 003 829, 1965.

Study examined interrelationships between adjustment, motive to achieve, motive to affiliate, acceptance of self and others, and acceptance of adult values. The California Test of Mental Maturity was used to select bright boys in grade 8, and the Wechsler Intelligence Scale for Children was used to confirm selection of 264 students who were interviewed and tested with the California Psychological Inventory. Grade point averages were obtained, and the Iowa Test of Basic Skills was also used. Dunn's Visual Discrimination Task was given to the high third and low third of the group. The author concluded that low achievers do not have as close ties with home, nor do they accept conventional values as much as do high achievers. Many of the findings concerning nonintellective characteristics of high and low achieving bright pupils confirmed previous studies.

10200.   Rodgers, P. C.   "The Effect of Organizational Climate on School Morale of Students in Selected Public Junior High Schools in Mississippi."   Ed.D. Dissertation, Mississippi State University, 1972.

Is there a significant difference between school morale of junior high school students in open and closed organizational climates when the factors of sex, grade level, participation in extracurricular activities, and nonparticipation in extracurricular activities are considered?   The Organizational Climate Description Questionnaire was used to identify the climates of the schools studied, and the School Morale Scale was used to assess the school morale of students. Analysis of the data showed that children in open climate schools had a significantly higher level of school morale than students in closed climate schools. A significant difference in morale was found between the mean scores of all students in open and closed organizational climates, between girls in the two climates, between boys, and between students in corresponding grades (7, 8, and 9). A significant difference also appeared between the mean scores of students participating in extracurricular activities in the two climates and between the students not participating in extracurricular activities. (See bibliography entries 10206 and 10213 for other organizational studies.)

10201.   Roffers, D. W.   "Kids Are Our Most Important Product.   Lincoln Learning Center Final Report." Minneapolis Public Schools, ERIC Doc. ED 016 007, August, 1967.

Discusses an experimental project to help junior high students of average or below average intelligence who have not performed well in normal classrooms. Report covers introduction and general description, philosophy, objectives, "candid cameraisms," calendar of significant events, the total team atmosphere, team experiments, mathematics units, communications units, schedule at the learning center through a typical day, a project hour schedule, conclusions, staff incentives, student incentives, and recommendations. Teams teach courses in American industry, home economics, science, math, communications, and fine arts.

10202.   Roistacher, R. C.   "Peer Nominations, Clique Structures, and Exploratory Behavior in Boys at Four Junior High Schools." Ph.D. Dissertation, University of Michigan, 1972.

The purpose of exploratory behavior is to discover new sources of information and new alternatives for behavior. Exploratory behavior in junior high school boys is viewed as a coping style for adapting to the high school. Author hypothesizes that the amount of such behavior a boy exhibits is a function of personal and environmental variables and that boys have a characteristic optimal level of information load and a characteristic marginal preference for risk. The research investigated the relation between exploratory behavior as measured by a peer nomination instrument and a questionnaire. Findings include the following: 1) Boys reputed to display relatively large amounts of exploratory behavior had larger and more diffuse sets of acquaintances.   2) Members of the largest cliques in each school were distinguished by greater participation in sports, greater reported conformity to peer group norms, and more concern with gaining status from school activities than nonmembers.

10203.   Roth, R.   "Developing positive attitudes toward junior high school." Bulletin of the National Association of Secondary School Principals, 63,424(1979): 119-122.

Principals can help students develop a positive attitude toward their school by 1) developing a school climate conducive to learning, 2) providing for students' individual success, 3) facilitating positive communication, and 4) having a multifaceted approach to discipline. See ERIC Abstract #EJ 196 069.

10204.   Rothman, G. R. "The influence of moral reasoning on behavioral choices." Child Development, 47,2 (1976):397-406.

Study examined how exposure to moral reasoning statements affected the subsequent behavioral choices of 144 seventh, eighth, and ninth grade boys at different stages of moral judgment. The subjects were divided into four experimental groups that attempted to isolate and relate behavioral choice and reasoning in specific ways. The presentation of reasoning had effects on the behavioral choices of subjects at two different stages. Author considers implications for developmental change and for a developmental analysis of the relationship between moral reasoning and moral behavior.

10205. Roe, V. and Tompkins, E. E. "Two-year junior high schools." Bulletin of the National Association of Secondary School Principals, 41(1957):24-44.

This survey reported that the two most prevalent grade patterns were the two-year (grade 7-8) and the three-year (grade 7-9) junior high schools. Of all the junior high schools in the United States, 74.2 percent were organized on a two-year plan. Among the 379 two-year junior high schools surveyed, 196 principals favored the 7-8 grade plan while the other 183 principals indicated a desire to change to the three-year (7-9) plan as soon as possible.

10206.   Roy, J. E. "Student Self-Concept and Attitude Toward School in Differing Junior High School Organizational Climates." Ed.D Dissertation, University of Missouri, Columbia, 1974.

Author studied teachers, principals, and students from twenty-five randomly selected junior high schools in Missouri. The Organizational Climate Description Questionnaire identified the three schools with the most open organizational climate and the three that were most closed. In these six schools a random sample of students responded to the self-appraisal inventory and school sentiment index. Findings showed no significant difference in the self-concept or in the attitudes of students in the two climates. (See bibliographic entries 10200 and 10213 for other organizational climate studies.)

10207.   Royer, J. S.   "Attitudes of Junior High School
Principals in the Los Angeles Unified District Toward
Possible Administrative Reorganizational Patterns."
Ed.D. Dissertation, Brigham Young University.   Dis-
sertation Abstracts International, 36 (3-A), 1228.
Order no. 75-19,700, 1975.

Survey of the seventy-five junior high school principals in the Los Angeles School District showed they
varied in responsibility and assignment, but their
responsibilities were more uniform than those of
their assistants, counselors, or deans.   Assistant
principals generally were responsible for discipline,
and deans were generally responsible for minor discipline.   Behavior modification was a minor role for
head counselors.   Principals who were older and had
more experience supervised personnel more closely
than the newer and less experienced principals.

10208.   Ruud, O. G.   "The Construction of an Instrument to
Measure Proportional Reasoning Ability of Junior High
Pupils." Ph.D. Dissertation, University of Minnesota,
1976.

Author developed a paper and pencil test of Piagetian
levels of proportional thinking of junior high students in physical science.   Junior high pupils' proportional reasoning ability is of special interest
because Piaget stated that 13 is the common age of
transition to formal thought levels and proportional
reasoning.   The present science curriculum in the
junior high school provides content such as density,
quantitative relationships of chemical reactions and
genetic ratios, and therefore science teachers could
use an established level of proportional reasoning
ability for this age group as a basis for a selection
of appropriate curriculum content materials.   The
author noted the problem of developing criterion-
referenced paper-pencil tests that could provide the
same kind and amount of information about proportional reasoning in physical science as could be
obtained through other types of examination.   To
develop this instrument and the description of its
characteristics, 2,027 students were tested.   Piagetian levels of concrete operational one, concrete
operational two, and formal operations one were
included in the final form.   The test results correlated positively with the task results of the
students who took tests.   The test also was found to
have a high reliability and good item descrimination
between proportional reasoning levels.

10209.   Samuels, S., Lyman, L., and Bahnmuller, M.   "The
Influence of Team Teaching and Flexible Grouping on
Attitudes of Junior High School Students.   Final
Report."   New York State Experimental and Innovative
Programs.   New Rochelle, N. Y.:   New Rochelle City
Board of Education, ERIC Doc. ED 041 370, December,
1969.

The social studies department of the New Rochelle
Albert Leonard Junior High School took part in an
experimental program to test student attitudes in
1965 and 1969.   Pupils in the experimental unit were
grouped heterogeneously for special class presentations and otherwise grouped homogeneously according
to individual needs.   In 1968, seventh graders were
housed separately, with specialized instruction for
incoming students.   The seventh grade school featured
team teaching and a swing teacher assigned to each
team.   A student opinion poll showed that students
with differing abilities grouped heterogeneously
developed significantly better attitudes than students grouped homogeneously in a program of traditional teaching.

10210.   Sanders, S. G.   "Differences in Mental and Educational Development From Grades 6 to 9 and Implications for Junior High School Organization."   Dissertation, University of Iowa, Iowa City, 1960.

Table 1 presents brief historical notes about grade
plans other than the 8-4 and 6-3-3:   1) 6-6,
advocated about 1900 by early reorganization committees, always common in smaller communities as a substitute for 6-3-3.   2) 7-5, existed in early 1900s.
prevalent in the South, where seven-year elementary
schools were common.   3) 6-2-4, advocated in the late
1800s, constantly common through the years.   4)
6-4-4, advocated in the 1940s (leading advocate was
Koos--see bibliography entry 10129), much recommended, seldom adopted.   5) 4-4-4, advocated in the
1950s (leading advocate, Woodring), received more
attention in the 1960s.   6) 5-3-4, advocated in the
1950s, most common in Texas and some cities of the
Northeast, now receiving support as more than an
expedient.

10211.   Sawyer, R. C.   "Evaluation of Alternative Methods
of Teaching Subtraction of Integers in Junior High
School.   Final Report."   Eastern Washington State
College at Cheney.   Washington, D.C.:   U. S. Office
of Education, National Center for Educational
Research and Development, Regional Research Program,
ERIC Doc. ED 073 944, 1973.

This study sought to determine if the method of subtraction of integers taught to seventh grade students

affected their mathematical achievement or retention.
Computation, concept, and problem-solving sections of
the California Achievement Test were given as pretests and posttests.   A test of the addition and
subtraction of integers was also used.   The project
was divided into two studies.   The first study
involved 140 students and three teachers and compared
the complement method of subtraction to the related
facts method.   Results showed that the group that was
taught the related facts method of subtraction had a
significantly greater understanding of mathematical
concepts.   See ERIC Abstract #ED 073 944.

10212.   Scarborough, G. E.   "An Investigation of Selected
Needs of Transescent Youth."   Ph.D. Dissertation,
University of Maryland, 1975.

Study examined eighth grade student perceptions of
what middle school practices were and how much the
school fulfilled their needs.   One significance of
the study lies in its effort to use information from
students to improve middle school programs.   A questionnaire containing fifty-three statements of the
transescent's needs was evaluated by fifty-two middle
school specialists who designated twenty needs as
most important.   These were included in a student
questionnaire administered in twenty-nine Maryland
schools. Findings: 1) Eighth grade students respond
to statements relating to their educational needs.
2) Educators are attempting to satisfy the transescent's needs, as identified by middle school specialists.   3) Overall mean scores for rural and urban
students differed only slightly.   4) Overall mean
scores for male and female students differed only
slightly.   Author concluded that in-service and pre-
service teachers need programs that help them understand and design activities to suit the physical,
social, emotional, and intellectual needs and characteristics of the adolescent.   Specifically, the
teacher needs help in understanding the middle school
child's peer group, human relations, and individual
learning style.

10213.   Schafer, C. "Teacher Attitudes Toward Students in
Differing Junior High School Organizational Climates
in Missouri."   Ed.D. Dissertation, University of
Missouri, Columbia, 1974.

Author identified organizational climates in twenty-
five Missouri junior high schools and then used the
Organizational Climate Description Questonnaire to
select the three schools with the most open organizational climate and the three schools with the most
closed organizational climate.   A class of students
was randomly selected for each participating teacher.

Findings: 1) The Minnesota Teacher Attitude Inventory showed no significant difference between the open and closed climates in attitudes of teachers toward students.   2) A relationship inventory showed that students' perceptions by their teachers' relationships with them were significantly more positive in the open climates than in the closed climates. (See bibliography entries 10200 and 10206 for other organizational climate studies.)

10214.   Schellenberg, J., et al.   "A Study of Self-Conceptions."   ERIC Doc. ED 089 189, April, 1974.

Study explored the possible impact of school, especially changes in school setting, upon self-concept.   Questionnaires were administered to 181 ninth graders at Burton Junior High School and Central High School in Grand Rapids, Michigan.   In the fall of the next year the same group, then in the tenth grade at Central High, was given a followup questionnaire.   The study shows no significant changes in general patterns of self-concept which can be considered a result of entering high school.   See ERIC Abstract #ED 089 189.

10215.   Schofield, J. W., et al.   "Social Process and Peer Relations in a 'Nearly Integrated' Middle School." Washington, D.C.:   U. S. Department of Health, Education and Welfare, National Institute of Education, ERIC Doc. ED 167 639, December, 1977.

Report reviews the literature on desegregation and intergroup relations and shows why intensive analysis of the social processes occurring in specific interracial schools is a much needed line of research. Authors describe the new interracial school in which this study was conducted, outline the methods of gathering and analyzing data on the development of relations between blacks and white students, and discusses findings about teacher and student attitudes, other aspects of the school's organization, and specific classroom activities and incidents.   Authors conclude that the Wexler Middle School has seriously attempted to provide an opportunity which fosters the educational attainment in all children in an atmosphere which respects the potential and individuality of each child.   There is a notable gap in the academic achievement between the average black and white students.   There is also a somewhat different behavior pattern of the two groups of students.   Two questions were considered in the study: 1) What is the result of interracial mixing when serious efforts are made to provide optimum circumstances?   2) What can be learned from Wexler's accomplishments and its problems?   The impact that Wexler had on students and the students' reactions to the school depended on a wide variety of factors, including many characteristics which the children brought with them into the school.

10216.   Schofield, J. W. and Sagar, H. A.   "Peer Interaction Patterns in an Integrated Middle School." Washington, D.C.:   National Institute of Education, ERIC Doc. ED 139 871, 1977.

This study viewed the interaction of black and white students in a new open-enrollment, desegregated middle school. The school had met most of the criteria specified through research as important in fostering positive intergroup relations. The cafeteria seating patterns observed during the school's first year of operation suggested: 1) Race is an extremely important grouping criterion even for students who have chosen a desegregated school.   2) In the sixth and seventh grades sex is an even more important grouping criterion.   3) Girls show more racial segregation than boys.   4) Racial segregation decreased over time in sixth and seventh grade but increased in the eighth grade which had a predominantly white accelerated academic track and a predominantly black regular track.

10217.   Schofield, J. W., et al.   "The Evaluation of Peer Relations in a Desegregated Middle School."   ERIC Doc. ED 179 481, 1979.

This study determined the evolution of students' attitudes toward a desegregated school over a three-year period. Ten black and ten white children were interviewed at the beginning, middle, and end of the period on 1) reactions to and feelings about attending new schools, 2) opinions on the academic life of the school, and 3) judgments of peer relations within the school. Ratings of the school and its academic program were generally positive. Answers to the peer relation question indicated that students perceived both a decrease in positive relations and a decrease in negative relations over time. See ERIC Abstract #ED 179 481.

10218.   Schonhaut, C. I.   "An Examination of Education Research as it Pertains to the Grade Organization for the Middle Schools."   Ed.D. Dissertation, Columbia University, 1967.

Author reviewed the literature on middle schools to establish the factors that influence and/or should influence grade organization. The factors were grouped into general categories: the pupil, the school, and the teacher. The research in each general category was organized and analyzed to determine to what extent it supported any specific pattern of grade organization. Conclusions: 1) The research on the physical, intellectual, psychological, and social growth of pupils seems to indicate that the years of greatest change and differences in pupil development occur in grades 6 to 8 for girls and grades 7 to 9 for boys. The 7-9 middle school would include more differences between students than any other three-year combination. 2) The research on schools covered educational reforms, school practices, curriculum, instructional aid, organizing for instruction, administration, guidance, and articulation. 3) The research on teachers indicates that there is a shortage of teachers for grades 7, 8, and 9 in the 6-3-3 system. Changing to 5-4-3 or 4-4-4 might have an adverse affect on the supply of qualified teachers for the middle school. General recommendation: where factors of housing and desegregation are not involved and there is currently a 6-3-3 system, that system should be continued. When cost is not a concern, 6-3-3 is recommended over 5-3-4, and 5-3-4 is recommended over 4-4-4.

10219. Schoo, P. H. "Students' Self-Concepts, Social Behavior, and Attitudes Toward School in Middle and Junior High Schools." Ph.D. Dissertation, University of Michigan, 1970.

Author selected at random thirty-one middle and junior high schools in Michigan. Of these, four were middle schools with grades 5-8, twelve were middle schools with grades 6-8, and fifteen were junior high schools with a conventional 7-9 grade organization. The student population of the schools ranged from a low of three hundred to a high of fourteen hundred. In each school, author sampled 10 percent of the students in each grade. A total of 1137 middle school pupils and 1334 junior high school pupils participated in the study. A three-part student questionnaire was used. The Social Behavior Scale portion of the questionnaire included five factors: dating, belonging, independence, vocational factors, and conformity. The Self-Esteem Inventory measured how students perceived themselves through the use of three subscales: self-measure, social measure, and school measure. The Student Opinion Poll II had five subscales: curriculum, teachers, peers, school, and all items. Questionnaire responses were analyzed with regard to type of school (5-8 middle school, 6-8 middle school, 7-9 junior high school) and also with regard to sex and grade level. Findings: 1) On the Self-Esteem Inventory, students in the 5-8 middle schools scored higher on the self-measure and school measure subscales than did students in 6-8 middle schools or junior high schools, indicating that the 5-8 middle school students had better self-concepts than the students in the other types of schools (the

6-8 and junior high school students did not differ significantly from each other). 2) On the social measure subscale students in 5-8 middle schools did not differ significantly from students in 6-8 middle schools or junior high schools while students in the 6-8 middle schools had self-perceptions significantly lower than those of the junior high school students. 3) Eighth graders in 5-8 middle schools exhibited less mature social behavior patterns than eighth graders in the other types of schools. 4) Middle school pupils in a 5-8 organization were more homogeneous in their behavior toward fellow students and in their attitudes, with no significant difference in response patterns found between male and female students.

10220.   School Information and Research Service. "Grade Organizational Plans." School Information and Research Service, no. 10, March, 1965.

Survey of school districts in Washington State examined which grade organizational patterns are used and why. A similar questionnaire could be useful in other states. Study found two interrelated and equally important reasons for changing grade patterns: better utilization of buildings and improvement of instruction. Most districts agreed that no grade pattern solved all problems. Ever present was the matter of articulation between and among units and also providing instruction to best serve the individual needs of youngsters and the just demands of society. Is any single plan inherently superior? Only research can help to answer that question. In the absence of research proof, is there a strong general conviction, based on principle or philosophy, concerning what is the best pattern? Such seems doubtful. Presently, debate centers largely on 6-3-3 versus 5-3-4, but other plans also have their adherents. In the main, districts appear to follow the established local divisions unless building conditions dictate a change. In some instances, however, changes are based upon positive convictions that another grouping of grades is educationally advantageous.

10221.   Schott, J. L.   "The practitioner's guide to research: maturity, pupils, and the middle school." Bulletin of the National Association of Secondary School Principals, 58,381(1974):94-98.

Study examined the intellectual, interest, emotional, and social maturity levels of fourth, fifth, sixth, and seventh grade pupils. Four hundred pupils were studied, half in middle schools and half in elementary schools. The Otis Quick Scoring Mental Ability Test and the California Test of Personality were

used. Findings: 1) Fifth graders scored significantly higher than fourth graders in intellectual and
emotional maturity. 2) Sixth graders scored significantly higher than fifth graders in intellectual
maturity. 3) Seventh graders surpassed sixth graders
only in intellectual maturity. 4) Middle school
students scored significantly higher than elementary
students on intellectual maturity for grades 6 and 7,
on interest maturity for grades 5, 6, and 7, and on
emotional and social maturity for grade 4. 5) Female
pupils were significantly more mature than male
students in intellectual maturity for grades 4 and 5,
in emotional maturity for grade 4, and in social
maturity for grades 4, 5, 6, and 7. Author concludes
that the middle school is becoming a constructive and
challenging alternative to the traditional junior
high school program in meeting the needs of pupils
moving from childhood to adolescence.

10222.   Schwartz, T. "An Evaluation of the Transitional
Middle School in New York City." Cleveland, Ohio:
ERIC Document Reproduction Service, Bell and Howell
Co., ERIC Doc. ED 011 020, 1966.

Professional observer teams assessed integration,
achievement, pupil-staff relationships, peer relationships, and student self-image perceptions in
seven middle schools. As part of a plan to promote
integration and quality education by establishing
middle schools in what had been a systemwide 4-4-4
grade distribution, seven junior high schools had
been selected to receive the new sixth grade. The
observers found that five of the schools were highly
segregated, and none were fully integrated. However,
schoolmates freely crossed racial and ethnic lines
for a variety of nonacademic activities. Recognizing
that the testing instruments were unreliable, the
observers still felt that no significant academic
improvement came about under the new scheme, and the
staff generally thought that the structure and curriculum impeded achievement. Teachers were not well
prepared for the transition, and many reacted negatively. Recommended are 1) better choices of future
middle schools to insure full integration, 2) interracial in-service programs for principals and staffs,
and 3) the development of suitable curriculum,
administrative procedures, parent-school cooperation,
and a single standardized measure to evaluate pupil
progress.

10223.   Schwer, W. E. "An Evaluation of the Effects of an
Open-Space Program on Selected Seventh Grade Pupils
and Their Teachers." Practicum report in National
Ed.D. Program for Education Leaders, Nova University,
ERIC Doc. ED 088 182, June, 1973.

In collaboration with a four-member teaching team, author studied an experimental group of twenty-five randomly selected seventh grade students in an open-space program and a similar control group. Findings: 1) The Comprehensive Tests of Basic Skills adminis-tered to both groups showed no significant differ-ences in cognitive achievement between the groups. 2) An attitude test showed a high level of favorable student attitudes. 3) Teachers found both advantages and disadvantages in an open-space arrangement. 4) The staff and students felt that the open-space program was working well and should be expanded into a new building.

10224. Scott, G. J. Statistics of State School Systems, 1971-1972. U. S. Department of Health, Education and Welfare. Washington, D. C.: U. S. Government Print-ing Office, 1975.

Table 7 presents the number of public schools by type (including one-teacher schools), and by state or other area in the United States for 1971 and 1972. At that time there were 2,080 middle schools and 7,750 junior high schools. Includes other interest-ing information.

10225. Secarea, R. V. and Olsen, L. K. "An Evaluation Instrument for Appraising the Health Knowledge of Seventh Grade Students Participating in a Special School Health Education Project." Paper presented at the Annual Meeting of the American School Health Association, New York, ERIC Doc. ED 164 559, October, 1974.

Describes development of a multiple choice test to assess how much students learn in the school health education curriculum project. Cognitive goals of the project were increased student knowledge, comprehen-sion, application, and evaluation. Trial tests administered to 159 students were reviewed for acceptable discrimination, difficulty, distractor functioning, skewness, and reliability. A forty-seven-item revised test resulted. Authors concluded that the sentence completion method of developing distractor responses for multiple choice items provided a practical means of obtaining the thoughts and vernacular of seventh grade students. See ERIC Abstract #ED 164 559.

10226. Seick, R. E., Jr. "The Reorganization of a Tradi-tionally Structured Junior High School to an Innova-tive Grade Level House Plan Concept." Practicum Report in Ed.D. Program, Nova University, 1976.

Report describes a year-long effort to reorganize a large urban junior high school according to the

"House Plan Concept," in which the school is organized administratively and geographically by grade level rather than by academic department. The five major changes were relocation of departments and classrooms in the building by grade level, reorganization and reassignment of staff by grade level, relocation and reorganization of support services, continued curriculum revision and innovation, and a major adjustment in the school day. The reorganization plan was implemented at the beginning of the 1975-76 school year and evaluated both internally and externally throughout the year. After a study of faculty and staff evaluations it was unanimously decided to continue the House Plan for 1976-77. The appendix contains detailed data on the attitudes of school staff members, students, parents, and members of an external evaluation team.

10227.   Sewell, A. F. and Dornseif, A. W.   "Controlled Multivariate Evaluation of Open and Traditional Education at the Junior High School Level. Preliminary Report." Paper presented at the Annual Meeting of the American Educational Research Association, New Orleans, ERIC Doc. ED 074 144, 1973.

Report provided midpoint results of a year-long educational evaluation project conducted at the Huth Upper Grades Center, Matteson, Illinois. (A final report was scheduled to appear at the end of the 1972-73 academic year.) Author studied 140 randomly assigned seventh and eighth graders in a single specially constructed classroom and an equal number of students in a control traditional departmental program. The teachers in the open plan follow an interdisciplinary curriculum. Authors measured academic achievement, personal growth, social development, and attitudes through pretests, midpoint tests, and posttests. Sections of this paper are: 1) The School District. 2) Development of the Oscar Program. 3) Oscar: Operational Phase. 4) Comment. 5) The Method of Study.   6) Students: Academic Achievement.   7) Students: Personal Growth.   8) Students: Social Development.   9) Students: Attitudes.   10) Teachers: Classroom Behavior.   11) Teachers: Attitudes.   12) Parents: Attitudes.   13) Preliminary Results.

10228.   Shannon, R. L.   "Student self-acceptance and curriculum organization in the junior high school." Bulletin of the National Association of Secondary School Principals, 44,259(1960):35-38.

An individual's perceptions of self and others have been shown to determine, to a considerable extent, what he does and what he believes. Persons who accept themselves as worthwhile individuals and who

perceive others in their peer group as being equally
self-accepting have been found to be better leaders,
more successful in academic pursuits, more responsible, and to have fewer physical complaints.
Evidence suggests that self-accepting persons are
better equipped for successful human relations and
for competent effective citizenship. Therefore, we
need research identifying those school experiences
which contribute to the development of self-accepting
persons. Author selected junior high schools which
illustrated three types of curriculum organization:
the departmentalized structure, the block departmental pattern, and the self-contained classroom.
Study used a device that measured the self-concept,
self-acceptance, and concept of the ideal self and
another device that measured perceptions of peers in
these categories. The findings cannot be construed
as definitive evidence. However, at the junior high
school level the self-contained classroom appears to
be more productive of persons who accept themselves
and perceive others to be self-accepting persons than
are either the departmental or block departmental
organizations. The departmental design seems to be
less successful than either the block departmental
plan or the self-contained classroom in encouraging
self-acceptance in junior high school students.

10229.   Shovlin, D. W. "The Effects of the Middle School
Environment and the Elementary School Upon the Sixth
Grade Students." Dissertation, University of Wash-
ington, 1967.

In the 1960s the traditional 6-3-3 organizational
pattern was under severe criticism for failing to
meet the needs of preadolescents and early adolescents. Among the alternatives, the middle school, a
new concept, was being employed as a possible solution with increasing frequency. There was, however,
a lack of hard data to support the establishment of
the middle school. Author conducted an experiment
with sixth grade students in the Lake Washington
School District to determine the effects of the
environment of the middle school and the elementary
school on academic achievement, self-concept, and
social behavior. The investigator hypothesized that
three events would occur as a result of assigning
sixth grade students to the middle school environment. The first hypothesis was that sixth grade
students would acquire a less positive view of self.
The study did not support this prediction. The
second hypothesis drawn from the literature was that
the sixth grade students in the middle school would
perform less well academically than their counterparts in the elementary school. This prediction did
not materialize. The third inference, that sixth
grade students in the middle school would tend to

emulate the more mature behavior of older students in the middle school, was generally substantiated. Author recommends that the school entrance age be manipulated for the different sexes in order to determine whether a more common maturation level will minimize the effects of the interaction of sex and environment. Author also recommends that sixth grade students be assigned to elementary schools under normal circumstances and to middle schools when elementary classrooms are in short supply.

10230.   Shriver, M. R. "An Evaluation of the Intermediate School in the 6-3-3 Organizational Structure of the South Bend Community School Corporation." Ed.D. Dissertation, Ball State University, 1976.

Author compared student achievement, attendance, and dropout rate in the two years prior to the implementation of an intermediate school program with the same results in the three years following implementation of the program. One questionnaire administered to the sample of Clay Middle School staff was used to establish the credibility of the middle school program. A second questionnaire was administered to Clay Middle School students in grades 7 through 9. Standardized tests were the Cooperative School and College Ability Tests and the Sequential Tests of Educational Progress from the Educational Testing Service. Findings: 1) The following basic middle school principles were implemented to a high degree: student services, exploratory and enrichment programs, continuous progress, auxiliary staffing, team teaching, use of multimedia, and physical experiences. 2) The following basic middle school principles were implemented to a low degree: student security factors, flexible schedule, intramural activities, and planned gradualism. 3) Most students held positive attitudes toward the open-concept intermediate school program. 4) Almost all students were able to become well adjusted and effectively oriented toward the school. 5) Most students considered the courses adequate. 6) A sizable minority of students were dissatisfied in regard to certain aspects of the courses. 7) Half the students considered the faculty and staff unresponsive and unavailable. 8) A majority of students had an overall positive feeling toward the school. 9) The physical layout was serviceable for the basic needs of the students. 10) The changes in student achievement were minor and could not be attributed to the program. 11) The changes in student attendance were minor and could not be attributed to the program. 12) The percent of ninth grade dropouts decreased as a result of the ninth grade being part of the intermediate school unit.

10231.   Sienkiewicz, H. S. "A Comparative Study to Determine the Relationship Between the Existing Practices
of Selected Middle Schools and Student Performance on
a Standardized Attitudinal Measure." Ph.D. Dissertation, Michigan State University.   Dissertation
Abstracts International, 34 (3-A) 1007.   Order no.
73-20,401, 1973.

Study compared practices observed in ten middle
schools scoring in the lowest quartile and ten middle
schools scoring in the highest quartile on the student attitude section of the 1971 Michigan Assessment
Test of Basic Skills.   Schools were visited and
responses elicited for a number of survey items.   Two
authorities on middle school education, William Alexander and Donald Eichhorn, were consulted to provide
an interview questionnaire.   There were no significant differences in the practices followed by middle
schools in the two quartiles.   Areas studied were
staff and organization, student activities, guidance,
instructional program, school plant, and equipment.
There also were no significant differences in social
class of the student population and events which may
have affected student attitude.   Teachers, students,
and administrators all agreed in their perception of
the practices of their respective middle schools.

10232.   Simmons, R. G. and Blyth, D. A. "The Impact of
Junior High School and Puberty Upon Self-Esteem."
Rockville, Md.: National Institute of Mental Health,
1977.

This longitudinal study measured the impact of
pubertal development, sex, race, and school type on
the self-esteem of children aged 12 and 13.   One of
the questions being investigated was whether the move
from a protected elementary school into a larger,
more impersonal junior high affected children's self-
image more negatively than did a move from sixth to
seventh grade within the same school.   Subjects were
798 children from eighteen elementary schools who
were interviewed privately once in sixth grade and a
year later in seventh grade.   There were three main
school populations in the sample: 1) K-8 schools, 2)
K-6/junior high schools with comparable social characteristics, and 3) K-6/junior high schools which
were predominantly black.   The interview consisted
primarily of multiple choice questions concerning
self-esteem, social behavior, and school behavior.
Findings: 1) White girls scored lower in self-esteem
than black girls or white and black boys.   2) Girls
moving into a junior high school were more likely to
show low self-esteem than girls remaining in a K-8
system.   3) Boys did not appear to be affected by
school type.   4) Physical maturation (as measured by
the presence of menstruation), achievement scores,

and dating behavior also affected self-esteem in girls. (See also bibliographic entries 10233 and 10234.)

10233. Simmons, R. G., Blyth, D. A., Van Cleave, E. F., and Bush, D. M. "Entry into early adolescence: the impact of school structure, puberty, and early dating on self-esteem." American Sociological Review, 44,6 (1979):948-967.

Authors followed 798 Milwaukee children from sixth into seventh grade under two different grade level patterns using survey interviews and nurses' measurements. The students were in either K-8 schools or moved from K-6 elementary schools to 7-9 junior highs. Findings: 1) In seventh grade, white adolescent girls who have entered the new environment of junior high school appear to be at a disadvantage in terms of self-esteem in comparison both to boys in general and to girls who do not have to change schools. 2) The girls with lowest self-esteem appear to be those who have recently experienced multiple changes, that is, who have changed schools, have reached puberty, and have also started to date. In contrast, early pubertal development is an advantage for self-esteem in boys. These data show how coping with a major role transition can be significantly affected by school environment, level of biological development and social behavior. While girls respond more strongly to the sharp environmental discontinuity of junior high school than to the physiological changes of puberty, boys seem to react to pubertal changes but not to those of the school environment. And whereas the self-esteem of girls is affected negatively by multiple changes in environment, physiology, and social relationships, while boys respond positively at least to pubertal changes. Whether the vulnerability evidenced by these early adolescent girls is merely a temporary reaction or reflects a long-term problem of coping with multiple, simultaneous changes is a question that will be addressed once the five-year followup is complete. (See also bibliography entries 10232 and 10234.)

10234. Simmons, R. G., Bulcroft, R., Blyth, D. A., and Bush, D. M. "The vulnerable adolescent: school context and self-esteem." Paper presented at the Society for Research in Child Development Meetings, San Francisco, March, 1979.

Authors studied 798 children identified as either more vulnerable or less vulnerable in sixth grade on various criteria to determine the effects of different school environments (K-8 and junior high school) on change in their self-esteem between sixth and

seventh grade.   The major hypothesis was that children already vulnerable or perceiving themselves as
doing poorly along one of a variety of ranked dimensions would respond less well to the sudden change
into a larger and relatively impersonal junior high
school.   Significant effects were found only for
girls, with junior high school girls consistently
experiencing a greater mean loss in self-esteem than
K-8 girls.   Similarly, more vulnerable children also
experienced a greater mean loss in self-esteem than
less vulnerable children.   Finally, these two variables were found to be additive in their deleterious
effects.   This study was conducted within the Milwaukee Public School System from 1974 to 1976.   Children
were interviewed privately in sixth grade and a year
later in seventh grade.   The main findings document
the importance of social structure or social context
for mental health.   That is, when the social entrance
into adolescence is sudden and discontinuous, girls
appear to have a greater difficulty in adjustment.
Prior vulnerability renders the student even less
capable of making this transition without damage to
self-esteem.   The student, particularly the adolescent girl, who in some significant way has not succeeded in her first environment, finds the next context more stressful in terms of the self-picture.
Therefore, the girl who has to make a radical
environmental change from an elementary into a junior
high school and who has not succeeded the year before
is the one most at risk.   Authors conclude that the
change from childhood to early adolescence is more
stressful for girls than boys, and it is particularly
difficult if it coincides with major environmental
discontinuity and if the girl has not mastered or
excelled in the tasks of childhood.   (See also bibliography entries 10232 and 10233).

10235.   Simpson, G. C. and Smith, G. J.   "Middle School
Survey of New York State."   Mid-Hudson School Study
Council.   New Paltz, N. Y.:   State University
College, 1967.

Researchers studying sixty New York school districts
with middle schools reported that the following services or activities were improved in the middle
schools in comparison to predecessor junior high
schools: guidance, corrective reading, speech correction, psychological services, clubs, musical
organizations, and team sports.   However, some of the
same problems and malaises that have plagued junior
high schools are plaguing middle schools in New York.
Teachers frequently lack special training for the
middle school, and those with special training want
an association with the senior high school.   Furthermore, the middle school organization has enabled some
traditional high school subjects to be offered

earlier, a development the authors regard negatively. Responses were 4 to 1 in favor of placing grades 5 and 6 in a middle school to help prepare pupils for college, another finding the authors consider a problem rather than an improvement.

10236.   Sinks, T. A., Bough, M., McLure, J., Malinka, R., and Terman, D. J. T.   "The middle school trend: another look at the upper midwest."   Clearinghouse, October 1975:52-56.

Since 1968 surveys of middle schools taken regularly in the upper Midwest states of Illinois, Indiana, Iowa, Minnesota, Wisconsin, and Ohio indicate a definite trend toward the modern middle school concept.   In 1970-71 the first three authors of this article took a five-state survey (Clearinghouse, November 1972).   That survey was repeated in 1973-74, and the state of Ohio was added.   The following is a report of the second survey: 1) The number of middle schools in the first five states has more than doubled in four years.   2) Ohio has the largest number of middle schools, with Illinois second.   3) Minnesota has the largest growth rate of middle schools.   Although the state has the fewest such schools, the number almost quadrupled between the studies.   4) The number of middle schools in Indiana has tripled in four years.   In each of the six states the state department of education was used to find the school districts.   Tables are: 1) A Distribution of Middle Schools.   2) Reasons Given for Establishing Middle Schools.   3) Grade Level Organization.   4) Teacher Learning Strategies of 157 School Districts. 5) Distribution of Scheduling Arrangements by Number of School Districts.   6) Curriculum Practices in Middle Schools.   The reduced number of required subjects is significant.   Although the number of elective courses did not show the same reduction, there was not the gain one would expect from such an increase in the total number of middle schools reporting.   These data appear to reflect a reduction in curricular offerings, probably a result of tightened financing and funding.   The effect of the reduced birth rate on school enrollment, reduction of public school budgets, and continued inflation in the economy all had their effects on schools.   Authors predict that the number of middle schools will continue to increase and the number of junior high schools will continue to decrease.   (See also bibliography entry 10237).

10237.   Sinks, T. A., McLure, J. W., Malinka, R., and Pozdol, M.   "What's happening to middle schools in the upper midwest?"   Clearinghouse, 51,9(1978): 444-448.

This is the third in a series of surveys of middle
schools in the upper midwest states of Illinois,
Indiana, Iowa, Minnesota, Wisconsin, and Ohio. The
first survey was done in 1970-71, the second in
1973-74, and the final one in 1976-77. In each survey the state department of education directed
researchers to the school districts that operate
public schools at intermediate grade levels, and a
survey was sent to these schools. Article is divided
into sections on organizational patterns, instructional practices, curriculum, and pupil reporting.
Findings: 1) The number of middle schools in the
upper Midwest states continues to increase, whereas
the number of junior high schools continues to
decrease.   2) The reasons for establishing middle
schools vary.   3) Some form of departmentalization
was used in most subject areas. Many times departmentalization and block-of-time structure of the
schedule worked hand in hand.   4) All of the 557
schools reporting required language arts, social
studies, math, science, and physical education, and
the most common electives offered were vocal music,
instrumental music, and band.   5) The seven special
programs listed by respondent were counseling, social
work, remedial reading, health services, programs for
the mentally handicapped, programs for the physically
handicapped, and learning centers.   6) Traditional
letter grades were still the most popular for reporting pupil progress.   Very few schools had only a
single method of reporting, though.

10238.   Smith, H. P.   "The relative efficiency of the
junior high school versus the conventional eighth
grade type school."   Journal of Educational Research,
29,4(1935):276-280.

This investigation of the Syracuse, New York, school
system reported the mean mental ages, intelligence
quotients, and composite scores on the Stanford
Advanced Examination for eighth graders in the
system's three-year junior high schools, junior high
school divisions of nine-year schools (elementary and
junior high school grades), junior high school
divisions of six-year high schools, and conventional
eighth grade schools.   Author concluded that the
pupils of the junior high school organizations tended
rather consistently to excel in the skills and
knowledges measured by this battery of tests.   A
graphic rating scale for habits and attitudes grouped
the pupils according to the same types of school
organization, and results suggested that in industry,
initiative, reliability, cooperation, and leadership,
students in the junior high school types of school
organization excelled compared to students in the
conventional type of school.

10239.   Smock, C. D. and Belovicz, G.   "Understanding of
Concepts of Probability Theory by Junior High School
Children.   Final Report."   Lafayette, Ind.:   Purdue
University, ERIC Doc. 020 147, February, 1968.

Authors studied: 1) students' understanding of variation and consistency in usage of quantitative language terms, 2) ability to generate possible combinations and permutations and recognition of all possible outcomes of a particular set of alternative
actions, 3) recognition and use of the concept of
independence of events, 4) preferences for low probability events, 5) ability to appropriately assess
and modify contingency relations in a complex set of
related events, 6) effect of a variation in event
structures of probabilistic event sets on estimation
of population parameters and on the subjective certainty of these estimations, and 7) relationship of
need for security to variation in event estimation
and subjective certainty. The results indicated that
junior high students failed to understand the basic
idea of probability theory and that further research
should be done on concepts such as permutation, correlations, and on determining the experience necessary for learning and using quantitative language
terms.

10240.   Soares, L. M., Soares, A. T., and Pumerantz, P.
"Self-perceptions of middle-school pupils."   Elementary School Journal, 36,6(1973):381-389.

There is little doubt that the reorganization of the
middle grades on the national level is one of the
most notable educational movements of the past
decade. Not only has there been significant growth
in the number of middle schools, but there has also
been considerable debate on the advantages of this
organization as against traditional school arrangements. Advocates of the middle school argue that it
could accomplish a wide range of purposes from
encouraging desegregation to opening the way to a
better curriculum. The reason most frequently
reported for establishing middle schools, Alexander
found, was to eliminate crowded school conditions.
Dissatisfaction in the junior high school is another
reason often given for the rise of the middle school.
Children in the middle grades are in the throes of
transition from childhood to adolescence--a crucial
time in preparation for adulthood. The traditional
junior high school may not be meeting the growth
needs of children in this period as well as it might.
Some believe that a middle school offers opportunity
for programs that will help students physically and
mentally to gain insight into their own personalities. The purpose of this study was to discover how
the middle school has influenced the way children in

grades 6, 7, and 8 look at themselves and to compare
their self-perceptions with those of children in the
same grade in comparable environments of traditional
schools. Four hypotheses were tested: 1) There
would be no difference between middle school and
traditional school groups in any of the self-
perception measures. 2) There would be no differences between boys and girls in either type of school
in any of the self-perception measures. 3) There
would be no differences in self-perception scores
among grades 6, 7, and 8 in either type of school.
4) There would be no differences between middle
schools and traditional schools in any of the self-
perception measures when pupils are grouped according
to grade and sex.

10241.   Spivak, M. L. "Effectiveness of departmental and
self-contained seventh and eighth grade classrooms."
School Review, 64,9(1956):391-396.

Data from Newark, New Jersey, reveal that departmentalized classrooms are not appropriate for seventh
and eight grade, especially in underprivileged areas.
Children entering the ninth grade of a junior high
school from elementary schools with self-contained
nondepartmental classrooms were matched with children
who had been in completely departmentalized seventh
and eighth grades in junior high school. It was
hypothesized that two years spent in the departmental
set of the junior high school should have given the
departmental children in the study the advantage, at
least with regard to academic achievement and school
adjustment, in the ninth grade at the same school.
Matching factors were sex, homeroom, course of study,
ninth grade subject teachers, intelligence quotient,
chronological age, eighth grade academic records,
eighth grade personality ratings by homeroom
teachers, and a family score derived from a simple
twelve-item questionnaire. Forty-one pairs remained
after all the matching criteria had been considered.
These pairs were then compared as they went through
the ninth grade at the junior high school. Their
academic achievement was recorded in terms of
teachers' marks in three major subjects. School
adjustment in the ninth grade was defined in terms of
personality ratings by homeroom teachers and a count
of the number of children in the homeroom who named
each child in the study as one of their three best
friends in the homeroom. School adjustment was
negatively defined in terms of the number of school
problems each child checked and in terms of the
number of times each child was referred to the office
or counselor for correction or advice. The hypothesis that the departmental children would do better
than their nondepartmental mates could not be
accepted in any respect.

10242.   Stanford   Research   Institute,   Educational   Policy
Research   Center.   "Survey of Basic Skills Programs
for   Adolescents   in   Seven   States."   Menlo   Park,
Calif., ERIC Doc. ED 155 299, July, 1977.

The purpose of this study was to determine what
federal, state, and local resources are being used to
assist   educationally   disadvantaged   adolescent
students and how programs for these students are
different from programs designed primarily for
elementary students.   The study covered Arizona,
California,   Michigan,   Missouri,   Nebraska,   South
Carolina,   and   Vermont.   Despite   substantial
obstacles, most secondary schools and their faculties
recognized the need for compensatory education for
adolescents and were willing to provide such help
when   strong   leadership   was   available.   Report
describes five common project designs for secondary
grades and reviews ways of selecting and training
staff members.   The appendix includes tables of Title
I participation by grade level and discusses the
study methodology and the concept of basic skills in
reading.   Reference lists are included.   See ERIC
Abstract #ED 155 299.

10243.   Stemnock, S. K. "Summary of Research on Size of
Schools and School Districts.   Research Brief."
Washington, D. C.:   Educational Research Service,
1974.

Report summarizes research on school size, on middle
schools, and on junior high schools.   Few references
to the optimum size for middle schools were found in
the literature reviewed for this 1974 paper--perhaps
because   middle   schools   were   relatively   recent
arrivals on the educational scene or because middle
schools were conceived as incorporating a number of
educational innovations designed to minimize the
detrimental effects of a small or large school.   A
table reports five recommendations found in the
reviewed literature.   The recommended range of middle
school enrollments is six hundred to eight hundred
pupils.

10244.   Stephens, C. E.   "Junior High Students' School
Satisfaction as a Function of Organizational Structure: A Study of Relationships."   Ph.D. Dissertation, University of Oregon.   Dissertation Abstracts
International, 33 (5), Sec. A, 2183, 1972.

This study involved 1) a comparison of seventh grade
students' satisfaction with school in an open-
flexible school and a traditional school, 2) testing
the relationship between measures of satisfaction
with school and achievement in mathematics, and 3)
analysis of incidents related to changes in student

satisfaction with school. Findings: 1) Significantly more positive attitudes toward the open-flexible school focused on the encouragement of students to participate in deciding how classes will be conducted. 2) The correlation coefficients of the mathematics tests with the factors of the attitude scales were predominantly nonsignificant. (In general, the group of students from the open-flexible school did score somewhat higher on the mathematics tests than the students from the traditional school, but no significant differences were found between any of the groups on the general ability level.) 3) In the open-flexible school certain incidents were related to a pronounced shift from October through May toward a more positive evaluation of the program in general. 4) The study found few attitudinal differences between the samples of seventh grade students from the open-flexible and the traditional schools. All significant differences favored the open-flexible school. The study concluded that the school environment did not have a major influence on student attitudes toward school. (See also bibliography entry 10245.)

10245.   Stephens, C. E. "A Multiple-Time Sequence Design Applied to Seventh Grade Student Attitudes Toward School in Two Schools with Contrasting Organizational Structure." Paper presented at the National Council on Measurement in Education Meeting, February 26-28, 1973.

One junior high school studied had made major modifications in its environment, the other maintained a more standard approach to education. At four time periods a multiple-time sequence design was employed to investigate the attitudes of students toward the schools. Author used two school attitude scales and a test of mathematics. While most correlations between attitudes and math achievement were not significant, the value of using a multiple-time sequence was most apparent. Had data been collected at only two points in time, the "culture shock" effect of the open-flexible school environment would not have been evident. Neither would the continuously divergent perceptions of students who were encouraged to participate in deciding how classes were conducted have been as evident. The two measures of student attitude toward school were 1) a forty-item scale developed by Fosmire and Associates at the University of Oregon to assess student expectations and preferences about school, and 2) a nine-item scale which was developed for this study and which focused on specific areas of peer relations. In addition, tests of mathematic concepts, computation, and problem solving (from the Metro 70, advanced form F) were used to measure achievement. Factor analysis of the two attitude scales identified fourteen factors in attitudes toward school. Differences between schools for each factor were tested by means of a two-by-four analysis of variance design. Changes in attitude over time were related to student-school, student-teacher, and peer relations. (See also bibliography entry 10244.)

10246.   Stewart, L. H. and Moulton, R. W. "Increasing the Academic Achievement of Culturally Disadvantaged Youth." University of California, Berkeley, 1966.

Fifty-five black junior high school boys from two schools in San Francisco formed a control group and experimental group that took pretests and posttests on insight and school attitudes. The control group experienced traditional group counseling procedures and the experimental group had small-group counseling. The experimental method did not prove superior to that of the traditional method in improving academic performance. It is important to study the black junior high school for three reasons: 1) Despite the potentially explosive social problems inherent in black slums and in the history of widespread discrimination against blacks, relatively little study has been made of them. Blacks have been excluded rather systematically from studies of academic motivation and socialization. 2) Technological changes make it necessary for the lower status black to find some means of radically upgrading his occupational skills in order to compete effectively in the labor market. Undoubtedly education is the main avenue toward such upgrading. 3) Evidence suggests, in general, that lower status blacks are not taking advantage of educational opportunities available to them. Instead, blacks underachieve in school and drop out at a high rate.

10247.   Stover, G. "An Analysis of the Changes Made by Sixth and Eighth Grade Students When Rewriting Arithmetic Word Problems." ERIC Doc. ED 171 568, 1979.

Thirty-five sixth and eighth graders enrolled in a program for the gifted in a large middle school individually rewrote arithmetic word problems to make them more understandable. Their format changes can be classified into twelve categories. Examples are included. See ERIC Abstract #ED 171 568.

10248.   Street, P., Powell, J. H., and Hamblen. "Achievement of students and size of school." Journal of Educational Research, 55(1962):261-266.

Authors studied achievement of students in grades 7 and 8 in two eastern Kentucky mining districts with

enrollments ranging from under 100 to 836. They
recommend an enrollment of 300 students for a junior
high school.

10249.   Strickland, V. E.   "Where does the ninth grade
belong?"   Bulletin of the National Assocation of
Secondary School Principals, February 1967:74-76.

Among the many factors to be considered in determining whether the ninth grade is placed better in
the 7-9 junior high school unit or in a 9-12 senior
high school unit is whether this has any effect on
the academic success of pupils.   Investigations
conducted in two Florida schools clearly showed that
difference in academic success in ninth grade does
not rest so much with its placement in either a
junior or senior high school as it does with the
program of instruction and instructional staff
involved.   This study does not support the idea that
ninth graders will necessarily experience either more
or less academic success in a junior high school.
Further, it appears from the data that ninth graders
in the junior high school value the importance of
school and schoolwork just as highly as ninth graders
in a senior high school.   The kinds of evidence and
the general procedures used were as follows: 1) a
statistical analysis of ninth grade scores obtained
from the statewide ninth grade testing program, 2) a
retest of the same ninth graders nine months later,
3) an analysis and comparison of pupils' scores
obtained from the retest with those achieved on the
initial test, 4) collection and analysis of pertinent
data on the personal and professional status of ninth
grade teachers participating, 5) collection and
analysis of socioeconomic data on pupils' home
situations through the use of the Carson-McGuire and
George White measures of social status, and 6) an
estimate of pupils' attitudes towards their school
through the use of the Grover-Tully attitude scale
called "How I Feel About School."

10250.   Taylor, G. R. and Jackson, M. H.   "School tardiness."   Southern Journal of Educational Research, 8,4
(1974):272-279.

Authors hypothesized that intervention initiated by
school personnel could successfully reduce the
tardiness rate in a Baltimore junior high school that
had habitual tardiness records in grades 7 and 8.
Data came from official school records, interviews,
and survey forms.   The results indicated that the
tardiness rate was significantly reduced at the end
of the ninth grade.

10251.   Thomas, B. "A Comparative Analysis of the Informal Communications Structure of Four Junior High
Schools." Ed.D. Dissertation, University of Washington, 1974.

This study of the effectiveness and efficiency of
informal school communications came from a sociometric questionnaire filled out by the professional
staffs of four schools. Measuring effectiveness
involved considering staff members' initial choices
and mutual choices of people to communicate with as
well as locating staff opinion leaders and isolates.
Findings showed no significant correlation between
the effectiveness of the informal communications
structure and the age of the school. However, there
was a significant negative correlation between the
efficiency of the informal communications structure
and the age of the school. The conclusion was drawn
that the informal communications structures of the
schools studied were less efficient as the schools
increased in age.

10252.   Thompson, P., Crawford, P., Virgin, A. E., and
Goode, R. C. "A Comparison of the Effects of Two
Physical Education Programs on the Physiological
Development of Adolescent Boys and Girls." Willow-
dale, Ont., Canada: North York Board of Education,
August, 1975.

The primary purpose of this study was to determine if
a specific daily indoor exercise program of six
minutes in length improved the aerobic fitness level
of junior high school students aged 12 to 14. A
minor purpose was to compare the performance of
participating students with Canadian norms for working capacity and fitness. Preliminary estimates were
made of normal values of cardiovascular respiratory
fitness for adolescent boys and girls. Researchers
hoped to find that both the boys and girls in the
experimental program would show greater gains on the
measures of aerobic fitness than boys and girls in
the control program and that there would be no
difference between students in the experiment and
control program in terms of nonaerobic measures of
strength, speed, and percent body fat. Five hundred
students in each of two New York junior high schools
took part in this study. The article describes the
program and the means by which strength and physical
fitness were measured. Both boys and girls in the
experimental school improved in aerobic fitness from
pretest to posttest, while control students declined.

10253.   Timmer, N. C. "An Investigation into the Degree
of Understanding of the Developmental Characteristics
of Pre- and Early Adolescents by Junior High and
Middle School Teachers." Ph.D. Dissertation,
Michigan State University. Dissertation Abstracts
International 38 (3-A), 1274. Order no. 77-18,556,
1977.

Advocates of the middle school state that an understanding of pre- and early adolescent physical,
intellectual, social, and emotional developmental
characteristics is a very important competency for
teachers of this age group. In this study, a questionnaire on teacher understanding of these characteristics was given to 161 middle school and junior
high school teachers. Comparisons of mean scores
were made between 1) junior high and middle school
teachers, 2) experienced and inexperienced teachers,
3) secondary certified and nonsecondary certified
teachers, and 4) teachers who desired to work with
pre- and early adolescents and those who preferred to
work with another age group. Findings: 1) Data
showed a slight but not conclusive trend toward
greater understanding by middle school teachers and
by teachers who choose to work with 10-to-14-year-
olds. 2) Nonsecondary certified junior high school
teachers had a better understanding of early adolescent characteristics than nonsecondary certified
middle school teachers. 3) In contrast, secondary
certified middle school teachers had a better understanding than secondary certified junior high school
teachers. Level of certification appears to be a
factor in understanding student characteristics,
although conclusions are difficult to state without
further investigation.

10254.   Tobin, W. "Seventh Grade Students in Two Pennsylvania Administrative Organizations, The Middle School
and the Junior High School." Ed.D. Dissertation,
Pennsylvania State University, 1969.

Study was done to determine 1) which of the two main
organizations where grade 7 is presently found--the
middle school housing grades 5-8 or 6-8 or the junior
high school housing grades 7-8 or 7-9--meets the
needs of seventh grade students with respect to
cocurriculum, curriculum, teachers, other students,
libraries, classroom situations, and their own personality. Principals' attitudes regarding grouping,
scheduling, location of seventh grade, and curriculum
for seventh grade students were explored as well as
teacher assessment of the curriculum, guidance and
counseling, cocurricular activities and educational
innovations in each type of school. Findings: 1)
Data showed no significant differences between middle
and junior high school students' opinions about

school.   2) The principals' attitudes and opinions evidenced no significant difference in any area.   3) The highest significant difference appeared in teacher assessment of the two types of schools, with reports of more innovations being carried out in the middle school.   Author concluded that differences in student adjustment do not exist between the Pennsylvania middle schools and junior high schools studied. Author made two conjectures: 1) A new school plant and a different atmosphere could provide the means to create more innovations in the curriculum, as was evident in the middle schools studied.   2) When a new middle school is in existence, a nearby junior high school should adopt some of its philosophy and thus create a different student atmosphere than might otherwise be evidenced in an older junior high school.

10255.   Trauschke, E.   "An Evaluation of the Middle School by a Comparison of the Achievement, Attitudes, and Self-Concepts of Students in the Middle School with Students in Other School Organizations."   Dissertation, University of Florida, Gainesville, 1970.

Miami Edison Middle School in Florida was compared to grades 7 and 8 of a junior high school and grades 5 and 6 of two elementary schools nearby.   Student populations were similar.   Fifty students were selected randomly in each grade of the middle school and in the control schools.   The Stanford Achievement Tests,   Gordon's   "How I   See Myself"   Scale,   and Battle's Student Attitudes Scale were used.   Hypotheses: 1) Achievement of middle school pupils on standardized test will equal or exceed that of pupils in conventional schools.   2) Middle school pupils will have more adequate self-concepts than pupils in conventional schools.   3) Pupils in the middle school will have more favorable attitudes toward school than pupils in the conventional schools.   Findings: 1) Middle school students showed more achievement, but only after at least two years of time spent in middle schools.   2) Middle school teachers had significantly more positive attitudes toward school.   3) There was no significant difference between middle school students and control students in self-concept and self-perception.

10256.   Travis, K. K.   "An Experimental Study to Determine the Impact of Career Exploration on Career Maturity and Attitudes Toward School of Junior High Students in Bullitt County.   Final Report."   Bullitt County Schools.   Frankfort: Kentucky State Department of Education, Bureau of Vocational Education, 1976.

This was one of the first research projects on the effects of the practical arts program by the Kentucky

State Department of Education. The results show
weaknesses and strengths in the program. Experimental and control groups of seventh, eighth, and
ninth grade students at Hebron Junior High School and
Mount Washington Junior High School responded to the
Career Maturity Inventory and School Sentiment Index
in the fall of 1975 and again in the spring of 1976.
The experimental program attempted to provide opportunities to explore a diversity of career roles in
classes that focused on occupational clusters. The
program also produced a career education evaluation
system consisting of a series of survey instruments
to obtain data from teachers, students, administrators, parents, and businesses. Recommendations: 1)
An advisory committee of parents and businessmen
should be organized to provide input into program
development. 2) In-service education should be
provided at least once a year for teachers and
administrators who are involved in career education
programs. 3) Schedule changes should be made to
provide ninth grade students more opportunity to
explore careers. 4) A full-time career exploration
coordinator should be placed in the schools. 5)
Additional materials and resources should be provided
from the state department of education. 6) Teachers
need to involve parents and business people in
teaching their career activity. 7) Teachers need to
provide additional out-of-classroom activities for
students.

10257.   Trimble, W. E. "The Effect of a Self-Evaluation
Environment on Growth in Self-Perception." Dissertation, Walden University, Naples, Fla., ERIC Doc. ED
076 907, July, 1973.

Study evaluated the effects of a special noncompeti-
tive program of physical education on the self-
concepts of underdeveloped junior high school boys.
Personality profiles of these boys were compared with
those of junior high athletes, with factor clusters
analyzed for variance within and between groups in
pretests and posttests (the National Physical Fitness
Test and the California Psychological Inventory). A
random sample of the underdeveloped boys received
additional verbal encouragement from the instructor
to see if further effects on personality were
evident. Author determined that allowing physically
underdeveloped boys to participate in an environment
using self-based evaluation standards rather than
competitively based standards contributed to gains in
emotional security and sense of personal worth.
Further research should be done on uses of self-
evaluation in more standard academic subjects. Most
of the underdeveloped boys in the study gained
significantly from the eight-month experience, as at
least one aspect of their environment allowed for

perceived self-growth. Initially, self-evaluation studies should be confined to curriculum areas where course objectives can be defined most clearly and where elements lend themselves to self-evaluation that gives students a chance to experience self-growth and achievement.

10258.   U. S. Office of Education. "Junior High School Facts." Misc. 21. Washington, D. C., 1955.

Of the 3,227 junior high schools in the United States in 1952, 2,395 (74.2 percent) were composed of grades 7, 8, and 9; 627 schools (19.4 percent) combined grades 7 and 8; and 150 (4.6 percent) combined grades 7-10. Vermont had no junior high schools, and five states had less than a dozen (Nevada 1, South Dakota 5, North Dakota 6, Maine 9, and Arizona 11). All of the junior high schools of four states--Maine, Nevada, Rhode Island, and South Dakota--consisted of grades 7, 8, and 9. This grade combination was prevalent also in many other states: Wyoming (79 percent); Maine (78 percent); New Hampshire (75 percent); Idaho (65 percent); Iowa (61 percent); Indiana (58 percent); Nebraska (56 percent); and Oregon (50 percent).

10259.   Waksman, S. A. "An evaluation of social learning procedures designed to aid students with conduct problems." Psychology in the Schools, 16,3(1979): 416-421.

Multiple measures were used to assess treatment effects of this middle school program. Teachers' reports on behavior checklists and daily ratings of targeted behaviors indicated improved conduct by nine out of the twelve consecutively referred students. A more conservative criterion of improvement on measures from two independent sources indicated improvement with seven students. All of the twelve students received improved scores on at least one outcome measure, and the program was well received by teachers.

10260.   Weber, N. "The grassroots: interviews with middle school students." National Elementary School Principal, 51,3(1971):55-59.

Study in Alachua County, Florida, had four purposes: 1) to discover how students adjusted to middle school education, 2) to discover how students made the transition from the self-contained classroom to multiage groups, 3) to identify the weak and strong points of middle schools, according to the students, and 4) to gather suggestions and comments from students. Author interviewed thirty students who were enrolled in the school system's first summer program for middle school students. She prepared for interviews by talking with a county supervisor and touring the facilities of the two schools. She grouped the students' comments, most of which are in their own words, according to subject: 1) Multiage groups: most seemed to get along well in their groups. Some of them attributed their quick adjustment to the fact that the older students in their groups helped them. The older ones felt that helping younger ones made studies more interesting. 2) More than one teacher: the idea of having several teachers was agreeable to the students. 3) Large or small groups: opinions seemed to be evenly divided. Those in favor of large groups felt that the members could help each other learn, that there was more freedom to move around and more sharing of ideas, and that work got done faster. Those favoring small groups liked to work more quietly, discuss things rather than just answer questions, and work more with the teacher. 4) Grading system: the schools used criterion referenced items for reporting. Parents received statements about the objectives, skills, and activities for their children and the teacher's evaluation of progress in each area. Some students were not enthusiastic about their grading system. Many students and parents did not fully understand the intent of the system. Other students liked being graded so that they would know how they were doing. Students at both schools expressed a dislike for tests. 5) Most interesting subject: the students did not hesitate a moment in naming their favorite subject. 6) Least interesting subject: the students were asked to pretend that they could choose one subject they would never have to take again. Their choices and the reasons behind them were not as varied or as well thought out as answers to the previous question. 7) Learning methods: more than half the students said they liked to learn best by having films in class.

10261.   Wegner, O. A.   "A Study of Student Attitude Towards School."   Ph.D. Dissertation, University of Iowa, Iowa City, 1976.

Author surveyed a large sample of students in an Ohio school district to measure their attitudes toward school, education, peers, subjects, and teachers. The problem: "Is there a point along the grade level continuum of a young person's formal educaton where a significant variation in student attitudes toward school occurs and can be detected?" Responses to a twenty-five-item questionnaire showed that elementary students in grades 1-6 had a significantly more positive attitude than did secondary school students. Grades 7 and 10 showed the least positive attitudes toward school in general, while grade 2 reflected the

most positive attitude toward school. Girls maintained a more favorable attitude toward school than
did boys.

10262.   White, J. W. "Differences Between Open and Traditional Elementary Students on Selected Characteristics and Changes in Same Characteristics After Six
Months in a Middle School." Ph.D. Dissertation,
University of Pittsburgh. Dissertation Abstracts
International, 34 (10-A), 6526-6527. Order no.
74-8693, 1974.

Fifteen students from an open elementary school and
thirty-seven from a traditional elementary school
responded to four questionnaires: the Self-Social
Symbols Tasks, General Self-Concept of Ability and
Grade Importance, Survey of Study Habits and
Attitudes, and a questionnaire on attitudes toward
different testing situations. Interviews were also
conducted with sixth grade teachers in the middle
school. Children from the traditional elementary
school showed less complex representations of self
than the open elementary students did after six
months in the middle school. The test anxiety of the
traditional elementary students lessened, indicating
they adjusted easily to a traditional middle school.
Esteem scores increased in the middle school for both
groups of students. It appeared that the children
from the open and traditional elementary schools did
come from the same population and there was little or
no change in study habits, self-concept, and test
anxiety after six months in the middle school.

10263.   White, W. D. "Pupil progress and grade combinations." Bulletin of the National Association of
Secondary School Principals, 51(1967):87-90.

This study demonstrates what seventh graders have
known for a long time: the lowest spot on the totem
pole is a hard one to operate from effectively. The
number of grades in the junior high school appears to
have an effect upon the progress of the pupils in the
school. This was the finding of research done in the
junior high schools of Jefferson County, Colorado
under the direction of the University of Denver.
Author studied the academic achievement, personal-
social adjustment, and activity participation of
seventh grade pupils from schools composed of two,
three, six, or nine grades and one experimental
school which contained only the seventh grade.
Matched groups of thirty-five pupils from each type
of school were compared after one year of experience
in their respective schools. Significant differences
were found between sample groups on eight comparisons. Findings: 1) Pupils who attended schools with
only one or two grades experienced advantages in

academic instruction over boys and girls enrolled in schools with three or more grades. 2) Junior high school pupils enjoyed some academic advantages when their instruction was organized and presented independently from the instructional program of older or younger pupils. 3) Pupils in the seventh grade were adversely affected in their adjustment to school-related problems when two or more grades were above the seventh in a particular school unit. More generally, when a majority of the pupils in the school were above a particular grade level, the participation of pupils in the lower grade group in school activities was likely to be less than in schools where that particular grade level was not overshadowed. 4) Somewhat in contrast with the above, greater participation in club activities was likely to be generated by bringing pupils from several grades together rather than by trying to maintain separate activity programs for each grade level. Overall, there appears to be an advantage in organizing the various grade groups in a junior high school so that faculty, administration, and the use of physical and other facilities can be focused on each grade group, independent of the other grades in the school unit.

10264. Whitehead, R. E. "School and District Size Related to Parental Attitudes, Achievement, and Expenditure." Ed.D. Dissertation, University of Illinois at Urbana-Champaign, 1973.

Parental attitudes, educational fund expenditures, and student achievement on standardized tests were examined in this questionnaire study of one hundred families in each of four junior high schools. The schools were of different sizes and were located in districts of different sizes. Findings: 1) There were no significant differences between any of the schools as measured by standardized student achievement tests. 2) Generally, in small schools and small districts, mean scores on parental attitudes were more positive. 3) School size is much more critical in large districts than in small districts. 4) Parents' attitudes toward the staff and their concern about the size of the school were the best predictors of overall final attitudes.

10265. Whitley, T. W. "Some Effects of a Locally Developed Program of Individualized Instruction on the Attitudes of Middle School Pupils Toward Various Aspects of the School Environment." Ph.D. Dissertation, Duke University, 1976.

The hypothesis of the study was that there would be no difference between an experimental group of middle school pupils in the fifth, sixth, and seventh grades and a control group of pupils in the same grades in their attitudes toward their teachers, learning processes, language arts, and mathematics after one school year of exposure to a locally developed program of individualized instruction. Findings: 1) There were differences between the scores of the two groups at each of the three grade levels. 2) The subjects in the experimental group indicated more favorable attitudes toward the aspects of the school environment examined in the study. 3) Exposure to individualized instruction had a positive impact on pupil attitudes.

10266. Wilcutt, R. E. "Individual differences: does research have any answers for junior high mathematics teachers?" School Science and Mathematics, 69,3 (1969):217-225.

In this study, half of a seventh grade class of 240 students was assigned at the beginning of the year to a single teacher who stayed with that group throughout the school year. Classes were heterogeneous, and each class operated independently of other seventh grade math classes. The other half of the grade was assigned to math classes on the basis of test results which indicated the students' proficiency in each separate subject unit of the course. A comparison of the results of two standardized mathematics tests for both groups at the end of the experiment showed that flexibly grouping students on the basis of a proficiency test before each new topic did not cause significant differences in academic achievement, but it did result in significantly more positive student attitudes toward mathematics.

10267. Wiles, J. W. and Thomason, J. "Middle school research, 1968-1974: a review of substantial studies." Educational Leadership, 32,6(1975):421-423.

Findings indicate little evidence by which to evaluate middle school education. A systematic approach emphasizing qualities distinctive to middle schools is greatly needed. This review of research identifies and summarizes studies which evaluated middle schools in a systematic way. Particular emphasis was given to comparative studies, and the search was restricted to sources readily available in the literature. Twenty-seven studies were reviewed, of which thirteen (seven dissertations and six school-sponsored studies) were found to be substantial in terms of research design, number of subjects assessed, and useful findings. Existing research on school education is of remarkably low quality. Most of the studies to date have been either the result of dissertation work or studies by junior high and middle school advocates whose research objectivity is questionable. Another problem is that most of the existing middle school research has been done in Florida, New York, Pennsylvania, and Michigan. This review utilizes studies from a total of seven states. Finally, most existing research on the middle school has been concerned with only four areas: academic achievement, attitudes, self-concepts, and facilities. It appears that other equally important questions have been ignored by researchers. In particular, the studies reviewed were limited in value because they did not precisely define the middle schools studied, did not consider how long the schools had been in existence, did not indicate how long pupils in the schools had experienced the middle school program, or did not indicate the reason for establishment of the schools. All of these factors could significantly affect the findings. Six of the studies reviewed compared middle school academic achievement to academic achievement in other forms of intermediate education. Most of the studies were based on national standardized tests. Three studies--Ehrlich and Murray, 1969 (see bibliography entry 10067); Glissmeyer, 1969 (see bibliography entry 1099); and Mooney, 1970 (see entry 10166)-- found no significant differences in achievement between students in middle schools and equivalent students in other forms of intermediate education.

10268.   Wilke, P. A.   "An Analysis of Factors Influencing Student Attitudes in Two Suburban Junior High Schools with Contrasting Organization for Instruction." Ph.D. Dissertation, University of Minnesota. Dissertation Abstracts International, 40 (06), Sec. A, 3222. Order no. 7926192, 1979.

Subjects for this research were 717 students in incoming seventh grade classes in two Minnesota schools: Central Junior High, organized on the traditional Carnegie Unit plan, and Westwood Junior High, with flexible modular scheduling. Student attitudes and feelings were determined by the Minnesota School Affect Assessment. A comparison of student attitudes and feelings was made on a pretest at the beginning of seventh grade and a posttest one year later. School organization proved not to be a major influence on student attitudes. (Author also studied the effects of sex and socioeconomic status on student attitudes.)

10269.   Willems, E. E.   "Sense of obligation to high school activities as related to school size and marginality of student." Child Development, 38(1967): 1247-1263.

Findings: 1) Overall, students from small schools reported more sense of obligation than students from

larger schools.   2) Marginal students in the small
schools reported as much sense of obligation as their
regular classmates, while marginal students in the
large schools were a group apart. 3) The impact of
school size appears to be upon marginal students.

10270.   Wood, F. H. "A comparison of student attitudes in
junior high and middle schools." High School Journal,
56(1973):355-361.

While the advocates of the middle school are promoting the 6-8 grade pattern in hopes that it will
produce more positive attitudes toward school and
learning, the findings of this study of a middle
school and three junior high schools do not support
such claims.   In fact, they suggest that the conventional junior high school organization where
seventh, eighth, and ninth graders mix during the day
generates student attitudes that are at least as
positive toward school, peers, professional staff,
and instruction as student attitudes in the middle
school.   Student attitudes in the junior highs using
seventh grade centers are significantly more positive
than student attitudes in the middle school.   The
conclusion that middle schools do not improve student
attitudes is strengthened by the fact that there were
no significant diffences with one exception, between
students in entry, middle, and exit grades in the
different schools or between grades within the school
organizations.   The results of this study cast some
doubt on the move to the middle school organization
if the goal for such a change is to improve student
attitudes toward school. However, the findings must
be viewed in light of the limited size of the school
sample.   This study does suggest that the middle
school may be another fad based upon assumptions
which cannot be substantiated. School administrators
might be well advised to postpone organizational
changes until these assumptions are tested.   In cases
where such changes are made, care should be taken to
assess the impact of this move on student feelings
about their school, especially when public support
and confidence are already shaken by educators'
inability to produce the results they promise.

10271.   Wright, G. S. and Greer, E. S.   The Junior High
School: A Survey of Grades 7, 8, 9 in Junior and
Junior-Senior High Schools, 1959-60.   U. S. Office of
Education, Bulletin 32. Washington, D. C.: U. S.
Government Printing Office, 1963.

This is a study of grades 7-9 as they were found in
junior and junior-senior high schools in the 48
states and the District of Columbia. Included in the
survey were junior high schools composed of grades 7
and 8 or of grades 8 and 9 as well as grades 7-9.

Questionnaire responses from principals tended to indicate that size had more to do with differences in educational practices at the junior high school level than type of school did. The school day for pupils, exclusive of lunch period, was typically six to six and a half hours. The school day for teachers was normally seven to eight hours. A school day of six periods each lasting fifty-five to fifty-nine minutes was reported more often than any other combination of number and length of periods. Of all junior high schools having class sections, 74 percent used homogeneous grouping as a basis for assigning pupils as compared with 60 percent of the junior-senior high schools. Large majorities of the schools grouped seventh and eighth grade pupils homogeneously in all four of the major subjects--English, social studies, science, and mathematics. Complete departmentalization as represented by a different teacher for each subject was found in 50 percent of the seventh grades, 60 percent of the eighth grades, and 80 percent of the ninth grades. Another third to a half of the schools assigned pupils the same teacher for two to three periods in seventh and eighth grades. Guidance was a function of the homeroom or activity period in 80 to 90 percent of the schools. Considerable time for study during the school day was provided in study halls and during regular classes. More than 90 percent of the schools had a central library and more than 80 percent had a full-time or part-time professional librarian in charge. All schools used various types of tests for pupil evaluation. Standardized achievement tests were the most common in all types of schools. Mental ability tests were the second most common, teacher-made tests third, interest tests fourth, and special aptitude tests fifth.

10272.   Zdanowicz, P. "A Study of the Changes that Have Taken Place in the Junior High Schools of the Northeastern U.S. During the Last Decade and the Reasons for Some of the Changes." Ed.D. Dissertation, Temple University. University Microfilms, Ann Arbor, Mich., 1965.

Findings: 1) The majority of schools returning usable questionnaires were grade 7-9 junior high schools, 15 percent were grade 7-8 junior high schools, 15 percent were grade 6-8 middle schools, and 3 percent were grade 5-8 middle schools.   2) Seven percent of the schools had enrollments of 300 pupils or less.   3) The typical school was a grade 7-9 junior high school with an enrollment of 601 to 900 pupils.   4) Of the 414 schools responding, 70 percent were in existence in 1953, ten years before this study.   5) More than half of the schools consisted of grades 7-9 in 1953.   6) Many schools had relatively small enrollments in 1953, and none had more than 1200 students.   7) The number of junior high schools of each type increased considerably during the decade of 1954-1963.   8) Seventeen percent of the schools studied changed their grade organization during this decade.   9) Of the grade 5-8 middle schools, 77 percent were either new schools or had changed to their grade organization in this decade. 10) Administrative necessity was the reason for change in the grade organization of 60 percent of these schools.   11) Nine percent changed their grade organization for strictly philosophical reasons, and 17 percent were contemplating a change because of philosophy.   12) The smaller the enrollment of a school the more likely it was to contemplate a change in grade organization.   13) Grade 7-8 junior high schools, more than any other type changed to their 1963 grade organization because of administrative necessity.

10273.   Zigler, J. T., et al.   "Application of a Cooperative University/Middle School Model to Enhance Science Education Accountability."   ERIC Doc. ED 103 281, 1975.

University science educators developed a model science program for public middle schools and presented it to thirty-nine teachers in the summer of 1973 at Ball State University.   Fourteen teachers took part in the followup project, using the model and the knowledge and skills gained during the summer institute and then reporting the results.   They developed instructional units consisting of specific performance objectives, pretests and posttests, and teaching strategies appropriate for meeting the needs of the students in their local school system. Results indicated that statistically significant learning by students using the model had taken place. See ERIC Abstact #ED 103 281.

11

Teacher Preparation and In-Service Training

11001.   Anderson, R. H. and Snyder, K. J. "Preparation of
staff for middle school implementation." Middle
School Journal, 10(1979):5.

Includes sections on recognizing the need for professional preparation, a middle school professional
development program, the school as an ecosystem,
educational leadership, action planning (the principal's task), school-wide planning (the school
community's task), staff development. Gone are the
days when dreamers can invent new systems of learning
and organization and expect others to carry out without training and/or assistance. Given the apparent
lack of preparation of middle school principals and
teachers, it is time for school districts to make a
major commitment to professional development. Such
training might include a change from thinking of the
school as a well-oiled machine to thinking of it as a
beehive thriving on goal-related activities and on
the dynamics of human interaction and educational
expectations. Educators need preparation that gives
them knowledge to make leadership decisions and
skills to determine how to get the task done. All
activity must reflect collaboratively defined goals
and provide the focus for continuous growth among
professionals and students. Such preparation will go
a long way toward building a sense of commitment to
the dreams of the Bedford Middle School Conference.

11002.   Armstrong, D. G. "Specialized training for middle
school and junior high school teachers: prescriptions, problems and prospects." High School Journal,
40,6(1977):247-254.

Author cites research showing differences in teacher
training, although certain themes are common. Author

considers teacher background in four broad areas that
contribute to success in working with intermediate
school students. He also evaluates responses to
suggestions that intermediate teachers receive
special pre-service instruction. See ERIC Abstract
#EJ 163 417.

11003.   Arth, A. A. and Weiss, T. M.   "University of
Wyoming: middle school teacher education." Journal
of Teacher Education, 28,1(1977):32-36.

At the University of Wyoming self-selection appears
to be a highly accurate screening device for levels
of teaching. It offers the opportunity for 384 hours
of classroom exposure prior to student teaching. See
ERIC Abstract #EJ 159 704.

11004.   Askov, E. N. and Dupuis, M. M.   "Guidelines for
in-service programs to teach reading in content
courses." Journal of Teacher Education, 30,5(1979):
16-18.

Authors suggest teaching methods to improve reading
skills within the context of junior high and senior
high school regular content reading. See ERIC
Abstract #EJ 213 560.

11005.   Augenstein, M. B. "A Comparative Study of Ratings
of Proposed Teacher Competencies for Middle School
English." Ed.D. Dissertation, Florida Atlantic University, ERIC Doc. ED 112 399, 1974.

Fifty teachers of middle schools, fifty educational
leaders, fifty high school teachers, and fifty
patrons of middle schools in the Broward County,
Florida, public school system were asked to rate the
importance of twelve general competencies and sixty
subcompetencies for training and certifying English
teachers. The procedure developed by this study
proved useful for determining the relative order of
importance assigned to the proposed teacher competencies for middle school English. See ERIC Abstract
#ED 112 399.

11006.   Baker, T. P. "What is an effective in-service education program?" Bulletin of the National Association
of Secondary School Principals, 35,177(1951):46-48.

Presents phases of the in-service education program
in the Austin, Texas, public schools.

11007.   Bantel, E. "Preadolescent: Misunderstood." Middle School Portfolio, Leaflet 11. Washington, D.C.:
Association for Childhood Education International,
1968.

For the average child in the 9 to 12 age group, behavior begins to assume neo-adult qualities, producing a stability and integration that will become the foundation for the ensuing period of youth and then adulthood. This article discusses the preadolescent's need for time, his capacity to understand or grasp temporal relations and function in relation to a time schedule which often leads to excessively demanding regulations and ordering of his behavior. It also discusses the need for time in the struggle for the self, and the child's growth in cognitive capacities. Hastening maturation may prolong childhood personality. The child must establish himself in these years, rather than be allowed to postpone the confrontation with himself as a human being growing toward adulthood. The article discusses the many difficulties in this age group, the moral code and values, the view of self, and the growth in cognitive capacity with references to Piaget.

11008.   Baughman, M. D.   "Patterns of staff personnel in Illinois junior high schools."   Bulletin of the National Association of Secondary School Principals, 43(1959):47-56.

Presents data from 129 checklists which dealt with what personnel are performing what services and functions.   Compares results with other recommendations and offers suggestions.

11009.   Baughman, M. D.   "Continuing Education for Junior High School Personnel."   Paper presented at the Annual Conference of the Junior High Association of Illinois, 1965.

Despite the striking increase in demands for competent junior high school teachers, they are in alarmingly short supply.   Article discusses the need for continued growth on the job in terms of 1) basic human needs, 2) the teacher as a professional, 3) principles of formal organization, 4) informal climate, 5) supervision for optimum growth, and 6) continuing education of the junior high school principal.

11010.   Baughman, M. D. Junior High School Staff Personnel --Their Preparation and Professional Growth.   Danville, Ill.:   Interstate Printers and Publishers, 1966.

Presents sections on pre-service education for junior high school teachers, in-service education for junior high school personnel, student teacher programs, and the importance of the home room and its teachers. Chapters are papers presented at the 1965 annual conference or the 1965 fall conference of the Junior High School Association of Illinois.

11011.   Belpre City Schools. "Project GIST (45-70-0260). ESEA, Title III, Project Termination Report." Belpre, Ohio, ERIC Doc. ED 086 670, 1973.

Study evaluates a two-year in-service teacher train-ing project in the Belpre Middle School. Objectives of the program included: 1) the change of teachers' roles, in terms of perceptions, procedures, and morale, from those in self-contained classrooms to those in cooperative teaching teams, 2) an increase of teachers' instructional ability as measured by their students on the Purdue Teacher Evaluation, and 3) a comparison of the academic achievement of sixth and eighth grade students with the norm groups on the Iowa Tests of Basic Skills. Workshops and confer-ences were held with an emphasis on organizing and administering a continuous individual program cur-riculum. Results showed that teacher morale improved for eleven teachers, remained unchanged for eight, and dropped for three. The PTE results showed an improvement in ratings for six teachers and a drop in rating for fifteen. It was concluded that the project was successful in helping to implement a continuous individual progress curriculum. See ERIC Abstract #ED 086 670.

11012.   Blackburn, J. E. "The junior high school teacher we need." Educational Leadership, 23(1965):206.

It is essential with children of junior high school age that the teacher be enthusiastic in his teaching and interested in both his work and his students. The successful junior high school teacher does not regard a junior high teaching assignment as a promo-tion from elementary nor a temporary delay on the way to high school teaching. He has a thorough under-standing of the preadolescent and early adolescent; he appreciates their wide range of differences; he likes this age group; and he has a sincere belief in providing the best education for all children.

11013.   Blackburn, J. E. "An unfinished dream: the junior high school." High School Journal, 48(1966):209-212.

Research shows that educators help the young adoles-cents in their process of becoming by working toward these goals: 1) accepting each pupil as he is, 2) providing opportunities for pupils to explore their own needs and interests and to relate these to their friends, their community, and their world, 3) pro-viding opportunities for pupils to develop problem-solving skills, 4) clarifying personal and social

ideals by exploring the values of democracy and providing opportunities for pupils to participate in
democratic decision making, 5) making social problems
more understandable and personal, and 6) fostering
positive attitudes toward change and the continuing
process of educaton.

11014.   Bondi, J.   "A new kind of teacher for the new
middle school." Resources in Education, ERIC Doc. ED
079 252, 1973.

Until now, the middle school teacher has received
in-service training at the elementary and secondary
levels. This method has proved to be inadequate, and
the rapid growth of middle schools has stimulated the
development of special pre-service education programs.   These programs in turn have stimulated an
investigation of the characteristics of the middle
school teacher. This new kind of teacher should not
only like working with 10-to-14-year-olds but should
also be sensitive to the emerging independence,
heightened insecurity, and divergent interests of
these students.   An internship period in the pre-
service education of the middle school teacher would
strengthen the student-teacher relationship.   Pre-
service education should help the middle school
teachers cooperate with other teachers, since team
teaching is common. The teacher should know how to
prescribe individually for the problems in reading
and communication that are prevalent in the middle
school.   The pre-service education program should
also include flexible scheduling because of the
various courses offered to the middle school student.
Activities and a model schedule from the De Soto
Middle School, Arcadia, Florida, are included.

11015.   Bosher, W. C., Jr.   "'To thine own self be true':
an antidote to melancholia: jh/ms idea factory."
English Journal, 67,7(1978):74-76.

Article discusses causes of teachers' poor self-
concept in junior high/middle school, including
administrative negativism and neglect, inadequate
preparation for the junior high/middle school,
absence of recognition for teacher accomplishments,
inferiority-superiority relationships, and failure of
professional organizations to be representative.

11016.   Bossing, N. L.   "Preparing teachers for junior
high school." High School Journal, 50(1966):150.

If the junior high school student is indeed an
individual with special needs in a school environment
that is neither elementary nor secondary, then the
teachers for the junior high school must be prepared

in programs that are different from those for elementary teachers and secondary teachers.

11017.   Brainard, E. "Junior high teachers: has training been adequate?" Clearinghouse, 38(1963):179-181.

Only 63 colleges and universities out of 812 investigated made any mention of a program to prepare junior high teachers. A review of the catalogs of the 246 institutions accredited by NCATE showed that only 36 had programs for the preparation of junior high school teachers.

11018.   Brogdon, R. E. "In search of competencies for preparing middle school teachers." Peabody Journal of Education, 55,2(1978):145-151.

Discusses Alabama middle school teachers' perceptions of competencies relevant to middle school teacher education programs. See ERIC Abstract #ED 176 578.

11019.   Brown, J. G. and Howard, A. W. "Who should teach at schools for the middle years?" Clearinghouse, 46, 5(1972):279-283.

Discusses findings of a study on the perceptions of junior high and middle school principals about the competencies, attitudes, characteristics, and training for teachers at the intermediate school level. See ERIC Abstract #EJ 050 119.

11020.   Brudy, H. F. "The Junior High School: A Philosopher's View." Highlights of the Tenth Annual Conference for School Administrators, Cornell University, School of Education, Ithaca, N. Y., 1963.

The middle grades teacher should be someone who has not yet fully incorporated the values of middle age, who shares the anxiety of students in coping with elders and officials, and who still has some of the youthful rebel in him. In other words, he should be still warm from the transitional state, albeit indubitably a member of the adult community.

11021.   Budde, R. "A study of the performance of 7th, 8th, and 9th grade teachers in Michigan." Bulletin of the National Association of Secondary School Principals, 46(1962):389-390.

The Michigan Teacher Personnel Study, in determining why there is such a turnover of teachers in the junior high school grades, concluded that in comparison to teachers in other grades, seventh, eighth, and ninth grade teachers were less permanent in teaching and less permanent at their grade level. They were

younger and they had fewer years of teaching experience. Many more of them were required to fill available positions in these grades. Many of them taught
in the junior high school grades for a few years and
then went on to positions in senior high school. The
reason most often given for disliking to teach at
this level was the problem of discipline, while professional and salary adjustment and the desire to
teach more challenging subject matter were the
reasons most frequently stated for moving to high
school teaching.

11022.   Burke, P. J. and Stoltenberg, J. C. "Certification
for the middle grades." Action in Teacher Education,
1,3-4(1979):47-52.

Sections are Introduction, The Schools, Learner
Styles, Teacher Styles, Teacher Needs, The Components, Residency, and Implications for Certification.
Special certification for teachers of transescent
students is recommended because of the uniqueness of
these students and of the tasks their teachers perform. These tasks include accepting students who have
experienced a child-centered learning program and
preparing them for a subject-centered environment,
moving students from a prescriptive disciplinary code
to a point of self-restraint and self-discipline,
insuring that students have mastered the basic skills
necessary to enter secondary school, and helping
students to identify strengths to be pursued. To do
this, schools can develop the following characteristics: 1) individualization of instruction, interdisciplinary teaching, and expanded curriculum concepts
in academic, vocational, and aesthetic areas, 2)
guidance and counseling services, 3) increasing standards for scholarly and personal achievement, 4) a
carefully planned learning environment, and 5) activities designed to promote social interests and
responsibilities. The authors coined the term JMI
schools as an abbreviation for junior high, middle,
and intermediate schools. A preparation program for
the initial and continuing certification of JMI
teachers could include requirements in the following
categories: 1) general education, 2) professional
education, 3) areas of concentration, 4) field-based
clinical experiences, and 5) a residency. The
article describes this residency and its implications
for certification at length.

11023.   Campbell, J. R.   "Cognitive and affective process
development and its relation to a teacher's interaction ratio." Journal of Research in Science Teaching, 8,4(1971):317-324.

Author identified direct and indirect teachers in
junior high school through Flander's Interaction

Analysis Technique. The findings concluded that students of indirect teachers were superior on affective and cognitive measures. Cognitive development was defined as the abilities to identify and define scientific problems, suggest or screen hypotheses, select valid procedures, interpret data and draw conclusions, critically evaluate claims or statements made by others, and reason quantitatively and symbolically. Research results from this and other studies suggest that teachers should not restrict students excessively. Teachers should conserve criticism and use it in consistently small quantities.

11024. Central State University, College of Education. "Oklahoma City-Central State University Cooperative Program in Teacher Education." Entry for the 1972 Distinguished Achievement Awards, American Association of Colleges for Teacher Education, Washington, D.C. Edmond, Okla.: Central State University, College of Education, ERIC Doc. ED 074 036, November 23, 1971.

This program provides future middle school teachers with an opportunity to integrate educational theories of learning and behavior with day-to-day public school experiences. They student teach for a semester with twenty-five students in a middle school, and at the same time they take three academic courses: educational psychology, child and adolescent psychology, and educational tests and measurements. A team of university professors spends half-days in the school building supervising student teaching and teaching. This document includes sections on the rationale, objectives, development, and description of the program, as well as administration, facilities, budget, academic course requirements, student teaching requirements, evaluation, discussion, conclusions, references for theoretical base, and bibliography.

11025. Chiara, C. and Johnson, E. "Is the middle school doomed for failure?" Clearinghouse, 46,5(1972):288-292.

Authors present positive and negative aspects of the middle school and discuss the skills and attitudes of the good middle school teacher. Such a teacher should understand the purposes of the middle school and relate them to the curriculum and organization of the middle school. The lack of teachers deliberately prepared to work with the preadolescent and early adolescent may be a significant factor in student frustration as evidenced in high schools and colleges in the 1960s and early 1970s.

11026.   Clarke, S. "The middle school specially trained teachers are vital to its success." Clearinghouse, 45(1971):218-222.

The most crucial course in the development of the prospective teacher in the middle school is the methods class.   If middle school teaching is to develop into an exciting, creative activity, then methods classes will have to become places where learning and thinking are engaged in actively, creatively, freely, and joyfully. Article presents eight principles by which a good middle school methods class functions.

11027.   Clasen, R. E. and Bowman, W. E. "Toward a student-centered learning focus inventory for junior high and middle school teachers." Journal of Educational Research, 68,1(1974):9-11.

An instrument was developed to assess the relative student-centeredness of junior high and middle school teachers.   The final version with sixteen semantic differential items had a reliability coefficient of .83.   It correlated .47 (substantial relationship) with principals' judgments of the student-centered-ness of junior high school teachers.   This study stems from the junior high versus middle school debate over which is better for meeting the educa-tional needs of pre- and early adolescents.   One claim made for the middle school is that it was designed to be more student centered than the tradi-tional junior high school which was deemed to be more subject centered.   Administrators could use the instrument in intake interviews of teachers who apply for jobs in middle schools or junior high schools. While a single score can never be used as the job determinant, the instrument should be used as one index in a series.   In addition, the individual's responses to various items could provide interesting insight into his or her philosophy of education.   If student-centeredness were to be articulated as a goal of a given middle or junior high school, the instru-ment could also help evaluate attainment of the goal by determining whether a teacher were behaving in a student-centered or subject-centered manner.   The instrument could be used either for pre-service screening or in-service education of teachers for pre- and early adolescents. Two operational defini-tions were used: student-centered teaching-learning transactions (transactions which are conceived, executed, and evaluated primarily to satisfy student needs) and subject-centered teaching-learning trans-actions (transactions which are conceived, executed, and evaluated primarily to transmit a body of knowledge).

11028.   College of Education, University of Kentucky. "Curriculum for Junior High School Majors." Lexington, Ky., 1972.

Presents requirements for teaching in junior high schools, different areas to specialize in, and the general studies component areas.

11029.   Commonwealth of Kentucky, Department of Education. "Guidelines for the Preparation-Certification for Junior High School Teachers." Teacher Education Circular 248. Frankfort, Ky., 1967.

Discusses basic beliefs regarding the preparation of teachers for junior high school aged children, the curriculum for junior high school teachers, teaching majors, semi-majors and minors approved for junior high school teachers, validity, renewal and effective dates, standard junior high school certificates, and fifth-year program for renewal or provisional teachers' certificates. The following beliefs are basic to the preparation program for junior high teachers: 1) The junior high school, generally speaking, should be composed of grades 7, 8, and 9 or other possible combinations, such as grades 6, 7, and 8. Organization will vary, but the underlying philosophy should consider the child of this age as the primary responsibility of the junior high school. 2) Junior high school teachers should meet all the personal and professional prerequisites of other teachers and in addition should understand the problems and needs of children this age. 3) The junior high school is not entirely a continuation of elementary school, and for this reason changes should be made in the preparation of teachers for this age student. 4) Junior high school teachers should understand the basic philosophy and problems of junior high schools and should also be thoroughly familiar with curriculum appropriate to the junior high school aged child. They should possess skills and knowledge in the subjects they teach. 5) In order to provide basic general education and to enable the program to fit in easily with the present approved program, the general education program currently required for secondary teachers should also be required for junior high school teachers.

11030.   Compton, M. F.   "How do you prepare to teach transescents?"   Educational Leadership, 31,3(1973): 214-216.

The preparation program for middle school teachers needs four elements: 1) early opportunity to make realistic professional choices, 2) content-filled preparation, 3) general education, and 4) professional preparation. An undergraduate program at the

University of Georgia includes an opportunity for
early professional choices based on experiences with
transescents. This field-based program is individually tailored to meet the needs of the prospective
teacher. This departure from a highly structured
program gives the prospective teacher a certain flexibility, which, it is hoped, will carry over into his
or her future planning of flexible programs for
transescents.

11031.   Conant, J. B. The Education of American Teachers.
New York: McGraw-Hill, 1963.

Conant has written specifically for middle grades
teachers. Chapters 5 to 9 would be useful for educators of middle school teachers. Chapters are: 1)
A Quarrel Among Educators. 2) Who Guards the Gates?
3) Patterns of Certification. 4) The Redirection of
Public Authority. 5) The Academic Preparation of
Teachers. 6) The Theory and Practice of Teaching.
7) The Education of Elementary School Teachers. 8)
The Education of Secondary School Teachers. 9) Continuing an In-Service Education of Teachers. 10)
Concluding Observations. Conant proposes some
radical alterations in teacher education. His book
is the product of a two-year study of certification
policies in sixteen state capitols and of teacher
training programs in seventy-seven institutions,
bringing to light the serious and now inescapable
questions that confront educators and the public
alike. He argues that the diversity of American education, a result of local controls and of the varying
programs of individual institutions, is of great
value and must be preserved. He covers many specific
questions: Who is responsible for the education of
teachers? Who ought to be responsible? How well do
state regulations protect the public against ignorant
or incompetent teachers? How much freedom should be
left to institutions preparing teachers? He also
discusses the scope and value of academic and professional courses and the time that should be devoted to
in-service education for teachers.

11032.   Conover, H. R. "The junior high school principalship."   Bulletin of the National Association of
Secondary School Principals, 51(1967):20-23.

Concerning the difference between junior high and
middle school principals, the person in the 5-3-4 or
6-2-4 type school was more likely to have moved from
teacher to principal, while the principal in the
6-3-3 type school was more likely to have been in
another administrative capacity before his present
position, according to this study by the National
Association of Secondary School Principals Committee
on the Study of Secondary School Principalship. The

study was underwritten by the Educational Testing Service, and the first part was presented at the National Convention of Secondary School Principals in 1964. According to this nationwide survey of principals of junior highs and middle schools, what is the ideal junior high school grade organization? Responses broke down as follows: 1) The 6-8 structure: most principals in this scheme considered it the ideal grade level organization. 2) The 7-8 structure: half the principals involved in this plan consider the 7-9 structure more desirable. Only one fourth thought their present 7-8 structure was the best. There was pronounced dissatisfaction. Many would like to annex the 6-9 grades, depending on the principals' educational background and orientation. 3) The 7-9 structure: three fourths of the principals thought their structure was the best.

11033.   Covert, W. O.   "A New Approach to Junior High Teacher Education."   Paper presented at the Annual Conference of Junior High Teachers in Illinois, 1965.

The success of any program of teacher education for the junior high school will depend on: 1) how well educators in the universities and the public schools can identify and attract people who are personally and academically qualified to teach the early adolescent, 2) how adequately we can organize our preparation program to help prospective teachers understand the purposes of school programs for the early adolescent and to inspire them to devote their professional lives to this age group, and 3) how well the junior high school professional staff accepts graduates of the program and helps them improve their professional practice.

11034.   De Vito, A.   "The middle of the muddle--in the middle school."   School Science and Mathematics, 75,7 (1975):621-626.

Author discusses middle school rationale and characteristics. He investigates the problems of science curriculum materials and preparation of science teachers for the 6-8 grade school. See ERIC Abstract #EJ 130 046.

11035.   DeVane, L. M., Jr.   "The qualities and qualifications of the excellent junior high school teacher." Bulletin of the National Association of Secondary School Principals, 46(1962):379-380.

Author surveyed 22 administrators, 213 teachers, and 1,212 ninth grade students from 11 junior high schools on the characteristics and qualifications of the excellent teachers. Study suggests a need for research and experimentation to develop programs of preparation for junior high school teachers.

11036.   Dean, S. E.   "Team-teaching: a review."   <u>School Life</u>, <u>44</u>(1961):5-8.

Article describes the roles of professionals in a school organized for team teaching.

11037.   Dixon, N. R.   "The search for JHS teachers." <u>Clearinghouse</u>, <u>40</u>(1965):82-84.

To move out of a fifty-year dilemma--the search for junior high school teachers--article offers several proposals. First, local, state, and national conferences can stimulate pre-service and in-service junior high school teacher education. These conferences can define teacher needs and draft broad policies for programs to meet these needs. The conferences should be joint efforts of professional organizations, state departments of education, and colleges and universities. A national committee composed of scholars of different disciplines and laymen could coordinate the national effort.   Second, research and experimentation should be done to determine the content and patterns of junior high school teacher education programs. A growing body of research offers findings that could be used as hypotheses.   Polemics and reports may also offer insight for developing hypotheses.   In addition, ideas about what an effective junior high school teacher is, as expressed by administrators, teachers, and pupils, might supply the data for research and experimentation. Third, as a result of the above proposals, pilot teacher-education programs should be instituted in selected colleges and universities on a state and/or regional basis.   Provisions should be made for pooling and disseminating data gathered in the conduct of the pilot teacher-education programs.   Fourth, even though there is some opposition to separate certification for junior high school teachers, the matter should receive deliberate study by the best minds available.   Fifth, state and regional accrediting agencies should develop evaluative criteria which reflect the specific purposes and functions of the modern junior high school and its teacher needs. All of the foregoing suggestions should supply guidelines for evaluating junior high school teachers.

11038.   Douglass, H. R. <u>Modern Administration of Secondary Schools</u>. New York: Ginn and Co., 1954.

The book contains sections on the selection of teachers for junior high schools, pp. 68-70, the teaching load in junior high schools, p. 94, and organization of the junior high school, pp. 555-559.

11039.   Dunn, R. and Dunn, K.   "Testing your diagnostic,
prescriptive skills." Bulletin of the National Association of Secondary School Principals, 63,424(1979):
95-101.

Examples help teachers test their abilities in
diagnosing the learning difficulties of a junior high
school student and prescribing the right kind of
instructional program.   See ERIC Abstract #EJ 196
064.

11040.   Dupuis, M. M., et al.   "The Content Area Reading
Project: An In-service Education Program for Junior
High School Teachers and Teachers of Adults.   Final
Report."   University Park: Pennsylvania State Uni-
versity, College of Education, ERIC Doc. ED 155 665,
September, 1977.

This project provides teachers with in-service workshops and on-site consultant assistance in content
area reading methods.   Chapter 1 discusses the need
for developing such a project.   Chapter 2 discusses
the in-service training model.   Chapter 3 outlines a
step-by-step diagnostic teaching model.   Chapter 4
describes the seven content strands that make up the
content component: diagnosis, linguistic differences, motivation, organization for instruction,
reading skills, selection of materials, and evaluation.   Chapter 5 discusses the results of the project.   Chapter 6 summarizes the project and presents
conclusions and recommendations. See ERIC Abstract
#ED 155 665.

11041.   Dupuis, M. M., et al.   "The Content Area Reading
Project: An In-service Education Program for Junior
High School Teachers and Teachers of Adults.   Appen-
dix A, The Instruments and Their Development:
Presentation and Analysis of the Findings.   Final
Report."   University Park: Pennsylvania State Uni-
versity, College of Education, ERIC Doc. ED 155 666,
September, 1977.

Instruments administered to teacher participants in
this content area reading project were: two attitude
surveys, a skill test, a questionnaire to obtain
demographic information, and the Purdue Teacher
Opinionnaire.   Appendix presents the instruments and
discusses the purpose, background, development,
reliability, and validity of each. See ERIC Abstract
#ED 155 666.

11042.   Dupuis, M. M., et al. "The Content Area Reading
Project: An In-service Education Program for Junior
High School Teachers and Teachers of Adults. Appendix B, Content Component Guidesheets. Final Report."
University Park: Pennsylvania State University, College of Education, ERIC Doc. ED 155 667, September,
1977.

Content guides in this content area reading project
include a bibliography of professional materials on
content reading, an annotated bibliography of junior
high school materials for reading development in ten
content areas, a list of materials useful in developing practical adult literacy, directions for administering group reading inventories, sample informal
reading inventories, sample grouping plans, and study
guides for helping teachers learn about black language and about language and culture. See ERIC
Abstract #ED 155 667.

11043.   Dupuis, M. M. and Askov, E. N. "Content area differences in attitudes toward teaching reading." High
School Journal, 62,2(1978):83-88.

Pretests and posttests were given to junior high
school teachers in a reading in-service program to
test their knowledge of reading instruction and
attitudes toward teaching reading in their content
classes.   Authors present results for English,
reading, social studies, science/math and related
arts teachers and draw implications for in-services.
See ERIC Abstract #EJ 199 054.

11044.   Dupuis, M. M. and Askov, E. N. "Combining University and School-Based In-service Education in Content
Area Reading." Paper presented at the Annual Meeting
of the National Reading Conference, St. Petersburg,
Fla., ERIC Doc. ED 166 646, 1978.

A university developed a content area reading project
that offered instruction to fifty-seven junior high
teachers at three schools.   The project tested
whether in-service education could improve secondary
teachers' knowledge of reading skills and help them
develop more positive attitudes toward teaching reading. The project provided field-based instruction by
university personnel, follow-up supervision in the
schools by trained supervisors, instruction using
various media to present content area reading concepts, and instruction in designing and using these
materials in the content area classroom.   While
morale of participants and a control group of non-
participants remained the same, project teachers
expressed significantly more positive attitudes
toward teaching reading in the content area than did
the comparison group. Pretest and posttest scores

indicated that reading skills knowledge of project teachers increased significantly. See ERIC Abstract #ED 166 646.

11045.   Edelfelt, R. A., et al. "Teacher-Designed Reform in In-service Education. Final Report." Washington, D.C.: National Foundation for the Improvement of Education, ERIC Doc. ED 137 256, January, 1977.

The rationale of the project on Teacher-Designed Reform in Teacher Education was that teachers should determine the content and design of in-service education at the school building level. Goals for staff development should be determined by the kind of staff needed to conduct the school program, and the school program should be decided by the needs and interests of students and parents. Results of this teacher education project were: 1) Teachers focused more on students. 2) Teacher-administrator working relationships were challenged. 3) New roles for professional associations were explored. 4) New ways of studying children and new avenues of communication between students and teachers were created. 5) The importance of the site for the project was determined. 6) Latent and subliminal hostility, conflict, and jealousy among professional personnel was uncovered. 7) Allotment of time given to duties other than teaching became a serious consideration. 8) New methods of changing school policy were discovered. 9) An overview of the project revealed the need for some changes in approach and implementation. See ERIC Abstract #ED 137 256.

11046.   Faunce, R. C. and Clute, M. J.   Teaching and Learning in the Junior High School. Belmont, Calif.: Wadsworth, 1961.

In this survey, principals from 135 Michigan junior high schools estimated the percentage of time devoted to 1) faculty affairs, such as staff committees and meetings, department meetings, hiring, and interviews, 2) student contacts, such as counseling, discipline, and planning student activities, 3) supervision of instruction, including conferences about instruction, classroom visiting, and preparing materials, 4) community contact, including PTA, other parent groups, and conferences with parents and advising committees, and 5) office routines, such as scheduling, correspondence, telephone, athletic management, budget, and reports. In describing the chief problems of the junior high school, the principals listed the following: 1) lack of trained and dedicated teachers, 2) poor building facilities or space, 3) lack of funds, 4) senior high pressure or control, 5) lack of understanding of function and

importance, 6) lack of status compared to senior
high, and 7) heavy teaching loads.

11047.   Fisk, R. S. "What is an effective in-service education program?" Bulletin of the National Association
of Secondary School Principals, 35,177(1951):43-46.

An in-service program can be evaluated in terms of
both its characteristics and its results.   While
undoubtedly there are other criteria, the prime
criteria arise out of the direct effect of the in-
service program upon the quality of the school's
education.

11048.   Flanders, N. A.   "Using interaction analysis in
the in-service training of teachers."   Journal of
Experimental Education, 30(1962):313-316.

In this nine-week in-service program, junior high
teachers studied classroom interaction between
teachers and their students.   No value judgments were
superimposed on the group.   The research showed: 1)
Two thirds of all class time is taken up by talking.
2) Two thirds of talking time is used by the teacher.
3) Two thirds of teacher talking is directive.

11049.   Folgate, C. C. "A teacher's responsibility in
child self-esteem: an administrator's view."
Illinois Teacher of Home Economics,   21,4(1978):173-
176.

Discusses the characteristics of a facilitative
student-teacher relationship and a "Know Thyself
Quiz."   See ERIC Abstract #EJ 178 854.

11050.   Ford Foundation.   Time, Talent and Teachers.   New
York, 1960.

An informal presentation of several Ford Foundation
staff utilization projects.   Emphasizes the instructional revolution and the flexible school with
examples from middle schools, and junior high
schools.

11051.   Fraser, D. W.   "What's ahead for preadolescence."
Childhood Education, 45(1969):24-28.

Fraser makes two basic points about the psychological
development of preadolscents.   First, he calls for a
revised concept of the preadolescent, emphasizing
increased cognitive skills, especially the fact that
preadolescence bridges the transitional period of
thought from concrete to abstract thinking.   Second,
we must adapt our environment more to the uniqueness
and individuality of each preadolescent.   Within
formalized educational settings, we must adapt our

teaching styles so that the learner can progress at
his own learning rate, a process that is psychologically sound.   Adapting teaching to student needs
requires a deliberate attempt to understand developmental and learning stages of the preadolescent.

11052.   Fritschel, A. L. "The Preparation of Teachers for
the Junior High School and Its Implications for the
Pre-Service Preparation College." Paper presented at
the Annual Conference of the Junior High School
Association of Illinois, 1965.

Describes eight problem areas in junior high teaching
preparation. First is the built-in time lag between
preparation and service--for the college student,
four years from the beginning to the end of school.
Second is the problem of defining what a junior high
school is.   Third, in many cases the junior high
school has been thought of as a building rather than
a program.   Fourth is the problem of certification.
Fifth, many students come to college not knowing what
a junior high school is.   A sixth issue concerns
trends--what programs actually are being dealt with
in the junior high school.   Seventh, advances in
technology, including television, suggest ways of
learning which we have not exploited and present
certain problems to the training institution.
Eighth, should we train junior high school teachers
for the 6-3-3 or 4-4-4 grade organization?

11053.   Gatewood, T. E. and Mills, R. C.   "Teacher education's most neglected area: middle school teacher
preparation."   Contemporary Education, 46,4(1975):
253-258.

Authors conclude that the middle school concept has
not and never will be successfully achieved unless
future middle school teachers are different from
their present-day counterparts. Authors feel this
can be achieved only through better pre-service and
in-service teacher education. See ERIC Abstract #ED
133 608.

11054.   Gatewood, T. E. "Middle School Teacher Education."
ERIC Doc. ED 180 957, 1978.

Article describes the educational program, curriculum
design, and degree requirements for six institutions
having outstanding middle school programs: Gordon
College in Massachusetts, Findlay College in Ohio,
Illinois State University, the University of Florida
the University of Georgia, and a new program at
Central Michigan University. See ERIC Abstract #ED
180 957.

11055.   George, P. S., McMillan, M., Malinka, R., and
Pumerantz, P.   "Middle school teacher certification:
a national survey."   Educational Leadership, December
1975:213-216.

The national survey reports the beginnings of a certification pattern that recognizes the special need
of the middle school.   Two prerequisites to effective
middle school teacher education are an adequate
number of already functioning middle schools where
the training can occur, and an adequate teacher certification pattern which will prompt initial effort
and lend continued long-term support to teacher
activities.   A questionnaire sent to the fifty state
departments of education asked: 1) How has the middle school movement expanded since 1968?   2) What new
developments, if any, have occurred in the area of
middle school teacher certification since 1968?   3)
What new developments, if any, have occurred in the
area of middle school certification for administrators and special personnel since 1968?   4) Are state
universities developing programs to complement state
middle school certification?   The study showed that
middle schools are functioning in all fifty states.
Arkansas, Montana, and South Dakota have already
developed accreditation standards for the middle
school.   An increase from two states to eight states
with special middle school teacher certification
within six years is encouraging.   With fourteen
additional states planning such certification or
studying the issue, the number offering middle school
certification is likely to continue to increase,
albeit slowly.   The number of universities responding
to the need to prepare middle school teachers is also
on the increase.   All these changes encourage the
belief that middle school staff development is assuming greater priority on the educational scene.   The
authors are hopeful that this trend, which seems
obvious when comparing the national scenes of 1968
and 1975, will continue.

11056.   George, P. S. and McEwin, C. K.   "Middle school
teacher education: a progress report."   Journal of
Teacher Education, 29,5(1978):13-16.

Authors propose guidelines for preparing teachers of
adolescents. See ERIC Abstract #EJ 191 488.

11057.   Gibb, E. G. and Matala, D. C.   "Study on the use
of special teachers of science and mathematics in
grades 5 and 6."   School, Science and Mathematics, 62
(1962):565-585.

Study indicated that special content area teachers
are more effective for student growth in grades 5 and
6.

11058.   Gillan, R. E.   "Middle School Certification--A
National Update."   Natchitoches, La.:   Northwestern
State University,   ERIC Doc. ED 152 720, January,
1977.

A definition of the middle school in this national
survey was "a school distinctively organized and
administered as a middle school with a combination of
grade levels 5 or 6 through 8."   Eleven states
reported no official definition, and in three the
middle school lacked legal status.   Fourteen states
required special middle school certification, and one
of these required special certification for middle
school administrators.   Thirteen states reported
action in developing such requirements for middle
school teachers, and four of these reported development of special administrator requirements as well.
Seventeen of the twenty-seven states reporting middle
school certification or proposals for the same
indicated that teachers and administrators helped
formulate the requirements.   See ERIC Abstract #ED
152 720.

11059.   Gillan, R. E.   "Teacher Preparation and Certification for the Middle School Grades."   ERIC Doc. ED 178
463, 1978.

Article discusses background of middle school teacher
preparation, and presents findings of studies concerning middle school teacher education and certification.   It also traces the history of the middle
school (emphasizing the special needs of students and
characteristics desirable in their teachers), and
reports on a state-by-state survey of middle school
certification requirements.   See ERIC Abstract #ED
178 463.

11060.   Gillan, R. E.   "The Middle School Questionnaire."
ERIC Doc. ED 160 617, 1978.

Article describes the development and field study of
the Middle School Teacher Questionnaire, which
includes a professional description survey, middle
school employment survey, middle school attitude
inventory, middle school concept list, and professional recommendations survey.   The questionnaire
identifies differences in attitudes and opinions
between forty-five teachers certified to teach at the
middle school level and forty-five middle school
teachers who had been certified at the elementary or
secondary level.   The teachers certified for middle
school had more positive attitudes toward the middle
school program, expressed greater job satisfaction,
and favored special preparation and certification of
middle school teachers.   Their concepts emphasized
the characteristics of the ideal middle school as

opposed to the traditional junior high school.   See
ERIC Abstract #ED 160 617.

11061.   Granite School District.   "An Interdisciplinary
In-service Model for Teaching Reading in the Content
Areas: Grades 7-9."   Salt Lake City, ERIC Doc. ED
122 223, 1975.

Describes an integrated approach to teaching content
reading skills to teachers, using methods and
materials applicable to text and media currently used
in classrooms.   These were produced by in-service
teachers in science, math, and social studies in a
Salt Lake City junior high school.   Included in this
document are the original proposal, a description of
the in-service model, an evaluation of the project,
teacher evaluations, and outlines of workshop
sessions.   See ERIC Abstract #ED 122 223.

11062.   Gross, E. and Popper, S. H.   "Service and maintenance orientation in a junior high school organization." Educational Administration Quarterly, 1(1965):
35-36.

Study suggests that training which gives prospective
junior high school teachers a professional orientation can help prevent technicism in the classroom.
Professionals who internalize a dedication to principles of their professional role are in less danger
of substituting mere technical means for ends.

11063.   Hannan, T. T.   "Middle school--the need to establish a unique identity."   Middle School Journal, 15
(1974):9-10.

The junior high has failed to serve the needs of the
adolescent learner because it has not firmly established itself as a unique institution.   The middle
school is now at a crucial point in its development
and may have better prospects of achieving this goal.
The great demand for change today, especially in
teacher education programs, means the opportunity to
develop and strengthen the middle school concept is
there, but more communication among the public
schools, universities and state departments of education is needed.   The promise of the middle school is
too great to let it fall aside for failure to develop
its own unique nature.   The traditional elementary
and secondary teacher preparation programs do not
provide the training necessary to meet the needs of
transescent learners.   Such training must have continuity, commitment, knowledge of the learner, and a
conspicuous lack of emphasis on subject matter per
se.   Continuity is needed to bridge the gap between
elementary and secondary and to develop the concept
of interrelatedness of ideas. Commitment to the

middle school and the transescent learner is essential, or the problems encountered by the junior high
will become paramount. Knowledge of the learner is
perhaps the most important feature of a preparation
program, especially since it has been given little
attention in the past. As for subject matter, the
direction is away from separate, distinct subjects to
broader fields that give teachers more opportunity to
work with students through flexible arrangements such
as team teaching. Most of these ideas apply not only
to the middle school but to all of education. However, it is at the middle school level that the
teacher plays the greatest variety of roles--guider,
motivator, catalyst, listener, director, diagnosti-
cian, and counselor. If the middle school is to
avoid being just another junior high school, sufficient emphasis must be placed on the preparation of
its teachers.

11064.   Harlan, H. "Preparing Teachers to Teach in the
Middle School Grades--Creating the Environment for
Learning."   Lincoln, Nebr.:   State Department of
Education, 1969.

Describes the excellent middle grade preparation
program adopted in September 1967 by the Nebraska
Council on Teacher Education, with broad bands being
established: elementary K-6, middle 5-9, and
secondary 7-12.

11065.   Hartman, R. D.   "Teacher Effectiveness: One
District's Approach."   Paper presented at the Annual
Conference on the Junior High Association of
Illinois, 1965.

Describes a program to evaluate junior high teachers
in Evanston, Illinois, using three main approaches:
1) the characteristics or traits approach--one of the
oldest research methods, 2) identifying effective
teachers by observing changes in student behavior,
and 3) observing and measuring the behavior of
teachers while they are teaching.

11066.   Harvey, P. J. "Teacher attitudes: subject matter
and human beings." Educational Leadership, 27(1970):
686-691.

Presents an opinionnaire designed to encourage
teachers to think of their pupils first as individuals rather than receivers-learners of factual subject matter. The opinionnaire can act as a spring-
board for discussion. Teachers are asked if they
agree or disagree with these statements: 1) The
textbook is the curriculum. 2) Attitudes are more
important than facts.   3) The teacher's primary
obligation is to the individual pupil.   4) Ability

grouping is an undemocratic procedure. 5) Rote memorization has little value. 6) Mastery of subject matter should be a primary goal in the classroom. 7) Textbook publishers should be more responsive to the wishes of teachers in the field. 8) Knowledge unrelated to goals is undefensible. 9) A nationwide standardized curriculum would be good. 10) Understanding of different points of view is more important than universal agreement. 11) Present teacher education programs encourage the inquiry or problem-solving approach to teaching and learning. 12) Minimum essentials of subject matter mastery are needed. 13) Teachers generally can do a better job when pupils are grouped by ability. 14) Most secondary school teachers are more highly skilled in subject matter than in human growth and development. 15) Each pupil as a person should be the paramount consideration of the teacher. 16) Elementary school pupils generally like school better than secondary school pupils do.

11067.   Havighurst, R. J. "Poised at the cross-roads of life: suggestions for parents and teachers of young adolescents." School Review, 61,6(1953):329-336.

Suggestions for junior high teachers on ways to help young adolescents learn best and cope with their problems in society.

11068.   Hayes, G. A. "Preparing teachers for block-of-time: the Glassboro Program." Core Teacher, April 1962:1-2.

The primary purpose of the program at the New Jersey State College at Glassboro is to prepare teachers to work in block-time classes or core programs, which are used in over half the junior high schools in the United States. In New Jersey, the state certification for junior high school teachers authorizes teaching majors in social studies, language arts, sciences, and mathematics in any combination (or individually in junior high schools not employing a block-time program). At Glassboro, in addition to a wide range of required specialized subject matter courses, junior high school majors can take forty-eight credit hours of restricted electives in general education, including choices in the social sciences, humanities, mathematics, and science, and twelve credit hours of free electives, six in the junior year and six in the senior year. The free electives give each student the chance to broaden his background as a potential core teacher or to strengthen himself in one particular field.

11069.   Heffner, C. P. "The student as teacher." Theory Into Practice, 13,5(1974):371-375.

Behind critical exteriors and sometimes unkind remarks and frequent obstinate behavior is something special that is lost in the short time it takes to grow from eighth graders to adults. It is an almost absolute honesty and a conviction that honesty is an ever-valuable commodity. Eighth graders realize the truth often hurts, but believe that in the long run it is the best possible choice. Embedded in that honesty is the greatest thing of all, a grain of innocence.

11070.   Hester, H. "Beginning junior high school teacher may benefit from seminar on discipline." Clearing-house, 37(1963):311-312.

New junior high school teachers can be aided by an in-service program 1) clarifies state laws related to the teaching process, 2) discusses the socioeconomic character of the city that students come from, 3) instructs the new teachers on unique characteristics of the junior high age youngster, and 4) provides conferences for the teacher as soon as school begins.

11071.   Hoats, W. R. "Junior high school teacher certifi-cation." Bulletin of the National Association of Secondary School Principals, 47(1963):44-48.

A study of certification practices for teaching on the junior high school level.

11072.   Hodges, M. F. "Teachers' Perceptions of the Con-gruence of Classroom Behavior with an Understanding of the Unique Characteristics of Transescents." Ph.D. Dissertation, University of Colorado at Boulder, 1978.

Author studies ten junior high/middle schools in Jefferson County, Colorado, and an equal number of teachers representing language arts, science, math, and social studies. The study was based on the idea that teacher education should emphasize the charac-teristics of the emerging adolescent and implications for classroom organization. School systems should attempt to place in the junior high/middle school teachers who not only recognize the characteristics of the transescent but are willing to adapt their programs to these characteristics. Questionnaire responses were grouped in two categories: 1) knowl-edge of physical, intellectual, and socioemotional characteristics of the transescent and 2) classroom behaviors responding to these characteristics. The categories were then correlated with six dependent variables: school, sex, age, years of experience, field of teaching, and number of courses in junior high/middle school education and/or early adolescent behavior. The greatest significant differences occurred in comparisons between teachers' professed knowledge and their classroom behaviors. Author sees a need for 1) greater emphasis on understanding transescent characteristics and learning ways to teach that reflect this understanding through professional growth seminars, teacher training, and in-service programs, 2) improvement in teacher-evaluation procedures, 3) hiring middle school and/or junior high schools teachers who understand transescent characteristics and who teach according to this knowledge, and 4) activity-oriented classes at the junior high/middle school level.

11073.   Hoover, K. H.   The Professional Teacher's Handbook.   A Guide for Improving Instruction in Today's Middle and Secondary Schools.   2nd ed.   Boston: Allyn and Bacon, 1976.

Book includes four units: 1) Preinstructional Activities.   2) Conventional Methods and Techniques: Focus upon the Individual.   3) Conventional Methods and Techniques: Focus upon the Group.   4) Contemporary Instructional Developments and Trends.   Each section includes a selective bibliography and lists films, filmstrips, overhead transparencies, and free and inexpensive learning materials.   Chapters 5, 15, 23, and 24 are of special interest.   They include basic information, a basic instructional procedure, values and limitations, and method illustrations in different subject fields.   Titles of all chapters in order are: 1) Gaining the Concept.   2) Establishing Instructional Objectives.   3) Planning for Teaching. 4) Motivational Activities.   5) Discipline Problems. 6) Providing for Individual Differences.   7) Independent and Semi-Independent Study.   8) Individualizing Instruction.   9) Value-Focusing Activities.   10) Encouraging Creativity.   11) Overview Strategies. 12) Sociometric Techniques.   13) The Sociodramatic Method.   14) The Case Method.   15) Developmental Reading Techniques.   16) Discussion Methods.   17) Debate.   18) Processes of Inquiry.   19) Small Group Techniques.   20) Group Processes.   21) Lecture Method.   22) Review Method.   23) Drill and Practice Procedures.   24) Measurement and Evaluation Techniques and Devices.   25) Evaluation and Reporting Procedures.

11074.   Howard, A. W.   Teaching in Middle Schools.   Scranton, Pa.:   International Textbook, 1968.

Author emphasizes practical experiences that experienced, effective, and successful teachers have found valuable.   Book discusses the argument for and against the middle school and the problems, controversies, and criticisms of middle schools and junior high schools.   Includes what research evidence was

available concerning middle school programs, earlier
adolescence and maturity, and supplements with statements of physicians and authorities on this age
group.   Discusses the fundamentals of successful
teaching, attitudes and characteristics of effective
teachers, classroom management, discipline, motivation, individual differences, and school law.
Devotes considerable space to explicit principles and
practices of planning, specific teaching techniques,
assignments, testing and test construction for the
middle grades classroom teacher, marking and grading,
and audiovisual aids.   A complete chapter is devoted
to school activities for middle school youngsters.

11075.   Hubert, J. B.   "A Survey of the Attitudes of
Prospective and Experienced Secondary School Teachers
Toward the Junior High School."   Masters Thesis,
University of New Mexico, 1969.

This sample of 172 teachers included 120 with one or
more years of experience, 17 who had just completed
student teaching but who had not yet taught, and 35
who had not yet been involved in student teaching.
Hubert reported: 1) Secondary education students
strongly preferred older students and higher grade
levels.   2) Later, student teaching was a definite
factor in the prospective teacher's age and grade
level preference.   Junior high student teachers were
far more receptive to the junior high age and grade
levels.   Those who had student taught at both the
junior high and senior high grade levels were the
only group which preferred the junior high age and
grades.   3) Teachers who had experience at the junior
high level were far more tolerant of that age and
grade level than were teachers without such experience.   4) Junior high school teachers were strongly
critical of the policy of identical preparation and
certification for junior high and senior high
teachers.   5) Those who had taught at the junior high
level showed strong support for a middle school
organization of grades 6, 7, and 8.   This feeling was
not expressed by teachers who did not have junior
high experience.   6) Completion of a course on the
junior high school positively affected attitudes of
respondents toward the junior high age and grade
levels.   Stated preferences of those who had not completed such a course were strongly for teaching in
the senior high school.

11076.   Hubert, J. B.   "Junior high image: how can it be
improved?"   Clearinghouse, 44(1970):373-377.

Article recommends: 1) All secondary education
students should be required to student teach at both
junior and senior high levels. 2) Junior high/middle
school teachers should be consulted on the curriculum

advisable for teachers at that level. 3) When preparation and certification for junior high/middle
school teachers is changed, a separate and special
course of studies should be required.   4) A middle
school plan involving grades 6-8 should replace the
traditional junior high plan of grades 7-9 as soon as
possible. 5) All secondary education students should
be required to take a course on the history, philosophy, and purpose of the junior high/middle school
and another on curriculum development and teaching
methods for this level.   The future of the junior
high or middle school movement is only as bright as
the outlook for securing a sufficient number of qualified and willing teachers. Many educators have long
recommended a special course of study to prepare prospective teachers for the unique curriculum, methods,
and subject knowledge necessary for successful teaching at the junior high level.   State certification
requirements are a related problem facing teacher
preparation programs.

11077.   Hubert, J. B.   "On preparing teachers for the
junior high and middle school: the teacher input."
Clearinghouse, 47(1973):550-554.

This survey of junior high/middle school teachers
focused on their educational background, career
plans, and attitudes toward their professional preparation. Conclusions were: 1) The preparation of
junior high/middle school teachers was primarily
oriented to high school.   2) Approximately half the
teachers preferred grades 9-12, which means they were
not teaching at their choice of grade level. 3) Most
advocated the 6-8 grade organization plan for the
middle years. 4) Most agreed with the statement that
"providing a school environment which specializes in
helping the student make a smooth transition from
childhood to adolescence is the primary purpose of
the school for early adolescents."   5) Most rejected
departmentalization as the major curriculum emphasis.
6) They were dissatisfied with the present undergraduate and graduate courses and programs available
to them.   7) Teacher training institutions should
develop special undergraduate programs for teachers
of early adolescents. 8) Teacher training institutions need to include specific, pragmatic courses and
experiences in their programs. 9) Colleges and universities which offer graduate courses and programs
in education should decentralize their programs and
offer more workshops and in-service training at
school locations.

11078.   Hyland, T.   "Affective Education in the Junior
High Schools: A Program for Staff Reorientation."
ERIC Doc. ED 102 158, February 21, 1975.

Author sees a need for greater emphasis on affective, social-psychological concerns in junior high school. Staff development for this purpose would involve teacher selection, teacher assignment, teacher development, and teacher release. Teachers hired should possess characteristics consonant with the determined goal. Inventories and interview techniques can measure these characteristics. Counselors can also give instruction in psychology to teachers. Teacher development would involve classes, clinics, workshops, and supervision. See ERIC Abstract #ED 102 158.

11079.   James, S. M.   "From In-service to Implementation: The Integrated Language Arts Curriculum for Middle School Level Students." Paper presented at the Annual Meeting of the Association of Teacher Educators, Atlanta, and at the Conference on Innovative Teacher Education--Pre-service and In-service, Atlanta, ERIC Doc. ED 135 763, January, 1977.

Author's research showed that many language arts teachers had background information on integrated programs but were unable to follow through in constructing such a program. To increase knowledge and develop methods of application, she conducted a summer workshop, four hours per day for five and a half weeks at a local middle school, using instruments that showed the individual teachers the extent of their background knowledge and the strengths and weaknesses of their professional experience. Conferences helped teachers to reach decisions regarding their needs and to determine learning objectives. The workshop included group meetings, lectures, and demonstrations. See ERIC Abstract #ED 135 763.

11080.   Jensen, B. H.   "The Influence of an In-service Teacher Training Reading-in-the-Content-Area Program on Student Reading Achievement." Ph.D. Dissertation, Florida State University. University Microfilms, Ann Arbor, Mich., ERIC Doc. ED 133 719, 1976.

Author studied the effect of teacher training in reading on 321 seventh, eighth, and ninth graders and on 26 teachers of English, math, science, and social studies in Wakulla County, Florida. The in-service training included a summer workshop that developed teacher competencies and educational materials, yearlong training of one regular teacher from each of the four content areas to provide assistance to the respective departments, monthly in-service sessions, and semester or year-long reading instruction in the content areas. Seventh grade students experienced a significant mean gain in comprehension, as did eighth and ninth grade students in vocabulary. Eighth graders, in a comparison of pretest and posttest scores, showed a significant gain in composite performances as well. See ERIC Abstract #ED 133 719.

11081.   Johnson, M., Jr. "The preparation of teachers for the junior high school." Teachers College Journal, 34,2(1963):57-59.

If we can accept the premise that our objective is the preparation of well-informed, thinking, creative teachers who will be committed to guiding the development of well-informed, thinking, creative individuals, then all of our efforts should jointly be directed toward creating the conditions in which such teachers can acquire competence and act upon this commitment. Those junior high schools which encourage individuality and creativity in teachers and pupils must be identified and brought into the teacher education process. Committed teachers must be encouraged to step forward and play a key role in efforts to multiply their number. As their tribe increases and they work with both prospective teachers and active colleagues, they will help junior high schools find the kind of teachers the schools need, and teachers will find the kind of junior high schools they want to teach in.

11082.   Johnston, J. H. and Markle, G. C. "What research says to the practitioner about teacher behavior." Middle School Journal, 10(1979):14-15.

Effective middle school teachers 1) have a positive self-concept, 2) demonstrate warmth, 3) are optimistic, 4) are enthusiastic, 5) are flexible, 6) are spontaneous, 7) accept students, 8) demonstrate awareness of developmental levels, 9) demonstrate knowledge of subject matter, 10) use a variety of instructional activities and materials, 11) structure instruction, 12) monitor learning, 13) use concrete materials and focused learning strategies, 14) ask varied questions, 15) incorporate indirectness in teaching, 16) incorporate success-building behavior in teaching, 17) diagnose individual learning needs and prescribe individual instruction, 18) listen. The image of the competent middle school teacher that emerges from this research is of a self-confident, personable professional who demonstrates awareness of both student needs and varied learning strategies. While this image is not unlike that which emerges from armchair listings of competencies, it has the added validity of empirical research. As the research base grows more detailed, the lines of the image are likely to grow more distinct.

11083.   Jones, P. and Garner, A. E. "A comparison of middle school teachers' pupil control ideology." Clearinghouse, 51(1978):292-294.

Authors expected no significant difference between the pupil control ideologies of teachers at various grade levels. They studied eighty-two teachers who were attending a university summer program and who taught in grades 5-8. Research showed that the lower the grade level, the more humanistic the pupil control ideology of the teacher. This finding probably reflects the teachers' training. Teachers in higher grades probably took more courses based on a subject-centered approach to teaching, while teachers of younger children learned more child-centered approaches. The authors saw a need for more research on the attributes needed for middle school teachers and the best type of classroom environment for middle school children.

11084.   Junior High School Workshop. "Duties and Respon-sibilities of the Junior High School Administrator." Hamilton, N.Y.:   New York State Association of Secondary School Administrators, Junior High School Committee, 1963.

The duties and responsibilities of the junior high principal are viewed by those who hold this position in New York State.

11085.   Kaback, G. R.   "An examination of teacher reaction to adolescent needs." Education, 76(1955):242-245.

To participate in the shaping of dreams and goals and future plans is the privilege of the teacher.   The degree of satisfaction which any teacher derives from this role, however, is closely related to his own personal needs. Perhaps the teacher must become more aware of his reaction to adolescent behavior before he can begin to fathom the complex relationships between his own physical, emotional, social, and intellectual needs and those of his students.   The article is divided into sections on the various needs.

11086.   Kelley, E. A. and Dillon, E. A.   "Staff develop-ment: it can work for you." Bulletin of the National Association of Secondary School Principals,   62,417 (1978):1-8.

Authors conclude that staff development activities should achieve both direct and indirect outcomes. Direct outcomes are staff behavior changes, and indirect outcomes are improvement in student achieve-ment.   Article describes how one junior high staff development program was initiated and carried out. See ERIC Abstract #EJ 175 594.

11087.   Kohut, S., Jr.   "Curriculum, Instruction, and
Communication in the Middle School." Carlisle, Pa.:
Dickinson College, ERIC Doc. ED 102 100, 1974.

Describes a University of Pennsylvania in-service,
competency-based graduate level workshop for middle
school teachers. The course examined the middle
school movement's innovations, curriculum, instruction, and communication dynamics. This document
includes a description of the course, the workshop
planning questionnaire, and a chart of workshop
objectives and procedures. See ERIC Abstract #ED 102
100.

11088.   Krinsky, J. L. and Pumerantz, P.   "Middle school
teacher preparation programs."   Journal of Teacher
Education, 23,4(1972):468-470.

Authors surveyed 241 NCATE-accredited teacher
training institutions in the United States to determine the current extent and nature of middle school
teacher preparation. They investigated 1) current or
planned pre-service undergraduate and graduate middle
school teacher preparation programs, 2) mandatory
student teaching programs in middle school units
only, and 3) in-service middle school training programs in local communities. The middle school was
defined as a separate intermediate school that combined one or more of the upper elementary grades (5
and 6) with the lower secondary grades (7 and 8).
The survey revealed that in 1969-70 only 37 (23 percent) of the 160 institutions responding had middle
school teacher preparation programs. Only 29 (18
percent) provided in-service programs geared to the
middle school concept. In most instances, programs
were confined to unstructured and limited staff consultant services. Only 18 institutions (11 percent)
had an undergraduate curriculum (either single course
or program) dealing with middle school education, and
19 (almost 12 percent) had a graduate middle school
curriculum (single course or program). Mandatory
student teaching in middle school units only was
required in 6 (4 percent) of the 160 responding
institutions. These figures show that teacher training institutions definitely lag in constructing valid
courses and establishing innovative, instructional
techniques appropriate for prospective middle school
teachers.

11089.   Lambert, P. D. "Junior high school, 1965." Clearinghouse, 39(1965):323-328.

Discusses teacher education for the junior high
school years, with an excellent list of footnotes and
a description of the state of the junior high school
in the mid-1960s.

11090.   Lawrence, G.   "Measuring teacher competencies for the middle school."   National Elementary Principal, 51,3(1971):60-66.

Describes research conducted to help build a competency-based approach for the preparation of middle school teachers. Article has four parts: An Introduction to the Competency Approach, A Rationale for Measuring Competencies, The Research Report, and A Discussion of Practical Implications of the Research.   Study used 1) measurement of abstract information, 2) conceptual measurement, and 3) dispositional measurement.   The TEAC Middle School teacher competencies to be measured were: 1) Personal qualities (positive view of self, flexibility and openness to change, respect for the dignity and worth of the individual, ability to interact constructively with others, and commitment to the education of transescents), 2) Understanding (of the transescent learner, the teaching-learning process, the American educational enterprise, and educational research and evaluation), and 3) Instructional skills.   What promise does the competency approach hold for teacher education and for middle schools? First, it offers little improvement over standard practices unless it builds on a solid rationale and a research base. Competencies are multidimensional and must be measured in several dimensions. Second, the ultimate test of a competency is the influence it has on the long-term growth of pupils and on the continued improvement of schools. To be satisfied that watching a teacher perform is a complete measurement of competency is to settle for a delusion. Finally, the competency approach seems well suited both to the middle school movement and to new pressures in teacher education. As colleges of education are being called on to make their teacher preparation programs more field oriented and more school based, the middle schools are developing new instruction programs that can accommodate greater numbers of teachers in training within the schools. Differentiated staffing, variable grouping, extensive use of community resource persons, and other trends in middle school programs open up needs for trainees to serve in the schools. Logic dictates that as teacher education moves farther out into the field, it must decentralize its curriculum.   Decentralization is exactly what the competency approach is capable of offering: self-pacing, self-instructing, self-check of progress, and a linkage with performance in actual school situations. And the competency approach, when based in the schools, is equally available and appropriate for in-service teachers.   Its potential now remains relatively unmined.

11091.   Lehr, J. B.   "Staff Development Needs in Middle
and Junior High Schools that Individualize Instruction."   Madison: University of Wisconsin, Research
and Development Center for Individualized Schooling,
ERIC Doc. ED 179 513, June, 1979.

This research identified in-service education strategies preferred by teachers and principals and
analyzed functional and dysfunctional aspects of
in-service programs.   Author visited schools and
interviewed school personnel following their response
to uniformly administered questionnaires.   Teachers
differed among themselves in identifying needed in-
service activities and preferences for program
designs.   The perceptions of the principals differed
considerably from those of the teachers. Methods for
improving staff development are considered. See ERIC
Abstract #ED 179 513.

11092.   Levenda, T. A.   "Developing a positive school
climate." Middle School Journal, 10(1979):8-9.

The principal becomes an effective instructional
leader by creating the proper school climate through
awareness, organization, communication, and recognition.   He should organize his and the school's
schedule to reflect the importance placed on the
worth of the individual by alloting daily time for
activities which emphasize the development of the
individual.   Having standard class periods for
specific subjects indicates to students the value the
school places on acquiring knowledge in those fields,
and so a period designated for learning about themselves tells transescents that the school feels they
are important.   The key to creating a positive
attitude in the school is to have people within the
school feel good about themselves.   This attitude
must emanate from those around them before it can be
internalized.   This is particularly true of middle
school children, who have great doubts about themselves due to the many changes taking place within
them.   Those who know that these changes are common
to this age group must consciously be understanding
and supportive. People in the middle need people in
the middle.

11093.   Licata, J. W. and Willower, D. J.   "The Consequences of Student Brinkmanship for the School
Organization." Paper presented at the Annual Meeting
of the American Educational Research Association,
Washington, D.C., ERIC Doc. ED 136 437, April, 1975.

Author studied two junior high schools, a traditionally organized one that emphasized custodial pupil
control and another with team teaching and modular
scheduling and an emphasis on humanistic control.

Authors used Osgood's semantic differential technique and the Pupil Control Ideology Form. They found that in the custodial school students were more euphoric about student brinkmanship in their everyday classroom life than were students in the humanistic schools. Teachers in the custodial school perceived acts of student brinkmanship as threatening to their social position in the school organization. See ERIC Abstract #ED 136 437.

11094.   Lincoln Public Schools. "An Overview of Goals and Models. Improving Learning Opportunities." IMPACT Series, no. 1. Lincoln, Nebr.: Lincoln Public Schools and University of Nebraska at Lincoln, Teachers College, ERIC Doc. ED 146 165, 1977.

Booklet describes the Teacher Corps Project at Goodrich Junior High School. Goals included: 1) use of diagnostic-descriptive teaching approaches, 2) development, implementation, testing, and refining of a comprehensive model for competency-based pre-service and in-service teacher education, and 3) integration and articulation of services to the pupil and family through the cooperation of community, university, and school. Booklet presents themes and diagrammatic models for each goal. Other booklets in the series present descriptive reports of the project themes and models. See ERIC Abstract #ED 146 165.

11095.   Lipsitz, J. S. "Growing up forgotten--must they?" Middle School Journal, 10,1(1979):3.

Early adolescence is a vibrant period in the lifespan, marked by changes that are critical to human development. This period is second only to infancy in velocity of growth and probably unique in intensity of growth and change. Biologically, early adolescence is that time of life marked by the adolescent growth spurt and the onset of puberty. Socially and emotionally, it is marked by processes of personal individuation, social commitment, and the beginning of the capacity for intimacy. Intellectually, early adolescence marks the beginning of the capacity to reason on the basis of symbols and contingencies, to hypothesize, to be conscious of one's own thinking. A result of a new concern for the early adolescent is the birth of the Center for Early Adolescence. The first goal of the Center is to improve the services offered to this age group by teachers, judges, juvenile officers, parents, police, recreation workers, doctors, social workers, librarians, and others in direct service roles. The second goal is to improve the decisions of policy makers, such as school administrators, legislators, hospital directors, government officials, and others who direct or affect this age group. To fulfill these

goals, the following objectives have been established: 1) to build a national constituency for this
age group, 2) to provide improved training for those
adults who serve this age group or make policy that
affects this age group, 3) to establish and maintain
various networks of adults who have professional
responsibility for this age group, in particular
through a clearinghouse function, and 4) to provide
technical assistance to those programs currently
serving or planning to serve the young adolescent.

11096.   Malinka, R. M.   "Teaching in the Middle School.
Implications Concerning Certification and Function."
Washington, D.C.:   U.S. Department of Health, Education and Welfare, Office of Education, ERIC Doc. ED
083 251, 1971.

Provides an overall view of the function of the
middle school staff, including teacher characteristics, number and kinds of personnel needed, criteria
for certification, and personnel functions.   Also
includes job descriptions for the principal, assistant principal, counselors, classroom teachers, and
noncertified personnel.   See ERIC Abstract #ED 083
251.

11097.   Malinka, R. M.   "A future for the middle school."
Junior High-Middle School Bulletin,   14,2(1976):Whole
Issue.

In December of 1972, steps were taken to recognize
the importance of providing middle grade certification in Indiana.   Article presents criteria for
middle school certification, including information on
general education requirements, subject matter concentrations, and professional education.

11098.   McCracken, R. A. (Ed.) "Supervision of Reading
Instruction in Junior High School."   Bellingham:
Western Washington State College, ERIC Doc. ED 046
638, 1968.

The purpose of this program was to improve the
performance of twenty junior high school teachers
who taught developmental reading as part of their
class assignment.   The program included a seven-week
summer training with four college courses in
individualized reading instruction, improvement of
reading instruction in the secondary school, observation and practicum in teaching reading at the junior
high level, and a seminar in reading education.   A
year of monthly seminars and supervised teaching of
developmental reading followed, with guidance offered
by two college supervisors and four reading experts.
This report includes summaries of the four summer
courses, participant reports of activities in the

teaching of reading, a summary of participant evaluations, evaluator reports, and a director's summary. See ERIC Abstract #ED 046 638.

11099. McCrory, D. L. (Ed.) "A Design for the Teacher Education Center." Beachwood, Ohio: Beachwood Middle School, ERIC Doc. ED 077 895, May, 1973.

Article describes a teaching center with open-space architecture, a team teaching organization, and flexible curriculum. Part I discusses assumptions about the community of teachers in the Beachwood Middle School, the community of teacher educators in the partner universities, the school as a field setting for teacher education experiences, and teachers in training from the partner universities. It also discusses implications and professional goals for the teacher education center, and criteria for creating professional growth. Part II discusses the organization of the teacher education center: societal, institutional, and instructional level decision making in the center, joint decision making by school and universities, and basic role expectations for personnel. Part III discusses planning in the teacher education center for comprehensive, specialized, and individualized teacher experiences. The faculty of this middle school believes that supervising teacher education students is of tangible benefit for the children in the middle school. The school provides a climate of continuous stimuli for veteran teachers and teachers in training and tries to provide experiences that all teachers should have, experiences that some teachers should have, and special experiences developed and directed by each individual teacher. The main idea of this school is that all teachers are responsible to and for each other.

11100. McGlasson, M. A., Manlove, D. C. and Weldy, G. R. "Summary of discussion of the junior high school regional conference--Indiana University." Bulletin of the National Association of Secondary School Principals, February 1963:39-40.

Principals at this conference were unanimous in their intention to seek specific improvements in qualifications, training, and certification of junior high school teachers. The junior high school should be regarded as a separate entity in the educational continuum and should have special teacher education requirements. Principals look to the National Association of Secondary School Principals for leadership in influencing states to provide special certification for junior high school teachers. While most agree that a special certificate for junior high school is needed, certification alone is not enough.

Professional educational associations must continue to encourage professional excellence.

11101.   Mechling, K. R.   "The preparation of junior high science teachers: by default or by design." School Science and Mathematics, 75(1975):395-398.

Author presents a position intended to stimulate interest in junior high school science teacher preparation programs. Several factors have contributed to lack of concern for this area. Author summarizes data from a survey of junior high school science teachers. See ERIC Abstract #EJ 121 553.

11102.   Meeks, J. W., et al. "Preparation for teaching reading in the middle school: a survey of current practices." Reading Improvement, 16(1979):301-303.

Authors present findings of a national survey to determine the extent of specialized preparation in reading for middle school teachers, including course offerings, course descriptions, methodology, and certification issues. Authors conclude that teacher training institutions are not formulating consistent policies for preparing teachers of middle school reading. See ERIC Abstract #EJ 212 208.

11103.   Morse, W. C. and Wingo, G. M. Readings in Educational Psychology. Chicago: Scott Foresman and Co., 1962.

Several sections of this book are relevant: Section 1: You as a Teacher. ("The Relevancy of Educational Psychology" by Coladrci. "What Psychology Can We Feel Sure About?" by Watson. "A Psychological Analysis of Vocational Choice: Teaching" by Englander. "Teacher Behavior Liked and Disliked by Pupils" by Leeds.) Section 2: What Goes on in Schools? ("Life Adjustment Education for Every Youth" by Office of Education. "Adjustment versus Education" by Smith. "Why is Education Obsolete?" by Mead. "An Anthropologist's View of Curriculum Change" by Henry.) Section 6: The Teenager. ("Developmental Levels of Character: A Theory" by Peck and Havighurst. "Psychological Health and Classroom Functioning: A Study of Dissatisfaction with School among Adolescents" by Jackson and Getzels. "Our Troubles with Defiant Youth" by Redl. "Adolescence--Implications for the Teacher" by Jensen.)

11104.   National Association of Secondary School Principals. Current Issues in Secondary School Administration. Bulletin of the National Association of Secondary School Principals, 37,192(1953):Whole Issue.

Describes the junior high school principal's many administrative tasks.

11105.   National Education Association.   "Teaching Reading.   Description of Teacher In-service Education Materials."   Cluster VI, includes 5 modules.   Washington, D.C.: National Education Association, Project on Utilization of In-service Education R and D Outcomes, ERIC Doc. ED 169 058, April, 1977.

Describes an in-service learning module for teachers interested in acquiring specific competencies for teaching English, language arts, and reading comprehension at the middle school level.   Outlines five modules and describes activites and resources involved in using this module.   See ERIC Abstract #ED 169 058.

11106.   Newlove, B. W.   "The 15-Minute Hour: An Early Teaching Experience."   Report Series 23.   Austin: University of Texas at Austin, Research and Development Center for Teacher Education, ERIC Doc. ED 040 154, September, 1969.

It has often been said that future teachers need actual teaching experience in their pre-service training.   This study was conducted to assess the effect of a one-time fifteen-minute teaching experience on teacher trainees.   The author hypothesized that this experience would help the teachers become more concerned with their pupils than with themselves and become more aware of the difficulties involved in teaching, while causing minimal disruption of school activities.   Twenty-three junior level students enrolled in this first professional education course taught for fifteen-minutes in a junior high school class. The novice teachers were filmed.   They later viewed the films of their own performance and received feedback on their performance from students and cooperating teachers.   Reactions of teacher trainees to this experience indicated greater respect for the teaching profession and an increased concern with student achievement resulting from their teaching.   See ERIC Abstract #ED 040 154.

11107.   Nordholm, H. and Bakewell, R. V.   Keys to Teaching Junior High School Music.   Minneapolis: Paul A. Schmitt Music Co., 1953.

Presents specific and practical suggestions for the junior high school music teacher.

11108.   Pabst, R. L.   "The junior high school teacher's certificate: something new in teacher education." Junior High School Newsletter, 1,1(1962):2-3.

Describes Indiana's endorsement for junior high on a four-year elementary certificate. This endorsement calls for six semester hours distributed among adolescent psychology, junior high school curriculum and organization, and developmental reading. It also requires twenty-four hours in the teaching field and two to three semester hours of supervised teaching in the junior high school.

11109.   Perkes, V. A.   "Junior High School Teacher Preparation, Teaching Behaviors and Student Achievement." Dissertation, Stanford University.   University Microfilms, Ann Arbor, Mich., ERIC Doc. ED 025 417, 1967.

Author studied the relationship between teacher characteristics and student achievement in junior high school science.   Information about teachers included the number of their science and science method credits, grade point average, recency of science course work, and years of teaching experience. Teaching behavior was recorded by trained observers using the Science Teacher Observation Instrument, or STOL.   Author observed 1) no significant correlation between specific teacher behaviors and their science credits, and 2) higher application scores and lower factual knowledge scores gained by students taught by younger teachers with higher science grade point averages and science method credits.   These teachers more frequently held student discussions and student activities, asked questions requiring students to speculate and hypothesize, used equipment in their classroom, and focused their lessons on principles of science.   Teachers whose students scored higher on factual information reversed this pattern and were older, held fewer science and methods credits, and had completed their college work earlier.   See ERIC Abstract #ED 025 417.

11110.   Pine, G. J.   "In-service Education: Collaborative Action Research and Teacher Emancipation."   Durham: University of New Hampshire, ERIC Doc. ED 180 946, 1979.

Author states that educational research must become classroom oriented instead of university oriented. This can happen if educators help teachers develop into practicing educational researchers as part of a staff improvement program.   Included are case studies of a New Hampshire junior high school's in-service research program and a bibliography.   See ERIC Abstract #ED 180 946.

11111.   Popper, S. H.   "Another look at the junior high school principalship."   Bulletin of the National Association of Secondary School Principals, 44(1960): 125-126.

Junior high principalships are usually taken by people who wish to move into high school administration. It is rare to find talented aspirants for administrative posts who are willing to accept the junior high school principalship as a lifetime career position.

11112.   Popper, S. H.   "Reflections of a troubled institution."   Bulletin of the National Association of Secondary School Principals, 53,337(1969):118-129.

The problem of early adolescent education is the failure of teacher training institutions to prepare teachers specifically for working with early adolescents. Consequently, junior high schools are staffed by teachers and administrators whose own values clash with the values of early adolescent education. They have internalized the values of a culture which conditions people to work hard, to compete, to display effort and optimism, and to practice deferred gratification in order to earn rewards. These values are institutionalized in professional school roles by means of preparation programs. The point of view of many teachers tends to be that the subject is of paramount importance, often overshadowing interest in the pupil. The author suggests that educators settle on a proper name for schools for early adolescents, fix by scientific means the institutionally correct pattern of organization, and demand from schools of education no less than a specially prepared professional for this particular school. If educators do this, they will begin to transform their own role from administrator to institutional leader.

11113.   Powell, W.   "Training teachers for the junior high and middle school."   Michigan Journal of Secondary Education, Fall 1967:22-26.

The real problem facing junior high and middle schools is that too little stress is laid on preparing teachers for a highly specialized task. The unique functions of the junior high school require a type of teacher education that recognizes the transitional role of the junior high/middle school, with its balance between the basic skills of the elementary school and the subject matter specialization of the senior high school. Students preparing for teaching at this level should take courses in the teaching of reading, instruction in guidance, information on conducting practical experience projects, psychology of adolescents, and sociology. Students should plan appropriate major-minor combinations such as English-social studies, math-science, or shop-arts and crafts, and certainly students should do their student teaching at the junior high or middle school level. Junior high schools and middle schools can also do their part to help train and retain teachers through orientation and in-service conferences and workshops emphasizing the school's point of view, visits to well-established schools in the area, coop- erative efforts or team teaching; curriculum study groups stressing adolescent needs, summer school classes in junior high education, proper supervision, faculty meetings, and visiting consultants.

11114.   Pumerantz, P.   "Relevance of change--imperatives in the junior high and middle school dialogue." Clearinghouse, 43(1968):209-212.

Author discusses a middle school rationale, status of the middle school, and strategies for change. Public school systems should 1) develop a functional model or a theoretical design for a middle school program and organization to help local planners formulate practices for their own communities, 2) reexamine the philosophical, social, and psychological bases for the education of children in the middle grades in terms of a dramatically changing American culture, so that any design for change is compatible with these understandings, and 3) conduct research within the community and especially in the schools that will yield data about local needs, so they can apply research findings directly to local problems and to the implementation of innovative programs. Youth in the 1960s may relate to society in a significantly different way than the youth did sixty years ago due to early maturation coupled with important cultural changes.   But since maturation is linked to socio- economic conditions, differences in individual com- munities will cause differences in student popula- tions. Designs for educational change must take into account these local differences, which may be quite apart from findings of research done with other pop- ulations.   Meanwhile, colleges of education should develop pre-service and in-service teacher prepara- tion programs for the middle grades. These programs should involve discipline and clinical approaches incorporating the comprehensive findings of research and experience. Colleges should stimulate a reexami- nation of education for children in the middle grades, carry out research and assist local communi- ties in evaluating their existing programs, and provide a forum where public school educators and professors of education can review opinions, experi- ence, and research dealing with the middle grades in order to develop relevant guidelines for planning. And colleges of education should establish regional centers for collecting information on middle grade education from the research and experience of school systems, from universities and colleges of education, and from the professional literature. This material

should be selected, indexed, abstracted, and distributed in such a way that those seeking guidance on the
middle school issue can translate information about
the approaches of others into relevant and workable
programs in their own communities.

11115.   Range, D. G.   "Staff Development: Still a Major
Challenge for Middle School Administrators."   Paper
presented at the Annual Meeting of the National
Association of Secondary School Principals, New
Orleans, January, 1977.

As the instructional leader of the middle school, the
principal faces the challenge of assisting both new
and experienced teachers in developing teaching
strategies that are consistent with the characteristics and needs of transescent students.   At the same
time, the principal must insure that the pressures of
the back-to-basics movement do not destroy the objectives of the middle school program.   The use of
sociodrama in teaching exemplifies a strategy that is
compatible with the philosophical goals of the middle
school and with the goals of the back-to-basics
movement.

11116.   Rice, A.   "What's wrong with the junior high
schools? Nearly everything."   Nation's Schools, 74
(1964):30-33.

Author's premise is that teachers are frequently dissatisfied with elementary school teaching and long
for the prestige and academic opportunities of the
senior high school setting.   Those who do not make it
in senior high teaching are sent to the junior high
school, where they attempt to teach at senior high
level in the interest of their own egos and to the
detriment of their pupils.   A plan developed in some
Indiana schools and partially backed by Indiana University involves special certification of junior high
school teachers and would help solve this problem.

11117.   Rock, D. A. and Hemphill, J. K.   "Report of the
Junior High School Principalship." Washington, D.C.:
National Association of Secondary School Principals,
1966.

In a 1965 study with 4,496 responding junior high
school principals, it was found that over 60 percent
considered courses stressing physical and emotional
development of the adolescent to be most essential;
43 percent believed that junior high school student
teaching is essential; over one third believed that
courses concerned with the teaching of reading are
essential; and there is a consensus among principals
about the need for a good background in psychology.
Course work concerned with teaching methods in

specific junior high school areas were considered essential by 37 percent of those replying. More than 70 percent of the principals favored extending the degree program to five years and including more liberal arts courses.

11118.   Rock, D. A. and Hemphill, J. K.   The Study of the Secondary School Principalship. Vol. II. Washington, D.C.: National Association of Secondary School Principals, 1966.

Presents some of the data from a survey of forty-five hundred junior high school principals in the United States during the 1964-65 school year.   Questions examined the principals' personal and professional backgrounds, their duties, activities, compensation, and their attitudes on current educational issues. Data are displayed in 170 tables that list responses according to such factors as geographical region, school size, per student expenditure, grade structure, rural or urban location, and job satisfaction.

11119.   Roper, S. S. and Nolan, R. R.   "Down From the Ivory Tower: A Model of Collaborative In-service Education." Occasional Paper 16.   Palo Alto, Calif.: Stanford University, Center for Research and Development in Teaching, ERIC Doc. ED 137 261, 1977.

Discusses an in-service education program of the Teacher Corps Project sponsored by the School of Education at Stanford University and a junior high school in San Jose, California.   The teachers determine the content of the in-service program and are also the in-service educators.   Paper presents a case study and shows how the collaboration between university and schools took place.   The model involves briefing the relevant community on the in-service program, outlining its dimensions, and correcting misconceptions, identification of needs by teachers, administrators, parents, students, and in-service educators, summarizing and cataloging pertinent literature, obtaining additional information from practitioners in the field, selecting and developing appropriate policies, adopting policies, evaluating policies, and disseminating information and writing articles for publication.   Paper includes sections on introducing the in-service topic, a model of collaborative in-service education, assessing specific needs, summarizing pertinent literature and research, and obtaining information.

11120.   Rose, H. C.   "A study of the competencies needed for junior high school principals." Bulletin of the National Association of Secondary School Principals, February 1962:405.

Author surveyed the educational literature to establish a comprehensive list of competencies desirable
for principals, then developed an opinionnaire and
sent it to selected principals and superintendents in
the geographical area covered by the North Central
Association of Colleges and Secondary Schools. The
administrators evaluated sixteen of the competencies
as more important for junior high school principals
than for senior high school principals. Ten of the
sixteen rated much higher for junior high school
principals: 1) knowledge of child growth and
development, 2) background of successful experience
as an elementary teacher, 3) background of successful
experience as a junior high school teacher, 4) background of successful experience as a junior high
school administrator, 5) background of successful
experience as an elementary school administrator, 6)
knowledge of development and function of the elementary schools, 7) knowledge of development and function of the junior high schools, 8) understanding of
current issues, problems, and practices of core
curriculum, 9) understanding of sound elementary
school curriculum practices, and 10) understanding of
effective block-time teaching techniques.

11121.   Rottier, J.   "Preparing teachers to make a
difference--for transescents." Middle School Journal,
7(1976):12-17.

During the 1972-73 school year the Division of Education faculty at Findlay College, Findlay, Ohio,
outlined a program to prepare teachers of transescents: 1) All students completing such a program
would also have to complete a regular elementary or
secondary certificate. 2) This program's goal would
be the preparation of teachers for transescents and
not the preparation of teachers for a special organizational structure such as the junior high school or
the middle school. 3) The sequence of professional
education courses for elementary and secondary certification would be examined to determine additional
competencies necessary for understanding and working
with transescents. 4) The content preparation of
elementary teachers and secondary teachers would be
examined to determine its appropriateness for
teachers of transescents. 5) Current teachers and
administrators would play a major role in planning
the specific components of this program. General
program competencies and components: a) to understand the social, emotional, physical, and intellectual development of the transescent, b) to develop an
initial feeling for the realities of a classroom of
transescent students, c) to understand oneself in
relation to the responsibilities of teaching transescents, d) to be capable of functioning as a teacher-
counselor with transescents, e) to recognize reading

problems of students and to provide corrective
procedures, f) to use various techniques of teaching
and be aware of instructional materials to maximize
learning possibilities, g) to have the breadth and
depth necessary to teach at least one subject area of
language arts, mathematics, science, or social
studies, h) to demonstrate the ability to teach
preadolescents.

11122.   Saunders, J.   "Job analysis--junior high school
principals." Bulletin of the National Association of
Secondary School Principals, 43,251(1959):46-55.

In connection with a Guide for Principals of Elementary Schools in New York City, the writer constructed
a checklist of duties and responsibilities of elementary school principals. This article, an extension
of that list, pinpoints the essential differences
between the jobs of junior high and elementary school
principals. The article describes two types of differences: those that are known and accepted and
those that are evident to the practicing junior high
school principal but probably need documentation and
statistical evidence.

11123.   Schniedewind, N.   "Group processes in education:
a cross-age affective education project." College
Student Journal, 12,1(1978):92-99.

Author discusses an affective education program which
taught group process and communication skills to
college students and middle school students at the
same time. Article describes the format of the
undergraduate course for pre-service teachers, the
field work component, teaching techniques, and
includes results of evaluations by students and their
instructors. The program met its goal for under-
graduates and for many of the middle school students.
Article contains many suggestions for pre-service
training, including successful techniques like developing awareness, interaction, responsiveness through
a magic circle, the eye message circle, and the use
of feedback. Article also describes two standard
formats that were helpful in planning an evaluation.
It elaborates on four aspects of the program 1) the
many foci of learning, 2) multidimensional learning
on the part of college students, 3) possible use of
the course as a model for teacher training, and 4)
the potential of a group for personal, professional,
and social change.

11124.   Shockley, R. E. and Shelly, A. C. "Staff Develop-
ment in the Middle School: A Systematic Approach."
Paper presented at Assembly of the Association for
Supervision and Curriculum Development, Atlanta,
March 30, 1980.

When school systems change from the traditional
junior high school to the middle school, a major
concern of superintendents, curriculum supervisors,
and building administrators, is the staff development
program. This article presents a systematic model
for such a program. While the focus of the article
is on middle school, the model could easily apply to
staff development at any level. Successful staff
development programs operate on these assumptions:
1) People learn best when they are learning by
choice. 2) A staff development program must respond
to identified needs. 3) A staff development program
should result in observable benefits for middle
school learners. 4) The program must have clear
goals and specific objectives. 5) Staff development
is a continuous process. 6) An effective program
requires commitment from leadership and staff in
design, implementation, and evaluation. 7) An
effective program requires feedback, follow-up, and
support. 8) Creativity and flexibility are key
elements. 9) Programs must be based on perceived
needs as well as identified needs. 10) Communication
between administration and staff as well as among
staff is essential. Sections of the paper cover
needs assessment, establishing program objectives,
implementation of the staff development program,
staff development evaluation, and feedback to staff.

11125.   Sizemore, R. W. "A Comparison of the Perceptions
of the Characteristics of Teachers by Black and White
Secondary Students in an Urban School District."
ERIC Doc. ED 174 729, 1979.

Teachers may fail with junior high school and black
students, because these groups differ from senior
high school and white students in their perceptions
of which teacher behaviors are important. Author
selected black and white ninth and twelfth graders
who were asked to select their three best and three
worst teachers and state the most important behavior
differences between the teachers. The students
identified 8,640 behaviors, which the author grouped
into three categories: warmth, organization, and
stimulation. Blacks and ninth graders more frequently perceived warmth as important. Whites and
twelfth graders considered organization and stimulation more important. The students identified twenty
specific behaviors as most important. Four of the
top five behaviors for each group were identical: 1)
ability or willingness to explain material adequately, 2) ability to present material interest-
ingly, 3) willingness to help students with work, and
4) caring attitude. See ERIC Abstract #ED 174 729.

11126.   Smith, M. C.   "Preparing and Keeping Junior High
Teachers."   Paper presented at the Annual Conference
of the Junior High Association of Illinois, 1965.

Author suggests two ways to insure excellent teaching
in the junior high school, both based on the premise
that if we have an insufficient supply of junior high
trained teachers entering that institution, we must
help the teachers who now find themselves in the
junior high school to become qualified for work at
this level. This can be accomplished through various
in-service avenues within the school and the school
district. Area colleges and universities can provide
extension courses, consultant service, institutes,
and workshops for the school district. The other
approach is through a master's degree program geared
specifically for the junior high teacher who is
prepared for the elementary or senior high and who
has decided he would like to remain at the junior
high level. Such a program should provide additional
work with his subject areas. Usually this teacher,
regardless of whether his education was directed
toward elementary or secondary, will not have sufficient subject matter depth to handle adequately the
two teaching areas normally expected of junior high
teachers. The other part of the curriculum would
fill in the voids in junior high school philosophy,
curriculum, history, guidance, and understanding of
the junior high age adolescent.

11127.   Smith, M. C.   "The case for teachers who are
specifically prepared to teach in junior high
school." Journal of Teacher Education, 17(1966):
438-443.

Results of questionnaires sent in 1964 to 291 superintendents and principals are as follows: 1) Administrators reported that junior high school teachers
who had joined their staff in recent years were
better prepared in subject matter than in professional education. 2) Very few administrators favor
any decrease in either subject matter or professional
education requirements. 3) The majority of administrators rate a teacher specifically trained for the
junior high school as more successful than one
trained for the elementary or secondary level. 4)
Teacher failure in the junior high school is due primarily to inability to cope with youngsters of this
age. Few teachers fail because of inability to
handle the subject being taught. 5) Qualified mathematics, science, English, and foreign language
teachers are the most difficult to acquire for the
junior high school. 6) Colleges and universities can
be of greatest service to junior high schools by providing teachers specifically trained for this level

and by furnishing leadership in conferences, workshops, institutes, in-service training, and research.
The middle school should be seen as a concept, an
idea, a school that recognizes the continued need for
change in the educational process. Some of the
frequently mentioned differences from other types of
schools include freedom from stresses of interschool
athletics and more emphasis on intramural activities,
more counseling services, more personal exploratory
experiences than the typical "exploratory" course
approach, freedom from Carnegie Unit pressures,
better use of specialists, and more emphasis on
independent study and self-reliant behavior.

11128.   Stainbrook, J. R., Jr. "Teacher Education for the
Intermediate School Staff."   ERIC Doc. ED 088 864,
1970.

Author analyzed the professional education of
Indiana's intermediate school teachers by comparing
data from 199 middle school and 289 junior high
school teachers in 44 schools as well as interviewing
five middle school and five junior high school principals. Author also compared junior high data with
findings from a similar study in 1959. Research
showed no major differences between the professional
preparation of junior high school teachers in 1969
and those of ten years before. The professional
preparation of middle and junior high school teachers
was quite similar, usually with an emphasis on the
senior high school. This preparation generally
lacked two important elements: course work in counseling and guidance and student teaching in either a
middle school or junior high school. In-service
college classes specifically related to the junior
high school were no more frequently a part of the
junior high school teacher's in-service activities in
1969 than they were in 1959. See ERIC Abstract # ED
088 864.

11129.   Stoneburner, L. "A Review of the Recent Litera-
ture on In-Service Training." Paper presented at the
Annual Conference of the Junior High Association of
Illinois, 1965.

Describes what various researchers have said about
the grave necessity of continuing in-service training
for junior high school teachers.

11130.   Thomas, W. "Trends and Problems in Preparing
Junior High Teachers." Paper presented at the Annual
Conference of the Junior High Association of
Illinois, 1965.

It is clear that the junior high school program
should differ from the elementary and secondary preparation programs in the following areas: 1) Junior
high teachers probably need more background in guidance than teachers at any other grade level.   The
social and emotional problems prevalent in early
adolescence bear directly on how much students learn
and should be the concern of every junior high school
teacher.   2) The junior high school teacher needs to
be better trained to teach the work-study skills that
become increasingly important beginning at this age.
3) The junior high teacher should have more preparation in reading than is usually found in programs for
secondary teachers.   4) The prospective junior high
teacher should study early adolescent psychology.   5)
Junior high teachers should study the purposes and
functions of the junior high school and how it
attempts to meet the needs of the early adolescent.
In addition, these prospective teachers should select
courses which will prepare them in at least two
teaching areas.   It is imperative that the student
teaching experience take place in a junior high
school under the supervision of an experienced junior
high school teacher.

11131.   Tobaygo, R.   "The 10 no matters."   Journal of
Teacher Education, 30,6(1979):28.

A tongue-in-cheek listing of junior high school
teaching experiences and student inattention to
teacher decisions and commands.   See ERIC Abstract
#EJ 215 110.

11132.   Toepfer, C. F., Jr.   "Who should teach in junior
high."   Clearinghouse, 40(1965):74-76.

Describes the University of Indiana at Bloomington
Pioneer Program in Junior High School Teacher
Education and Certification.   Also describes other
undergraduate and graduate programs for junior high
school teacher education.   If the junior high school
student is unique, his teachers must be educated in
programs distinctly different from those for prospective elementary and senior high school teachers.
Such programs must teach awareness of the important
ways that junior high preadolescents and later
adolescents differ from students in other age groups.
Programs must prepare teachers to organize instruction to meet the educational needs of their students,
to understand the importance of student exploration
in planning curricula, and to use techniques of
instruction that differ from those of the elementary
or senior high school level.

11133.   Toepfer, C. F., Jr.   "Must middle grade education
consist of cast-offs?"   Educational Leadership, 31
(1973):311-313.

Pioneering efforts by the Educational Leadership
Institute have created six new multimedia information
packets for teachers who work with emerging adolescents.   The ASCD working group on the emerging ado-
lescent learner, composed of leaders in junior
high/middle school education, has developed this
presentation on the adolescent learner in the middle
grades.   The topics and their authors are: 1)
"Implications of the Curriculum: Boyce Medical
Study" by Dr. Donald Eichhorn, Group Chairman,
Assistant Superintendent of Schools, Upper St. Clair,
Pennsylvania.   2) "Educating Emerging Adolescents:
Some Operational Problems" by Dr. Conrad Toepfer,
Jr., Associate Professor of Education, State Univer-
sity of New York at Buffalo.   3) "The Nature of the
Emerging Adolescent" by Dr. Mary Compton, Associate
Professor of Education, University of Georgia,
Athens.   4) "Learning Strategies for the Emerging
Adolescent" by Dr. Bruce Howell, Superintendent of
Schools, Tulsa, Oklahoma.   5) "Adult Models for the
Emerging Adolescent" by Dr. Thomas Sweeney, Associate
Professor of Education, Ohio State University,
Columbus.   6) "The Impact of Social Forces on Chil-
dren" by Dr. James Philips, Director of Secondary
Education, St. Paul, Minnesota, and Dr. Philip
Pumerantz, Program Editor and Associate Professor of
Education, University of Bridgeport, Connecticut.
Inquiries concerning this program should be directed
to Educational Leadership Institute, Inc., P.O. Box
863, Springfield, Massachusetts, 01101.

11134.   Trachtman, G. M.   "The role of an in-service program in establishing a new plan of elementary school
organization."   Journal of Educational Sociology, 34
(1961):349-354.

Description of in-service programs necessary for
teachers beginning to work in an upper elementary
school that uses core concept organization.

11135.   Underwood, B. and Underwood, R.   "Concerns of
junior high school and middle school teachers: a
framework for in-service."   Clearinghouse, 51,1
(1977):36-37.

Authors analyze the concerns of junior high and
middle school teachers and offer three recommendations to improve in-service activities for them.
See ERIC Abstract #EJ 169 093.

11136.   University of Georgia. "Instructional Improvement
in Middle and Junior High Grades for 250 Teachers
Districts.   Director's Report."   Athens: University
of Georgia, ERIC Doc. ED 050 843, August 31, 1970.

This project used summer conferences, seminar activities, and biweekly contact with University of Georgia
staff for a full year to assist 120 teachers of disadvantaged students in ten local school districts.
The project's most important contributions were to
guide implementation of more appropriate instructional methods, to help teachers update their content
areas, and to change self-attitudes.   Five formal
evaluative devices were used.   The major strength of
the project lay in its conduct in the field rather
than under laboratory conditions.   See ERIC Abstract
#ED 050 843.

11137.   Upper Midwest Regional Educational Laboratory.
"Teacher Competence for the Middle School Years."
Report of a conference, University of Minnesota at
Duluth.   Minneapolis: Upper Midwest Regional Educa-
tional Laboratory, ERIC Doc. ED 044 369, 1967.

This report contains the following presentations made
at this conference on teacher competence for middle
school years: 1) "Our Goal: Improving Education for
the Middle School Years" by Clifford Hooker. 2) "The
Special Case of Early Adolescents" by Samuel H.
Popper.   3) "Teachers for the Middle Schools" by
William W. Wattenberg.   4) "Learning Through Dis-
covery in Fifth Grade" by R. E. Meyers.   5) "Teaching
Thinking on the Synthesis Level" by Burton L. Grover.
6) "What a Middle School Might Be Like" by William
Alexander.   7) "Establishing Objectives for Individ-
ualized Instruction" by John Downs.   8) "Team Teach-
ing and the Block-Time Class" by Lloyd Johansen.   9)
"Flexible Scheduling for the Middle School Years: the
Fluid Block Plan" by Almon Hoye.   10) "Preparing
Teachers for the Middle School Years" by Emmett L.
Williams.   11) "Summary of Conference Results and
Directions for the Future" by Clifford Hooker.   The
conference focused on three questions: Do some
teaching strategies and staff utilization patterns
hold promise for improving education in the middle
school years? Do teachers who would work with middle
school students need special competencies?   If so,
can better programs be provided to prepare such
teachers?

11138.   Usdan, M. D. and Bertolaet, F. (Eds.) Teachers for
the Disadvantaged. Chicago: Follett Publishing Co.,
1966.

Though not specifically related to middle grades
education, most task force material would be useful

for teacher educators. Task Force 1: Description of Desirable Behaviors for Teachers in Depressed Areas. Task Force 2: The Development of Teacher Education Curricula for Teachers of the Disadvantaged. Task Force 3: Criteria for Evaluating Teacher Education Programs. Report includes sections on new ways of preparing teachers for urban schools, the professional sequence for preparing urban teachers, some suggestions for evaluating the outcomes of the school-university teacher education project, ways of observing teacher behavior in classrooms, and evaluating educational outcomes by means of formal behavioral science instruments.

11139.   Vars, G. F.   "Preparing junior high teachers: A prof's eye view."   Clearinghouse, 40,2(1965):77-81.

The distinguishing characteristics of a good junior high school teacher is that he finds success and satisfaction in working with young adolescents. Both the challenges and the joys of working with this age group should be highlighted in recruitung teachers for this level. Pre-service preparation of junior high teachers should differ in emphasis rather than kind from either elementary or secondary preparation. The present practices of accepting either elementary or secondary certification at the junior high level should continue, provided that both programs include some junior high student teaching. The student teaching should be under the direction of a teacher committed to this level and in a school that exemplifies at least some of the better contemporary practices. A special junior high endorsement on either certificate should indicate completion of a program that includes a broad general education, some depth in at least two teaching fields, and some special attention to the nature of the young adolescent, the teaching of reading, the teacher's role in guidance and counseling, and the history and philosophy of the junior high school. New York State, in revising certification standards, includes a requirement that all permanent elementary certificates incorporate five years of study and a thirty semester hour minimum in a department or interdepartmental plan of liberal arts studies. A special junior high endorsement on this K-9 certificate is awarded for thirty-six hours of work in English or social studies, forty-two in science, or twenty-four in mathematics, and at least eighty of the three hundred clock hours of supervised student teaching must be in the junior high grades. Unfortunately, no specific work in junior high school education, not even adolescent psychology, is listed as part of the required semester hours in professional education.

11140.   Vars, G. F.   "Teacher preparation for the middle
school."   High School Journal, December 1969: 172-177.

The effective middle school teacher is a reasonably
cultured individual of good character who understands
and enjoys working with youngsters in this age range,
knows something worth teaching to young people, and
knows some effective ways to teach.   The uniqueness
of junior high and middle school teaching stems in
part from the diversity and rapid change that charac-
terizes young people as they approach and pass
puberty.   A second source of uniqueness is the
in-between status of the school itself.   It receives
students from an institution concerned primarily with
common learning, especially the basic skills, and
passes them on to one that stesses specialization and
at least the beginning of vocational separation.   Why
are not more colleges preparing teachers for the
middle school?   At least part of the difficulty
appears to come from five false antitheses rampant in
the field of teacher education: 1) encounter vs.
professional skill training, 2) subject matter vs.
method, 3) depth vs. breadth, 4) program vs. certification, and 5) push vs. pull.   That is, at what point
should the effort be applied to secure qualified
middle school teachers?   Should college educators
push hard to get programs established?   Should school
administrators and hiring officials exert more pull
on college administrators and certification officials?   Obviously, it is going to take concerted
effort by everyone to solve the middle school teacher
problem.   Interested individuals can have an impact,
but action is more likely if organizations of
teachers, administrators, curriculum supervisors, and
others bombard the colleges and the state certification authorities with demands for change.   In the
meantime, interested college staff members should
push from within to change existing teacher
preparation programs or to establish new ones.

11141.   Walker, J. G.   "Instructional Difficulties of
Beginning Junior High School Science Teachers in
Arkansas, 1972-73."   Ed.D. Dissertation, University
of Arkansas, ERIC Doc. ED 094 972, 1973.

Through the use of a questionnaire, author obtained
data concerning sources of assistance, professional
preparation, teaching assignments, and instructional
difficulties of sixty beginning teachers.   Author
suggests possible solutions to the difficulties and
makes recommendations for upgrading junior high
school science teaching and programs.   The majority
of teachers are not adequately prepared to teach
science at this level or to handle the unique
problems of junior high school.   Problems included
coping with reading difficulties, stimulating

critical thinking, providing enrichment experiences,
and encouraging students to do independent study.
Teachers were hindered by lack of encouragement,
assistance, supervision, and financial support from
their administrators. See ERIC Abstract #ED 094 972.

11142.   Wattenbarger, J. L.   "Competencies needed by core
teachers."   Educational Research Bulletin, 32(1953):
181-185.

Ratings by core teachers in Florida of forty-eight
competencies drawn from published descriptions of the
work of core teachers.

11143.   Willink, R. J.   "In-service training of junior
high school teachers."   Bulletin of the National
Association of Secondary School Principals,   43,251
(1959):13-17.

Describes an exemplary in-service training program
for junior high school teachers.

11144.   Wilson, M. T.   "Better training for junior high
and middle school teachers." Bulletin of the National
Association of Secondary School Principals,   58,382
(1974):164-170.

Author suggests creative partnerships between school
and teacher training institutions to assure better
prepared beginning teachers.   See ERIC Abstract #EJ
098 804.

11145.   Wood, C. W.   "The Development and Implementation
of a New Model for the Preparation of Teachers for
Junior High School Youth."   Project 2-75 of the Educational Coordinating Council of the State of Oregon.
Corvallis: Corvallis School District 509J and Oregon
State University, School of Education, ERIC Doc. ED
072 036, November 26, 1971.

This project provides a sequence of personalized
educational experiences for teacher trainees prior to
and after student teaching.   The sequence consists of
four training levels.   Three levels (tutorial, student assistant, and teacher associate) are included
in this project.   The fourth level is a year-long
resident experience that comes after student teaching.   Sixty-five students were enrolled at the
various levels of this project.   Questionnaires,
journals, and progress reports to the Educational
Coordinating Council of the Oregon Board of Education
provided evaluation of the project.   See ERIC
Abstract #ED 072 036.

12

Discipline and Problem Behavior
in Schools for Early Adolescents

12001.   Adams, W.   "Mental Health in the Schools: Parent
Training."   Paper presented at the Annual Convention
of the American Psychological Association, Toronto,
Ontario, ERIC Doc. 166 589, August, 1978.

Discusses a training program run by teachers for
parents of school children who are creating problems.
Ten couples rated their child's at-home behavior by
means of a checklist, participated in teacher-led
group sessions with a focus on ways of dealing with
student behavioral problems, and then rated their
child's at-home behavior after group sessions.   The
control group also filled out the behavior checklist
at the beginning and the end of the period.   Teachers
rated children whose parents attended the group
sessions more positively in overall classroom
behavior whereas control group children's ratings
remained unchanged.   See ERIC Abstract #ED 166 589.

12002.   Ainsworth, L. and Stapleton, J. C.   "Discipline at
the junior high school level."   Bulletin of the
National Association of Secondary School Principals,
60,397(1976):54-59.

Recent data gathered from a junior high school
(grades 7, 8, and 9) suggest there is no one way to
tackle the problems of discipline.   Some current
approaches include humanizing the school, behavior
modification, logical consequences, punishment, or a
discipline code.   Developing an effective discipline
program at the junior high level requires involvement
by all segments of the school community.   Effective
discipline is not synonomous with control.   Discipline refers to the total school environment and its

relationship to student behavior.   Existing procedures and ideologies should be extensively analyzed
in any plan for improvement.

12003.   American Friends Service Committee.   "A Report on
Short-Term, Out-of-School Disciplinary Suspensions in
the   Junior   High/Middle   School   and   High   Schools of
Richland   County   School   District   1,   1975-1976   and
1974-1975."   Columbia, S. C.:   American Friends Service   Committee,   South   Carolina   Community   Relations
Program, ERIC Doc. ED 127 663, August, 1976.

Short-term suspensions are a severe disciplinary tool
that can be used by school officials for one to five
days   at   their   discretion.   In   addition   to   the
negative impact of suspension on students, districts
lose   some   state   financial aid   when   students are not
in school because they have been suspended.   The
report contains basic data over a two-year period on
seven high schools, two junior high schools, and nine
middle schools.   See ERIC Abstract #ED 127 663.

12004.   Bergland, B. W. and Chal, A. H.   "Relaxation
training and a junior high behavior problem."   School
Counselor, 19,4(1972):288-293.

Discusses   behavioral   counseling   with   a   junior   high
school student who was a heavy drug user.   Systematic
desensitization is particularly effective in helping
individuals overcome fears of specific situations and
has been used well with teenagers.   The paradigm consists of three components: a) construction of hierarchy   of   anxiety-arousing   scenes,   b)   training   in
relaxation, and c) pairing relaxation with visualiza-
tion of scenes from the hierarchy.   This article
could be very useful to junior high school counselors
working with drug users.

12005.   Blair, A. S. and Burton, W. H.   Growth and Development of the Preadolescent.   New York: Appleton-
Century-Crofts, 1951.

Serious   behavior   problems   and   delinquency   are   more
likely to originate during preadolescence than during
early adolescence.

12006.   Borland, G. F.   "LaFollette High School student
vandalism committee."   ERIC Doc. ED 181 017, 1978.

Article describes the development of an antivandalism
program   in   which   volunteer   junior   high   school   students operate an educational program for children in
lower grades.   A reward system for information leading to the identification of vandals added significantly to the effectiveness of the program.   See ERIC
Abstract #ED 181 017.

12007.   Brodbelt, S.   "The epidemic of school violence."
Clearinghouse, 51,8(1978):383-388.

Examines the research on school violence, its history, and its peculiar difficulties. Article reports
on interviews with a school chief of security, five
junior high principals, and two senior high principals who discuss the Baltimore public schools. See
ERIC Abstract #EJ 182 787.

12008.   Campbell County School District 1.   "Alternatives:
Alternative Discipline and Suspension Program Hand-
book, Campbell County Junior High."   Gillette, Wyo.,
ERIC Doc. ED 172 460, 1979.

Booklet explains a program of discipline and suspension for students who come in conflict with school
policy.   The Alternative Discipline and Suspension
Program operates in an environment of strict adherence to set rules where a student must earn advancement through and eventually out of the program back
to regular classroom attendance.   The booklet
includes the basics of the program and the four
phases, which include a final phase of transition
back to the classroom.   Students are referred to this
program for infractions such as theft, drug use, and
discipline.   See ERIC Abstract #ED 172 460.

12009.   Commonwealth Learning, Inc.   "Morse Crisis Inter-
vention Center: Project Advance.   Title III Project
Final Evaluation Report."   Alexandria, Va.:   District
of Columbia Public Schools Department of Research and
Evaluation and Commonwealth Learning, Inc., ERIC Doc.
ED 103 732, July, 1974.

Project Advance provides supplemental services to the
Morse Crisis Intervention Center in the Washington,
D.C., Public School System.   Students are sent to
this center because of disruptive behavior in the
public junior high schools.   This project provided
psychotherapy to alleviate or minimize disturbing
behavior, individualized instruction using an open
classroom technique, and enrichment activities to
relieve hyperactivity and tension.   Four courses for
staff development were required during the current
project year: 1) the open classroom, 2) methods and
materials for teaching the nonmotivated learner, 3)
guided group interaction, 4) concepts of crisis
intervention and providing prevocational skills
training within the content areas.   This evaluation
reports on interactional activities and on-site visitations and includes parent and student interview
data, sections on counseling therapy and enrichment
activities, and a project awareness questionnaire.
Conclusions were not clearly delineated in the report
due to lack of good pretest and posttest data.

12010.   Commonwealth Learning, Inc. "Morse Crisis Inter-
vention Center: Project Advance. Title III Project
Final Report. "Alexandria, Va: District of Columbia
Public Schools Department of Research and Evaluation,
ERIC Doc. ED 117 157, June, 1975.

The Morse Crisis Intervention Center is a program of
survival for the youth of the D.C. Public Schools who
have been removed from the public junior high school
because of disruptive behavior. The Center's ongoing
activities were supplemented by Project Advance in
these areas: 1) Psychotherapeutic services were provided to alleviate or minimize disturbing behavior.
2) Individualized instruction was provided, using a
modified open classroom technique. 3) Enrichment
activities were provided the students. The project
director and staff developed twenty-three standards
which emphasized affective, behavioral and educational objectives. These standards form the basis
for the program evaluation. See ERIC Abstract #ED
117 157.

12011.   Crane, R. L. and Jacobson, M. E. "Self-
instruction: an experimental program." Educational
Leadership, 6(1973):563-565.

In an experimental project at Webber Junior High
School in Saginaw, Michigan, pupils study in a self-
instruction center. The project is formally called
the Adjusted Study Program. Webber, like most junior
high schools of its size, has a number of students
experiencing behavioral as well as learning difficulties. As in many other urban settings during the
past years, the number and seriousness of these
difficulties has been growing. The rate of this
growth is out of proportion to increasing enrollment.

12012.   Damico, S. B., et al. "A Comparison Between the
Self-concepts as Learner of Disruptive and Nondisrup-
tive Middle School Students." Paper presented at the
Annual Meeting of the American Educational Research
Association, San Francisco, ERIC Doc. ED 128 710,
1976.

Study compares the academic self-concept scores of
disruptive and nondisruptive middle school students
in grades 5-8. The Florida Key and the School-
Academic subscore of the Coopersmith Self-esteem
Inventory were used to obtain scores with 3,254
students enrolled in four middle schools. Authors
surveyed 208 students who had been removed from the
learning environment two or more times during the
first six months of the 1973-74 school year. The
study showed no significant effect of race, sex, or
school on academic self-concept and no significant
interactions between these variables. However, those

students identified by their behavior as disruptive had significantly lower inferred and professed academic self-concepts than did students identified as nondisruptive. Authors concluded that negative feelings about oneself as a learner may be a contributing factor in student disruption. See ERIC Abstract #ED 128 710.

12013.   Dysinger, D. W. "Title VIII Student Support Program: Minneapolis Public Schools. Final Evaluation Report." Minneapolis: Minneapolis Public Schools, Department of Research and Evaluation, ERIC Doc. ED 118 643, July, 1975.

This Student Support Program was initiated in 1971-72 and ran until 1974-75. Report describes the final year and includes descriptions and some comparisons from previous years. The program was designed to reduce the student dropout rate for grades 7-12 at two junior high schools and two senior high schools in inner city Minneapolis. The program had three components: 1) education, 2) student and family support, and 3) work experience. See ERIC Abstract #ED 118 643.

12014.   Feldhusen, J. F. "Behavior problems in secondary schools." Journal of Research and Development in Education, 11,4(1978):17-28.

Article discusses antisocial student behavior in schools, from talking out of turn to violent attacks on fellow students and teachers. It attempts to identify causes while examining programs and procedures for changing or preventing such behavior. Author concludes: 1) Federal and state governments should support the development and rigorous evaluation of a variety of comprehensive programs to deal with social behavior of junior high school youth. These programs should be developed as theoretical models based on the best research available, and the research evaluation must be sound. 2) Schools with severe problems of violence, crime, vandalism, and truancy should organize task forces of teachers, parents, administrators, and students to survey the problems and develop plans for corrective programs. 3) In-service programs should help teachers and administrators learn how to deal effectively with youth behavior problems. Behavior management techniques are especially promising. 4) Teachers, students, parents, and administrators should cooperate in developing and enforcing school rules. 5) School curricula should be carefully examined in relation to discipline problems. 6) Educators should not condone illegal behavior in the schools. 7) Basic skills should be stressed and taught effectively. 8) The

principal must take the lead in developing a positive, humanistic climate. 9) Special classes should
be developed within the school for short-term treatment of severe discipline problems.   10) Explicit
efforts must be made to involve youth in developing
self-direction and self-control.   11) Special vocational and career education programs should be developed.   12) Each school should have a system coordinated by guidance counselors to plan programs for
severe discipline cases.   13) There should be much
recognition of positive behaviors of students.   14)
In schools with severe and widespread behavior problems, security devices and personnel should be
employed.   15) Schools of education should bolster
teacher training in the area of classroom management.

12015.   Finnegan, H. "Discipline Study." Spokane, Wash.:
Spokane School District 81, ERIC Doc. ED 122 450,
April 30, 1976.

In this survey citizens, parents, students, teachers,
counselors, and principals listed the most important,
second most important, and third most important problems regarding discipline and provided examples of
each. This report discusses responses concerning the
junior high school, which fell into sixteen categories: attendance, class size, discipline, discrimination, external influence, lack of parental guidance,
lack of respect, miscellaneous, parent-teacher cooperation, physical abuse, rights and responsibilities,
smoking, drugs, alcohol, staff behavior, student
attitude, too much freedom, vandalism, and theft.
See ERIC Abstract #ED 122 450.

12016.   Fiordaliso, R., et al. "Decreasing Absenteeism on
the Junior High School Level."   Paper presented at
the Annual Meeting of the American Educational
Research Association, San Francisco.   Silver Spring,
Md.:   Institute for Behavioral Research, ERIC Doc. ED
123 764, March, 1976.

Study conducted with the Preparation through Responsive Educational Programs suggests that no general
statements can be made about the relationship among
school absenteeism, juvenile delinquency, and other
measures of school performance. The special approach
used to reduce absenteeism did work for two groups of
student subjects.   One group was enrolled in the academic phase of this program, which included individualized instruction in reading, math, and English.
The other experimental group participated in the
social skills component of the program.   A third
group participated in no special activities.   Attendance data for these junior high students from the
year before indicated which ones had been absent the
most.   This approach entailed calling parents or

sending them letters when students had been present
for a certain number of days instead of contacting
parents only when students were absent.   See ERIC
Abstract #ED 123 764.

12017.   Fuchs, J. E., et al. "An approach to student misbehavior."   Bulletin of the National Association of
Secondary School Principals, 62,414(1978):98-103.

Discusses a pilot program in small-group counseling
designed to change attitudes of junior high school
students with serious behavior problems.   See ERIC
Abstract #EJ 171 520.

12018.   Glasser, W.   "Schools Without Failure, 1977:
Glasser's Approach to Discipline--Realistic and
Working."   Paper presented at the Annual Meeting of
the American Association of School Administrators,
Las Vegas, ERIC Doc. ED 137 958, February, 1977.

Glasser presents a ten-step approach to school discipline based on his book Reality Therapy and discusses
preliminary results of this approach.   He surveyed
twenty-four schools: fourteen elementary, five
junior high, and five high schools.   See ERIC
Abstract #ED 137 958.

12019.   Hall, R. V., et al.   "Modification of Disputing
and Talking Out Behaviors, with the Teacher as
Observer and Experimenter."   Paper presented at the
Annual Meeting of the American Educational Research
Association, Minneapolis.   Lawrence: University of
Kansas, Bureau of Child Research, ERIC Doc. ED 039
298, March, 1970.

Authors studied "disputing and talking out behaviors"
of individual pupils and entire classroom groups in
special education classes and regular classes from
white middle class areas and from black disadvantaged
areas ranging from first grade to junior high school.
The classroom teacher was the experimenter and primary observer.   Various means of recording behaviors
were used.   After baseline rates were obtained,
extinction of inappropriate disputing or talking out
behaviors and reinforcement of appropriate behavior
with teacher attention, praise, and desired classroom
activity brought a decrease in undesired behavior.
See ERIC Abstract #ED 039 298.

12020.   Hardesty, L. "Pupil Control Ideology of Teachers
as It Relates to Middle School Concepts."   Paper presented at the Annual Meeting of the American Educational Research Association, Toronto, Ontario, ERIC
Doc. ED 150 722, March, 1978.

In this study of 252 teachers, junior high school
teachers were significantly more custodial than
either elementary or senior high teachers. A two-way
analysis of variance showed statistically significant
main effects. Author sees this result as supporting
middle school ideas about pupil control. See ERIC
Abstract #ED 150 722.

12021.   Harlem Consolidated School District 122.   "Reduc-
ing Dropouts Through Achievement Motivation.   End of
Project Report.   Title III, ESEA."   Rockford, Ill.,
ERIC Doc. ED 117 265, June, 1974.

Discusses a program for preventing dropout attitudes
from developing in middle schools in grades 6, 7, and
8.   The three major goals: 1) training staff to lead
project activities, 2) developing materials to help
teachers in the project activities, and 3) providing
of teacher-led circle discussions for the students.
Sections are included on student and teacher data,
evaluative techniques, and the effects of the project
on the clientele.   Two major goals were met: staff
training and the provision of circle discussion
activities for all middle school students. See ERIC
Abstract #ED 117 265.

12022.   Havighurst, R. J.   "Problem youth in the junior
high school."   Bulletin of the National Association
of Secondary School Principals, 42,237(1958):367-372.

The junior high school should have a program for slow
learners which is geared to their ability and also
gives them a reasonably clear pathway to growth.
Work experience and opportunity is an essential for
these boys and girls, who can generally get the feeling of successful growing up by earning money and
doing usual work, even if their school performance is
a source of discouragement to them.   In a rural area,
the work experience can usually be obtained on a farm
or in a farm household.   But in towns and cities,
there should be a patient, persistent program of
finding jobs and supervising the program of these
young people.   The principle things which the society
can do directly for such youth are two: One is to
examine carefully the existing child labor laws to
find out whether, under present industrial conditions, they may not be unnecessarily limiting the
opportunity of boys and girls aged 14 and over to get
wholesome work experience.   The other is to develop
and enlarge programs for wholesome recreation of
teenage youth, giving them an opportunity to get
excitement and adventure and pleasure under circumstances that do not deprive them.

12023.   Hayden, B. S., et al. "The alienated student: an effort to motivate at the junior high level." Journal of School Psychology, 8,3(1970):237-241.

Program for alienated junior high school boys attempted to increase motivation, cooperation, and the desire to remain in school beyond the age of 16. Results showed positive changes in self-reported personality measures and school achievement after one school year. See ERIC Abstract #EJ 026 322.

12024.   Irwin, J. R.   "Doubters, Delinquents, and Dropouts --Can They Be Helped Through Improved Self-Concepts?" Paper presented at the Annual Meeting of the National Association of Secondary School Principals, Anaheim, Calif., ERIC Doc. ED 150 730, February 11, 1978.

Discusses programs to improve student achievement through improved self-actualization in Rev. Jesse Jackson's Operation PUSH, the Youth Incentive Entitlement Pilot Project Program, the New Pride Experiment, the Michigan Expeditions Program, and the John Dancy Street Academy.   Contains biographical sketches of approximately eighty outstanding blacks who have achieved success.   Educators are encouraged to give students a stake in their schools so that the percentage of those who make trouble remains low.   In many cases, the delinquent and the dropout do not suffer from a lack of self-confidence, but rather lack confidence in a school's relevance to their own life.   See ERIC Abstract #ED 150 730.

12025.   Jenkins, A. E., III.   "Reducing Classroom Discipline Problems Among Twenty Selected Classroom Teachers at Hamilton Junior High School."   Ed.D. Dissertation, Nova University, Fort Lauderdale, Fla., ERIC Doc. ED 136 413, July, 1976.

The author, a former principal, isolated students and faculty who were involved in the most discipline referrals.   He then initiated a program that put these students and teachers together in an interdisciplinary cluster.   He discusses the performance objectives for both students and teachers, the teacher development program, and the students' curriculum.   The teacher development program focused on self-evaluation and teaching methods that take into consideration student attitudes and abilities.   See ERIC Abstract #ED 136 413.

12026.   Jones, F. R. and Swain, M. T.   "Self-concept and delinquency proneness."   Adolescence, 12,48(1977): 559-569.

Research project investigated differences in self-concept among 12-to-14-year-old junior high school

delinquent-prone and nondelinquent-prone bright boys
in an inner city setting. Contrary to the theory of
the homeostatic model of self-concept, engaging in
antisocial or prosocial behavior did not cause shifts
in self-concept. The subjects generally did react to
manipulation by engaging in reparative behavior, as
expected, but the delinquent-prone and nondelinquent-
prone bright boys did not view themselves differently. Authors postulate that if shifts did occur
for the delinquent prone it would be after they left
school and left the delinquent-prone subculture of
their school years.

12027.   Kelly, D. H.   "The role of teachers' nominations
in the perpetuation of deviant adolescent careers."
Education, 96,3(1976):209-217.

Recent works on social typing and labeling suggest
that teachers may play a critical role in perpetuat-
ing deviant adolescent careers. Author studied sixth
and seventh grade students and teachers in middle
schools in western New York State. A comparison of
the teachers' nominations for placement of students
in remedial reading with the reading specialist's
evaluations indicates that many nominees do not meet
the minimal criteria for placement. Further analyses
indicate that selected nonacademic criteria such as
past enrollment in remedial reading play a significant role in the nomination process.

12028.   Kvaraceus, W. C.   "Meeting the serious behavioral
problems in junior high schools."   Bulletin of the
National Association of Secondary School Principals,
43(1959):347-353.

The junior high school by itself can have very little
effect on the more serious problems of youth. It is
more likely to help students if it works in conjunction with other school units and coordinates its
resources with those of other community agencies.
However, this will not come about until the delinquent or predelinquent feels that the school staff
likes him, wants him, and is interested in him. And
it will happen only when he likes them; only when the
school spots the potential delinquent and gives him a
second look and a helping hand; only when the school
can work to change the concerns of the cultural
milieu in which most delinquents breed; only when the
school involves the delinquent in solving his own
problems; and only when the community is willing to
pay for more and better schools and community programming in behalf of all youth.

12029.   Linton, H. W. and Chavez, C.   "Behavior checklist
for junior high students."   <u>Bulletin of the National
Association of Secondary School Principals</u>,   <u>63</u>,431
(1979):119-121.

Junior high school teachers can use this checklist,
which gives immediate feedback on specific items to
control individual behavior problems of students.
See ERIC Abstract #EJ 211 026.

12030.   Lufler, H. S., Jr.   "Discipline: a new look at an
old problem."   <u>Phi Delta Kappan</u>, <u>59</u>,6(1978):424-426.

Author calls for increasing the severity of punishment and discusses the failure of schools in dealing
with discipline problems.   He sees schools as a con-
tributor to the problems.   See ERIC Abstract #EJ 171
616.

12031.   McCaffery, J. F. and Turner, D.   "Discipline in
the innovative school."   <u>Clearinghouse</u>, April 1970:
491-496.

With adequate planning, orientation for students, and
in-service for staff, the traditional school can make
the transition into a more innovative program.
Teachers, administrators, and students who have
experienced the excitement of working with modular
scheduling and independent study agree that the
problems of such new programs are solvable, and the
benefits greatly outweigh the deficits.

12032.   McCurdy, B., et al.   "Human relations training
with seventh grade boys identified as behavior
problems."   <u>School Counselor</u>, <u>24</u>,4(1977):248-252.

Training procedures including videotape and facilitative communication were used to improve the self-
esteem of twelve seventh grade boys who were causing
behavior problems in a class of underachievers.
Authors concluded that both quasi-structured and
highly structured procedures were effective.   The
adolescent males in the study were able to learn
facilitative communication and showed an improvement
in human relations skills after training sessions.
The human relations group experience seemed to affect
classroom behavior positively, as evidenced by a
decrease in behavior problems. Human relations
training also seemed to offer considerable benefits
to all concerned when it was taught to students
individually.

12033.   Metz, M. H.   "Clashes in the classroom: the
importance of norms for authority."   <u>Education and
Urban Society</u>, <u>11</u>,1(1978):13-47.

Author interprets the literature on the nature of authority and discusses the character of authority between teacher and student in four desegregated junior high schools. See ERIC Abstract #EJ 193 516.

12034. Middle School Journal. "Responsibility: discipline inside out." Middle School Journal, 11,1(1980): 8-9.

Discusses responsibility in middle school students: 1) Taking on responsibility is risky, so middle school youngsters will only attempt it when they feel in control and safe from failure. 2) Responsible behavior demonstrates concern for others. Middle schoolers will learn to be responsible in a context of caring relationships with teachers and peers, where interdependence is as important as independence. 3) Responsibility emerges from personal success and responsible roles. Middle school learners need opportunities to be successful and productive in authentic ways. 4) Responsibility is holding up your side of a commitment. Middle school kids need practice in making and being held accountable for their commitments. 5) Responsible individuals take initiative. They are independent rather than dependent. Middle school kids need the time, opportunity, and encouragement to go it alone. 6) The capacity for responsibility grows slowly, and public schools are not necessarily designed to promote real responsibility taking, so teachers have to fight both nature and the system. Article includes sections on groundwork (changing the big picture), bringing out the best in kids (tips for teaching responsibility), rules (reasons for responsibility, what to say, when and how), and responsibility in learning.

12035. Moyer, D. H. "Aggressive and delinquent adolescent behavior patterns: effective curriculum adjustments in the middle school." Clearinghouse, 49,5 (1976): 203-209.

Discusses effective curriculum adjustments developed by the staff of the Bayard Middle School in Wilmington, Delaware, to deal with both aggressive and delinquent adolescent behavior. See ERIC Abstract #EJ 137 241.

12036. Moyer, D. H. "Discipline in the urban middle school: a rehabilitative process." Bulletin of the National Association of Secondary School Principals, 62,416(1978):68-74.

Discusses discipline in an urban middle school as a rehabilitative process requiring accurate adult perception of the kinds of behavior problems which

interfere with student achievement.   See ERIC
Abstract #ED 173 581.

12037.   Muir, M. S. and deCharms, R.   "Personal Causation
Training and Goal Setting in Seventh Grade."   Paper
presented at the Annual Meeting of the American Educational Research Association, Washington, D.C., ERIC
Doc. ED 106 725, April, 1975.

Study divided 122 seventh grade students in an inner
city school district into experimental and control
groups.   Motivation training was given to teachers,
and then the authors and the teachers together
designed training units emphasizing feelings of
personal causation.   The teachers used these units in
their classrooms.   Effects of the motivation training
on the experimental children were not significant in
the sample.   Two subscales that measured intrinsi-
cally relevant motivation and imposed motivation
accounted for significant portions of variance in
motivation beyond that accounted for by intelligence.
See ERIC Abstract #ED 106 725.

12038.   National Education Association, Research Division.
"Discipline in the Public Schools."   Washington,
D.C., December, 1957.

This bibliography of discipline techniques has a
section on junior high schools.

12039.   Newsweek magazine.   "Remaking the city schools."
Newsweek, 63,21(1964):100.

Newsweek described the issue of ninth grade behavior
problems as considered by a special panel recommend-
ing a new organization for New York City.   If the
ninth grade were separated from the earlier grades,
creating a middle school for these earlier grades,
the younger students would begin their exposure to
secondary education earlier, yet not be subjected to
the undesirable peer models provided by so many ninth
graders.   This is one response to the extraordinary
discipline problems in many New York junior highs.

12040.   Oden, W. E.   "A Plan for Improving Student Attendance at Brownsville Junior High School."   ERIC Doc.
ED 155 807, 1978.

This project was undertaken to raise the percentage
of student attendance to 95 percent or above at
Brownsville Junior High School in Miami, Florida.
The program included the use of community resources
and incentives.   The project is considered successful
because schoolwide attendance was up 2 to 4 percent,
with pupils making a greater effort to get to school

on time and expressing more self-pride.   See ERIC
Abstract #ED 155 807.

12041.   Page, D. P. and Edwards, R. P.   "Behavior change
strategies for reducing disruptive classroom behavior." Psychology in the Schools, 15,3(1978):413-418.

Examines the effects of independent and group
arrangement for academic work on the disruptive
classroom behavior of junior high school students.
Free time was given on a contingency basis to
individuals and to the class as a whole. See ERIC
Abstract #EJ 183046.

12042.   Petruzielo, F. R.   "Organizing and Using Resource
Personnel to Improve Student Behavior."   Ed.D. Dis-
sertation, Nova University, Fort Lauderdale, Fla.,
ERIC Doc. ED 136 373, 1976.

This plan to improve the behavior and attitudes of
misbehaving junior high school students involved
having resource people like guidance counselors, work
experience coordinators, and a substance abuse
specialist work with each student in a target group
for nine weeks during the 1975-76 school year.   A
personal visit to each child's residence was made and
a cumulative guidance record was reviewed. A study
of results showed that disciplinary referrals to the
assistant principal for each student were reduced by
50 percent, classroom conduct grades for each student
and the overall group improved markedly, and attitudes of participants were generally more positive at
the conclusion of the program. See ERIC Abstract #ED
136 373.

12043.   Reese, S. C., et al.   "Behavioral Effects Within
and Between Individual and Group Reinforcement Proce-
dures."   Paper presented at the Annual Meeting of the
American Educational Research Association, New York.
Silver   Spring,   Md.:   Institute   for   Behavioral
Research, ERIC Doc. ED 143 106, April, 1977.

Outlines the effects of a large-scale behavioral
program called Preparation through Responsive
Educational Programs, or PREP. It involves students
with academic or social deficits from a 1350-student
junior high school.   Program effectiveness was
assessed by examining total school grades, grades in
non-PREP classes, school attendance, number of suspensions, and standardized test scores. Researchers
discovered that successive reinforcement system
phases did not produce significant changes in either
behavioral ratings or class attendance. The program
was successful in promoting increases in school
grades and attendance and in decreasing the amount of

school suspensions for the experimental group of students. See ERIC Abstract #ED 143 106.

12044.   Reynolds, C.   "Buddy system improves attendance." Elementary School Guidance and Counseling,   11,4 (1977):305-306.

Discusses a cooperative effort of the pupil services staff in reducing chronic absenteeism by helping middle and junior high school pupils understand the importance of good attendance, a major guidance objective for counselors. See ERIC Abstract #EJ 158 417.

12045.   Richland County Board of Education.   "Project: Prevent Delinquency, Underachievement, and Dropout." Mansfield, Ohio, ERIC Doc. ED 037 858, June, 1968.

In this study of six school districts, the Nye and Short Self-reporting Delinquency Scale indicated exceptionally high rates of delinquency for one of seven elementary schools (grades 5 and 6), normal rates for only one of the five junior high schools, and normal rates for only one or possibly two of the five high schools.   The Hall-Waldo Inventory of Attitudes toward law and toward school and teachers was administered to sixty-seven hundred students. The Teachers Situation Reaction Inventory was administered to 654 teachers.   See ERIC Abstract #ED 037 858.

12046.   Riessman, F.   "Low income culture, the adolescent, and the school." Bulletin of the National Association of Secondary School Principals, 49(1965):45-49.

The school organizes learning in certain ways established by the "school culture."   It is often presumed that this is the only way you can learn.   This is not the case.   The school emphasizes speed a great deal. It emphasizes being able to answer questions in class very quickly.   It emphasizes certain styles of learning and deemphasizes other styles of learning.   The article discusses the physical style of learning, special talents and thinking, and a new approach to guidance for high school youth who might become dropouts.

12047.   Robinson, J. V., et al.   "Project Probe: A Student-Conducted Study of Truancy.   A Project Report."   ERIC Doc. ED 180 110, June, 1979.

Five current truant, five former truant, and five nontruant junior high school students helped develop a questionnaire used in the Iowa City Community School District.   The survey showed that most student and teacher respondents believed that truancy was highly related to peer influence and that improved relations and communication between students, teachers, and parents would result in improved attendance. See ERIC Abstract #ED 180 110.

12048.   Rogers, J. W.   "A Report of the Team Teaching, Team Governance Program at Rockland Junior High." Rockland, Mass.:   Rockland Public Schools, ERIC Doc. ED 083 123, 1972.

Report describes the low student morale, absenteeism, discipline, and vandalism that prompted the principal and staff to adopt a team teaching format which led to restructuring the school and turning control over to the teachers.   Paper discusses the changes and procedures involved, including the adoption of an experimental curriculum, a six-day cycle, and five schools within a school.   Tables and statistics chart the results of the project, which included a reduction in student absenteeism, vandalism, and suspension.   See ERIC Abstract #ED 083 123.

12049.   Sanders, S. G. and Yarbrough, J. S.   "Bringing order to an inner-city middle school."   Phi Delta Kappan, 58,4(1976):333-334.

A school was reorganized and teachers specially trained for Project Order, which was based on organization for responsibility, dependability, education, and reality.   Objectives of the program included: 1) improving the general school atmosphere as perceived by faculty, students, and parents; 2) improving pupil behavior, 3) improving the teaching/ learning environment so that affective gains could contribute to cognitive gains.   Discipline problems went down 63 percent, referrals to the principal went down 17 percent; corporal punishment went down 93 percent, and suspensions went down 20 percent.   These were measured benefits of the Project and were achieved at a minimum cost in dollars.   Project Order was effective in developing constructive, orderly, and acceptable behavior through reorganization.   The system's motto provided a structure and guide for the planning, implementation, and evaluation of all aspects of school reorganization, along with an adaptability that allowed for changes as the project developed. Organizational and administrative arrangements that were aimed directly at the number one secondary school problem, poor discipline, were highly successful.

12050.   Scott, W. C.   "A middle school's plan for an after-school detention program."   Bulletin of the National Association of Secondary School Principals, 63,424 (1979):55-58.

An after-school detention program was developed to help students increase their self-awareness, understand and respect the rights of others, and increase their ability to relate to their peers, teachers, and other adults. See ERIC Abstract #EJ 196 057.

12051.   Sheridan School District 2. "Project Outreach for Optimum Growth of Alienated Youth Who Reject School: Continuation Application, Dropout Prevention Program, 1972-73." Englewood, Colo., ERIC Doc. ED 074 201, March 15, 1972.

Project Outreach was designed to provide meaningful educational experiences in Sheridan School District for all students and specifically for alienated youth who were potential dropouts or had already rejected school. This project involved basic and widespread changes in organization, curriculum, pupil services, and teacher training. Among the six program components, the Outreach Center is providing services to hard-core dropouts, while the middle school, high school, and pupil personnel services components modified their practices to help students develop improved self-concepts, and the staff training component was designed to provide in-depth training to the project staff and key personnel within the system. See ERIC Abstract #ED 074 201.

12052.   Smith, G. "Rx for curing dropout." Catalyst for Change, 4,2(1975):22-24.

Discusses the value of administering an interest inventory to junior high school students. Also discusses developing an educational program that is geared to student interests and uses a variety of school and community resources. See ERIC Abstract #EJ 110 976.

12053.   Taylor, E. N., et al. "Procedures for Surveying School Problems: Some Individual, Group, and System Indicators. A Manual." Alexandria, Va.: Human Resources Research Organization, ERIC Doc. ED 106 375, 1974.

Describes three instruments for surveying mental health problems in schools (two questionnaires, called the School Problem Area Survey--Staff and the School Problem Area Survey--Students, and an interview guide called the Demographic Information Form) as well as procedures for their use. The questionnaires were designed to obtain information about potential problems which may be treatable through programs carried out by mental health consultants and members of the school staff. See ERIC Abstract #ED 106 375.

12054.   Theimer, W. C., Jr.   "Black Urban Students' View
of Themselves and Their Counselors." Speech given at
the American Personnel and Guidance Association
Convention, New Orleans. Philadelphia: Philadelphia
School District, Office of Research and Evaluation,
ERIC Doc. ED 040 247, March 25, 1970.

In interviews with thirty-nine junior high school
dropouts and twenty-six parents, school and teachers
were rated as adequate, but some teachers were rated
as lacking knowledge of how to deal with students,
and respondents viewed course content as often
irrelevant and uninteresting.   Students wanted new
programs that would help them find jobs and develop
their own identity. The desire to graduate from high
school was not associated with regular attendance,
nor was the desire to move into semiprofessional and
professional occupations.   Students saw lack of
needed courses as the greatest obstacle to finishing
high school. See ERIC Abstract #ED 040 247.

12055.   Upshur, B.   "Analysis of Satellite Program for
Disruptive Children.   Final Report."   Washington,
D.C.: Department of Health, Education and Welfare,
National Institute of Education, Career Education
Program, ERIC Doc. ED 136 468. (No year given.)

This study concerned the influence of special vs.
traditional class placement on forty-three maladjusted junior high students. The Satellite Program
involved some students in a self-contained setting
and some in a traditional departmentalized program.
The Piers-Harris Children's Self-Concept Scale, the
Metropolitan Achievement Test, and the Tennessee
Self-Concept Scale were administered to the students.
Attendance data were also considered.   The control
group had more positive feelings about their behavior
than those in the Satellite Program, and there were
no statistically significant differences in reading
gains by the two groups. Authors recommended special
class assignments for disruptive students. See ERIC
Abstract #ED 136 468.

12056.   West, E. L., et al. "The COOL Connection: alternative to suspension."   Middle School Journal, 9,4
(1978):10-11.

Discusses suspension and expulsion in High Point,
North Carolina, schools.   Alternative learning
centers were established in each junior high school
to combat these problems. See ERIC Abstract #EJ 190
422.

Author Index

Abramowitz, M. W.
  4001, 7001
Adams, C. W.
  10001
Adams, J. F.
  1001
Adams, L.
  7002
Adams, W.
  12001
Adcock, D.
  9001
Ahrens, M. R.
  1002
Ainsworth, L.
  12002
Albert, N.
  10002
Alberty, E. J.
  7160
Alberty, H. B.
  7252
Aldrich, J. C.
  7003
Alessi, S. J.
  4002
Alexander, W. M.
  1003, 1004, 1005, 1130,
  1290, 2001, 2002, 10003
Allegheny Intermediate
  Unit.
  7004
Allen, F. B.
  7005
Allen, R. E.
  7006

Alley, L. E.
  8001
Almen, R. E.
  7007
Alpren, M.
  7008
American Association for
  the Advancement of
  Science.
  7009
American Association of
  School Administrators.
  7010
American Council of Learned
  Societies and National
  Council for the Social
  Studies.
  7011
American Federation of
  Teachers.
  2003, 6001
American Friends Service
  Committee.
  12003
American Industrial Arts
  Association.
  7012
American School Board
  Journal.
  5001, 5002, 5003, 5004,
  5005, 7013
American School and
  University.
  5006, 5007, 5008
Amundson.
  5032

Anastasiow, N. J.
  1006
Anderson, H. S.
  7014
Anderson, J. G.
  10004
Anderson, L. D.
  8002
Anderson, R. H.
  6002, 6003, 6043, 11001
Anderson, W. G.
  2004
Andreen, E. P.
  3001
Andriette, W. R.
  10005
Anes, L.
  1098
Arends, R. H.
  10006
Arey, C.
  7015
Arizona Teacher.
  2005
Arlin, M.
  10007
Armstrong, D. G.
  11002
Arnspiger, R. H.
  7016
Arth, A. A.
  7017, 7202, 11003
Askov, E. N.
  7079, 11004, 11043,
  11044
Association for Childhood
  Education International.
  2006
Association for Supervision
  and Curriculum Develop-
  ment, 1964 Yearbook
  Committee, Doll, R. C.
  (Ed.)
  6006
Association for Supervision
  and Curriculum Develop-
  ment.
  2007, 2008, 2009, 3002,
  4003, 6004, 6005
Association of Wisconsin
  School Administrators.
  8003
Athey, I. J.
  10008
Atkins, N. P.
  1007

Atkins, T. A.
  1008
Augenstein, M. B.
  11005
Backer, R.
  10009
Bahner, J. M.
  6007
Bahnmuller, M.
  10209
Baillie, J. H.
  7018
Bair, M.
  6008
Baker, J. A.
  6009
Baker, L. G.
  10010
Baker, T. P.
  11006
Baker, V. K.
  6010
Bakewell, R. V.
  11107
Baldwin, G. H.
  2010
Ballinger, T. O.
  7019
Bannen, J.
  7020
Bantel, E.
  11007
Bardwell, R. W.
  6051
Barker, R. G.
  1009
Barnes, D. E.
  2011
Barnes, D. G.
  8004
Barnett, L. J.
  1010
Barratt, B. B.
  1011
Barrett, R. E.
  6011
Barrington Middle School.
  2012
Barrow, L. H.
  10011
Baruchin, F.
  1012, 10012
Baruth, L. G.
  4004
Bates, P.
  7020

Batezel, W. G.
 1013
Battlick, D. H.
 1015
Bauer, F. C.
 1016
Bauernfeind, R. H.
 3056
Baughman, M. D.
 1016, 3003, 11008,
 11009,11010
Baur, M. S.
 10013
Baxter, B.
 8005
Bayley, N.
 1159
Baynham, H. D.
 1310
Beals, L.
 3004, 4005
Beane, J. A.
 2013, 6012
Beard, E. M. L.
 7021
Beasley, W. M.
 10159
Beaton, V. L.
 10191
Beavers, W. S.
 4006
Beck, A. T.
 10002
Belcher.
 10052
Bell, E.
 7022
Belovicz, G.
 10239
Belpre City Schools.
 11011
Bender, L. W.
 7023
Benish, J.
 1017
Bennett, H. K.
 5081
Benson, P.
 7024
Berdan, N.
 7049
Berg, L. L.
 10114
Bergland, B. W.
 12004
Bergmann, S. P.
 4007

Berkeley Unified School
 District, Berkeley,
 Calif.
 9002
Berman, S.
 1018
Bernard, J.
 1019
Berns, B.
 10078
Bertis, E.
 7049
Bertolaet, F.
 11138
Bettelheim, B.
 7025
Bick, L. W.
 5009
Bidwell, W. W.
 2032, 7062
Bienenstok, T.
 7026
Billings, R. L.
 2014, 10014
Bingham, N. E.
 7188
Birkmaier, E. M.
 7027
Bishop, D. W.
 6013
Bishop, W. J.
 10015
Blackburn, J. E.
 2083, 11012, 11013
Blair, A. S.
 12005
Blakslee, R. W.
 10016
Blanc, S. S.
 7028
Bloom, J. R.
 7232
Bloomington Metropolitan
 School District, Ind.
 5010
Blyth, D. A.
 10017,10018,10019,10233,
 10234
Bocolo, J. M.
 7029
Bogner, W. F.
 5026
Bohlinger, T.
 4008
Bondi, J.
 1020, 2015, 10020,
 10021,11014

Bonekemper, H. G.
    10022
Bonnar, C. F.
    10023
Booth, N.
    7030
Booth, W.
    9003
Borland, G. F.
    12006
Bortner, D. M.
    7031
Bosher, W. C., Jr.
    10024,11015
Bossing, N. L.
    3005, 7032, 7033, 7034,
    7084, 8006, 11016
Bothwell, K. H.
    5011, 10061
Botts, R. E.
    8007
Bough, M.
    1021, 1022, 2016, 10236
Boutwell, W. V.
    1023
Bouvier, J.
    7035
Bowden, W.
    4026
Bowman, F. H., Jr.
    4035
Bowman, W. E.
    11027
Boy, A.
    4009
Brackett, R. D.
    3006
Braham, R. V.
    8008
Brainard, E.
    11017
Brandt, R.
    1024
Brandwein, P. F.
    7036
Breckenridge, M. E.
    1025
Bretzing, B., II.
    10034
Briggs, T. H.
    1026
Brimm, R. P.
    1027, 1028, 3007
Brinkopf, J. W.
    3008

Briskin, A. S.
    10025
Broadhead, F. C.
    10026
Brod, P.
    2017, 2079, 4010
Brodbelt, S.
    12007
Brodinsky, B.
    1029
Brogdon, R. E.
    11018
Brooks, K.
    10027,10028
Brough, J. R.
    4011
Broward County School
    Board.
    7037
Brown, B. F.
    7038
Brown, E. D.
    6014
Brown, F.
    7039
Brown, I. S.
    8009
Brown, J.
    7040
Brown, J. G.
    11019
Brudy, H. F.
    11020
Brueckner, L. J.
    7041
Bryan, C.
    10029,10184
Bryan, J. N.
    7042
Bryan, K.
    10030
Buchmiller, A. A.
    9004
Budde, R.
    1030, 11021
Budke, W. E.
    7043
Buell, C. E.
    1031, 3009
Buffie, E. G.
    6015
Building Design and
    Construction.
    5012
Buker, M.
    1133

Bulcroft, R.
  10234
Bulletin of the National
  Association of Secondary
  School Principals.
  1032, 3010, 6016
Bureau of Field Studies and
  Surveys.
  3011
Burke, P. J.
  11022
Burkhart, P.
  7044
Burks, J. B.
  4015
Burnett, L. W.
  7045
Burston, N.
  10088
Burt, C. W.
  9005
Burton, D. L.
  7046
Burton, W. H.
  12005
Busaker, W. E.
  4035
Bush, D. M.
  10018,10019,10233,10234
Bush, P. I.
  3012
Butler, C. H.
  7047
Byers, R. S.
  3013
Byhre, E. B.
  6017
CEFP Journal.
  5013
Caldwell, B. M.
  10068
Caldwell, W. E.
  1170
California Association of
  Secondary School
  Principals.
  3014
California Journal of
  Secondary Education.
  3015
California State Department
  of Education.
  1033
Calvert County Board of
  Education.
  9006

Cambridge Independent
  School District 911.
  2018
Cammarota, G.
  7008
Campanale, E. H.
  3016
Campbell County School
  District 1.
  12008
Campbell, J. R.
  11023
Campbell, R. E.
  10031
Canadian Teachers'
  Federation.
  1034
Canady, R. L.
  6032
Canning, J. A.
  10032
Cantlon, R. J.
  1035
Capehart.
  7048, 7049
Caplan, G. (Ed.)
  1036
Carbonell.
  5080
Cardellichio, T. C.
  1037
Carefoot, J.
  1038
Carlson, R.
  1039
Carlson, R. E.
  7050, 10033
Carroll, J. L.
  10034
Carson, M.
  7051
Case, D.
  10035
Case, T. N.
  7052
Casmey, H. B.
  2072
Casteel, J. D.
  4012
Castore, G. F.
  4013
Caul, J. L.
  10036
Cawelti, D. G.
  6082

Center School District 58.
  7053
Center for Early
  Adolescence.
  1040, 1041, 1042, 4014
Central State University,
  College of Education.
  11024
Chal, A. H.
  12004
Chalender, R. E.
  3017
Chall, J. S.
  1043
Chambliss, J.
  10168
Chandler, A. M.
  10037
Charles, A. D.
  2019
Chavez, C.
  12029
Chiara, C.
  7054, 11025
Chismar, Sister M. H.
  10038
Chop, W. C.
  2020
Christenson, G. A.
  10039
Church, J.
  1286
Clapp, F. W.
  5026
Claremont Graduate School.
  6018
Clark, L. H.
  4015
Clarke, D. H.
  1044
Clarke, H. H.
  1044
Clarke, S.
  11026
Clasen, R. E.
  11027
Clear Creek Independent
  School District.
  1045
Clearinghouse.
  3018
Clinchy, E.
  5014, 6019
Clute, M.
  8010, 11046

Cobain, H.
  10040
Cockfield, D.
  7161
Coe, T. R.
  1046
Cole, L.
  1047
Coleman, J. S.
  1048, 1049, 1050, 8011
College of Education,
  University of Kentucky.
  11028
Collins, D.
  8012
Collister, E. G.
  1173
Commission on Secondary
  Schools and Commission
  on Research and Service.
  3019, 3020, 3021
Commission on the Reorgani-
  zation of Secondary
  Education.
  1051
Committee for Economic
  Development, Research
  and Policy Committee.
  6020
Committee on Adolescence,
  Group for the Advance-
  ment of Psychiatry.
  1052
Commonwealth Learning, Inc.
  12009, 12010
Commonwealth of Kentucky,
  Department of Education.
  11029
Commonwealth of Virginia,
  Department of Education.
  9007
Compton, C.
  2021
Compton, M. F.
  1053, 2022, 2023, 2024,
  11030
Conant, J. B.
  1054, 8013, 10041, 11031
Connecticut State Depart-
  ment of Education.
  2025, 3022
Conover, H. R.
  11032
Constant, G. A.
  1055

Cook, D. H.
  1056
Cook, P.
  7055
Cook, R. F.
  6096
Cooper, C.
  9001
Coplein.
  7141
Coppock, N.
  1057, 2026
Corbally, J. E.
  1058
Corbett, L. H.
  4012
Corbett, W. T., Jr.
  4012
Costantino, P. S.
  10042
Costantino, R.
  7056
Costar, J. W.
  4016
Cotterell, J. L.
  10043
Cottingham, H. F.
  4017
Council for Administrative
  Leadership.
  6021
Council for Basic
  Education.
  7057
Council on Junior High
  School Administration.
  3023
Covert, W. O.
  11033
Craig, M. L.
  7058
Cramer, R. V.
  3005, 7059
Crane, R. L.
  12011
Crawford, P.
  10252
Creamer, J. K.
  4018
Creamer, R. C.
  4018
Creek, R. J.
  10044
Croft Educational Services.
  1059, 2027

Cronin, R. L.
  8014
Crosby, H. H.
  7060
Crouter, A.
  10088
Crow, L. D.
  1060
Cuff, W. A.
  2028, 2029
Cunningham, G. S.
  7021
Curtis, R. L., Jr.
  10045,10046
Curtis, T. E.
  1061, 1062, 2030, 2031,
  2032, 7061, 7062, 10047
Cutler, M. H.
  2033, 5015, 5016, 5017
Cutler, S. J.
  8058
Cyphert, F. R.
  7063, 7064, 7065
Dacus, W. P.
  10048
Dade County Public Schools,
  Fla.
  7066, 10049
Damico, S. B.
  12012
Daniels, L. M.
  3024
Darien Public Schools.
  1063
Darling, G.
  1064
Dasenbrock, D. H.
  10050
Davey, E. J.
  7067
Davis, E. L.
  10051
Davis, H. S.
  6022, 6023, 7068
Davis, R. B.
  1065
Davis.
  10052
Dayton University, Office
  of Educational Services.
  10053
De Bruler, L.
  10181
De Vito, A.
  11034

deCharms, R.
   12037
DeFrancesco, I.
   7069
DeVane, L. M., Jr.
   11035
DeVita, J. C.
   2034
Dean, A. O.
   5018
Dean, S. E.
   11036
Dearborn, Mich., Public
   Schools.
   9008, 10054
Deaton, J. C., Sr.
   7070
Delavan, F. E.
   6024
Delaware Valley School
   District.
   7071
Deller, D. K.
   7072
Denman, T.
   7073
Dennis, E. G.
   10055
Denton, W. D.
   3025
DesJarlais, L.
   1066
Detjen, E. W.
   4019
Detjen, M. E. F.
   4019
Detjen, N. G.
   10056
Dettre, J. R.
   2035
DiVirgilio, J.
   1067, 2036, 6025, 7074,
   7075
Diamond, H. J.
   6038
Dillon, E. A.
   11086
Dippo, J.
   7076
Disinger, J. F.
   10057
District of Columbia Public
   Schools, Department of
   Research and Evaluation.
   10058

Division of Instructional
   Learning Systems,
   Charleston, West
   Virginia.
   9009
Dixon, N. R.
   11037
Docking, R.
   6026
Donovan, B.
   9010
Dornseif, A. W.
   10059,10227
Dorr, M.
   1122
Dougherty, A. M.
   4020
Dougherty, J. H.
   6027
Douglass, H. R.
   1112, 3026, 3027, 3035,
   7101, 10060,
   10144,10145,11038
Douglass, M. P.
   6028
Downing, L. L.
   10061
Doyle, D.
   10114
Drake, J. C.
   5019
Drash, A.
   1068
Dravatz, B.
   7077
Drummond, H. D.
   6029
Duchi, S. A., Jr.
   10062
Duffy, G. G.
   7078
Duffy, S.
   9026
Dugan, C. L.
   10063
Dukelow, D. A.
   8015
Dunn, J. A.
   8046
Dunn, K.
   11039
Dunn, R.
   11039
Dunn, S. V.
   6030

Dupuis, M. M.
    7079, 11004, 11040, 11041,
    11042, 11043, 11044
Durall, E. P.
    10064
Duran, L. A.
    5020
Dysinger, D. W.
    12013
Dyson.
    7141
Eash, M. J.
    8016
Eckstein, W.
    1069
Edelfelt, R. A.
    11045
Edgerly, R. F.
    4021
Edgmon, A. W.
    7080
Edling, J. V.
    6031
Education, U.S.A.
    2037
Educational Equipment and
    Materials.
    2038
Educational Facilities
    Laboratories.
    2039, 2040, 5021
Educational Leadership
    Institute.
    2042, 2043
Educational Leadership.
    2041, 3028
Educational Products
    Information Exchange
    Institute.
    7081
Educational Research
    Council of Greater
    Cleveland.
    3029
Educational Research
    Services.
    10065
Edwards, C. H.
    10066
Edwards, R. P.
    12041
Egnatuck, T.
    2044
Ehrlich, V.
    10067

Eichhorn, D. H.
    1070, 1072, 1073, 1074,
    1170, 2045, 2046, 2047,
    2048, 2049
Eichorn, D. H.
    1071
Elardo, P. T.
    10068
Elicker, P. E.
    3030
Elie, M.
    10069
Elkind, D.
    1075, 1076, 1077
Elliott, R. W.
    1078
Ellis, J. R.
    3031, 7082, 10070
Elwell, W. C.
    8034
Emmert, B. A.
    10071
English, J. J.
    6032
Epstein, H. T.
    1079, 1080
Epstein, J. L.
    10072, 10073
Ericksen, J. K.
    7144
Erikson, E.
    10029, 10184
Erie County Board of
    Education.
    7083
Ernst, L.
    5022
Espenschade, A.
    1081
Essex, M. W.
    10074
Estrada, R. J.
    7024
Evans, C. L.
    8017, 10075, 10076
Evans, R. C.
    7288
Eve, A. W.
    2050
Everett, F. U.
    7058
Everhart, R. B.
    3032
Ewert, B.
    10143

Fairfield Public Schools.
    9011
Fallon, J. P.
    10077
Farran, D. C.
    6033
Farris, L. P.
    1082
Faunce, R. C.
    7084, 11046
Faust, M. S.
    1083
Fazzaro, C. J.
    6034
Feld, M.
    10078
Feldhusen, J. F.
    12014
Felmlee, D.
    10103
Fenwick, J. J.
    1084
Ference, C.
    4022
Ferguson, W. J.
    1085
Ferrer, T.
    10079
Fine, B.
    1086
Finkelstein, E. L.
    10102
Finley, R.
    2051, 6035
Finnegan, H.
    12015
Fiordaliso, R.
    12016
Fisher, D. L.
    6036
Fisher, L.
    10080
Fisk, R. S.
    11047
Flanders, J. N.
    4023
Flanders, N. A.
    11048
Flanigan, M. C.
    7085
Fleming, R. F.
    6037
Fletcher, B. J.
    4024, 4060
Flinker, E.
    2052

Florida State Department of
    Education.
    2053, 2054, 5023
Fogg, W. F.
    6038
Folgate, C. C.
    11049
Ford Foundation.
    7086, 11050
Ford, E. A.
    1087
Ford, P. M.
    10006, 10040
Forst, C. F.
    10081
Fournet, G. P.
    7097
Fox, D. F.
    10082
Fox, D. J.
    2055
Fox, J. H., Jr.
    1088
Fox, L. H.
    7087
Frank, J., Jr.
    8018
Frank, L. K.
    1089
Frankel, E.
    10083, 10084
Fraser, D.
    2056
Fraser, D. M.
    7088
Fraser, D. W.
    11051
Frazier, G. W.
    1090
Frederick, O. I.
    1281
Frederick, R. W.
    8019
Freeman, E.
    7195
Fresno County Schools.
    5024
Frey, S. H.
    10085
Friedman, R. M.
    7089
Fritschel, A. L.
    11052
Fryklund, V.
    8020

Frymier, J.
  10086
Fuchs, J. E.
  12017
Fuller, K. A.
  8021
Fuller, M.
  10188
Furlong, C. B.
  2057
Gabel, D.
  10087
Gabor, G. M.
  7090
Galano, R. W.
  2106
Gallina, M. N.
  2058
Garbarino, J.
  10088
Garcia, G. B.
  10089
Gardner, G. A.
  7091
Garner, A. E.
  6039, 11083
Garstens, H. L.
  7092
Garty, R. H.
  10090
Garvelink, R. H.
  2059, 2060
Gastright, J. F.
  10165
Gastwirth, P.
  1091, 1092
Gatewood, T. E.
  2061, 10091, 10092, 10093,
  10094, 11053, 11054
Gaumnitz, W. H.
  1093, 1094, 10095
Gauvain, M. T.
  10096
Gay, G.
  1095
Gee, T.
  7093
Geisinger, R. W.
  10097
George, P. S.
  1096, 2062, 2063, 3033,
  6040, 10098, 11055, 11056
Georgia State Department of
  Education.
  7094, 9012

Georgiady, N. P.
  1097, 2064, 2065, 2110,
  7095
Gerard, G. K.
  8022
Gerber, D.
  10182
Gesell, A.
  1098
Gibb, E. G.
  11057
Gibbs, J.
  7096
Gibson, J. T.
  1099
Gillan, R. E.
  11058, 11059, 11060
Glancy, P. B.
  6041
Glass, J. M.
  1100
Glasser, W.
  12018
Glatthorn, A.
  1101, 1194
Glenn, E. E.
  6042
Glines, D. E.
  1102
Glissmeyer, C. H.
  10099
Godbold, J. V.
  7097
Golub, L. S.
  7098
Goode, R. C.
  10252
Goodlad, J. I.
  6043, 6044
Gordon, J.
  10100
Gorman, F. H.
  6027
Gorwood, B.
  1103
Grady, J. B.
  8023
Graham, G.
  8024
Grambs, J. D.
  3034
Granite School District.
  11061
Grant, W. R., Sr.
  4025

Gray, R.
  1104
Green, D. R.
  6045
Green, R. C.
  10101
Greenfeld, N.
  10102
Greer, E. S.
  10271
Grimm, R. L.
  7215
Groden, A. F.
  1105
Grooms, A.
  1106
Grooms, M. A.
  2066
Gross, E.
  11062
Gross, R.
  5025
Gross, S.
  10059
Grosse Point, Michigan,
  Public School System.
  1107
Grossnickle, F. E.
  7099
Gruhn, W. T.
  1108, 1109, 1110, 1111,
  1112, 1113, 3035, 7100,
  7101
Gulf School Researcher.
  1114
Gump, P. V.
  1009
Hackett, D.
  7102
Hagstrum, A. A.
  6003
Hale, C. J.
  1115
Hale, N.
  1057
Hall, H. L.
  4026
Hall, R. V.
  12019
Haller, C. E.
  4027
Hallinan, M.
  10103
Hallman, C. L.
  7027

Ham, I.
  9003
Hamblen.
  10248
Hamm, R. L.
  1022, 3036, 7103
Handel, G.
  1010
Hannan, T. T.
  11063
Hansen, J. C.
  4029
Hansen, J. H.
  2067
Hanson, J. W.
  4028
Hanson, N. G.
  1116
Hantula, J.
  7104
Hardcastle, K.
  10030
Hardesty, L.
  12020
Hargreaves, A.
  1117
Harlan, H.
  11064
Harlem Consolidated School
  District 122.
  12021
Harmer, E. W.
  7105
Harnett, A. L.
  7106
Harper, T.
  10104
Harries, E.
  7107
Harrington, H. L.
  3037
Harris, D. E.
  10105
Harris, J. D.
  10034
Harrison County Continuing
  Education Council and
  Teacher Education
  Center.
  9013
Harrison, R.
  1089
Hartman, R. A.
  10106
Hartman, R. D.
  11065

Hartwig, K. E.
    6024
Harvell, H.
    7108
Harvey, J. P.
    1118
Harvey, P. J.
    11066
Hatch, M.
    8025
Hatley, R. V.
    10107
Haueter, L. R.
    7109
Havighurst, R. J.
    1119, 1120, 1121, 1122,
    11067, 12022
Hawke, S.
    7110, 7111
Hawn, H.
    10086
Hayden, B. S.
    12023
Hayes, G. A.
    11068
Hayes, M.
    4030
Heald, J. E.
    2110
Hearn, A. C.
    2067, 7112
Heathers, G.
    6046, 6047, 6048
Hedberg, J. D.
    1263, 10108
Hedgecock, L.
    1123
Heffernan, H.
    1124
Heffner, C. P.
    11069
Heilbron, P. D.
    1125
Hein, F. V.
    8015
Heironomous, N. C.
    1126
Heller, R. W.
    1127, 4029
Hellersberg, E.
    1089
Hemphill, J. K.
    11117, 11118
Henrich, M.
    7113

Henry, N. B.
    6049
Hergebroth, E. H.
    7114
Herrick, J. H.
    5026
Herring, L. H.
    8026
Herriott, M. E.
    1128
Herron, J. D.
    10087
Hester, H.
    11070
Hickerson, J.
    7115
Hicks, J. A.
    4030
Hiebert, R.
    10107
High School Journal.
    3038
Highline Public Schools.
    7116
Hiles, D.
    7117
Hill, R.
    9003
Hillson, M.
    1129
Hillyer, J. L.
    10109
Hines, V.
    1130, 2068
Hinkley, G.
    9014
Hinrichs, R. S.
    7118
Hoats, W. R.
    11071
Hobbs, M. E.
    1131
Hodges, A.
    7049
Hodges, M. F.
    11072
Hoffman, A. J.
    7119
Hoffman, J.
    5027
Hoffman, N. L.
    7119
Hoffmann, E. B.
    6050
Hogan, D.
    6026

Holliston Public Schools.
    2069
Holloway, W. H.
    10107
Holmes, J. A.
    10008
Holmgren, C. A.
    10110
Holyoak, O. J.
    7006
Hood, C. E.
    2070
Hoover, K. H.
    11073
Hoover, N. R.
    8027
Hopke, W. E.
    4017
Hoppe, A.
    7120
Horrocks, J. E.
    1132, 1133
Hott, L.
    7121
Houston, L.
    7122
Houtman.
    10052
Howard County Board of
    Education.
    7126
Howard, A. W.
    1134, 1135, 1288, 7123,
    7124, 7125, 10111,11019,
    11074
Howard, E. R.
    6051
Howell, B.
    1136
Howell, C. E.
    10112
Huber, J. D.
    1137, 2071
Hubert, J. B.
    11075,11076,11077
Hughes, C. L.
    1279
Hughes, D. E.
    3039
Hughes, F. W.
    10113
Hughes, W. O.
    7127
Hull, J. D.
    1093

Hull, J. H.
    1138, 1139
Human Development Training
    Institute.
    4031
Hunt, J. J.
    10114
Hunt, J. T.
    1140
Hunter, M.
    1141
Hurd, P. D.
    7128, 7129
Hurley, B.
    6037
Hurlock, E. B.
    1142
Hutson, P. W.
    10023
Hyland, A.
    6052
Hyland, T.
    11078
Hynes, M. E.
    10136
Ikeda, K.
    8058
Ilg, F.
    1098
Illinois State University.
    1143
Illinois Teacher of Home
    Economics.
    7130
Imhof, H. E.
    9015
Inhelder, B.
    1144
Institute for Development
    of Educational
    Activities.
    6053
Instructional Objectives
    Exchange.
    7131
Instructor.
    5028, 6054
Irwin, J. R.
    12024
Isacksen, R. O.
    1145
Jackson, M. H.
    10250
Jacobs, J. W.
    10115

Jacobson, M. E.
  12011
James, S. M.
  7132, 11079
Jenkins, A. E., III.
  12025
Jennings, H. H.
  4032
Jennings, W.
  1146, 7133, 7134
Jensen, B. H.
  11080
Jensen, H. L.
  10116
Jensen, J. T.
  1058
Jensen, K.
  1147
Jensen, L.
  6071
Jersild, A. T.
  1148
Jester, J. F., Jr.
  10117
Joan, D. R.
  1149
Joans, R. L.
  10118
Johns, F.
  2131
Johnson, E.
  1150, 11025
Johnson, E. G.
  4033
Johnson, H.
  9003
Johnson, L.
  4034
Johnson, M., Jr.
  1151, 1152, 1153, 1154,
  1155, 1277, 3040, 4035,
  11081
Johnson, S. C.
  1156
Johnston, E. G.
  8028
Johnston, J. H.
  10100,10119,11082
Johnston, R. J.
  2072
Joint Commission on Mental
  Health of Children,
  Committees on Education
  and Religion.
  1157

Jones, C. K.
  2073
Jones, D. R.
  2074
Jones, F. R.
  12026
Jones, M. C.
  1158, 1159
Jones, P.
  11083
Jordon, J. W.
  8029
Josselyn, I. M.
  1160, 1161
Journal of School Health.
  1162
Junior High School Association of Illinois.
  7135, 8030
Junior High School
  Workshop.
  11084
Jurenas, A. C.
  1163
Jurich, A. P.
  7251
Jurjevich, J. C., Jr.
  7136
Justman, J.
  10120
Justus, J. E.
  5029
Kaback, G. R.
  11085
Kagan, J.
  1164, 1165
Kaiser, D. W.
  7137
Kalamazoo Public Schools.
  7138
Kaspert, J.
  7117
Katzenmeyer, C. G.
  10136
Katzer, W. D.
  8031
Kaufman, J. F.
  7034
Kealy, R. P.
  1004, 10121
Keck, M. B.
  4036
Keedy, M. L.
  7139
Kehas, C. D.
  10122

Keliher, A. B.
  6037
Kelley, E. A.
  11086
Kelly, D. H.
  12027
Kennedy Junior High School.
  6055
Kenny, F. X.
  4037
Kerr, R. D.
  1166
Kesner, P. M.
  4038
Ketron, S. R.
  4039
Khan, M. W.
  10123
Kibblewhite, S.
  7140
Kidder, F. R.
  10124
Kindred, L. W.
  1167
Kindred.
  7141
King, D. C.
  7142
King, M. J.
  10125
Kinghorn, J. R.
  2098
Kittel, J. E.
  1168
Klein, I. R.
  5030
Klein, R. L.
  4015
Knopp, M. A.
  7143
Knowles, P. L.
  10126
Knudsen, G.
  4040
Koepsel, E. A.
  10127
Kohen-Raz, R.
  1169
Kohl, J. W.
  1170
Kohlmann, E. L.
  7144
Kohut, S., Jr.
  10128,11087
Kokomo Consolidated School
    Corp.
  7145

Konicek, R.
  7146
Koos, L. B.
  1171, 1172, 1281, 3041,
    10129
Kopp, O. W.
  10130
Kops, P.
  10088
Kramer, L.
  9016
Krevolin, N.
  7147
Krinsky, J. L.
  11088
Kroenke, R. G.
  7148
Krug, E. A.
  6056
Kruger, J. M.
  10131
Kuhlen, R. G.
  1173, 1174
Kunzweiler, C. E.
  2075
Kurth, R. J.
  7149
Kurtz, V. R.
  7150
Kvaraceus, W. C.
  12028
LaRoe, M. E.
  7151
LaRue, C. J.
  7056
Lagana, J. F.
  2122
Lahaderne, H. M.
  10132
Lambert, P. D.
  11089
Landers, J.
  1175
Landes, J. L.
  5075
Landman, J.
  6057
Larson, C. O.
  9016
Larson, J. C.
  9017
Lasseigne, M. W.
  10133
Lauchner, A. H.
  1176, 7152, 10134

Lavender, J.
  7153
Lawhead, V. B.
  6058, 7154
Lawrence, G.
  1177, 11090
Lawson, A. E.
  10135
Laycock, F.
  8058
Lazzaro, E.
  4041
Lee, B. J.
  1174
Lee, F.
  3042
Lee, J.
  4042
Leeds, W. L.
  7155
Leeper, R. R.
  2076
Leggett, S.
  5031
Lehr, J. B.
  11091
Leigh, T. G.
  6059
Leipold, L. E.
  1178
Leonard, J. P.
  1179, 7156
Lerrigo, M. O.
  4043
Lesyk, C. K.
  10136
Levenda, T. A.
  11092
Lewis, G. M.
  1180, 10137
Lewis, J.
  4044
Licata, J. W.
  11093
Liddle, C.
  6056
Liederman, E.
  3043
Lifton, E.
  7117
Lincoln Public Schools.
  4045, 11094
Linebarger, D. E.
  10138
Linton, H. W.
  12029

Lipka, R. P.
  2013
Lipsitz, J. S.
  1181, 10139, 11095
Little Rock Public Schools.
  9018
Livingston, H.
  1182
Livingston, S. A.
  10140, 10141
Lloyd-Jones, E.
  4046
Loepp, F. L.
  10142
Logsdon, D. M.
  10143
Long, D.
  7245
Long, F. E.
  3044
Loomis, M. J.
  1183, 1184
Loost, W. R.
  1185
Lounsbury, J. H.
  1186, 1187, 1188, 1189,
  1318, 2077, 3045, 3046,
  3069, 10144, 10145, 10146
Lovetere, J. P.
  6060
Low, C. M.
  1190
Lowe, A. D.
  6061
Lowe, J. Y.
  8032
Lowry, A.
  7157
LuPold, H. G.
  6062
Ludden, W.
  8033
Lufler, H. S., Jr.
  12030
Lulich, M.
  1263
Lum, S.
  7158
Lumpkin, D.
  7159
Lurry, L. P.
  7160
Lutes.
  5032
Lyman, L.
  10209

Lynch, J. J.
  2078
MacConnell, J. D.
  5033
MacKenzie, W. J.
  8034
Macari, C. C.
  7001
Macauly, G.
  1191
Machek, K.
  7161
Machover, K.
  1089
Madon, C. A.
  2079
Magid, M. K.
  5034
Maguire, H. P.
  5035
Malinka, R.
  10236,10237,11055,11096,
  11097
Malm, M.
  3047
Man/Society/Technology.
  7162
Mandersheid, R. W.
  4061
Manitoba Department of
  Education.
  1192
Manlove, D. C.
  3048, 1193, 11100
Manolakes, G.
  6037
Manone, C.
  1101, 1194
Marani, J. B.
  10146
Marascuilo, L. A.
  10147
Marcus, L.
  10148
Mari.
  10052
Maring, G. H.
  10149
Marion County Board of
  Public Instruction.
  6063
Markle, G.
  10100,11082
Marshall, D. L.
  10150

Martin, E. C.
  1195
Martinson, F. M.
  1196
Martorana, S. V.
  10151
Maryland State Department
  of Educational Curric-
  ulum Studies.
  1197
Mason, E. P.
  10152,10153
Massachusetts Association
  of Health, Physical Education and Recreation,
  Research in Education
  Commission.
  8035
Massialas, B. G.
  8036
Matala, D. C.
  11057
Matthews, L.
  9003
May, D. C.
  10154
Maybee, G. D.
  1198
Mazza, P.
  7163
McCaffery, J. F.
  12031
McCaig, T. E.
  10155
McCann, C. K.
  10119
McCarthy, R. J.
  2080, 2081, 6064
McClure, J.
  2016
McClurkin, W. D.
  5036
McCormick, M. J.
  1199
McCracken, R. A.
  11098
McCrory, D. L.
  11099
McCurdy, B.
  12032
McDonald, W.
  2082, 10156
McEachen, H. D.
  8037
McEwin, C. K.
  11056

McGee, J. C.
2083
McGlasson, M.
1200, 1201, 3048, 3049,
10157,11100
McGuffey, C. W.
9019
McHugh, E. A.
2084
McLeary, R. D.
5026
McLure, J.
10236,10237
McMahon, M. P.
1202
McMillan, J. H.
10158
McMillan, M.
11055
McNally, M.
2131
McNamara, J. A.
9035
McNassor, D.
1203, 1204
McNeil, E. B.
1205, 1206
McPartland, J. M.
10072,10073
McQueen, M.
1207
McTeer, J. H.
7164, 10159
Mead, M.
1208, 1209, 1210
Means, L. E.
8038
Mechling, K. R.
11101
Meehan, M. L.
8039, 10160
Meeks, J. W.
11102
Mehit, G.
1211
Meister, R. W.
7165, 10161
Meleny, H. E.
1081, 1212
Mellinger, M.
2085
Mercurio, C.
1175
Merenbloom, E. Y.
6065, 8040

Merritt, D. L.
7166
Merz, W. R.
1213
Metz, M. H.
1214, 12033
Michigan Association of
School Boards.
1215
Mickelson, J. M.
7167
Mickelson.
7141
Middle School Journal.
12034
Midjaas, C. L.
2086, 5037, 5038
Miles, D.
4044
Miles, L. C.
7168
Miller, C. S.
2058
Miller, D.
7266
Miller, D. R.
10162
Miller, F. M.
10163
Miller, J. F.
10164
Miller, L. P.
4047
Mills, G. E.
5039
Mills, R. C.
11053
Millu, M. J.
5038
Milwaukee Public Schools,
Office of the Super-
intendent of Schools.
1216
Mindess, D.
2087
Minkler, M.
7169
Minnesota Instructional
Materials Center.
7170
Minnich, W. K.
10165
Mirsky, A. F.
1043
Mitchell, E. D.
8041

Mitchell, J. J.
    1217
Mitchell, W. E.
    7171
Modern Schools.
    5040, 5041, 5042, 5043,
    5044, 5045, 5046, 5047,
    5048, 5049
Moeckel.
    5080
Mooney, P.
    2128, 10166
Moore, J.
    2088
Moos, R. H.
    10167
Morrison, W.
    2089
Morse, W. C.
    1218, 11103
Mortimore, D. E.
    3050
Moseley, P. A.
    7149
Mosher, R. L.
    1219
Moss, H. A.
    1165
Moss, T.
    1220, 1221, 2090
Mott, K.
    7172
Moulton, R. W.
    10246
Mowrey, L.
    1193
Moyer, D. H.
    12035, 12036
Muir, M. S.
    12037
Mullen, D. J.
    5050
Muller, D.
    10168
Murphy, J.
    2091, 5025
Murphy, L. B.
    1222
Murray, J. N.
    1223
Murray, K.
    10067
Murray, M.
    7173
Murwin, S.
    7173

Muus, R. E.
    1224
Myers, J. D. V.
    1297
Myers, N. K.
    10169
Nampa School District 133.
    7174
Nanuet Public Schools.
    6066
Napier, G.
    9026
Nardelli, W.
    7175
Nashville-Davidson County
    Metropolitan Public
    Schools.
    7176
Nation's Schools.
    2092, 2093, 2094, 3051,
    5051, 5052, 5053, 5054,
    5055, 5056
National Association of
    Secondary School Prin-
    cipals, Committee on
    Junior High School
    Education.
    1225, 1226
National Association of
    Secondary School
    Principals.
    3052, 7177, 7178, 8042,
    10170,11104
National Association of
    State Directors of
    Teacher Education and
    Certification and Ameri-
    can Association for the
    Advancement of Science.
    7179
National Council of
    Teachers of Mathematics.
    7180
National Council on School
    House Construction.
    5057
National Education
    Association Journal.
    7185
National Education
    Association, American
    Association of School
    Administrators.
    10175

National Education
    Association, Department
    of Superintendents.
    7182
National Education
    Association, Educational
    Policies Commission.
    7183, 8043
National Education
    Association, Educational
    Research Service.
    10176,10177
National Education
    Association, National
    School Public Relations
    Association.
    1227
National Education Associa-
    tion, Project on the
    Instructional Program of
    the Public Schools.
    7184
National Education
    Association, Research
    Division.
    10178,10179,12038
National Education
    Association.
    6067, 6068, 7181, 9020,
    9021, 10171,10172,10173,
    10174,11105
National Elementary
    Principal.
    7186
National School Board
    Association.
    9022
National Study of Secondary
    School Evaluation.
    1228, 4048
Nebraska State Department
    of Education.
    10180
Neel, R. S.
    10181
Neill, S. B.
    7187
Nelson, B. H.
    4049
Nelson, C.
    7113
Nesbitt, D. R.
    7188
Nesset, B. C.
    4050

New Hampshire State Depart-
    ment of Education.
    1229
New Jersey State Department
    of Education.
    1230, 2095, 6069
New Mexico State Department
    of Education.
    9023
New York City Board of
    Education.
    7189, 9024, 9025
New York State Education
    Department.
    7190, 7191
Newlove, B. W.
    11106
Newsweek.
    12039
Nickerson, N. C., Jr.
    1231, 6070
Nickols, B. S.
    7192
Nield, J. B.
    9026
Nielsen, A.
    10182
Noall, M. F.
    6071, 7193
Noar, G.
    1232, 1233
Nolan, M.
    9027
Nolan, R. R.
    10096, 11119
Nordholm, H.
    11107
North Dakota State Board
    for Vocational Education
    at Bismarck.
    7194
Noyce, C. G.
    3034
O'Brien, J. L.
    10183
O'Connell, W. I.
    6072
O'Dell, F. L.
    4051
Oakley, J. P.
    8044
Odell, W.
    1234, 9028
Oden, W. E.
    12040

Odetola, T.
    10184
Oestreich, A. H.
    1235
Office of Public
    Instruction.
    6074
Office of Secondary and
    Vocational Education,
    St. Paul, Minn.
    3053
Office of the County
    Superintendent of
    Schools.
    6073
Ogletree, E. J.
    1236
Ohio School Counselors
    Association.
    4052
Ohles, J. F.
    1237
Olds, H. F.
    6085
Olsen, F.
    6075
Olsen, L. K.
    10225
Olsen, M.
    7017
Olson, A. T.
    7195
Olson, C.
    10185
Olson, J. C.
    9029
Olson, N. G.
    2096
Olympia Public Schools.
    9030
Omaha Public Schools.
    2097
Onofrio, J. E.
    10186
Oregon Consolidated
    Schools, Wis.
    6076
Orloff, J. H.
    7196
Osmon, R. V.
    3054
Otto, A. C.
    7197
Otto, H. A.
    1238

Otto, S. T.
    1238
Ovard, G. F.
    1239
Overly, D. E.
    2098, 5058
Overton, H.
    7198
Overview.
    2099
Ovsiew, L.
    7199
Pabst, R. L.
    11108
Pace, V.
    1201, 10157
Page, D. P.
    12041
Page, W. R.
    7200
Palminteri, P.
    7201
Pansino, L. P.
    1240
Paparella, P.
    1241
Paradis, E. E.
    7202
Parker, F.
    1242
Parkin, D.
    7117
Partin, C. S.
    1243
Passow, A. H.
    1244
Patrick, J. J.
    6077
Patterson, F.
    1245, 3034
Paxson, W. M.
    9031
Peetoom, A.
    7203
Pence, W. R., Jr.
    6078
Pennsbury School Board.
    9032
Pennsylvania School Study
    Council.
    2101
Pennsylvania State Depart-
    ment of Education,
    Bureau of Curriculum
    Services.
    7204

Pennsylvania State
   Department of Education.
   2100
Perkes, V. A.
   11109
Perry, I. L.
   2102
Peterson, J. L.
   10070
Petruzielo, F. R.
   12042
Phi Delta Kappan.
   3055
Philadelphia Public
   Schools.
   7205
Philadelphia School
   District, Office of
   Curriculum and
   Instruction.
   7206
Philadelphia School
   District.
   5059, 5060
Philadelphia Urban League.
   9033
Phillips, C. A.
   6027
Phillips, M. W.
   4004
Piaget, J.
   1144
Pianko, N.
   2052
Piele, P.
   2103
Pierce, L.
   9003
Pine, G.
   4009
Pine, G. J.
   11110
Pingry, R. W.
   7207
Pink, W. T.
   10187
Pint, R. F.
   6079
Pitkin, V. E.
   1246, 8045
Pittsburgh Public Schools.
   2121
Pittsfield Public Schools.
   9034
Ploghoft, R. E.
   7208

Plumley, D. L.
   8046
Plutte, W.
   1247
Politzer, R. L.
   7209
Pontiac City School
   District.
   7210
Popper, S. H.
   1248, 1249, 1250, 1251,
   1333, 2104, 11062,11111,
   11112
Portland Public Schools.
   7211
Post, R. L.
   1252
Powell, A.
   7212
Powell, G. J.
   10188
Powell, J. H.
   10248
Powell, R. H.
   10189
Powell, W.
   6080, 11113
Powers, L. S.
   7213
Pozdol, M.
   10237
Prawat, R. S.
   10190
Pray, H. E.
   9035
Prescott, D. A.
   1253
Preston, R. L.
   2098
Progressive Architecture.
   5061, 5062, 5063
Pumerantz, P.
   1254, 2034, 2105, 2106,
   10240,11055,11088,11114
Purkey, W. W.
   1255
Putnam, R.
   1256
Putney, E.
   2107
Rabinowitz, F. M.
   10191
Rabuck, J.
   7228
Rackauskas, J. A.
   2085

Radov, C.
    10078
Ramsey, M.
    9036
Range, D. G.
    11115
Rankin, H. J.
    10192,10193
Rankin, S.
    7214
Rash, A. M.
    7215
Ray, W. E.
    7216
Raymer, J.
    6081
Read, B.
    10194
Reagan, E. E.
    1257
Redl, F.
    1258, 1259, 1274, 4053
Reece, J. L.
    10195
Reed, C.
    7217
Reese, S. C.
    12043
Reese, W. M.
    4054
Rehage, K.
    6044
Reichert, J. L.
    8047
Reid, J. L.
    5064
Reid, M.
    7246
Remmers, H. H.
    3056
Research for Better
    Schools, Inc.
    7218
Reum, E.
    8048
Reynolds, C.
    12044
Reynolds, L. J.
    3057
Rice, A.
    11116
Richardson, J. A.
    2108, 6082
Richardson, S. K.
    1274

Richland County Board of
    Education.
    12045
Richter, M. G.
    5065
Riegle, J.
    2109, 2065, 8049, 10196
Riessman, F.
    12046
Riggs, N. D.
    1260, 10197
Riley, H. W.
    6045
Riley, R. D.
    10198
Ringers, J., Jr.
    5066
Ringness, T. A.
    10199
Rist, F. H.
    9037
Ritz, J. M.
    1261, 7219
Rizzo, M. E.
    8050
Robertson, J. C.
    3034
Robertson, W.
    10189
Robinson, A. A.
    3024
Robinson, G.
    1262
Robinson, J. V.
    12047
Robinson, L. S.
    4055
Robinson, M.
    7220
Robinson, M. Z.
    1122
Robinson, W. M.
    6003
Rock, D. A.
    11117,11118
Rodgers, P. C.
    10200
Roe, V.
    3066, 10205
Roehler, L. R.
    7221
Roffers, D. W.
    10201
Rogers, H. J.
    3058

Rogers, J. W.
  12048
Roistacher, R. C.
  10202
Roman, R. J.
  7222
Romano, L. G.
  1097, 1263, 2064, 2065,
  2110, 6083, 7095
Roper, S. S.
  10096, 11119
Rose, H. C.
  11120
Rosenfeld, G.
  7223
Rosser, M. A.
  3059
Roth, R.
  10203
Rothman, G. R.
  10204
Rottier, J.
  11121
Rowe, F. A.
  4056, 8051
Rowe, R. N.
  1264
Roweton.
  10052
Roy, J. E.
  10206
Royal Oak City School
  District.
  4057
Royer, J. S.
  10207
Ruud, O. G.
  10208
Ryan, F. L.
  7224
Ryan, M. K.
  4058, 4059, 4060
Sagar, H. A.
  10216
Samuels, S.
  10209
Samuelson, E. V.
  3060
San Diego Unified School
  District.
  7225
Sandefur, W.
  1265
Sanders, S. G.
  1266, 7226, 10210, 12049

Saunders, J.
  11122
Savannah-Chatham Public
  Schools.
  7227
Sawyer, D. J.
  1267
Sawyer, R. C.
  10211
Scannella, A.
  7228
Scarborough, G. E.
  10212
Schafer, C.
  10213
Schaller, G. W.
  7229
Schein, B.
  2111
Schein, M. P.
  2111
Schellenberg, J.
  10214
Schenk, Q.
  6056
Scherer, J.
  6084
Schipper, J. F.
  5067
Schmuck, R.
  1268
Schneyer, J. W.
  7286
Schniedewind, N.
  11123
Schofield, J. W.
  10215, 10216, 10217
Schonhaut, C. I.
  10218
Schoo, P. H.
  1269, 10219
School Executive.
  1270
School Information and
  Research Service.
  10220
School Management.
  2112, 5068, 5069, 5070,
  5071, 5072, 5073, 5074
School Science Review.
  7230
Schott, J. L.
  10221
Schreiber, D.
  8052

Schubert, D. G.
    7231
Schuller, C. F.
    7259
Schuncke, G. M.
    7232
Schutter, C. H.
    1271
Schwartz, B.
    7233
Schwartz, T.
    10222
Schwer, W. E.
    10223
Scott, F. C.
    7234
Scott, G. J.
    10224
Scott, W. C.
    12050
Scrofani, E. A.
    1272
Seagren, A.
    1104
Secarea, R. V.
    10225
Seefeldt, V.
    7235
Seick, R. E., Jr.
    10226
Senn, M. J. E.
    4043
Sewell, A. F.
    10059,10227
Shane, H. G.
    1273
Shannon, R. L.
    10228
Shaplin, J. T.
    6085
Sharpe, W. C.
    7023
Shaw, R. A.
    7236
Shawnee Mission Public
    Schools.
    7237
Shelly, A. C.
    11124
Sheridan School District 2.
    12051
Sheviakov, G.
    1274
Shipp, F. T.
    1275

Shirts, N. A.
    1276
Shockley, R. E.
    7238, 11124
Shovlin, D. W.
    10229
Shriver, M. R.
    10230
Sienkiewicz, H. S.
    10231
Sigurdson, S. E.
    7239
Silbergeld, S.
    4061
Simmons, R. G.
    10018,10019,10232,10233,
    10234
Simney, L.
    6086
Simone, M. W.
    8036
Simpson, D.
    4044
Simpson, G. C.
    10235
Singer, H.
    7240
Sinks, T. A.
    2016, 6087, 10236, 10237
Sizemore, R. W.
    11125
Skill Development Council.
    2113
Skogsberg, A. H.
    1277
Slater, R. D.
    7241
Slawski, E. J.
    6084
Slimak, P.
    7242
Smith, M.
    1124
Smith, B. F.
    1278
Smith, C. W.
    4062
Smith, G.
    12052
Smith, G. J.
    10235
Smith, H. P.
    10238
Smith, M.
    1279

Smith, M. C.
11126,11127
Smitherman, B. J.
7243
Smock, C. D.
10239
Sneed, L. C.
7244
Snooks, L.
7245
Snow, R.
7246
Snyder, K. J.
11001
Snyder, R. A.
7247
Soares, A. T.
10240
Soares, L. M.
10240
Society of State Directors
of Health, Physical
Education, Recreation.
8053
Sonstegard, M.
7121
Soroka, D. J.
7077
Southard, H. S.
4043
Spaights, E.
1280
Spaulding, F. T.
1281
Spayde, P. E.
10074
Spencer, H. B.
1282
Spivak, M. L.
10241
Spokane School District 81.
7248
Spring Branch Independent
School District.
2114
Springfield Public Schools,
Middle School Study
Committee.
9038
Springfield, C. A.
6088
Stafford, E.
7249
Stahl, R. J.
4012

Stainbrook, J. R., Jr.
11128
Stalnaker, E. M.
4063
Stanavage, J. A.
1283
Standley, L. L.
1279
Stanford Research
Institute, Educational
Policy Research Center.
10242
Stanley, J. C.
7087
Stanton, W. W.
4064
Stapleton, J. C.
12002
State Committee on Core and
General Education.
6089
State University of New
York.
7250
Staub, F.
1058
Stein, A.
9044
Steiner, M.
1089
Steinmann, A.
7251
Stelle, A.
6090
Stemnock, S. K.
2115, 10243
Stepanovich, M. M.
6091
Stephens, C. E.
10244,10245
Stephens, W.
2088
Stephens, W. R.
1284, 1285
Stevic, R.
4041
Stewart, H.
7252
Stewart, L. H.
10246
Stier, S.
2116
Stillwater Junior High
School.
7253

Stockhaus, S.
  7254
Stoddard, G. D.
  6092, 7255
Stoltenberg, J. C.
  11022
Stone, J.
  1286
Stone, W. J.
  6093
Stoneburner, L.
  11129
Storen, H. S.
  1287
Stoumbis, G.
  1135, 1288
Stover, G.
  10247
Stradley, W. E.
  2117, 2118
Strahan, D.
  10100
Strang, R.
  1289
Stranik, E.
  5027
Street, P.
  10248
Strehle, J.
  7241
Strickland, J. H.
  1290
Strickland, R. G.
  7256
Strickland, V. E.
  1291, 7257, 10249
Struthers, A. B.
  1309
Stuart, H. C.
  1292
Suess, A. R.
  7258
Summers, A. A.
  6094
Sumption, M. R.
  5075
Sur, W. R.
  7259
Swain, M. T.
  12026
Sweeney, M. E.
  10187
Swenson, G. A.
  3061
Tannebaum, A. J.
  7260

Tanner, J. M.
  1293
Taormina, F. R.
  6095
Task Force on Intermediate
  Education.
  2119
Taylor, E. N.
  12053
Taylor, G. R.
  10250
Taylor, H. A.
  6096
Teacher Education
  Resources.
  2120
Teachers' College Journal.
  6097
Teachers' College Record.
  3062
Tegarden, R. S.
  1294
Teicher, J. D.
  1295
Teitel, M.
  9004
Tenoschok, M.
  5076
Tepper, S. S.
  1296
Terman, D. J. T.
  10236
Texas Education Agency.
  5077
Texas Study of Secondary
  Education.
  3063, 3064
Thayer, L. Y.
  3065
Theimer, W. C., Jr.
  12054
Thibadeau, G.
  2122
Thiel, K. S.
  10019
Thomas, B.
  10251
Thomas, J. K.
  4065
Thomas, W.
  11130
Thomas-Tindal, E. V.
  1297
Thomason, J.
  10267

Thomasson, A. L.
  4066
Thompson, L. J.
  2123
Thompson, M.
  7261
Thompson, P.
  10252
Thornburg, H. D.
  1298, 1299, 1300, 1301,
  1302, 1303, 1304
Tierno, M. J.
  2082
Tiffany, B. E.
  1305
Times Educational
  Supplement.
  9039
Timmer, N. C.
  10253
Tinsley, T.
  7146
Tobaygo, R.
  11131
Tobin, M. F.
  2124
Tobin, W.
  10254
Tocco, T. S.
  10021
Today's Education.
  2125
Todd, S.
  2126, 7212
Toepfer, C. F., Jr.
  1080, 1306, 1307, 1308,
  2127, 4002, 7262, 8054,
  11132,11133
Tompkins, E.
  1113, 3066, 6098, 10205
Topeka Public Schools.
  9040
Torrance Unified School
  District.
  9041
Touton, F. C.
  1309
Trachtman, G. M.
  11134
Trauschke, E.
  2128, 10255
Travis, K. K.
  10256
Treacy, J. P.
  2129

Trimble, W. E.
  10257
Tripp, R. L.
  7263
Tritzkaw, P. T.
  7264
Trowbridge, L. W.
  7265
Truesdell, W. H.
  5078
Trump, J. L.
  1310, 1311, 1312, 1313,
  3067, 3068, 7266
Tucker, B.
  7267
Tullock, B. (Ed.)
  7268
Turnbaugh, R. C.
  2130
Turner, D.
  12031
Tyler, R. W.
  7269
Tyrrell, R.
  2131, 2132, 7270
U. S. Department of Health,
  Education and Welfare,
  Office of Education.
  10258
U. S. Office of Education.
  7271
Underwood, B.
  11135
Underwood, R.
  11135
University of Georgia.
  11136
University of Michigan,
  Survey Research Center.
  8055
University of Oregon at
  Eugene.
  2133
University of the State of
  New York, State
  Education Department.
  7272
University of the State of
  New York.
  1314
Upper Midwest Regional
  Educational Laboratory.
  11137
Upshur, B.
  12055

Urell, K.
  1315
Usdan, M. D.
  11138
Van Cleave, E. F.
  10233
Van Hoose, J.
  1316
Van Noy, F.
  3057
Van Riper, B. W.
  4067
Van Til, W.
  1317, 1318, 3069
Vannote, V. G.
  4068
Vars, G. F.
  1189, 1319, 1320, 1321,
  2077, 2134, 2135, 3069,
  7273, 7274, 7275, 7276,
  7277, 11139,11140
Vincent, E. L.
  1025
Virgin, A. E.
  10252
Vogel, F. X.
  4069
Volpe, R.
  4070
Vredevoe, L. E.
  9042
Wagner, G.
  3070
Waksman, S. A.
  10259
Waldrep, R.
  6100
Walker, G. H., Jr.
  10094
Walker, J. G.
  11141
Walker, L.
  10184
Wallace, H.
  6090
Walton, R. E.
  1322
Ward, D. E.
  9026
Warren.
  10052
Warwick, D.
  1117
Washington Evening Star.
  7278

Washington State Coordinating Council for Occupa-
  tional Education, Voca-
  tional Education, Home
  and Family Life Section.
  7279
Watkins, J. H.
  8056
Watson, G. E.
  7280
Wattenbarger, J. L.
  11142
Wattenberg, W.
  1323, 1324, 1325, 1326,
  4053
Waukegan Community Unit
  School District 60.
  7281
Weaver, J. F.
  7282
Webb, R.
  6101
Weber, E. (Ed.)
  1327
Weber, N.
  10260
Wegner, O. A.
  10261
Weiss, T. M.
  11003
Weldy, G. R.
  11100
Weser, H.
  1010
West, E. L.
  12056
West, G.
  5079
White, J. W.
  10262
White, W. D.
  10263
Whitehead, R. E.
  10264
Whiteside.
  5080
Whiting, R.
  6102
Whitley, A. C.
  6103
Whitley, T. W.
  7283, 10265
Whyte, W.
  3071
Wichita Public Schools.
  9043

Wilcutt, R. E.
  10266
Wild, P. H.
  7115
Wiles, J.
  2136, 6104, 10020, 10267
Wiley, R. B.
  1328
Wilke, P. A.
  10268
Wilklow, L. B.
  2034
Willems, E. E.
  10269
Williams, E.
  1005, 1329, 1330, 1331,
  7284
Williams, G.
  7285
Williams, S. W.
  1332
Williamson, E. G.
  8057
Willink, R. J.
  11143
Willower, D. J.
  11093
Willson, M. F.
  7286
Wilson, H. L.
  4062
Wilson, L. S.
  6105
Wilson, M. A.
  2137
Wilson, M. T.
  1333, 2138, 11144
Wilson, R. E.
  5081
Wilson, W. E.
  1334
Winget, L.
  7193
Wingo, G. M.
  1218, 11103
Wisconsin Cooperative Planning Program, Super-
  intendent of Public
  Instruction.
  7287
Wixson, E. A.
  7288
Wohlers, A. E.
  5082
Wolf, R. E.
  1335

Wolfe, B. L.
  6094
Wolff, M.
  9044
Wolfson, B. J.
  6106
Wolin, R. B.
  5083
Wolotkiewicz.
  7141
Wood, C. W.
  11145
Wood, F. H.
  10270
Wood, M.
  10168
Woodin, R. J.
  7043
Woodring, P.
  1336
Woodward, R. G.
  6008
Wren, F. L.
  7047
Wright, B.
  7289
Wright, G.
  7290, 7291, 10271
Wright, J. E.
  7072
Wynn, R.
  1337
Yager, R. E.
  7292
Yale-Fairfield Study of
  Elementary Teaching.
  1338
Yanofsky, S. M.
  6033
Yarbrough, J. S.
  12049
Yinger, J. M.
  8058
Young, I. F.
  1339
Zachry, C. B.
  1340
Zdanowicz, P.
  1341, 2139, 9045, 10272
Zigler, J. T.
  10273
Zupfer, J.
  7293

Subject Index

Academic Achievement--See
    Student Achievement
Accreditation
    1201, 2023, 2053, 2083,
    2100, 3007, 3009, 3026,
    3027, 3048, 3049, 3060,
    7178, 7238, 11037,11055.
    See also--School
    Evaluation.
Activities
    1047, 1048, 1067, 1072,
    1091, 1110, 1112, 1135,
    1160, 1184, 1193, 1208,
    1230, 1260, 1279, 1305,
    1314, 1332, 1334, 2004,
    2022, 2031, 2052, 2057,
    2065, 2069, 2073, 2077,
    2083, 2087, 2089, 2113,
    2115, 2128, 2138, 3005,
    3009, 3011, 3016, 3017,
    3020, 3041, 3053, 3068,
    3069, 4002, 4015, 4019,
    4029, 5082, 6039, 6065,
    6073, 6091, 7138, 7141,
    7168, 7226, 7253, 7270,
    8004, 8005, 8006, 8007,
    8008, 8009, 8010, 8014,
    8016, 8018, 8019, 8021,
    8023, 8025, 8027, 8028,
    8029, 8030, 8031, 8032,
    8033, 8034, 8042, 8044,
    8045, 8048, 8049, 8050,
    8057, 9008, 9017, 9030,
    9034, 9036, 9038, 9040,
    10018,10041,10072,10085,
    10089,10092,10098,10105,

Activities--continued
    10111,10129,10150,10155,
    10174,10186,10195,10200,
    10228,10235,10237,10263,
    11074.
Administration
    1022, 1135, 1167, 1193,
    1226, 1326, 1332, 2005,
    2007, 2012, 2014, 2030,
    2031, 2034, 2036, 2037,
    2040, 2044, 2061, 2082,
    2083, 2085, 2088, 2089,
    2090, 2117, 2121, 3003,
    3007, 3013, 3023, 3048,
    4016, 4029, 4039, 5068,
    6013, 6021, 6061, 6083,
    8026, 8031, 9015, 9034,
    10012,10015,10027,10047,
    10053,10065,10084,10085,
    10111,10112,10129,10157,
    10172,10197,10218,10226,
    10237,10272,11008,11058,
    11084,11104,11127. See
    also--Principal.
Administrative Personnel--
    See Administration
Articulation
    1007, 1013, 1078, 1101,
    1109, 1112, 1170, 1215,
    1230, 1237, 1247, 1290,
    1332, 2001, 2002, 2019,
    2022, 2024, 2031, 2038,
    3008, 3011, 3013, 3016,
    3022, 3025, 3046, 4025,
    4026, 4039, 6004, 7071,
    7122, 10041,10043,10047,

Articulation--continued
    10081,10085,10086,10088,
    10150,10174,10183,10186,
    10218,10220,12031. See
    also--Curriculum.
Athletics Interscholastic
    1067, 1101, 1139, 2073,
    3007, 3009, 3044, 7124,
    7212, 8001, 8003, 8011,
    8013, 8015, 8020, 8022,
    8038, 8041, 8043, 8047,
    8051, 8053, 8054, 9023,
    9030, 9036, 9038, 10041,
    10098,10150,10174,11127.
Athletics Intramural
    2052, 2069, 3044, 7124,
    7157, 7212, 8003, 8022,
    8038, 8047, 8051, 8053,
    8054, 8056, 9030, 9036,
    10150.
Behavior Problems--See
    Student Behavior
Bibliography
    1017, 1025, 1034, 1040,
    1057, 1076, 1140, 1142,
    1240, 1242, 1307, 2026,
    2030, 2041, 2043, 2085,
    2100, 2101, 2102, 2103,
    2115, 2119, 2133, 2139,
    3021, 3050, 5009, 5036,
    6022, 6030, 7068, 7143,
    7275, 9003, 10092,10169,
    10197,11042,11073,11110,
    12038.
Block Time
    1002, 1109, 1256, 1319,
    1334, 2097, 2135, 3005,
    3016, 3019, 3020, 3034,
    4036, 6016, 6048, 6056,
    6062, 6069, 6074, 6076,
    6086, 6089, 6093, 6098,
    7023, 7033, 7045, 7105,
    7154, 7229, 7264, 7271,
    7275, 9030, 9038, 10094,
    10134,10144,10237,11068,
    11137. See also--Core
    Curriculum.
Brain Growth--See Student
    Cognitive Development
Building Innovation
    2012, 2033, 2071, 2091,
    2131, 2132, 5002, 5003,
    5004, 5005, 5006, 5007,
    5009, 5010, 5012, 5013,
    5014, 5015, 5016, 5017,
    5018, 5019, 5020, 5022,

Building Innovation--
    continued
    5023, 5024, 5025, 5029,
    5030, 5032, 5033, 5034,
    5035, 5038, 5039, 5040,
    5041, 5042, 5044, 5045,
    5046, 5047, 5048, 5049,
    5051, 5055, 5056, 5058,
    5059, 5061, 5062, 5063,
    5064, 5066, 5067, 5069,
    5070, 5071, 5072, 5073,
    5074, 5078, 5079, 5080,
    5081, 6019, 6084, 9015.
    See also--Facilities.
Classroom Environment
    2075, 2111, 2126, 10022,
    10167,11083,11103. See
    also--School Environ-
    ment.
Classroom Organization
    1141, 2116, 3005, 3041,
    3057, 6090, 10163,10266.
    See also--School
    Organization.
Cocurricular Activities--
    See Activities
Cognitive Abilities--See
    Student Cognitive
    Development
Community Involvement
    1163, 1167, 2015, 2083,
    5013, 5017, 5018, 5034,
    5066, 5076, 5079, 5081,
    7023, 7039, 7072, 7086,
    7245, 9012, 10022,10078,
    10098,10104,10137,11046,
    11114,12052.
Comparison of Jr. High/
    Elementary School
    10238.
Comparison of Jr. High/
    Middle School
    1004, 1012, 1016, 1021,
    1023, 1024, 1027, 1028,
    1030, 1038, 1053, 1064,
    1091, 1096, 1097, 1099,
    1102, 1104, 1107, 1116,
    1136, 1146, 1153, 1154,
    1168, 1189, 1198, 1199,
    1200, 1207, 1213, 1221,
    1231, 1257, 1269, 1283,
    1312, 1317, 1321, 1331,
    1333, 1341, 2005, 2014,
    2027, 2077, 2078, 2082,
    2084, 2085, 2097, 2115,
    2123, 2129, 9031, 9045,

Comparison of Jr. High/
  Middle School--continued
  10010,10012,10029,10042,
  10051,10069,10076,10081,
  10091,10092,10094,10098,
  10105,10111,10166,10184,
  10192,10235,10254,10255,
  10270,11074.
Comparison of Middle
  School/Elementary School
  10032,10109,10166,10255.
Core Curriculum
  1002, 1112, 1233, 1334,
  2090, 2134, 2135, 3005,
  3019, 3041, 3053, 3069,
  4026, 5029, 6004, 6005,
  6013, 6048, 6058, 6100,
  7031, 7032, 7033, 7034,
  7045, 7048, 7049, 7054,
  7057, 7059, 7063, 7065,
  7070, 7084, 7091, 7101,
  7103, 7105, 7108, 7133,
  7134, 7136, 7138, 7154,
  7155, 7156, 7160, 7165,
  7167, 7189, 7193, 7198,
  7199, 7205, 7233, 7264,
  7269, 7271, 7273, 7274,
  7275, 7276, 7277, 7280,
  7290, 10074,10094,10134,
  11134,11142. See also--
  Block Time.
Counseling
  1005, 1032, 1051, 1057,
  1067, 1068, 1072, 1101,
  1107, 1112, 1135, 1136,
  1160, 1170, 1179, 1183,
  1189, 1199, 1229, 1230,
  1231, 1256, 1260, 1314,
  1332, 1341, 2012, 2014,
  2017, 2027, 2034, 2038,
  2041, 2048, 2056, 2064,
  2065, 2073, 2074, 2085,
  2089, 2090, 2094, 2097,
  2104, 2106, 2109, 2113,
  2121, 2135, 2137, 3003,
  3005, 3017, 3022, 3023,
  3025, 3034, 3039, 3041,
  3044, 3053, 3054, 3069,
  4002, 4003, 4004, 4005,
  4006, 4007, 4008, 4009,
  4010, 4011, 4013, 4014,
  4015, 4016, 4017, 4019,
  4020, 4021, 4022, 4023,
  4024, 4025, 4026, 4027,
  4028, 4029, 4030, 4032,
  4033, 4034, 4035, 4037,

Counseling--continued
  4038, 4039, 4040, 4041,
  4042, 4046, 4048, 4049,
  4050, 4051, 4053, 4055,
  4056, 4057, 4058, 4059,
  4060, 4061, 4063, 4065,
  4066, 4067, 4069, 4070,
  5027, 7023, 7082, 7106,
  7154, 7260, 7280, 8026,
  9006, 9008, 9017, 9037,
  9041, 10016,10034,10039,
  10041,10049,10051,10074,
  10074,10075,10079,10085,
  10093,10098,10099,10113,
  10126,10128,10129,10134,
  10145,10174,10196,10228,
  10246,10271,11022,11046,
  11078,11121,11127,11128,
  12004,12009,12017,12042,
  12044,12046,12051,12054.
  See also--Values
  Clarification.
Curriculum
  1004, 1010, 1013, 1017,
  1022, 1035, 1037, 1057,
  1091, 1102, 1107, 1110,
  1111, 1112, 1124, 1167,
  1169, 1193, 1199, 1207,
  1230, 1252, 1288, 1289,
  1320, 1321, 1323, 1332,
  1334, 1334, 2004, 2005,
  2007, 2010, 2011, 2012,
  2013, 2014, 2017, 2019,
  2020, 2021, 2022, 2026,
  2027, 2028, 2032, 2033,
  2034, 2035, 2042, 2044,
  2047, 2048, 2048, 2052,
  2053, 2055, 2058, 2059,
  2061, 2063, 2064, 2066,
  2067, 2069, 2069, 2074,
  2076, 2076, 2077, 2077,
  2079, 2085, 2088, 2089,
  2090, 2099, 2112, 2113,
  2114, 2115, 2117, 2118,
  2119, 2136, 3005, 3011,
  3020, 3031, 3033, 3041,
  3044, 3058, 3065, 3068,
  3069, 3070, 4029, 4054,
  4055, 5010, 5028, 5082,
  6009, 6031, 6033, 6039,
  6043, 6053, 6056, 6060,
  6065, 6076, 6091, 6102,
  7001, 7013, 7017, 7023,
  7026, 7051, 7061, 7062,
  7062, 7071, 7075, 7082,
  7083, 7088, 7100, 7120,

Curriculum--continued
    7121, 7129, 7135, 7147,
    7152, 7166, 7184, 7200,
    7203, 7241, 7253, 7263,
    7280, 7287, 8026, 9003,
    9006, 9009, 9013, 9019,
    9029, 9032, 9036, 9038,
    9040, 10009, 10012, 10025,
    10028, 10042, 10047, 10049,
    10053, 10065, 10072, 10074,
    10075, 10079, 10081, 10083,
    10085, 10091, 10098, 10105,
    10111, 10115, 10123, 10128,
    10129, 10146, 10151, 10201,
    10222, 10228, 10236, 10254,
    11022, 11029, 11066, 11087,
    11088, 11099, 11103, 12011,
    12046, 12048. See also--
    Articulation.
Curriculum Design--See
    Curriculum Planning
Curriculum Development--See
    Curriculum Planning
Curriculum Evaluation
    2124, 2133, 3054, 6091,
    7043, 7134, 7141, 7245,
    7262, 10063, 10161, 12023.
Curriculum Planning
    1004, 1005, 1010, 1020,
    1022, 1048, 1074, 1084,
    1085, 1097, 1101, 1146,
    1149, 1153, 1175, 1180,
    1210, 1235, 1254, 1260,
    1290, 1299, 1308, 1310,
    1314, 1326, 1327, 2001,
    2003, 2004, 2011, 2015,
    2021, 2025, 2029, 2030,
    2034, 2035, 2036, 2038,
    2042, 2047, 2050, 2053,
    2056, 2058, 2063, 2076,
    2077, 2078, 2080, 2082,
    2087, 2098, 2104, 2110,
    2116, 2123, 2124, 2134,
    3002, 3003, 3005, 3006,
    3021, 3039, 3040, 3043,
    3046, 3050, 3053, 5027,
    5037, 5039, 6020, 6025,
    6047, 6052, 6078, 6092,
    6104, 7052, 7062, 7071,
    7074, 7080, 7095, 7141,
    7162, 7190, 7206, 7212,
    7222, 7234, 7238, 7260,
    7262, 7279, 8031, 9001,
    9033, 9036, 9037, 10009,
    10015, 10161, 10186, 10192,
    10212, 10226, 11054, 11132,
    11133, 12035.

Curriculum, Art
    1261, 2097, 7019, 7069,
    7096, 7114, 7140, 7161,
    7177, 7185, 7217, 7219,
    7291.
Curriculum, Business
    Education
    7175.
Curriculum, Careers
    4045, 4064, 7044, 8039,
    8046.
Curriculum, Core--See Core
    Curriculum
Curriculum, Drama
    4007, 8027.
Curriculum, English
    2006, 2067, 4026, 6017,
    6055, 6100, 7004, 7016,
    7035, 7046, 7078, 7085,
    7132, 7220, 7227, 7256,
    7267, 7284, 10149, 11005,
    11105.
Curriculum, Foreign
    Language
    7027, 7029, 7186, 7201,
    7209, 7261.
Curriculum, Health
    1005, 2067, 2077, 3005,
    7058, 7106, 7145, 7177,
    10011, 10225.
Curriculum, Home Economics
    1261, 7002, 7004, 7006,
    7024, 7037, 7076, 7117,
    7125, 7130, 7144, 7170,
    7190, 7197, 7211, 7216,
    7219, 7243, 7246, 7279,
    7285, 9043.
Curriculum, Industrial Arts
    1027, 1261, 7012, 7066,
    7067, 7094, 7116, 7123,
    7137, 7153, 7162, 7173,
    7194, 7210, 7216, 7219,
    7250, 7258, 7285, 8002,
    10142.
Curriculum, Language Arts
    2021, 2057, 2066, 2067,
    6087, 7053, 7093, 7172,
    7176, 7186, 7227, 7237,
    7255, 10117, 11105.
Curriculum, Math
    2021, 2047, 2057, 2066,
    2067, 6017, 6055, 6087,
    7004, 7005, 7010, 7021,
    7041, 7047, 7073, 7078,
    7087, 7090, 7092, 7099,
    7109, 7112, 7121, 7122,

Curriculum, Math--continued
7129, 7139, 7150, 7180,
7182, 7186, 7187, 7195,
7207, 7213, 7215, 7236,
7239, 7278, 7282, 7288,
10006,10032,10037,10064,
10122,10124,10211,10247,
10266.
Curriculum, Music
2097, 7022, 7060, 7127,
7214, 7257, 7259, 11107.
Curriculum, Outdoor
Education
7050.
Curriculum, Physical
Education
1005, 2067, 2077, 2097,
2099, 3005, 3034, 7124,
7157, 7235, 7247, 7249,
7272, 7288, 8022, 8035,
10239,10252,10257.
Curriculum, Reading
1319, 2006, 4054, 6045,
6080, 7078, 7079, 7098,
7113, 7148, 7149, 7159,
7174, 7192, 7202, 7204,
7221, 7225, 7231, 7240,
7242, 7244, 7252, 7281,
7286, 8040, 10006,10008,
10032,10038,10141,10149,
11004,11040,11042,11043,
11044,11061,11073,11098,
11102,11105.
Curriculum, Sex Education
7131, 7146, 7169, 7211,
7251.
Curriculum, Science
2006, 2021, 2047, 2066,
2067, 6017, 6055, 6087,
7004, 7009, 7014, 7015,
7018, 7020, 7028, 7030,
7036, 7042, 7055, 7056,
7078, 7081, 7087, 7121,
7123, 7128, 7129, 7177,
7186, 7188, 7213, 7230,
7242, 7265, 7268, 7278,
7292, 7293, 9041, 10005,
10006,10050,10122,10135,
10208,10273,11034,11141.
Curriculum, Social Studies
2006, 2021, 2047, 2066,
2067, 4026, 6017, 6055,
6077, 6087, 7003, 7004,
7008, 7011, 7016, 7020,
7025, 7077, 7078, 7097,
7102, 7104, 7107, 7110,

Curriculum, Social Studies
--continued
7111, 7115, 7117, 7119,
7126, 7129, 7151, 7163,
7164, 7172, 7181, 7183,
7186, 7191, 7224, 7228,
7232, 7248, 7254, 7255,
7266, 7289, 8036, 10090,
10117,10141,10147,10159.
Delinquency
1223, 2104, 10013,10039,
10182,12006,12007,12015,
12016,12024,12026,12028,
12035,12045. See also--
Student Behavior.
Departmentalization
1002, 1004, 1013, 1051,
1129, 1138, 1139, 1143,
1179, 1231, 2017, 2028,
2041, 2052, 2072, 2073,
2074, 2112, 2129, 3009,
3017, 3022, 3037, 3041,
5010, 5025, 5070, 5071,
6004, 6015, 6027, 6048,
6092, 9040, 10026,10051,
10059,10075,10083,10094,
10099,10108,10111,10117,
10174,10177,10197,10241,
10271,11057,11077. See
also--School Organiza-
tion, Student Grouping.
Discipline
1032, 1047, 1132, 1205,
1214, 1223, 1239, 1274,
1300, 1321, 2085, 2087,
2113, 2114, 2138, 3054,
3071, 4015, 4035, 4051,
5079, 6011, 6031, 6033,
6065, 6091, 6092, 10043,
10066,10070,10203,11073,
11074,12002,12005,12007,
12008,12009,12010,12011,
12012,12013,12014,12015,
12018,12021,12022,12023,
12025,12028,12030,12031,
12033,12034,12036,12038,
12039,12041,12046,12048,
12049,12050,12055,12056.
See also--Student
Behavior.
Educational Administration
--See Administration
Educational Environment--
See Classroom Environ-
ment

Educational Goals--See
    Middle School Objective,
    Junior High School
    Objectives
Educational Needs--See
    Student Needs
Educational Objectives--See
    Middle School Objec-
    tives, Junior High
    School Objectives
Educational Park
    1264, 6030, 9002, 9044.
Educational Program--See
    Curriculum
Educational Purpose--See
    Middle School Objec-
    tives, Junior High
    School Objectives
Educational Theory--See
    Middle School Philos-
    ophy, Junior High School
    Philosophy
Eighth-Grade Placement
    1105, 2041, 2079.
Enrichment--See Exploration
Exploration
    1003, 1004, 1005, 1015,
    1033, 1107, 1135, 1143,
    1170, 1207, 1216, 1243,
    1291, 1314, 2012, 2026,
    2030, 2031, 2057, 2065,
    2077, 2083, 2084, 2117,
    2128, 3011, 3017, 3019,
    3022, 3023, 3036, 3053,
    3069, 4035, 4039, 6073,
    6088, 7023, 7043, 7082,
    7144, 7147, 7168, 7176,
    7212, 7253, 8026, 8049,
    9023, 9040, 10006,
    10093,10146,10151,10186,
    10202,10230,11127.
Extracurricular Activities
    --See Activities
Facilities
    1017, 1021, 1067, 1091,
    1102, 1114, 1135, 1170,
    1193, 1207, 1225, 1310,
    1322, 1334, 1341, 2011,
    2012, 2017, 2020, 2027,
    2030, 2033, 2050, 2052,
    2056, 2058, 2074, 2075,
    2078, 2079, 2083, 2086,
    2088, 2089, 2092, 2094,
    2095, 2098, 2099, 2106,
    2110, 2112, 2119, 2121,
    2124, 2131, 2132, 3017,

Facilities--continued
    3021, 3042, 3048, 3068,
    5001, 5002, 5003, 5004,
    5005, 5006, 5007, 5008,
    5009, 5010, 5011, 5012,
    5013, 5014, 5015, 5016,
    5017, 5018, 5019, 5020,
    5021, 5022, 5023, 5024,
    5025, 5026, 5027, 5028,
    5029, 5030, 5031, 5032,
    5033, 5034, 5035, 5036,
    5037, 5038, 5039, 5040,
    5041, 5042, 5043, 5044,
    5045, 5046, 5047, 5048,
    5049, 5050, 5051, 5052,
    5053, 5054, 5055, 5056,
    5057, 5058, 5059, 5060,
    5061, 5062, 5063, 5064,
    5065, 5066, 5067, 5068,
    5069, 5070, 5071, 5072,
    5073, 5074, 5075, 5077,
    5078, 5079, 5080, 5081,
    5082, 5083, 6006, 6019,
    6084, 6102, 7013, 7043,
    7052, 7270, 8035, 9009,
    9011, 9012, 9015, 9019,
    9022, 9032, 9037, 9041,
    9043, 9045, 10041,10053,
    10065,10083,10084,10098,
    10111,10111,10123,10166,
    10177,10186,10192,10228,
    10254,10260,10263,10267,
    11046. See also--
    Building Innovation,
    House Plan.
Fifth-Grade Placement
    1023, 1029, 1130, 1180,
    1220, 1251, 2005, 2016,
    2087, 2091, 2112, 6007,
    7026, 10035,10044,10081,
    10106,10109,10221.
Flexible Scheduling
    1107, 1135, 1216, 1252,
    1257, 2012, 2022, 2036,
    2053, 2057, 2065, 2073,
    2080, 2109, 2111, 2125,
    2128, 2138, 3007, 3034,
    3067, 5001, 5010, 6014,
    6017, 6026, 6032, 6035,
    6059, 6068, 7001, 7013,
    7159, 7242, 7253, 9003,
    9008, 9040, 10035,10051,
    10063,10075,10099,10130,
    10138,10150,10155,10174,
    10196,10230,10268,11014,
    11093,11137,12031. See
    also--Scheduling.

Grade-Level Pattern
1023, 1029, 1032, 1038,
1046, 1051, 1059, 1062,
1078, 1082, 1086, 1110,
1113, 1134, 1141, 1191,
1194, 1198, 1220, 1225,
1239, 1246, 1249, 1250,
1271, 1275, 1277, 1294,
1311, 1317, 1323, 1328,
1332, 1338, 2036, 2044,
2076, 2077, 2079, 2080,
2091, 2108, 2112, 3003,
4010, 6070, 6090, 7062,
7262, 9005, 9010, 9020,
9021, 9024, 9028, 9032,
9039, 9042, 10048,10060,
10079,10081,10083,10084,
10091,10109,10128,10175,
10218,10229,10236,10237,
11032,11052. See also
School Organization.
Grade-Level Pattern
Consequences
1005, 1010, 1012, 1018,
1030, 1031, 1172, 1180,
1202, 1251, 1266, 1270,
1281, 1306, 1322, 1326,
1339, 2017, 2045, 3016,
3041, 9016, 9022, 9035,
10017,10018,10019,10046,
10058,10077,10078,10129,
10139,10155,10169,10170,
10233,10234,10254,10263.
Grade-Level Pattern
National Trends--See
Grade-Level Pattern
Surveys
Grade-Level Pattern Surveys
1004, 1054, 1087, 1092,
1093, 1114, 1168, 1260,
1262, 1281, 1330, 1337,
2001, 2006, 2016, 2023,
2024, 2028, 2037, 2062,
2063, 2069, 2074, 2085,
2093, 2105, 2129, 3035,
3066, 7212, 10003,10012,
10027,10095,10114,10121,
10130,10139,10145,10151,
10170,10171,10172,10173,
10176,10177,10178,10179,
10194,10197,10205,10220,
10224,10258,10267,10271,
10272.
Grading--See Student
Evaluation

Graduate Teacher Education
1085, 1290, 2017, 11009,
11077,11087,11088,11098,
11102,11126.
Guidance--See Counseling
Heterogeneous Grouping
2074, 6026, 6038, 6057,
6066, 6073, 10024,10147,
10209. See also--
Student Grouping.
Homogeneous Grouping
1109, 1280, 2074, 6038,
6045, 6080, 6097, 7087,
7187, 10024,10092,10094,
10099,10147,10148,10187,
10209,10219,10271. See
also--Student Grouping.
House Plan
2069, 2099, 3033, 5020,
5027, 5069, 5072, 6009,
6018, 6038, 6103, 7206,
9002, 10063,10226. See
also--Facilities.
Individualized Instruction
1003, 1004, 1005, 1007,
1252, 1254, 1324, 2001,
2020, 2029, 2032, 2053,
2056, 2073, 2074, 2081,
2096, 2116, 2125, 2128,
5010, 5014, 6006, 6009,
6020, 6026, 6046, 6049,
6087, 6088, 6106, 7007,
7017, 7056, 7071, 7110,
7141, 7148, 7158, 7200,
7215, 7283, 8040, 9023,
10009,10035,10050,10093,
10128,10146,10174,10186,
10265,11022,11091,11137,
12009,12010. See also--
Instruction, Student
Grouping.
In-service Teacher Educa-
tion
1057, 1088, 1091, 1170,
1175, 1192, 1216, 1254,
2003, 2008, 2009, 2015,
2028, 2034, 2054, 2058,
2083, 2089, 2098, 2116,
2120, 2125, 4006, 4008,
4055, 6040, 6047, 6083,
6105, 7016, 7043, 7062,
7079, 7089, 7098, 7113,
7174, 7181, 7196, 7210,
7212, 7215, 7225, 7240,
7260, 8031, 9013, 9032,
9033, 9040, 10033,10049,

In-service Teacher
  Education--continued
  10084,10108,10126,10157,
  10212,10222,10273,11002,
  11004,11006,11009,11010,
  11011,11014,11031,11033,
  11037,11040,11042,11043,
  11044,11045,11047,11048,
  11053,11055,11061,11070,
  11078,11080,11081,11083,
  11086,11087,11088,11090,
  11091,11094,11099,11105,
  11110,11113,11114,11119,
  11124,11126,11127,11128,
  11129,11134,11135,11143,
  12009,12021,12025,12049,
  12051.
Instruction
  1004, 1017, 1035, 1050,
  1065, 1149, 1167, 1175,
  1218, 1235, 1288, 1289,
  1290, 1310, 2006, 2007,
  2030, 2031, 2035, 2039,
  2050, 2053, 2054, 2061,
  2063, 2088, 2102, 2106,
  2115, 2117, 2124, 2136,
  3007, 3011, 3039, 3069,
  5082, 6025, 6027, 6031,
  6033, 6053, 6055, 6067,
  6077, 6080, 7040, 7062,
  7075, 7080, 7104, 7119,
  7154, 7200, 7226, 7240,
  9009, 10004,10096,10098,
  10100,10123,10146,10161,
  10164,10186,10197,10218,
  10249,11013,11067,11074,
  11087,11107,11131,11133,
  11136,12046. See also--
  Individualized Instruc-
  tion, Team Teaching.
Instructional Staff
  1007, 1010, 1013, 1057,
  1067, 1091, 1106, 1112,
  1135, 1163, 1167, 1189,
  1193, 1214, 1229, 1279,
  1310, 1320, 1332, 1333,
  2002, 2004, 2010, 2026,
  2034, 2044, 2052, 2053,
  2056, 2058, 2076, 2082,
  2089, 2090, 2094, 2098,
  2100, 3007, 3020, 3023,
  3029, 3034, 5071, 6002,
  6034, 6064, 7052, 7212,
  9001, 9009, 9011, 9033,
  9041, 9043, 9044, 10012,
  10028,10029,10053,10065,

Instructional Staff--
  continued
  10081,10083,10091,10128,
  10129,10151,10249,11001,
  11008,11050,11091.
Interdisciplinary--See Team
  Teaching
Junior High School
  Historical Development
  1022, 1026, 1051, 1063,
  1090, 1112, 1126, 1135,
  1145, 1152, 1171, 1186,
  1188, 1189, 1201, 1231,
  1232, 1242, 1284, 1285,
  1317, 1318, 1332, 2050,
  2090, 3007, 3035, 3036,
  3069, 6072, 9023, 10139,
  10195,10210.
Junior High School Objec-
  tives
  1002, 1016, 1026, 1028,
  1034, 1035, 1061, 1063,
  1099, 1154, 1155, 1176,
  1178, 1187, 1193, 1209,
  1233, 1243, 1254, 1287,
  1291, 1297, 1313, 1319,
  1323, 1328, 1332, 2031,
  2114, 3004, 3005, 3010,
  3011, 3015, 3018, 3021,
  3028, 3036, 3038, 3045,
  3046, 3051, 3055, 3059,
  3062, 3068, 4031, 6091,
  7083, 7195, 10029,10041,
  10091,10112,10157,11037,
  11052,11130.
Junior High School Philosophy
  1026, 1030, 1035, 1061,
  1073, 1094, 1099, 1100,
  1102, 1109, 1110, 1111,
  1112, 1135, 1143, 1152,
  1155, 1176, 1186, 1187,
  1193, 1209, 1229, 1244,
  1254, 1287, 1297, 1319,
  2004, 2031, 3004, 3005,
  3010, 3015, 3018, 3020,
  3028, 3031, 3033, 3035,
  3036, 3038, 3042, 3046,
  3048, 3054, 3055, 3057,
  3062, 3071, 5026, 5031,
  6072, 7086, 9037, 10157,
  11029,11037,11052,11130.
Junior High School Survey
  10172,10263,10271.
Junior High School Theory--
  See Junior High School
  Philosophy

Large Group Instruction
    1004, 1257, 2020, 2022,
    2052, 2096, 2106, 5010,
    5020, 5028, 5082, 6023,
    6039, 7158, 10071, 10138.
    See also--Student
    Grouping.
Library--See Media Center
Longitudinal Studies
    10008, 10107, 10138, 10244.
Media Center
    1023, 1193, 1229, 1314,
    2033, 2074, 2089, 2107,
    2121, 3007, 3034, 3048,
    5015, 5018, 5025, 5028,
    7064, 7068, 7132, 7208,
    9007, 10129, 10271.
Media Specialist--See Media
    Center
Methods Courses
    2028, 2049, 11026, 11117.
Middle School Historical
    Development
    1029, 1057, 1063, 1088,
    1117, 1200, 1201, 1249,
    2034, 2067, 2078, 2090,
    2098, 2102, 2116, 2119,
    9023, 9034, 10092, 10121.
Middle School Objectives
    1008, 1010, 1013, 1016,
    1016, 1017, 1024, 1028,
    1034, 1061, 1062, 1063,
    1072, 1091, 1099, 1105,
    1108, 1127, 1131, 1136,
    1154, 1163, 1169, 1182,
    1193, 1248, 1249, 1254,
    1294, 1301, 1313, 1331,
    1333, 2008, 2009, 2014,
    2024, 2025, 2030, 2031,
    2032, 2034, 2038, 2043,
    2053, 2054, 2060, 2061,
    2066, 2067, 2070, 2073,
    2076, 2077, 2078, 2082,
    2095, 2097, 2098, 2102,
    2120, 2121, 2127, 2129,
    2133, 2139, 7078, 9007,
    9012, 9013, 9030, 9034,
    9040, 9041, 9044, 10003,
    10027, 10028, 10029, 10044,
    10091, 10092, 10093, 10097,
    10100, 10130, 10157, 10174,
    10186, 10196, 10240, 11060.
Middle School Philosophy
    1013, 1017, 1061, 1063,
    1073, 1091, 1099, 1102,
    1103, 1105, 1108, 1111,

Middle School Philosophy--
    continued
    1117, 1127, 1131, 1137,
    1152, 1166, 1182, 1193,
    1211, 1229, 1248, 1249,
    1254, 1294, 1330, 2002,
    2005, 2006, 2007, 2008,
    2009, 2010, 2012, 2014,
    2020, 2021, 2022, 2024,
    2026, 2027, 2030, 2031,
    2034, 2040, 2043, 2046,
    2049, 2050, 2051, 2052,
    2054, 2057, 2058, 2060,
    2063, 2065, 2067, 2069,
    2072, 2073, 2078, 2079,
    2085, 2086, 2091, 2095,
    2100, 2102, 2104, 2120,
    2133, 2134, 4010, 4029,
    5054, 5082, 6039, 6079,
    6090, 7071, 7078, 8054,
    9007, 9008, 9009, 9012,
    9013, 9034, 9037, 9044,
    9045, 10028, 10047, 10065,
    10069, 10075, 10092, 10097,
    10121, 10157, 10174, 10240,
    10254, 11060, 11063, 11114.
Middle School Survey
    2109, 2115, 2127, 6079,
    10027, 10028, 10065, 10093,
    10109, 10111, 10150, 10177,
    10180, 10196.
Middle School Theory--See
    Middle School Philosophy
Minorities
    1001, 1012, 1027, 1095,
    1164, 1175, 1278, 2086,
    2116, 2130, 6084, 6094,
    7023, 7100, 7142, 7260,
    8052, 8058, 9002, 9004,
    9024, 9025, 9029, 9033,
    10031, 10032, 10035, 10049,
    10054, 10061, 10079, 10082,
    10083, 10084, 10099, 10104,
    10113, 10126, 10152, 10153,
    10162, 10215, 10216, 10217,
    10222, 10232, 10242, 10246,
    11125, 11136, 12054.
Ninth-Grade Placement
    1030, 1045, 1059, 1069,
    1105, 1230, 1266, 1269,
    1276, 1282, 2076, 2079,
    2091, 2128, 5064, 6050,
    10047, 10048, 10051, 10060,
    10081, 10169, 10230, 10249.
Non-Graded School--See
    School Organization

Paraprofessionals
  1193, 2003, 2065, 2084,
  2090, 2098, 3071, 5027,
  7013, 10230,11008.
Parental Attitudes
  2001, 7039, 7195, 7203,
  10029,10065,10104,10264.
Parental Involvement
  1116, 1169, 1185, 1268,
  1302, 2011, 2013, 2015,
  2082, 2096, 2098, 3016,
  4016, 4021, 4024, 4040,
  4059, 4060, 5079, 6065,
  7017, 7089, 7098, 7158,
  7203, 8052, 9011, 9026,
  10020,10045,10086,10088,
  10104,10113,10137,11094,
  12001,12013,12015,12047.
Peer Relationships
  1032, 1052, 1084, 1133,
  1157, 1161, 1185, 1205,
  1258, 1298, 2013, 4008,
  4014, 4022, 4040, 6010,
  7071, 7171, 7196, 9011,
  9017, 10010,10019,10020,
  10035,10045,10061,10071,
  10076,10168,10202,10215,
  10216,10217,10222,10261,
  10270,12050.
Physical Plant--See
  Facilities
Policy Development
  1010, 1021, 1152, 1167,
  1181, 1227, 1234, 1336,
  9017, 9027, 9028, 10078,
  10084,11045,11095,11119.
  See also--School Board.
Pre-service Teacher Education
  1020, 1084, 1088, 1175,
  1192, 1244, 1333, 1334,
  2041, 2049, 2058, 2102,
  2105, 2117, 2121, 7181,
  7200, 7223, 10097,10100,
  10212,11001,11002,11003,
  11010,11014,11016,11017,
  11018,11019,11028,11029,
  11030,11031,11034,11035,
  11037,11052,11053,11054,
  11055,11056,11062,11063,
  11064,11068,11072,11075,
  11076,11077,11081,11088,
  11089,11094,11097,11100,
  11101,11102,11106,11108,
  11109,11112,11113,11114,
  11117,11121,11123,11127,

Pre-service Teacher Educa-
  tion--continued
  11128,11132,11137,11138,
  11139,11140,11141,11144.
Principal
  1008, 1022, 1057, 1109,
  1233, 1248, 1251, 1260,
  1279, 2002, 2052, 2084,
  2115, 2133, 3001, 3027,
  3029, 3034, 3040, 4008,
  4066, 5027, 7052, 7178,
  9017, 10028,10041,10060,
  10115,10128,10130,10207,
  11032,11046,11084,11092,
  11111,11115,11117,11118,
  11120,11122. See also--
  Administration.
Program Appraisal--See
  School Evaluation
Program Evaluation--See
  Curriculum Evaluation
Pubertal Development--See
  Student Physical
  Development
Reading in Content Areas--
  See Curriculum, Reading
Scheduling
  1007, 1013, 1072, 1167,
  1332, 2034, 2069, 2077,
  2082, 2083, 2084, 2085,
  2089, 2095, 2111, 2121,
  2124, 3030, 3053, 3057,
  5065, 5080, 6004, 6011,
  6032, 6036, 6038, 6039,
  6050, 6056, 6064, 6080,
  6083, 6091, 6093, 6101,
  6102, 6103, 7052, 7222,
  7264, 9008, 9011, 9038,
  10053,10129,10146,10201,
  10236,11092. See also--
  School Organization,
  Flexible Scheduling.
School Architecture--See
  Facilities
School Board
  1088, 1116, 2005, 2072,
  4016, 9015, 10041. See
  also--Policy Develop-
  ment.
School Budget--See School
  Finance
School Climate--See School
  Environment
School Environment
  1013, 1040, 1056, 1072,
  1151, 1157, 1170, 1185,

School Environment--
  continued
  1215, 1216, 1248, 1301,
  1303, 1309, 2013, 2056,
  2073, 2075, 2089, 2099,
  2125, 2126, 2128, 2131,
  3032, 5011, 5029, 5045,
  6006, 6040, 6078, 6082,
  7036, 7270, 9011, 10006,
  10010,10046,10055,10063,
  10066,10078,10080,10123,
  10125,10146,10148,10184,
  10200,10213,10229,10234,
  10245,10251,10257,10261,
  10265,11009,11051,11077,
  11092,12049. See also--
  Classroom Environment.
School Evaluation
  1017, 1085, 1130, 1135,
  1170, 1193, 1228, 2002,
  2004, 2005, 2064, 2068,
  2098, 2116, 2124, 2136,
  3003, 3011, 3014, 3021,
  3023, 3026, 3027, 3033,
  3048, 3052, 3054, 3064,
  4040, 7178, 7238, 9007,
  9017, 9038, 10021,10059,
  10080,10123,10130,10227,
  10230,10244,10255,10267.
  See also--Accreditation.
School Finance
  1067, 1085, 1092, 1114,
  2002, 2083, 2113, 3027,
  3068, 4008, 5024, 5036,
  8036, 9001, 9009, 9014,
  9032, 9033, 9036, 10078.
School Organization
  1003, 1007, 1008, 1009,
  1013, 1024, 1030, 1045,
  1051, 1054, 1057, 1062,
  1067, 1070, 1084, 1085,
  1091, 1096, 1099, 1102,
  1106, 1110, 1114, 1116,
  1129, 1137, 1138, 1152,
  1154, 1156, 1168, 1171,
  1180, 1210, 1226, 1237,
  1239, 1240, 1246, 1249,
  1251, 1264, 1273, 1290,
  1306, 1334, 1336, 2001,
  2005, 2010, 2011, 2012,
  2014, 2025, 2028, 2036,
  2037, 2045, 2046, 2047,
  2048, 2050, 2057, 2058,
  2061, 2066, 2067, 2069,
  2071, 2072, 2074, 2075,
  2076, 2079, 2080, 2081,

School Organization--
  continued
  2082, 2083, 2084, 2090,
  2095, 2097, 2100, 2101,
  2105, 2109, 2111, 2112,
  2116, 2121, 2125, 2128,
  2131, 2134, 2135, 3003,
  3007, 3021, 3023, 3039,
  3041, 3048, 3071, 4034,
  4050, 5006, 5010, 5027,
  5060, 5065, 5067, 5069,
  6002, 6011, 6013, 6015,
  6020, 6021, 6024, 6026,
  6034, 6035, 6037, 6038,
  6040, 6043, 6044, 6046,
  6047, 6051, 6053, 6064,
  6068, 6072, 6075, 6083,
  6084, 6091, 6092, 6093,
  7038, 7052, 7086, 7141,
  7141, 7184, 7264, 8037,
  9001, 9003, 9004, 9008,
  9018, 9024, 9025, 9027,
  9033, 10003,10018,10019,
  10022,10030,10035,10053,
  10059,10061,10074,10075,
  10081,10083,10086,10091,
  10094,10095,10096,10100,
  10105,10107,10108,10111,
  10114,10129,10130,10139,
  10155,10161,10173,10175,
  10177,10179,10184,10186,
  10210,10213,10220,10223,
  10226,10245,10268,10270,
  11009,12020,12048,12049.
  See also--Grade-Level
  Pattern, Departmental-
  ization, Self-Contained
  Classroom, Team Teach-
  ing, Scheduling, Student
  Grouping, Classroom
  Organization.
School Orientation--See
  Articulation
School Personnel--See
  Instructional Staff,
  Paraprofessionals,
  Administration
School Size
  1009, 1225, 2115, 3019,
  3037, 4039, 6001, 6021,
  6030, 6093, 6102, 9015,
  10043,10089,10105,10105,
  10108,10115,10172,10176,
  10243,10248,10264,10269,
  10271,10272.

Self-Contained Classroom
    1013, 1143, 1231, 2017,
    2028, 2030, 2039, 2041,
    2052, 2066, 2072, 2074,
    2097, 2112, 5071, 6004,
    6005, 6015, 6045, 6047,
    6048, 6080, 6090, 6092,
    7277, 9040, 10035,10075,
    10094,10096,10177,10241,
    10260,11011,12054,12055.
    See also--School Organi-
    zation, Student
    Grouping.
Seventh-Grade Placement
    1032, 1082, 1105, 2041,
    2079, 2093, 10221.
Six-Year High School
    1082, 10023,10195.
Sixth-Grade Placement
    1023, 1032, 1105, 1130,
    1220, 1251, 1269, 2041,
    2045, 2076, 2079, 2087,
    2093, 2097, 2112, 2133,
    3017, 6007, 9008, 10018,
    10044,10048,10060,10099,
    10106,10221,10229.
Small Group Instruction
    1257, 2020, 2022, 2096,
    2106, 2126, 4042, 5010,
    5020, 5082, 6023, 6039,
    10005,10022,10094,10138,
    10163,11073.   See also--
    Student Grouping.
Staff Development--See
    In-service Teacher
    Education
Student Achievement
    1012, 1024, 1069, 1076,
    1089, 1165, 1255, 1267,
    1272, 1280, 1302, 2013,
    2075, 3011, 3024, 4011,
    4037, 4057, 6011, 6024,
    6050, 6080, 6087, 6094,
    7078, 7086, 7089, 7090,
    7100, 7137, 7138, 8011,
    8012, 8052, 8058, 10009,
    10010,10024,10029,10032,
    10033,10035,10039,10056,
    10059,10063,10064,10065,
    10067,10070,10083,10084,
    10087,10096,10106,10117,
    10120,10138,10138,10141,
    10155,10157,10163,10166,
    10168,10190,10191,10195,
    10199,10211,10222,10223,
    10227,10229,10230,10241,

Student Achievement--
    continued
    10244,10245,10246,10248,
    10249,10255,10263,10264,
    10266,10267,10271,11022,
    11080,11106,11109,12023,
    12024,12045.
Student Activities--See
    Activities
Student Adjustment
    1159, 1199, 1239, 1279,
    1289, 2022, 2121, 4015,
    4047, 10044,10073,10241,
    10260.   See also--
    Student Behavior.
Student Attendance
    1214, 4051, 6024, 7226,
    8052, 9029, 10013,10039,
    10056,10065,10166,10181,
    10182,10230,10250,12008,
    12015,12016,12040,12043,
    12044,12047,12048.   See
    also--Student Behavior.
Student Attitudes
    1012, 1015, 1074, 1123,
    1132, 1148, 1158, 1180,
    1195, 1254, 2001, 4013,
    4023, 4034, 4057, 6006,
    6047, 6077, 6079, 7007,
    7039, 7110, 7117, 7195,
    7200, 7226, 7283, 9017,
    10007,10010,10029,10032,
    10043,10049,10054,10058,
    10063,10065,10067,10070,
    10076,10087,10096,10107,
    10108,10116,10118,10132,
    10133,10146,10147,10162,
    10184,10203,10204,10206,
    10209,10215,10217,10219,
    10223,10226,10227,10228,
    10230,10231,10238,10244,
    10245,10255,10257,10261,
    10267,10268,10270,12015,
    12017,12042,12048.
Student Behavior
    1003, 1052, 1079, 1132,
    1159, 1165, 1199, 1298,
    2083, 4006, 4013, 4031,
    4041, 4055, 4061, 4068,
    5037, 6027, 6078, 7006,
    7086, 7089, 7117, 7218,
    7226, 7232, 7272, 8052,
    9017, 9026, 9034, 10021,
    10026,10029,10037,10042,
    10063,10066,10096,10126,
    10131,10132,10189,10199,

Student Behavior--continued
   10202,10204,10232,10259,
   11048,11065,11093,12001,
   12004,12010,12014,12017,
   12029,12032,12034,12035,
   12037,12039,12041,12042,
   12043,12049.   See also--
   Student Attendance,
   Delinquency, Discipline.
Student Characteristics
   1004, 1007, 1020, 1022,
   1041, 1057, 1068, 1073,
   1074, 1076, 1097, 1120,
   1140, 1174, 1190, 1216,
   1222, 1229, 1238, 1254,
   1258, 1301, 1315, 1325,
   1334, 2004, 2005, 2012,
   2020, 2021, 2026, 2034,
   2036, 2044, 2046, 2047,
   2053, 2053, 2058, 2060,
   2061, 2065, 2069, 2072,
   2076, 2081, 2086, 2090,
   2090, 2095, 2099, 2100,
   2115, 2117, 2118, 2121,
   2124, 2129, 3001, 3031,
   3034, 3046, 3056, 3061,
   3063, 3067, 3068, 4016,
   4030, 5077, 6034, 6049,
   7095, 7100, 7280, 7287,
   8024, 8055, 9036, 10008,
   10015,10021,10023,10059,
   10071,10088,10100,10102,
   10128,10137,10212,11070,
   11072,11133.   See also--
   Student Self-Concept,
   Student Sex Role, Stu-
   dent Physical Develop-
   ment, Student Emotional
   Development, Student
   Social Development,
   Student Cognitive
   Development.
Student Cognitive Development
   1001, 1011, 1012, 1021,
   1041, 1043, 1065, 1068,
   1072, 1073, 1075, 1076,
   1077, 1079, 1080, 1089,
   1110, 1118, 1125, 1132,
   1144, 1151, 1152, 1169,
   1181, 1192, 1197, 1202,
   1203, 1204, 1217, 1219,
   1224, 1236, 1248, 1255,
   1267, 1269, 1286, 1291,
   1294, 1298, 1301, 1302,
   1307, 1308, 1324, 1325,

Student Cognitive
   Development--continued
   1327, 1329, 1333, 2005,
   2010, 2017, 2026, 2030,
   2046, 2047, 2048, 2051,
   2054, 2058, 2061, 2065,
   2066, 2073, 2088, 2112,
   2115, 2124, 2128, 2129,
   2130, 2135, 3017, 3036,
   3054, 3061, 3068, 6034,
   6063, 7021, 7036, 7040,
   7052, 7097, 7141, 7245,
   8017, 8036, 9011, 9017,
   9030, 9034, 9036, 10010,
   10050,10057,10069,10073,
   10082,10091,10109,10110,
   10119,10124,10135,10147,
   10165,10169,10187,10192,
   10194,10208,10221,10223,
   10225,10238,10239,11007,
   11023,11051,11095.   See
   also--Student Characteristics.
Student Emotional Development
   1005, 1030, 1036, 1047,
   1058, 1072, 1073, 1110,
   1118, 1119, 1140, 1151,
   1152, 1161, 1169, 1181,
   1192, 1203, 1205, 1215,
   1217, 1218, 1241, 1254,
   1259, 1295, 1302, 1316,
   1325, 1327, 1329, 1335,
   2026, 2032, 2046, 2047,
   2051, 2054, 2061, 2124,
   2129, 2130, 3020, 3021,
   3036, 4018, 4031, 4035,
   4037, 4043, 4048, 7095,
   8036, 9012, 9017, 9030,
   10002,10016,10018,10019,
   10021,10025,10048,10057,
   10069,10082,10100,10109,
   10122,10137,10148,10169,
   10190,10194,10212,10221,
   11023,11072,11117,12053.
   See also--Student Characteristics.
Student Evaluation
   1003, 1112, 1279, 2003,
   2006, 2011, 2018, 2022,
   2054, 2065, 2066, 2068,
   2078, 2084, 2089, 2116,
   2137, 3005, 3007, 3039,
   3044, 3069, 3071, 4013,
   4054, 4063, 6039, 6053,
   6064, 6068, 6091, 7143,

Student Evaluation--
    continued
    8036, 8058, 9006, 9008,
    9009, 9012, 9013, 9034,
    9037, 9040, 10002,10024,
    10081,10087,10134,10196,
    10237,10257,10271,11073,
    11138,12021.
Student Grouping
    1007, 1072, 1076, 1109,
    1129, 1215, 1260, 1273,
    1280, 1320, 1323, 1324,
    2006, 2012, 2013, 2029,
    2036, 2039, 2048, 2052,
    2053, 2056, 2072, 2080,
    2081, 2087, 2088, 2089,
    2091, 2096, 2115, 2132,
    3007, 4010, 4013, 5001,
    5072, 6007, 6020, 6032,
    6038, 6041, 6045, 6050,
    6055, 6064, 6066, 6068,
    6073, 6080, 6083, 6097,
    7013, 7232, 7238, 10017,
    10028,10035,10038,10041,
    10075,10087,10094,10111,
    10118,10122,10134,10148,
    10177,10189,10238,10260,
    11090. See also--School
    Organization, Large
    Group Instruction, Small
    Group Instruction,
    Departmentalization,
    Self-Contained Class-
    room, Team Teaching,
    Individualized Instruc-
    tion, Homogeneous Group-
    ing, Heterogeneous
    Grouping.
Student Intelligence--See
    Student Cognitive
    Development
Student Interest
    1015, 1111, 1132, 1142,
    1143, 1158, 1170, 1180,
    1203, 1216, 1291, 1315,
    2002, 2053, 2066, 2081,
    2111, 3005, 3012, 3020,
    3036, 3046, 3047, 4019,
    4044, 4057, 7052, 7164,
    7255, 9011, 10093,10109,
    10221,12052.
Student Morale--See Student
    Attitudes
Student Needs
    1004, 1013, 1016, 1020,
    1033, 1037, 1040, 1085,

Student Needs--continued
    1099, 1101, 1106, 1111,
    1118, 1124, 1128, 1136,
    1143, 1170, 1183, 1204,
    1205, 1216, 1233, 1239,
    1253, 1299, 1301, 1314,
    1334, 2002, 2025, 2032,
    2034, 2038, 2042, 2052,
    2054, 2079, 2082, 2091,
    2094, 2095, 2100, 2113,
    2121, 2124, 2129, 2138,
    3012, 3020, 3031, 3041,
    3048, 3061, 3069, 4019,
    4030, 4038, 4040, 4044,
    6002, 6065, 6081, 7007,
    7052, 7062, 7074, 7082,
    7163, 7227, 7238, 7243,
    7245, 7284, 9008, 9009,
    9011, 9013, 9023, 9037,
    9040, 10023,10098,10123,
    10155,10212,10220,11051,
    11085,12051.
Student Perceptions--See
    Student Attitudes
Student Physical Develop-
    ment
    1005, 1006, 1021, 1024,
    1025, 1028, 1041, 1043,
    1044, 1047, 1052, 1055,
    1059, 1060, 1068, 1070,
    1071, 1072, 1073, 1074,
    1079, 1081, 1083, 1084,
    1089, 1098, 1110, 1115,
    1118, 1121, 1125, 1132,
    1140, 1142, 1147, 1150,
    1152, 1159, 1160, 1162,
    1164, 1169, 1177, 1181,
    1184, 1192, 1197, 1204,
    1212, 1215, 1217, 1219,
    1224, 1226, 1231, 1254,
    1267, 1269, 1292, 1293,
    1294, 1295, 1296, 1300,
    1301, 1303, 1307, 1308,
    1321, 1324, 1325, 1327,
    1329, 1340, 2005, 2017,
    2026, 2031, 2032, 2045,
    2046, 2047, 2048, 2051,
    2054, 2061, 2065, 2073,
    2097, 2112, 2124, 2128,
    2129, 2130, 3020, 3021,
    3036, 3046, 3047, 3054,
    3061, 3063, 4035, 4043,
    4048, 4065, 7095, 7141,
    7211, 7280, 9011, 9030,
    9034, 10021,10047,10048,
    10068,10069,10077,10100,

Student Physical
    Development--continued
    10139,10148,10168,10169,
    10194,10212,10232,10233,
    10252,11072,11095,11117.
    See also--Student Char-
    acteristics.
Student Progress--See
    Student Evaluation
Student Relationships--See
    Peer Relationships
Student Self-Concept
    1012, 1030, 1039, 1084,
    1121, 1122, 1148, 1180,
    1238, 1243, 1245, 1255,
    1265, 1280, 1289, 1329,
    2013, 2030, 2057, 2106,
    2126, 4015, 4017, 4031,
    4044, 6040, 7007, 7121,
    7141, 7143, 7160, 7200,
    7224, 7243, 8036, 10010,
    10018,10024,10032,10035,
    10039,10044,10054,10055,
    10056,10065,10067,10069,
    10070,10076,10077,10096,
    10113,10127,10138,10150,
    10158,10168,10190,10206,
    10214,10219,10222,10228,
    10229,10232,10234,10240,
    10255,10267,11049,12012,
    12024,12026,12032.   See
    also--Student Character-
    istics.
Student Self-Esteem--See
    Student Self-Concept
Student Self-Identity--See
    Student Self-Concept
Student Sex Role
    1001, 1052, 1084, 1121,
    1142, 1150, 1165, 1174,
    1183, 1196, 1206, 1210,
    1272, 1293, 1294, 1295,
    1298, 1299, 1300, 1301,
    1325, 1340, 3047, 4020,
    4043, 7051, 9030, 10032,
    10048,10070,10073,10076,
    10189,10233.   See also--
    Student Characteristics.
Student Social Development
    1005, 1006, 1009, 1012,
    1016, 1019, 1024, 1032,
    1033, 1044, 1047, 1049,
    1052, 1056, 1058, 1060,
    1068, 1072, 1073, 1076,
    1083, 1084, 1091, 1118,
    1119, 1132, 1133, 1140,

Student Social Development
    --continued
    1142, 1144, 1149, 1152,
    1159, 1164, 1169, 1173,
    1174, 1183, 1184, 1192,
    1197, 1199, 1205, 1206,
    1207, 1208, 1215, 1217,
    1218, 1226, 1231, 1259,
    1269, 1278, 1295, 1296,
    1301, 1303, 1315, 1316,
    1325, 1327, 1329, 1333,
    1335, 2010, 2022, 2032,
    2046, 2047, 2048, 2051,
    2054, 2061, 2065, 2104,
    2128, 2129, 2130, 3020,
    3021, 3036, 3046, 3063,
    4011, 4021, 4048, 7071,
    7280, 8010, 8017, 9012,
    9017, 9030, 9034, 10018,
    10019,10021,10025,10044,
    10048,10068,10069,10075,
    10076,10081,10099,10103,
    10109,10111,10137,10139,
    10148,10155,10169,10194,
    10196,10212,10219,10221,
    10229,10232,10233,10259,
    10263,11072,11133,12053.
    See also--Student Char-
    acteristics.
Student Teachers--See
    Pre-service Teacher
    Education
Student-Teacher Relation-
    ships
    1013, 1035, 1123, 1141,
    1160, 1268, 1289, 1303,
    2123, 4034, 4036, 6021,
    6064, 7017, 7071, 7203,
    8048, 9011, 10001,10022,
    10029,10043,10055,10072,
    10089,10108,10131,10142,
    10213,10222,10261,10270,
    11023,11046,11049,11069,
    11083,12033,12047,12050.
Teacher Attitudes
    1341, 2001, 2087, 6006,
    6047, 6079, 7039, 7071,
    7113, 7195, 10010,10041,
    10065,10123,10213,10226,
    11011,11015,11019,11021,
    11025,11044,11060,11066,
    11074,11075,11077,11135,
    11136.
Teacher Behavior
    1102, 1233, 1289, 2126,
    2132, 3057, 3061, 4037,

Teacher Behavior--continued
5037, 6064, 6078, 7025,
7141, 10022,10041,10042,
10063,10131,10146,11013,
11023,11025,11027,11048,
11051,11065,11073,11082,
11085,11093,11098,11103,
11109,11125,11138,12015,
12020,12027. See also--
Teacher Evaluation.
Teacher Certification
1320, 1334, 2028, 2035,
2062, 2063, 2074, 2105,
7212, 9043, 10098,10174,
10180,11022,11029,11031,
11037,11052,11055,11058,
11059,11060,11068,11071,
11076,11096,11097,11100,
11108,11116,11121,11139,
11140.
Teacher Characteristics
1096, 1106, 1138, 1149,
1161, 1190, 1192, 1301,
1303, 1322, 1341, 2010,
2017, 2050, 2063, 2069,
2076, 2077, 2106, 2117,
3017, 6094, 7025, 7141,
10004,10041,10057,10089,
11012,11014,11019,11020,
11021,11025,11027,11029,
11030,11033,11035,11037,
11062,11065,11074,11077,
11078,11082,11085,11090,
11096,11109,11125,11137,
11139,11140.
Teacher Competencies
1032, 1096, 3021, 7098,
7195, 7240, 10022,11002,
11005,11012,11016,11018,
11019,11025,11027,11029,
11035,11039,11072,11077,
11081,11082,11087,11090,
11100,11105,11113,11121,
11130,11137,11140,11142.
See also--Teacher
Evaluation.
Teacher Education--See Pre-
service Teacher Educa-
tion, In-service Teacher
Education, Graduate
Teacher Education
Teacher Evaluation
3017, 6091, 10009,11061,
11065,11072,12025. See
also--Teacher Selection,
Teacher Performance,

Teacher Evaluation--
continued
Teacher Behavior,
Teacher Competencies.
Teacher Perceptions--See
Teacher Attitudes
Teacher Performance
1022, 1047, 1169, 6038,
6091, 7098, 7273, 10004,
10022,10029,11013,11021,
11023,11025,11027,11039,
11051,11082,11090,11096,
11098,11125,11131,12025.
See also--Teacher
Evaluation.
Teacher Preparation--See
Pre-service Teacher
Education
Teacher Selection
2078, 2121, 11038.
Teacher-Student Relation-
ships--See Student-
Teacher Relationships
Teacher Training Institu-
tions
1325, 2049, 2063, 2131,
4059, 10180,11003,11017,
11031,11033,11054,11055,
11063,11077,11088,11090,
11102,11114,11121,11132,
11144.
Teaching--See Instruction
Team Teaching
1023, 1067, 1096, 1107,
1129, 1135, 1136, 1141,
1204, 1252, 1290, 1310,
1319, 1333, 1336, 2012,
2021, 2034, 2038, 2041,
2044, 2052, 2057, 2062,
2065, 2073, 2080, 2081,
2091, 2094, 2098, 2099,
2106, 2107, 2109, 2122,
2125, 2128, 2132, 3067,
4057, 5001, 5002, 5010,
5021, 5029, 5065, 5080,
6003, 6007, 6008, 6009,
6012, 6014, 6015, 6018,
6019, 6020, 6022, 6023,
6025, 6028, 6029, 6039,
6041, 6042, 6044, 6052,
6054, 6063, 6064, 6065,
6067, 6071, 6075, 6076,
6079, 6081, 6083, 6085,
6090, 6092, 6095, 6096,
6102, 7013, 7020, 7056,
7110, 7159, 7242, 7270,

Team Teaching--continued
    9003, 9008, 9017, 9034,
    9038, 10035,10051,10093,
    10094,10098,10099,10117,
    10128,10138,10150,10161,
    10174,10184,10196,10197,
    10201,10209,10223,10230,
    11011,11014,11036,11063,
    11093,11099,11113,12048.
    See also--Instruction,
    School Organization,
    Student Grouping.
Unified Arts
    2069, 7138, 7165, 7173,
    8002.   See also--Core
    Curriculum.
Values Clarification
    1180, 1238, 2057, 2123,
    2138, 4001, 4012, 4015,
    4018, 4037, 7051, 7160,
    7218, 10020,10116.   See
    also--Counseling.

About the Compilers

DALE A. BLYTH is Assistant Professor of Psychology at Ohio State University in Columbus. He has written several book chapters and has contributed to *Youth and Society, American Sociological Review, Sociology of Education, Journal of Early Adolescence*, and other journals. He was formerly Director of the Schools and Adolescent Development Research Program at the Boys Town Center at Omaha.

ELIZABETH LUEDER KARNES is Supervisor of Curriculum and Instruction for the Boys Town School System in Nebraska. Her articles have appeared in such publications as *The Gerontologist*.